A HISTORY OF
SOUTHEAST ASIA

THE BLACKWELL HISTORY OF THE WORLD

General Editor: **R.I. Moore**

A HISTORY OF SOUTHEAST ASIA

CRITICAL CROSSROADS

ANTHONY REID

WILEY Blackwell

This edition first published 2015
© 2015 Anthony Reid

Registered Office
John Wiley & Sons, Ltd, The Atrium, Southern Gate, Chichester, West Sussex,
PO19 8SQ, UK

Editorial Offices
350 Main Street, Malden, MA 02148-5020, USA
9600 Garsington Road, Oxford, OX4 2DQ, UK
The Atrium, Southern Gate, Chichester, West Sussex, PO19 8SQ, UK

For details of our global editorial offices, for customer services, and for information about
how to apply for permission to reuse the copyright material in this book please see our
website at www.wiley.com/wiley-blackwell.

Library of Congress Cataloging-in-Publication Data

Reid, Anthony, 1939– author.
  A history of Southeast Asia / Anthony Reid.
    pages   cm
  Includes bibliographical references and index.
  ISBN 978-0-631-17961-0 (cloth : alk. paper) – ISBN 978-1-118-51300-2 (pbk. : alk. paper)
1. Southeast Asia–History.   2. Southeast Asia–Foreign relations.   I. Title.
  DS525.R45 2015
  959–dc23

                                                           2014040544

A catalogue record for this book is available from the British Library.

Cover image: Detail from a Burmese illustrated manuscript (parabaik) showing the
merit-making festival of light patronized by King Mindon, in the period 1853–7, with
orchestra in the foreground. British Library, Or 13681, folio 3r.

Set in 10/12pt Plantin by SPi Publisher Services, Pondicherry, India
Printed and bound in Malaysia by Vivar Printing Sdn Bhd

2   2016

for
Kate and Daniel
who shared the highs and lows

CONTENTS

LIST OF TABLES

LIST OF MAPS

LIST OF ILLUSTRATIONS

SERIES EDITOR'S PREFACE

There is nothing new in the attempt to understand history as a whole. To understand how humanity began and how it has come to its present condition is one of the oldest and most universal of human needs, expressed in the religious and philosophical systems of every civilization. But only in the last few decades has it begun to appear both necessary and possible to meet that need by means of a rational and systematic appraisal of current historical knowledge. Until the middle of the nineteenth century history itself was generally treated as a subordinate branch of other fields of learning – of literature, rhetoric, law, philosophy, or religion. When historians began to establish its independence as a field of scholarship in its own right, with its own subject matter and its own rules and methods, they made it in practice not the attempt to achieve a comprehensive account of the human past but the history of the European nation-states and of the societies created by European expansion and colonization. In laying the scholarly foundations of their discipline they also reinforced the Enlightenment's belief in the advance of "civilization" (and, more recently, of "Western civilization"), and made it in this form, with relatively minor regional variations, the basis of the teaching of history almost everywhere for most of the twentieth century. Research and teaching of the histories of other parts of the world developed mainly in the context of area studies like those of ancient Greece and Rome, dominated by philology, and conducted through the exposition of the canonical texts of their respective languages.

While those approaches prevailed, world history as such remained largely the province of thinkers and writers principally interested in constructing theoretical or metaphysical systems. Only toward the end of the twentieth century did academic historians begin to recognize it as a proper and even urgent field for the application of their knowledge and skills. The inadequacy of the traditional parameters of the discipline is now widely acknowledged, and the sense is growing that a world facing a common future of headlong and potentially catastrophic transformation needs its common history. The realization of such a history has been delayed, however, by simple ignorance on the one hand – for the history of enormous stretches of space and time has until very recently been known not at all, or so patchily and superficially as not to be worth revisiting – and on the other by the lack of a widely acceptable basis upon which to organize and discuss what is nevertheless the enormous and enormously diverse knowledge that we have.

The first of those obstacles is now being rapidly overcome. There is almost no part of the world or period of its history that is not the subject of energetic and sophisticated investigation by archaeologists and historians. The expansion of the horizons of academic history since the 1990s has been dramatic. The quality and quantity of historical research and writing have risen exponentially in each decade, and the advances have been most spectacular in some of the areas previously most neglected. The academics have not failed to share the results of their labors. Reliable and accessible accounts are now readily available of regions, periods, and topics that even twenty years ago were obscure to everyone but a handful of specialists. In particular, collaborative publication, in the form of volumes or sets of volumes in which teams of authors set forth, in more or less detail, their expert and up-to-date conclusions in the field of their research, has been a natural and necessary response to the growth of knowledge. Only in that way can non-specialists, at any level, be kept even approximately in touch with the constantly accelerating accumulation of information about the past.

Yet the amelioration of one problem exacerbates the other. It is truer than it has ever been that knowledge is growing and perspectives multiplying more quickly than they can be assimilated and recorded in synthetic form. We can now describe a great many more trees in a great deal more detail than we could before. It does not always follow that we have a better view of the wood. Collaboration has many strengths, but clarity, still less originality of vision, is rarely among them. History acquires shape, structure, relevance – becomes, in the fashionable catchphrase, something for thinking with – by advancing and debating new propositions about what past societies were like, how they worked and why they changed over long periods of time, how they resembled and why they differed from contemporaneous societies in other parts of the world, and how they interacted with one another. Such insights, like the sympathetic understanding without which the past is dead, are almost always born of individual creativity and imagination. Each volume in this series, therefore, embodies the work and vision of a single author. Synthesis on such a scale demands learning, resolution, and, not least, intellectual and professional courage of no ordinary degree, and we have been singularly fortunate in finding scholars of great distinction who are willing to undertake it.

There is a wealth of ways in which world history can be written. The oldest and simplest view, that it is best understood as the history of contacts between peoples previously isolated from one another, from which (as some think) all change arises, is now seen to be capable of application since the earliest times. An influential alternative focuses upon the tendency of economic exchange to create self-sufficient but ever expanding "worlds" which sustain successive systems of power and culture. Another seeks to understand the differences between societies and cultures, and therefore the particular character of each, by comparing the ways in which their values, social relationships, and structures of power have developed. The rapidly emerging field of ecological history returns to a very ancient tradition of seeing interaction with the physical environment, and with other animals, at the center of the human predicament, while insisting that its understanding demands an approach which is culturally, chronologically, and geographically comprehensive. More recently still "Big History," led by a contributor to this series, has begun to show how human history can be integrated with that not only of the natural, but of the cosmic environment, and better understood in consequence.

The Blackwell History of the World seeks not to embody any single approach, but to support them all, as it will use them all, by providing a modern, comprehensive, and accessible account of the entire human past. Each volume offers a substantial overview of a portion of world history large enough to permit, and indeed demand, the reappraisal of customary boundaries of regions, periods, and topics, and in doing so reflects the idiosyncrasies of its sources and its subjects, as well as the vision and judgment of its author. The series as a whole combines the indispensable narratives of very long-term regional development with global surveys of developments across the world, of interaction between regions and what they have experienced in common, or visited upon one another, at particular times. Together these volumes will provide a framework in which the history of every part of the world can be viewed, and a basis upon which most aspects of human activity can be compared across both time and space. A frame offers perspective. Comparison implies respect for difference. That is the beginning of what the past has to offer the future.

R.I. Moore

SERIES EDITOR'S ACKNOWLEDGEMENTS

The editor is grateful to all the contributors to the *Blackwell History of the World* for advice and assistance on the design and contents of the series as a whole, as well as on individual volumes. Both editor and contributors wish to place on record their immense debt, individually and collectively, to John Davey, formerly of Blackwell Publishers, without whose vision and enthusiasm the series would not have been initiated, and to his successor Tessa Harvey, without whose energy, skill, and diplomacy it could not have been realized.

PREFACE

Southeast Asia was and is a distinct place, but one of infinite variety. The region's unique environment, combining a hot, wet, monsoon climate, dense forest cover and extensive waterways with periodic natural catastrophes, has preserved exceptional diversity while resisting large unifying organization. It has not been congenial to the kind of empires that elsewhere dominated and integrated substantial territories, and thereby too much dominated historical narratives. Its coherence has lain in the fact of diversity, and its genius in managing it. Legal-bureaucratic states came late to the region and would dominate its history only in the twentieth century. Maintaining the balance between the two contrasting phenomena of diversity and distinctiveness without allowing the one to obscure the other is the challenge of a book such as this.

Southeast Asian history merits the attention of the people who are its heirs for all the usual reasons, and because much of that history offers a route around and beneath the brittle nationalist preoccupations of many of their textbooks. It merits the attention of the rest of the world for three crucial reasons, in addition to the often-acknowledged diversity. Its dangerous tectonic interfaces can determine the world's climate and the survival of our species; its women were more autonomous economically and socially than those in other societies whose histories are known; and its societies had other mechanisms for cultural and economic coherence than those of the states which dominate much history elsewhere. These factors help to make the region a "Critical Crossroads."

The world's two most destructive volcanic eruptions of modern times occurred at Tambora in Sumbawa (1815) and Krakatau (1883), situated at opposite ends of the extremely eruptive zone of Java, Bali, and Lombok, also famous for their high fertility. They darkened and cooled the whole planet and produced years without summer in Europe, though this causation has only recently been understood. The only disaster thought to have seriously endangered the survival of humanity (*Homo sapiens*) since its African origins occurred in Sumatra – the eruption that created the crater of Lake Toba 74,000 years ago and caused six years of global winter. Climate research has recently identified other sudden cooling episodes causing crises in the northern hemisphere, notably in 535, 1258 (probably caused by a mega-eruption in Lombok), and the 1580s. These probably had their origins in tropical volcanoes, which alone have the capacity to affect the whole planet through prevailing wind patterns. Southeast Asia's are the prime suspects.

Southeast Asia's gender pattern was strikingly different from that of its neighbors and trade partners in China, India, and the Middle East. Up until the nineteenth century, Southeast Asian women played economic roles equivalent to though different from those of men, and therefore had more latitude and agency than their European, Chinese, Indian, or Arab counterparts. They monopolized textile and ceramic production, shared agricultural tasks (dominating planting, harvesting, and foraging), and most importantly did most of the marketing and business. The status concerns of Southeast Asian men made them particularly inept in managing money and marketing. European and Chinese male traders dealt largely with local women, and found their own local sexual partners extremely helpful in their business.

Historians of the current post-nationalist era are increasingly aware that their profession arose with modern nation-states and made its principal business the chronicling of those states. Our fixation on the spectacular successes (and failures) of those states in modern times has led us to look for comparable institutions or at least ancestors in times and places where they played no such dominating role, and to marginalize themes and actors that cannot be narrated in state terms. Not only have stateless societies thereby become "people without history," but systems of social organization based on kinship, religion, the arts and performance, or ritual and economic reciprocity are classified as primitive and doomed, when not wholly ignored. The challenge is how to do better, when the modern state has educated us since childhood and generates, classifies, and preserves our knowledge. Our globalized era, however, is one that can no longer afford nationalist history that ignores our past entanglements and present common responsibility for the planet. In building a different history with other themes, Southeast Asia is an excellent place to start.

In this region of forest and water, the legal-bureaucratic state with which we are familiar has been an alien intruder, with little purchase over its peoples until the twentieth century. The history thus far written about many areas relates only to port-cities on the trade routes, while the population was overwhelmingly in the fertile uplands. The highlands were freer of malaria and other diseases, safer from maritime raiding and tsunamis, and easier than the densely forested lowlands to tame for both irrigated rice agriculture and the swidden pattern of shifting cultivation through burning-off fields in rotation.

There is, however, also a political factor, whereby populations appear to have consciously opted for their own pattern of social organization through kinship and ritual, evading the trade-based river-states to practice "the art of not being governed," as James Scott (2009) puts it. The argument that statelessness was an informed choice, which I had been tentatively advancing with particular reference to the Islands, has now been powerfully made by Scott for "Zomia" – the highlands of Mainland Southeast Asia and Southwest China. His plea for acknowledging the importance of these non-state choices was elegantly balanced by the monumental scholarship of Victor Lieberman (2003; 2009). He pointed out that Mainland Southeast Asia, like France, Japan, and other Eurasian "Protected Rimlands," underwent its own relentless process of state expansion and consolidation, punctuated by ever shorter disruptions that indeed suggest "Strange Parallels" across Eurasia. He demonstrated Southeast Asia's utility in undermining dichotomous East-West history and ideas of European exceptionalism. I am much indebted to both these treasured colleagues, as to an army of others. They have made it easier for me to plot a course that acknowledges both the benefits nation-states have brought and the ingenuity and achievement of those who preferred to live outside them. History appears to be leading us beyond state-based nationalisms toward a shared recognition that non-state histories are equally important to our evolution.

Even in Europe the mountains were a refuge of liberty and autonomy from the states, but in Southeast Asia the upland valleys were also in many ways more successful in building healthy, populous, complex societies. In the Peninsula and parts of the Philippines, aboriginal populations who rejected violence and authority, even of a kinship type, survived remarkably into the twenty-first century by retreating into the forest cover whenever threats approached, and avoiding dependence on agriculture that was vulnerable to natural as well as political disasters.

In seeking to understand, therefore, the entrenched pluralism of Southeast Asia we must abandon assumptions from European or Chinese history (though questioned even there) about the rise in tandem of civilization and the state. Societies such as the Batak, Bugis, Tagalog, and Shan developed writing, irrigation, metallurgy, and complex religious systems without the benefit of any unified polity. Other "kings" of culture areas not dominated by a single river system or port, like Balinese, Malays, and Minangkabaus, had a ritual and magical prominence rather than a legal-bureaucratic one. Stateless interior societies traded extensively with the more hierarchic monarchies of the coast and even incorporated these into their myths and rituals. Yet they neither allowed themselves to be incorporated into the political hierarchies of the coast, nor even imitated them as a means of self-defense.

Earlier scholars examining the evidence of Chinese Imperial reports, Sanskrit inscriptions, and archaeological remains were much too inclined to assume substantial kingdoms ruling over subject populations. Since this interpretation was at odds with the diffuse power structures Europeans encountered in the late nineteenth century, they resorted to presumptions of decline and decadence. Today's prehistorians, informed by a wealth of careful anthropological work about the nature of political relations in more recent times, have read more critically both Chinese reports of barbarian "kingdoms" sending tribute, and the grandiloquent Indic titles of many inscriptions. In reality the polities we know by these means appear to have been characterized by a plurality of fluid centers, and an emphasis on supernatural means of mobilizing populations for war or temple-building. Astonishing Buddhist temples like those of Borobudur in Java and Pagan on the Irrawaddy should inspire us with awe about the popular piety that built them, in the absence of evidence of a coercive state.

This volume seeks not to deny the importance of charismatic and powerful individuals in shaping their times, but to correct distortions imposed by reading back modern concepts of state into times and places where they do not belong. Dethroning the state allows more room for environmental, religious, social, cultural, demographic, health, and intellectual changes, usually of greater importance to the inhabitants than the doings of kings. In particular, the third major point of interest in Southeast Asia for outsiders, its distinctive gender pattern which generally balanced the role of men and women in the economy, needs much more attention by a world which imagines itself only now discovering gender equality. The Southeast Asian pattern is one in which modernity gradually imposed patriarchy, as first the scriptural world religions, and then European models of state, corporation, and marriage, gradually become marked as "modern," while Southeast Asian complementarity became marked as rural, poor, and superstitious.

Since we are all brought up on modern maps that divide the world into differently colored national blocks, there is a seductive pressure to use these known contemporary boundaries to describe locations in an earlier period, thereby encouraging the inappropriate reading-back of national units into the past. When discussing the period before the nineteenth-century European demarcation of boundaries, I will endeavor to use geographical features such as islands and river catchment areas, notably the Irrawaddy, Chao Phraya, Mekong, and Red Rivers that dominate the pattern of human settlement in Mainland Southeast Asia. When other options fail, it will sometimes be necessary to refer to "what is today...". The narrow, mountainous peninsula which extends the Eurasian Mainland a further 1,300 km southward has been a refuge for exceptional pluralism throughout recorded history, making it particularly inappropriate to extend the nineteenth-century British label "Malay Peninsula" beyond the twentieth-century politicization of the term "Malay" (Montesano and Jory 2008). I have therefore called it the Southeast Asian Peninsula, or more frequently simply "the Peninsula."

Ethnic terms have had a way of shifting their meanings over time, usually beginning as exonyms applied by others but often ending as politicized and emotive signifiers in the nationalist era. I have sought to use language labels where these are known to express both specific groups and large language families such as those of Austronesian (Malayo-Polynesian) and Tai. "Thai" is restricted to those Tai further unified by the state commanding the Chao Phraya River. Ethnonyms do enter the literature before modern national identities, but I have sought to illustrate the nature of their usage by quotation rather than assuming that they have independent meaning.

I use Viet for lowland speakers of the language I call Vietnamese, though their own way of distinguishing themselves from "non-civilized" neighbors was (confusingly) as Han until the nineteenth century, while in the twentieth century Kinh (town-dweller) became officially accepted. The Viet kingdom in Tongking I call Dai Viet, and the southern Viet kingdom of the Nguyen that blossomed in the seventeenth and eighteenth centuries, Cochin-China (as did foreigners at the time).

Variants of the vernacular terms "Myanma," the written form, and "Bama," the spoken form, have become as controversial as Burma's politics. The English name for the country stabilized as Burma by the 1880s, and I have used that term for the state in all eras, despite Myanmar having been adopted by the country's military rulers (but rejected by the then-suppressed opposition) in

1989. The name of the largest language and ethnic group within that state was often also called Burmese, though Burman was used by some when the ethno-linguistic distinction needed emphasis in a multi-ethnic state. Recent official usage has favored Bama as the term for the lowland majority language (though less so ethnicity), and I have adopted it in this book as an appropriate linguistic and ethnic self-designation.

This book is intended to be lightly referenced, which has prevented me from adequately acknowledging the mountain of observation, insight, and scholarship on which it relies. If I were to begin to thank those from whom I have learned about Southeast Asia's countless peoples and experiences there would be no end to it. Let me simply thank those who have read some or all of the text and helped me get the balance right – Mary Somers Heidhues, John Sidel, Eric Tagliocozzo, Bob Moore, David Marr, Craig Reynolds, Li Tana, Pierre van der Eng, and Nicholas Cheesman. As always Helen was an indispensable support, companion, and gentle critic.

Bob Moore was patient beyond all reasonable expectation in waiting for this long-promised book in the series, and immensely helpful in steering it in an accessible direction. Tessa Harvey, Georgina Coleby, and their colleagues at Blackwell (which became Wiley Blackwell over the years) were most helpful in the publication process. Karina Pelling of CartoGIS at ANU drew wonderful maps. I am once again grateful to ANU's College of Asia and the Pacific for providing a generous welcome home for me since 2009. The Center for Southeast Asian Studies in Kyoto (2009–10) and the Wissenschaftskolleg zu Berlin (2012–13) provided wonderfully supportive and stimulating environments in which to do much of the writing.

GLOSSARY

A – Arabic; B – Bama; C – Chinese; D – Dutch; I – Indonesian; J – Javanese; Jp – Japanese; M – Malay; P – Portuguese; S – Spanish; Sk – Sanskrit; Tag – Tagalog; Th – Thai; V – Vietnamese.

áo dài (V)	modernized (1920s) form of Vietnamese female dress
bangsa (M/I)	modern race or nation, from older descent or caste
bangsawan (M)	modern staged theater in Malay, on Indian model
belacan (M)	garnish of fermented shrimp or other seafood
bissu (Bugis)	transsexual shamanic priest
blijver (D)	stayer (migrants), as opposed to transient sojourners
bungkus (M)	lit. "bundle"; home-made cigarettes with maize-leaf wrapper
casado (P)	locally domiciled [Portuguese with family]
cash	base Chinese-style coin with square hole for stringing. Anglicization of Portuguese *caixa*
chao (Th)	lord of a *muang*
chat (Th)	race or nation
cultuurstelsel (D)	[forced] cultivation system, of export crops primarily in Java
dalang (J)	puppeteer-narrator
Đàng Trong (V)	"the inner region"; Cochin-China or southern Viet Nam
dharma (Sk/Pali)	cosmic law or order; in Buddhism, the teaching, way, or duty
Đôi Mới (V)	"new change", Viet Nam reform program from 1986
Han (C/V)	common self-identification of Chinese, Koreans, Vietnamese having adopted "civilized" norms (of the Han and other dynasties)
hát bội (V)	Chinese-derived classical Viet Nam theater
hui (C)	(Chinese) association or society
ilustrado (S)	enlightened, in particular of elite Spanish-educated Filipinos
Indië (D)	India (the Indies, Indonesia)
Jawi (A)	Southeast Asian Muslim
kadi (M/I)	Islamic judge

kaum muda (M/I)	young group
kebaya (M)	light female upper garment; blouse
keroncong (I)	hybrid musical style featuring a ukelele-like instrument
kiwi (M)	traveling merchant, or crew with share in cargo
komedi (M)	commercial popular performance (from French *comédie*)
kongsi (C/M)	a partnership or cooperative association, particularly for business or mutual support (pinyin *gongsi*)
kretek (I)	clove cigarette (onomatopoeic)
kris (M/J)	wavy-bladed dagger
lingga (Sk)	symbolic male phallus, particularly emblematic of Shiva, often paired with female *yoni*
lukjin (Th)	Sino-Thai, typically with Chinese father and Thai or local mother
mestizo (S)	mixed, creole, particularly of Chinese-Filipino hybridity
Minh Hương (V)	"Ming exiles"; long-settled or hybridized Chinese in Viet Nam
muang (Th)	autonomous polity based on a single irrigated rice area
nagara (Sk)	town, city, Indic-style state
nakhoda (M)	supercargo or commander of a ship
Nanyang (C)	South Seas; Southeast Asia
nat (B)	unseen spirits, ubiquitous in Burma
negeri (M)	settlement, trade center, river-mouth state
nôm (V)	hybrid Viet-Chinese script (from *chữ nôm* = southern characters)
Nusantara (M)	The island world comprising today's Indonesia and Malaysia (from Malay *nusa* = islands; *antara* = between)
orang laut (M)	sea people
orangkaya (M)	merchant aristocrat (lit. rich person)
padi (M/I)	bunded rice field, flooded during growing season
parian (Tag)	Chinese quarter (of Manila)
peranakan (M)	local-born (of foreign fathers), particularly of hybridized Chinese Indonesians
pongyi (B)	(Theravada Buddhist) monk
raja (M/Sk)	king, ruler
rantau (M)	migrate, frontier of migration
romusha (Jp)	volunteer, the term used for forced laborers deployed by the Japanese
sangha (Pali)	the brotherhood of monks in Hinayana Buddhism
sarsuela (Tag)	light opera, musical romance (from Spanish *zarzuela*)
sarung (M)	wrap-around lower garment
sawah (M/I)	bunded and flooded rice field
sawbwa (B)	Shan hereditary chiefs of *muang* (from Shan *Saopha*)
seishin (Jap)	spirit
shari'a (A)	Islamic law
siwilai (Th)	civilized, or civilization
tarekat (M/I)	a mystical order with similar ritual practice, from *Tariqah* (A: way, method)

Tatmadaw (B)	National Armed Forces
totok (C)	China-born, or by extension Europe-born for Europeans
trepang (M/I)	sea-cucumber or bêche de mer, an echinoderm living on the sea floor.
ulama (A/M)	scholar and teacher of Islamic texts (plural of '*alim*, though used also as singular in Southeast Asia)
uleebalang (Aceh)	hereditary territorial chief in Aceh
Volksraad (D)	"People's Council," legislative assembly of Netherlands India, 1918–41
wayang (J/M)	theater
wayang kulit (J/M)	"leather theater"; Javanese shadow puppet theater
wujuddiyah (A)	a monist strain of Sufi mystical belief
yoni (Sk)	symbolic vagina, representing female procreative energy and matching male *lingga*
zhang (C)	miasma; diseases attributed to dangerous atmosphere of tropics

ABBREVIATIONS

ABRI	Angkatan Bersenjata Republik Indonesia; Armed Forces of the Indonesian Republic
AFPFL	Anti-Fascist People's Freedom League
ASA	Association of Southeast Asia
ASEAN	Association of Southeast Asian Nations
BCE	Before the Common Era (BC)
CE	Common Era (AD)
DRV	Democratic Republic of Viet Nam
GCBA	General Council of Buddhist (from 1920 Burmese) Associations
ICP	Indochinese Communist Party
ICS	Independent Chinese Schools (Malaysia)
ILO	International Labor Organization
ISEAS	Institute for Southeast Asian Studies, Singapore
JAS	*Journal of Asian Studies*
JSEAS	*Journal of Southeast Asian Studies*
KMT	Kuo Min Tang (pinyin *Guomindang*) "National Peoples' Party," the ruling nationalist party of China before 1949, and thereafter in Taiwan
KPM	Koninklijke Paketvaart Maatschappij (Royal Packet Navigation Company)
MCP	Malayan Communist Party
NGO	Non-Government Organization
NIT	Negara Indonesia Timur; State of East Indonesia
NU	Nahdlatul Ulama
PKI	Partai Komunis Indonesia
PNI	Partai Nasionalis Indonesia
PRB	Partai Rakyat Brunei; Brunei People's Party
PRC	People's Republic of China
PRRI	Pemerintah Revolusioner Republik Indonesia (Revolutionary Government of the Indonesian Republic – rebels of 1958–9)
SEAC	South-East Asia Command
SLORC	State Law and Order Restoration Council (Burma)
UMNO	United Malays National Organization
VOC	Vereenigde Oost-Indische Compagnie; [Dutch] United East India Company

[1] PEOPLE IN THE HUMID TROPICS

BENIGN CLIMATE, DANGEROUS ENVIRONMENT

Both the diversity and the coherence of the Southeast Asian story begin with its geology. Its scatter of islands and rivers emerged from the collision of continental plates. The northward-moving Australian and Indian plates, and the westward-moving Pacific plate, pushed up the chain of volcanic mountains that almost surround the region. Within these mountains lies the relatively stable Sunda shelf, which united Sumatra, Java, Borneo, and the Philippines with the Mainland during periods of global cold temperatures and low water levels. During the latest of these, in the ice age that preceded the global warming that made possible humanity's ascent in the last 10,000 years, Southeast Asia's equatorial environment must have been one of the world's most habitable, and the land bridges then carried the larger Eurasian mammals such as elephant, tiger, rhinoceros, monkey, deer, pig, and buffalo, as well as man, into all of the vast area now divided by the Java Sea and southernmost South China Sea. As the world's largest area of monsoonal humid tropics, Southeast Asia shared a pattern of rainforest and water that provided a background for human economic and social activity.

The region lies almost wholly within the tropics, and enjoys relatively even daytime temperatures around or a little below 30 degrees centigrade throughout the year. The exceptions are the northernmost parts of the region that do experience a mild winter in December/January when temperatures can fall below 20 degrees. Except in the dry zone of the upper Irrawaddy valley, rainfall is everywhere generous, between 100 and 400 cm a year, though with a variability that caused difficulties for settled agriculture. Although Southeast Asia's climate has been benign for humans, it is unusually prone to natural disasters in the long term, which may be a factor reversing population growth at certain periods. The great arc of mountains formed by the subduction of the northward-moving Australian plate beneath Sumatra, Java and the Lesser Sunda Islands curves northward to Sulawesi, Maluku, and the Philippines where the tectonic pattern is more complex. Farmers were attracted by the rich volcanic soils, giving most volcanically active Java and Bali the densest

A History of Southeast Asia: Critical Crossroads, First Edition. Anthony Reid.
© 2015 Anthony Reid. Published 2015 by John Wiley & Sons, Ltd.

population in the region and non-seismic Borneo the sparsest. Yet periodic mega-eruptions darkened the skies, poisoned the water, and covered the land with ash, causing crops to fail and populations to plummet.

Earthquakes wrought havoc on stone temples, but caused relatively little damage to houses built overwhelmingly of wood and thatch until modern times. The tsunamis that followed the worst events were a different matter, capable of wiping out coastal settlements and ports, and small-island populations. The destructiveness of the 2004 tsunami that claimed over 200,000 lives in Sumatra (chiefly), the Peninsula, and beyond, has been shown to have regular precedents every few centuries. Typhoons wreak havoc on coastal settlements in the Philippines and modern-day Viet Nam. El Niños having severe effects on Island Southeast Asia have been documented as far back as those of 1618, 1652, and 1660, and appear to have recurred with varying severity and periodicity at least once in a decade. They caused rainfall as low as a third of normal levels, and prolonged dry seasons that drove people out of settled areas in search of water and food. Despite the severity of these El Niños for the region (as demonstrated by the modern ones of 1982/3 and 1997), the smaller proportion of the Southeast Asian population dependent on settled rice agriculture rendered it somewhat less exposed to the severest El Niño famines than China and India. As discussed below in this chapter, the periodic volcanic eruptions of the island arc between Sumatra and Luzon devastated the populations dependent on a seasonal crop cycle, and thereby prolonged a balance with hunter-gathering and shifting agriculture that had disappeared elsewhere.

Seasonality in these humid tropics is marked above all by the monsoon winds. The warming and cooling of the great landmass to the north creates dependable winds from the northeast across the South China Sea in November–March, but in the opposite direction in the middle of the year. In the Bay of Bengal the winds are easterlies in November–March, and westerlies in the middle of the year. This dependable pattern of alternating wind-flows was highly favorable for sailing within Southeast Asia and the whole of the equatorial Indian Ocean, making this area the world's major cradle of commercial navigation. The same monsoonal alternation governs the variable patterns of rainfall.

The center of the region – its long central peninsula, southern and eastern Sumatra, Borneo, and western Java – as well as the eastern Philippines, has predictable high rainfall all year round (Map 1.1). This non-seasonal climate supported a lush growth of evergreen forest, through which the sun seldom penetrated. For human settlement it was in general discouraging, especially in the coastal marshes. The soils in this region are clays of poor fertility except where improved by recent volcanic activity – as in Java and west Sumatra. The nutrients falling as leaves are more quickly broken down in tropical conditions, and recycled through the forest biomass rather than building up topsoil suitable for agriculture. The equilibrium of these forests is therefore precarious, and removal of the canopy can quickly lead to leaching of the remaining nutrients and subsequent erosion by the combined effect of sun and torrential rain. Such forests also contain relatively few edible wild plants and suitable game. Without a dry season, clearing and burning the forest presented a major obstacle, and many crops could not ripen satisfactorily. Until the late eighteenth-century era of immigration and commercial agriculture, therefore, most of this central equatorial zone remained very thinly peopled.

In most of the Mainland, on the other hand, there is a marked dry season around January–April. In the mountainous parts of this region the streams continue to run through the dry season, because the mountains attract more rain and groundwater returns to the streams as their level drops. The dry season and the cooler temperatures provide a more open forest pattern with lower bushes, ferns, and grasses suitable for a variety of larger mammals. The higher land of these Mainland dry-season zones supported a large population of deer, pigs, elephants, tigers, and rhinoceros, as well as smaller animals. To a much greater extent than in the equatorial forests of perennial rain or the smaller islands, these Mainland regions provided both meat for hunters and deerskins, ivory, and rhinoceros horn for the export trade.

In the deltas of the great rivers of this zone, the land dries out completely during the dry season except in immediate proximity to the great rivers themselves. These deltas provide excellent conditions for rice-growing, as the alluvial soil is annually enriched by flooding and the wet season provides abundant water for one or even two crops. At least since the sixteenth century, large

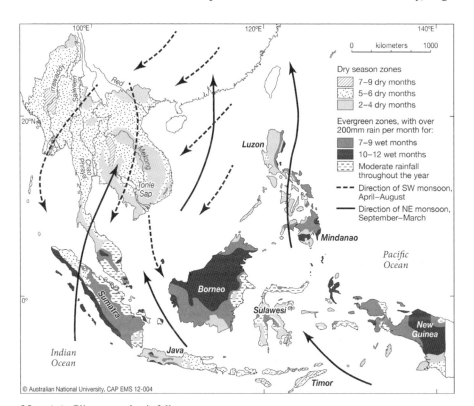

Map 1.1 Climate and rainfall.

surpluses were garnered from varieties of rice which grew two or three meters tall as the flood waters rose each year in the flood plains of the Mekong, Chao Phraya, Salween, and Irrawaddy Rivers.

Unfortunately these deltas are not so suitable for human settlement. In the wet season vast regions disappear completely under water. A million hectares are annually flooded in the Chao Phraya delta alone. In the dry season there is no fresh water at all. Only along the natural banks of the rivers was settlement convenient before the era of modern drainage and irrigation methods. What population there was in these deltas before 1800 was concentrated almost wholly along the riverbanks.

Only the Vietnamese mastered the difficult task of intensive delta agriculture before the nineteenth century. Applying similar techniques to those used in many Chinese deltas, Vietnamese began already to tame the Red River delta at least a thousand years ago, building dykes along the river to prevent flooding, and a complex pattern of irrigation that enabled them to grow rice during the dry season.

The eastern part of Java and the Lesser Sunda Island chain to its east experience an even more marked dry season from May to September, in places extending to more than six months. The volcanic soil of some of these islands is highly suitable for agriculture, and in Bali and Lombok in particular there are streams and springs flowing throughout the year which have for many centuries been directed into bunded rice fields on the sloping foothills of the mountains. Further east, rice is more difficult to sustain in the progressively drier terrain, and the eastern Indonesian islands subsisted chiefly on tubers, sago, or millet until the advent of American maize. For commercial crops such as cotton, however, the prolonged dry season was a distinct advantage.

While the eastern Philippines facing the Pacific experiences year-long rain comparable to Malaya and Sumatra, the western areas of that archipelago have a pattern similar to the Mainland with a marked dry period between December and March. The volcanic soils and the gently sloping terrain of the central valley of Luzon provided excellent conditions for rice-growing in river-fed bunded fields, and traces of rice husks have been found in the Cagayan Valley from the second millennium BCE. This has led Bellwood (2005) to hypothesize that it was the earliest Austronesian-speakers to migrate southward from Taiwan to Luzon and beyond more than 3,000 years ago who introduced rice cultivation to the islands.

FORESTS, WATER, AND PEOPLE

For most of the 60,000 or more years in which *Homo sapiens* inhabited these humid tropics, the dense forests and warm shallow seas and waterways provided the sole livelihood and context for life. While forest-dwelling and seaborne foragers have proved unusually able to retain some of these lifestyles even amidst modern changes, it is a mistake to equate the modern "tribal" peoples of the Peninsula and elsewhere with the original pre-agricultural populations of 8,000 years ago. Anthropologists have carefully documented the intense interactions of survival strategies, languages, and cultures between agricultural and non-agricultural people. Since foraging was always more rewarding around the fecund coastlines and the forest fringes than in the dark primary forest, hunter-gatherers have never been isolated. Southeast Asia is uniquely penetrated by water among major world zones, most of its land surface being within 200 km of tidewater. Canoeing around rivers and coastal waters probably pre-dated agriculture as a necessary aid to foraging. The tropical forest had unique assets in terms of plant resources and refuge from attackers coming usually by water. But for ancient as for modern populations, dwelling wholly in the deep forest was not undertaken by choice.

Some things can be deduced about the past, however, from studies of contemporary forest-dwellers. Firstly, that the humid forests of year-round rainfall in Central Southeast Asia were difficult but not impossible for human populations, which probably first settled areas of less dense forest in the northern Mainland and the eastern islands. It was also in areas of a significant dry season and open forest that fire became useful as a tool in taming the forest, and that the earliest domestication of plants and animals took place. The primary forest did, however, provide one key tool for pre-metal hunter-gatherers in the blowpipe, and the dart dipped in vegetable poisons to stun the monkeys, mouse-deer, or other small prey of the forest. Many types of rattan and palm of the forest also provided the equipment for fish-traps and baskets for the abundant sea life of the coasts.

Secondly, hunter-gatherer and beach-foraging societies tended to remain small-scale as long as they did not make the shift to agriculture. Any large concentration of population could quickly impoverish the coastal or forest food stocks on which hunter-gatherers depended. Hence there was always high mobility, as particular kin-groups either moved as a whole in search of resources, or split up as the younger families sought their own territories to exploit elsewhere. Agriculturalists and hunter-gatherer societies have coexisted and interacted in Southeast Asia for at least 5,000 years, and the choice of means of livelihood was as much about the scale of social unit particular communities preferred to operate in, as about the technologies involved.

Prior to the Holocene warming of 10,000–12,000 years ago, the occupants of Southeast Asia were chiefly what Bellwood calls Australo-Melanesians, occupying a territory much less watery than it became with the glacial melting. There remained even in the glacial period the deep trench of the "Wallace line" to the east of Borneo and Bali, which they somehow crossed to populate also the easternmost islands including New Guinea and Australia. In New Guinea they independently developed tuber-based agriculture while in Australia they retained a hunter-gatherer lifestyle better adapted to the environment. These pre-Holocene settlers in Southeast Asia are presumed to be the ancestors of modern groups labeled *negritos* by earlier ethnographers on the basis of their dark skin, crinkly hair, and short stature. They had succeeded, in the Philippines and the Peninsula, in avoiding conquest or absorption by incoming agriculturalists by clinging to a stateless hunter-gatherer lifestyle, though their interaction with the agriculturalists was extensive enough that they adopted Austronesian languages in the Philippines and Mon-Khmer ones in the Peninsula, followed by a recent Malay overlay.

In the Philippines, where they are estimated to have comprised as many as 10% of the population around 1600, a Spanish chronicler described them as:

> A barbarous race who live on fruits and roots of the forest. They go naked, covering only the privies with some articles ... made from the bark of trees.... They have no laws or letters, or other government or community than that of kinsfolk.... The Spanish call them Negrillos because many of them are as much negroes as are the Ethiopians themselves, both in their black colour and in their kinky hair ... In one of the large islands there are so many of them, that it is for that reason called the island of Negros. Those blacks were apparently the first inhabitants of these islands, and they have been deprived of them by the civilized nations who came later by way of Sumatra, the Javas, Borneo, Macassar (Colin 1663, cited Minter 2010, 37–8).

In 2000 there were still over 30,000 such people in Luzon, Palawan, Mindanao, Panay, and Negros, the best survivors being the Agtas of Northeast Luzon and Aetas of the Mount Pinatubo area of Western Luzon. There were about another 6,000 in the Peninsula, largely Semang or Sakai clustered on both sides of the current Malaysia-Thailand border.

From Sumbawa eastward to Timor and in the islands eastward of Sulawesi there is a gradation of mixings between the older settlers and Austronesians, though most now speak Austronesian languages. At least in Flores, the Australo-Melanesians appear to have interacted with the *Homo floresiensis*, of whom a group of skeletons were discovered in 2003 and quickly dubbed "hobbits" because they were little more than a meter tall. Although some have argued that they merely represent a pathological malformation of *H. sapiens*, they seem more likely to have been a distinct species. Perhaps they were related to the *Australopithecus* or *H. erectus*, the result of the first migration out of Africa over a million years ago, of which skeletal remains have been turning up in Java since they first caused a stir in 1891 as "Java-man", and more recently also in Flores. Whichever way the controversy is resolved, the survival of *H. floresiensis* alongside modern *H. sapiens* much later than had been experienced elsewhere on earth dramatically demonstrates the capacity of the humid tropics to retain a unique degree of biological diversity.

WHY A LOW BUT DIVERSE POPULATION?

Only in the twentieth century did censuses provided comprehensive population data for Southeast Asia. To estimate earlier populations we must combine surviving reports from travelers (often relying on royal head-counts since lost), backward projection from the known figures, and the trends from those few limited areas for which long-term data are available (in particular areas relatively tightly controlled by the Dutch or Spanish). These methods suggest an overall Southeast Asian population of less than 25 million around 1600, with major concentrations already in Java, Bali, and the Red River delta, but densities in most other places below five per square kilometer. Yet humans had been continuously present in the Asian tropics longer than in most parts of the planet, surviving the last ice age there, and developing agriculture some 5,000 years ago.

Why then did Southeast Asia's demographic catch-up with the denser populations of Europe, India, China, and Japan occur only in the last two centuries? Natural disasters may be a factor in the island chain from Sumatra to Luzon. It is fertile in volcanically enriched soils but also exposed to natural disasters from its location on the most active tectonic interface of the whole Pacific "ring of fire" (Map 1.2). Because geological research in this dangerous region lags behind that in the affluent world, the pre-twentieth-century record is largely guesswork except for the two mega-eruptions that grabbed the world's attention, Tambora (1815) and Krakatau (1883). Major tectonic traumas certainly punctuated Island Southeast Asia's history, but we still know more about them from ash deposits on the polar ice caps and human records in the northern hemisphere than about their poorly researched effects at their origin. Tsunamis may not have as great a demographic impact, but they destroyed coastal ports and fishing communities, deterring later settlement along these exposed coasts. The Philippine archipelago has also a tragic history of typhoons. More than most, therefore, agricultural population of Southeast Asia's Islands must be understood to have flourished during the benign intervals, such as the period 1840–2000, between major natural disasters.

The same factor helps explain Southeast Asia's remarkable human and biological diversity, particularly evident in the most exposed arc of tectonic subduction around the region's southern and eastern rim. It was in highly volcanic Flores that the "hobbit" was discovered to have survived the advent of

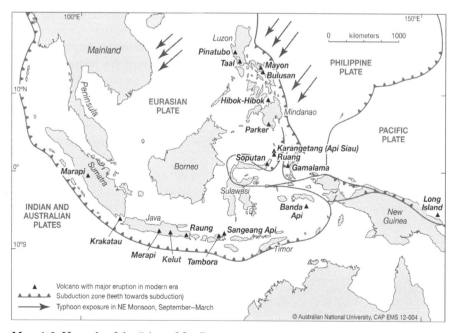

Map 1.2 Hazards of the "ring of fire."

modern humans. The principal areas of Negrito survival are also in areas exposed to mega-disasters, notably Pinatubo and Kanlaon volcanoes in Luzon and Negros, respectively, and the east coast of Luzon most exposed to terrible typhoons. Disasters may have checked the expansion of their agriculturalist rivals. The Austro-Melanesian Aeta people reacted to Pinatubo's 1991 eruption, which destroyed a quarter of a million homes and livelihoods in Luzon, with a flexibility and mobility in locating food sources that settled populations could not. After typhoons, it had been noted, poor agriculturalists sought to marry into Aeta families for survival. It seems likely, therefore, that just as rapid expansion of agriculture and population has threatened the extinction of hunter-gatherers in the last two hundred years, similar expansions threatened them in the past only to be checked by natural disaster.

Southeast Asia's biological, as well as human, diversity was also protected by these periodic setbacks to agriculture from natural crises. The transition to agriculture itself appears to have been unusually complex and gradual in the Asian tropics. Modern studies have shown that a greater range of plants is domesticated in Southeast Asia than in any other world region. This makes it almost certain that some of them were independently domesticated there, not introduced as part of a migrant "package." Likely candidates are yams, taro, Job's tears, betelnut (areca), banana, sago, and even sugar cane.

Even non-seismic Mainland Southeast Asia was much less densely settled than China and India, however, so broader causes must also be at play. One may have been changes in sea level, some 50 meters below its present level during the last ice age 10,000 years ago, but between 2.5 and 6 meters *higher* than at present only 4,000 years ago. At that latter date the major river deltas that today support much of Southeast Asia's population were under water. Another factor may paradoxically have been the benign warmth and high rainfall itself, which produced dense forest and facilitated modes of production that did not require population concentration. The systems of forest and seashore foraging, nomadic shifting cultivation, and low-level warfare and raiding without strong states all made relatively light labor demands but required mobility and the capacity to survive frequent crop failures. Especially when combined, as it usually was, with the need for constant vigilance against raids from neighboring communities in a stateless environment, this system encouraged small family size. Many Southeast Asian societies practiced infanticide or abortion to space and limit childbirth.

Apart from the exceptional Viet development of the Red River delta, the earliest centers of intensive rice-growing appear to have been in upland valleys of the dry-season zone, and in the sloping foothills of the island massifs. In the first category are Irrawaddy tributaries of the dry zone of Burma, the northern tributaries of the Chao Phraya around Chiang Mai, Nan, and Sukhothai, and the upper Mekong valley basins centered on Vientiane and Luang Prabang. By the thirteenth century all these valleys were practicing a form of wet-rice agriculture in bunded fields watered by upland streams and rivers. The early development of such centers of irrigated rice fields supports the view that the bulk of the Tai (the language family embracing modern Thai, Lao, and Shan) population up until the fifteenth century was far up these rivers, not in the lower Chao Phraya as it is today. The ruler of Luang Prabang enumerated 300,000 male Lao subject to corvée as well as 400,000 non-Tai under his authority in 1376, while another successful Lao ruler around 1640 enumerated 500,000 male subjects capable of bearing arms. Such figures suggest a Tai population well over a million in the northern valleys at a time when the lower Chao Phraya was an unmanageable swamp.

Whenever strong rulers maintained internal peace and encouraged sedentary agriculture, population appears to have grown rapidly, as in fifteenth-century Dai Viet, Siam, and Lan Na (Chiang Mai). Dai Viet, adopting some bureaucratic, military, and agricultural innovations encountered in the brief Chinese occupation of 1405–27, acquired the demographic base in Red River delta agriculture to put armies in excess of 200,000 in the field against Champa in the south, Tai-Lao kingdoms in the west, and even Yunnan. The Siamese kingdom took shape around Ayutthaya, which used the hitherto malarial lower Chao Phraya River as a base for both rice agriculture in the flood plain, and a vigorous external trade. Lan Na (literally, "million rice fields"), and in the following century Lan Sang (Vientiane), profited from strong rulers and advanced rice agriculture to become important population centers in the upper Chao Phraya and Mekong, respectively.

Population increase of this type did not usually long outlast the ruler who provided stable conditions. Wars and periods of disorder caused death rates to rise and birth rates to fall, not so much through battle casualties as displacement, destruction of food stocks, inability to get in the vital harvests, and disease. A ferocious civil war between 1545 and 1592 appears to have reduced the Vietnamese population by about a fifth. The Burmese conquest of Siam in 1567 is thought to have caused population losses not made good for two centuries, while the sixteenth-century heartland of a flourishing Burmese kingdom around Pegu was in turn reduced to a wasteland by war and the resulting famine and disease in 1598–1600.

During the fifteenth and sixteenth centuries the vigor of international trade brought prosperity to coastal ports and power to their rulers. The population that had in most places (except Dai Viet) been concentrated in upland valleys congenial for both agriculture and human life began to shift toward the coast. People moved to the vicinity of the port-capitals to share in their prosperity, but many were also brought there involuntarily by the better-armed and organized states. In this period the demographic center of gravity which had previously been in upland Siam and Burma, and in the Angkor area of Cambodia, shifted downstream to the areas around the port-capitals of this period – Pegu, Ayutthaya, and Phnom Penh, respectively. Whereas there were several flourishing Tai-speaking states in the upper reaches of the Chao Phraya and Mekong Rivers in the sixteenth century, all were subordinated to the major lowland states by 1820, and experienced little further population gain until the nineteenth century. In Burma, the same southward shift occurred during the heyday of Pegu in the fifteenth and sixteenth centuries, but was reversed with the devastation of Pegu and the return of the capital inland around 1600. Only 26% of the population lived in Lower Burma (the southern third of the modern country) at the Burmese census in 1785, though 58% did so at the first British census in 1891.

In Java, the northern coast that boasted such new ports as Gresik, Surabaya, Demak, Japara, Cirebon, and Banten became the center of civilization and population for the first time. Elsewhere, other wealthy port-cities like Melaka, Aceh, Banten, Makassar, and Spanish Manila increased their population by attracting or coercing the nomads and shifting cultivators of their hinterlands to come and serve them. But these Early Modern cities were relatively unhealthy places (like pre-modern cities everywhere) and could only remain populous by a constant influx of migrants and captives. This gunpowder age, moreover, increased the scale of warfare, and the population loss it caused. Long-term political stability reached most rural areas only in the nineteenth century, and only then did serious population increase begin.

Southeast Asia began its modern demographic transition (a decrease in mortality followed several generations later by a decrease in fertility) as an alien model of bureaucratic state established internal order during a relatively benign period for natural disasters. This happened first in the Philippines (eighteenth century), then in Java and the major states of the Mainland (nineteenth), and finally in Laos and many areas of Indonesia outside Java, where colonial conquest around 1900 coincided with the onset of sustained population growth (see Chapter 13).

AGRICULTURE AND MODERN LANGUAGE FAMILIES

The diverse language families that today dominate Southeast Asia moved southward out of what is today southern China and the eastern Himalayas. The fact that Asians first made the transition to rice agriculture in the lakes area just south of the middle Yangzi appears the main reason why Chinese or proto-Chinese people gradually pushed southward the peoples not willing to be absorbed into the Chinese Empire. Whereas cultural features largely link Southeast Asians to South Asia, therefore, genetic and linguistic ones make it closer to East Asia.

Peter Bellwood (2005), building on the linguistic hypothesis of Blust (1995), has been the most persistent synthesizer of archaeological, linguistic, and recently genetic data on the likely origins of the contemporary Southeast Asian population. His argument for Southeast Asia and the Pacific, like Colin Renfrew's (1987) for Europe, is that the population advantage enjoyed by the pioneers in the transition from hunter-gathering to agriculture is the best explanation for the very wide dispersal of some language families – notably the Indo-European and the Austronesian. Not only did agriculture provide higher and more reliable nutrient products for effort expended and encourage permanent settlement in sizable (and therefore militarily effective) communities, it encouraged higher fertility by reducing the mobility of women and by providing soft weaning foods (such as rice porridge) which reduced the need for several years of breast-feeding and thereby reduced the necessary intervals between births. In their expansion southward at the expense of older hunter-gatherer inhabitants of Southeast Asia, the Neolithic (agricultural) pioneers may often have used the force of their larger communities, including the incorporation of hunter-gatherer women. Fundamentally they simply out-populated their rivals.

Bellwood's scheme has rice agriculture originating in the Middle Yangzi valley about 7,000 BCE and gradually spreading southward to other headwater areas in Guangdong by 3,000–4,000 BCE and parts of Yunnan somewhat later. This diffusionism must be balanced, however, with recent genetic evidence that the two main strains of modern cultivated rice, Japonica and Indica, were separately domesticated, the first in south China and the second in India and/or Mainland Southeast Asia. At any event, peoples practicing "a widespread Mainland Southeast Asian Neolithic expression," including rice agriculture and common patterns of red-incised pottery, appear at sites dated between 2300 and 1500 BCE in the middle levels of Red, Mekong, and Chao Phraya river systems (Bellwood 2005, 131). These peoples appear also to have brought a related set of languages we now call the Austroasiatic family, including the ancestors of Mon and Khmer in one branch and Vietnamese and Muong in another. This family dominated these river systems until the arrivals of speakers of Tai and Tibeto-Burman languages several millennia later, and continues to dominate lowland modern Cambodia (Khmer). Vietnamese is controversial, many seeing it as somehow surviving a thousand years of Chinese overlay, though recent scholarship proposes it assumed its essential shape only in the tenth/eleventh centuries CE as a hybrid of proto-Viet-Muong with a southern dialect of middle Chinese previously dominant (Map 1.3).

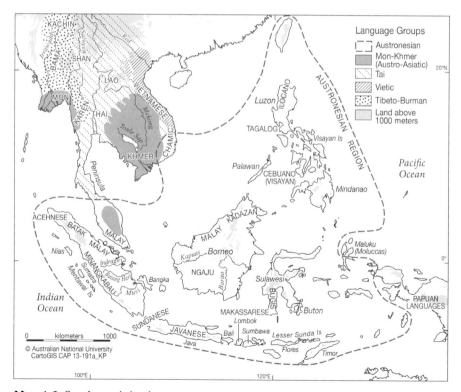

Map 1.3 Southeast Asian language groups.

The older human settlers who had lived in the tropical areas for 40,000 years or more, since before the ice age, and shared characteristics of darker skin, round eyes, and frizzy hair with the peoples of Australia and New Guinea, appear to have been largely assimilated or wiped out in this process, though in complex ways involving long-term interaction between foraging and agricultural lifestyles. Only in the southerly island arc, as explained above, did some remarkably survive as hunter-gatherers.

The Austronesian language dispersion is one of the world's most remarkable, having apparently spread in less than a thousand years from Taiwan throughout Island Southeast Asia and into Melanesia and western Polynesia. The ancestor of this language family, including both aboriginal Taiwan and Malayo-Polynesian languages, may have arrived in Taiwan from the mainland as early as 3500 BCE, although the evidence of its having carried rice agriculture with it comes from only 2500 BCE. The evidence of similar pottery types to those of Taiwan, with rice grains indicating agriculture, is then found in the northern Philippines from about 2000 BCE, and spread very quickly to eastern Indonesia, Melanesia, and as far as Samoa by 1400 BCE. Sumatra, Java, and southern Borneo, by this reckoning, formed a different dispersion network, dominated by different types of ceramics, but which similarly spread rice agriculture very rapidly from its Taiwan source.

It was this south-western dispersion that was the most complete, almost obliterating the previous population in Borneo, Sumatra, Java, Bali, and Sulawesi. It would appear that the dense forest cover had sustained only a sparse hunter-gatherer population previous to the Austronesian dispersion, and they were readily absorbed. The only survivals as hunter-gatherers in these islands, the Kubu in central Sumatra and the Punan of eastern Sarawak (Borneo), appear to have once also been agriculturalists, but less successful or aggressive ones, who retreated into hunter-gathering activity in the forest fringe under pressure from other agriculturalists. In the Philippines, on the other hand, the Negrito Agtas of highland Luzon and the Batak of Palawan appear to have retained hunter-gatherer lifestyles consistently, but under increasingly desperate conditions. They long ago adopted variants of the Austronesian dialects of the newcomers. Yet although the Austronesian immigrants were highly successful in absorbing or obliterating their predecessors, they became diversified among themselves, with many distinct Austronesian languages surviving into modern Indonesia, the Philippines, and southern Viet Nam.

The dominant populations of the Irrawaddy valley today, Bama, Chin, and Kachin, are part of a very diverse family usually known as Tibeto-Burman, comprising also several hundred languages in the eastern Himalayas. Like the other language families discussed, this one may have originated with the pioneer rice-cultivators in the region of the middle Yangzi, and it shares a tonal system with Chinese, Tai languages, and Vietnamese (though not the older Mon-Khmer). It has also been linked to Chinese in a Sino-Tibetan umbrella group, but the distance is there much greater. Karens, now occupying the higher ground around the current Thai-Burma border, also speak a range of dialects problematically linked to this family. The spread southward of Bama occurred probably only about a thousand years ago – before 1112 AD, when the Myazedi inscription was written in four languages (Pali, Mon, Pyu, and Bama). The diversity of this language family, however, suggests long occupation of the mountainous Himalayan borderlands on the borders of what are now China, India, and Southeast Asia.

Finally, the second most widespread language family of modern Southeast Asia, the Tai or Austro-Tai speakers, appear to have arrived, or at least made their presence known through the first evidence of an inscription (at Nakhon Sawon), only in 1167 AD. Tai-speaking groups, including those speaking today's Thai and Lao national languages and the Shan of Burma's northeast, are widespread also in southern China from Yunnan to Guangdong, and may have had their origin further north in the area of earliest rice agriculture in the middle Yangzi valley. Carrying their languages, an efficient form of upland rice agriculture involving some channeling of small rivers, and a pattern of numerous autonomous *muang* (small polities) centered on a fortified citadel and a charismatic leader, they must have moved southward in the eleventh to thirteenth centuries. A final impetus for military and political elites to move south may have been the expanding southward under aggressive Mongol rule (1279–1368) of the border of Chinese-style bureaucratization, but the process of settlement must have been taking place imperceptibly over a longer period. Many older Mon- and Khmer-speaking communities were absorbed, but others continued in their separate valleys, creating a mosaic of pluralities in the highlands of Mainland Southeast Asia. In the late thirteenth century, Tai-speaking rulers, in alliance with Theravada Buddhism, very quickly established a series of *muang* dominating the upper Chao Phraya and middle Mekong river valleys, and in the fourteenth even making their mark throughout the highly plural Peninsula.

THE RICE REVOLUTION AND POPULATION CONCENTRATION

For almost all Southeast Asians except the Viet, the relative lightness of population pressure on the land made swidden or shifting cultivation the favored method of producing food crops. As was reported of sixteenth-century Maluku (east Indonesia), the farmers "make clearings, which they burn off; and with pointed sticks they make holes in them, in which they put two or three grains, covering them with the foot or hands" (Galvão 1544/1971, 133). The ash left by the burn-off added enough nutrients to the soil to allow a harvest of dry rice, millet, or various root crops. Little weeding was done, and rice sheaves were cut individually as they ripened among the other new growth. This means of cultivation was profligate of land, since it required a fallow period of ten years or more before the forest had regrown enough to allow the farmer to return to repeat the process in the same area. But in upland soils it gave the highest return of any method for a family's input of labor. Moreover, root crops and vegetables could be grown alongside the main rice crop or after it, which increased the self-sufficiency of a family and its security against the failure of any particular crop. Until the nineteenth century the majority of Southeast Asia's farm population was occupied with this swidden method, and until well into the twentieth it affected a larger area than did permanent irrigated agriculture.

By the thirteenth century we can, however, point confidently to some irrigated areas of intensive wet-rice agriculture, producing rice surpluses which in many cases supported complex urban life and culture. It seems likely that especially in northern Southeast Asia these developed as part of the process that Mark Elvin (1973, 113–45) has described as an "agricultural revolution" in southern China, whereby more intensive rice-growing techniques were developed and then generalized in roughly the ninth to thirteenth centuries. These changes were much better documented in China than in Southeast Asia, but it is clear that improvements were not limited to one written culture (though Chinese agricultural manuals may have helped generalize techniques between China and Viet Nam), but passed back and forth wherever they were found useful. Some techniques, including double-cropping, terracing, and some irrigation devices, were almost certainly older in parts of Southeast Asia than in China. The best-known new variety of rice in south China was said to be from Champa (in what is now south-central Viet Nam), introduced through Dai Viet and Fujian and popularized widely on imperial orders in the eleventh century because it ripened faster and could cope with poorer soils and dryer conditions than other types.

The chief elements of this agricultural revolution were the plough, capable when pulled behind a buffalo of turning over the soil, not simply scratching it; transplanting seeds from a carefully prepared and protected seed-bed; quick-ripening strains of rice making double-cropping easier; and improved techniques of irrigation through damming streams, partitioning and flooding fields as seedlings grew, and moving water through a variety of bucket devices or pumps. The effect of these improvements in rice cultivation in China was to shift the balance of population from the wheat-growing north, which contained three-quarters of China's population in the third to fifth centuries, to the rice-growing south, which contained more than three-quarters by the thirteenth century. Mainland Southeast Asia experienced the same transformation.

Upriver Mainland Southeast Asia underwent a particularly rapid expansion in population and in wet-rice agriculture in the period of benign climate between about 1400 and 1550, following the expansion of Tai-speaking populations and the disruptive intervention of Ming Chinese troops. Chinese observers in the sixteenth century noted that the rice fields of the upper Mainland rivers were more productive than any they knew in China. The use of the plough was widespread, as were two wet-rice crops per year. The golden age of fifteenth century expansion enjoyed by the northernmost Tai-speaking *muang* such as Lan Na and Ahom in Assam, as well as by Dai Viet, owed much to superior rice technology making possible a rapid rise in Tai and Viet populations, respectively, though also to the introduction of more advanced firearms from China.

Analysis of the rice husks left at archaeological sites has revealed a shift by the ninth and tenth centuries from a round-grain type of rice resembling modern *Japonica* types to the long-grain *Indica* rice strains that have dominated modern Southeast Asia. This seems to coincide with the effective use of dry zones for irrigated agriculture in Upper Burma, the Khorat plateau, and the Angkor plain. It may also indicate a shift from reliance on broadcasting seed prior to the annual floods of the larger rivers, to a more labor-intensive system of creating bunded fields away from the disaster-prone flood plains.

In the Archipelago, the earliest evidence of wet-rice agriculture in irrigated fields comes from inscriptions in upland parts of Java and Bali, where small rivers, especially the higher tributaries of the Brantas River in east Java, point to the cooperative digging of irrigation canals as early as the ninth and tenth centuries. As in the Mainland, these are intramontane valleys in an upland area with a substantial dry season. In the Java uplands there is the additional factor of nearby active volcanoes (Mounts Kelud, Kawi, Arjuno, Penanggungan), which added to the fertility of the soil but caused periodic traumas that included changes to the river courses. In Bali there is evidence for the existence of the self-regulating irrigation associations or guilds (*subak*) as early as 1022.

In southern and central Sumatra, as in the Malay Peninsula and Borneo, the relative constancy of rainfall, with no substantial dry season, created a thick forest less favorable to early elaborations of irrigation systems for rice. The exceptions were in the mountain valleys of the Batak, Minangkabau, Korinci, Rejang, and Besemah, where there is only half the rainfall of the west coast and a dry season of three months or more, and along the north coast of what is now Aceh, the most conducive coastal area of Sumatra for wet-rice. Pollen evidence suggests that rice was being cultivated in the highlands around Lake Toba and Lake Korinci more than 2,000 years ago. The principal concentrations of population in the central "wet" zone of Southeast Asia (Sumatra, Malaya, Borneo) before colonial intrusion were in fact in these high valleys (above 500 m) of the western mountain spine of Sumatra, and in the Hulu Sungei area over 100 km up the Nagara River in south Borneo, not in the coastal areas known to travelers and therefore to historians. When the first European observers penetrated into these valleys in the early nineteenth century they were astonished at the sophistication and intensity of irrigated rice fields. The earliest physical remains of civilization have been found not in the coastal ports which sustained the well-known states (Palembang/Sriwijaya, Jambi, Siak), but nearer the headwaters of the east Sumatran rivers. The megaliths of the Besemah plateau, and Dongson-like bronzes near the highland lakes of Kerinci and Ranau, go back to the first five centuries of our era. And even in the period after the seventh century, when there were maritime states near river-mouths known to the world outside, some of the most important Buddhist temple sites were in highlands very far up the Barumun (Bila), Inderagiri, and Batang Hari Rivers, where there is little historic evidence for states.

THE AGRICULTURAL BASIS OF STATE AND SOCIETY

The state-resisting tendency we noted above was rooted in the environment and demography of the region. It was most marked in the Archipelago minus Java, the coastal forests of which were thinly populated, inhospitable, and impenetrable. Access to the more populous upland areas was only through the numerous rivers, each of which had a larger or smaller port-state near its mouth. This port-state could to some extent dominate the interior economically by channeling imports and exports, but with its small population of maritime traders it had no capacity to dominate militarily, and its agents seldom even penetrated into the stateless highlands. Moreover, the pattern of shifting cultivation described above was antithetic to the development of states. The availability of a storable and taxable rice surplus required a settled and concentrated population cultivating irrigated fields.

Earlier scholars examining the evidence of Chinese Imperial reports, Sanskrit inscriptions, and temple remains were inclined to assume substantial kingdoms ruling over subject populations. Since this interpretation was at odds with the diffuse power structures Europeans encountered in the nineteenth century, they resorted to presumptions of decline and decadence. Today's historians, informed both by archaeological evidence for relatively dispersed settlements, and by better understandings of pre-colonial polities, have read more critically both Chinese reports of barbarian *kuo* (countries, polities, or cities) sending tribute, and the grandiloquent Indic titles of many inscriptions. In reality such polities as took shape in the first millennium CE featured a multiplicity of autonomous centers with shifting loyalties, as one focus of trade could readily give way to another.

The earliest Chinese reports of *kuo* in Southeast Asia appear to be entrepôts along the main trade routes, though often linked with areas where a simple flood recession form of rice growing could be practiced along rivers. Thus Chinese records give us Funan (c.250–540 CE), which modern archaeology has associated with settlement sites and canal formations between Oc Eo, the point on the Gulf of Thailand most accessible to the lower Mekong, and Angkor Borei. They also record Linyi (and later Champa) at a similar period in what is today central Viet Nam, probably to be associated with sites excavated at Tra Kieu; and Langkasuka covering portage routes across the Peninsula, now associated with temple remains and settlements near Chaiya on the east coast and Takuapa on the west.

Despite the greater trade of most of these centers with China than with India, and the much greater knowledge shown by Chinese than Indian sources about them, when they began to speak for themselves it was in Sanskrit, for reasons explained in Chapter 2. Indian traders carried religious images, texts, and ritual specialists with them, so important were their gods to them as the basis for commercial trust. There is later evidence from the tenth and eleventh centuries of how Tamil merchant guilds used particular temples, images, and rituals to bind a network spanning the Indian Ocean. Traders and power-holders at Southeast Asian ports sought to command the same access to cosmic power and retribution, borrowing the new writing as a language for the gods.

The favorable position of Champa for trade and piracy on the sea route to China was matched by that of Sriwijaya in the Straits of Malacca area, through which traders and pilgrims between China and India had to pass. During the Song Dynasty (960–1279), when China-Southeast Asia commercial links began to flourish through the medium of the "tribute" trade, the three chief beneficiaries were Dai Viet (76 tribute missions in the period), Champa (62), and Sriwijaya (26). The remaining Southeast Asian states barely managed twenty missions between them, accurately reflecting the value of the China trade for these three polities.

Sriwijaya is again a term imposed by historians on what is now seen as a loose polity of rival river-ports. When it first sent embassies to China in the mid-seventh century it was probably centered in Melayu, near Jambi on the Batang Hari River, but later near modern Palembang. At times during a long career that endured until the thirteenth century this maritime civilization brought lesser ports throughout the Peninsula, Sumatra, and parts of Java into its orbit by funneling their exports to China.

These maritime centers, however, left relatively modest temple remains, and probably had shifting populations of traders who could be fed without major supplies of rice from irrigated fields. The most impressive temples requiring thousands of laborers are invariably located in the interior, at points where a large rice surplus could be conveniently concentrated. The earliest of these were in the Mataram area on the southern slopes of Mount Merapi near modern Yogyakarta, between the eighth and tenth centuries. A vast Buddhist stupa such as the Borobudur temple, along with nearby temples such as Sewu and Kalasan, must have required the coordinated labor of thousands over a substantial period. The Sailendra kings conventionally understood to have ruled this area were not conquerors like the Egyptian pharaohs, however, and are not mentioned as patrons of Borobudur. Piety and ritual obligations, rather than force, appear to have mobilized the necessary labor for building these monuments much as they provide the manpower for Balinese temple festivals today.

Nevertheless, Mataram does foreshadow the kingdoms that are more characteristic of Southeast Asia after the tenth century, when the exalted ideas of kingship associated with the foreign-influenced port-cities combined with a large population fed by some interior center of irrigated rice agriculture.

The two most northerly states of the region, in the Red (Hong) River delta and the upper Irrawaddy, were economically distinct from the pattern elsewhere and few generalizations can apply to them. The delta of Tongking was ruled by the Chinese Empire for most of the first millennium, and developed a type of deltaic agriculture common in southern China but virtually absent elsewhere in Southeast Asia. The extensive dykes built to control the annual flooding of the river required a relatively high degree of social control, but in return provided stable conditions for dependable annual yields supporting the most dense populations in pre-modern Southeast Asia. The most stable of the region's capitals had become established on the site of modern Hanoi by the seventh century. After the collapse of the Tang Dynasty in China, an independent Viet dynasty gradually took shape, occupying Hanoi in 1007 and withstanding subsequent Chinese invasions. From the thirteenth century it emulated Imperial methods of competitive examinations in the Chinese classics to build a state-serving bureaucracy. After a Ming occupation in 1406–28, a dynamic new Le Dynasty sought to remake Viet Nam as a centralized bureaucratic polity on Confucian lines, though the difficulty of the task is indicated by its repetition by other new dynasties, in the seventeenth and nineteenth centuries.

Irrigated, settled agriculture also developed early in the dry zone of Upper Burma, the exceptional area of below 60 cm rainfall through which the Irrawaddy flows between Mandalay and Pagan. It was the manageable Irrawaddy tributaries that flowed into this zone, the Mu River from the north, and the complex of four rivers of the Kyaukse area from the south, which proved ideal and dependable for the development of early irrigation systems from the time the first pre-Bama capitals arose in the seventh century CE. Their water came from areas of high rainfall outside the dry zone, but the gradient through the northern plains was gradual enough for most of the nutrients to be retained there. A complex series of canals and weirs was developed in the Kyaukse region in the eleventh to thirteenth centuries, making possible the civilization associated with Pagan (see Chapter 2). Modern estimates suggest that the Kyaukse irrigated area alone may have produced about 80,000 metric tons a year in this period, enough to feed half a million Burmese.

The agricultural basis of the Angkor complex in Cambodia, which was a major power center in the lower Mekong from the eighth century to the thirteenth, remains a matter of controversy. The older argument of Groslier and others was that the great artificial reservoirs (*baray*) of Angkor supplied a constant flow of water to multiple-cropped bunded fields capable of sustaining a concentrated population of up to a million people. More recent studies have ruled out irrigation of this type as the purpose of the reservoirs, suggesting that they were primarily for ritual purposes, as in India, and for water security through the dry season. There *were* permanently irrigated fields in Cambodia during Angkor's heyday, but they were probably not concentrated in one place as once thought. Like Pagan, in an unpromising area of the dry zone, the Angkor temple complex may have been primarily a ritual center, whose fluctuating population could be fed by transporting by boat and bullock-cart the abundant fish of Tonle Sap lake and the rice of a number of small-scale irrigated areas (see Chapter 2).

FOOD AND CLOTHES

The chief items of consumption and trade in pre-modern Southeast Asia were foodstuffs and wearing apparel. Diet was relatively plain, focused on rice and fish, differing only in opulence and variety for the rich and powerful.

Southeast Asia contributed its share of edible staples to the world's food supply. Three key sources of starch – bananas, yams (*Dioscoria alata*), and sago trees (*Metroxylon sagu*) – were native to Southeast Asia and were domesticated there as part of the Neolithic revolution. Taro (primarily *Colocasia esculenta*) was one of the earliest domesticated crops, perhaps first in India and Burma, and has been useful in swampier areas of the region for thousands of years. These four items were carried to the rest of tropical Asia, Africa, and the Pacific, at least in part by early Austronesian navigators, to form a large proportion of starch needs everywhere. Their widespread availability meant that most Southeast Asian villagers had direct and year-round access to at least one of these, as well as to forest foods in the wild. These remained important default foods when the preferred rice supply failed, so that "failures of crops or grains are never attended with those dreadful consequences which more improved countries ... experience" (Marsden 1811/1966, 64). Their cultivation could also be a preference for stateless hill peoples, since these dispersed crops could not be expropriated by a state as could a rice harvest on the valley floor. The prominent place occupied by taro in the highland areas of Java, especially Sundanese west Java up to 1800, may indeed have been motivated as much by the desire to be free of state levies as by soil types. In the Visayan Islands also taro remained important into the seventeenth century.

Poorer areas too dry, arid, or brackish to sustain rice made do with sago or yams as a starch, often adjusting to maize when that hardy crop spread through the region from the Americas around 1600. By that time, however, rice had become everywhere the preferred food for taste, for nutrition (as an almost complete food), and for ritual purposes. The wealthiest areas which could not grow their own rice, such as cities, spice-exporting areas, and some productive fishing grounds, could still eat imported rice produced in the most abundant of the rice bowls in central and east Java, and the flood plains of the Chao Phraya, Irrawaddy, and Salween.

The principal daily garnish of rice was not meat but fish. Fishing was undoubtedly the second industry after agriculture at all times before the twentieth century. Those close to fishing grounds along the coasts and in fish-rich lakes and rivers could eat their seafood fresh. Sources of meat, on the other hand, were relatively limited. There was as little of a pastoral or herding tradition as was possible in the great grasslands of Eurasia, and Europeans found in many areas that their demands for regular meat supplies quickly exhausted the supply. Feasting was the time for meat-eating, with a sacrificial slaughter preceding immediate distribution and consumption. Before the norms of Islam and Theravada Buddhism made a major impact (in accessible lowlands generally around the long sixteenth century), pigs were widely preferred for this purpose, whether domestic or hunted in adjacent forests.

At least by the seventeenth century, there were significant grasslands in areas where there was a marked dry season (the northwest and southeast margins of the region in particular), and where shifting cultivation had been practiced so intensively that grasslands had become permanent. As Islam came to rule out hunting wild pig in the forest, there is evidence that such grasslands were made permanent by deliberate human intervention, burning off in each dry season to ensure that either domestic cattle or wild deer for hunting had enough pasture to flourish. There were for example "savannahs" in the hills near seventeenth-century Aceh where herds of buffaloes were maintained for sale in the city market. From as early as the fourteenth century there was a trade in livestock from the dryer islands in the east – Bali, Madura, Sumbawa, and Sumba – to the population centers in Java, profiting from the grasslands in the former. In south Sulawesi and parts of southern Borneo deer were hunted on horseback for their meat and for the excitement of the chase, while in the more open forests of Laos, Cambodia, and northern Siam they were vigorously hunted for their hides, to provide an export trade to Japan in the sixteenth and seventeenth centuries.

Nevertheless, meat remained a less important item of diet in Southeast Asia than in most of Eurasia. As Islam spread in the fifteenth and sixteenth centuries, meat-eating was probably further reduced, goats and chickens not being able to substitute for the once-popular pig, and for the dogs, snakes, and frogs also eaten by pre-Muslim Indonesians. All Southeast Asians considered that meat was to be eaten only on ritual occasions when large numbers of people gathered for a feast. The slaughter of animals had a sacrificial character long after such rituals were officially discouraged by Islam, Christianity, and Theravada Buddhism, and solemn rituals continued to be performed to offer the blood of an animal to the ancestral spirits. For marriages, puberty rituals, village purifications, and even the holy days of the new religions, but above all

Figure 1.1 Dress of a Thai woman, as sketched in the 1680s. Source: Simon de la Loubère 1693/1969.

for death-feasts where the spirits were especially dangerous, animals would be ritually slaughtered and the meat distributed. Hence it was always eaten fresh, not dried or salted as Europeans and Chinese did. Chicken and pork were the most popular meat sources in non-Muslim areas; chicken and goat for Muslims; with buffaloes slaughtered for the great feasts.

While rice, salt, pickled fish, livestock, palm wine and betelnut (areca) were traded up and down rivers and along coasts, the biggest item of long-distance import from very early times must have been cloth. Southeast Asian texts seldom discuss housing, tools, or utensils, but they seem preoccupied with beautiful cloth. One missionary noted that "in the food, beds and houses of the Burmese, they are as parsimonious as they are splendid and extravagant in their dress" (Sangermano 1833/1966, 159), and the same could be said of most Southeast Asians. Personal wealth was most readily used and demonstrated in cloth and other items of personal adornment such as gold ornaments. As the next chapter makes clear, these were the keys that unlocked the region to the wider world.

Southeast Asians were much slower than their neighbors to adopt sewn garments that required the production or acquisition of needles. Only in the Red River delta that nurtured Sino-Vietnamese culture were sewn silk tunics, blouses, or trousers common before the sixteenth century. Throughout most of Southeast Asia the essential items of dress until the great upheaval of the "age of commerce" were simple woven cotton cloths. They were used first and fundamentally as a wrap-around lower garment fastened through folding, known in modern times as Malay *sarung*, Thai *panung*, or Bama *longyi*. Another cloth would often drape the upper body, either for warmth or a modicum of modesty over the breasts (Figure 1.1).

Sewn upper garments and trousers of course made their entry quite early from China, north India, and the Muslim world. We are particularly well informed when European accounts become available after 1500 of their attempts to sell tunics and jackets of various sorts. These items were to some extent taken up by those who could afford them, initially as a curiosity or status symbol. Yet even with the pressure of Islam and Christianity after 1500 to cover it, the carefully oiled and perfumed skin of the upper body remained in many areas the ultimate sign of cultivation. Even in the nineteenth century John Crawfurd could say of long-Islamized male Javanese that "when in full dress, they are almost naked" (Crawfurd 1820, I, 29). Even at a time of great cultural borrowing among the elite, the contrast between this cultivation of the body as ornament with the head-to-toe costumes of Muslim Indian, Christian European, and Chinese traders in their midst was evident to outside observers (Figure 1.2).

WOMEN AND MEN

A relatively low population density before the nineteenth-century expansion was one of the key features which determined Southeast Asian social structure. The forests were perceived as limitless. What created wealth was not possession

Figure 1.2 Notables of Banten, as sketched by a Danish trader in the 1670s. Indian Muslim (l) and Chinese (r) traders engage a Javanese aristocrat. Source: A.J.P. Cortemünde, Dagbog fra en Ostindiefart, 1672–5, ed. H. Henningsen, Kronborg: Handels-og sjøfartsmuseet, 1953.

of land but control of people. Only the labor of men and women could "open" the forest to productive cultivation; only the military power of men and the reproductive power of women could increase the number of one's followers. A Chinese report on the Malay states around 1500 remarked that "they say that it is better to have slaves than to have land, because slaves are a protection to their masters" (cited Reid 1988, 129). In comparison with either of its neighbors, India and China, Southeast Asia was a region where bureaucratic states had limited purchase over the lives of individuals, and both wealth and security were obtained by direct control over people.

A vertical bond between leader and follower, or master and slave, was the key to social integration in this world. States as they grew stronger sought to homogenize their subjects in this region as in others, but only in Dai Viet did the bureaucratic state succeed before the nineteenth century in replacing the essentially dyadic bonds between individuals as the principal social cement. Relations between equals were charged with competitive danger. The abundant personal pronouns of Southeast Asian languages demonstrate that relationships that acknowledged patronage on one side and obligation on the other were perceived as the most comfortable. There was no "free" labor until the late nineteenth century, except among immigrant Chinese, because laboring for another was inherently part of one's obligation, whether through kinship, debt, inherited status, or forced enslavement. Slaves, in the sense of a clearly servile labor category identified as property to the extent of being saleable, were most clearly a feature of expanding urban centers incorporating captive labor. Elsewhere it is wiser to use terms such as clients or bondsmen.

Warfare was a constant feature of pre-colonial Southeast Asia, and lack of security for property the major inhibition against its development in a capital-rich or capitalist direction. Headhunting and raiding for slaves or women was a feature of most of the stateless societies of the highlands, while raiding and piracy by sea was a standard tactic for ship-owners not directly tied into the tribute system of the major ports. The object of most of the warfare, of both large and small scale, was to capture people, not to kill them. "In all the countries of Below the Winds [Southeast Asia] ... when the natives ... wage war, they are extremely careful and the struggle is wholly confined to trickery and deception. They have no intention of killing each other or inflicting any great slaughter because if a general gained a real conquest, he would be shedding his own blood" (Ibrahim 1688/1972, 90). The defenders of cities tended to draw off into the surrounding forest and wait for attackers to loot and move on, so that there were few bitter sieges by European or Chinese standards. Deaths on the battlefield had much less severe an impact in restricting population and capital accumulation than the disruptions, plunder, diseases, and crop failures caused by the constant movement of captives or refugees.

The environment favored light, airy houses of wood and thatch, elevated on poles for safety, coolness, and cleanliness – the refuse falling through the floor cracks to the animals below. Only as wood supplies became scarce in the areas of highest population and state control – northern Viet Nam and Java by the sixteenth century, Maluku by the nineteenth – were houses built on the ground and sometimes with stone or brick bases. Elsewhere it was the pattern of insecurity and mobility that particularly discouraged investment in bricks and mortar. Most houses could be rebuilt by a family in a week from materials available in the forest, so that flight, fire, or pillage was not an overwhelming disaster. Capital was conserved rather in gold, jewelry, and cloth that could be buried or carried away.

Although the temple-studded ancient cities of Angkor, Pagan, and early Mataram must at their peak have incorporated the labor of tens of thousands of men and women, this form of social organization supporting Hindu-Buddhist royal cults has to be seen as exceptional. For most Southeast Asians in most periods before the nineteenth century, security was sought on the one hand from the armed strength of the household, its kin, or its patron, and on the other by the supernatural order. Evil or inappropriate actions would be punished by the retribution of the spirits, sometimes assisted by human agents. Similarly, one could protect one's family, crops, and property by correct ritual manipulations of the spirits, often including the sacrifice of some animal at a major feast. The power of kings and warriors, the validity of contracts, the credibility of evidence in a trial (usually by ordeal), were all understood to be underwritten by supernatural powers. More modern forms of both secular and religious authority, relying on written codes, bureaucratic hierarchies, and more predictable and egalitarian moral universes, certainly made major advances within the cities of the region at various periods. These advances should be seen, however, against a background neither of savagery nor of anarchy, but rather of unstable vertical alliances in both the human and the spiritual worlds.

The respective roles of men and women must also be understood before describing the effects of growing commercial interaction from the fifteenth century. As in many other respects, Southeast Asia differed, and still differs, sharply from both China and India in its gender relations. We can speak of a "Southeast Asian" pattern of relatively balanced roles and economic autonomy for women and men, even if Confucianism, Islam, Buddhism, and Christianity carried external models of male dominance into the region. Southeast Asian ritual and belief systems (except where altered by those scriptural religions) typically emphasize the complementarity of male and female principles, part of the dualism that imbues much ritual life. The ancestral figures representing the creation myth of many a pre-modern village are a primal pair, male and female, representing respectively the upper world and the watery lower world whose union created mankind.

Houses were often divided into male and female spheres, while the spirits of plants, animals, metals, and fields insisted that either men or women conduct particular tasks. The male sphere included all that pertained to metals and large animals, including hunting, ploughing, metalwork, felling trees, and opening new land. Women were believed essential for transplanting and harvesting rice, growing vegetables, weaving, and in most cases pottery-making. As spirit mediums they were as active as men in religious spheres. Women and men each had their own economic autonomy, and marriage by no means rendered women dependent on men. Marital property was held jointly, marital residence was more often with the bride's than the groom's parents, descent and inheritance was bilateral, and women's claim on property was sufficiently secure to allow them to be the initiators of divorce as often as men. Attractive as this pattern seems in modern terms, it could be argued that the absence of male primogeniture, which cruelly concentrated wealth in particular dynastic lines in Early Modern Europe and China, was one of the reasons that Southeast Asians did not accumulate capital as those centers did.

Of particular relevance for commercial patterns was the expectation that women should control the money income of the household and do its marketing. The local view would have been rather that men were concerned with other things, notably status. Gambling, especially on cockfights, was a particular male passion, partly designed to show his indifference to winning or losing money. Haggling over a price was appropriate behavior only for women and foreigners, who thereby dominated commercial transactions.

This pattern proved advantageous for the Indian, Arab, Chinese, and European traders who knew how to profit from it. Temporary wives were an accepted part of the trading system for these foreigners. They were the ideal cultural brokers, they created (at least in Southeast Asian eyes) bonds of kinship and reciprocity with the host community, and they brought knowledge of the market and marketing which a foreign male could not hope to have. As a Chinese visitor remarked of the central Vietnamese port of Hoi An, "The women were very good at trade, so the traders who came here all tended to marry a local woman to help them with their trading" (Da Shan 1699/1993, 58). Some local women, including those of the ruling circle and wives of particularly powerful foreign traders, became major commercial figures and ship owners. But like the foreign traders, they flourished in commerce because they were outside the male world of power and status. Their ability to transform that world in a capitalist direction was inherently limited.

It is remarkably fitting that one of the earliest and finest bronze artefacts known to have been produced in Southeast Asia depicts not an Indic god but a familiar female figure (Figure 1.3). She takes a break from her everyday task of weaving on a backstrap loom, such as is still found in many corners of the region, to suckle her child. She wears a simple wrap-around cloth garment such as she may have woven herself, though only by sewing two or three widths of her narrow product together. Though her upper body is bare in terms of clothing, one is struck by the intense care with which it is adorned. The hair is elegantly braided, and rich jewelry hangs from her neck and ears. The 26-cm statue was found in eastern Flores and dated to the sixth century CE. From similarities with other bronzes of the period it is thought it may have been

Figure 1.3 Bronze statue of a female weaver and child, sixth–seventh century CE, found in Flores but possibly of Borneo manufacture. 25.8 × 22.8 × 15.2 cm. Source: Reproduced by permission of the Australian National Gallery.

produced in eastern Borneo. The woman is distinctively Southeast Asian, but her appearance in an area not known otherwise for the early availability of copper, tin, or bronze technology makes one wonder whether she had become the wife or muse of some hybridized foreign trader familiar with bronze-casting techniques for religious purposes.

NOT CHINA, NOT INDIA

Southeast Asia is often seen as the awkward residue after the great civilizations of India and China have been studied, or at best as the sphere of interaction between the two. It must be repeated that the region has its own distinct environment that produced many common features of material culture and social structure, and preserved political and cultural diversity by limiting the extent to which foreign models could assimilate what had gone before. Fundamentally, Southeast Asia appears to have derived most of its modern gene pool and language stocks from the north, in the Asian mainland now occupied by China, and its religions and written cultures (except the Viet) from the west. The limits to these two crucial interactions, however, should be made clear.

Chinese civilization has been unique in human history for the longevity, scale, and bureaucratic strength of its state system, reconstituting itself on a similar organizational base after each traumatic foreign conquest or internal collapse. While China was the first large area to ban the private carriage of arms in favor of a state monopoly of force, Southeast Asia was among the last. The definition of Chinese-ness before the twentieth century was that of civilization itself, whereby the civilized insiders defined themselves as people of Ming, or Tang, or in more modern times of the "middle kingdom" (*zhongguo*), making their subjecthood inseparable from their civilization. Its boundaries were therefore uniquely clearly demarcated, as the point where the authority stopped of officials appointed from the imperial center on the basis of their knowledge of the Chinese classics. China's boundaries with Viet Nam in the south and Korea in the north have been stable for a thousand years, in sharp contrast to the Southeast Asian world of charismatic, personal, and relatively ephemeral power.

China's greatest contribution to Southeast Asian population was not the imperial subjects who migrated south from the thirteenth century and were identified by southerners as "Chinese". Rather, it was the diverse populations who moved south to escape absorption into that bureaucratic empire who brought agriculture and Southeast Asia's modern set of languages into the region. "Greater Southeast Asia" is a term that has been used for the vast regions of "not yet China" south of the Yangzi River, before the border of Chinese-ness moved south. These diverse peoples were indeed not "China" until absorbed by the empire, and their languages, cultures, and social relations were within the spectrum of diversity found in Southeast Asia. Yet since I am defining Southeast Asia largely in terms of a humid tropical environment, I accept migrating peoples as "Southeast Asia" only as they enter that environment on their movement southward.

Four major factors defended the state-light domain of Southeast Asia from the long-term expansion southward of successive Chinese empires. The first may be called the low exportability of Chinese civilization, tied as it was both to a difficult writing system (in contrast with alphabetic Indic scripts) and to the control of imperially appointed officials versed in the classic literature expressed in those ideograms. The second is the sea, which the Chinese state (as opposed to many enterprising merchants of its south-eastern coasts) showed no taste for subjugating. Even an island as close and strategic as Taiwan was not securely brought under imperial control until the Manchu conquest in 1683, contrasting strikingly with the achievements of the stateless Austronesians, maritime peoples who expanded from Taiwan eventually to the vast oceanic zone from Madagascar to Easter Island. It was only the world-conquering Mongol expansion that carried China into maritime adventures to Japan (1274, 1281) and to Java (1292–3). The Chinese regime that succeeded the Mongols, the Ming, briefly emulated its predecessor's world-encompassing vision, in its first, energetic phase (1368–1424). The awesome but still-mysterious maritime initiatives under the eunuch admiral Zheng He (1405–24) were not sustained or sustainable, however, since they appear to have been concerned with ideology rather than exploiting the benefits of trade.

The third factor protecting the Southeast Asian world of low population and relative statelessness was the environment of James Scott's "Zomia," the mountainous region where modern China meets Southeast Asia. The mountain barrier was itself a major obstacle for Chinese civilization, dependent on its southward expansion for finding fertile river valleys that could be irrigated for wet-rice agriculture. The transport and supply of armies also became much more difficult the further they sought to march from their supply bases in the rice-growing valleys. In their critical battles with Tai and Bama opponents in the eighteenth century, Chinese military advantages of numbers and firearms technology tended to be negated by the terrain. The most crucial factor, however, was the balance of the microbes. Chinese expansion southward had the usual advantages of compact agricultural populations that smallpox and other diseases had become endemic to them, but wrought havoc on their opponents who were too dispersed to have gained the same immunity. But in the tropics, diseases unfamiliar to the Chinese, notably malaria and cholera, balanced this advantage with a greater obstacle.

Ever since the initial Han expansion to the southern areas (including today's Viet Nam), Chinese sources routinely attribute their setbacks to the basket of tropical diseases they labeled *zhang*, often translated as "miasma." It is presumed to include malaria, but perhaps also water-borne diseases such as cholera. This mysterious disorder routinely killed more troops than did the enemy, and terror of it became a further factor deterring troops even from setting out. When the Ming Hongzhi Emperor (1488–1505) sent millions of troops to settle the southern frontier in Guangxi, most reportedly died of *zhang* and the rest fled. But while Guangxi and Yunnan were eventually subdued, Burma and Tongking were not. The mighty Qianlong Emperor (1736–95), who took the Manchu Empire to its greatest extent even at the expense of Tibet, lost his crucial campaign to subdue Burma in the 1760s for similar reasons. After the debacle the Emperor swore off such adventures with the words: "The land of Burma is awful. Human beings cannot compete with seasons of heaven and water and soil. It is very pitiful to see that our crack soldiers and elite generals died of *zhang* for nothing" (translated in Yang, 2010).

The fourth barrier to Chinese expansion southward were the ancestors of the Vietnamese, who controlled the most natural avenue for such expansion across the Red River delta (Tongking). The Tongking Gulf was a major maritime trading zone, and the Red River one of the trade arteries into Guangxi. The first documented kingdom in the region, which Chinese sources labeled Nanyue, embraced both Tongking and what is today Guangdong in south China, in the second century BCE. This came under the control of the expanding Han Empire that laid the basis of Chinese power in 111 BCE. Direct Chinese rule came in 43 CE, putting down resistance led by the first of Viet Nam's long list of nationalist heroes, the Trung sisters. Tongking therefore became "Chinese" in administration and written culture earlier and more thoroughly than much of modern China. In 679, at the peak of the success of the Tang Dynasty, this civilized status was recognized by the creation of a "Protectorate of Annan" in the delta.

During the thousand-year Chinese rule of the Tongking area, a literate ruling class, schooled in Chinese methods of reporting and accountability, acquired the essential tools for its remarkable ability to turn back Chinese expansion. In 939, during China's troubles between Tang and Song dynasties, this elite took charge of its own affairs and formed an independent polity, labeled Jiaozhi by the Chinese. While other such polities were eventually reabsorbed into the next successful Chinese dynasty, Jiaozhi twice turned back invasions by the Song (981 and 1077), and thrice more by the Mongols ruling China as the Yuan Dynasty (1257, 1285, 1287). Although the Mongols succeeded each time in occupying the Dai Viet capital (modern Hanoi), they eventually withdrew under pressure from the *zhang* diseases mentioned above, guerrilla resistance from the Viet, and a skillful Viet policy of agreeing to send tribute to China in return for effective independence.

The fifteenth century was decisive in transforming Dai Viet into a military power that could henceforth hold China at bay. The Ming Dynasty, in the same exceptional world-conquering moment that had sent Zheng He on his massive foreign adventures, occupied Dai Viet for two decades (1406–27). This occupation was achieved by one of the first systematic uses of gunpowder technology in Asia, but a consequence was that Vietnamese turned the same technology against the Chinese to drive them out. After this military success of 1427, the Le Dynasty of Dai Viet set the pace of firearms technology in Southeast Asia, able to expand at the expense of previous rivals in Champa and Laos, as well as holding out China. Underlying these military successes was the social transformation of Vietnamese society. Chinese techniques of dyke-building helped Tongking become the rice bowl that it has remained, and the population more than doubled during the century. In this way Dai Viet prevented further Chinese expansion along the coastal plain. Instead it was the Viet who carried the Chinese model of intensive delta agriculture,

Confucian-style administration, and a reverence for the Chinese classics ever further southward in the ensuing four centuries (Chapter 9).

India might seem more difficult to disentangle from Southeast Asia, since the European imaginary before the nineteenth century saw all the littoral of the Indian Ocean as "India." For mediaeval Europeans this exotic place was the source of the spices they badly needed, and these turned out to be as much in Southeast as in South Asia. The Dutch and Spanish believed that their major bases in Asia were in India, and called the people of the island world "Indians" (Dutch *Indiër*; Spanish *Indio*) until the twentieth century. Unlike China this was clearly not a state but a region of many states and non-states large and small.

Asians never suffered this confusion. Despite much shared culture the geography seemed distinct, with a serious sea voyage the only practical means of communication across the Bay of Bengal and the jumble of mountains between the Bhramaputra and Irrawaddy deltas. The Vedic texts labeled Southeast Asia *Suvarnabhumi*, "gold-land," while early Southeast Asian texts were aware of the source of Buddhism in *Bharat* or *Gurjaradesa*. Islamic traders around the Indian Ocean were clear about the geographic distinction between "Below the Winds" (Southeast Asia) and "Above the Winds" (South and West Asia). Southern India, like southernmost China, was "Southeast Asian" in its pluralities and resistance to imperial absorption. Most of Southeast Asia's maritime exchanges that created the "Sanskrit cosmopolis" were with the southern regions outside the control of the successive powers in the Ganges valley. In the political sense we used for "not-China," it was only with the late eighteenth-century British unification of the sub-continent that Southeast Asia was clearly also "not-India."

Even before the advent of British rule in India, religion had created a further dichotomy between it and Southeast Asia. The *dwidharma* of Buddhism and Saivism had united Southeast Asia and India in the first millennium CE, so that Indian culture was vastly more influential than Chinese everywhere except Dai Viet (Chapter 2). But by the fifteenth century Buddhism had virtually died in India, while the Burmese, Tai, and Khmer worlds had adopted the strict Theravada Buddhism of Sri Lanka. Islam, a minority almost everywhere in India, became in the island world the religion of states at about the same time, and ultimately a kind of orthodoxy that excluded the Hindu gods from every domain except literature, dance, and mythology.

[2] Buddha and Shiva Below the Winds

Debates about Indic States

The habits of both European and Northeast Asian historians have encouraged a quest for early state formation in Southeast Asia, as the principal theme for the proto-historic period before written sources become abundant. Chinese sources from the third century of the Common Era report the existence of states that sent tribute from the tropical regions in the south, and scholarship focused on how to connect the Chinese toponyms so recorded with material remains in Southeast Asia, to determine the site of these kingdoms. Recent archaeological work in Viet Nam, Thailand, and Malaysia in particular has identified relatively complex societies from about the beginning of the Common Era, leaving evidence of pottery, metalwork, elaborate funerary arrangements, and trade as represented by imported beads, coins, and metalware. Until the sites speak for themselves, however, through inscriptions in Indian languages from about the sixth century, the naming of sites, let alone "kingdoms," is highly speculative. Even in the period of relatively abundant inscriptions and temple remains from the eighth to thirteenth centuries, the labeling of kingdoms, cities, and ethno-linguistic communities on the map of Southeast Asia rests on rather fragile foundations. Economic and religious activity is well documented in the material evidence, but political structures and identities much less so.

This chapter will take a more conservative approach to the identifying of states than is common among historians, preferring to trust the evidence of the archaeologists as to what can be known. In particular, the Chinese record on the arrival of missions from barbarian southern "kingdoms" is extremely important in regard to commercial networks, production, and exchange, but should not be translated into modern assumptions about states. Traders understood that the best means of access to the huge market of China was to present themselves as tribute-bringers from a barbarian kingdom, particularly one that was recognized at the Chinese court from older documents regardless of whether it represented any continuing reality.

A History of Southeast Asia: Critical Crossroads, First Edition. Anthony Reid.
© 2015 Anthony Reid. Published 2015 by John Wiley & Sons, Ltd.

The deciphering of inscriptions in scripts, imagery, and often languages derived from India began a major debate about the nature of the "Indianization" which appeared to have transformed Southeast Asia between the sixth and fourteenth centuries. The Greater India school of the 1930s raised excitement in India about the spread of Indian culture outward through colonization – a wording particularly unacceptable to nationalist Southeast Asian of the 1950s and 1960s. Much post-war scholarship was devoted to seeking to show that it was local genius and adaptation rather than foreign colonization that built the states and their temples. This debate had the unfortunate effect of dividing Indian from Southeast Asian scholarship, and these have only begun to find each other again in the current century.

For western scholarship the classic text was George Coedès' 1944 synthesis of the history of the *états hindouisés*, usually translated as "Indianized states," of the region (Coedès 1968). It was widely relied upon by D.G.E. Hall (1968) and later authors. These pioneers constructed a coherent narrative of how "kings" may have succeeded one another, at the cost of beguiling later writers into a simplified idea that the same few "states" built the temples, left the inscriptions, and conducted relations with China.

An exemplary case is Funan, hailed by Coedès, Hall, and subsequent text-book-writers as "the first Indian kingdom." Funan appears in Chinese records from the third century CE, though no such place-name occurs on the ground in Southeast Asia. Coedès (1968, 36) proposed a derivation from the old Khmer word *bnam* (modern *phnom*), "mountain," making this an essentially Khmer state and antecedent of Angkor. Others argued it was a maritime state and therefore Austronesian. Coedès ingeniously linked the various stories about Funan in Chinese sources of the third to sixth centuries with later echoes in inscriptions from the sixth century, to propose the existence of a kingdom born in the first century CE in the Mekong delta region, but expanding through conquests in the third century until it dominated much of southern Indochina and the Peninsula (Coedès 1968, 36–42). Later historians and text-book writers developed this idea to the point where the first six centuries of the Common Era are explained as "the Funan Age," as if the whole introduction of Indian religious ideas and writing was centered on this state.

The success of this Funan idea owed much to the fact that the first archaeological site of that period to be analyzed scientifically was at Oc Eo, today about 25 km from the Gulf of Thailand in the westernmost frontier of southern Viet Nam. Louis Malleret explored this walled city in the early 1940s as Coedès was preparing his book, and the two men agreed that this site, with its abundance of Roman and other coins, glassware, and medallions, must have been the port of the state of Funan. Since then there has been much more archaeological work, including other sites nearly as old as Oc Eo in the Mainland, the Peninsula, and West Java. There was trade and exchange, but were there states? Even the later temple-building civilizations that scholars labeled Angkor, Champa, Sriwijaya, and early Mataram have become less unitary and state-like as we learn more from archaeology. Oliver Wolters came to believe that in the early centuries of the Common Era "a patchwork of small settlement networks of great antiquity stretched across the map of Southeast Asia" (Wolters

1999, 16). There is plenty of evidence for a sophisticated bronze culture but little for states being responsible for it.

BRONZE, IRON, AND EARTHENWARE IN THE ARCHAEOLOGICAL RECORD

The remarkable dispersion of large bronze drums around Southeast Asia gave rise to some of the earliest scholarly work on the distinctive pattern of Southeast Asian proto-history. How metals technology spread in Southeast Asia in the earliest periods is a matter of long-standing debate, more intense since the excavations at Ban Chiang near the middle Mekong River in the 1970s raised the possibility that bronze-working there may have been as old as that in China. The earliest Ban Chiang periodization has now been largely discredited, however, and a consensus is emerging that the Southeast Asian bronze age, including vitally important sites in what is now southern Yunnan but was then very distinct from the older "Chinese" tradition of the Yellow River, began less than 4,000 years ago. Unlike the other major bronze traditions of Eurasia, the spread and development of sophisticated metallurgy in Southeast Asia involved not states nor even urban settlements but village communities linked by complex exchange networks. Bronze was adopted for ornamental and functional forms already familiar in the region in stone, ceramics, or shells. Bronze items joined the repertoire of prestige goods buried with the dead. Yet these burial sites suggest not hereditary chieftainship let alone kingship, but rather the honoring of individual men and women of achievement – including female potters buried with their tools.

The first millennium of this distinctive Southeast Asian tradition included production sites in Yunnan, the Red River area, the Khorat plateau, the middle and lower Mekong, and upper Chao Phraya. There is much overlapping of stone, bronze, and iron tools, although bronze axes, arrowheads, chisels, and adzes dominate in the first millennium BCE. Many of the finest surviving bronze and iron artefacts, together with ornamented pottery, have been found in burial sites, which demonstrate some complexity of ritual even in the small and scattered communities that are the hallmark of the region. There were settlements that specialized in pottery or bronze casting, and others that mined the copper and tin necessary for bronze casting from deposits hundreds of kilometers apart. Although there is no evidence of substantial cities before the Common Era, or of any overarching political authority, there must therefore have been extensive networks of trade and exchange between specialized settlements over long distances. The reciprocities that existed between coastal and interior producers, agriculturalists, fishermen and hunters, miners and metalworkers provided the basis for "civilization without cities" that was a distinctive long-term feature of Southeast Asia.

In the humid center of Southeast Asia, including Sumatra, the Peninsula, and western Java and Borneo, there is predictably little evidence of bronze working at all before the Common Era, as conditions for settled agriculture were difficult except in some highland valleys. The earliest evidence of bronze arte-facts in Island Southeast Asia occurs in the last centuries before the Common Era, as traded items from the Mainland. The most spectacular finds dating back to this period are the large "Dongson" bronze drums apparently traded to settled agricultural communities in the uplands of Sumatra and Java and in Bali. The drums found in Sumatra were in some of the lakeside highland val-leys furthest from the east coast, where they appear to have given stylistic inspiration to a number of megaliths and stone tombs assumed to be of the same period. These drums were therefore traded over large distances, from the Red River valley production centers by sea to Palawan, Borneo, and as far as Java. Some went to Trengganu and Pahang in the Peninsula. From there they were evidently carried by portages across the Peninsula, where others have been found in Selangor, and again by ship and land across the Malacca Straits and up the long eastern rivers of Sumatra to Besemah (Pasemah) and other high-land centers of agriculture. Through this arduous trade route they must have assumed great value, which implies relatively complex societies to buy them. Numerous smaller drums, perhaps made in the Islands, were traded through-out the south-easternmost islands (Sumbawa, Flores, Timor, Alor) at a later period, perhaps beginning in the second century CE.

The finest productions of these non-state societies of the Islands before the Common Era were ceramics, with distinct traditions probably dispersed southward from Taiwan along with the Austronesian seaborne migrations. A cave site in Palawan (western Philippines) revealed a "soul boat" burial jar dated to about 800 BCE, linked in style to the findings of a similar period in other islands and the adjacent Indochina mainland. In this period the Islands were importers of complex bronze drums from the Mainland centers of the Red River, but not yet producers.

The earliest evidence of bronze casting in the Islands has been found in Bali and Palawan, dated to the third and second centuries BCE. Copper does occur in Palawan and nearby northern Borneo, and is distributed widely also in Sumatra, west Java and western Borneo, but tin, the other essential for making bronze, is available only in the seam down the whole Peninsula and ending in Bangka and Belitung off eastern Sumatra. For bronze to be cast in Bali and Palawan, therefore, there must have been exchange networks already in place around the Archipelago. As well as copper and tin, gold and iron were widely mined, smelted, traded, and worked into ornaments and utensils by this period. We must wait for the first centuries of the Common Era, however, for specialist bronze production centers close to sources of copper and tin to emerge in the Archipelago, producing such gems as the bronze weaver discussed in Chapter 1. Iron-smelting may have been a little older, since the discovery at one of the major portages across the Peninsula, in Bujang Valley, Kedah, of a major iron-smelting site active from the third to sixth century CE suggests already considerable complexity in the smelting and trading of iron tools.

In early times, Austronesians were among the Asian pioneers in boat-building and navigation, and there seems little doubt that their activity linked the islands of Southeast Asia to each other, to the Mainland, and to India and China well before the Common Era. Austronesian traders from Southeast Asia appear to have reached Madagascar and the east coast of Africa by the onset of the Common Era, gradually colonizing the former in the following centuries. Enough of these pioneer navigators may have carried with them the gold of Sumatra and the Peninsula for the region to become known as *Suvarnabhumi* (gold-land) in the Indian epics as early as the third century BCE.

With the exception of this gold, and the tin of the Peninsula, metals remained less exploited in the region than in its better-populated neighbors, China and India. Travelers from Europe and China found that their everyday nails, knives, and needles were in great demand from the locals, chiefly because the sparse population in the vicinity of most of Southeast Asia's minerals required a smaller scale of production, and therefore less efficient methods of both mining and smelting than developed in China. As trade developed in the second millennium of the Common Era, the flourishing Southeast Asian ports found it cheaper to import everyday metal items from afar, and their own local traditions of mining and smelting gradually retreated to the less accessible interiors.

Bronze statuary is one of the defining legacies of Indic religion everywhere, but many of the earliest Buddhist and Hindu images produced in Southeast Asia were in gold or terracotta. Bronze in the region was by no means first or primarily used for these universal religious purposes, but for everyday tools, ornaments, and celebrations of the dead.

THE BUDDHIST ECUMENE AND SANSKRITIZATION

The process once called the "Indianization" of Southeast Asia has been better explained by Sheldon Pollock (2006) as the rapid spread of a Sanskrit cosmopolis from a few priestly centers in northern India throughout all the commercially linked power centers of South and Southeast Asia. Having been for centuries a sacred "language of the gods," taught to a few priestly men so that they could recite the activities of the gods in the Vedas, Sanskrit embarked on a new career as a universal legitimating language of power around the beginning of the Common Era. We might explain this as the first stage of globalizing religion, contemporary with the Roman Empire giving birth to Christian universalism in the West and with Han power extending a Chinese cosmopolis through Northeast Asia. While no comparable political power center arose in Southeast Asia at this or any other time, those engaged in the multiple maritime exchanges which ultimately linked Roman and Han Empires must have been unusually receptive to universal ideas. To judge by the inscriptions, by the fifth century CE Sanskrit had expanded not only throughout Southern India and Sri Lanka but also to Southeast Asian sites in Borneo, Java, the Peninsula, the lower Mekong and the centers of Chamic (Austronesian) settlement in what is today central Viet Nam. So successful did it become as a "celebration of aesthetic power" that its two new genres of courtly poetry (*kavya*) and royal eulogies (*prasasti*) spread to peoples of multiple languages and habits throughout South and Southeast Asia. It marked the beginnings of writing, of kingship (presented as universal, not bounded power), of scriptural religion (primarily through Buddhism), and of literature.

This expansionary impetus was facilitated by the mobility of Buddhism. Although early Buddhism rejected Sanskrit as identified with the established hierarchical order, by the third century CE there had been a return to using the universal language, now purged of its offensive features. For various reasons early Buddhism established a symbiosis with trading networks which made possible a considerable expansion of Indian Ocean trade in the first centuries of the Common Era. Buddhist advocacy of detachment from worldly engagement had the effect of rendering caste distinctions less restrictive, and breaking the caste taboo against travel by sea. The organization of the *sangha* (monkhood), and various practices of lay support for it, proved able to be transplanted readily across barriers of place and culture. Although the earliest contacts of China with Buddhism were through Central Asian overland routes, some of the earliest Chinese pilgrims discovered in India that it was easier to return by sea. Faxian did this round trip in the early fifth century, and by the time of Yi Jing (635–713) the sea route was well established. In 671 he set out by sea from Guangzhou, and traveled along the trading networks already established by Southeast Asia–based traders. Of the 24 years (671–85) he devoted to studying, traveling, and collecting scriptures along the route to the holy places in India, ten were spent at the place he called Shilifoshi, evidently the most important base for the Buddhist trading network in Southeast Asia. There, he wrote, "there are more than a thousand Buddhist priests whose minds are bent on study and good works … their rules and ceremonies are identical with those in India" (cited Coedès 1968, 81). He therefore recommended Chinese pilgrims to use this multicultural Buddhist center to learn their Sanskrit and Pali.

Historians have equated Yi Jing's Shilifoshi with the Sriwijaya mentioned in some inscriptions, and estimated modern Palembang, 60 km up the Musi River in south Sumatra, to be its likeliest location. Certainly there was a major trade center there, at an important junction between sea routes through the two major straits and river supplies of rice from the well-cultivated south Sumatran highlands. It remains puzzling, however, that Palembang offers no major Buddhist remains comparable to Java's Borobudur or even other Buddhist sites in Sumatra – Muara Jambi, Muara Takus, and Padang Lawas. Certainly there were religious and commercial connections between various Sumatran, Javanese, and Peninsula sites which shared the cosmopolitan cultures of early Sriwijaya, and Palembang may be best understood as primarily a node of interaction between rice-growing centers in highland Sumatra, Java, and Cambodia and the trade and pilgrimage to China and India. Buddhism made Sriwijaya a key player in Asian interaction from the seventh to tenth centuries. Some of the foreign monks expelled from China in 741 traveled to Southeast Asia and Sri Lanka, of whom the most famous, Amoghavajra (Bukong in Chinese, 705–74), returned to China in 750 with hundreds of texts and became one of China's most influential Buddhist teachers. A ninth-century copperplate found at the great center of Buddhist scholarship and devotion in Nalanda, northeast India, records the endowment of five villages there for the upkeep of a monastery built by the Sailendra king of Suvarna Dvipa (Sumatra), to accommodate visiting monks from the "four quarters." The famous Bengal-born monk who established Vajrayana Buddhism in Tibet, Atisha (980–1054), had apparently learned that doctrine while studying in Sumatra, at the feet of a famous teacher. Southeast Asian ports and sacred sites in this period were part of a pan-Asian ecumene of Buddhism. As a ninth-century Javanese Sanskrit text put it, "a constant flow of people" came to Java from places in India and Cambodia, "bowed low with the devotion to the Buddha" (Pollock 2006, 127).

The earliest Buddhist imagery understandably occurs along the major trade routes connecting China and India, notably at some of the trans-Peninsula portages and in southern Sumatra and tin-producing Bangka. By the sixth century, Buddhist networks were established from India through Southeast Asia to China. Buddhist statues and inscriptions found in Southeast Asia in this first phase (up to the seventh century) are exclusively religious in character. No king or state is mentioned as commissioning them, though one from the Peninsula notes that it was engraved by a ship-master (*mahanavika*). They share a number of features, including a small range of favored Buddhist texts repeated in many inscriptions, and three common genres of standing Buddhas and Avalokitesvaras. Their Sanskrit writing also evolved in a common way distinct from the Indian original, demonstrating the importance of intra-Southeast Asian Buddhist networks and pilgrimage.

The gods of Hinduism were not left behind, however, in this expansion of Buddhist imagery and Sanskrit language. Images of Vishnu with a characteristic miter on his head occur at some of the earliest Buddhist sites in Java and Cambodia, and all the associated inscriptions make claims to royal power. It appears, therefore, as though Buddha and Vishnu traveled together along the trade routes, with Buddhism a more popular belief system uniting traders from different parts of Asia, while Vaishnavism was taken up by those seeking legitimacy for novel forms of hierarchy and kingship in Southeast Asia. Vishnu was the preeminent deity of the Gupta Emperors who ruled northern India from the fourth to sixth centuries, so it was not surprising that his royal cult should appeal to the ambitious. One of the earliest such Sanskrit inscriptions, from the late fifth century, was far up the Mekong in what is today southern Laos, about a king named Devanika who built a reservoir and claimed to have inaugurated a kingdom emulating the gods of the Mahabharata. Another such was Mulawarman, who left seven stone pillars at a site in Kutai, 30 km upriver from the eastern coast of Borneo, with Sanskrit inscriptions, estimated by style to be fourth or fifth century, claiming to have conquered other kings. The Pendawa king-conqueror of the Mahabharata saga is thus made the legitimation for a novel concentration of power in Borneo, perhaps inspired by a Brahmin traveler who could provide an Indic form of consecration. Similarly in Java, the earliest dated inscription, from 732 CE, records the erection of a *lingga*, the preeminent symbol of Shiva, in the Kedu plain of south-central Java by one King Sanjaya who evidently used this Sanskrit and Shaivite legitimation for the first definite claim to kingship in the Javanese-speaking area.

Sanskrit courtly genres such as poetry and eulogies spread to peoples of multiple languages and habits from Gujarat in the west to Java and Cambodia in the southeast, praising local kings in exemplary Sanskrit as learned, beautiful, brave, just, and generous. An exalted rhetoric threatening cosmic curses for defiance but rewards for obedience became the principal weapons of big men seeking to rise above the established networks of reciprocity and kinship. Even Tang China, which accepted "tribute" implying trade access only from a single Java "king," acknowledged there were in fact 28 "small countries" in that island.

The earliest centers of Indian religious ideas in Southeast Asia were naturally along the routes of trade from the Indian Ocean to China. The watery world where the Mekong's many mouths meet the sea was evidently a key part of this route in the earliest centuries of the Common Era, as were portages across various parts of the Middle and Upper Peninsula. From the seventh century, inscriptions became numerous here, both Sanskrit ones addressed to the gods and Khmer ones dealing with everyday affairs. One Chinese report told of "Funan" having been established by a Brahman from India, who sought to unite people into villages around a reservoir or tank, rather than digging individual wells. The religious ideas from India do indeed appear to have established a Khmer pattern of settlement clustered around a tank or reservoir which maintained essential water supplies through the dry season, and a sacred shrine, *lingga*, or stupa which might incorporate both the new idea of merit-making through religious devotion and reverence for the ancestor-figures who had founded a particular community. The inscriptions show that many communities included both an elite of priests and rulers who administered the rites to these sacred places and a variety of bonded people who served the former in a great variety of modes of slavery or loyalty.

In this complex world of interconnected but independent villages, one larger temple complex was built in the seventh century at Isanapura (now Sambor Prei Kuk, near modern Kampong Thom), midway between Angkor, the royal capital from the ninth century, and the greatest concentration of more ancient sites on the rivers below Phnom Penh. The main temple among the more than a hundred constructed within the complex is to Shiva, and there is a king, Isanavarman, associated with it in the inscriptions. But it was popular piety that built the temples, while the kings achieved their power by association with the sacred site. Perhaps the people were inspired by *pasuputa*, wandering ascetic Brahmans who became a feature of southern Asia in the fifth and sixth centuries, and appear to have preached devotion to Shiva as the ultimate form of cosmic protection. Along with Mahayana Buddhist monks, they were the agents of broader unities of culture, convincing an increasingly mobile population that in addition to local deities of place and ancestry, universal protectors were also needed to ensure fertility, security, and prosperity. Because cosmic forces were everywhere, the goal of all was to realize the divine within, and the king, who by definition must have concentrated more of the sacred, was thereby an exemplar.

In the Irrawaddy River region we know today as central Burma, colonial and nationalist scholarship had posited a city, kingdom, and center of Mon-speaking Theravada Buddhist civilization named in later chronicles as Thaton, somewhere in the Irrawaddy delta. Archaeological research failed to find it, however, but rather located a pattern of small walled towns centered in the dry zone of the middle Irrawaddy, conventionally known as the Pyu civilization. Michael Aung-Thwin (2005) has effectively demolished Thaton as a latter-day myth, and proposed rather that we accept the Pyu civilization in most of the first millennium CE as the builder of a Buddhist shared civilization in what later became Burma.

Many earlier scholars assumed that the wonderful ninth-century monuments of south-central Java, including the Buddhist Borobudur and the Shaivite Prambanan, must have been built by powerful kings. The problem of two religions was resolved through the notion of a Sumatran invasion under a Buddhist Sailendra Dynasty that gave rise to the Buddhist monuments. More careful study of the physical evidence, however, suggests Hindu and Buddhist shrines coexisted, while there was no great urban center or palace complex such as might elsewhere be associated with temple-building kings. Most of the early monuments of the Mataram area are in fact Buddhist constructions, and no inscriptions have been found attributing their construction to a king. The earliest, Candi Sari and Candi Kalasan, built in the area of later Prambanan in the late eighth century, are massive-walled shrines to the Buddha, or the female bodhisattva Tara, with two stories intended also as dwellings for monks, devotees, or pilgrims. Candi Sewu, a great mandala of 240 Mahayana Buddhist temples and stupas, was erected at a similar period, evidently through the piety and devotion of a numerous population in this fertile rice bowl of Java. The only inscription mentioning the greatest of all such mandalas, Borobudur, is one dated 842 near to the temple site, recording the name of a woman who bestowed land to sustain it. A high degree of social cohesion must have been required to organize the labor and skills for these vast and exquisite building projects, but it appears to have been provided by charismatic religious leaders rather than kings.

The extent of popular enthusiasm for making merit and escaping the wheel of suffering through the teachings of Buddhism can be measured by the exceptional proliferation of stone buildings that have survived from the eighth and ninth centuries. Rather than states building temples, some state formation probably arose on the back of the temple-building effort, by controlling access to the popular pilgrimage sites or manipulating their charisma. The Shaivite temple complex at Prambanan was built on the very edge of Candi Sewu mandala a few decades later, and, unlike the Buddhist complexes, it contains inscriptions lauding the king who presided over the building.

Religion appears the strongest unifying factor in civilizations such as that of Java, but irrigation cooperatives and market cycles also played a role. Except for the Chinese model, extended to the Red River delta (Tongking) during the first millennium, Southeast Asia appears the antithesis of a "hydraulic state" where the control of large river systems required a kind of despotism. Local cooperative arrangements channeled the watercourses of upland valleys rather than the mighty rivers themselves, as is still a marked pattern in Bali. Market cycles also operated in ancient Java and other areas according to a five-day cycle, so that the women who largely operated them could travel to five neighboring villages on successive days, at least one of which was connected to a broader cycle of large villages. Within this world the kings who associated themselves with the most sacred centers of pilgrimage and devotion were sustained much as the temples themselves were maintained, by particular villages accepting a divinely sanctioned obligation to provide rice, thatch, ceramics, or labor whenever needed.

SHIVA AND NAGARA IN THE "CHARTER ERA," 900–1300

The Buddhist ecumene had particularly flourished when China's Tang Empire had stimulated both trade and pilgrimage through the passages of Southeast Asia. Sriwijaya around the Straits of Malacca, south-central Java, and Champa on the main route to China had been particular beneficiaries of this Buddhist era, though without a strongly established pattern of hereditary kingship. Recent discoveries show the Buddhist trade diaspora and Indic scripts as more widespread than once thought. The Laguna copperplate inscription in Luzon of 900 CE, in an Austronesian vernacular with old-Javanese script, released a lady and her brother from a debt. Buddhist images and inscriptions have also surfaced in Mindanao and in Sulawesi.

The major trade centers all suffered disruption in the tenth century, probably more because of natural disasters than the disruption of China trade at the fall of the Tang (907). The silencing of the Mataram civilization in south-central Java after 928 is difficult to explain without natural disruptions such as one or more major volcanic eruptions.

The next phase of the expansion of civilizational cores coincided largely with the prosperous Song Dynasty in China (960–1127) but appeared much less dependent upon it. The period from the tenth to thirteenth centuries was dominated in Mainland Southeast Asia by polities I will call *nagara*, as they called themselves. This Sanskrit term essentially means a city or town and all that pertains to urban sophistication. Angkor and Pagan on the Mainland, and Majapahit in Java, saw themselves as foci of civilization as well as sacred centers. They had no boundaries, and have been labeled *mandala* or galactic polities by others, because they dominated a penumbra of smaller centers that emulated and deferred to them. Lieberman (2003, 23–5) has suggestively labeled this the "charter era" because each *nagara* established a vernacular civilization that survived subsequent vicissitudes as a sense of collective identity. Each *nagara* was made possible by one or more compact centers of wet-rice cultivation that provided a secure surplus to feed it. This was the period of the "rice revolution" discussed in Chapter 1, when rice surpluses began to be produced by more intensive methods in the areas that gave rise to *nagara*. Coinciding with the medieval anomaly of warm climate in Europe, this period was also favorable for rainfall in Mainland Southeast Asia.

Contributing to the disruption of the older trade centers on the route to China was the only maritime military intervention from India into Southeast Asia known to pre-modern history (balancing the two from China in the 1290s and 1400s). This was from a southern and maritime Tamil polity, not from the empire-builders of the Gangetic plain. The Chola Dynasty since 985 had risen with the increase in trade from the Indian Ocean to Song China, although it was aggressively Shaivite rather than Buddhist. Its partner and potential rival in exploiting this trade was Sriwijaya, which sponsored the building of a Buddhist *vihara* (monastery) at the principal Chola port of Nagapattinam in 1005, as Tang China had done a couple of centuries earlier, to facilitate pilgrims following the trade route. But the south Indian traders sought the greater profits that would flow from direct access to China. The Chinese court recorded the first "tribute" from the Cholas in 1015, among a flurry of Sriwijayan ones. Ten years later the Chola king Rajendra made his move, claiming that he sent many ships to capture the treasures of Sriwijaya including its "gate of large jewels" (perhaps a metaphor for the gateway to China), among a dozen ports in the Malacca Straits area. Sriwijaya's sway over rival ports relied on supernatural charisma (loyalty was sanctioned by Buddhist-tinged oaths), patronage, and privileged access to China rather than armies or laws. What little it had accumulated by way of administrative capital was lost with the Chola raid.

The new era favored centers that could combine a domestic rice surplus with control of trade arteries, without being exposed to direct naval attack. Popular Buddhism remained a key mobilizing factor, but kings were increasingly able to channel it for their own accumulation of sacred power. And for such kings, even while patronizing the Buddhist pilgrimage centers, the hierarchies of Hinduism were indispensable. They required a corps of Brahmins to conduct the rituals of enthronement and legitimation as godlike *devaraja* or "king of the gods," elevated far above others by the accumulation of supernatural power.

In linguistic terms, to judge by the inscriptions, this period marked a vernacularization of the earlier "language of the gods," Sanskrit, into what is recognizably Bama, Khmer, Cham, Javanese, and Malay, each with its own adaptation of an Indic script. This shift occurred throughout the Indic world, slightly earlier in south India than in Southeast Asia. By the end of this period each had congealed as a distinct high-culture tradition with which the literate elite of religious scholars and court officials had to be familiar. Sanskrit and Pali were still known to scholars, but no longer served as the essential mark of a universal civilization. On the ground, of course, numerous spoken dialects differed markedly throughout this sprawling region, from each other and from the written high culture. But the pattern of pilgrimage to sacred sites of piety and learning, rather more than the pull of charismatic kings, laid some basis for the broader cultural integrations that would follow.

Angkor and the Khmer. The most puzzling case for historians, and the first to emerge as a major power center in the new era, was the civilization we know as Angkor (the term itself a localization of *nagara*). The idea of cosmically powerful kings identified with Shiva and the *lingga* cult appears to have become established in the Khmer area of the lower Mekong and Tonle Sap Rivers in the ninth century. It may have come from the islands in the south, since the first Khmer to claim himself (according to much later inscriptions) as a *devaraja* representing the power of Shiva appears to have brought this idea from "Jawa." In the time of one of his descendants called Yosadharapura (reigned c.889–910) a city was established at Angkor. This was not, or not yet, a "state" that could be inherited or captured by a king.

The astonishing development of Angkorean civilization in two centuries that followed, 950–1150, certainly requires more explanation than the *sakti* of Shaivite kings and their Brahmin advisors, however. The awe-inspiring temple complexes of Angkor Wat (c.1140) and Angkor Thom (c.1200), the vast reservoirs, and the straight roads fit for armies to march hundreds of kilometers, inspired earlier scholars to presume that here, at least, was a true oriental despotism organizing a complex hydraulic system. Subsequent research has shown, however, that Khmer agriculture rested rather on thousands of autonomous village irrigation systems. The core of the Angkor *nagara* in the plain north of the Tonle Sap lake was extremely favored by the lake's prolific fish and its habit of doubling or tripling its extent in the wet season when Mekong flood waters filled it to capacity. The Khmer method of agriculture required dykes to slow the retreat of the water and direct it into bunded rice fields. Traces of more than 3,000 temples have been discovered in this flood plain, each served by a community that cooperated to build its dykes. The system did not require state control, yet at its peak may have contained one or two million people, probably more than 5% of the total Southeast Asian population of the time. The uniquely favorable location attracted people to the Angkor area where they flourished for two centuries.

This concentration gave Angkor the potential manpower to dominate over an unprecedentedly large hinterland. It became a militarized state only after a fleet of the more maritime-oriented Chams sailed up the Mekong and plundered the riches of Angkor in 1177. The leader who drove the Chams out, known as Jayavarman VII (r.1181–1220), was understandably obsessed with military power, and became the conqueror and builder *par excellence* of Khmer history. In religion he was also exceptional. He adopted Mahayana Buddhism, perhaps as a way to rise above the pluralities of the old Shaivite order. His reign was all conquests and building projects, estimated to have exceeded those of all previous rulers combined. While in many respects he does look the stereotype of the "oriental despot," his power was not structural but personal, an extreme case of what Wolters (1999) called the "man of prowess" phenomenon in Southeast Asia, where dynastic and bureaucratic continuities were relatively low. His massive building projects were not sustainable, including the rapidly built Bayon (Figure 2.1) and what appear desperate enlargements of the water reservoirs. His Buddhism was rejected by his successors, though it later made a comeback. His excesses probably hastened the demise of the system.

Pagan and the Bama. In the Irrawaddy valley a typically Southeast Asian fragmentation of power continued through the tenth century, during which ethnically Bama migrants from the north (perhaps driven by a rising Nanchao in Yunnan) appear to have joined and eventually dominated the older Pyu settlements. They probably brought with them some of the new techniques of irrigating and ploughing rice fields. By the eleventh century, Pagan on the central Irrawaddy had emerged as the preeminent center of Buddhist pilgrimage and temple-building. It was adjacent to the Irrawaddy valley's most sacred pre-Buddhist pilgrimage site, the volcanic cone now known as Mt Popa, from which the *nats* of the Burmese spirit world are believed to have emerged.

Figure 2.1 Buddha-like faces on the Bayon, perhaps intended also to represent its patron, Jayavarman VII, the most powerful and most Buddhist of Angkor's kings (1181–1218). Source: Wikimedia Commons. Photograph by Mackay Savage.

Pagan's great founder-king, Anawrahta (r.1044–77), was also by tradition the great synthesizer of Buddhism and *nat*-worship. He canonized 36 ancestral and nature spirits (almost equally male and female) from Mt Popa, and an additional one to represent the Hindu god Indra, by including their images at the base of the great Buddhist stupa, Shwezigon, he built near Pagan to contain a tooth relic from Sri Lanka. Pagan also had some practical advantages through its ability to attract rice supplies from upriver settlements such as Kyaukse and Minbu, as well as the Irrawaddy trade artery between the Indian Ocean and footpaths into Yunnan. Anawrahta for the first time appears to have established a kind of Buddhist peace over the whole of the Irrawaddy valley.

During the following two centuries, Pagan grew ever more important as a center of Buddhist piety. As many as 10,000 brick structures may have arisen in the plain of Pagan, and 3,000 remain as marvels of this charter period. The inscriptions show that most were built not by kings but by a landed elite, typically donating rice land for the building and upkeep of the temples. Not without reason did a Burmese envoy tell the Chinese Emperor in 1286 that Pagan's glory derived more from religion than from military power. This temple building peaked around 1200, when tens of thousands of acres were donated each year, and collapsed quickly toward 1300. The cause of the rise and fall of this pious building is controversial, as in Angkor, but it must have accompanied an expansion of population and profitable rice-growing. A favorable climate and rainfall in the period had much to do with both phenomena, as did improved technologies of rice-growing and metal-working and the growth of trade during the prosperous Song Dynasty in China.

Java-Bali. Although the Buddha-Shiva civilization of the Mataram area south of Mount Merapi in Java was abandoned in the tenth century, it had sown the seeds of a distinctive Java-Bali culture. The two great Indian epics were both "Javanized" into a poetic form of old Javanese, the Ramayana as early as the ninth century and the Mahabharata in the tenth. The Ramayana was also popular enough to be displayed graphically, at the Prambanan temple and on one of the gold items discovered in a buried hoard from this period. Elements of the same cultural complex began to appear in the intra-volcano valleys of east Java (around modern Malang and Kediri, divided by the active Kelut volcano), and in southeast Bali, of which the earliest dated inscriptions are tenth century. As the inscriptions cease in central Java they become more numerous in east Java and Bali. The period of this flowering of a Hindu-Buddhist culture in their upland valleys in the eleventh to fourteenth centuries can be seen as a charter era of similar type to that in the Mainland. It also profited from similar techniques of wet-rice agriculture, including the plough, and thereby built another pocket of concentrated population with a comfortable rice surplus. Some of the legendary hero-kings of this era continued to be celebrated in subsequent literature and performance. The fourteenth-century Pararaton rendered immortal the story of Ken Dedes, "the princess with the flaming womb" of an earlier era, and her low-born but supernaturally powerful lover Ken Anggrok. The first two state universities of the east were named in the 1950s after two eleventh-century "men of prowess," Airlangga in Java and Udayana in Bali. Even the first of independent Indonesia's universities, Gajah Mada in Yogyakarta, was named not for a personality of that region but for the most powerful chancellor of east Java's fourteenth-century Majapahit.

A Javanese culture was being formed in these valleys through such stories, and the cycles of markets and pilgrimage to the sacred sites of Buddha and Shiva. The economy was commercialized and monetized in a trade boom of the tenth to thirteenth centuries, but never unified politically. The Brantas River that curls its way from the valleys between volcanoes to the coast near Surabaya was not able to unify as the Irrawaddy and the Tonle Sap began to do. The inscriptions of kings such as Airlangga and Kertanagara (1254–92) suggest that they promoted irrigation, conquered rivals, and attracted holy men and artists to their courts, but could build only a temporary primacy.

The unprecedented maritime expedition of "a thousand ships," 20,000 men and horse-mounted cavalry that Kublai Khan sent from China to Java in 1292–3, evidently failed in its objective to establish Mongol authority. The Chinese force was exploited by a man claiming to be Kertanegara's son-in-law, who used it to establish a new capital only 50 km from the mouth of the Brantas River, and thereby to control the foreign trade of all the fertile uplands. This became Majapahit, which in the fourteenth century established a true charter *nagara* by combining Java's overseas connections with the politically autonomous upland valleys. The most remarkable document to emanate from Hindu-Buddhist Java was a text written in 1365 by Majapahit's "superintendent of Buddhist affairs," Mpu Prapanca, rediscovered in a single old Javanese text at the Dutch conquest of Lombok in 1894, and known in its two English translations as *Desawarnana* or *Nagarakertagama*. This lengthy poem is dedicated to honoring the king known to history as Hayam Wuruk (b. 1334; r.1350–89), as the divine figure who supernaturally unites all of Java and the known world. "He is Shiva and Buddha, embodied in both the material and the immaterial; as King of the Mountain, Protector of the Protectorless, he is the lord of the lords of the world" (Robson 1995, 26). Prapanca tells in vivid poetry the earliest history of Java we have, explaining that it is through women that the dynasty was established and legitimized. The founder of Majapahit who allied with the invading Mongols married all the daughters of the former king Kertanegara to establish his legitimacy. One of these wives, Rajapatni, is described as so adept in yoga and Buddhist meditation that she could arrange the succession of her daughter on the throne, and later of that daughter's son, Hayam Wuruk himself.

This Mongol/Chinese intervention in 1292 helped move the balance of power in east Java toward the coast and commerce. The emergence of east Java and its north coast ports as a hub of Southeast Asian trade in the following century was made possible in part by the technology brought by defectors and captives from the Mongol fleet. A new type of large Sino-Southeast Asian trading vessel, known to sixteenth-century European observers as a junk (Javanese *jong*), came into use at this time. The literary evidence of Hayam Wuruk's reign shows that Majapahit knew the trade centers of the *Nusantara* world (Peninsula and Archipelago), and regarded them as part of the universe protected by Majapahit's divine king. These extended from the spice-producing islands of Maluku in the east to the newly Muslim port of Pasai (Sumatra) in the west. Siam, Cambodia, Champa, Dai Viet, and some Indian ports were listed as "always friends." This brief interval of peace and prosperity consolidated a formidable literary, musical, and theatrical culture that would survive much subsequent disunity.

Prapanca and the other great writer/monk of the period, Mpu Tantular, celebrated not only their own Buddhist faith but the other two crucial elements of Java's inherent balance – the Shaivite priests essential to Indic ideas of kingship, and the indigenous tradition which honored the sacred power of the volcanoes, the sea, and the ascetics (*resi*) who lived hermit lives in the forest. In southern Java and Bali royal rituals appeased both the male gods of the mountains and the female deities of the sea. The Shaivite kings of Singhasari positioned themselves between volcanoes, naming the most active one Smeru for the Meru of Indic myth, and the others Bromo (the Hindu Brahma) and Arjuna. A mark of Hayam Wuruk's divine status was that the active Kelut volcano erupted at his birth in 1334, while the earth shook with earthquakes.

The *Desawarnana* tells us that the royal citadel of Majapahit was surrounded by the priests of Shiva in the east, under their Brahmaraja, the Buddhists in the south, under their Abbot, and the royal relatives and officials in the west. It became a theme of Javanese mysticism that different ritual paths to enlightenment were only external expressions of an inner oneness. The state motto of contemporary Indonesia (*Bhinneka Tunggal Ika*) derives from a fourteenth-century mystical poem, the *Sutasoma*, in which Mpu Tantular pondered the essential oneness beneath surface differences, such as those between Buddhism, Shaivism, mountain cults, and the new, still marginal presence of Islam: "the truth of Jina (Buddha) and the truth of Shiva is one; they are indeed different, but they remain one [*Bhinneka Tunggal Ika*], as there is no duality in Truth" (Santoso 1975, 578).

AUSTRONESIAN GATEWAY PORTS – THE NEGERI

The Malay and Cham polities experienced not a "charter era" in this period but rather an intensification of rivalry between strategically placed ports along the trade routes supplying Song and Yuan China. Just as Sriwijaya fell before the Cholas in 1025, the Champa capital of Indrapura (modern Tra Kieu, near Hoi An), probably including its ridge-top temple sites of My Son, fell before a Dai Viet attack around 1000. The subsequent four centuries of increasingly lively trade were a time of opportunity for trade-based societies, but of a different type. These had never been *nagara* unified by a single river system and the rice surplus of an extensive irrigated core, but rather what we will call by the Malay term *negeri* – rival ports strategically situated as gateways for upriver communities along the trade route of the Malacca Straits and the mountainous eastern coast of the Mainland. The model of multi-centered loose polities has been described by such metaphors as mandala, archipelago, galaxy, or more prosaically federation, but these may exaggerate the political stability of the model. What held these societies together were essentially commonalities of religion, language, and material culture, and the pragmatic need to trade with China as if they were a single polity presenting "tribute" from a recognized barbarian kingdom. Kings continued to build Shaivite temples (in Champa) and Mahayana Buddhist, often Tantric, stupas in Sumatra, with inscriptions suggesting their aspirations to be protectors of the various regions within their realm. A 1070 Cham inscription notes that the king "has protected the ten regions from fear." In times of outside threat, which Champa suffered repeatedly from Dai Viet and Angkor, kings did indeed attempt to act this way. But their sanctions remained supernatural for the most part, threatening cosmic retribution in the afterlife for those who disturbed the royal order. The ports that succeeded in this period were highly cosmopolitan, embracing Chinese, Indian, Arab, and Malay traders, Hindu, Buddhist, and Muslim teachers.

In its own inscriptions Champa appeared to recognize five Sanskrit-named regions or centers spread along the coast. Having lost the northernmost, Indrapura, to Dai Viet, a new successful center emerged in the twelfth century named Vijaya (near modern Quy Nhon), until this was also lost to Dai Viet in 1471. Chinese and Sino-Viet sources recognized at least ten centers, however, while one Champa mission to China claimed that Champa had "105 places" protected by the king. The polity continued to be among the most frequent "tribute"-bearers to China, but also traded increasingly eastward, to Java and Butuan (Mindanao). To a greater extent than the Malay ports of the Malacca Straits, each region had its own small rice-growing valley, profiting from the annual flooding of the riverine plain. Indeed, "Cham rice" was introduced to southern China during the Song period as a superior strain.

During the first millennium of the Common Era, the Cham ports had profited by being "not China," free ports close to the great empire and its flourishing southern maritime province of Jiaozhi, but not subject to its restrictive regulation of maritime trade. Once a Viet polity emerged from the collapse of the Tang in the tenth century, it became a rival for Champa. From the eleventh through the thirteenth centuries there was much conflict between ambitious rulers of Angkor, Champa, and Dai Viet, each anxious for dominance in the flourishing trade with Song China. In the fourteenth century, however, when the *nagara* of Pagan and Angkor were in crisis, Champa, like Majapahit in Java, reached an unprecedented peak of external power. The key to this was evidently its large fleet and crucial location, not only for the trade bound for China, but in acting as the export center for Vietnamese ceramics, then at their peak of distribution virtually throughout Southeast Asia. When the ambitious Che Bong Nga came to the Champa throne in 1361 relations with Dai Viet broke down, and the great Cham fleet turned to raiding the Red River delta. In a sequence of ten separate raids before 1383, the Vietnamese capital was sacked three times. This aggression ended when the Vietnamese successfully deployed newly acquired firearms to kill Che Bong Nga as he was on the point of his greatest success in 1390. This loss proved crucial, since the Viet were better able ultimately to profit from the Chinese invasion and occupation of their homeland in 1406 to create a military/bureaucratic state of Chinese type, and thereby definitively to shift the balance against Champa in the fifteenth century (Chapter 9).

Malay ports around the Straits of Malacca also flourished during the trade boom of Song and Yuan, but were even less united than the Champa ones. After the Chola raid on the Sriwijaya capital at Palembang, the China trade shifted to the Batang Hari River further north under the pretext of continuing the "tribute" of Sriwijaya. One Buddhist temple complex was developed at Muara Jambi, near the mouth of that river, whereas others were built hundreds of kilometers up Sumatran rivers, at sites such as Pagarruyung in Minangkabau, Muara Takus, and Padang Lawas. By contrast, a major port site of the eleventh to fourteenth centuries has been excavated at Kota China, near modern Medan, without much evidence of sacred buildings. Marco Polo visited the north Sumatran coast in 1292, as Islam was beginning to make its mark in the Sumatran ports, and declared that there were eight "kingdoms" in Sumatra, each with its own language. In the Peninsula, meanwhile, archaeological sites at the portages reveal increased activity from the eleventh century, with seemingly autonomous Buddhist city-states around modern Chaiya, Nakhon Sithammarat, and Trang.

Sumatra had extensive contact and conflict with the Hindu-Buddhist centers of east Java in this period, giving rise to a cluster of inscriptions and Buddhist constructions found almost exclusively in the highlands. The highland areas today speaking dialects very similar to modern Malay, from Minangkabau in the north to Rejang in the south, had already established a written culture based on a south Indian type of script. About 30 inscriptions from this period relate to the figure of Adityavarman, a Buddhist prince evidently sent from Majapahit in the fourteenth century to exploit the gold-producing area Majapahit knew as Melayu. The majority of these inscriptions are in the higher reaches of the Batang Hari river system and at Pagarruyung, the later supernatural center of essentially stateless Minangkabau. They show Adityavarman attempting to accumulate cosmic power in this area, but do not mention his undoubted interest in the region's gold and rice. The fourteenth century also marks the first Malay manuscript (on paper rather than as a bronze inscription), preserved on bark-paper in the highlands at Kerinci. This contained a compilation of laws, in Old Malay but with a Sanskrit introduction.

The fourteenth-century manuscript in question also contains a more everyday document of similar age in both the ancient Pallava script and the *ka-ga-nga* alphabet which became widespread in Sumatra. In short, Buddhist civilization, and writing for both sacred and prosaic purposes, had already extended to the highlands of Sumatra by the fourteenth century. So had notions of sacred kingship expressed in tantric Buddhist form, though this feature appears to have survived Adityavarman's death in the 1370s only as the lofty charisma that continued to surround the "kings" of Minangkabau at Pagarruyung for several centuries. Once deprived of the opportunity to control trade through a single river-mouth or privileged access to the China market, however, the highlands returned to an essentially stateless mode of civilization. The many ports of eastern Sumatra and the Peninsula, in turn, appear to have developed Malay in the direction of a lingua franca between them, even before Islam and its Arabic loan-words transformed the language in the fifteenth century.

DAI VIET AND THE BORDER WITH CHINA

Dai Viet in the tenth to thirteenth centuries was also a charter polity in the sense of establishing the first distinct Vietnamese written identity, a permanent capital (Southeast Asia's most enduring), and a concentration of population around irrigated rice cultivation. But far from vernacularizing an Indic language and script, its perilous achievement was to build in a Chinese written idiom a polity that was not China. Its predecessor, Jiaozhi, had been the "jewel in the crown" of the Tang Dynasty, occupying all three sides of the Tongking Gulf and making of it China's vital southern trade centre. Indeed, throughout the first millennium CE the Red River delta was more clearly enmeshed in the Sinic world than most parts of what we now call China. As the Tang collapsed in the tenth century, however, Jiaozhi broke into competing fragments, among which only Dai Viet succeeded in having its separate legitimacy recognized by Chinese dynasties. It thereby drew a boundary against the further southward expansion of Chinese imperial order that proved decisive for the definition of Southeast Asia in the long term.

Dai Viet's state aspirations were always Chinese/Confucian rather than Indic/Shaivite, so it cannot be called a *nagara*. Popular Mahayana Buddhism was, however, crucial to its earliest stage of state formation, as it was in the charter *nagara*. This was the achievement of some warrior chiefs from a redoubt at Hoa-lu, on the southern edge of the Red River delta, who harassed the remaining elements of collapsing Tang imperial control, gained recognition from the interim Southern Han Chinese regime, and established a degree of local order. But only their alliance with Buddhist monks literate in Chinese, and aware of the basic principles of Chinese bureaucratic order, made possible the re-establishment of a court at the old Tang-era capital of Thang-long (modern Hanoi) in 1010. The monks managed the essential tributary relationship with the Song court, supervised the building of Buddhist monuments, and enabled the Ly Dynasty of kings (1009–1225) to produce a body of laws and court rituals. Buddhism (rather than Confucianism) was essentially the mark of civilization, but like their equivalents at Pagan, the Ly systematized the powerful local spirits into a kind of royal cult. The Tongking Gulf maritime area profited from Song China's prosperity on the one hand and relative military weakness on the other, to become a much more fluid zone of competing ports. The Ly also launched several raids on Champa to the south and on competing "bandit" groups to its north. The long-term consequence of China's diminished control of the Tongking Gulf, however, was to make Guangzhou (Canton), and especially Quanzhou in Fujian, the favored access ports to China, which would lead by the fifteenth century to the isolation of Dai Viet and the whole Tongking Gulf from long-distance Asian trade.

Maritime trade was still vigorous enough in the thirteenth century, however, to enable the Tran clan to use its fleet to seize power and establish a new dynasty in 1225. Its great innovation was to inaugurate a Chinese-style examination system for officials. While Buddhism remained dominant, these examinations on Chinese literary classics provided a growing cadre of literati for whom the norms of Tang and Song Chinese statecraft were a model. These literati were instrumental in enabling Dai Viet to survive the threat from an aggressive Mongol China, which occupied Thang-long in 1257 before being driven back. The task of the literati was then to try to convince successive rulers of China in the language of the classics that Dai Viet was a separate place, equal in civilization and dignity to China itself. One of them, Le Van Huu, was commissioned to write the first narrative of Dai Viet history. His *Dai Viet Su Ky* of 1272 rejected as unsatisfactory past rulers who called themselves only by the Chinese term for king, and reached back to a legendary declaration of a southern ruler opposing the Han that he was equal to the great emperor himself. The status of an emperor, Le declared, lay in his virtue (*duc*), not his territory or armies.

The Tran Dynasty did not survive the deadly struggle with Che Bong Nga's Champa in the 1370s and 1380s, and the takeover of "usurper" Ho Quy Ly in the 1390s provided the pretext for Ming China to invade in favor of the "legitimate" Tran in 1406, inaugurating a complete transformation of the country. Already for some decades beforehand, however, the order provided by the Buddhist monkhood and an alliance of warrior-chiefs was dissolving in Dai Viet's own version of a fourteenth-century crisis. It had done enough, however, to mark a clear national identity for subsequent generations of Vietnamese.

THE STATELESS MAJORITY IN THE CHARTER ERA

The charter civilizations that succeeded in combining a rice surplus from a core area with control of a vital artery of trade occupied only small enclaves of a vast, heavily forested region (Map 2.1). The cosmopolitan port-cities along the trade routes made even less impact on the overall environment. The overwhelming majority of Southeast Asian space, sheltering a probable majority of its people, comprised primary forest, grasslands in some drier areas, and the secondary forest resulting from the shifting agriculture described in Chapter 1. Population throughout this area was lightly dispersed around the coastal strand and upland waterways where food was relatively easily harvested from sea, river, and forest fringe, as well as the palm and fruit trees, vegetables, tubers, and hill rice planted by scattered village communities. As James Scott (2009) has demonstrated, irrigated rice baskets such as Kyaukse in upper Burma, the Red River delta, or the stream-fed upland pockets of east Java both required and facilitated a high degree of organization and peace, to ensure that the high yields of the harvest season were safeguarded for the remainder of the year. Coordination was required, if not through a state then through a kind of irrigation association like the Balinese *subak*. Peaceful conditions and high rice yields per hectare boosted the population of these rice bowls during the charter era, and permitted leisure time for a rich ritual and cultural life. The ease with which discontented or dispossessed farmers could open an alternative agricultural frontier outside state control created definite limits to oppression.

Outside these denser enclaves, scattered village communities engaged with a network of other communities both through reciprocal trade, pilgrimage, feasting and the exchange of tribute for protection, and in sporadic raiding. Their freedom was real, but came at the cost of insecurity and constant readiness to fight or run, which kept populations low. The contrast between such mobile, stateless societies and the cities and irrigated-rice cores became progressively sharper after 1400, as Confucian, Islamic, and Christian notions of civilization created boundaries between those within and without – as detailed in Chapter 5. In the charter era, however, the civilization of written culture and shared ritual was carried in the first place by a Buddhist monkhood that knew few boundaries, and spread its habits of scholarship also to forest retreats and hilltop sacred places. As we have seen in the Sumatran case, the highlands were by no means isolated from the spread of these elements. Even those peoples regarded as most clearly outside the civilized world in the nineteenth century – highland Bataks (Sumatra), Torajans (Sulawesi), Ifugaos (Luzon), and Karens (Mainland) – absorbed key elements of Indic and Buddhist civilization, including Sanskrit terms for cosmic forces. Bataks kept alive through centuries of subsequent isolation their enthusiasm for chess, introduced before Islam from India and Persia.

Writing was an essential tool of states whether for law or for narratives of legitimacy. The many peoples of Southeast Asia who did not have a system of writing until the advent of the roman script at western hands were seen as stateless and backward. Yet many such peoples, including the Hmong, Karen,

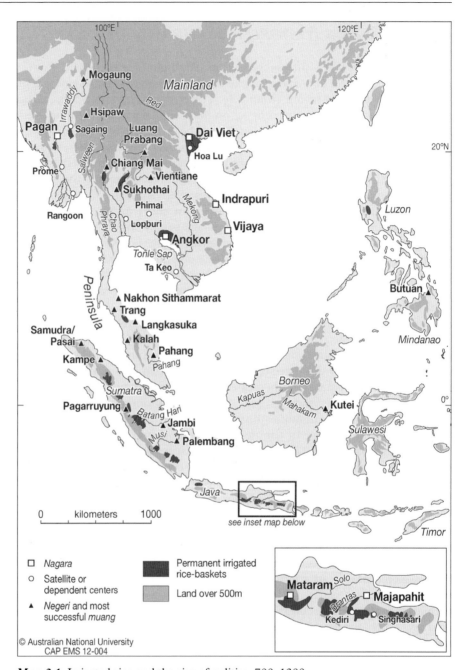

Map 2.1 Irrigated rice and the rise of polities, 700–1300.

Chin, and Yao in the upland Mainland, and Kadazan/Dusun, Kayan, and Kenyah in Borneo, retain vivid stories of how their sacred book and the keys to reading it were lost, stolen, or destroyed in a mythical past. In earlier stages of the spread of writing at Buddhist hands, the barriers were low to sharing or accepting that writing across the still-embryonic boundaries between civilized and barbarian, believers and pagans. Once writing became associated with both alien religion and alien state power, on the other hand, those barriers became substantial. Nevertheless, the spread of a particular type of *ka-ga-nga* alphabet around stateless societies of Island Southeast Asia is a remarkable exception to the widespread association of writing with states and scriptural religions. That this script of straight lines to cut across the fibre of bamboo or palm-leaf with a stylus was first adapted from Indic models in Sumatra during the "charter era" of vernacularization is suggested by the fourteenth-century Sumatran text described above. A similar alphabet had spread throughout highland Sumatra, to south Sulawesi and much of the Philippines by the sixteenth century. It was used, Spanish missionaries in Luzon noted, not for religion or government, but by women even more than men for exchanging notes and commercial and ritual information. In parts of Sumatra the exchange of love notes between young men and women was an essential part of the mating game, and the probable reason for exceptionally high levels of literacy.

This pervasiveness of Buddhist civilization was even more evident in the Mainland during this charter era. Its first carriers appear to have been monastic networks expressing themselves through inscriptions in Mon (the Austroasiatic language of the Irrawaddy delta), and through a style of religious art known as Dvaravati, from the sixth to ninth centuries. This Buddhist culture influenced not only the *nagara* of Angkor and Pagan, but also the diversity of Tai-speaking peoples who gradually moved into Mainland Southeast Asia from the north during the eighth to twelfth centuries. They developed a predominately Theravada style of Buddhism, but suffused also with Mahayanist elements and the *lingga* cult of Shiva, present in most of the autonomous rice-growing Tai *muang* (a group of interrelated villages) of the Mainland. These *muang* were clearly very successful in organizing the irrigation of upland valleys for rice, and their population grew accordingly. They appear to have recognized each other as part of a coherent world probably sharing agricultural technologies, trade networks, and a similar pattern of dominating the irrigable valley floors while operating in symbiosis (mutual raiding as well as exchange of essentials) with longer-established swidden farmers of the hills.

As the *nagara* crumbled in the thirteenth and fourteenth centuries, Tai *chao* (lords), war leaders or men of prowess, emerged to challenge Angkor or Pagan through strategic raiding expeditions, while using some of the Shaivite rhetoric and imagery of the old charter order. Hso Hkan Hpa features as such a figure among the Shans of the upper and eastern Irrawaddy basin. In the period 1152–1205, the chronicles claim, he led Shan forces to attack "China" (probably meaning the Nanchao *nagara* of the Yunnan area), Assam, and eventually Pagan itself. Despite these legends, the essential Shan level of polity remained the autonomous *muang*, sharing a written culture and extensive market networks, but never developing into a bureaucratic state. Since the unifying factor of the Irrawaddy trade artery was in Bama hands, the more successful Shan *muang*, like Mogaung and Hsipaw, tended to acknowledge the Bama *nagara* when it was strong, and raid it when it was weak, rather than developing a unifying state of their own.

Mangrai, who created the Tai kingdom of Lan Na and founded its capital at Chiang Mai during an energetic reign (1259–1317), was clearly skilled both as war leader and diplomat. His chroniclers claimed that alone among the lords of neighboring *muang*, he had the legitimacy that came from Indic rituals of enthronement and supernatural regalia, while in the course of his reign he acquired famously potent images and relics of the Buddha from older-established Mon and Bama cities. In 1287, Mangrai mediated a dispute between two other ambitious *chao*, of Phayao and Sukhothai respectively, which ended in an agreed alliance to fight not each other but the threatening Mongol/Chinese armies from the north.

King Ram Khamhaeng, who ruled Sukhothai from 1279 to 1298, appeared from both chronicles and inscriptions to have created a still more remarkable sphere of influence within his short reign, extending to Tai *muang* throughout the Chao Phraya valley and even into the Peninsula as far as Nakhon Sithammarat (whose chronicle improbably claims that Ram Khamhaeng came to rule the city for two years). His secret appears to have been to offer to an array of diverse peoples a distinctly Theravada discipline of the Buddhist monkhood, and a model of consensual kingship more compatible with *muang* autonomy than that of overstretched and declining Angkor. His famous multilingual inscription of 1283, the authenticity of which has been doubted because it was almost too good to be true for its nineteenth-century modernizing discoverer, explained Ram Khamhaeng's kingship by the Angkor-like things it did *not* do.

> When any commoner or man of rank dies, his estate – his elephants, wives, children, granaries, rice, retainers and groves of areca and betel – is left entirely to his son … When he [the king] sees someone's rice he does not covet it, when he sees someone's wealth he does not get angry … If anyone riding an elephant comes to see him to put his own country under his protection, he helps him, treats him generously, and takes care of him (cited Wyatt 1982, 54–5).

Sukhothai has elements of a charter state in the model of Thai-ness (now more specifically referring to Siam rather than Tai in general) it left, notably including the vernacular Thai script and the close identification with Sri Lanka's Theravada style of Buddhism. But it also bequeathed a loose personal pattern in which heads of small *muang* acknowledged one other's legitimacy in an ever-shifting hierarchy of rivalry or temporary deference.

Strategically placed on the upper Chao Phraya, Sukhothai provided the Tai within its orbit with some of the distinctiveness of the people of a state, taken further in subsequent centuries by Ayutthaya near the mouth of the river. We may thus begin to call them Thai or Siamese – a distinct variant of Tai. The tributaries of the Irrawaddy were not similarly unifying for the Shan, and the middle Mekong also less so than the Chao Phraya. The Lao counterpart of Ram Kamhaeng, Fa Ngum, therefore remained in the category of a man of prowess, unifying ephemerally for war purposes. With his more successful but less remembered son Un Huan he built a major capital at Luang Prabang between 1353 and 1416. Fa Ngum invites comparison with his Sumatran contemporary Adityavarman in bringing some of the ritual and imagery of a Shaivite charter state into the stateless territory of Tai *muang* and upland shifting cultivators. Fa Ngum's state, like Adityavarman's, was too Angkor-like to last, and he was overthrown in favor of his son in 1373. Un Huan was more diplomatic, and in his cordial relations with more powerful neighbors he claimed to be king of 300,000 Tai (organized in irrigated rice-growing *muang*) and 400,000 other peoples presumably distinguished by their swidden cultivation. The prominence of these rulers died with them, but subsequent state-builders in the nineteenth and twentieth centuries cultivated their memory.

It is more difficult to describe the probable majority of Southeast Asians who continued to live the life of shifting cultivators, fishermen, and hunter-gatherers outside the fixities that irrigated rice brought. Occasional Chinese references suggest that the *nagara* did incorporate such people through various types of bondage. Zhou Daguan described how the Angkor elite used "savages" as slaves in the 1290s, and regarded sexual relations with them as disgraceful. In one intriguing passage he distinguishes between two kinds of savage, of which the first "know how to deal with people," are useful as slaves and were probably in the process of assimilation into the dominant society. The second were "very ferocious" hunter-gatherers, who "have no homes to live in, but move from place to place in the mountains" (Zhou 1297/2007, 61).

The savage/civilized dichotomy came easily to Chinese, Arab, and later European observers, but Southeast Asian sources have no such sense of boundary. They mention different peoples distinguished by dress and language, and various types of subordination to a lord or patriarch. The dichotomies that do appear are those between upland and lowland, mountain and sea, forest and settled wet-rice agriculture. But the former categories of these dyads have their own spiritual potency, exemplified by mountain shrines, forest monks, and local spirits. Vernacular Buddhism drew no boundary to exclude them. Even in the later period when boundaries were drawn (see Chapter 5), the interdependence and synergy between these dyads would remain part of the fabric of Southeast Asia.

THIRTEENTH/FOURTEENTH-CENTURY CRISIS

There has been much discussion of the reasons for the eclipse of the temple-building *nagara* in the thirteenth and fourteenth centuries, and the apparent fragmentation of power among trade-based *negeri* and relatively compact but autonomous Tai *muang*. Among causes favored are the invasions of Yuan (Mongol) China into Burma and Java in the 1280s and 1290s, the southward migration of Tai-speaking peoples under pressure of agricultural expansion in south China, and the growing importance of new religions. The Theravada Buddhist *sangha* (monkhood) in the Mainland, and Islamic teachers in the Islands, increasingly dominated the supernatural resources which kings had sought to attract to themselves through Shaivite cults and the Sanskrit cosmopolis.

Much progress has been made recently in understanding global patterns of climate, of disease, and of volcanic and tectonic disturbance. No historian of the long term can now fail to grapple with these expanding fields, even though most of the new data and the debates concentrate on temperate zones in the northern hemisphere. In that context it is now clear that the Eurasian expansion of Mongol power in the thirteenth century was followed by a Eurasian pandemic of bubonic plague in the 1340s, halving populations in some intensive-agriculture areas. It is likely that parts of Southeast Asia joined the common disease pool of Eurasia at about the same time, suffering initial heavy losses in the pockets of dense population, but eventually acquiring in them the status where smallpox and plague were endemic rather than epidemic, and therefore less destructive. The shift of rice-growing population to the swampy flood plains of the Mainland river deltas was long restricted by malaria and other water-borne diseases, but in the fourteenth century delta rice agriculture appears to have reached the point where the anopheles mosquito did not survive the harsh sunlight of continuous *padi* fields. An early Siamese chronicle records a myth that appears to link the fourteenth-century establishment of the capital on the lower Chao Phraya River with the conquest of a disease that looks like malaria. An exiled Chinese prince was leading his fleet from place to place in search of an appropriate new settlement. When he came to the island of Ayutthaya in the Chao Phraya River he was told by a hermit that no settlement could be built there unless the dragon (*naga*) in a marsh there was first vanquished, which "on being disturbed blew poisonous saliva from his mouth. This brought about such an epidemic that everybody around there died of the stench." Once the dragon had been killed and the marsh filled in, "the land has been free from epidemics" (van Vliet 1640/2005, 200–1).

The "Mediaeval warm period" in about 900–1250 facilitated agricultural production in Europe and China in this period, and its reversal toward cooler weather contributed to northern-hemisphere famines in the fourteenth century. Tree-ring analysis, in its infancy in the tropics, now suggests that the warmer weather in northern Europe was connected with more reliable monsoon rainfall patterns in Mainland Southeast Asia. Thereafter there were some substantial periods of drought. One colossal eruption creating the crater of Rinjani (Lombok) in 1257 must have disrupted weather patterns and deposited poisonous ash on a wide area. These critical changes in weather disrupted agriculture in general and the complex systems that sustained Pagan and Angkor in particular. Thereafter markedly dryer conditions are shown by recent tree-ring analysis, notably in the mid-fourteenth century and the extremely dry years 1401–4. What made these worse was the occurrence also of extremely wet years, the wettest of them occurring in 1257–8 and 1453, the years of the two biggest tropical volcanic eruptions. Floods appear to have damaged the hydraulic system of Angkor so much that its agriculture was unable to cope with the dry periods. These conditions also made the dry-zone agriculture of Upper Burma less viable. There was a shift of population to the wetter regions of the Irrawaddy delta, which also profited more directly from the flourishing maritime trade. The Mons of the coastal areas by 1300 had their own polity no longer in awe of Pagan. The Pagan *nagara* itself had been distracted by Mongol/Chinese expansionism in its northern hinterland from 1277 to 1301, and eventually fell to Shan raids in 1359–68 much as Angkor succumbed to other Tai-speakers in the Southeast.

This climatic data confirms a long-held hypothesis that the population density that had developed in Angkor through reliance on regular rainfall and flooding of the Tonle Sap proved no longer viable in the worsened climatic conditions of the mid-fourteenth century. The overstretched military empire and construction program of Jayavarman VII was impossible to maintain, and royal power appears to have begun to decline even before his probable death in 1218. The Angkor described by Zhou Daguan in the 1290s offered an agreeable urban life with an honored place for learning, but the Shaivite cult of kingship had lost the power it had to inspire devotion. The people were all Buddhist of distinctly Theravada type, with a temple in every village. In the countryside "as a result of repeated wars with the Siamese the land has been completely laid to waste" (Zhou 1297/2007, 79). The Thai conquest and looting of the capital, probably in 1431–2, only confirmed the massive shift away from the pattern of agriculture and sacred statecraft already long untenable.

Did the archipelagos experience a similar period of environmental crisis separating Buddhist from Muslim-Christian eras? Unfortunately the best tree-ring sequence explored so far, in Java teak forests, began only in 1514, and in their absence caution is appropriate on how to relate humid tropical islands to northern-hemisphere climatic patterns. Tectonic mega-events including tsunamis, and volcanic eruptions that darken skies and induce major crop failures, are likely to be more important factors.

Since the devastating tsunami of 2004 along the northwest coast of Sumatra, however, the advances in understanding this "subduction zone" have been spectacular. By examining and carbon-dating layers of sand deposited by previous tsunamis, and dating the death of coral through the uplift that accompanies major tectonic releases such as that of 2004, geologists have given us a degree of certainty about the last major events of equal or bigger scale than 2004. These probably multiple events occurred in the period 1340–1450, affecting both the northern (Aceh and Nias) and central sections of the west Sumatran coast. This provides an additional reason for the absence of Hindu-Buddhist remains on the tectonic west coast of Sumatra, and probably also the south coast of Java, in addition to the strong surf that reduces the number of safe harbors. River-mouth ports probably did facilitate international interactions in the several-century intervals between major tsunamis (as again during the relatively benign nineteenth and twentieth centuries), but a major tsunami would have eliminated most of the evidence.

The newer scientific research makes clear that there was relatively high discontinuity in the long-term pattern of Southeast Asian history, caused by climatic disruption, volcanoes, and tectonic releases. To this we should probably add diseases, in the period from the tenth to the fourteenth century, when the concentrated pockets of population were in the process of incorporation into the great Eurasian disease pool. Unlike the Americas and Australia, even

Island Southeast Asia did not suffer horrendous mortality with the coming of Europeans in the sixteenth century, meaning that smallpox and other diseases had become endemic earlier. But there are enough memories preserved in mythology about cataclysmic epidemics associated with the previous five centuries to make it likely that smallpox, plague, and cholera did arrive with the large Chinese fleets of the 1290s and early 1400s, or the smaller-scale Indian contacts, and became endemic after initial traumatic epidemics. This discontinuity is the background to Southeast Asia's still-low population of the sixteenth century, at only one-eighth the density of India or China.

[3] TRADE AND ITS NETWORKS

THE first two chapters of this book would have made little sense without reference to trade connections around the tropical seas. The presence of Chinese ceramics, Dongson (Red River valley) bronzes and Indian statues in seemingly remote corners of Southeast Asia from the beginning of the Common Era shows that long-distance trade affected them vitally for centuries before we have historical records. Nevertheless, the growing importance and measurability of trade in the age of commerce after 1400 makes this the point for a more systematic discussion of how it operated. The horizontal bonds of trust formed by different trading networks served both to integrate the civilizational patterns built by religion and written language and to link them with the broader worlds of Eurasia.

LAND AND SEA ROUTES

The commercial symbiosis of upstream agricultural centers and downstream ports appears to have been a feature of the river systems of the region for at least two millennia. As a missionary described the pre-Spanish Philippines:

> The inhabitants of the mountains cannot live without the fish, salt, and other articles of food ... of other districts; nor, on the other hand, can those of the coast live without the rice and cotton of the mountaineers (Loarca 1582, 121).

The trade centers near river-mouths or other strategic waterways could usually not provide themselves with rice. This was shipped down to them on the rivers from the more fertile and productive uplands. In return, however, all upland populations had need of salt, produced in tidal ponds for the most part. In exchange for their rice and other agricultural products, they also received dried fish from the downstream centers, and a variety of imported goods – precious metalware, ceramics, and cloth in particular, often produced as far away as India and China.

The movement of Tai peoples into northern Southeast Asia and the adjacent area of Yunnan in the thirteenth and fourteenth centuries, together with the

A History of Southeast Asia: Critical Crossroads, First Edition. Anthony Reid.

expansive energies of Yuan (Mongol) and early Ming (1368–c.1450) rule in China, created a lively traffic across the mountain passes of the region. What is best documented (from Chinese sources) is the tributary trade, with 250 overland missions from the Ming Dynasty to the Tai and other principalities of the northern highlands, and double that number of "tributary" missions in reply. The emissaries from the south presented slaves, elephants, horses, ivory, rhinoceros horn, gold, spices, and gems, and received in return a generally greater value in silver and silks, as well as paper money no doubt used to purchase trade goods. Tai and Viet chronicles also attest to the large amount of trade in the form of diplomacy in the late fourteenth and early fifteenth centuries between the principalities in northern Southeast Asia and Yunnan.

The increased population in Yunnan as silver mining was expanded under the early Ming appears also to have stimulated a lively private trade, illegal for the Ming rulers but very profitable for local officials. From the Tai and Bama principalities came cowries (used as base currency in the whole area until the seventeenth century), gems, ivory, cotton cloths (both local and Indian), raw cotton (from Burma), fish products, and salt, as well as spices and sandalwood from the Archipelago. In return the Southeast Asians sought Yunnan silver and copper, and Chinese silks and other manufactures. Human carriers were much the quickest way to traverse these mountains, and thousands of mostly Tai porters frequented the routes between the upper reaches of the rivers.

The long dry season and relatively open terrain of northern Southeast Asia made these overland routes somewhat less hazardous than was the case in the rainforests covering the center of the region, where roads were few and short-lived before the twentieth century. As against that disadvantage, a large and increasing proportion of the population lived within a day's walk of some navigable waterway. Even the population of upland valleys where much of the early rice-growing was concentrated tended to cluster around rivers and lakes used for transportation and fishing as well as irrigating the fields. Familiarity with boats was therefore almost universal.

Small islands were, along with alluvial valleys, a favored area for early settlement because of their abundance of fish and coastal palms, and the defensive advantages which local knowledge of reefs and passages provided. Many of the major river estuaries, on the other hand, were dangerously malarial until tamed for permanent rice fields. This left a role in some of the crucial sea-lanes to the boat- or island-dwelling *orang laut* (sea people). The ability of successive Malay-speaking regimes – Sriwijaya, Melaka, and Johor – to control the Straits of Malacca and attract trade to their ports may have owed much to their magical-charismatic hold over the otherwise piratic *orang laut* inhabiting the innumerable islands off the east coast of Sumatra.

The important arteries of global trade that passed through the region were a further stimulus for commerce. Although it was possible to trade between China and India, the Middle East, and Europe by land (along the so-called "silk road"), the maritime routes through Southeast Asia were far quicker and more cost-effective at any time when they were not terrorized by pirates or rapacious states. The maritime route became dominant in the period of prosperity and enhanced trade associated with China's Song Dynasty (960–1279), and remained so except for the remarkable moment when the Mongols united central and west Asia with China in the thirteenth/fourteenth centuries.

The earliest traders from whatever origin no doubt stayed relatively close to the coastlines, navigating primarily by familiar landmarks, currents, and shoals, and secondarily by the stars. By the ninth century the Arabs had established direct routes across the Arabian Sea to Indian ports such as Quilon or Calicut, and from the Falk Straits between Sri Lanka and India directly to the northern tip of Sumatra, touching only at the Nicobar Islands. Chinese Buddhist pilgrims to India had already followed this route in the seventh century.

The most convenient route further east was through the Straits of Malacca and Singapore when pirates or monopolists did not bedevil them. A more difficult sea passage was available down the west coast of Sumatra and through the Sunda Straits between Sumatra and Java. When the Portuguese dominated the Malacca Straits through control of Melaka in the period 1511–1641, the shipping of their enemies – first Muslim, later Dutch – preferred the Sunda Straits route, which favored the west Java seaports of Jakarta Bay and Banten. The other option, to cross the Peninsula by one of the difficult portages, was most used when the Straits were unsafe and when Siam was strong enough both to act as an entrepôt between east and west and to ensure order on the portages – as in the fourteenth century and the seventeenth. A dozen different routes across the Peninsula were known, but the most important were those between Kedah and Patani (used by Muslim traders), between Trang and Nakhon Sithammarat (more favored by Buddhists), and higher up the Peninsula from Tenasserim into the Siamese heartland (Map 3.1).

In the South China Sea the usual routes went from the Singapore Straits and Pulau Tioman to the Champa coast of what is now southern Viet Nam, and thence across the Gulf of Tongking to Hainan and the Chinese ports. The main route of the first millennium CE through the river arteries of the Red River delta became a branch route by the fifteenth century, rendering the Vietnamese less active in trade. A more dangerous eastern route to China ran northeast from the Straits along the northern coast of Borneo and the western coasts of the Philippines to southern Taiwan and eventually the ports of Fujian. This may have been pioneered in the Song Dynasty (960–1279) when Butuan in Mindanao and Brunei in Borneo were reported as Chinese "tributaries." In the mid-fourteenth century, traders using it were the likeliest candidates to have begun to commercialize the trade in cloves and nutmeg from Maluku. Some time in the following century it dropped into disuse, so that Chinese contacts with the Philippines and Borneo were carried out chiefly through the entrepôt of Melaka. It revived with a vengeance when the Spanish made Manila the major Asian market for American silver in the 1570s.

SPECIALIZED PRODUCTION

Within the region the ease of communication by water encouraged specialized centers of production of cloth, metals, salt, and ceramics. Unlike the pattern in Europe or China, specialized market-oriented production was as often in

Map 3.1 Trade routes, by sea, river, and land.

female as in male hands. Textile and ceramic production were the preserve of women (except where Chinese example was strong), while metalworking was done by men. Some of these production centers expanded in step with commercialization of the economies in the long sixteenth century, but many of the coastal and urban centers were undercut by increased quantities of cheaper or higher-quality imports from manufacturing centers in China, Japan, India, and eventually Europe.

The earliest weaving of cloth was probably from plant fibres such as the *abaca* (*Musa textilis*) native to the wetter parts of the Philippines. The export of such cloth from the Philippines was mentioned in the thirteenth century and continued to modern times. Cotton, native to India, spread to Southeast Asia in the first millennium CE, and flourished in the areas with a substantial dry season – central Burma, Tongking, Cambodia, western Luzon, eastern Java, Bali, Sumbawa, and south-western Sulawesi. At the time for which we first have detailed information, in the sixteenth century, these areas were providing cloth to other parts of the region and to China through an established pattern of exchange. Indian cotton cloth was nevertheless a valued import ever since the Buddhist expansionary phase at the beginning of the Common Era. Its dyes were more colorful, its patterns more sophisticated, while Indian frame looms more efficiently produced in bulk than the back-strap looms used by Southeast Asian women.

Ceramics and metal tools followed textiles in importance among long-distance imports. Since prehistoric times specialized villages close to suitable sources of clay provided ceramic cooking utensils, containers, and water jars to the surrounding area. By the fifteenth century, at least, water transport had made it possible for the produce of northern Java ceramic centers to be marketed around Maluku and Borneo and for the huge Pegu jars (martabans) of southern Burma to travel throughout Southeast Asia and India. That such exchanges were not limited to luxuries is suggested by an English report of the 1680s, that almost 100,000 cheap Vietnamese bowls had been transported at great profit to west Sumatra in a single shipload.

The high-temperature glazes of China were in particular demand from the twelfth century. Much of the finest trade ware entering the international art market in recent years has been from burial sites in the Philippines and eastern Indonesia, and the retrieval of shipwrecked cargoes from around the South China Sea. These show large quantities of quality Chinese ware being imported to Southeast Asia in the twelfth to fourteenth centuries. In the fifteenth, however, there was a "Ming gap" apparently caused by tighter export restrictions. There was no diminution of fine ceramics circulating in Southeast Asia, but the Chinese ware was largely replaced by high-temperature glazed ceramics of hybrid styles from new kilns in the northern Mainland. A transfer of technology, and perhaps of artisans themselves, wrought magnificent results in what the contemporary trade knows as Sawankhalok and Annamese ware.

Accessible sources of iron, copper, tin, and lead were unevenly distributed around the region, and were another key basis for the specialization of function and the development of trade. The richest sources of copper were probably in the northern hills of Viet Nam, where output in excess of 500 tons a year was reported in the eighteenth century. Many other centers were being exploited in north and central Sumatra, in west Java, and among the Igorots of the Luzon Cordillera, who were still able in the nineteenth century to mine and smelt the copper more economically than Spanish engineers. That copper working was even more widespread than copper mining is illustrated by the fine bronzes of Bali, cast from imported metal since neither copper nor tin occurs on the island.

Iron was found in the northerly areas of the Mainland, and in the hills between Siam and Burma, as well as in central Sumatra, Belitung, western Borneo, and central Sulawesi in the Islands. Weapons, tools, and plough-tips manufactured in these places had to circulate to many other populous centers, such as Java and Bali, where iron was not found. The famous *kris* (dagger) manufacture of Java had to draw its metal supplies from as far away as Borneo and Sulawesi. But Chinese ironwork began by the fifteenth century to take over the markets accessible by sea. A great trading city like Melaka around 1500 was provided principally from China with copper, iron, ... cast iron kettles, bowls, basins, ... plenty of needles of a hundred different kinds, some of them very fine and well made ... and things of very poor quality like those that come to Portugal from Flanders (Pires 1515/1944, 125).

These items could be produced more cheaply in China because of more advanced methods and economies of scale, so that Southeast Asian mining and metalwork tended to retreat with time to less accessible areas in the interior.

While the long-distance trade of Southeast Asia is better documented, as the vital link between the Indian Ocean and the eastern seas, the goods carried locally must always have been more voluminous. The river-systems were highways of interaction. The biggest of all the region's river arteries, the Irrawaddy, could be navigated by substantial sailing vessels for 1,400 km, from the sea to Bhamo. The Mekong, even longer but more interrupted, had major navigable stretches of about 500 km in its middle reaches and 460 km in its lower ones, which formed the arteries for Lao and Khmer interaction respectively. But in between, the Khone falls were impassable, and only very rarely did traders attempt the arduous task of dragging their boats around them. Where rivers could not serve, over mountain passes and portages, humans were the most efficient and widespread carriers over frequently washed-out tracks. Shan porters serving the uplands between the Irrawaddy valley and the upper Mekong, for example, were reported to carry 36 kg about 24 km a day. Bullock-carts were of course in use over short distances, particularly in drier and flatter terrain, but only sporadically did such polities as Angkor, Pagan, and Mataram maintain an effective network of roads and bridges for them.

INTEGRATION OF THE ASIAN MARITIME MARKETS

Because the region was a major crossroads of world trade, Southeast Asia's products found their way early onto world markets. Striking evidence comes from Indonesian cloves found in the excavation of a pantry securely dated to 1700 BCE in the Mesopotamian town of Terqa. Until the eighteenth century CE cloves grew only in Maluku (the Spice Islands). Literary evidence for a trade in cloves as a medicinal item is available from ancient Rome and Han China. Until the commercial expansion that began around 1400, however, Southeast Asian contributions to the world's trade were almost entirely items that grew wild in the tropical forests or shallow seas of the region. With the exception of the surface mining of gold and tin, Southeast Asia's export economy was based on foraging, providing luxury items such as incense, aromatic woods, spices, ivory, and medicines.

The exceptional increases in productivity of China under the Song Dynasty (960–1279), which McNeill (1982, 25) has argued "tipped a critical balance in world history" in the direction of market-regulated behavior, undoubtedly created favorable conditions for the "charter era" described in Chapter 2. The Southern Song (1127–1279), having lost the northern capital and the main overland routes westward through Central Asia, devoted unprecedented attention to sea-going links to the south. From this period Southeast Asians began to see the effects of the technical progress made in domestic water-transport under the Song, as Chinese shipping joined the trade networks of the region. Chinese reportage on the southern "barbarians" also took a giant step toward more factual commercial manuals such as that of Chau Ju-kua (*pinyin* Zhou Rugua, 1170–1228), a port official in thirteenth-century Fujian.

In the thirteenth century the Eurasian trade system became more integrated than ever before, with all three of the major east-west routes functioning effectively. The Mongols established unprecedented ease of communication through Central Asia around 1300, which then collapsed in the mid-fourteenth century. Southeast Asia, we saw (Chapter 2), indeed underwent a kind of crisis in the late thirteenth and fourteenth centuries, but for climatic and political reasons rather than a collapse in the maritime trade that was its life-blood. Indeed, the fall of Baghdad (1258) and the break-up of the Mongol Empire ensured that the seaborne route through Southeast Asia would thenceforth dominate east-west traffic.

The most persuasive evidence that the sea routes through Southeast Asian waters continued to grow in scale and sophistication in the period 1300–1500 is the shift in power in that period from temple-building agrarian states to maritime trading centers dominated by Islam and Theravada Buddhism. The "charter era" gave way to what I call an "age of commerce" (Chapter 4), from the fifteenth to seventeenth centuries, dominated by a range of more compact trade-based *negeri*, the most successful of them becoming "gunpowder empires" that expanded rapidly with the new weapons (Chapter 5). The first of these arose along the trade routes in the fourteenth and early fifteenth centuries – Pegu in Mon-dominated southern Burma, Ayutthaya in the Tai world, Phnom Penh as the new center for Cambodia, Pasai, Aru, Baros, Palembang, and Melaka in the Straits area, Gresik, Japara, Tuban, and Banten in Java, and Brunei, Cebu, Manila, Ternate, and Banda further east. By the time European ships arrived in Southeast Asia (1509), these were the dominant political forces, sustained by a highly organized system of entrepôt trade.

China was the dominant external variable on this system between about 1000 and 1600. The prosperity and technological progress of the Song extended swiftly to Dai Viet, which learned quickly from its threatening neighbor. Although the Ming authorities banned private trade during their first century (from 1368), the loopholes for evasion were many and increasing. There was reason for the Sultan of Melaka to declare in 1468, "All the lands within the seas are united in one body, and all living things are being nurtured in love; life has never been so affluent in preceding generations as it is today" (cited Kobata and Matsuda 1969, 111).

AUSTRONESIAN AND INDIAN PIONEERS

The pioneers of long-distance navigation in Asian waters were Southeast Asians. As befits their modern name, the Austronesians (southern islanders) linked Asia's offshore islands with each other and the Pacific between 3,000 and 1,000 years ago. The dispersal of Austronesian-speakers is the widest of any language group in the pre-modern world, from Madagascar in the west to Easter Island (eastern Pacific) in the east and Taiwan in the north, embracing all the islands of Southeast Asia in between. They established commercial beachheads along the north coast of New Guinea, and eventually colonized also those parts of the Asian Mainland most strategically placed on the trade routes, notably the Peninsula, Champa on the Mainland, and Hainan. The prosperous Song Dynasty recorded 44 seaborne missions coming to it from Champa, twenty from Sriwijaya, and nine from other Austronesian trading centers in Island Southeast Asia such as Butuan, Java, and Brunei. Most of the 38 other seaborne missions were listed as Arabs (*Da-shi*) coming by sea through Southeast Asia from ports further west.

The older view that Austronesian settling in Madagascar and the more distant Polynesian islands was the result of some chance accident is no longer sustainable. Archaeological, genetic, and botanic evidence suggests that Austronesian traders were in contact with the East African coast and operating an exchange network between New Guinea and Fiji 2,000 years ago. Some peoples of the Indonesian Archipelago appear to have retained commercial contact with Madagascar from the initial settlement in the first Christian millennium until halfway through the second. The first generation of Portuguese travelers to Madagascar encountered the memory of this long-distance trade by people described as from "Jawa." It is appropriate that the Malay culture hero, Hang Tuah, is depicted in epic stories as a great mariner sailing for his master, the ruler of Melaka, to Siam, India, the Middle East, and China. The Portuguese reported Malays, Javanese, Chams, and "Luzons" (natives of the commercial centers of north Borneo and the Philippines) still regularly trading to China in the early 1500s, at a time when China-based private trade was forbidden by the Ming.

Since the first millennium CE, people of the Indian sub-continent and Sri Lanka, predominately Tamils, were also engaged in Indian Ocean trade. Autonomous Tamil communities of maritime merchants played a major role, perhaps sharing capital on the basis of common ritual obligations like later merchant castes such as the Chettiars. Such communities, often likened to European medieval guilds, erected monuments regulating their religiously sanctioned trade arrangements in many parts of India, but also in the ninth century at Takuapa on the Peninsula, in the tenth in south-central Java, and in the thirteenth in Pagan (Burma) and Quanzhou (south China). The most compelling evidence for the way such communities operated in Southeast Asia is the large column they erected in the camphor port of Barus (northwest Sumatra) in 1088. Written in good Tamil by the Ayyavole guild of 500 Tamil merchants, the inscription prescribed, in the name of the patron god Durga, a tax in gold for each ship wishing to trade in the port. It should be paid by both *nayana* (supercargo or captain) and *kevi* (traveling small merchants or crew), probably ancestors of the *nakhoda* and *kiwi* encountered in Melaka documents of the fifteenth to sixteenth centuries and discussed in Chapter 4.

Around 1500, when we begin to have more abundant sources, the most spectacularly successful of the diaspora capitalists in Southeast Asia were

Hindu commercial castes, notably the Chettiars of south India and the Gujarati Sharafs of the north. In each of the major sixteenth-century cities of the region – Pegu, Ayutthaya, Melaka, Pasai, and Banten – there were a few Chettiars able to draw capital from a communal temple fund, and linked to each other through a system of letters of credit (*hundi*). The Portuguese were in awe of the wealth and skill of these money-managers. The leading financiers and ship-owners of both Melaka and Pasai around 1500 were Chettiars well known in the sources, partly because they were as ready to use Portuguese as they had been Muslim shipping ventures for their investments. Naina Suradewana, probably the wealthiest of these, financed about eight large ships a year on the eastern route from Melaka to Java and Maluku. Another, Nina Chatu or Setu Nayinar, in 1513–14 partnered with the new Portuguese masters of Melaka to send large ships (junks) to Siam (twice), Pegu, Bengal, Coromandel (the Tamil coast), Palembang, Maluku, and China.

As conflict between Muslims and Christians grew intense in the sixteenth century, these Hindu networks tended to lose out in the Muslim ports to Gujarati Muslims. Less secretive and exclusive than the Chettiars, but with similarly advanced accounting methods, their rise may be seen as a step toward generalizing Indian commercial skills in Islamic Southeast Asia.

THE EAST ASIAN TRADING SYSTEM OF *1280–1500*

We have seen that "Chinese" traders traveled to Southeast Asian waters in significant numbers from the Southern Song period (1127–1279). The ports of Quanzhou and Canton had become very cosmopolitan centers, and one must assume that the earliest Chinese voyagers drew on the example of Arab, Malay, and other shippers in their midst. The massive Mongol-Chinese invasion fleet sent to Java in 1292–3 reversed the flow by leaving hundreds of Chinese behind in Java and western Borneo. On both sides of the South China Sea there was intermittent ethnic mixing and cultural borrowing from this point onward. The suppression of a Muslim rebellion in the Fujian ports (1357–66), followed by the Ming ban on foreign trade in 1368, must have forced many China-based traders, especially Muslims, to move their base to Southeast Asia (see Chapter 5).

In the imperial world-view of Ming rulers, anxious to demonstrate the centrality of the Emperor under Heaven, the tributary system was the only valid relation between themselves and barbarian kings. They regarded the gracious acknowledgement of tribute missions, rewarding their gifts with Chinese products at least equal in value, as an important manifestation of imperial virtue. Such missions were sporadic at best, however, as long as they depended upon the commercial tactics of Southeast Asian or Arab traders in seeking access to a market. Only when the more ambitious world-ruler Kublai Khan sent imperial expeditions against Pagan (Burma) by land and Java by sea did the court gain first-hand knowledge of the southern countries, and expect them to send regular tribute according to prescribed norms. Following the Chinese seizure of Pagan in 1287, competing Tai and Bama rulers in the upper Irrawaddy and

Chao Phraya river systems sent a steady stream of missions to the imperial court in the years 1290–1330. The system reached its peak during the first four reigns of the Ming Dynasty, covering the period 1368–1435, when envoys from a dozen Southeast Asian countries were received virtually every year.

The Ming system was put in place in the first instance by the large military missions despatched by the Hong-wu (1368–98) and Yong-le (1403–24) emperors, using a mixture of force and inducement to have tribute missions sent in return. But the trade advantages of tribute missions were such that continued coercion was not necessary. In addition to enjoying generous gifts, the envoys in both directions brought along their own trade goods, which were in 1384 granted freedom from taxation. The authenticity of tribute missions was established by a system of tallies stamped with a character and a number, each split in half so that the sending court had one set which had to be matched against the other kept in the Chinese port. In practice, particularly in Java where Chinese or Sino-Javanese merchants appear to have organized the tribute trade, this system probably strengthened the hand of particular Chinese shipping families that understood and controlled the tallies.

The extraordinary intensity of official relations between China and Southeast Asia in the early Ming period stimulated both the external trade of the region and the rise of the series of port-states along the trade routes that would dominate the politics of the next two centuries. The six imperial expeditions sent out under the eunuch Zheng He between 1405 and 1433 were unprecedentedly large, with as many as 48 junks and 27,000 men in the biggest of them. These expeditions created a new demand for Southeast Asian produce such as pepper and sappanwood, both of which were taken back to China in sufficient quantities to be used as part of the salary of hundreds of thousands of government officials. They thereby made the transition from elite luxuries to items of mass consumption. Ports which took early advantage of the Chinese missions, like Ayutthaya (Siam), Melaka, Brunei, Sulu, and Manila, gained the edge over their rivals not only by becoming entrepôts for the China trade but also through the prestige, and occasionally power, emanating from the Middle Kingdom. The map of Southeast Asia was refashioned by these rising ports, which in the course of the fifteenth century came to dominate their respective hinterlands.

The same Ming emperors who authorized this unprecedented official involvement with Southeast Asia imposed a ban on any private overseas trade. Southeast Asian traders other than those on official missions became a rarity in the Chinese ports, while Chinese traders had to engage in subterfuge. When the emperor moved his capital north from Nanjing to Beijing in 1421 he quickly lost interest in the exotic procession of foreign kings and envoys, and by the 1440s was writing to instruct Javanese rulers to send their missions less often. As the tribute trade waned, some of the demand for foreign goods was made up by smuggling through the many islands of the Fujian and Guangdong coasts. Another "legitimate" channel was provided by the island kingdom of Ryukyu (Okinawa), which became a base for Fujian merchants to trade between Southeast Asia, China, and Japan in the guise of Okinawa's tribute trade to the two latter states. Ryukyu sent ships annually to the key Southeast Asian ports for about a century beginning in the 1420s. Each ship was provided with a letter full of compliments in Chinese from the Ryukyu king to his Siamese, Javanese, or Melakan counterpart, not requiring or giving tribute as in the China case, but expressing the hope "that all within the four seas will be regarded as brothers and that friendly relations will be maintained for ever through our intercourse" (Kobata and Matsuda 1969, 159).

Table 3.1 sets out the frequency of these East Asian exchanges as they are recorded in documents of China and Ryukyu respectively. This provides the earliest quantitative evidence of the relative importance of different ports in the century before the arrival of European ships. Siam, Champa, and Java were the long-term heavyweights in this traffic, though Champa's missions may have been boosted above its commercial importance by its strategic position as a stopover for Chinese ships and its need for protection against the expansive Vietnamese.

The importance of Siam and Cambodia in the early Ming period reflects new concentrations of power around Chinese communities at their respective river-ports. "Siam" was a new Tai state, founded (according to legend in 1351) at Ayutthaya, situated at the limit of navigability for ocean-going ships on the Chao Phraya River, through the interaction of a hybrid Chinese merchant community and local Tai *muang*. Its rise owed much to the ability of its Chinese or Sino-Thai traders to mount missions not only to China but also to Korea, Japan, and Ryukyu in the following half-century. "Cambodia" was no longer the ritual and agricultural complex of Angkor, losing its long struggle with the Tais through the fourteenth century, but the new port-city of Phnom Penh at the confluence of Mekong and Tonle Sap Rivers. There too Chinese were prominent among the merchant community, which took only what it needed from the Angkor tradition of god-kings.

Java missions were sent from the ports of Majapahit situated in the Surabaya-Tuban area, and most appear to have been led by Sino-Javanese with Chinese names but Javanese titles. One of the same enterprising Chinese who had

Table 3.1 Frequency of seaborne official "tribute" missions to China (main figures) and of trade missions from Ryukyu (in brackets).[a]

From	Siam	Cambodia	Champa	Java	Melaka	Brunei	Pasai
1369–99	33	13	25	11	0	1	1
1400–19	17	7	14	14	11	7	10
1420–39	14 (24)		19	21 (6)	8	2	8
1440–59	5		12	10	5		
1460–79	5 (10)		7	3	3 (15)		1 (3)
1480–1509	7 (2)		8	2	2 (2)		3

[a]Date periods given are those for tribute missions to China. The Ryukyu data for 1419–42 is inserted against the category 1420–39, for 1464–81 against 1460–79, and for 1490–1509 against the category 1480–1509.

opened Siamese relations with Japan and Korea showed up later as an envoy of Java to Japan in 1406 and again in 1412 (Kobata and Matsuda 1969, 149–50). Melaka's rise in the early part of the fifteenth century was largely due to its eagerness to exploit the China connection, its three first rulers making between them five royal visits to the Chinese capital between 1411 and 1434. By the successful reign of Sultan Mansur (1459–77) Melaka had made itself so strategically central that trade from its old rivals, Brunei, Pasai, and even Java, came to it for the China and Ryukyu trade, rather than attempting to trade directly. Thereafter Melaka appears to have declined again in relative importance due to internal conflict.

Among the first witnesses to the Chinese diaspora in Southeast Asia was Zhou Daguan, who visited Angkor (Cambodia) on a Mongol/Chinese mission in 1296/7. He recorded that

> Chinese sailors do well by the fact that in this country you can go without clothes, food is easy to come by, women are easy to get, housing is easy to deal with, it is easy to make do with a few utensils, and it is easy to trade. They often run away here. (Zhou 1297/2007, 81).

Many Chinese members of the Mongol expeditions to Java were shipwrecked, captured, or lured away. A group of several thousand Cantonese, reportedly refugees from the Ming takeover in 1368, took control of Palembang, and grew rich like the Sriwijaya rulers before them on the Malacca Straits trade. Zheng He quarreled with their leader in 1407 and had him executed, installing another Palembang Cantonese as "pacification commissioner." Not recognized as kings by China, this regime nevertheless managed to send envoys to Japan and Ryukyu in the 1420s, and received at least eight trade missions from Ryukyu in the period 1428–40.

In the key Java ports of Tuban, Gresik, and Surabaya there were also thousands of wealthy Cantonese at the time of the Zheng He visits, one of them reportedly the ruler of Gresik. The missions such men organized from "Java" were initially welcomed, but by the 1440s Chinese sources complained that they were troublesome and a burden on imperial finances. Official missions came very seldom after 1453, unauthorized ones were punished, and the direct Java-China link seems to have been abandoned in favor of trade via the entrepôt of Melaka. By the time of the Portuguese reports after 1500, "Chinese" as a separate category had virtually disappeared in Java. The dynamic class of trader-aristocrats the Portuguese encountered on the Java coast were described as "Javanese," as the similar class of the Manila Bay area and Brunei were called "Luzons," and those of the Sumatran ports "Jawi" or "Malay." But Portuguese chroniclers reported that on the male side their origins and many of their institutions were Chinese.

In the jerky trajectory of commercial activity in Southeast Asia, there is reason to see an important upward turning point around 1398–1430 associated with these Chinese missions and renegades. Chinese or Sino-Southeast Asians appear to have been the first traders systematically to exploit the cloves of Maluku in the fourteenth century, encouraging commercial planting. Sumatra, which would dominate the world market of pepper from the sixteenth to the nineteenth century, began commercial production at about the same time, presumably responding to a new demand from the Chinese voyages. In the mid-fifteenth century there was, however, a "bullion famine" in China and much of Eurasia, and another downturn in trade, so that we are on safer ground identifying the new commercial boom of the Early Modern period with the long sixteenth century.

The expansion of Chinese shipping to Southeast Asia after its legalization and licensing in 1568 was part of this age of commerce, discussed in Chapter 4.

THE ISLAMIC NETWORK

The Arabian Sea had long been dominated by merchants based on its western shores, around the Persian Gulf and Red Sea. The rise of Islam unified both these regions by 700, and the traders were among the first to accept the new religion. "Arabs," as the Muslim subjects of the Umayyad (Damascus, 661–750) and Abbasid (Baghdad, 750–1258) Caliphates were known, dominated the Arabian Sea and began to appear in Southeast Asian and Chinese ports from the eighth century. One Arab trader, Sulayman, visited the then greatest port of Guangzhou (Canton) in 851, and described a self-governing Muslim community there where a Chinese-approved *qadi* administered Muslim law. From the ninth century comes concrete evidence of direct Arab trade through Southeast Asia to China in the form of the wreck of an Arab-style vessel, with a sumptuous cargo of Chinese ceramic and precious metal objects designed for Middle Eastern customers, discovered off Belitung Island in 1998. Far south of the shortest Malacca Straits route, it was probably on its way to Java or Sumatra as an intermediate port. As early as the tenth century, Chinese chronicles report tributary envoys from the key Southeast Asian intermediate ports of Sriwijaya and Champa who bear Islamic names with the Chinese-style "surname" Li, perhaps Shi'a (Alid) refugees from Umayyad and Abbasid Sunni orthodoxy.

Islamic communities around the Indian coast and in the ports of Southeast Asia provided a remarkable network in which traders of many different ethnic origins could feel secure. With the fall of Baghdad (1258) the Arab label tended to yield to more diverse categories like Persian, Turkish, Gujarati, and Chulia, though Arabic remained one of the great world languages into the sixteenth century, holding this mercantile community together. The travel books of the Venetian Marco Polo at the end of the thirteenth century, and of the Moroccan Ibn Battuta in the middle of the fourteenth, are marvelous witnesses to the coherence of the essentially Islamic network of the Indian Ocean trade, increasingly intersecting with the other networks based in the ports of China.

Many of the earliest Muslim traders settling in South and Southeast Asia were Arabs from Hadhramaut or Persians from the Gulf, but they married locally and produced a localized progeny who attracted many other local traders to join their ranks. Islam in that time and place seemed the natural religion of commerce, with its established vocabulary and legal framework governing loans, partnerships, slavery, commenda, and commission agents. Where the older Hindu, Taoist, and animist faiths were tied to particular localities, tombs, and ritual centers, and Buddhism counseled renunciation of the concerns of this world, Islam provided a completely portable set of regulations appropriate to the traveling merchant. The Malay legal code first compiled around 1500 in the entrepôt of Melaka took most of its commercial and financial provisions from Islamic law, though not those dealing with the place of the king or with civil and criminal codes.

Self-ruling Islamic trading communities began to appear on the south Indian coasts from the tenth century, but the first to be authenticated in Southeast Asia were in northern Sumatra at the end of the thirteenth, paradoxically in a chronological order largely east to west – Aru, Perlak, Pasai, and Lambri (Aceh). These became useful footholds for Muslim merchants on the eastern side of the Indian Ocean, and entrepôts for manufactures from China and spices from Maluku. The Chinese imperial fleets of the early 1400s appear if anything to have stimulated the role of Islam as the religion of trade, for Zheng He and many of his leading commanders were Yunnan Muslims, and most of the Chinese left behind by them assimilated into the cosmopolitan Muslim society of the ports rather than the Hindu-Buddhist-animist ones of the interior. In the early 1400s Islamic communities were established and partly self-governing in the ports of Java and Champa, the rising dynasty of Melaka decided to throw in its lot with Islam, and even the elites of clove-producing Ternate and Tidore and nutmeg-producing Banda began to assimilate Islamic culture. The prominence of first Pasai and then Melaka as Islamic entrepôts in the fifteenth century confirmed the Malay they spoke as the language of commerce throughout the Archipelago and many of the Mainland ports. Southeast Asians from whatever background who joined the cosmopolitan community of the trading cities were likely to assimilate to both Malay speech and the Islamic religion.

In the West the commercial nexus between Venice and Cairo became dominant to the point of monopoly as the northern hemisphere began its recovery from the Black Death of 1346–8. A commercial treaty between these two powers in 1345 ensured that the seaborne route from the Indian Ocean through the Red Sea to Cairo and Alexandria carried the lion's share of Asian produce destined for the Mediterranean through the fifteenth century. The Venetian Republic and the Mamluk regime in Egypt became prosperous and indeed dangerously comfortable on this monopoly, as subsequent events would show. But further east there was vigorous competition between the different Islamic ports and carriers bringing the pepper and spices of the East to Egypt. Southeast Asian ports such as Pasai (Sumatra), Melaka and Tenasserim (Peninsula), Gresik and Japara (Java), and Banda (Maluku), like those on the south Indian coast, had to treat the Muslim traders well or lose them to their rivals.

By the end of the fifteenth century the Islamic trading network had developed considerable efficiency in carrying spices and pepper to the increasingly prosperous markets of Europe and the Middle East. Malukan spices were arriving in Venice in the late 1490s in many times the quantity of a century earlier. By the 1490s these spices were traveling in Javanese and Malay ships from their source in Maluku to the Java ports and Melaka, from there to south India in

Indian and Malay ships, and across the Arabian Sea in Arab and Gujarati ships. Pepper shipments to Venice grew more modestly, but Southeast Asia's share in them grew from nothing in 1400 to a significant share by 1500, since the new production from Sumatra, stimulated by the China demand, was also shipped westward to add to the Indian pepper in the markets of the sub-continent.

The Portuguese onslaught on Muslim shipping after 1500 caused enormous disruption, so that the amount of pepper and spices reaching Venice through the Muslim route plunged to less than half in the following decade. But the Islamic route proved resilient. Once the Portuguese began to settle into a pattern of trading rather than raiding, and the Muslim ports reconstructed their network to avoid centers of Portuguese strength, the Muslim route proved more effective than ever. In the 1560s unprecedented quantities of pepper and Malukan spices reached Venice through Egypt, controlled by the powerful Ottomans since 1517. The period 1560–1600 marked the apogee of the Muslim route, and of direct connections between the heartland of Islam and the ports of Southeast Asia (see Chapter 5).

THE EUROPEANS

European enthusiasm for the spices of Indonesia had been one of the motors driving the growth in this Islamic trade route. Venice reached its florescence in the fifteenth century as it funneled an ever-increasing flow of pepper, clove, nutmeg, and cinnamon to a Europe growing in wealth and population, and apparently insatiable in its desire for garnish of its meat, fish, desserts, and drinks. European pepper consumption may have grown only about 25% in this century, but the increase in specifically Indonesian spices, cloves and nutmeg particularly, was in the region of 155%. Cut out of this crucial trade by Venice's monopoly agreements with the Mamluks in Egypt, Genoa stepped up its financing of Spanish and Portuguese exploration of alternative routes. In 1498 these efforts were crowned with success, when Vasco da Gama reached the major south Indian entrepôt of Calicut from Lisbon. Thereafter Antwerp formed an even more important partnership with Lisbon, providing German silver and arms in exchange for eastern spices.

By 1504 Lisbon had eclipsed Venice as the European conduit for Asian spices. The disarray in Venice was exacerbated by conflict in Egypt, only ending with its conquest by Turkey in 1517. This entry of European ships into the Indian Ocean seriously disrupted the established pattern of trade. The ferocity that had long characterized naval warfare in the Mediterranean was introduced to a much vaster commercial network hitherto experienced only in combating low-level piracy. The Portuguese brought nothing that Asians wanted to buy except precious metals and firearms, neither of which they were much inclined to part with. But they claimed a right to plunder Muslim ships and cities as a continuation of the centuries of religious warfare they had conducted in recovering Portugal and penetrating West Africa. Their ships were small but well-armed and maneuverable by Asian standards. In their first twenty years in Asia, when they sent an average of eleven ships a year eastward, they wrought havoc on Muslim shipping. Until about 1519, nevertheless, the volume of spices and pepper that they were able to carry to Lisbon did not equal that which had been reaching Venice. Some of the precious goods were no doubt lost at sea, but most of the loss to Europe was probably diverted to safer markets in India and China.

This disruption was short-lived. To survive in Asia the Portuguese had to fortify some defensible strongholds (Diu, Hormuz, Muscat, Goa, Cochin, Melaka, Ternate) and to make local allies. By mid-century they were just another element in the pattern of Asian trade, distinguished by their strong fortresses and ships but very small numbers, and by a novel attempt to control trade on particular routes through a license system. The spice trade was in theory monopolized by the Crown, but in practice the greatest profits came from private partnerships with Asian merchants, of whom the wealthiest were south Indian Chettiars.

East of India the Portuguese had little military strength, and the long-term effect of their joining the competition for goods was predominately positive for Southeast Asian economies. Their major disruption was in capturing the great entrepôt of Melaka in 1511, and subsequently fortifying and holding it against a series of Islamic counter-attacks. But the Muslim trade established new routes and markets, notably in Aceh, Banten, Johor, Patani, and Makassar, creating a more developed urban culture than had existed earlier. Pepper-growing expanded in Sumatra and elsewhere, as the Muslims, and later the Dutch, avoided Portuguese interference in the previous pepper-coast of Kerala. Even the Portuguese began buying pepper from Southeast Asia, which became the major world supplier in the late sixteenth century. By then both Muslim and Chinese networks were more important than Portuguese in the rapid expansion of the region's trade.

Beyond Melaka, the Portuguese established forts in Ternate and Ambon (for cloves), and Solor and Lifao, Timor (for sandalwood). Unlike their Dutch successors, however, they were never able to control more than a fraction of these products. In 1570 their heavy-handedness in Ternate produced a reaction that forced them to flee this principal center of the clove trade, and they thereafter played an even smaller role from neighboring Tidore. In Mainland Southeast Asia, Portuguese shipping played a useful minor role in the trade to Japan and China, and Portuguese mercenary soldiers helped to spread the new European military techniques.

The Spanish in 1492 had hoped to reach the fabled spices of Asia by setting out westward. In 1521 Magellan's expedition achieved this, calling at Cebu in the central Philippines, where its commander was killed, as well as Brunei and Tidore in Maluku. Despite the 1529 Treaty of Saragossa, which allocated virtually all of Southeast Asia to the Portuguese sphere, the Spanish continued to be tempted by the wealth of Asia, sending periodic missions westward from Mexico. In 1565 Miguel López de Legazpi began at Cebu the permanent Spanish occupation of the Philippine Archipelago. He moved his headquarters in 1570 to Manila – more strategically situated both for the China trade and for the Pampangan rice bowl.

Although the Spanish were the least commercially active of the major European networks, the foundation of Manila and the annual galleon voyage which tied it to Mexico wrought massive change in Asia. The American silver annually shipped from Acapulco made Manila the most popular Southeast Asian destination for Chinese ships, which in turn ensured the prosperity of the city. Its customs revenue already surpassed that of Portuguese Melaka by 1600 and peaked at over 70,000 reals per year around 1612. Papaya, chili, maize, and tobacco were introduced from the Americas to Asia through Manila, transforming habits of consumption within two decades. For a time during the union of Spanish and Portuguese crowns (1580–1640) Spanish forces from Manila also attempted to sustain the Portuguese enterprise in Maluku, but never succeeded in taking a major share of the cloves.

The Iberians were remarkably successful for a century, through a mixture of force and secrecy, at preventing other Europeans from intruding into their lucrative Asian routes. In 1596 a Dutch expedition broke this monopoly by sailing directly to the Indonesian Archipelago, returning with a rich cargo of pepper, cloves, and other spices. This opened the floodgates, with 22 Dutch ships departing for Southeast Asia in 1598, and the English, French, and Danes not far behind. While the Portuguese had concentrated what military strength they had in the Arabian Sea, leaving their Southeast Asian possessions always vulnerable and isolated, the newcomers made directly for the pepper and spice ports in the Archipelago. The Dutch, English, and Danes each formed chartered companies to operate their commercial ventures in the East, though the Dutch version, the United East-India Company or VOC, with a founding capital of 6.5 million guilders in 1602, was ten times the size of its rivals.

By capturing Ambon in 1606 and the Banda Archipelago in 1621 the VOC became the dominant factor in clove and nutmeg respectively. Its monopoly of both key items was effective by mid-century. Pepper was much more widespread, and the Dutch always had to compete with English, Chinese, Islamic, and Portuguese networks who kept the buying price relatively high. In 1619 the VOC took control of Jakarta, an outpost of the major Java pepper-port of Banten. Renamed Batavia (after a Roman-era territory now in the eastern Netherlands), it became the headquarters of the whole Dutch Asian trade network. With far more ships at its disposal than other networks – an average of 148 in the 1620s and 257 by the 1660s – and methods of capital mobilization and bookkeeping as advanced as any in the world, the VOC represented a wholly new kind of commercial power spanning half the world.

[4] CITIES AND PRODUCTION FOR THE WORLD, 1490–1640

SOUTHEAST ASIA'S "AGE OF COMMERCE"

Southeast Asia played its most central role in world history as a crucible for the birth of modernity and the unification of world markets. During the long sixteenth century, roughly 1480–1630, it owed this centrality less to its people, then a much smaller proportion of the world's population than its 10% today, than to its maritime location and its spices. This was a critical period of commercialization and global encounters for many parts of the world, but exceptionally so for Southeast Asia, indeed its preeminent "age of commerce." China's direct "discovery" of Southeast Asia in the Zheng He period after 1400, Europe's from 1509, and Japan's from the 1580s, brought these powerful economies together with one another and the Muslim traders of the Indian Ocean in the ports of Southeast Asia. They were there in part to buy the pepper, spices, and aromatics of Southeast Asia, to which they had become addicted in the preceding centuries. But they also used Southeast Asia's ports to exchange the goods of one another. In particular China, having converted to a silver-based cash economy during the Song and Yuan periods, had an insatiable demand for further silver throughout the Ming Dynasty (1368–1644). It met this in large part by buying American silver in Manila, Japanese in Hoi An, Cambodia, and Ayutthaya, and European (often also from American mines) in Banten, Batavia, and Melaka. European and Indian demand for Chinese silks and ceramics was met in the same ports, while the cottons of India were in enormous demand in all ports to its east.

World silver production increased ninefold in the sixteenth century, from about 42 metric tons per annum in 1493–1520 to 380 tons throughout the peak period 1581–1620. Thereafter there was a steady decline to the 1670s, and the inflow of silver into the world economy did not regain the boom levels of around 1600 until the 1720s. The main contribution to this world boom came from the Americas, but more important for eastern Asia was the increase in output of Japanese silver mines, which developed the much more efficient mercury

A History of Southeast Asia: Critical Crossroads, First Edition. Anthony Reid.
© 2015 Anthony Reid. Published 2015 by John Wiley & Sons, Ltd.

extraction technique at almost the same time as those of Peru. Until 1600 Europe was exporting silver and gold to pay for spices and other Asian goods, though most of this went first to ports in India and the Arabian Sea. By contrast the small amounts brought from Mexico by the Manila galleon before 1600, and those exported by Japan, all went to Southeast Asian ports initially, albeit ultimately to China. All these sources peaked in the 1620s, when the Japanese were exporting as much as 130 tons a year by some estimates, the Manila galleon bringing in about 23 tons, while the Dutch and English were now shipping at least 20 tons a year directly to Southeast Asian ports. All this fueled an enormous expansion of commerce and urban life in the peak of this age of commerce between 1580 and 1630, after which the decline was dramatic (Chapter 7).

Part of the reason for Southeast Asia's centrality in these exchanges was its geography; part was the peculiar trade situation of China. Although it was the world's largest economy Ming China severely restricted private economic exchanges beyond its borders. In the early Ming period tribute missions from the "barbarian" states to its south were the only officially sanctioned means of exchanging goods. The frequency of these tribute missions declined sharply after 1430 (Table 3.1), as the empire shifted focus to its northern defenses, moved the capital to Beijing, and passed through its own mid-century monetary crisis. Private traders based in Southeast Asia and Ryukyu filled part of the gap in that difficult period, operating under conditions of uncertainty moderated by bribery. From about 1470, as gold and silver began to flow back into the world system, Southeast Asia-based traders became the chief beneficiaries of the better conditions in the China trade. But during the sixteenth century they were edged out by China-based shippers.

In 1567 a new Ming Emperor, Muzong, finally accepted the inevitability of maritime trade and began a system of officially licensing it. This greatly increased the security of Chinese shippers, who had unique advantages in negotiating bureaucratic hurdles in Canton and the Fujian ports. Japanese, Southeast Asian, Muslim, and European shippers therefore contented themselves with buying from the Chinese in Southeast Asian ports. Chinese shipments to the south rapidly increased in frequency as the junk captains sought to bring home not just the exotic spices and aromatics of the region but the growing supply of silver now available. Fifty ships a year were licensed in 1567, and by 1597 this had grown to 118. Although the licensing system gradually broke down thereafter, there were estimates of several hundred Chinese junks in the trade in the 1610s.

Manila was the most attractive port for this expanding Chinese shipping because of its silver supplies, attracting nearly half the Chinese vessels in many years. From around 1600, when Nguyen Hoang made his southern Viet state of Cochin-China effectively independent, its port of Hoi An became another important destination for the silver traders, with Ayutthaya and Cambodia the next most important Mainland ports for the Chinese. Further south, south Sumatra and west Java were the main Chinese sources of pepper, with Dutch Batavia soon after its 1619 foundation usurping the role played for a century by Javanese Banten. The Chinese records, however, show a variety of small ports, beyond those permitted to play the old tribute trade game, now acknowledged officially as destinations for the seventeenth-century ships. In the Peninsula, Patani, Pahang, Melaka, and Johor were mentioned; in Sumatra, Jambi and Palembang; in Borneo, Brunei, Sulu, and Banjarmasin.

Japan's great opening to world trade began around 1580, as its ships carried silver and metalware southward to exchange with Chinese and Southeast Asians. The Tokugawa shogunate also adopted a system of annual licenses to sail to different Southeast Asian ports, and that data reveals a similar hierarchy, with Hoi An in the lead followed by Manila. Siam and Cambodia were less convenient for this Japan-China exchange, but did offer a great supply of deerhide, for which Japan developed an insatiable demand in the seventeenth century as the inner lining for gloves and armor. The ports of Dai Viet became steadily more important for Japan during the seventeenth century, as an alternative to inaccessible China as supplier of silk.

A still greater variety of ports serving the international trade were mentioned by the European chroniclers, beginning with Tomé Pires around 1515, including those serving the Indian Ocean rather than the South China Sea. Pires described four trading *negeri* on the coast of Pegu (modern Burma), seven on the Peninsula, a dozen in Sumatra, eight in Java, and a host more in the eastern islands. In the peak period a century later a few ports, such as Aceh, Banten, Batavia (from 1619), Pegu (until 1598), and Ayutthata (Siam), became dominant. These nodal points of the global trade routes became the centers of economic and social innovation discussed below. They not only exposed a significant proportion of newly urbanized Southeast Asians directly to global products and ideas, but indirectly brought a larger number of rural producers and consumers into contact with the world market.

CROPS FOR THE WORLD MARKET

Until the fifteenth century the overwhelming majority of Southeast Asian exports derived from foraging in the seas or forests. Chinese imports of Southeast Asian exotic luxury items had expanded tenfold during the southern Song boom, but in items such as elephant tusks, rhinoceros horns, pearls, aromatic woods, and incense. Such expansion entailed the development of settled ports and markets, where the goods of forest and sea were exchanged for manufactured items from China, but not yet of cash crops.

Even cloves and nutmeg, traded from Maluku around the world as medicines throughout the Common Era, had for centuries been plucked from trees growing wild in the islands. Only in the fifteenth century, according to the first Portuguese account (Pires 1515/1944, 219), did production gradually shift from wild to cultivated trees, "in the same way that wild plums become cultivated plums and wild olives become cultivated olives." The other products shipped to China, India, and the Muslim World were largely aromatic woods (sappanwood, gharu, sandalwood, cinnamon), and gums and resins (camphor, benzoin, frankincense, dammar) collected from trees in the forest, or the product of forest-dwelling fauna (lac, rhinoceros horn, ivory, bird of paradise, birds-nest). The same foraging process had delivered a variety of products of the sea, notably pearls and tortoiseshell.

The change to a totally different scale of commercial agriculture appears to have begun around 1400. The last years of the fourteenth century provide the first evidence of regular and substantial shipments of clove and nutmeg into Europe's Mediterranean ports – at about 30 tons of clove and 10 of nutmeg each year. Pepper, which was not among the exports of northern Sumatra in the 1350s, had begun its spectacular career there by the 1420s. Though numerous factors contributed to a global increase in trade at this time, the most important single development for Southeast Asia was the unprecedentedly active southern policy of the first and third Ming emperors in China (Chapter 3). Their fleets brought back such large amounts of pepper that the demand attracted from India to Sumatra the cultivation for the first time of round or black pepper, *Piper nigrum* (as opposed to the long pepper already grown), much closer to the China market along the established trade route.

Between 1400 and 1650 the expansion in pepper and Malukan spice exported from the region was spectacular, as competition from all quarters drove prices higher. Europe alone was importing about 200 tons of cloves and nearly 100 tons of nutmeg in the early 1600s. European pepper imports grew threefold in the same period, and whereas all had come from India in 1400, most came from Southeast Asia by 1620. All three of these items became organized plantation crops covering a large amount of land – cloves first in northern Maluku and later Ambon; nutmeg in the Banda Archipelago; pepper in Sumatra, west Java and the Malayan Peninsula. In addition, cane sugar became an important cash crop in the southern Viet kingdom, Siam, Cambodia, and Java in the seventeenth century, as did benzoin in northern Sumatra, Laos, and Cambodia. Cotton production for local use was very widespread, but export was already extensive by 1600 to the areas too wet or infertile to grow their own.

As Table 4.1 shows for the two exports easiest to quantify, production of pepper and cloves expanded rapidly after 1560 to meet the growing demand from Europe. The influx of silver and the competition among buyers drove prices up spectacularly, until the Dutch Company (VOC) succeeded in establishing a partial monopoly of cloves and nutmeg in the 1620s and a total one by the 1650s. The arrival of Dutch and English competitors in the early 1600s drove prices in free-market entrepôts like Banten and Makassar to all-time highs of around 160 Spanish dollars per ton for pepper and 1,000 for cloves in the 1640s (Bulbeck et al. 1998, Table 2.15). The cumulative effect of the increased exports of these and other Southeast Asian products was not only to divert large populations to specialized cash-cropping, but to encourage the growth of trading cities, of a commercial culture, and of profound changes in values.

Southeast Asian economies had never been static and subsistence-oriented, but only at this time can we begin to quantify the extent of their dependence on the world market. The total value of Southeast Asian long-distance exports at the peak of the trade boom in 1630 was around 8.6 million Spanish dollars, representing nearly half a Spanish dollar per head of population. This magnitude enriched the trading centers and increased the scale of internal exchanges,

Table 4.1 Estimated growth of two key Southeast Asian long-distance exports.

	Cloves exports: tons		Value	Pepper exports: tons		Value
	To Europe	Total	$000	To Europe	Total	$000
1500–09	30	170	5.9	50	950	47
1530–39	50	200	20	300	1300	78
1560–69	70	230	115	1300	2700	189
1590–99	140	250	150	1400	3400	340
1620–29	330	450	360	1500	3800	551
1640–49	205	308	308	2100	3800	602

Source: Derived from Bulbeck et al. 1998. Quantities are decade averages per year in metric tons; values are in thousands of Spanish dollars (reals), based on prices at Southeast Asian entrepôts. All are estimates, though the best data comes from Europe.

carrying foodstuffs, cloth, ceramics, and metal goods from port to port, upstream to downstream.

If we exclude rice, traded over shorter distances within Southeast Asia, pepper was the largest export crop both by quantity and by land area of its cultivation. Pepper-growing was established by 1500 along the north coast of Sumatra, though smaller amounts were produced in west Java, and in Kedah, Patani, and Pahang on the Peninsula. By 1600 the original gardens were exhausted, and the main source was along the west coast of central Sumatra, and in Lampung (southern Sumatra) and west Java. In the subsequent half-century Sumatran pepper-growing was taken further inland by Minangkabau growers who now exported their crops through Palembang and Jambi. The older pepper fields on the west coast were finished by 1700, though new frontiers opened further south around (British) Bengkulu, in the Banjarese area of south Borneo, around Nakhon Sithammarat (Ligor) in the Peninsula, and in the southern Viet kingdom of Cochin-China.

The primary reason for this constant shifting of the areas of production was the exhaustion of the soil on which pepper was grown. Sumatrans sought primary forest to open a new pepper garden, as near as possible to some port. The forest would be cut down and burned, and a crop of dry rice grown in the first year. Stakes of chingkareen (*dadap duri*) were planted to provide living support and shade for the pepper vines, which produced their best yield between their seventh and tenth year. A new patch of forest would therefore be cut down after the tenth year to replace the deteriorating old one. Pepper would never be replanted on the old garden, which no longer had enough nutrients to sustain cultivation. It was left either to regenerate slowly as secondary forest, or very frequently to turn into grassland (*alang-alang*, Imperata cylindrica) – still a feature of Aceh and Lampung.

In the seventeenth century the Peninsula and western Archipelago became the dominant source of the world's pepper. Total exports increased to a peak of 6,500 tons in the 1670s, by which time about a tenth of the then population of Sumatra, the Peninsula, and Borneo must have been economically dependent on this single export crop. The key figure in this expansion was usually the aristocratic entrepreneur, who either controlled labor directly or was able to use his or her capital to acquire it. Some were already established trader-officials in a port-capital; others became rajas of a pioneer *negeri* devoted to pepper production. Such entrepreneurs would send cultivators into the selected forest areas with tools and a supply of rice. At least initially, these producers were less than free, bonded to a powerful entrepreneur either by their debt or by their purchase or seizure as slaves.

One of the consequences of cash-cropping for the international market, particularly in pepper, was to shift population from established rice-growing areas in the uplands to coastal areas more accessible to the ports. These forested areas had been neglected by rice-cultivators for good reason – frequent flooding, constant rainfall, and great dangers from malaria and water-borne diseases. In much of the central Southeast Asian area of no dry season (Sumatra, the Peninsula, and Borneo) it was pioneer pepper-growers, joined in the nineteenth century by gambier-growers, who gave their lives to tame the hostile forest for agriculture. As an Aceh poet observed, "The Lord has created the desolate *rantau* (frontier); there man goes wrong ... You know how it is in the *rantau*, it is misery everywhere. When you are ill, there is no end to your laments ... If you are in luck you will return; if not you will die in the *rantau*" (Drewes, 1980, 10–11).

Sugar, which became Southeast Asia's greatest export crop in the nineteenth century, began its career there in the seventeenth. Previously, palm sugar and honey had been the staple sweeteners of the region, but around 1600 the cultivation and refining of cane sugar was brought southward by Teochius from southern China. Japan, too cold itself for cane cultivation, was the great market for Southeast Asian sugar. Teochiu immigrants began growing and refining the cane in the Quang-nam area of Cochin-China, and Japanese shippers took it home from Hoi An. In the same period, Chinese began cultivation in the low hills above the flood-plains of Siam and Cambodia respectively, and in Banten in west Java. When the Dutch Company established its headquarters in Batavia in 1619 it soon took an interest in the Chinese sugar industry established in nearby Banten. Chinese growers and millers were encouraged to move to the outskirts of Batavia, where about 23 small mills were operating in the 1640s. Further expansion occurred to the east of Semarang on Java's north coast, where there were 36 mills operating in 1686. Production levels were highest in the 1640s and 1650s, when more than a thousand tons were shipped to Europe in the best years, in addition to the 400–500 tons regularly sent to Japan and Persia.

A large proportion of the world's tin is concentrated in the chain of hills that runs down through the whole Peninsula to the islands of Bangka and Belitung in the south. By the tenth century the Peninsula was supplying most of Asia's tin needs, and a series of Arab travelers extolled the importance of the west coast tin mines they located in Kalah. The trade boom of 1580–1640 witnessed a great increase in mining of this tin to supply the busy markets of India, China, Siam, and Java. Up until the seventeenth century the ports of the western coast of the Peninsula – Junkceylon (Phuket), Kedah, Perak, and Selangor – supplied India and the Arabs, while Nakhon Sithammarat, Patani, and Pahang on the eastern coast supplied China.

Local inhabitants of the Peninsula may have been mining for hundreds of years as a subsidiary to agriculture and foraging. Mining sites were located and supervised by a shaman who could mediate with the spirit of the tin. Men dug the ore and earth out of flooded pits, while women separated the tin ore with their fingers. The "casting" was a primitive form of smelting by mixing burning charcoal with the tin ore until the metal ran out into the mold. These slabs of about 20 kg weight were then floated down the rivers to port, where the port-ruler usually took the largest share of the profits of selling it.

By 1500 the *negeri* of Melaka had risen to control most of the tin of what is today Kedah, Perak, and Selangor in the western Peninsula, and sold it to Indian merchants to take back to their markets. The amounts coming onto the market appear to have been less than 100 tons a year around 1500, up to 300 tons in 1600, and over 1,000 tons in a peak year such as 1638. The Portuguese occupants of Melaka (1511–1641) had to contest the supply of tin with Muslim traders, and they lost badly after their great Muslim enemy, Aceh, conquered the Perak and Kedah fields in 1575. The Dutch, who in turn conquered Melaka in 1641, hoped to use the port to monopolize the supply of tin, and they were in a much stronger position to do so. The largest amount they ever succeeded in acquiring was 380 tons in 1650, however, and the effect of their heavy-handed system of fixed prices and quotas appears only to have been to drive the tin industry of the Peninsula into decline in the second half of the century. It began its modern rise a century later, largely at Chinese hands (Chapter 9).

SHIPS AND TRADERS

The annual alternation of wind patterns made the different sectors of the sailing routes (described in Chapter 2) relatively dependable for a few months of each year and almost impossible at others. From December to March the monsoon winds blow reliably southward from the Asian landmass; from April to August they blow northward, or northeast in the Indian Ocean (Map 1.1). The entrepôts that arose at different junctions of the routes were therefore essential not just for provisioning but to await a favorable wind for the return voyage. Most Southeast Asian maritime cities, and all those which served the long-term trade with India and China, had hectic periods when merchants from both China and India were in port, which reminded Europeans of the trade fairs of their continent. The ports around the Straits of Malacca and Sunda, or serving the trans-Peninsula portages, were particularly prone to this pattern, with huge temporary populations of traders arriving with one monsoon and leaving with another. Melaka, which cornered a large share of the trans-Asian exchange trade in the period 1450–1511, was aptly described by its Portuguese conquerors as:

> a city made for merchandise, fitter than any other in the world; the end of monsoons and the beginning of others … The trade and commerce between the different nations for a thousand leagues on every hand must come to Melaka (Pires 1515/1944, 286).

The variety of shippers visiting Southeast Asian ports was reflected in the variety of ships, considerably more diverse than those in the Mediterranean or Atlantic. Technological borrowing was a constant process. Ships were built in Southeast Asian harbors to the specifications of Javanese, Chinese, Gujarati, or Arab masters. Southeast Asian vessel types had been derived from an iron-scarce environment. Instead of using nails, shipbuilders constructed a hull by joining planks together very tightly with wooden dowels, adding the strengthening frame only afterward. The smaller vessels all had an outrigger for stability, and the depictions on the ninth-century Borobudur temple in Java reveal that even large ocean-going ships at that time used them. Southeast Asian ships had a quarter rudder on either side of the stern, lateen sails, and a system of internal rooms or divisions (*petak*) between the ribs of the ship's frame. Descendants of vessels of this type, typically of less than 50 tons, still carry the freight of the islands as they have for more than a millennium.

By contrast, the river-based shipping tradition of China had used a flatter bottom, planks nailed onto a series of bulkheads which took the place of a frame, and split-bamboo sails mounted on two or three masts. The vessels of the western Indian Ocean resembled Southeast Asian ships in their lateen sails, and in being built up from a keel by attaching one plank to another, but the system of attaching was not wooden dowels but coconut-fibre ropes. These vessels proved no match for European ships in naval warfare, and Gujarati and other Indian shipping began to emulate the Iberian galleons from the sixteenth century.

The period between about 1290 and 1500 saw the evolution of a hybrid Sino-Southeast Asian style in shipbuilding as in many other spheres. The thousands of Chinese sailors, soldiers, and traders who made their home in Southeast Asia following the interventions of Kublai Khan in the 1290s and the Yung-lo Emperor in the early 1400s, helped to create the new port-cities of Southeast Asia, and also their shipping techniques. The large ships known to Europeans and Arabs as junks were hybrids, using the keels, quarter-rudders, and lateen sails of the Austronesian tradition, but with the large size (80–700 tons), several masts, and multiple hulls of the Chinese tradition.

The term junk occurs from the fourteenth century in foreign accounts, though the Javanese term *jong* from which it derives is older. One Old Javanese poem refers to a new type of *jong* copied from the Chinese at the time of the Mongol invasion of Java. Although the disappearance of these large Southeast Asian junks around 1600 shifted the meaning of the term in English to a specifically Chinese ship, there is no doubt that it was the Southeast Asian variant (with part-Chinese ancestry) which dominated the seas and most impressed Europeans when they first arrived in the region. Figure 4.1 illustrates the Javanese and Chinese junks observed in 1596, as the former was becoming scarcer.

CITIES AS CENTERS OF INNOVATION

The rapid trade expansion gave rise to substantial cosmopolitan cities at the nodal points where monsoons met. Until the fourteenth century food supplies were probably the main constraint on the growth of such cities. The irrigated

Figure 4.1 Vessels of the Java coast, as sketched by the first Dutch expedition, 1596. Clockwise from left: Javanese junk, small Javanese trading vessel, Chinese junk, local fishing boat. Source: *De eerste schipvaart der Nederlanders naar Oost-Indië onder Cornelis de Houtman 1595–1597*, Vol. I, eds. G.P. Rouffaer and J.W. Ijzerman. The Hague: Nijhoff for Linschoten-Vereniging, 1915.

upland areas that produced a ready rice surplus were far from the key straits and portages where entrepôts were located. In turn, the Champa coast, the Peninsula, eastern Sumatra, and west Java were strategically placed as shipping hubs, but lacked rice-growing areas. The success of Thai migrants in the fourteenth century in taming the malarial swamps of the lower Chao Phraya River and developing highly productive rice strains which grew as fast as the river flooded, was one important key to providing a source of rice for maritime cities. Javanese cultivated the lower Brantas delta to provision Gresik and Surabaya and to export to Maluku. Cities such as fifteenth-century Melaka, sixteenth-century Patani, Johor, and Pahang, or seventeenth-century Batavia, Banten, and Aceh could not have survived without these new sources of exportable rice.

Throughout Eurasia cities grew in response to the silver influx and resulting trade boom of the long sixteenth century. Edo (Tokyo) and Beijing were among the biggest with around a million inhabitants. In the mid-seventeenth century it seems likely that Ayutthaya (the Siamese capital) had more than 150,000 inhabitants, and Aceh, Makassar, and Banten each close to 100,000. The largest cities were those at the centers of populous gunpowder empires that had used trade wealth and the new firearms to attract or coerce a dependent population to its temporarily glittering capital. At their respective peaks, Thang-long (Hanoi) around 1460, Pegu (the Burmese capital) around 1570, and Mataram (Java) around 1640 may have reached 200,000. Each of these very large cities was able to tap an adjacent rice-surplus area. In all, there were about a million urban dwellers (in a dozen cities over 30,000) in Southeast Asia at its commercial peak around 1630 (Map 4.1). This relatively advanced urbanism, contrasting with its later peasantization, was at its most evident in the Peninsula, at least 20% urban through its many entrepôts and sparse agricultural land.

Cities Below the Winds combined elements of both the chessboard regularity of many Eurasian imperial civilizations and the huddled confusion of many Islamic and European commercial hubs. In the Buddhist cities of the Bama (particularly), Khmer, and Tai the state seemed better able to cast its ordered imprint on the city. Pegu, Ava, and Chiang Mai, like Angkor before them, were all walled cities with a palace at the center, many temples, and a grid of streets within, while foreigners and the busy life of the market were typically outside the walls. In Archipelago and Viet cities the walled area was essentially only the royal palace or citadel – even if larger city walls were later built as defenses against Europeans. Muslim cities such as Banten, Demak, and Aceh built the market into the central planned area, comprising a large central square, the palace to its south, mosque to its west (the direction of Mecca), and market to its north. Beyond this, however, the pattern was determined by rapid commercial accretion rather than royal plan. Aceh, Makassar, and Banten, as well as Ayutthaya, grew fastest at times of low state authority, and the cities became agglomerations of rich men's extensive and often fortified compounds surrounded by the

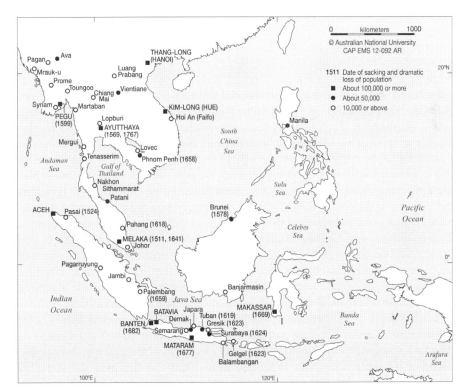

Map 4.1 Urban populations at their sixteenth- to seventeenth-century peak.

urban poor. Sixteenth-century Aceh was reportedly dominated by rich merchant-aristocrats with large, fortified houses. In Banten, the Dutch described the interior of these fortified compounds, each containing a small open space, a prayer-hall, a nearby well for washing, storerooms, shops, and guardrooms where slaves lived to ensure protection of the buildings at night.

To European, Chinese, or Arab eyes, even the walled cities of Siam and Burma seemed astonishingly green. The unwalled ones, like Aceh and Makassar (Figure 6.1), appeared to them as an agglomeration of villages within a forest, so dominant were the coconut and fruit trees, and so absent any constraints imposed by walls. The only treeless and congested quarters of these cities were the Chinese or European quarters, which often became pestilential with time – as eighteenth-century Batavia notoriously was. Before the nineteenth-century advent of piped water it seems likely that Southeast Asian cities shared the universal pattern of higher death than birth rates, though they were better protected than European counterparts from urban epidemics by their high rainfall, frequent bathing, and open wooden houses. The greatest danger was seen to be fire, since almost all buildings were light and wooden.

With the exception of some briefly inflated conquest capitals, these cities were by no means the parasites of the oriental despotism image. The majority of their imported supplies were paid for from the benefits of trade, not tribute. In addition, the great centers of population and wealth naturally became the centers also of craft production, where ceramics and metalware were fashioned for the court elite but also for the surrounding hinterland. The initial process was often involuntary, as craftsmen were brought to the capital by conquerors to serve their ostentatious purposes. Iskandar Muda (1607–36), the most powerful of Aceh's rulers, reputedly had three hundred goldsmiths at his palace in addition to other craftsmen. Such power did not always outlast the ruler, but permanent specialized craft districts did develop in the larger cities, where gold, iron, copper, and clay were manufactured to meet the needs of a diverse urban population. An extreme case was Nagara, the capital of the Banjar kingdom on Borneo's Barito River before its sixteenth-century conversion to Islam. When the capital moved downriver to the trade center of Banjarmasin, the craftsmen appear to have stayed in Nagara, which became the prime metalworking center of Borneo over the following two centuries. In Java also the centers of sixteenth- and seventeenth-century kingdoms remained as specialist centers of metalworking thereafter – Kota Gede (Yogyakarta), Surakarta, Tuban, Sidayu, and Gresik. Goldworking reached levels of skill matched in few other crafts except boat-building. One seventeenth-century French missionary to Cochin-China related how, 24 days after presenting a Parisian chiming clock with a silver face to the king, the royal goldsmith produced a replica indistinguishable from the original, and which kept equally good time.

In the larger cities there were whole quarters dedicated to particular crafts. Particularly famous for this pattern was the Tongking (Dai Viet) capital of Thang-long, divided administratively into 36 quarters, most of which bore the name of the particular craft practiced in it. Even the city over the water in Brunei had two quarters for ironworkers and one each for *kris* (dagger) makers, bronzeworkers, and oil processors. As the Burmese capital moved from Ava to

Amerapura to Mandalay the specialist craft villages which sustained urban life remained in place at different points along the river. Most large cities had quarters for ironworkers, bronzeworkers, gold- and silversmiths, shipwrights, furniture-makers, arms manufacturers, potters, weavers, and *arak* distillers. In Thang-long there were also paper-makers and silkworkers.

The Makassar chronicles are unusually informative about the rapid progress of that city in developing different skills, under the influence of the rapid influx of foreign traders and new technologies during the commercial boom. Under King Tunipalangga (1548–66), bricks, gunpowder, and large cannons were first manufactured. Under Tunijallo' (1566–90), *kris* makers and chronicle-writers made their appearance; under the regent and chancellor Matoaya of Tallo' (1593–1636), irrigation works were first undertaken, a gold and lead coinage minted, and muskets and war galleys first made, as well as other innovations in shipbuilding including the use of nails. From foreign sources we know that this technological innovation went further under the chancellor Pattingalloang (1639–54), discussed in Chapter 6.

Nevertheless, the system of labor organization in most Southeast Asian cities limited the extent to which innovation could be rewarded and encouraged. Manual labor was associated with servitude and inferior status even when it involved skilled craftsmanship. The booming cities of the long sixteenth century offered abundant opportunity for upward mobility, the object of which was to escape such manual labor as craftsmanship, or acquire one's own slave to perform it. War captives usually performed the roughest forms of construction labor, but craftsmen too were typically bonded to some powerful figure. As late as 1822, Crawfurd (1828/1967, 322) complained that in the Siamese capital "every mechanic of skill is immediately seized upon, and becomes the retainer of the king, or of some courtier, or other man in authority." The only labor market was that of Chinese immigrants to cities where they were numerous, or that of slaves hired out at rates much higher than a free market would have allowed. A Persian visitor to Aceh and Siam noted "it is their custom to rent slaves. They pay the slave a sum of money, which he gives to his master, and then they use the slave that day for whatever work they wish" (Ibrahim 1688/1972, 177–8).

Trade, Guns, and New State Forms

The age of commerce brought with it substantial benefits for a new kind of maritime state: the revenues from trade; improved military technologies; foreign minorities willing to act as mercenaries; and new ideas of statecraft and religion which could be used to legitimate absolutism. There were two stages to this state-forming. Around 1400 it was Chinese intervention that provided enormous advantages to a distinct type of port-state that played the Chinese tribute game. In the second stage, the sustained trade boom of the long sixteenth century introduced more lethal firearms and a competitive world-contest that was both ideological and economic. In this environment some trade-based *negeri* became expansive gunpowder states with enough state centralization to lay the basis of some of the region's modern ethnic identities.

In the first, city-state, phase, Ayutthaya, Melaka, Pasai, Brunei, Manila, and the Javanese ports of Gresik and Demak were the great winners from the unprecedented Ming Dynasty interest in southern barbarian tributaries in the period 1368–1424. Melaka and Brunei gained special privileges by sending their kings to Nanjing for investiture, while Ayutthaya sealed its dominance in the Tai world by becoming the one port in the Gulf of Thailand to be recognized by China. As well as channeling the trade of Southeast Asia to China, these ports benefitted from the defection of thousands of Chinese mariners – both anti-Ming Cantonese and Muslims who did not wish to return after the change of dynasty, and direct defectors from the massive fleets of Zheng He. The Javanese ports appear to have become a base for Chinese of both sorts, many of them Muslims long associated with the Arab-descended maritime communities of Quanzhou. Palembang and Patani, on the other hand, became the havens for thousands of anti-Ming Cantonese, and never achieved Ming recognition as properly respectful barbarian kingdoms.

With the exception of Ayutthaya, which conquered Angkor in 1432 and set about dominating the longer-established northern Tai polities, these all remained essentially port-states in the fifteenth century, with little purchase over the interior. The Bay of Bengal ports of Pegu – Bassein, Syriam, Martaban, and Ye – owed little directly to the Chinese but showed a similar pattern of maritime prosperity with relative autonomy in the fifteenth century. Under the benign Mon Buddhist rule of Queen Shinsawbu (1453–72), and the monk she selected to succeed her as King Dammazeidi (1472–92), Pegu became a very successful center of both trade and Theravada Buddhism, little interested in territorial expansion. In a different category was Dai Viet, which the expansionist Ming had occupied for two decades (1407–28). Once Le Loi mobilized the country to expel the Chinese, his new Le Dynasty provided the Tongking (Red River delta) area with Southeast Asia's most bureaucratic and regulated state on the Confucian model. Although the fifteenth was Viet Nam's great century of ceramic export, this was the only Southeast Asian state of the period that flourished for reasons other than its cultivation of seaborne trade (see Chapter 9).

The second stage may be equated with the sixteenth century, when maritime commerce accelerated and new military techniques became central to the rise of what might be termed gunpowder empires. These had similarities with those that arose all over Eurasia in the period, but were more brittle, personalized, and short-lived than their better-known Moghul, Safavid, Ottoman, or Hapsburg contemporaries. Various kinds of cannons had begun to influence Southeast Asian warfare from around 1400, introduced chiefly from China but also from Islamic sources in the Middle East. In particular, the countries bordering China needed to acquire Chinese gunpowder technology to fight the expanding Chinese state, and did so through defectors and smugglers. The Ming minister of war complained in 1444 that Chinese firearms had been smuggled into all the northern polities of Southeast Asia, making them more resistant to absorption. Dai Viet and the northern Tai state of Lan Na were particular beneficiaries of Chinese-style gun technology.

The Portuguese arrival in 1509, and their spectacular conquest of Melaka two years later, nevertheless began a more fundamental military revolution in Southeast Asia as elsewhere. Although the Portuguese conquerors reported that they found a great store of firearms in Melaka, as well as skilled gun founders, these appear not to have been effectively used in defending the city. At least the Malay chronicle of Melaka's loss, written a century after the event, preferred to remember the defenders as dumbfounded at the effectiveness of the Portuguese artillery onslaught. "The people of Melaka were more and more astonished to see the effect of this artillery; they said 'What is this weapon called that is round, and yet so sharp that it kills?'" (*Sejarah Melayu* 1612/1938, 182). Whereas the Chinese technology was stagnating, Portugal was an active participant in the competitive military revolution just beginning to transform Europe, and Portuguese gunners were immediately identified as the preferred mercenaries. The most successful Southeast Asian gunpowder empires of the long sixteenth century – Pegu, Ayutthaya, Aceh, Banten, and Mataram – were able to exploit the possibilities of unprecedented trade wealth, new military technology including Portuguese or Muslim mercenaries, and imported ideologies of statecraft.

Mainland Buddhist rulers were the chief beneficiaries of Portuguese merce- naries, because the most ambitious Islamic states were on the other side of Portuguese-Muslim polarization. The Bama ruler of Toungoo, Tabinshweihti (r.1531–50), was the quickest to adopt the new firearms, using Muslim as well as Portuguese mercenaries to conquer Pegu and its wealthy ports on the Bay of Bengal. He was criticized in the Burmese chronicles for being excessively close to his dissolute Portuguese mercenaries, whereas his successor Bayinnaung extended the new technology throughout his army. From a prosperous and cosmopolitan base at Pegu he conquered the whole Irrawaddy basin for the first time, and established Bama hegemony over the trade-oriented Mon of the south as well as the Shan *muangs* in the north. He also conquered his strongest Tai rivals – Chiang Mai and in 1569 even Ayutthaya, which had undergone its own military revolution with the help of Portuguese mercenaries.

In the Archipelago, Muslim adventurers and mercenaries played a similar role as disseminators of the new technology. Although most of these were car- ried to Southeast Asia by the usual factor of trade, the Ottomans provided a unique moment of great-power intervention into the Indian Ocean on the Muslim side. Aceh was the chief initiator and beneficiary of an alliance with Turkey that marked the summit of Ottoman global ambitions (Chapter 5). Turkish gunsmiths and artillerymen made an important contribution to Aceh's sixteenth-century rise, but Turks were also noticed among Islamic forces in the conflicts of Java, along with Gujaratis and Malabaris from India, and Muslim Chams and Filipinos. Aceh, Johor, Banten, Patani, and Makassar all possessed giant cannon deemed impractical in Europe, but prized, personalized with names, and given supernatural powers in the internal literature. Several of these gunpowder empires at their peak possessed hundreds of cannon large and small.

In Java, the autonomous, polyglot, predominately Muslim ports of the north coast gradually got the better of the Hindu-Buddhist interior in the fifteenth century, and the last capital of the Majapahit Dynasty, at Kediri, probably fell to Muslim forces in the 1520s. The center of gravity remained on the coast throughout the sixteenth century, though Demak was not able to centralize power as effectively as Pegu did in Burma. Other north-coast city-states such as Gresik, Surabaya, and Tuban continued to enjoy a virtual autonomy that was undoubtedly advantageous to their commerce. Only in the early seventeenth century, as the coastal *negeri* were weakened by Europeans taking over the most lucrative branches of commerce, did Mataram use the demographic weight of the rice-growing interior to create a brief moment of centralized power in Java – the work of Sultan Agung (r.1613–45).

Other potent Archipelago states of the sixteenth century were creations of that period's trade boom and adoption of firearms. After the Portuguese conquest of Melaka in 1511 the Muslim trade sought other centers, preferably strong enough to withstand Portuguese bullying. The new sultanates of Aceh, Johor, Pahang, Patani, and Banten were the result, each centered in an important entrepôt but also commanding a particular river system or pepper-growing littoral. Further east, Makassar began to unite the populous southwest peninsula of Sulawesi in the same period. It became Muslim only in 1605, attracted Malay and Portuguese traders needing protection against Dutch monopoly, and produced a rice surplus for the Maluku spice trade.

On the Mainland, both Cochin-China and Arakan can be considered analogous maritime states, arising in a commercially advantageous location on the strength of trade wealth and firearms. Arakan had only a century of successful autonomy (c.1540–1640), using the trade of its port-capital, Mrauk-U, and the skills of Portuguese mercenaries to hold off the ambitions of both Bengal and Burma. Cochin-China, known to its inhabitants as "the inner region" (*Dang Trong*), was established on the southern frontier of Viet settlement by Nguyen Hoang around 1600. While proclaiming loyalty to the powerless Le Dynasty in Hanoi, he refused to accept the claims of the Trinh Dynasty that had seized effective control of Tongking in 1592. For almost two centuries (c.1600–1777) the Nguyen Dynasty governed a rival southern Vietnamese state, borrowing from its *negeri*-like Cham predecessors on this crossroads both a commercial orientation and a pluralist style of mediating between upland producers of export produce and the outside world.

In virtually all the states of Southeast Asia in this period except Tongking and the landlocked northern Tai polities, trade provided the principal source of royal revenues. The Melaka sultanate has been calculated to have drawn the equivalent of two tons of silver a year from its customhouse around 1500, which must have constituted at least 90% of state revenue. In general port duties amounted to 5–7% of the value of imports, though compulsory gifts to powerful officials could distort this pattern in disorderly ports. Rulers and key merchant-aristocrats made most of their income through selling their own export items like pepper, tin, jewels, and sappanwood, often insisting on a monopoly of the supplies coming from their own domains. Speaking particularly of Siam, one French observer correctly observed that "These kings are all merchants, and are only wealthy to the extent that they engage in commerce" (Le Blanc 1692 II, 219).

This commercial interest distinguished Southeast Asian rulers from most of their counterparts on the Eurasian mainland. Although royal chronicles were designed to show the supernatural origin and legitimacy of a dynasty, they acknowledged that a mark of the successful ruler was a port full of foreign ships. But this closeness to commerce did not necessarily create conditions favorable for commerce to flourish. There was always tension between royal greed and mercantile interests, between the palace and the marketplace. Because states rose and fell so quickly, this dynamic period provides a fascinating laboratory of the birth pangs of capitalism.

On the positive side there was progress in a number of places toward royal absolutism and rule of law, central requirements for the growth of capitalism in the Europe of the same period. Both in Siam under Naresuan (1590–1605) and Aceh under Iskandar Muda (1607–36) the king radically centralized authority at the expense of the nobility, who were killed, expropriated, or intimidated into royal service. The new prominence of foreigners, Christian, Muslim, and Chinese, enabled ambitious rulers to rely on mercenary troops and quasi-monopolist buyers of export produce to reach over the heads of their own over-mighty subjects. To some extent this process did give rise to royal officials dependent on the king rather than on local revenues (particularly in Dai Viet from the fifteenth, and Burma and Siam from the seventeenth centuries), and to courts which enforced increasingly codified laws (particularly in Burma, Siam, and Aceh).

This progress was not accompanied by political theories or institutions that guaranteed the property of subjects against their kings. The very newness of absolute power encouraged its abuse. The new religions, Islam, Theravada Buddhism, and Spanish Catholicism, were used by the ambitious to override local pluralisms rather than to build the rights of subjects into the system. The more analytical of the European observers identified the rapaciousness of rulers as the chief reason that Southeast Asians of the seventeenth century did not accumulate capital except in forms that could be readily hidden, like gold and jewelry, or in manpower that could protect them against their rivals. "This is the reason they get as few immovables as they can, and that they always endeavour to conceal their movables from the knowledge of their king" (La Loubère 1691/1969, 52).

The most successful states commercially, if not always militarily, were those that incorporated, by accident or design, an element of oligarchy into their theoretically absolute kingship. The most dynamic, if disorderly, period of Banten's commercial growth came when the kings were children over most of the period 1580–1620. Several port-kingdoms in the Archipelago institutionalized a dualistic symbiosis between an upstream and a downstream ruler. Other dualities were built into contractual form – between Malay king and Bugis "junior king" in Riau-Johor, between the front palace and the main palace in Siam, and most successfully between Goa and Tallo' dynasties in Makassar. The preference shown for queens, despite Islamic strictures against them, in Aceh (1641–99), Patani (1584–c.1690), and a number of other Archipelago port-states, can be seen in a similar light. Female rule proved congenial to peaceful commerce, but as queens succeeded each other there was a tendency for their power to diminish to the point they could no longer act as effective referees between the mercantile oligarchs, so that the system declined into disorder.

One of the major commercial functions of the state was to regulate the market and issue standardized currency that could be used in it. Southeast Asian rulers provided for markets, both at the center of the capital and at the harborside, and at best regulated its affairs through commercial courts, market officials, and a systematic leasing of booths to sellers. But as commerce grew, these markets expanded in scale rather than sophistication, remaining preeminently the sites where prices were established through a process of bargaining. The minting of coins by rulers must be one index of the increasing monetization of the societies in question, but it shows a curiously discontinuous pattern. Arakan, the Mon and Pyu kingdoms of Burma, and the Dvaravati kingdom of the Chao Phraya basin had all minted their own silver coinages from around the fifth century, but these disappeared from Burma and Siam in the ninth century and from Arakan in the eleventh. The charter polities of Angkor, Pagan, and Champa (ninth to fourteenth centuries) issued no true coinages, using instead as measures of value rice, cloth, Chinese coins, or, for large transactions, gold and silver by weight. In Java, Brunei, and other Archipelago states there were coins of gold and silver between the ninth and twelfth centuries, but in the thirteenth these disappear, their place taken by a large influx of base Chinese coins.

One of the features of Southeast Asia's age of commerce was the great influx of Chinese copper *cash*, with a square hole in the middle to facilitate compiling strings of 600–1,000 coins. They became the base coinage of Java around 1300, perhaps as a result of the Mongol naval expedition of the 1290s, and of some parts of the Philippines soon after. In the fifteenth century they became still more widespread, probably as a result of the intense Chinese interaction associated with the early Ming interventions. Kingdoms such as Dai Viet, Champa, Melaka, Pasai, and Brunei became so dependent on the coins during the Ming visitations that they began minting their own when the ships stopped coming around 1430. Despite widespread local production, Southeast Asia could never get enough of these *cash*. The local manufacture initially used the more abundant tin, but this proved uncompetitive once China, around 1590, began producing for the Southeast Asian market low-grade *cash* made primarily of lead rather than copper. English and Dutch companies began supplying lead to manufacturers in the islands and copper to Dai Viet in the 1630s, and the tonnage of metal imported provides some measure of the base money supply. By calculating that the small lead coins deteriorated to nothing within about five years, while the Vietnamese copper ones lasted somewhat longer, one must assume that over a billion *cash* must have been in circulation in Southeast Asia at this time (Reid 1993, 98–9).

For higher values, gold coinage re-entered the Archipelago with Islam. North Sumatran kingdoms continuously minted a small gold *mas* of 0.6 grams in the ruler's name, from Pasai around 1300 through to Aceh around 1700. Similar coins were issued in the seventeenth century by Johor, Kedah, Banten, Makassar, and Patani. Cambodia produced both a silver and a gold coin from the sixteenth century. Silver was historically more favored, and more available, in the Mainland. Arakan reintroduced a silver coinage at least by the 1530s. In the Tai and Burmese states, large transactions continued to be by weight of silver, but Ayutthaya (Siam) by the sixteenth century had produced a standard kidney-shaped lump of silver weighing 14.6 grams, the long-lasting *baht*, which functioned as a currency even though not marked with the ruler's name.

These attempts at managing the money supply through domestic coinages must be understood against the background of the massive influx of silver to the region after 1570. Increasingly this was in the form of the Spanish *real*, which quickly became the international currency of the whole region. The gold coinages issued by the port states of the Archipelago fought an unequal battle in the marketplace, despite periodic draconian attempts to enforce their use. Because of the popularity and abundance of silver, and the large quantities of it brought in by foreign buyers, no ruler in the Archipelago could maintain effective control over the money supply. By 1620 the international currency was the *real*, and local gold coinages were chiefly used for internal taxes and fines that touched the ruler directly.

ASIAN COMMERCIAL ORGANIZATION

As the major point of interaction of Indian, Arab, Chinese, and European commercial methods, Southeast Asia represents an important laboratory in the development of financial techniques. Each commercial network or diaspora in the region operated by its own rules of trust. Each of them also contributed elements to the distinctively Southeast Asian commercial system that evolved during the fifteenth and sixteenth centuries, particularly in the Malay idiom.

Before the great commercial revolution of the Early Modern period brought about the incorporation of a host of foreign terms and concepts into Southeast Asian trade, there was already a long tradition of commerce, exchange, and borrowing at interest. Thus the dictionaries compiled in the early 1600s for the Visayan language include a range of indigenous terms for such things as a business partner (*bakas*), a business partnership (*samahan*), buy on credit (*gamit*), and for a variety of types of exchange. Vernacular concepts of interest were well established through the metaphor of the flower (*bunga* in Malay, *dok* in Thai) produced by a tree. The profit of a transaction was expressed in the Austronesian languages of the Archipelago by the ancient term *laba*.

In the sixteenth and seventeenth centuries, the preeminent financial managers were Gujarati Muslims, inheriting some of the capital accumulation methods of the Hindu *sharafs* (described in Chapter 3) with the universal aspirations of Islamic commercial law. A Florentine merchant with the Portuguese in Melaka conceded that the Gujaratis there were "astute and clever merchants, as good as us in all business matters; their cargo ledgers with their lists of bales taken and discharged are all in perfection" (cited Reid 1993, 113). European merchants in Islamic ports found it difficult to cope with the complexity of currencies, weights, and prices unless they employed a Gujarati broker who could work the system. Many Indian terms, like capital (*modal*), were adopted into Southeast Asian languages at this time, as the methods of these Indian commercial specialists were followed by a broader group of urban merchants. Arab commercial terms came into Malay usage through Islamic law, which was partially adopted into Malay law codes to govern such matters as bankruptcy (*muflis*) and the Islamic disapproval of usury (*riba*).

Chinese commercial practice was influential in the system of weights used throughout Southeast Asia. The maritime practice on board Sino-Southeast Asian shipping was largely shared by the Chinese vessels from Fujian, though the interactions between Chinese, Tamil, and Southeast Asian practice in the period were so constant that we should assume hybridity rather than single origins. Aboard the seagoing junks in this region, whether Chinese, Malay, or Javanese in ownership, the hold was divided into a series of partitions, and traveling merchants, captain, and crew all had a stake in one or more of these partitions. The term adopted in the Malay maritime code for these traveling merchants (*kiwi*) may be of Fujian (*Kheh-ui* in Amoy dialect) or Tamil (*kevi*) origin, or perhaps from some more complex set of interactions.

The peak of Southeast Asian commercial activity in its age of commerce was also a period of exceptional cosmopolitanism. It is easy to be misled by the prominence of foreign merchants at every major port to imagine that Southeast Asia lacked a commercial group of its own. The reality is that in this period foreign merchants were constantly being incorporated into local society through the medium of marriage and adoption of local language and dress norms. It remained an advantage to be foreign and mobile, because jealous kings were less likely to try to cut down a powerful merchant if he was seen as outside the system. The Malay word for commerce, *dagang*, indeed had a prior meaning as foreign. But among the most important "foreign" commercial minorities in every port by 1600 were Southeast Asians operating outside their own area – Javanese, Malays, Bandanese, Chams, Mons (from Pegu, southern Burma), and "Luzons" (from Manila and Brunei). All these terms referred to peoples of cosmopolitan origins, with a strong Chinese element in those labeled Javanese and Luzons; Javanese, Chinese, and Indian in those labeled Malays; Javanese and Malay in those labeled Bandanese, and so forth.

As sites of interaction of these diverse commercial traditions, Southeast Asia's ports gave rise in this period to their own hybrid commercial minorities and commercial methods, adopting the most serviceable of the foreign techniques. In addition to features of the junk itself, Javanese and Malay navigators incorporated the Chinese compass and chart-making into their navigational methods, which in coastal waters were heavily dependent on recognition of tides, winds, and land features.

The crucial evidence for Southeast Asian commercial and maritime methods comes from complementary Malay and Portuguese sources. Two Malay law codes were probably first drawn up for the Melaka sultanate in the late fifteenth century, and are known to us from later texts such as the *Undang-undang Melaka* (Melaka Laws; Liaw 1976) and the *Undang-undang Laut* (Maritime Code). The first generation of Portuguese also described the local Indian financial systems and Javanese, Malay, and Mon navigation on which they relied for their own voyages. These sources show the *nak-hoda* on Southeast Asian vessels acted as both captain and supercargo. The *Undang-undang Laut* was drawn up by five leading *nakhoda* of Melaka, reportedly in consultation with all the others, and endorsed by the sultan of the day with the words, "you *nakhoda* are like kings in your respective junks." On shipboard the *nakhoda* held powers of life and death, and his authority was supported by officers expected to enforce his will – a master, several deck officers (*tukang*), helmsmen, and boatswains (*jurubatu*) to look after the anchor and leadline. In the typical large junk of around 200 tons there would be 50–100 crew members, some of whom would be slaves but others active traders. The pilot was in a class alone as the *malim*, a term also used for a learned Muslim teacher. He was the possessor of arcane knowledge both technical and mystical, and thereby responsible for the survival of all.

The *nakhoda* was supreme in commercial matters, with the right to buy and sell onshore first, at the most favorable prices. He acted also as diplomat, carrying letters and news between the courts and ports of the region. Besides his own goods he would be entrusted with the cargo of several stay-at-home merchants at a rate of return agreed beforehand. For Melaka ships sailing to Java, the conventional return on such commenda transactions was 40%, to Pegu or Siam 50%. More common, however, was the system whereby the stay-at-home merchant rented one or more of the divisions (*petak*) into which the cargo was divided, either for a fixed charge or for a percentage of the cargo's value – 20% on some Archipelago routes. The merchant then sent his own men to manage the cargo and trade it. In each of these cases the investor would lose everything if the ship were wrecked.

The traveling merchants, probably including those working for a stay-at-home investor, were known as *kiwi*. Their spokesman (*maula kiwi*) had to be consulted by the *nakhoda* on matters affecting the commercial outcome of the voyage, especially if cargo had to be jettisoned. A typical ship would have as many *kiwi* as crew, each sleeping with his goods, and perhaps his wife, in one or more cargo partitions. While an allowance of rice was provided for the slave crew, the officers and freemen were given no salary but an entitlement to trade. In this respect, as in most other shipboard arrangements, the Melaka-based ships were very similar to the ocean-going ships of the south China coast, but quite unlike those of India. Although there are unfortunately no surviving examples of commercial contracts from the sixteenth century, we know that Malay, Javanese, Mon, and Vietnamese merchants recorded their obligations in writing. As the first Dutch expedition noted of Banten:

> The rich merchants usually remain at home, and when a ship is about to sail they give to those travelling with it a sum of money on [the promise of] a double return, more or less, when the voyage is complete, of which they make an obligation, and if the voyage is successfully completed then the investor is paid, following the contract. ... These writings, like all others, are written on leaves of a tree [palm-leaves] (Lodewycksz 1598/1915, 120).

It was not ignorance of financial techniques that restrained the development of capitalist structures in Southeast Asia, but a lack of security of capital. In comparison with cities that took a faster capitalist track (in parts of Europe, Japan, and China), Southeast Asian merchants were apt to suffer from the commercial orientation of their rulers. Rulers took a very active interest in commerce as the source of their power. Paradoxically, the much greater reliance on landed wealth on the part of feudal aristocracies in Europe and Japan provided more breathing space for mercantile enclaves than was the case in Southeast Asia. None of the cities of the region solved the problems of insecurity, though on the whole merchants fared better in the somewhat chaotic periods between strong rulers.

The most powerful rulers of the age of commerce were those who succeeded in drawing the maximum wealth of the port into their own hands, both by trading on monopolistic or advantageous terms, and by outright confiscation of the goods of potential rivals. The rapid rise of many states on the back of commerce and gunpowder tended to erode traditional legal conventions and aristocratic privileges, making it possible for kings to rise to high but brittle pinnacles of personal power, usually giving rise to a reaction after their death. Sultan Iskandar Muda of Aceh (r. 1607–36), one of the most successful tyrants of this type,

> makes great gains from confiscating the property of those whom he has executed every day. Most often these are the great lords who have incurred his displeasure. ...
> I noted two reasons which cost the lives of various *orangkaya* [merchant-aristocrats]. One was the good reputation which they had among the people; the other was their wealth (Beaulieu 1622/1996, 215–16).

The consequences of this insecurity were a shortage of capital, its concentration in the hands of those who could protect it, and consequently high interest rates. European observers in all the trading cities of the region complained at how difficult it was to find merchants who had significant supplies of goods on hand. Foreign merchants whose capital was protected by their mobility had to advance funds on one voyage and return later for the goods. Chinese traders were more adept at establishing networks that could collect goods from a large range of small providers. The European companies, however, with their large overheads, were driven to deal with the rulers, and thereby to accentuate the absolutist tendencies already evident in the period.

Interest rates in seventeenth-century Southeast Asia were far above those in Amsterdam, the world's leading capital market, and even above the leading Indian cities such as Surat. The minimum rates quoted were at 2% a month (24% p.a.), but these were only available to rulers, the European Companies, the largest foreign merchants, or one's own close kin – in other words, either those who could be trusted to repay, or those whose power enabled them to dictate terms. These rates were cited at enough cities around the region to suggest that this was an optimum standard sought by these large borrowers in dealing with each other. Elsewhere in the mobile, insecure world of commerce borrowing rates could rise as high as 200–400% a year.

In short, Southeast Asian societies in this period were relatively heavily exposed to commerce, in relation to other times and places, but failed to develop an institutional base for capital accumulation in private hands. The chief inhibition to such accumulation was insecurity, caused by the lack of political or legal safeguards. The political problems were made more difficult by the presence of a monopolistic Dutch Company in the seventeenth century, but the Company itself is not an adequate explanation for the failure to develop durable capitalist institutions.

[5] RELIGIOUS REVOLUTION AND EARLY MODERNITY, 1350–1630

THE explosion of contacts in the age of commerce accompanied a new universalism of ideas, a quest for cosmopolis akin to that which had spread Buddhist universalism in the previous millennium. Now the mood spanned the globe, ushering in what has been aptly labeled the "Early Modern era" in world history, in which nobody could escape the collision of rival universalisms. Elsewhere I have labeled this period a "religious revolution" for Southeast Asians, which established the ways in which they would identify themselves as individually responsible members of universal cultures. Each of the new scriptural religions brought a sense of its own core and its own boundaries, conscious of being in competition with other universalisms. While the impetus that drove Southeast Asians to adopt such religions was similar – a commercial, cosmopolitan, competitive environment that shook the foundations of older local beliefs – embracing these religions put them on paths that would ultimately diverge. Unlike the changes brought by Buddha and Shiva, which created further patterns of interaction across the region and beyond, the new universalisms divided the region into five modes of modernity. Over the following centuries the Islamized south, the Theravada Buddhist north, the Christianized east, and Confucianized Viet culture grew gradually more distinct from each other and from the fifth mode, the remaining adherents of an older Southeast Asian religious pattern.

This last-mentioned category was the most fundamental layer of Southeast Asian belief. At the outset of this revolution it may have been almost universal, coexisting naturally with both the popular Mahayana Buddhism of wet-rice growing communities and the Shiva cults of ambitious kings. It even survived the religious revolution, as it does today, not only in holdouts against the new, such as the Batak, Toraja, Ifugao, Chin, Hmong, and Karen, but in partnerships suffusing the scripturalisms and supplying what they lacked.

A History of Southeast Asia: Critical Crossroads, First Edition. Anthony Reid.
© 2015 Anthony Reid. Published 2015 by John Wiley & Sons, Ltd.

SOUTHEAST ASIAN RELIGION

Because of problems associated with terms such as animism and shamanism, I have chosen to label this older pattern simply "Southeast Asian" religion, though this should not be understood as implying uniqueness. Certainly there is no geographical boundary to this mental universe. Some of its ideas may indeed have had near-universal currency, arising simply from the contrast with organized modern "religion," a concept that took hold later in Southeast Asia than in Europe, China, and India. The most reliable descriptions of the system from the age of commerce itself come from Christian missionaries who needed to understand what they were up against, and reported most abundantly from the Philippines, but the more systematic work of modern ethnographers in many areas is also very helpful.

The spiritual realm was immanent and pervasive, inseparable from the practical or everyday. European missionaries found the system crassly materialist, interested only in gain, but they quickly realized that if they could not appear to cure ailments, safeguard life passages, and make the rains come on time, they could not compete with traditional rituals. Spirits were everywhere there was power, and keeping those spirits content and well-disposed was the business of the specialist. A distinction was widespread between the dangerously mobile spirit or soul-essence of living individuals (Malay *semangat*, Thai *khwan*, Bama *leikpya*), which needed to be ritually brought back or reconcentrated in the body at various life crises, and the myriad spirits (Thai *phii*, Bama *nat*) of nature and of deceased humans that governed the inhabited world. Austronesian terms for the latter are too numerous to record, though many are cognates of *anita* (*anitu*, *hantu*), and Arabic-derived *roh* has become a generalized term in Malay. The dead continued to influence the living for better or worse. Illness in the living might be attributed to inadequate or incorrect death rituals for a relative recently passed on, and health and prosperity similarly attributed to appropriate manipulation of the powerful spirits of ancestors, heroes, or powerful animals. Even the most important agricultural spirit, that residing in the rice plant, was often humanized as originating from a virtuous maiden sacrificed for the good of humanity.

Among all the panoply of rituals for every life passage, those for death were the most elaborate. An acute seventeenth-century observer noted how Southeast Asians "do not only believe that they may be helpful to the dead; ... they think also that the dead have the power of tormenting and succouring the living; and from hence comes their care and magnificence in funerals; for it is only in this that they are magnificent" (La Loubère 1691/1969, 121). No feast was more important, and since feasts were the only occasion for meat-eating, the sacrifice of a pig, chicken, or buffalo was intimately linked to the ritual. Dancing and consumption of alcohol were often part of such feasts, to the horror of moralists of all the scriptural religions, because it was necessary to reaffirm life amidst death and to assure the deceased that legions were gathered to celebrate his or her name.

This pattern can be generalized by contrast with the modern and scriptural, but observers were bewildered by its diversity, noting the extraordinary abundance of spirits particular to each village or even each household. There was also a necessary experimentalism amidst the abundant options. Those whose enterprises prospered and whose crops and children were abundant were assumed to have adopted the right rituals, and others would seek to find the ritual formula kept secret by the beneficiary. Hence when Muslims and Christians appeared among them who appeared successful in both trade and warfare, their ritual secrets were also keenly sought. Some decided they should spurn pork simply because this seemed the key Muslim formula, while the holy water used by Catholics in the sacraments was sought after as a healing remedy. This fundamental openness in the system made it a ready field for "conversion," though, at least initially, without abandoning the assumptions of the old system.

One striking difference between the old and new religious systems was in their gendering. Southeast Asian religion was balanced and dualistic, with the female gods of the earth, rice, moon, and the underworld matching the male ones of the sky, iron (which ploughs the earth), sun, and upperworld. Women were indispensable in ritual as healers and mediators with the spirits. In some areas like south Sulawesi the particular potency of the male-female mix ensured that the most powerful shamans were of a third gender, the transsexual *bissu*. By contrast, scriptural religions were brought to the region by exclusively male specialists with developed concepts of the maleness of their gods and prophets, of a celibate male ascetic ideal, and of female impurity and ritual pollution. Not surprisingly, it was men who most readily adopted the new faiths, often relegating the old rituals to women's business, however necessary they may still have been to ensure fertility and health. Women were often the most determined opponents of the new monotheisms, as best reported in the Philippines. The Christian stress on lifetime monogamous marriage attracted women disproportionately in the Confucian-influenced zone, but often deterred women accustomed to the widespread Southeast Asian pattern of monogamy within marriage but relatively easy divorce and remarriage. One Visayan lady told a missionary "it was a hard thing if unhappy with one's husband one could not leave him, as was the custom among them" (Chirino 1604/1969, 313).

THERAVADA COSMOPOLIS AND THE MAINLAND STATES

New religious universalisms were fostered by the gunpowder empires that broke with tradition in the age of commerce, because they provided a justification for unprecedented expansion of state power in the name of a foreign orthodoxy. In this they differed profoundly from the popular Mahayana Buddhism that had spread writing and civilization in earlier periods. The rulers of the Mainland who chose Theravada Buddhism as their new orthodoxy did some of the things their Mahayana predecessors had done, accumulating merit by building and ornamenting temples and sacred places and patronizing their monks. Sri Lankan Theravada, however, enabled them to unify in a more profound way, by enforcing ritual uniformity for the beloved monks, especially in their ordination.

It is difficult to date the beginnings of the adoption of externally validated, Sri Lankan ordination rituals and practices, known today as Theravada Buddhism. Though consolidated as orthodoxy by the commercial intensification of the long sixteenth century, Theravada clearly began in a pre-1300 wave of trade expansion in which Sri Lanka played a more important role. Later Burman chronicles sought to give the credit to the semi-legendary Pagan king-conqueror Anawhrata (1044–77), but the evidence of architecture, inscriptions, and texts from the period suggests rather the 1170s. One impetus may have been a Sri Lankan military expedition as far as Pagan, in defense of its trade with Cambodia, reported by the Sinhalese chronicle *Chulavamsa* for 1165. In Cambodia, Theravada-style monks, who "shave their heads and dress in yellow … leave their right shoulder uncovered … and go barefoot," were described by Zhou Daguan (1297/2007, 52–3) in the 1290s, though they were not patronized by the Khmer court of the day, and the word Zhou used for them (*zhugu*) appears to be Tai. Mon traders in the ports of the Pegu coast were probably the initial mediators of this Sri Lankan contact for other Southeast Asian peoples, and their conquest by the Bama of Pagan probably dispersed these ideas more widely. Particularly ambitious kings such as Mangrai in Chiang Mai (1292–1317) and Ram Kamhaeng in Sukhothai (c.1279–98) favored the foreign orthodoxy as a means to override local particularities.

Before the age of commerce, religious practice remained extremely varied, and local sacred places more important than any national uniformity. Sri Lanka-inspired ritual uniformity allied with potent gunpowder kings to change that. Thirty-nine Tai and Mon monks were reordained in the Mahavihara Monastery in Sri Lanka in 1423, and on their return persuaded a succession of Southeast Asian rulers to ally with their type of reformism. King Tilokaraja in Chiang Mai (1441–87), and his contemporary Trailok in the rising port-state of Ayutthaya (r.1441–87), were the great unifiers of the Tai-speaking *muang* in the name of the Mahavihara ordination. Control of the Chao Phraya and foreign wealth and weaponry generally gave Ayutthaya the advantage. But King Trailok, one of the first great Ayutthaya expansionists, used religion even more effectively than warfare. He abdicated the throne in 1464, became a monk for two years and invited his rivals to support with land donations the great monastery he had built near the capital. His great rival, Tilokaraja, responded by building ever-greater Buddhist edifices, including the seven-spired Wat Chet Yod built on the model of the Mahabodhi Temple in Bodhgaya, India, to host the Eighth World Buddhist Council he convened in Chiang Mai in 1477. The following half-century was indeed devoted more to religious than military competition, with Ayutthaya, Chiang Mai, Sukhothai, Vientiane, and Luang Prabang all seeking to unite inherently fragmented upland valleys through the splendor of their temples and their devotion to the popular *sangha*.

In the Irrawaddy valley the initial motives may have been more pious than political, as the two great rulers of the flourishing coastal state of Pegu, devout

Queen Shinsawbu and the monk-king Dammazeidi (1472–92), used the wealth and contacts of their ports to purify and unify the *sangha*. Dammazeidi called a Buddhist council, despatched another mission to Sri Lanka for reordination, and on its return insisted that all monks be reordained according the Mahavihara rituals or cease to be recognized. He left an inscription declaring that more than 15,000 did so. The rulers of the rival ports of Arakan followed suit, sending their own repeated missions to Sri Lanka in the mid-fifteenth century.

Throughout Southeast Asia the period 1550–1680 saw the apogee of the gunpowder kings. The mightiest of them, King Bayinnaung of Pegu (r.1551–81), used Theravada uniformity and the purity of the *sangha* as his justification for relentless campaigns to unify all the "Shans, Mons and Bama." The two-century domination of the northern Irrawaddy by the *muang*-centered and Tai-speaking Shan was thereby ended, along with the human and animal sacrifices and spirit worship of which they were accused. Bayinnaung's military power was unprecedented, not only employing Portuguese and Muslim artillerymen to good effect, but integrating firearms throughout his army. An Italian visitor spoke very highly not only of his cannons and 80,000 harquebuses, but of the skill of his soldiers: "the king will have them shoot every day at the Plank, and so by continual exercise they become most excellent shot" (Frederici 1581/1907). Theravada orthodoxy helped Bayinnaung subordinate what Lieberman (2003, 152) rates "probably the largest empire in the history of Southeast Asia." It included not only the Irrawaddy valley – from the rich trading ports of the delta to the rice-bowls of Kyaukse and Minbu and the gem-rich gateway to Yunnan and China – but also extended at its greatest to almost the whole Tai-speaking world, embracing the Shan areas, and modern Laos and Thailand.

His conquest of the Thai commercial metropolis of Ayutthaya in 1569 briefly eliminated any rival, and enabled Bayinnaung to declare himself truly a world-ruler (*cakkavatti*) in the Buddhist tradition. Bayinnaung was fondly remembered by the modern Burmese military, and statues of him dot the contemporary landscape. The empire he built was inherently fragile and personal and could not outlast his death, but his world-conquering ideology in the name of Theravada orthodoxy would echo down the subsequent centuries.

Ayutthaya had in the long term the greater resources for such a religious and military unification project. Van Vliet (1640/2005, 155–8) estimated that there were 20,000 monks in the 400 monasteries of the flourishing capital alone in the 1630s, a quarter of those in the whole of Siam. More monasteries meant more literacy, and it was through this process that cultural cohesion increased in the Chao Phraya basin, well in advance of political control. The Burmese conquest of Ayutthaya in 1569 was devastating to religious life, but the logic of Ayutthaya's position quickly drew trade and population back to the site. Independence from a collapsing Burma was recovered by the warrior-king Naresuan (r.1590–1605), the temples were rebuilt, and successive kings placed themselves at the center of religious life by patronizing but also disciplining the *sangha* through uniform standards of training and ordination.

Post-Angkor Khmer-speakers also found cultural coherence through the Theravada monks, who made up in devotion and asceticism what they lacked in wealthy royal patronage. A Dominican missionary of the 1560s thought that every third male in Cambodia was a monk, and "the common people have a great confidence in them, with great reverence and worship." Where Buddhist rulers elsewhere sought to ensure their own centrality between rival monasteries, Cambodia at this time already had a national patriarch (*mahasangharaja*) more respected than the king (da Cruz 1569/1953, 61–2).

The new Cambodian kingship at the strategic junction of Mekong and Tonle Sap was indeed short on charisma in comparison with its Shaivite predecessors. Like other port-capitals of the age of commerce, Phnom Penh was dependent on the foreign traders but frequently threatened by them. When a Siamese (Ayutthaya) invasion drove him from the capital in 1594, one king appealed to the Spanish and Portuguese traders for military help. They obliged by killing the Siam-imposed king, and eventually brought from Vientiane the son of the deceased exiled king, and installed him on the throne. The quarrelsomeness of the Christian adventurers, however, provoked the Muslim traders to massacre them all in 1598, and later to kill the young king himself. Buddhist kingship was again only restored with Siamese assistance, leaving the Muslim traders as the most effective upholders of Cambodian independence. They later became the chief rivals of the Dutch Company in the trade of Cambodia, and after this conflict exploded into murderous violence in 1642–4, the king threw in his lot with the Muslims by converting. For the period 1644–58, Cau Bana Cand became the Muslim ruler of the port-capital, known as Ramadhipati to his Theravada Khmer subjects but Sultan Ibrahim to the Islamic world. He was eventually removed only by a Cochin-China invasion as Cambodia became a Viet-Thai battleground.

ISLAMIC BEGINNINGS: TRADERS AND MYSTICS

Prior to the long sixteenth century, the carriers of Islamic beliefs and customs to Southeast Asia had little to do with states. They began as trading networks and diasporas, albeit also as effective warriors with some of the same superiorities of weapons, solidarity, and motivation as the Europeans who joined them in the sixteenth century. The Islamic networks described in Chapter 3 enabled traders of various Asian origins to escape the restrictions of place, belief, and status by assimilating into this effective diaspora. Initially they learned enough Arabic for essential acts of devotion, but soon developed hybridized languages expressed in the Arabic script. Malay was the key example in Southeast Asia, its utility as a trade language spreading it far and wide.

By the late thirteenth century, dated Muslim tombstones began to appear in northern Sumatra and the portages of the Peninsula, and some declared themselves rulers of their trading communities. The Muslim ruler of Pasai in north Sumatra, the first Southeast Asian landfall for many travelers across the Indian Ocean, described himself to Ibn Battuta in the 1350s as an Islamic warrior (*ghazi*) leading his people in righteous warfare against surrounding pagans. Ibn

Battuta also encountered a well-placed and educated Muslim "princess" in a non-Muslim port now identified as Cham, but no other Muslim communities until he reached the great Chinese port of Quanzhou.

The flourishing multi-ethnic community of many thousand Quanzhou Muslims was thrown into chaos in 1357, the beginning of a rebellion or coup by a Mongol garrison of Muslim soldiers who appear to have been primarily Persian and Shi'a in origin. A very confused period of fighting ensued for control of the plural city, into which its different communities were inevitably drawn. The Mongol rulers of China sought to gain control after 1366 by allying with a Persian general, who presided over a wholesale massacre of the Sunni population. Massacres of Muslims continued in the violent collapse of the Mongol (Yuan) regime's authority, before the new Ming regime gradually established control after 1368. This terrible period marked the end of Quanzhou's dominance of maritime trade. All fled the city who could, including large numbers of Sunni Muslims involved in the trading networks of Southeast Asia and the Indian Ocean.

The withdrawal of these wealthy cosmopolitan traders to the closest alternative trading bases in Champa, Java, Sumatra, Brunei, and Manila Bay accounts for the many "Chinese" Muslims identified by the Muslim chronicler of the Zheng He voyages, Ma Huan (1433/1970), in the ports of north Java in particular, and for the greater incidence of apparently elite Muslim tombs in Java, Brunei, Trengganu on the Peninsula, Barus, and elsewhere in Sumatra. In the 1970s, outrage was expressed by Indonesian Muslims over the idea that Islam came to Java from China. Much of this was stimulated by the publication by a Sumatran Muslim engineer, Mangaradja Parlindungan (1964), of a racy memoir with data from his well-connected father including a mysterious "Chinese" source that gave Chinese names and origins to the "nine walis" credited in popular memory for the Islamization of Java. While further discussion of this topic was forbidden by the Suharto government, there were enough surprising facts in the book to intrigue serious scholars engaged in uncovering similar data. The truth appears to be that a wealthy, partly Sinicized group of Muslim traders from Quanzhou did play a major role in the spread of Muslim communities in Java and several other parts of Southeast Asia in the years after 1368.

Alongside the trading communities there arose intellectual communities associated with particular lineages of Sufi mystics, often the sheikhs of Sufi *tarekat*. The first use found thus far of the term al-*Jawi* to designate a Muslim from Southeast Asia is in a fourteenth-century Sufi hagiographic text from Hadhramaut, which lists Abu Abd Allah Mas'ud al-Jawi as a great saint and miracle-worker, famed for his ability to speak beyond the grave to past Sufi masters. This Mas'ud was probably born in one of the spice ports of Southeast Asia in the late thirteenth century, though he became a renowned Sheikh in Hadhramaut, where he probably died. This confirms that Sufi orders were already active in Southeast Asia during the first century of Muslim port-states.

By 1500 there were a handful of Southeast Asian *negeri* serving the long-distance trade that were ruled either by foreign Muslims or nominally Islamized local dynasties –Melaka and several other river-mouth *negeri* on the Peninsula;

Pasai, Pidië (Pedir), Lamri, Perlak, and Aru competing in northern Sumatra; Gresik and Japara in Java. In Brunei (Borneo), the Cham ports, Siam, Pegu [Burma], and Cambodia, the Muslim traders were rich and powerful enough in their respective quarters to be treated with respect and care. This outer picture of an Islam brought by the foreign traders was one that was evident to the first wave of European observers in the early 1500s, and was frequently described by them. What they could not see happening at about the same time was the creative cultural adaptation into Malay of Islamic mystical ideas of oneness with God, and of Persian and Arabic popular poetry.

The poetry of Hamzah Fansuri epitomized this creative fusion. He was thought to have died in the 1590s until a grave bearing his name and the date equivalent to 1527 was discovered in Mecca. His use of the name al-Fansuri suggests he originated in the camphor port of Fansur in western Sumatra, though he also identified himself as a *Jawi* (Muslim Southeast Asian) from Sharnawi, the Persian name for the Siamese capital of Ayutthaya. We know he was the most popular of Sumatran poets in the better-known seventeenth century, but this earlier date suggests he had already been influential for a century. His poetry beautifully expressed the aspiration for unity with an immanent God.

> He is the greatest of kings…;
> He constantly conceals himself within a slave…;
> He is both mother and father;
> Now he is a traveller;
> Now a comrade working the fields
>
> (Fansuri 1986, 98).

The monism of classic Arab authors such as al-Hallaj, and especially the Andalusian Sufi Ibn al-Arabi (1165–1240), was particularly popular Below the Winds because it could build on ascetic practice and meditative innerness already developed by Buddhists. Hamzah and his fellow mystics translated into a local idiom the Sufi doctrines of progression through seven layers of meaning toward the ultimate hidden oneness that is God. Popular stories about the legendary "nine *wali*" of Java's fifteenth- and sixteenth-century Islamization highlight the attraction of this mystic side of Islam. Java had an already deep tradition of meditative ascetics (*tapa*, from the Sanskrit), and many of them appear to have embraced Sufi ideas of ultimate oneness to make a smooth transition. Reports reached the Portuguese of 50,000 celibate, mendicant *tapa* in Java at the height of the religious transition, apparently revered by Muslim, Buddhist, and Hindu alike (Pires 1515/1944, 177). Another Sanskrit term to make the transition was *santri* (and their hermitages, *pesantren*), to denote first Hindu-Buddhist adepts and later piously observant Muslims.

Among the most beloved of the *wali* apostles in the tradition of Java was Siti Jenar, a martyr to hidden inner truth perhaps modeled on al-Hallaj in Arabic literature. The conflict between his style of monistic mysticism and the more literal versions propounded by the greatest of Arab theologians, al-Ghazali (1059–1111), was played out in Java as elsewhere, but it is only through the *wali* legends that we catch glimpses of the process. Some stories describe a meeting of the *wali* where all gave their views about the true nature of unity. They were concerned that Siti Jenar was growing very popular by teaching the secret knowledge which should not be publicly revealed, and that in consequence his followers neglected the Friday prayer as unimportant. When they summoned Siti Jenar to join them he insisted that Siti Jenar did not exist, only God existed. When they criticized his followers for not attending Friday prayer, he replied that "there is no Friday, and there is no mosque." Sunan Kali Jaga, one of the warrior *wali*, then drew his sword and beheaded Siti Jenar, giving rise to various miraculous stories about how he vanished, and had no grave like the other *wali*.

As the site of the most complex Hindu-Buddhist civilization in the Archipelago, Java did not go without a fight, and the chronicles are full of the battles of the sixteenth century transition. On the surface, almost the whole of the Javanese-speaking culture area became Muslim in this period, in marked contrast with the Muslim conquests of the same period in India, where the subject majority remained Hindu, or even Sumatra and Sulawesi, where hill peoples reacted against the militant Islam of gunpowder empires. Java could appear to be more fully Islamized than elsewhere because the new religion was so successfully merged with older patterns. The quest of Sultan Akbar for a unifying religious system was a failure in Mughal India, but the analogous project in Java eventually succeeded under the Mataram kings by declaring the necessary cultural compromises simply "Islam," and by driving the holdouts to Bali.

Around 1500, according to Portuguese reports, Islam was still limited to the coastal trading cities of what had been the Majapahit kingdom. Demak was then the strongest of these Muslim port-states, while its erstwhile patron, Hindu Majapahit, was in disarray. Dynastic upheavals after 1486 led to the move of its capital further inland, to Kediri, where it lost influence over all the coastal ports except Tuban. The wealth of Demak had been built by the trading fleet of a hybridized (partly Chinese) trader from Palembang, dominating the spice trade from Maluku and the supply of Java rice to Melaka. He was not himself a ruler so much as a politically astute merchant, who married his daughters to several of the key coastal kings. His descendants became rulers of Demak, and made it the leader of the Islamic alliance and the major power of the Java Sea. He or his son must have been one of the historical identities whose memory went into the construction of the legendary Javanese hero Raden Patah ("the conqueror"). In the eighteenth-century Mataram historical epic, *Babad Tanah Jawi*, this figure was used to legitimate the non-Javanese Muslims from the coast as appropriate heirs of Majapahit. He was made the son of the last Majapahit Hindu ruler by a Chinese princess, banished to Palembang as a child and brought up by a client ruler there. His conquest of Majapahit, in the also legendary year 1478 (the Javanese year 1400, thought appropriate for a change of dynasty), could therefore be reimagined as a restoration of the Majapahit lineage.

The first historically clear ruler of Demak was known posthumously as Sultan Trenggana, son or grandson of the Sino-Malay shipping magnate. He may have come to the throne around 1505, and legitimized his leadership by building or rebuilding the great mosque of Demak in 1507, and making a great cannon in the year of his final conquest of the Hindu capital at Kediri, 1527. His long reign coincided with the transition of Javanese Islam from a cosmopolitan commercial enclave situation to the dominant religion of Java, although it was not until Sultan Agung (r.1613–46) that the Javanese-speaking area was briefly unified in the name of Islam (see below).

The contest for spiritual legitimacy in this period also concerned sacred sites, such as the holy hills on which shrines, stupas, and temples had long been built. Although the Islam of scriptural purists may have had no time for such traditions, the Sufi tradition had its own pattern of sacred tombs of the wonder-working mystical sheikhs. Each of the *wali* is associated with a sacred place where they were thought to have taught, and where their tomb is located. In Java the architecture of the earliest such holy tombs continued the older pattern of sacred building today still seen in Hindu Bali, and often they must have been on sites already made sacred by the older religions. In Aceh the oldest surviving mosque is that of Sanskrit-named Indrapuri, presumably built on the site of a pre-Islamic temple.

Prior to 1511 and the entry of a new Portuguese element in the mix, Islam advanced in the intensely plural and cosmopolitan atmosphere of the ports. Their lifeblood lay in welcoming different kinds of merchants, each religious group playing its necessary role in the trade. Though Muslim shipping (of many languages and persuasions) was dominant, every port needed also the financial services of specialist Hindu castes and therefore the Hindu temples essential to their operations. Every port also welcomed the Chinese merchants with their plural religious traditions. It was said of Melaka that 84 languages could be heard in its streets. Frequently voyages were equipped using crews who were Muslim and Buddhist, and finance capital that might be Hindu or Jewish. In this early stage even port-states with Muslim rulers were plural and permissive, with legalist Muslims a tiny minority.

Muslim influences had also traveled to those trade centers of the eastern islands best connected with trade routes to southern China on the one hand and to the clove-producing centers of northern Maluku on the other. The undated genealogies of Sulu have been interpreted to mean that a Muslim trader and adventurer from Sumatra began an Islamic lineage there around 1400. Brunei, Sulu, and Manila were the three easternmost "tributaries" of Ming China in the early 1400s, probably because some of the Muslim traders from Quanzhou had settled there in the 1360s. By the time of the first European reports, around 1520, Brunei was a flourishing sultanate seeking to dominate trade along the whole route from Manila to Melaka. In Cebu (central Philippines) a Muslim trader was on hand to warn the local raja against the dangers of Magellan's expedition while Manila had a Muslim chief in alliance with the traders. In Maluku it appears that Javanese buyers of the precious clove crops of Ternate and Tidore, and the nutmeg of Banda, began to establish stable Muslim communities there in the late fifteenth century. The dynasties of Ternate and Tidore trace their Muslim origins to the same period.

In all these eastern islands Muslims remained a minority who did not present an obstacle to the favorable reception of the European spice-seekers. The Iberians were at first welcomed everywhere as alternative buyers of the local spices, driving up the prices. Only as they sought local domination or monopoly, or like Magellan tried to impose Christianity at the first encounter, did the lines gradually become established between supporters of the Iberians and of the Muslim traders.

POLARIZATIONS OF THE FIRST GLOBAL WAR, 1530–1610

The Portuguese brought to the Indian Ocean a crusading habit that was new to it. A tight fit between national self-interest and religious zeal had propelled the Portuguese southward in a long series of battles with Islam, first to complete the reconquest of Portugal itself, and then to carry the fight to the coast of Africa. Once into the Indian Ocean, in 1498, their objective was to locate the sources of pepper and spices and seize control of them from the Muslim traders by whatever means it took. It was not a missionary imperative but a crusading one, justifying plunder as part of a military-political struggle with Islam.

The first two Portuguese fleets, of Vasco da Gama (1498–9) and Cabral (1500–1), seized or sank enough Muslim shipping to make their intentions plain. The Muslim traders of Calicut and Gujarat appealed through their partners in Cairo to the Mamluk rulers of Egypt to send a military force to combat this new threat. In 1502 and 1504 they did so, joining their Asian allies to fight a number of battles along the western coast of India. They could not prevent the Portuguese entrenching themselves in fortified strategic points, initially at Calicut but more permanently at Goa (1510), Melaka (1511), and Hormuz (1515). This onslaught forced the trade of the Indian Ocean to adjust in a variety of ways. While Hindu and Buddhist actors worked out modes of operating with the Portuguese, the dominant Muslim trade was obliged to arm itself more effectively, and to regroup around stronger rulers able and willing to confront the Portuguese threat.

The key political institution of Indian Ocean trade in the fifteenth century had been city-states like Melaka, Pasai, Japara, Gresik, and Ternate, and Calicut and Cochin in south India, cosmopolitan port-polities dedicated to maritime trade and dependent on it. They tried to stay aloof from the warfare of continental powers, buying their autonomy when necessary by sending tribute to those in a position to threaten. Dependent for even their rice staple on imports by sea, they suffered particularly from the unprecedented naval attacks launched by the Portuguese. It was as Muslims that the traders had been attacked, and it was naturally as Muslims that they responded. Their complex links with Hindu rulers or financiers were called into question by the Portuguese challenge, and they transferred their support to rulers strong and willing enough to defend them against Portuguese attack. In the sixteenth century the cosmopolitan city-states gave way to gunpowder empires like Aceh, Banten,

Pegu, and Ayutthaya, which rode the new commercial, military, and religious opportunities to unprecedented power.

The north-western tip of Sumatra, the first Southeast Asian landfall of Indian Ocean traders, spawned several lively port-states, mostly Muslim by the fifteenth century. In 1509 the Portuguese began seeking a foothold in the two largest of them – Pidië (modern Sigli) and Pasai (near modern Lhokseumawe). They succeeded only in destabilizing the ruling dynasties and alienating the Arab and Indian Muslim merchants. The latter transferred their support to upstart Aceh, further west, which proceeded to drive the Portuguese from Pidië and Pasai in the early 1520s, and to unify the whole north Sumatran coast under a militantly Islamic and anti-Portuguese dynasty. From that point Aceh provided a secure base for Muslim traders and scholars, who gradually developed new routes avoiding the centers of Portuguese power. Throughout the remainder of the century, Aceh was the most consistent enemy of the Portuguese, reaching across the Indian Ocean for friends and protectors in the Middle East, and frequently laying siege to the Portuguese fortress in Melaka.

The rise of Banten in northwest Java, eventually the strongest maritime sultanate in Java, had a similar origin. Still Hindu at the Portuguese arrival in 1512, west Java's ports were seen by the Portuguese as a promising source of pepper and slaves. Their establishment of a base at a port, later known as Jakarta, in 1522 provoked a quick Muslim riposte. Its leader was a militant *wali* known to Javanese tradition as Sunan Gunung Jati, by origin a Sumatran from Pasai. Angered by the blunt intrusion of the Portuguese there, he set off to Mecca to study. On his return three years later he looked to Demak in Java for leadership of Muslim forces, and reputedly married the sister of its ruler, Sultan Trenggana. Portuguese intrusion in Jakarta helped him win the support of Demak and other Muslim allies for a holy war against the infidels. He conquered both Banten and Jakarta in 1527, and his descendants became Sultans of Banten. The north coastal strip of west Java became distinct, by its Javanese language and its literal Islam, from the Sundanese of the interior, but also a formidable rival of the Javanese state centered eventually in Mataram (Map 5.1).

The rise of a few powerful gunpowder empires in the sixteenth century at the expense of less defensible commercial ports was a wider phenomenon than the Indian Ocean world, and Muslim-Christian rivalry was by no means the only factor at work. The military revolution making more effective use of cannon and other technologies spread unevenly, and assisted some military innovators in becoming unprecedentedly strong. Portugal's invasion of the Indian Ocean coincided with the rise of the Ottomans in the Middle East as a maritime force and aspirant for global leadership. The Ottomans extended their power to the Indian Ocean by annexing Egypt in 1517, the Hejaz and Hadhramaut soon thereafter, and the Iraqi ports on the Persian Gulf in the 1530s. They thereby controlled all the land passages of the old Islamic spice route, as well as the holy places of Islam, making them the first credible claimant for several centuries of a universal Islamic Caliphate. Asian traders and political actors with a stake in the Muslim spice trade like Gujarat, Bijapur (south India), and Aceh wasted little time in appealing to Istanbul to lead a concerted Islamic response to the Portuguese threat.

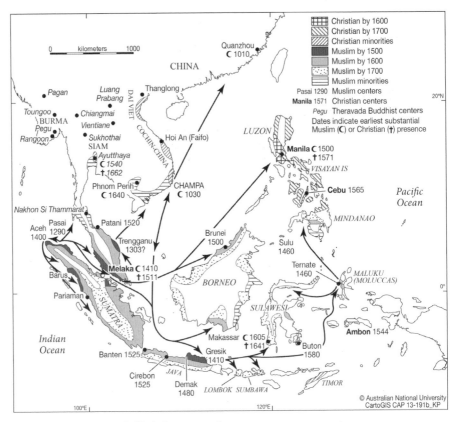

Map 5.1 Muslim and Christian expansion.

The first large Ottoman fleet set out to assist Gujarat in 1518, and thereafter "Turks" were reported in most of the conflicts of the Indian Ocean even if many of them would earlier have been classified as Arab or Persian. The strongest of the Ottoman rulers, Suleiman "the Magnificent" (1520–66), was able to turn his attention to a concerted anti-Portuguese campaign in 1537, and began assembling another major fleet in the Red Sea. Aceh had by then become a strategic partner of the Ottomans and Gujarat in reviving the Muslim spice route, shipping its pepper via the Islamic Maldives directly to the Red Sea. It seems likely that the first Acehnese attack on Portuguese Melaka, in 1537, was partly motivated by the Ottoman initiative. From this point onward, Portuguese sources are full of references to Turkish soldiers and weapons playing a key role in Aceh's campaigns, against both the neighboring Hindu/animist Bataks and the Portuguese in Melaka.

The sultan who assumed the Aceh throne during this crisis, Ala'ud-din Ri'ayat Syah al-Kahar, then ruled until 1571, and became the major scourge of the Portuguese in the Malacca Straits. Alliances between the Portuguese and Aceh's rivals in northern Sumatra increased the militant *jihad* quality of al-Kahar's expansion strategy. The important Muslim states all along the Indian Ocean trading route, including the Mughals, Bijapur, Golconda, the

Mappilas of Kerala, and the port-states of Southeast Asia, became committed in this period to orthodox Sunni Islam. To a greater or lesser extent they accepted the leadership of the Ottoman sultan as Caliph of Islam.

The peak of this great power rivalry in the Indian Ocean came in the 1560s, partly at Acehnese initiative. Turkish records have preserved some of Aceh's letters of this period, not only pleading for the sultan's help as Caliph to protect Muslim pilgrims and merchants on the way to the holy places, but even begging to be considered an Ottoman subject like governors of Egypt or Yemen. A new Ottoman sultan, Selim II, responded vigorously to aid these distant vassals. In decrees of September 1567 he commanded an expedition of seventeen vessels, with guns and gunsmiths, to proceed to assist Aceh to crush the Portuguese and take Melaka. The promised fleet was diverted to suppress a rebellion in Yemen, but Portuguese and Acehnese both record some Turkish help arriving in Sumatra. Turkish soldiers were involved in Aceh sieges of Portuguese Melaka in 1568 and 1570, in the joint offensive of Indian sultanates that destroyed Hindu Vijayanagar in 1566, and in concerted attacks on Portuguese positions in India in 1570. This was one of the most difficult moments for the Portuguese in Asia. Even in remote Maluku, where the multiple local alliances and conflicts had initially made it easy for outsiders to insert themselves as one more factor, the mid-sixteenth century marked a polarization between Muslims and Christians. The tenuous Portuguese alliance with the nominally Muslim kings of Ternate, leaders of one side of age-old rivalries throughout Maluku, finally broke down completely in 1570. The Portuguese murdered their supposed ally Sultan Hairun, and his son Baab Ullah led an effective Muslim alliance to throw the Portuguese out of Ternate and to impose Islam as the principal symbol of loyalty to his cause. He reigned until 1583, and is credited with spreading the faith as far as Buton and Selayar (both in southern Sulawesi), and southern Mindanao.

In Java a similar militant mentality had seemed to motivate Demak in the years before Sultan Trenggana's death in battle in 1546. He intervened in Banjarmasin to secure the victory of Islam there, and led a military campaign against the remnant Hindu kingdom of Pasuruan in Java's east. The semblance of Muslim unity did not outlast Trenggana, and Java became again a patchwork of local chiefdoms. Pajang, near contemporary Surakarta, claimed authority over much of central Java including Demak itself in the third quarter of the century, but in the fourth Mataram emerged as a center. This area around modern Yogyakarta had sustained the first great temple-building civilization of Java before the disasters around the tenth century. Now Panembahan Senopati used its volcanic fertility as a new power base at the end of the century. A later Dutch visitor reported that he used Islam to make a clean break with the old Hindu aristocracy and kill all rivals from that quarter, while staking his claim to a new kind of legitimacy based nominally on Islam – though no Islamic monuments are associated with him. He "made war until the end of his life" in 1601, having subdued the older centers of Pajang and Demak, as well as Kediri and Madiun (van Goens 1656/1956, 177).

Senopati is remembered as the founder of the last strong Javanese state; a conqueror who returned power to the interior by mastering the new type of warfare introduced by Muslims, Portuguese, and Chinese on the coast. His

Mataram appears to have been a pioneering military camp in a fertile area underpopulated through past eruptions and earthquakes, with most of its early population forced to shift there as soldiers or captives from other areas. The models both for Islamic learning and for the partially Islamized Javanese court culture were now in the commercial cities of the north coast. Surabaya inherited from Demak the cultural task of building a new civilization which could reconcile the needs of international Muslims of the port communities with Javanese aristocratic tradition. Senopati failed to incorporate the coastal ports, and it was his grandson, Sultan Agung (r.1613–45), who defeated Surabaya in a series of campaigns in 1620–5. The reign of this Javanese sun-king molded the synthesis between the old Java of Hindu Majapahit and the new Java of the Muslim coastal cities. The eclipse of the latter, under the military pressure of Mataram and the commercial inroads of the Dutch and English into their formerly lucrative spice trade, brought an end to a remarkable chapter in Javanese history. During the sixteenth century Java had been as exposed to the cosmopolitan and commercial influences of the Muslim ecumene as had other parts of the Indian Ocean littoral. By the end of Agung's reign those influences were limited and controlled, and a Javanese synthesis in place that could incorporate even the most Indianized elements in Javanese society (Chapter 8).

The Islamization of south Sulawesi in the short period 1603–11 is better documented. The Bugis and Makassar peoples in the populous, south-western arm of Sulawesi had developed irrigated rice-growing and a written culture in an Indic script closest to those of Sumatra and the Philippines, despite being only lightly touched by Buddha and Siva. They had great reverence for their heaven-descended royal lineages, and a priesthood of transsexual *bissu* as special mediators between the kings and the upperworld of the gods, whose prehistory was elaborately described in the La Galigo epic. The abundant Chinese, Vietnamese, and Thai ceramics buried in grave sites of the fifteenth and sixteenth centuries indicate that it was already integrated into the Asian trading world before Islam, largely as a rice supplier for traders in Malukan spices. Their dozens of ruling lineages were familiar with both Islam and Christianity in the sixteenth century but resisted conversion that might diminish their supernatural status, not to mention interfere with their pattern of religious feasting with pork and palm wine.

Pious traditions credit the rapid Islamization to Sumatran missionaries, but royal chronicles suggest a pattern of consultation among key rulers to ensure Muslim–Christian conflict did not disrupt their societies. Karaeng Matoaya of Tallo', the more trade-oriented side of the Goa-Tallo' partnership, led the Makassar aristocracy into Islam in 1605, and then requested all the Bugis states to follow suit. A war of conquest would follow if they refused, but the generous offer of autonomy for each state that submitted helped produce the desired result within a few years. Hence Makassar at its height differed from other gunpowder states in respecting traditional autonomies, as well as the older aristocratic culture. The cosmopolitan port and capital of Makassar, until it fell to the Dutch in 1669, was also a remarkable beacon of tolerance of all faiths, presenting itself in that period as the free antithesis of the monopolistic Dutch. While Catholic worship was forbidden in the Dutch settlements, there were three Catholic churches in mid-century Makassar, and a well-regarded Portuguese trading community of several thousand.

In the first stage of Islamization in these maritime realms, force had been a minor factor and the community was essentially a commercial one living as an enclave minority in a very plural world. The sixteenth-century polarization made holy war seem the appropriate response to the Portuguese onslaught. New gunpowder empires arose on the back of trade wealth and firearms, and adopted a militant vision of Islam as the rationale for their expansion. The new faith was embraced by many, and rejected by some, explicitly because it was a universal system with its political leadership in Istanbul and its sacred center in Mecca. This universalism encouraged some rulers in trade centers such as Aceh, Banten, Brunei, and Makassar to accept (selectively) the scriptural literalism of foreign-born *ulama*, since it enabled them to satisfy the foreign traders and overrride cherished local autonomies. In the period 1550–1650, when the reach of Islam expanded dramatically, we also find literal applications of scripture not evident before or for a long time thereafter – rulers sending missions to Mecca, setting up religious courts, imposing *hudud* penalties such as amputation of limbs for theft and the execution of alleged apostates and heretics. As we shall see in Chapter 8, this phase ended with the vernacularizations and syntheses of the later seventeenth and eighteenth centuries, which affected both Islam and Christianity.

RIVAL UNIVERSALISMS

The initial crusading zeal of the Portuguese had not involved great interest in preaching or proselytizing, and most of their early converts were their wives, children, or close allies for whom this was the mark of identity. Their global conflict with a Turkish-led Islamic world, however, became caught up in the European reformation and counter-reformation, and thereby with Early Modernity. Although the Catholic reforms of the Council of Trent (1545–63) were stimulated largely by the Protestant challenge in Germany, their most faithful agents, the Jesuits, saw their great mission as to the east. Ignatius Loyola had made a pilgrimage to Turkish-ruled Jerusalem before establishing the Society of Jesus in 1534 (approved by the Pope in 1540), and always saw Asia as the greatest challenge for Christendom. His closest friend, Francis Xavier, was sent to Asia on a Portuguese ship at the first opportunity, and wasted no time in translating texts and preaching to every Asian society he could. Little more than two of his ten Asian years were in Southeast Asia (1545–7), but he transformed the Christian approach by preaching and teaching in Malay and baptizing thousands in Melaka, Ambon, and the other islands of Maluku. Before moving on to more ambitious targets in Japan and China, he introduced Jesuit methods and personnel to Southeast Asia, and inspired the older preaching orders, Augustinian, Franciscan, and Dominican, to adopt a similar rigor.

This serious missionary impetus had its effect also on enclaves such as Melaka – Portugal's primary Southeast Asian base. Portuguese who were living with Asians were pressured to Christianize and marry them. The women in turn had to adopt Portuguese norms of decency in dress. At a 1532 census of the settlement only 75 Christian women were enumerated, whereas there were thousands by the end of the century. On the other hand, this increasing Christianization of the Portuguese presence distanced them further from the pluralism inherent in Asian ports. Since the 1511 conquest the Portuguese had attempted to govern their non-Christian traders through a former Malay official, the *bendahara*, who faced terrible problems mediating between Portuguese and Asians. The conversion of the last *bendahara* to Christianity in 1564 marked the end of the influence of the once-powerful Indian communities in Melaka.

When Philip II of Spain (r.1556–98), the mightiest Christian monarch of the day, decided that Spain should establish a permanent presence in Asia, the counter-reformation mind-set was wholly different from that of the Portuguese crusaders, or of the conquistadors of the Spanish Americas a century earlier. The expedition Philip commanded to sail from Mexico to the Philippines (already so named in his honor) in 1564 was motivated partly by Southeast Asian spices, but "the most important thing His Majesty desires is the spread of our Holy Catholic Faith and the salvation of the souls of those infidels," as Legazpi was instructed (Zaide 1990, 408). Its command had been entrusted to Fr Andrés de Urdaneta, navigator turned Augustinian priest, but when he refused this he became instead the spiritual guide of the mission alongside Legazpi as military commander. Six Augustinian priests went out on this mission, which began the colonization of the Philippines at Cebu in 1565, transferring the center to Manila in 1570. The number of missionary priests rose to 94 by 1586 and 267 by 1594, more than tenfold the numbers the Portuguese sent to the rest of Southeast Asia. They translated and printed devotional texts in Tagalog and Visayan, and by 1650 had accomplished the Christianization of lowland Luzon and the Visayas.

Though markedly peaceful by the standards of Latin America, the Spanish presence in Manila was also influenced by the global struggle referred to above. Alarmed at the success of Islamic teachers from Ternate and Brunei, Spanish Manila sent expeditions to Mindanao and Sulu, and in 1578 succeeded in sacking Brunei and curbing that city's role as a hub of trade and Islamization for the Philippines. Henceforth the sultanates based on the island of Sulu and the Pulangi river basin of Magindanao would be the primary political upholders of Islam and of resistance to the Spanish in the Philippines. The greatest defensive strength of both states was the dispersion of power among many chiefs, which made it impossible for the Spanish to turn their military superiority and periodic victories into permanent influence. Only the long reign of Sultan Qudrat in Magindanao (c.1619–71) produced a strong political center for Islam in this period, partly thanks to Dutch commercial support.

Some of the reasons why Filipinos embraced Christianity so rapidly were similar to those that persuaded others to embrace Islam in the same period. The rapid economic expansion of Southeast Asia's long sixteenth century pulled many away from their local agricultural roots, and made a portable, universal religious code attractive. The scriptural religions also countered the pervasive and terrifying power of malign spirits with their predictable, rationalized moral code. The abundant Spanish missionary accounts of the conversion of the Philippines are rife with descriptions of the "demons" that terrorized the inhabitants until conquered by the power of the cross and the sacraments.

If the motives for the "religious revolution" of Early Modernity were similar, the modalities of Muslim and Christian proselytizers were strikingly different. Muslim traders and scholars married locally, even if already married at home, and their families provided a built-in mechanism of localization. But the counter-reformation Catholic Church was determined to enforce the discipline of a celibate clergy as the sole mediator of sacramental power. This tended to keep the church European in leadership and orthodox in faith in its early stages. The clergy's monopoly of spiritual power was particularly unpalatable for Southeast Asian rulers, whose main source of power had been as mediators with the cosmic order. The Portuguese made many attempts to baptize kings as Christians, but all failed once it became clear that their conversion destroyed their former spiritual potency without giving them access to the supernatural power of the Christians. By contrast, Muslim and Theravada Buddhist rulers found numerous ways to manipulate the new religion to enhance their eminence. Arabic terms such as *dawla* (the state) and *wahy* (the divine inspiration revealed in the Prophet) were used to give an Islamic legitimation to the supernatural potency uniquely claimed by rulers, in Malay (*daulat*) and Javanese (*wahyu*), respectively. The newly potent gunpowder kings, moreover, were able to use the new externally validated religions to override the highly plural contractualism of many Southeast Asian societies.

The long sixteenth century brought Early Modernity to Southeast Asia in the sense that all elites became aware of the competing universalisms of Islam, Christianity, and Buddhism, and the need to choose among them. If the Muslim–Christian conflict had begun with brutal raiding and warfare in the early 1500s, by the latter part of that century it had acquired intellectual and spiritual dimensions as both scripturalisms were creatively translated into vernaculars. Muslim literary creativity was particularly striking in the century 1580–1680, effectively creating what we now call classical Malay literature. In the first stage, up through the fifteenth century, the lingua franca of Islamic commercial communities around the Indian Ocean had been Arabic. The Melaka chronicle noted that the people of fourteenth-century Pasai all spoke Arabic, whereas in fifteenth-century Melaka the commonest spoken and written language was Malay with Arabic script. In its story of the Portuguese conquest of 1511, the same chronicle mentions the *Hikayat Muhammad Hanafiah* and the *Hikayat Amir Hamzah*, Malay verse versions of two famous Arab stories of warrior heroes of the Prophet's time, as inspirations for the young Melaka nobles to fight the Portuguese courageously.

Hamzah Fansuri had felt the need to say that he was writing in Malay so that the Muslims who did not know Arabic or Persian could understand his mystical message. Many of the key writers of the seventeenth century read and quoted Hamzah, and like him taught and wrote in Aceh, the principal domesticator of Arabic and Persian ideas into the Malay world. Foreign Muslim scholars, presumably writing in Arabic, are mentioned by name arriving in Aceh from the Red Sea and Gujarat on the pepper-ships in the 1570s. The great works of the seventeenth century were in Malay by local-born scholars, such as the prolific Pasai-born Shamsud-din al-Samatrani, who advocated a mystical monism influenced by the Naqshabandiah Sufi order. His chief tool for proselytization was a Malay catechism of 1601, in the form of 211 questions and answers, the *Mi'rat al-Mu'min*. He is also thought to have been the *kadi* or Sheikh ul-Islam of Aceh ("bishop," to the English), who was able to use his Arabic to discuss matters with James Lancaster's first English fleet in 1602.

The contest between Hapsburg-led Catholic Christendom and Ottoman-led Sunni Islam ended quickly in the seventeenth century. The most implacable enemies of Catholic Portuguese after 1600 were not Muslims but Protestant Dutch, who initially sought Muslim powers like Aceh and Banten as allies against the Portuguese. Dutch and English success in shipping spices and pepper around Africa completely eclipsed the Muslim trade route through the Red Sea by the 1630s. Together with the slow decline of Ottoman (and Spanish) power, this broke the direct link of Southeast Asian with Middle Eastern Muslims. The seventeenth-century economic crisis (Chapter 7) was followed by a new phase of vernacularization of religious and cultural identities, discussed in Chapter 8.

PLURALITIES, RELIGIOUS BOUNDARIES, AND THE "HIGHLAND SAVAGE"

In the evolution of Southeast Asian pluralities, this religious revolution was a major turning point. It might be said of this region, as of others, that homogeneities were eventually imposed on the natural diversity of spatially separate peoples by the twin forces of scriptural religion and bureaucratic states. These forces were slower in Southeast Asia than elsewhere to overcome the environmental barriers to integration, with Southeast Asia retaining a high degree of pluralism up to very recent times. In the age of commerce, however, the competing universalisms just discussed confirmed some of the enduring boundaries in the region, not only between Muslim, Buddhist, Christian, and Confucian. They also created a new boundary between "civilized" lowlanders and "savage" highlanders.

How did this latter distinction arise? The most fundamental differences were between modes of production – hunter-gatherers, forest and sea exploiters, shifting cultivators, settled wet-rice growers, and urban traders. Each mode endured in Southeast Asia, where tropical forests dominated until the twentieth century, because each had its advantages in relation to particular environments and market conditions. There are myriad examples from past and present of combining modes and shifting between them. Only settled rice-growers provided what Scott (2009, 73) calls a "state-accessible product," compatible with state control and exploitation, but the open frontier ensured that most agriculturalists could escape oppressive state control by moving further into the forest. The older indigenous sources do not suggest any sense of binary division between highland and lowland or savage and civilized.

Three imported dichotomies did, however, consolidate the idea of the highland savage: Chinese ideas of civilized and barbarian; the growing reach of states; and the behavioral boundaries of the scriptural religions. Chinese civilization had for millennia defined itself in contrast to the barbarians outside imperial control. Viet literati elites shared the idea, at least in their fifteenth- and nineteenth-century phases of neo-Confucian zeal. Civilized was equated with the controlled space of imperial bureaucracy, and state ideology sought to prevent populations escaping their taxable status by emphasizing the savagery of non-state peoples outside their control. Vietnamese (like Chinese and Koreans) referred to themselves as *Han*, in contrast to barbarian, until the nineteenth century. The now fashionable term *Kinh* (literally "city people") later became an acceptable ethnic marker for Viet nationalists, as the opposite of *Thuong* or "upland people." Although Viet lowlanders had much more interaction with highlanders than did Chinese, the civilizational mind-set was stronger there than elsewhere in Southeast Asia. There was even a wall built between civilized *Han* and savage *Thuong* in the Quang Ngai area in 1819, as if in emulation of Chinese rather than Southeast Asian concepts.

A similar dichotomy was first expressed elsewhere in Southeast Asia from Chinese observers who, like later Europeans, may have imposed their own assumptions on a more complex reality. Zhou Daguan (1297/2007, 59, 61) provided a particularly stark picture of Angkor in the 1290s, where "savages ... from the mountains" were bought to serve as slaves and were so despised that sexual relations with them were scandalous. There was a second kind so savage that they could not be taken as slaves or communicate with the city-dwellers. These were "very ferocious" and warlike. They had "no homes to live in, but move from place to place." In reality they were almost certainly similar in language and appearance to the lowland Khmer, whom Zhou (54) had already described as "course people, ugly and very black." It was their statelessness and weakness that made them savages and slaves in these Chinese eyes. The Muslim Chinese chronicler of the Zheng He expeditions, Ma Huan (1433/1970, 93–4), made similar distinctions between the clean and proper Chinese and Muslim inhabitants of the coastal port-cities of Java and the dirty, unkempt people of the country who "loved savagery and ferocity." Early Southeast Asian sources, on the other hand, refer not to savages but to uplanders, or forest or rural people, or use ethnic or place terms. The uplanders often appear as supernaturally powerful, in recognition that the spirit world they inhabited reflected an older reality of the lowlands.

Beyond the Sinified world, the state factor was most marked in the Philippines, where Spanish control had expanded throughout the lowlands of Luzon and the Visayas by 1650, in tandem with Christianity. The limits to Spanish control were logistic. With a very small number of soldiers, they could not sustain supply lines for an extended campaign in the hills far from Manila against significant resistance. Those who resisted therefore tended to focus in the Cordillera that runs down the middle of Luzon. Even though the island's most valuable asset from a Spanish viewpoint, gold, was chiefly in the Cordillera, the early Spanish campaigns to reach it were unsuccessful, and they gave up trying by the mid-seventeenth century. The most widespread revolt against Spanish control occurred in northern areas of Ilocos and Pampanga in 1660–1. Some highlanders participated, and the unreconciled holdouts naturally retreated to join them in the hills when it was suppressed. Pre-Spanish highlanders were already less literate, less hierarchic, and less sedentary than the lowlanders, but these distinctions became far more marked with Spanish control of the lowlands. Spanish officials and priests suppressed petty warfare, head-hunting, and elaborate death-feasts in the lowlands, and established Iberian Catholic patterns of marriage and dress, as well as homogenizing the main language groups through the introduction of printing. The Cordillera remained diverse in language and religious practice, and the continuation of low-level warfare and head-taking made it seem increasingly wild and dangerous to Spanish and Chinese, and eventually to the lowlanders themselves.

Recent advances in dating the spectacular rice terraces built by the Ifugao in their section of the Cordillera suggest that they began to be built subsequent to Spanish control of the Cagayan valley floor below (Acabado 2009). The most probable explanation for the sequence of carbon dates obtained is that wet-rice agriculturalists from that rice bowl of Luzon retreated rather than surrender their religious and social habits for those of the Spanish. Accustomed to intensive rice-growing in permanent flooded fields, they developed the characteristic rice terraces in the hills of the region, which sustained a larger population than the shifting cultivation of long-term hill-dwellers (Figure 5.1). If this is the explanation for Ifugao rice terraces, a similar process probably gave rise to the irrigated terraces of the upland Toba Batak in northern Sumatra and Toraja in Sulawesi. But here the factor pushing irrigated rice–growers up into the highlands is likely to have been Islamic rather than Christian.

From the thirteenth century to the sixteenth, the term Batak appears as a place or even a kingdom, presumably representing the point on the coast where foreign traders encountered the then majority peoples of northern Sumatra. About 1515, before the rise of Aceh, Tomé Pires (1515/1944, 145–6) described a "kingdom of Bata" on the northeast coast of Sumatra, the "king" of which had grown rich by salvaging the rich cargo of the ship Afonso de Albuquerque had sent homeward with the booty he seized in conquering Melaka (1511). He had also accommodated the foreign traders by calling himself Muslim, like his neighbor to the south in Aru. But the Islam of both these "kingdoms" was of so different or superficial a type as not to be accepted as Muslim at all in the polarized atmosphere that followed the rise of Aceh and its bitter conflict with the Portuguese. Bata and Aru sided with the Portuguese in that conflict, and whatever "Bata kingdom" there was on the coast was probably an early victim of Aceh expansion.

By the 1540s Muslim Aceh already commanded the northern coast, "Batak" had become an ethno-religious label, and "the King of the Bataks" had his port-capital on the west coast. Mendes Pinto (1578/1989) tells a tragic story of a militant Aceh sultan, supported by Turks and Gujaratis, offering only Islam or death to his Batak rival despite the latter's attempts at accommodation. When his sons were murdered, his troops defeated, and help from the Portuguese was not forthcoming, the embittered "king" moved further up into the hills and abandoned his commercial links with the outside world. This appears to mark a

Figure 5.1 Ifugao rice terraces in highland Luzon. Source: © Rangzen – Fotolia.com.

turning point, after which the term Batak was used to define uplanders in terms of their resistance to Islam and the coastal states that represented it, rather than by any particular language or location. By mid-century the Portuguese were reporting that Sumatra was divided between indigenous animists and Muslims derived from foreign traders, who took over the coastal areas over the previous century and a half and created Islamic states. Those who rejected Islam left the coast and became known as upland savage Bataks who ate human flesh.

Images of savage Southeast Asian cannibals go as far back in the European imaginary as Ptolemy, and had been specifically linked to the term Batak since the fourteenth century, though scarcely mentioned in local Malay sources. Although there is indeed strong evidence of rituals in which the flesh of defeated enemies was consumed, this practice appears to have been exaggerated by latter-day Bataks in their dealings with outsiders in order to discourage intruders from proceeding inland.

The Batak story has parallels wherever rapid military expansion by aggressively Muslim states in this period provoked a new sense of different highland identity. Nearby, the seemingly primeval megalithic culture of Nias, in villages perched high on ridgetops, is now estimated by carbon-dating and oral genealogies to extend back only to the seventeenth century. Whether a new beginning was made in response to the first Aceh raids against them, or in the aftermath of a terrible tsunami, has yet to be determined.

The Toraja of Sulawesi are another such case. Their language, culture, and ritual are very close to those of the neighboring Bugis of the lowland but they appear to have deliberately chosen freedom from Islam and the coastal Bugis states that sought to impose it. The Toraja memory as still chanted at feasts in modern times is of an alliance of those who swore an oath of resistance to Muslim Bugis attack, and "held back the mountain of Bone" (*untulak buntuna Bone*). The attack was probably that of the most powerful of Bone's kings, Dutch ally Arung Palakka, who sought to subjugate the highlands in the 1680s. Those who joined the resistance oath are remembered as ideal ancestors, "people of the same dream." In the chants it is remembered also that "the harvest of the earth was abundant at that time, and human beings multiplied" (Waterson 1997, 73–6). This memory of an agricultural golden age suggests that the seventeenth century was the time when the Toraja, probably including many wet-rice growing Bugis lowlanders who chose freedom from Islam and state, began to carve their hillsides in beautiful terraces of irrigated rice, just as did the Ifugao.

The closest analogy in Java to the Islam-induced upland statelessness of the Batak and Toraja were the people who came to be known as Sundanese, after the Sunda polity which left inscriptions in the region of modern Jakarta and Bogor as early as the seventh century. Even Javanese sources attribute early kingship and civilization to this western third of the island, although it seems likely that its demographic and civilizational prominence was reversed by a volcanic disaster in the eleventh century or later. The expansion of Muslim Demak, described above, established Muslim power along the whole northern coast as part of the same polarized phase of religious expansion. A Sundanese kingdom or sacred center survived near modern Bogor only until 1567 when that in turn fell to the Banten sultanate. Banten, however, could not, any more than Aceh, extend this power into the highlands. The population that resisted Islam or coastal control became a distinct highland people, reproducing a productive rice economy without apparent benefit of a state. Although Banten in the sixteenth century, and Mataram in the seventeenth, claimed a nominal primacy over the Sundanese, the latter insisted that they were autonomous and equal. Like the highlanders of southern Sumatra, however, the Sundanese gradually accepted Islam in the eighteenth and nineteenth centuries, as Batavia encouraged coastal control over the highlands for its own purposes. Its fertile and lightly populated lands became the first extensive venue for the Dutch-controlled coffee industry.

In the Javanese-speaking eastern two thirds of the island, the synthesis achieved by Sultan Agung succeeded in absorbing even uplanders rather than forcing a hard choice. But the political and religious elites moved east in face of the attacks from Muslim Demak in the polarized sixteenth century. Pasuruan and Balambangan in the furthermost east of Java held out for some time, but in the seventeenth century only Bali remained as the bastion of an older Hindu-Buddhist civilization. Its high population and elaborate irrigated-rice system, as well as its literature and arts, undoubtedly owe much to migrations from Java at this time. Though differing from highlanders in their hierarchic social system and elaborate literary culture, Balinese also encouraged their reputation for ferocity, for they knew the dangers the Muslim states posed to them long before they understood the potential danger of Europeans.

Mainland Southeast Asians followed a different historical rhythm, though with some of the same long-term results. At moments of neo-Confucian success and assertiveness among the Viet, in the fifteenth and early nineteenth centuries and to a lesser extent the seventeenth, state attempts to enforce

Confucian norms bureaucratically did create reaction and rejection in the highlands. But in the remainder of the Mainland, Theravada Buddhism expanded through the charismatic power of its sacred centers and its *sangha*, with little sense of boundary against the unbeliever or savage. There were certainly aggressive campaigners against the old spirit religion in the sixteenth century, of whom the Burmese conqueror Bayinnaung was paramount. The chronicles show him building Buddhist temples throughout the areas of Upper Burma that he conquered, unifying their diverse religious calendars with his own, and outlawing human and animal sacrifices. Yet he only destroyed shrines to the spirits (*nat*) if he deemed they had failed to aid him in his campaigns, and belief in them remained universal in Burma until the twentieth century. Earlier (1527), Luang Prabang had destroyed its great shrine to the local spirit at the meeting of its rivers and built there a Buddhist pagoda, yet a Portuguese source a little later described a great diversity of cults and of blood sacrifices still thriving there.

The upland communities that survived and developed a separate identity from lowlanders in the mainland did so chiefly by pragmatically sending some form of symbolic tribute to the lowlanders with whom they traded, invoking their intervention only when it seemed necessary to fend off rival lowland centers. Until the nineteenth century the Jarai in the hills between Khmer and Viet territory exchanged gifts with each King of Cambodia, in acknowledgement of a symbiosis symbolized by their possession of a sword inherited from ancient Cham rulers, of which the Khmer held only the scabbard. But in return for being acknowledged as suzerain, the Cambodian king sent presents of far greater value than he received – not unlike the rulers of China.

The people now known as Karen occupy the hills between two lowland Theravada cultures – the Bama and Mon in the deltas of the Irrawaddy and Salween, and the lowland Thai of the Chao Phraya basin. They were typically diverse stateless communities trading their forest products and hill crops to the lowlands, and often content to see it interpreted as tribute. Although as usual their history is poorly known, in the late eighteenth century the missionary bishop Sangermano (1833/1966, 36) singled them out in his account of Burma:

> although residing in the midst of the Burmese and Peguans, they not only retain their own language, but even in their dress, houses, and everything else are distinguished from them; and what is more remarkable, they have a different religion.

This suggests that despite their great internal diversity, many Karen uplanders had consciously begun to distinguish themselves from lowlanders. At least since the mid-nineteenth century an origin myth had been shared among them, whereby the founding ancestor entrusted with the book of knowledge by the creator-god had lost it through carelessness, and thereby left the Karen without writing as their neighbors forged ahead. Baptist missionaries in the 1830s found that the Karen were exceptionally receptive because they understood the Karen Bible as a return to them of their lost writing, and confirmation of their position as elder brother to the Bama (Chapter 11).

[6] ASIAN EUROPEAN ENCOUNTERS, 1509–1688

THE EURO-CHINESE CITIES

As we saw in Chapter 4, cities set the cultural and political pattern of the long sixteenth century. Among them, the cities refashioned by European conquerors after 1511 were relatively small and culturally marginal, but nevertheless revolutionary in the three new elements they introduced. They were strongly fortified against a hinterland presumed to be hostile; part of an international network of posts all subject to the same authority; and governed by regularly replaced administrators. These factors combined to provide a relatively stable environment in which commercial considerations were usually paramount, thereby minimizing the perennial Southeast Asian risks to traders of tyranny on one side or anarchy on the other. In many other respects, however, these new cities continued the commercial techniques and ethnic complexities of their forebears.

The successful formula was certainly not discovered overnight, and it was as much due to good luck as to good management that it was found at all. The Portuguese introduced in the period 1500–25 a chain of conquered and fortified posts along the major arteries of Asian maritime commerce, but they notably failed to attract a major share of the Asian trade to these centers. Titling himself "Lord of the conquest, navigation and commerce of Ethiopia, India, Arabia and Persia," King Manuel I (r.1495–1521) sought the military destruction of the hitherto largely unarmed Muslim commerce of the Indian Ocean, and its replacement by a Portuguese state monopoly of the key items of trade. Afonso de Albuquerque was responsible for the seizure of the three key ports of Goa (1510), Melaka (1511), and Hormuz (1515).

In Southeast Asia, where Portuguese power was always more tenuous than in the Arabian Sea, Melaka was the only major stronghold, though forts were also episodically maintained in Ternate from 1520 and in Ambon, Solor, and Timor from mid-century. Given the belligerence with which the Portuguese had set out to attack Muslim shipping, the Muslims who dominated the Indian

A History of Southeast Asia: Critical Crossroads, First Edition. Anthony Reid.
© 2015 Anthony Reid. Published 2015 by John Wiley & Sons, Ltd.

Ocean trade had little appetite to settle in these fortified settlements even on the occasions they were admitted. On the contrary, they specifically sought out alternative ports strong enough to confront the Portuguese. The attempt to monopolize trade in the hands of the Portuguese crown or merchants licensed by it was counter-productive. The Portuguese made their largest profits where they were too weak to contemplate these monopolies, particularly in their easternmost footholds in Macao and Nagasaki.

Portuguese Melaka contained only a fraction of the population or the commerce of its Malay-ruled predecessor. The military resources of the city depended largely on its Portuguese or *mestizo* population, never amounting to more than a few hundred. Portuguese policy encouraged soldiers to marry locally, Christianize their local wives, and become permanent householders (*casados*). Even at its height, around 1612, there were only 300 such *casados* living within the fortified city along with 7,400 Christianized Asians mostly living outside the walls, alongside a probably smaller number of Hindus, Muslims, and Buddhists. The Muslim Malay population of Melaka's ruling group had largely moved out at the conquest, along with the Indian Muslims. The Javanese, the largest ethnic component of population under the Sultans, also soon fell out with the Portuguese and had gone by 1525. The Asian population that did eventually assemble in Melaka was predominantly of non-Muslim Indians, Chinese from Fujian (particularly after 1567), and a variety of Southeast Asians who had had dealings with the Portuguese.

Chinese trade with Southeast Asia changed fundamentally in 1567, when for the first time scores of private junks were annually licensed to trade southward. Whereas in earlier periods Arab or Southeast Asian ships had been responsible for a large portion of China's maritime trade, between 1567 and 1840 this was overwhelmingly in the hands of Chinese ships, mainly based in Fujian. In this period, European ports would become so heavily reliant on the visits of Chinese ships, and the admission of skilled Chinese migrants, that we may reasonably label them Euro-Chinese cities.

Manila was the first of the European settlements to profit from this influx, and remained for its first two centuries absolutely beholden to it. This boon was pure good fortune for the Spanish. The friars and conquistadors sent westward to claim the Philippines for Spain in the 1560s were thinking of spices and souls, but had virtually no idea of the potential of trade with China. Their commander, Legazpi, soon became aware of the thriving port of Manila and of the rich Chinese trade that had begun to focus on it. The expedition he sent to reconnoitre it in 1570 found four Chinese ships anchored off the Muslim-ruled trading settlement, and had the wit to treat them well. Once Legazpi moved his capital to Manila in 1571, the ships from Fujian came in ever-greater numbers, for the Spanish had what the Muslims had not – a steady supply of cheap silver from the mines of Mexico and Peru. By 1575 there were fifteen ships a year arriving, and the colony's economic viability was firmly established. Chinese silks and porcelains were sent to Acapulco on the returning Spanish galleons that became Manila's lifeline to Mexico.

With one of the best natural harbors in the world, Manila became, almost despite itself, the biggest Southeast Asian market for Fujian traders between

1580 and 1640. It thereby provided a magnet for Japanese traders (banned from direct access to China) to obtain the silk and other goods they needed from China. Manila was also their most popular destination until surpassed by Hoi An (the port of Cochin-China) around 1610. Distinct Chinese and Japanese communities developed in the city, and the craftsmen brought there to service the needs of Chinese traders soon became indispensable to the whole city. Governor Ronquillo, in 1581, first assigned them a specific district and silk market, the *parian*, just east of the walled city on the south bank of the Pasig River. Though burned down seven times between 1588 and 1642, it was regularly rebuilt more handsomely. Ronquillo also began the lucrative practice of taxing the Chinese, imposing an initially moderate 3% tariff on all goods imported from China, later raised to 6% in 1606.

Bishop Salazar, who adopted a protective stance toward the Chinese residents in the hope of using them for the conversion of China, commented in 1590 that:

> This Parian has so adorned the city ... that no other known city in Spain or in these regions possesses anything so well worth seeing as this; for in it can be found the whole trade of China, with all kinds of goods and curious things which come from that country. These articles have already begun to be manufactured here, as quickly and with better finish than in China. ... They make much prettier articles than are made in Spain, and sometimes so cheap that I am ashamed to mention it (Blair and Robertson 1903–9 VII, 224–5).

Others were more critical, complaining that Chinese industry caused both Spanish and Filipino inhabitants to abandon whatever skills they had and leave craftsmanship to the Chinese. The sheer dependence of the Spanish colony on Chinese enterprise gave rise to fears that bordered on paranoia, frequently endangering the whole enterprise. A city census of 1586 showed already 750 Chinese shopkeepers, and a further 300 craftsmen with an amazing range of skills, while there were only about 80 Spanish citizens, 200 Spanish soldiers, and 7,500 Filipinos outside the walls. There were reported to be 20,000 Chinese residents in Manila in 1603, when mutual suspicions got out of control and the Spanish, Japanese, and local populations joined a ghastly pogrom which killed three quarters of the Chinese. Although the bloodthirsty victors were rewarded by the distribution of 360,000 pesos' worth of Chinese trade goods, "the city found itself in distress, for since there were no Chinese there was nothing to eat and no shoes to wear" (Morga 1609/1971, 225).

The China-based trade was uninterrupted by these grisly events, and the population quickly built up again despite oft-repeated regulations to limit Chinese migration. In 1640 there was another horrific pogrom in which 20,000 Chinese were thought to have been killed, and in 1662 yet another. Thereafter Spanish vigilance and the declining fortunes of the city combined to prevent its Chinese population from growing beyond about 20,000, still always far outweighing the Spanish. By the 1660s about a quarter of the Chinese were Christian, most of them married residents. Their Filipina wives deserve more credit than they have been given for integrating the Chinese into a Southeast Asian society.

Piracy, smuggling, and the constant wars with the Dutch between 1609 and 1648 took a big toll on the glittering profits of the Manila galleons and the Chinese ships that supplied them. Nevertheless, the number of Chinese ships reaching the port seldom fell below twenty a year before 1644, when the fall of the Ming Dynasty ended the golden age of Manila by reducing the flow to an average of only seven a year. The crown sought to impose a limit (*permiso*) on the value of the cargoes sent annually to Acapulco in the two licensed ships, in order to protect Spanish silk manufacture and to limit the outflow of silver from Mexico. In 1593 the *permiso* was first set at 250,000 Spanish dollars' worth of purchases in Manila, or double that amount of sale value in Mexico. This was raised gradually to 500,000 in 1734 and 750,000 in 1776. Since this limit was always exceeded, the Manileños had an interest in not recording the real amounts. About two million Spanish dollars must have been carried to Acapulco each year in more prosperous times, such as the 1590s and early 1600s, and again periodically after 1690.

The Dutch Company (VOC), profiting from Spanish and Portuguese experience, set out far more deliberately to establish an entrepôt that would attract Chinese and Southeast Asian traders. Jan Pieterszoon Coen (1587–1629) was the most determined advocate of establishing a Dutch stronghold at a strategic place, and he eventually found it at Jakarta. A site adjacent to the Sunda Straits between Sumatra and Java was ideal for the Dutch strategy of approaching the Spice Islands not through India like the Portuguese, but directly along the roaring forties of the southern Indian Ocean and then northward to Java. This territory was dominated by Banten, at whose capital both Dutch and English first made their eastern base. Jakarta was a weaker eastern dependency of Banten, and Coen managed to conquer the small town in May 1619. There he built a fort that would withstand all conceivable attacks and laid the basis for an Asia-wide trading strategy.

Coen renamed the city Batavia, and envisaged it as the principal site in Asia for solid Dutch householders and private traders, on the model of Portuguese *casados*, who would defend the settlements without the need for expensive professional soldiery. However, European women were almost never sent to the east. The VOC sent 978,000 men to Asia in the period 1602–1795, of whom only a third ever returned, against a few hundred women in one failed experiment. Dutch mores were less accommodating than Portuguese (and much less than Chinese) to intermarriage with Asians, and the Company's shareholders opposed the idea of sharing its lucrative monopolies with private traders. When the city faced its gravest hour against the attacks of Mataram in 1628–9, it was defended by only about 230 Dutch "citizens," as against 470 Company soldiers, 700 Chinese residents, 260 Company slaves, and 200 slave-descended Christian freemen (*mardijkers*) and Japanese. The Dutch-speaking Protestant European and *mestizo* communities declined steadily in demographic significance as the city grew, until it was less than 1% after 1770, but their economic and social position as a pampered and powerful endogamous elite was steadily enhanced.

To a far greater extent than the Portuguese or Spanish, the Dutch relied on slaves from eastern Indonesia, southern India, and Arakan as a labor force and female population for their early Asian cities. At the 1632 enumeration there were 2,724 slaves in the city, a third of the population, in addition to 495 *mardijkers*, some of whom already had their own slaves. Most slaves then belonged to the Company, working in the warehouses and on building sites, but already there were 735 belonging to Dutch citizens. After initial difficulties in finding supplies, Batavia from 1660 to 1800 became much the largest importer of slaves in Southeast Asia. About 500 a year were introduced in 1660–90 and the number rose to about 4,000 during the eighteenth century. The great majority were purchased in south Sulawesi, Bali, and the islands further east. Slaves in the city (both inside and outside the walls) numbered over 30,000 in 1729 despite enormous mortality and the manumission of a high proportion of second-generation slaves. The numbers were even higher in the eighteenth century, though as a proportion of the total population they dropped to a quarter. By then slaves were no longer of great significance as a labor force, becoming overwhelmingly domestic and largely related to the needs of the European elite for status and of the disproportionately male population for sexual partners.

Although Coen's policy for Dutch settlers was a failure, his other strategy proved its salvation both in the short and the longer term,

> to establish a place where so great a concourse of people would come to us, Chinese, Malay, Javanese, Klings and all other nations, to reside and trade in peace and freedom under Your Excellency's [VOC] jurisdiction, that soon a city would be peopled and the staple of the trade attracted, so that [Portuguese] Melaka would fall to nothing (Coen 1616, in Coen 1919 I, 215).

It was particularly Chinese settlers and Chinese trade that Coen attempted to lure or bully to Batavia from the moment of the city's foundation. He once threatened that no Chinese junk would be permitted to leave Batavia for China until it had provided 100 men for the city.

Before the end of 1619 more than 400 Chinese had made the move to the new city, providing its first labor force before the advent of significant numbers of slaves in 1623. By 1632 there were 2,390 Chinese in the city and they furnished 45% of the free adult male population. As in Manila, they were engaged in service industries, construction, craft production, and provisioning, as well as trade. Unlike Manila, however, the Chinese did not need to become Christian to be trusted, but were encouraged to maintain a distinct identity under their own Dutch-appointed leaders. So Bingkong was already made head (later Captain) of the Batavia Chinese in 1619, and his authority was reinforced with the right to certain monopoly revenues in what became an entrenched pattern of Sino-Dutch economic organization. He farmed the right to run the city's weighing-house from 1620, while another prominent Chinese, "Jancon," took the lucrative monopoly on Chinese gambling. By mid-century, Chinese operated the lion's share of the revenue farms in Batavia and other Dutch cities, including port duties, and the revenue they thereby generated represented a quarter of total VOC income in Asia, second only to VOC trading.

The disruption caused by the fall of the Ming Dynasty (1644) and the 30-year struggle thereafter for control of China's seaboard put a damper on Chinese trade and emigration to Batavia. The four to five junks that had annually visited Batavia from Fujian ports in the 1630s dropped to almost nothing. In the 1670s a trickle of Fujian junks began to rebuild the trade connection, but only in 1683 did the Manchus sufficiently control the Fujian coast and Taiwan to allow normal trade. Chinese vessels poured southward from Xiamen (Amoy). Batavia became their most important foreign destination after Nagasaki (Japan's only open port), with an average of fourteen large junks a year arriving throughout 1691–1740. The Chinese population of the city built up quickly to 14,800, or 17% of the population, by 1739. Given the large numbers of increasingly unproductive slaves, this was the most valuable population group in the city, responsible for most of the manufacturing, construction, and service industry, as well as sugar milling and market gardening.

Indonesians, and especially Javanese, were initially distrusted by the Batavia administration as potentially hostile, and it was only in the 1650s that they began to feature significantly in any but the slave categories. Batavia, unlike Manila, began as an enclave economy entirely provided by sea. The most economically important of the Southeast Asian categories in the seventeenth century were Muslim Malays, an essentially diasporic trading community having its roots in the former emporia of Melaka (before 1511), Patani, Johor, Makassar, and Palembang. The office of Malay Captain was established in the 1640s, and its first three occupants were all wealthy merchants from Patani. The Malay group numbered 2,000–4,000 in the period of the city's commercial apogee between 1680 and 1730, and was the most important ship-owning community after Chinese and Europeans, with ships double the size of other Indonesian craft.

Javanese farmers began to be tolerated in the outer districts in the latter decades of the seventeenth century and to provide the city with some of its food needs, while a growing number of Islamized Balinese ex-slaves assimilated with them. By the end of the century this was the largest single ethnic category in Batavia, which was beginning to lose its enclave quality. Growing beyond 100,000 in the 1720s, Batavia's population nevertheless remained modest in comparison to the extraordinary reach of its commercial transactions throughout maritime Asia. It was not the largest of Southeast Asia's cities during its heyday in 1650–1740, but certainly the wealthiest and most strategic. It was a hothouse of cultural interaction and mutual learning.

WOMEN AS CULTURAL MEDIATORS

The exclusively male traders, sailors, and soldiers who came to Southeast Asia from elsewhere before 1800 formed mutually beneficial partnerships with Southeast Asian women. The open and cosmopolitan nature of the ports gave wealthy long-distance traders high status as sexual partners, and particular value for women accustomed to dominating most areas of their own markets. Rather than the prostitution practiced in other areas, Southeast Asian ports offered the visiting trader the much more valuable opportunity for a temporary marriage, which

> lasts as long as he keeps his residence there, in good peace and unity. When he wants to depart he gives her whatever is promised, and so they leave each other in friendship, and she may then look for another man as she wishes, in all propriety, without scandal (van Neck 1604/1980, 225).

The more balanced power equation between women and men Below the Winds encouraged serial monogamy and easy divorce for both parties. The Asian outsiders – Chinese, Indian, and Muslim – had little difficulty fitting this pattern into their concept of polygyny, with a different wife in every port. European Christians had more difficulty accepting the system without guilt or scandal, but wherever individual Europeans escaped the social control of their home community they found the system congenial. Hybridity was therefore the norm for these cities, up to the point when communication with the homeland became so well established that its prejudices were imported. In the nineteenth century such interracial unions came to be looked down upon as lower class by the commercial immigrants themselves, though less so by Southeast Asians.

Southeast Asian women were therefore the pioneers of cultural interaction with outsiders, a creative role honored by neither nationalist nor imperialist authors. The first areas in which they showed their adaptive skills were naturally in language and in trade, both crucial to the sexual exchange system. As actors in the local marketing system, the women of the commercial centers could advise their foreign partners of market conditions, and act for them when they were away.

> If their husbands have any goods to sell, they set up a shop and sell them by retail, to a much better account than they could be sold for by wholesale, and some of them carry a cargo of goods to the inland towns, and barter for goods proper for the foreign markets that their husbands are bound to ... but if the husband goes astray, she'll be apt to give him a gentle dose, to send him into the other world a sacrifice to her resentment" (Hamilton 1727/1930, 28).

Particularly in the early stages, we can assume that it was women who explained to visiting Chinese, Europeans, or Arabs how the system of weights, measures, and currencies worked, and how to develop hybrid ways of doing business between different systems. Money-changers were usually women as long as this profession was dominated by locals.

In the formation of permanently creolized cultures (*peranakan* or *mestizo*) of locally born "Chinese" in cities such as Melaka, Manila, and Batavia, the Southeast Asian mothers of the first generations were crucial. Chinese in Melaka and Manila appear to have found their partners among locals, while in more isolated Batavia, slave or ex-slave women provided most of the early partners. The small exiled Japanese Christian community disappeared by assimilation within a century, their daughters largely marrying Europeans, and their sons Christianized Indonesian ex-slaves. Chinese who settled in seventeenth-century Batavia were likely to marry women from Bali or Borneo (who could share their taste for pork). Some of the sons of the most successful might be sent to China for education, but the daughters never were, and the latter tended over time to be the preferred marriage partners of the more established Chinese, thus re-establishing the endogamy of the hybridized group. In 1648 the Captain of the Batavia Chinese died and his Balinese-born wife took over his duties, despite protests from Chinese men. Unlike those of Manila, Christian Chinese in Batavia were rare and little encouraged even among hybrid *peranakan*. It was the ancestral cults and cycle of temple festivals that held the Chinese community in the Indies together.

The tightly organized European ventures into the Indian Ocean in their initial military stage allowed fewer opportunities to profit from Southeast Asian female partners. Individuals escaping from official control certainly did so, however, to their great advantage in adapting to Southeast Asia. The very first Portuguese expedition to Southeast Asia, that of Diogo Lopes de Sequeira in 1509, believed it owed its survival to a woman from the large Javanese community of Melaka, "the lover of one of our mariners, who came by night swimming to his ship" and warned the Portuguese of the Bendahara's plans to seize them at a banquet (Albuquerque 1557/1880, 73–4). After his 1511 conquest of Melaka, Afonso de Albuquerque sent three ships to the east to discover the sources of nutmeg and cloves. Its most successful member was its deputy commander, Francisco Serrão, who had the good sense to marry a local woman while provisioning in the Java port of Gresik. Although his ship was wrecked in Maluku, he and his wife, with a few mixed followers, managed to win the friendship of the Sultan of Ternate and lay a basis for Portugal's intimate relations with the sultanate, which endured until the religious polarization of the 1560s. Virtually all Portuguese in outposts such as those in Maluku, and on the Mainland, had local wives or concubines who played a crucial mediating role as the Portuguese gradually adapted to Asian commercial methods. Among the better-known progeny of these unions were the three sons (as well as one well-married daughter) of Juão de Erédia, who in 1545 sailed away with his Bugis princess rather than confront her reluctant father, the raja of Suppa in south Sulawesi. The couple became pillars of Melaka society. Two sons were leading priests in the city, while the third, Manuel Godinho de Erédia, became a great chronicler and discoverer with a claim to have been the first to map the southern continent of Australia.

The female pioneers in the understanding of Europeans, as in understanding the Chinese before them, naturally became also interpreters and negotiators. Indeed, there is evidence from the Archipelago of their use as negotiators even when language facility was not the issue, presumably because women were accustomed to bargaining and compromise by their commercial roles, where aristocratic men were constrained by fear of compromising status. The first Dutch mission to Vietnamese-speaking Cochin-China found itself dealing extensively with women. The interpreters for the royal court were two elderly women who had formerly lived in Macao as the wives of Portuguese. The Dutch bought their pepper chiefly from another woman who had traveled down from the trade center to meet them.

In Ayutthaya (the Siam capital) the VOC owed much of its success in obtaining advantageous trading conditions in the 1640s to an enterprising woman known to them as Osoet Pegu. Though born into the Mon trading community of the capital, she learned Dutch as a child from frequenting the Dutch traders there. As an adult she became the indispensable link between the Dutch and the court and was taken on as "wife" (in the local rather than Dutch sense) by three successive Dutch agents. Until her death in 1658 she remained a wealthy trader and intermediary with great influence with the Thai queen and key officials. Arguing with her most senior ex-husband, Jeremias van Vliet, for control of their children, she was able to make her case in Batavia by sending an elephant as a gift to the Governor-General. Few subsequent Dutch agents obtained Siamese royal permission to remove their offspring, so that there were in 1689 seventeen Dutch-Siamese children being partly supported by the Dutch post there.

Such key marriage alliances were part of the stuff of Southeast Asian diplomacy, and could extend to the royal courts themselves, which might give and receive daughters in marriage as a means to cement alliances with powerful foreigners. Chinese, Arab, and Indian traders had long understood these relationships and used them to create local cultural hybridities, as did Europeans away from their controlling group. The powerful Sultan Iskandar Muda of Aceh tried to cement his relations with Siam by acquiring a Thai princess as a wife, and also proposed to the English agent Thomas Best that the Company should send English women to him.

> If I beget one of them with child, and it prove a son, I will make him king of Priaman, Passaman and of the coast from whence you fetch your pepper, so that you shall not need to come any more to me, but to your own English king for these commodities (Best, cited Reid 1993, 239–40).

This pattern gradually broke down in dealing with Europeans. Christian insistence on lifetime monogamous commitment, along with the group solidarity of often beleaguered company outposts and increasing racial prejudice, handicapped Europeans in making use of this channel. By the late eighteenth century marriage with even high-born Asians was disapproved by colonial society.

What did keep the European presence viable in cities like Batavia was concubinage for ordinary Dutch soldiers and traders, and marriage within the Christian Eurasian community for the elite. The hundreds of thousands of Europe-born men who came to Asia suffered a mortality rate about four times that of those who stayed at home, dying from malaria, smallpox, and various water-borne diseases that proliferated in the dense urban settlements they built. Mortality for Europeans was typically above 10% a year in Dutch Southeast Asian settlements, but rose to a staggering 36% once malaria became endemic in Batavia in 1733. Mortality among the local-born was primarily in childhood, so that the women available for marriage to immigrant Europeans had some immunity as adults, and often outlived several husbands. The Eurasian women also imbibed some healthy habits from their mothers, such as bathing daily and chewing betel (which provided protection against parasites and digestive ailments), and from Chinese acquaintances by drinking their water boiled in the form of tea. In the early phase of Portuguese and Dutch settlements Asian women could rise spectacularly from slave or illegitimate origins to immensely wealthy widows. By the second and third generations more care was taken to keep large fortunes within the elite of Batavia and other settlements. Ambitious men then gained fortunes by marrying the Eurasian widows of well-placed VOC men. A restricted group of well-married Eurasian women became central in controlling the fortunes of Batavia. Their ethnic origins were extremely diverse, their common languages Portuguese and Malay rather than Dutch, but their most important common ritual was weekly attendance at the Protestant church to which they processed in splendor, a slave in attendance carrying a parasol.

Among the most vital mediating roles of Southeast Asian women in relation to the broader evolution of renaissance knowledge were those in botany and human health. Women had always been in charge of child birthing and abortion practices, and the collecting, exchanging, and application of medicinal plants. They astonished early European observers with the abundance of medicinal herbs they sold in the market. They were also prominent as masseurs, bone-setters, and mediums with spirits held to be the cause of mental and nervous disorders. In marked contrast to the European surgeons sent out on Company ships, they knew from long experience how to survive in the tropics. They taught reluctant European men to wash daily as the price of access to sex. When European writers condescended to acknowledge the source of their remedies it was usually from female herbalists. The pioneer of tropical medicine Jacobus Bontius (Jacob de Bondt, 1591–1631) reported that "every Malayan woman is her own physician and an able obstetrician and (this is my firm conviction) I should prefer her skill above that of a learned doctor or arrogant surgeon" (cited Sargent 2013, 149). In India and China the comparable European pioneers had little contact with women and were led into theoretical discussions with male Ayurvedic and humoral specialists, whose theories were of little practical help. Medical theory in Southeast Asia had not been formalized into any such male-dominated intellectual system with more prestige than effectiveness. At a practical level, Southeast Asian medicine depended much on herbal antiseptics and cures, where "their botanic knowledge ... is far more advanced than our own" (Bontius, cited Sargent 2013, 148). This knowledge was most explicitly formalized by Rumphius (Georg Eberhard Rumpf, 1627–1702), the great savant of Ambon, whose exploration of Southeast Asian herbs aided the development of scientific botany in Europe. Like Bontius, he had a high opinion of his female informants, but especially of his Malukan wife tragically killed in the great tsunami of 1674, whose vital role in his knowledge of medicinal plants he graciously acknowledged.

CULTURAL HYBRIDITIES

The Portuguese language, with its various creole variants, became one of the key mediators between East and West in the trading cities of Asia, important even in seventeenth-century Dutch Batavia where Portuguese power and Catholic worship were forbidden. Its interaction with the Malay lingua franca provided the field for cultural transfer and interaction in the creative cities of the sixteenth century. Arabic vocabulary had begun entering earlier, and Hokkien Chinese and Dutch were added to the mix in the seventeenth century. Thus while most of the days of the week were taken from Arabic, Sunday (*minggu*, also the word for week itself) is from Portuguese. The Dutch pastor and writer Francois Valentijn was among the first to point out the difference between the written high Malay of Muslim texts and palace diplomacy, "which is not understood even on the Malay coast … apart from Muslim kings, rulers and priests" and the low or hybrid Malay, *bahasa kacukan*, which "is derived from many nations … sometimes mixed with some words from Portuguese, or from any other language" (trans. Maier 2004, 9).

Female dress was one of the items most rapidly changed by the foreign male gaze, whether Arab, Chinese, or European. Cloth and clothing, especially the colorful styles imported from India, were the most conspicuous items of extravagance in Southeast Asia, perhaps because the low-born were not inhibited by sumptuary laws from exhibiting their wealth this way. So although Europeans and Chinese were surprised at what they considered indecently light clothing, with usually bare feet and heads, and with little more than a scarf above the waist, the extravagance of adornments was equally surprising. Even into the nineteenth century, Javanese, Balinese, Thais, and Bugis considered a bare upper body carefully prepared with oils, perfumes, cosmetics, and jewelry the most appropriate dress for both sexes on high ritual occasions. Yet in protecting the genitals from view, Southeast Asians were more fastidious than most of the visitors, obliging French soldiers, for example, to wear a *sarung* when bathing in the river of Siam.

A major effect of the commercial boom was the expansion of imported cloth from India, and experimentation with finery from all quarters of the world. Traders were pressed to provide rare and exotic items, particularly opulent clothing or ornaments for the bodies of the wealthy. Since sewn and fitted clothing had been rare until this revolution, European or Middle Eastern jackets and Indian trousers were in demand as novelties. The Makassar rulers greeted visitors in the seventeenth century with European cloth coats over their otherwise bare upper torso. Gradually, however, sewn upper garments more appropriate to the climate were devised and requested from India or sewn locally. The very different ideas of female propriety of Muslim, Christian, and Chinese males became influential selectively, beginning in the commercial cities where such men were concentrated. In Portuguese Melaka the local partners of Portuguese men, even when Christianized and attending church, continued to wear flimsy upper garments and bare heads until the Jesuits arrived and forced them into more Portuguese-style dress in the mid-sixteenth century. In the Philippines also, Christian converts were pressured to adopt a

Spanish style of dress, fully covering the female body. But the most influential innovations were the hybrid styles which maintained the wrap-around cloth for the lower body (Malay *sarung*), but added first a breast-cloth, somewhat less revealing than the scarf, and eventually a sewn blouse or tunic. In the Malay-speaking world of Southeast Asia's port-cities, many of the words for sewn garments were of foreign origin – *kemeja* (shirt), *celana* (trousers), and *sepatu* (shoes) from Portuguese, and later *jas* (jacket) and *rok* (skirt) from Dutch. The urban women who interacted with foreigners in the ports developed a Portuguese-influenced distinctive upper garment, the *kebaya* (though the word may be derived from Arabic), often so fine as to be transparent, making the *sarung-kebaya* combination the hybrid female dress par excellence of the region.

Performance had long been the cultural form of choice in Southeast Asia. Localized Indian stories of the Mahabharata and Ramayana, alongside some local traditions, were learned and loved not through reading but by experiencing as dance and theater. In the stateless societies held together largely through ritual and religious ceremony, feasting was always accompanied by music and dance, intended to link the living with the spirit world as well as to entertain and provide opportunities for matchmaking. Weddings, religious occasions, and funerals were all enlivened by music and dance, while the river-boatmen sang to keep time as they rowed. Where royal courts arose, they demonstrated their eminence as cultural exemplars. There, performance reflected both their religious centrality and their cosmopolitanism. Foreign visitors were sometimes entranced by this activity, but often complained that they had time for little else than to witness dances and dramas lasting through the night.

In this regard, too, the age of commerce was a period of great innovation and borrowing. The port-capitals that became great centers of cultural exchange rejoiced in their eclecticism. Stringed instruments were introduced from the Middle East, China, and Europe to expand the ancient Southeast Asian mix of bronze percussion instruments and flutes. Each foreign community was expected to provide its style of entertainment for court and public occasions. A Malay text from Sumbawa, too far east for the major commercial encounters, nevertheless showed its cosmopolitanism by listing "all kinds of entertainments like Indian dances, Siamese theatre, Chinese opera, Javanese puppet theatre and music of the viol, lute, kettledrum, flute, bamboo pipe, flageolet, *kufak* and castanets" (*Hikayat Dewa Mandu*, 257). Most of the "traditional" theatrical forms were created in this period out of the encounter of older patterns and the new religious and social norms. The shadow theater (*wayang kulit*) of Java certainly had older origins in religious ritual, but both it and the masked drama (*wayang topeng*) assumed their familiar modern form in the cosmopolitan ports of north Java during the sixteenth century, presumably as a way of telling the popular Indian stories in oblique ways not explicitly confronting Islam. The shadow theater spread to the Mainland, but was there confined to a more esoteric ritual role, while Thai masked drama (*khon*) developed for the beloved Jataka stories about the life of the Buddha, and Java-derived unmasked dance drama (*lakhon*) for the highly popular stories of both Indian and local origin. The Vietnamese national dance drama (*hat boi*) was also developed and popularized around 1600 by the addition in the south of Cham and other themes to the older Chinese-inspired northern opera.

Clifford Geertz (1980, 123–5) aptly remarked that Southeast Asian rulers were engaged in a "continual explosion of competitive display" to demonstrate their exemplary status through public theater and ritual. Whatever power each state possessed derived from "its imaginative energies, its semiotic capacity to make inequality enchant." In the port-states that set the cultural tone in the long sixteenth century, the foreign traders were essential to the demonstration of royal success and status. The English factor in Banten, Java's preeminent such state of the time, described the challenge of doing at least as good a job as the Dutch in making a spectacular display to honor the circumcision ceremonies of the boy-king, which dominated the city throughout the trading season from March to July 1605. The Europeans had little chance to impress in comparison with Chinese opera, fireworks, and acrobatics, and all manner of Javanese processions with hundreds of splendidly adorned women and men, pageants, and floats, including mock forts and battles, ships laden with gifts, dragons and

> "many sorts of beasts and fowls, both living and also so artificially made that … they were not to be discerned from those that were alive", theatre and dance, all kinds of music, and "significations of historical matters of former times, both of the Old Testament and of chronicle matters of the country and kings of Java. All these inventions the Javans have been taught in former times by the Chinese; … and some they have learned by Gujaratis, Turks and other nations which come hither to trade" (Scott 1606/1943, 154–6).

The first generation of rough European trader-soldiers had little to contribute to the mix, though any ship that did carry musicians, like Francis Drake's in Ternate and Java in 1579–80, found them in great demand to join the competitive performance of the ports. In the longer term the European contribution to Southeast Asian music was considerable. Catholic Church music was one of the great attractions of that new faith in the island world in general, and Filipinos became extremely proficient in Gregorian chanting and instrumental music. They and the Portuguese-influenced communities of Melaka were in demand as performers throughout the region, and spread European instruments and themes everywhere. Dutch and English Protestants placed less emphasis on music, but found in the singing of the psalms of David, as the first English voyage was requested to do in Aceh, a point of intercultural contact with Muslims. In Dutch Batavia the great households had their slave orchestras, whose descendants spread the knowledge of instruments and melodies much further afield. The violin was so valued for its virtuosity that it had spread widely by the eighteenth century. Thomas Forrest (1729–1802), an unusually cultivated country trader, regularly ingratiated himself with the local elite where he traded by exchanging performances with them and presenting key allies with violins. Muslim Magindanao was outside the bounds of Spanish control or Christian influence, but in 1776 he found the heir apparent to its throne (*raja muda*) was a violinist who showed great interest in Forrest's demonstration of musical notation.

Rumphius was a rare case of acknowledging the role of his local wife in his discoveries, but we must assume that many of the important "European" accomplishments of the period were born from intense interaction with a well-informed local woman. One such was the Mon-Siamese Osoet Pegu, mentioned above. The father of her three daughters, the VOC's Jeremias van Vliet, was also the best-informed foreigner of his day on Siamese history and culture, and his three precious works on the subject could not have been written without her.

ISLAM'S "AGE OF DISCOVERY"

Muslim voyaging in the fifteenth century was no state enterprise but the business of individual entrepreneurs of many different ethnicities and cultures, communicating with each other through the religious and legal commonalities of Islam. As maritime peoples in southern Asia were drawn into cosmopolitan relations through the boom of the long sixteenth century, many saw in Islam a new universal. It asserted strongly that there was only one God for the whole planet, one true path, and one revelation in a particular language – Arabic. Even more than Pollock's "Sanskrit cosmopolis" of the first millennium, the "Arabic cosmopolis" of the fifteenth to seventeenth centuries created a global imperative above place and culture. With it came a network of scholars and manuscripts, as well as story-tellers and their tales, translating the idioms of Arabic and Persian into Malay and Javanese. Malay was transformed in the process, adopting a modified Arabic script and a host of terms from the Arabic and Persian. Whereas the older Indic-derived manuscripts had been written on palm-leaf, paper was more appropriate to the swirls and dots of the Arabic script. Large quantities of it were imported to Southeast Asia, mainly from China in the fifteenth century but Europe by the seventeenth. Yet it was Arabic words for paper, pen, and ink that were adopted by Malay, and in the case of paper even into Thai.

This Indian Ocean world was the largest venue of Eurasian exchange in the fifteenth century, but European knowledge was peripheral to it. That changed when the Ottomans conquered Constantinople with its legacy of Greek learning in 1453. Their extraordinary expansion continued to the key portages of Eurasia's maritime routes – the rich prize of Egypt in 1517, and the keys to the Persian Gulf and the Red Sea in 1537. The Ottomans became a bridge more effective than the Portuguese between the Mediterranean and Indian Ocean worlds. Their "Age of Discovery" was able to combine European and Arab knowledge of maritime discoveries. In 1516, Ali Akbar's "Book of Cathay" (*Hitayname*) was presented to Sultan Selim, with a first-hand account of a trading voyage to China more informative than any European account of the time. Not long after Selim took control of Cairo in 1517 he was presented with the even more remarkable world map of Piri Reis, intended to inform the sultan about the potential of the Indian Ocean and its spices, to which Turkey now had easier access than the rival Europeans.

How technical advances were exchanged in the East is not always clear. Muslim traders in the Indian Ocean certainly made use of charts before the encounter with Europeans, and some of them must have learned very quickly of the Portuguese discoveries in the Atlantic. When Afonso de Albuquerque conquered Melaka from its Muslim Malay dynasty in 1511 he acquired from a Javanese pilot there a map he considered the finest he had ever seen. It showed the Portuguese discoveries including Brazil and Africa, as well as Europe, Muslim routes from the Red Sea to Maluku, and Chinese ones from Fujian and Ryukyu. Unfortunately it was lost with other treasures being sent home to King Manuel in the wreck of the *Flor de la Mar*.

Despite the Turkish failure to expel the Portuguese from their Indian Ocean strongholds (Chapter 5), they had more direct influence on the peoples of the Indian Ocean littoral than did the Portuguese. The fundamental difference between the two contenders was that the Portuguese fleets represented from the beginning a state-funded and directed monopoly, as outsiders in Asia with few natural allies. The Ottomans were drawn into the Indian Ocean by appeals from the established commercial centers like Gujarat and Aceh for military protection against the Portuguese intrusion. The Ottomans had laid claim to a universal Caliphate in 1518, immediately after conquering Mecca, and this added to Asian hopes for protection. The Islamic cosmopolis peaked in the second half of the sixteenth century at a time when religious polarization highlighted universal norms at the expense of the local. Islamic books, like the parallel Catholic ones in the Philippines, introduced to the southern islands a new pattern of text-based scholarship, using written texts on paper to translate and explicate the sacred canon. Ottoman subjects also transferred navigational, shipping, and military technologies to the Muslim ports.

Southeast Asians had long been literate, but popular piety had primarily been expressed visually in the form of statuary and theatrical performance. The Islamic cosmopolis brought a new emphasis on the written word and its texts, debates, and erudition. From the 1560s Aceh became the Southeast Asian hub of this cosmopolis, welcoming learned *ulama* from South and West Asia and producing a number of its own. The tradition of scholarly writing in the Malay language was effectively created in Aceh during this key century, with important offshoots in cosmopolitan ports like Banten, Makassar, Demak, and Patani. While the great majority of surviving translations and commentaries were in the Islamic scholarly tradition, the works of the sixteenth and early seventeenth centuries were consciously innovating in their attempts to reconcile scriptural norms with the inner-directed mystical and ascetic traditions of earlier periods. A few texts on technical and scientific matters have also survived, and the transfer of Turkish military and naval technology to centers such as Aceh, Johor, and Makassar was extensive.

The European contribution to this cosmopolitan moment was not limited to military technology, although that was the first to make an impression. By the seventeenth century the Jesuits were representing the best of European mathematics and astronomy to Asia. Alexandre de Rhodes was the best known (thanks to his writings) of their scholar-missionaries in Southeast Asia, and described his discussions with the elites in Makassar (see below) and Tongking.

He gained access to the northern Viet court by presenting the king with a Jesuit rendering into Chinese characters of how Euclid's sphere worked, which so interested the ruler Trinh Trang (1623–52) that he talked mathematics and astronomy for two hours with the Jesuit and gave him permission to stay and build a church. The Jesuits in Cambodia found themselves in competition with knowledgeable Chinese, and urged their peers to make sure they made no mistakes in predicting lunar eclipses so as not to be ridiculed. The Dutch were also competitors in science, presenting or trading telescopes and clocks to the leading trade centers – even as far as the Lao capital of Vientiane.

European paper was becoming popular by 1600, replacing the palm-leaf of the older era to make possible the explosion of new writing on Islamic subjects especially. But printing was not so quickly taken up. Printing presses were introduced by the Spanish to the Philippines in 1593, followed by the Dutch in the Archipelago and French missionaries in the two Viet states. In each case European missionaries printed texts in a roman alphabet they devised to replace older alphabets for Tagalog, Malay, and Vietnamese, respectively. In the long run each of these printed roman alphabets was hugely influential, becoming the national languages of great modern countries and opening the door to the eventual rise of a European cosmopolis. At the time, however, the printing presses sparked surprisingly little interest except in Christianized circles. The explanation must be sought in the broader distrust of missionary printing presses for reproducing the sacred texts of Islam and Buddhism, a distrust that would endure until the twentieth century.

SOUTHEAST ASIAN ENLIGHTENMENTS – MAKASSAR AND AYUTTHAYA

The Asian-ruled cities most visited by curious Europeans were the best documented examples of how cosmopolis worked. Makassar was the leading port in eastern Indonesia from about 1580 to its capture by the Dutch in 1666. Before its rise, the Makassarese corner of Southwest Sulawesi was as politically fragmented as the Bugis societies to its north. Both were primarily rice-growing agricultural peoples, governed by a proud heaven-descended aristocracy whose relations with one another were governed by contracts supernaturally sanctioned by oaths. Writing in an Indic-derived script appeared to have been introduced only in the fifteenth century, and was largely used to record genealogies. Malay/Muslim traders began visiting the area in large numbers in the 1540s, and were persuaded to make their base near modern Makassar in mid-century. The reason may have been in part Portuguese attempts to convert rulers in their earlier settlements further north, but also the skill of the Makassar kings in guaranteeing key autonomies to the Muslim trading community.

Politically Makassar flourished as a partnership between Gowa, on the larger Jeneberang River that provided the sovereign, and Tallo', a more maritime center to its north that provided the Chancellor of the kingdom and managed its trade. It was two Tallo' figures in particular who guided Makassar as

Chancellor through its most successful period: Karaeng Matoaya in 1593–1637, and his son Karaeng Pattinggalloang in 1639–54. Matoaya led Makassar into Islam in 1605, at a time when both Sunni Islam and Catholic Christianity were well known, while the Protestant Dutch and English had begun to make their presence felt as opponents of Portuguese Catholics. Islam was the means by which Makassar established its primacy over all the Bugis and Makassarese polities of south Sulawesi, but both Makassar and Bugis chronicles show Matoaya explicitly recognizing their traditional autonomies. Although the dress code and manners of the Makassarese were changed by Islam, they remained no less open to the Europeans. Matoaya was reported to be very dutiful with his five daily prayers after his conversion, and only had to miss them when he went to an Englishman to cure his swollen foot, who treated him with alcohol. Another Englishman reported in 1612 that "It is a very pleasant and fruitful countrye, and the kindest people in all the Indias towards strangers ... The King is very affable and true harted towards Christians" (cited Reid 1999, 144). Indeed one of the sultan's wives was Portuguese, and the son of this union, Francisco Mendes, became an indispensable, trilingual "Portuguese secretary" to the court in the 1640s. At that time Muslim Makassar had four Catholic churches to cater for Jesuits, Franciscans, Dominicans, and the secular clergy expelled from Melaka (Figure 6.1).

Makassar's prosperity depended on being a spice port open to all comers, at a time when the VOC was using every means to assert a monopoly over both clove and nutmeg. All other traders found Makassar the safest place to buy their spices, as long as small boats could evade Dutch blockades to get the spices to Makassar, and the city itself was strong enough to deter a Dutch conquest. Some hundreds of Portuguese were based there in the 1620s, and several thousand after the Dutch took their major base of Melaka in 1641. To the VOC's demands for monopoly Makassar insisted on even-handed freedom for all. "God made the land and the sea; the land he divided among men and the sea he gave in common. It has never been heard that anyone should be forbidden to sail the seas" (Sultan Ala'ud-din 1615, cited Stapel 1922, 14). But Makassar's position was only viable if it was strong, and the elite were intensely interested to learn key military techniques from Portuguese, English, or Muslims. The Makassar chronicle, which reads as a litany of innovations, declares that Karaeng Matoaya was the first to introduce the manufacture of cannons and muskets, and was himself "skilled at making gunpowder, fire-works, flares, and fireworks that burn in the water, as well as being an accurate marksman" (cited Reid 1999, 138).

Karaeng Pattinggalloang, who succeeded his father as Chancellor of the joint kingdom, was an even more remarkable "renaissance man." He had all of his father's intellectual curiosity, but the added advantage of a cosmopolitan upbring-ing that gave him fluency in Portuguese as well as Makassarese and Malay, and at least a reading knowledge of Spanish and Latin. He pestered visiting European ships for novelties, but particularly for books of which he built up a considerable library. The fullest first-hand account we have of him is that of the French Jesuit scholar Alexandre de Rhodes, who wrote of his time in Makassar in 1646:

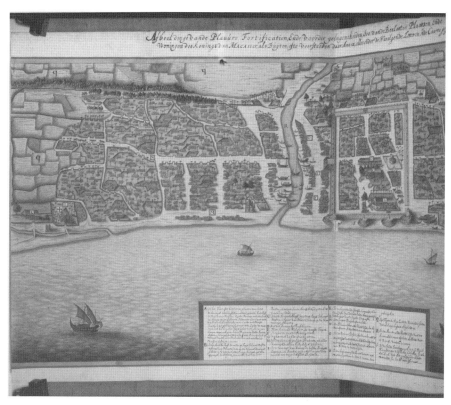

Figure 6.1 Makassar in 1638, as drawn by van der Hem for the "Secret Atlas of the VOC." The citadel at right contains: the Sultan's palace (B) on wooden pillars, the former palace (C), royal warehouses (D), and royal mosque (E). The channel to its left was newly dug as an outlet to the Jeneberang River, with Portuguese (F) and Gujarati (G) quarters beside it. To left of the channel are the Portuguese church, Market (M), English (L) and Dutch (K) lodges. Source: Anthony Reid, "Southeast Asian Cities before Colonialism," *Hemisphere* 28:3 (1983), 144–5.

The high governor of the whole kingdom … I found exceedingly wise and sensible, and apart from his bad religion [ie Islam], a very honest man. He knew all our mysteries very well, had read with curiosity all the chronicles of our European kings. He always had books of ours in hand, especially those treating of mathematics, in which he was quite well versed. Indeed he had such a passion for this science that he worked at it day … and night. To hear him speak without seeing him one would take him for a native Portuguese, for he spoke the language as fluently as people from Lisbon itself.

Seeing that he was pleased to talk of mathematics, I began conversing with him on the subject, and God willed him to take such pleasure in it that he wanted to have me at his palace as a matter of course thereafter. It happened that I predicted an eclipse of the moon to him a few days before it took place … This so won him over he wanted me to teach him all the secrets of this science (de Rhodes 1653/1966, 208–9).

Although the Dutch were the chief threat to his kingdom, they acknowledged Pattinggalloang's remarkable scientific mind and did their best to supply his demands for the latest world maps and globes. A telescope of the latest Galilean kind had also been requested from the English in 1635 in the name of the sultan, but this sadly arrived only years later when the Chancellor was dead and this enlightenment moment gone with him.

Although this remarkable Chancellor was only one unusual man, there were wider indications of a court culture of curious cosmopolitanism. Makassar offers the best evidence we have for the translation on Southeast Asian auspices not only of religious texts but also of European and Turkish technical manuals. Surviving manuscripts in both Makassarese and the quite different (but generally better preserved) Bugis language provide translations and summaries of works on gunnery, gunpowder, and ballistics by Spanish, Portuguese, Turkish, and Malay authorities. The practical consequences of this were seen after Pattinggalloang's death, when twelve large iron cannons of over a tonne weight, 34 smaller bronze cannons, and 224 culverins defended Makassar against a massive Dutch assault in 1669. Pattinggalloang's interest in maps appears also to have stimulated an unusual south Sulawesi tradition of map production.

The influence of Arabic and Persian models of history-writing, verse-epics, and literature spread through Islamic trading networks in this innovative Early Modern period. Chinese example was strongest through the spectacle of Chinese (usually in fact Hokkien) Opera, staged at festivals wherever there was a substantial Chinese trading community – certainly in Banten, Patani, and Hoi An by 1600. European models were more important in Makassar, where a habit began in Pattinggalloang's time of carefully recording important events in a state diary. Each day's date was given in both Muslim and Christian form. A genre of historical chronicle unusually matter-of-fact by Southeast Asian standards also developed in the sixteenth and seventeenth centuries. The Goa (Makassar) chronicle began with an explanation of why it was important that future generations remember the past, "to avoid the twin dangers, either of our thinking that we were all great kings, or of others alleging that we were worthless" (*Sejarah Goa*).

The placing of a high value on personal freedom is often thought a key feature of the European Enlightenment, and, ever since Herodotus, has been stereotyped as alien to Asia. It is therefore significant that south Sulawesi society, following this enlightenment moment, appears to have been one that particularly prized its freedom. The rise of the gunpowder empire of Makassar was carefully balanced by traditional south Sulawesi contractualism, expressed in the idiom of freedom (*merdeka*) as the opposite of slavery. At least in the Bugis kingdom of Wajo', rituals of inaugurating a new king required him to guarantee the personal freedoms of speech, property, and movement of his people – by which was meant, as in ancient Greece and Jeffersonian America, his free people, not their slaves.

The Siamese capital of Ayutthaya during the remarkable reign of King Narai (r.1656–1688) is the second example, alongside Makassar, about which there is enough information to be able to show the effects of cultural exchange at this exceptional moment. The cosmopolitan capital attracted "a great multitude of strangers of different nations, who settled there with the liberty of living according to their customs, and of publicly exercising their several ways of worship" (La Loubère 1691/1969, 112). La Loubère estimated about 3,000 each for the number of Indian Muslims, Portuguese, Malay Muslims, and Chinese, with influential pockets also of Dutch and French (the two who left the best records), English, Japanese Christian refugees, and Mon Buddhists. The king was a cosmopolitan modernizer, though a ruthless autocrat internally, and surrounded himself with educated people, including even the multilingual Greek adventurer Constance Phaulkon, who served him as effective minister for foreign relations in the 1680s.

The scientific curiosity of King Narai was first served by the VOC, to which he had granted extraterritorial rights in 1664, ending a period of mutual suspicion. Thereafter the Company was the most consistent provider of European expertise, sending him not only military assistance with artillerymen and gunpowder manufacturers, but also clocks, telescopes, a glassblower, goldsmiths, sculptors, and medical men. The French sought to top this with an elaborate royal mission in 1685, accompanied by six of the most learned Jesuits in France. They arranged to be in Siam for a total eclipse of the moon on December 10, 1685, with the double purpose of impressing the king and calculating more accurately the meridians of Paris and Siam. The Jesuits reported how curious the court circle was to exploit these scientists, frequently sending their own scholars to pose questions about the nature of the sun, the winds, and so forth. The king requested that a larger team of Jesuit "mathematicians" be sent out to Siam, and agreed to build for them a handsome observatory, never realized because of his overthrow and death in 1688. In literature, too, Narai's reign demonstrated remarkable innovation, with the first truly secular histories and poetry.

GUNPOWDER KINGS AS AN EARLY MODERN FORM

One is struck in reading the accounts of seventeenth-century travelers in Southeast Asia how well they understood the basic form of polity they encountered. They seemed to be dealing with courts and cities familiar enough to appreciate, in contrast with their nineteenth-century counterparts who saw at best eccentric exoticism, at worst decay, self-indulgence, and incompetence. Early Modern kings in many parts of the world were aware of their interdependence as well as competition, and understood that they surmounted fragile pinnacles of power that needed to be demonstrated and legitimated theatrically. Presiding over rapidly urbanized port-capitals, they impressed with extravagant forms of state theater, even more than by ambitious building projects and the accumulation of weapons. They exchanged envoys to impress and manipulate each other, but also to discover how the game was played elsewhere.

At both ends of Eurasia, elites were impressed with new discoveries, marvels, and curiosities from afar. European rulers assembled them in curiosity cabinets or *wunderkammer* to demonstrate not the vastness of their empires (as in the nineteenth century), but their cosmopolitan sophistication as people who understood the new world. No less in Southeast Asia did the elite display their status in this period by the possession of rarities. The age of commerce was made possible by the enthusiasm of Southeast Asians everywhere for colorful India-produced cloth, readily selling their spices and tropical exports in return for these imports. Nothing better defines the end of this period in the seventeenth century (Chapter 7) than the turn against foreign cloth and exotic fashions.

The rulers of the age of commerce eagerly questioned arrivals from afar, anxious both to measure themselves against their global peers, and to use distant connections for their own purposes. A feature of gunpowder kings everywhere was their dependence on foreign traders, financiers, and mercenaries. Envoys who brought an authentic letter from their monarch were received with great ceremony at the courts of Southeast Asia, the letter being carried in procession by caparisoned elephant ashore or gilded galley on the river. One of the last such exhibitions of royal theater, the reception of a French mission to Siam in 1687, assembled about 3,000 men in 70 decorated galleys, with musicians and dancers, to accompany the Ambassador up the river. The addition of European envoys to the Asian diplomatic mix led to embassies in response. Aceh in 1601–3 and Siam in 1607–8 sent envoys to Prince Maurits in Holland, but after beginning its career of conquest in 1619, the VOC refused to allow future envoys further than Batavia. Later embassies were therefore sent in hope of help against the Dutch. Banten sent one celebrated embassy to Charles II in England (1682), and Siam a series of embassies to Louis XIV in response to French initiatives, in 1680, 1684, and 1686–7. The fall in Asia of the monarchs who sent them, and a loss of interest in Europe, ended this phase of curious exchange.

The theater of state reached a peak during the long sixteenth century in the form of elaborate processions to honor the accession or death of the king, or of some wedding or religious festival over which he presided. At the same time as Europe developed the royal parade into an allegory of state power at such grand moments as the entry of Charles V into Rome (1530), Henry IV into Paris (1628), or Elizabeth (1588) or James I (1604) into London, Southeast Asia's gunpowder kings also altered the great public rituals from religious themes to those essentially celebrating themselves. The "theater state" concept was developed by Clifford Geertz (1980) to explain nineteenth-century Bali politics, but it applies even better to the gunpowder kings of the age of commerce. In Aceh the processions awed the watching crowds with the abundance of richly adorned elephants (260 at the last such grand occasion, in 1641), exotic creatures like rhinoceros and Persian horses, and thousands of armed men. In the Mainland river-capitals and those of Borneo, the greatest such processions were of galleys on the river. As a Dutch resident described an annual ritual in Siam,

> In front go about 200 mandarins, every one with his own beautiful boat and sitting in a small pavilion which is gilded and decorated according to the rank of the owner. These boats are rowed by 30 to 60 rowers ... In the finest boat the king is seated under a decorated canopy ... surrounded by nobles and courtiers who pay him homage at the foot of his seat ... The total number of boats amounts to 350 to 400, and 20,000 to 25,000 persons take part in the procession (van Vliet 1640/2005, 119).

In the later seventeenth century such grand occasions declined quickly, in Asia as in Europe, as monarchs no longer controlled the resources for them, new firearms made rulers dangerously vulnerable in them, and royal theatrical energies were redirected to more elegant and introverted occasions within the palace walls.

These parallels are more than coincidence, but reflect a certain ecumene, in which kings in different corners of Eurasia saw themselves as competitors within a moral order to some extent common. There was more contact and knowledge than in earlier periods, more mutual respect and curiosity than in later ones. One reflection of the time was the popularity of the literary genre known as "Mirrors of Princes," or *Mirat al-Muluk* in Arabic, mediated to Asia largely in its Islamic form. Familiar in both Christian and Islamic worlds from the eleventh century, this genre became both more popular and more widespread in the long sixteenth century when gunpowder kings needed guidance in how to surmount the unsteady pinnacles of power to which they had been projected. An explicit borrowing from Persian and Arabic sources into Malay was the *Taj as-Salatin* (Crown of Sultans) dedicated to the Aceh sultan by Bukhari al-Jauhari in 1603. This in turn was emulated in other Malay texts like Raniri's *Bustan as-Salatin* (Garden of Sultans, 1643), translated into Javanese and widely cited in the following period. Like much of the best of the genre in the same period in Europe and the Middle East, it condemns tyranny with colorful examples, and extolls the centrality of reason for a good king. Reason was the first thing God created, the essential virtue for guiding the conduct of king and commoner.

> Reason in the human body resembles the sun in the sky, of which the rays illuminate every corner of the world. ... Everything, good or evil, is apparent to those endowed with reason, just like colours, white or black, are clearly discernible in the light of the sun. Therefore you should glorify reason, so that your reign may become perfect (trans. Braginski 2004, 437).

Subsequent events would erect walls between cultures, and dull the interest for learning from one another. Nevertheless, Early Modernity had begun.

[7] THE CRISIS OF THE SEVENTEENTH CENTURY

THE GREAT DIVERGENCE DEBATE

The foregoing chapters have traced a robustly expansionary period in which Southeast Asian elites interacted as equals with Europeans and others. All sides of the exchange appeared eager to learn from the cultural differences that newly confronted them. This picture is difficult to square with the more abundant evidence from the nineteenth and early twentieth centuries, when Southeast Asians, even more than Asians in general, appeared unable to compete with the Europeans commercially, militarily, scientifically, or politically. That a divergence between East and West occurred between the sixteenth century and the nineteenth was clear; its causes were far less so. For the past century debate has raged around this issue, between colonial and nationalist apologists, between Marxist economic determinism and cultural explanations, between European exceptionalism and theories of Asian decline. Southeast Asia provides a critical forum for this wider debate about the relative impoverishment of what became the twentieth century's Third World. The boom and bust of its spice trade and its entrepôts makes it one of the world's more dramatic cases.

In the colonial period, European agency was thought to be central, for better or worse, reducing the Asian actors to helpless victims of European advance. The relentless monopolies of the VOC in the seventeenth century had crushed Asian commercial dynamic, causing the decline of states, cities, and welfare. Serious empirical quantification began in the 1960s, led by Chaunu (1960) and Magalhães-Godinho (1969) on Iberian data, but extending later to the copious records of the VOC. Japanese scholarship helped complement the European data with Japanese and Chinese evidence that Japanese silver and Chinese shipping were essential to the commercial boom of 1567–1644. It became more apparent that Southeast Asia formed part of a larger global pattern of massive expansion of silver production and trade in the long sixteenth century, followed by a faltering or crisis in the mid-seventeenth.

A History of Southeast Asia: Critical Crossroads, First Edition. Anthony Reid.
© 2015 Anthony Reid. Published 2015 by John Wiley & Sons, Ltd.

In the 1990s, the historiographic frontier was able to shift to more balanced empirical explorations of Eurasia as a whole, escaping from theories of West European, Chinese, or Japanese uniqueness. The fundamental point of Victor Lieberman (2003, 2009) is hard to deny, that the whole Eurasian world has evolved over the past thousand years in ways that show more parallels than divergences. Like Kenneth Pomeranz (2000), he rejects Europe/Asia dichotomy in favor of specific comparisons between different parts of Eurasia that have the most useful parallels. Lieberman (2009, 77–92) helpfully summarizes nine fields of interaction across Eurasia which help to explain the "strange parallels" he perceived between the Southeast Asian pattern and that of other parts of Eurasia. These may be further summarized under five heads to which I will return: changes in climate; disease patterns; military innovation, notably cavalry and firearms, tending to favor stronger states; global commercial cycles; and intellectual trends, borrowings, and reactions.

My own intervention in these debates was to argue that the radical changes affecting Southeast Asia in the mid-seventeenth century strengthened the case already proposed by Geoffrey Parker (1978; 2013), that the European crisis associated with the "little ice age" of the seventeenth century was in fact a global crisis (Reid 1990; 1993, 270–311). Victor Lieberman (1995) explicitly rejected this thesis for Mainland Southeast Asia, and his focus on the territorial consolidation of the major Mainland states led him to posit rather regime crises across the region in 1560–1600 and 1750–1800, which nevertheless produced ever-stronger state integration thereafter (Lieberman, 2003).

The question of when or how Asia's impoverishment relative to Europe came about was not Lieberman's concern, but was taken up by Kenneth Pomeranz (2000). He shifted the crucial moment of economic divergence between Europe and Asia to the period 1750–1850, and the critical cause to the exhaustion of resources of land and energy (especially timber) in the most dynamic Asian cores such as the Yangzi delta, whereas western Europe (especially England) had access to coal at home and abundant agricultural and forest resources in the New World. His impressive argument implicitly discounts the importance of the Chinese crisis associated with the shortage of silver and fall of the Ming Dynasty in the 1640s, but has little to say about this crisis elsewhere in Asia. Southeast Asia remains a periphery rather than a core in his scheme, with too low and dispersed a population to encourage proto-industrialization in the manner of England, the Netherlands, or parts of China.

I had argued that there was an important seventeenth-century crisis in Eurasia as a whole, but that Southeast Asia was more profoundly affected because of its high exposure to the expanding trade cycle in the long sixteenth century, and its vulnerability to VOC monopoly strategies and the withdrawal of the Japan-China silver-for-silk exchange from the region's economy (Reid 1993, 288–9). That there was a decisive change in the region at this time appears to me indisputable, in the direction of reduced engagement with the long-distance trade and with foreign ideas. The remainder of this chapter seeks to summarize this change and address the more intractable problems of its fundamental causes and its effects.

SOUTHEAST ASIANS LOSE THE PROFITS OF LONG-DISTANCE TRADE

There is a global synchronicity in the upward movement of prices, particularly for grain but also for labor, throughout the sixteenth century, followed by a decline in the middle decades of the seventeenth. Many authors have pointed as an explanation to the reduced amounts of silver being sent to both Europe and Asia (via the Manila galleon) from the New World silver mines after 1628, after more than a century of expansion. For Asia, the remarkable fact that Japanese silver exports also boomed in the period 1570–1630, and thereafter dramatically collapsed to less than half the peak levels by the 1640s, was even more persuasive as a factor in the collapse of China's Ming Dynasty (1644) and the problems of many Southeast Asian entrepôts.

Throughout the century from the 1540s to the 1640s China placed a markedly higher value on silver (in comparison with gold or key trade goods) than the rest of the world, as a result of the decay of China's paper money system and the need for currency for the expanding population and economy of Ming China. This highly profitable trade of silver from Southeast Asia and elsewhere to China came to an end when the influx of a large share of global silver output into China finally eliminated the price differential. This reduced both real value of revenues collected by the Chinese government in silver, but also, more drastically, the profits of the trade which had been conducted in Southeast Asia.

This factor is understood to have played a role in the fall of the Ming Dynasty, but it had an even more dramatic effect in Southeast Asia, as the venue for most of China's trade with the rest of the world in the period. The region's ports and urban centers had benefited more than most from the trade boom of 1570–1630. International demand for its products reached a peak in the 1620s, when Southeast Asian pepper and spices accounted for more than half of the value of European homeward cargoes from Asia. China and Japan had also traded with each other and with the maritime world at large in Southeast Asian ports. In 1635 Japanese ships stopped coming, while Chinese demand was reduced drastically by the crisis of the 1640s and the embargo on foreign trade imposed by the new Qing regime until the 1680s. For Europeans the initial concentration on Archipelago spices and pepper was replaced by other Asian interests, notably Indian cloth and indigo. Malukan spice and Southeast Asian pepper together dropped from 68% of Dutch homeward cargoes in 1648–50 to 23% in 1698–1700, and from the bulk of English cargoes before 1640 to about 2% after the loss of access to Banten in 1682 (Reid 1993, 288–9).

The small but significant technical disadvantage of Southeast Asian ships in naval encounters with Europeans was one of the military factors that had some profound effects on trade and shipping. The situation described by Portuguese and Italian writers in the early 1500s, and confirmed by marine archaeology, was that the South China Sea shipping was dominated by large "junks" of 300–500 tons, primarily based in Melaka, Java, and Siam though often built in Pegu. The Portuguese described these ships as Javanese or Malay, though their hybrid Sino-Southeast Asian design suggest the likelihood that they emerged from Chinese-Southeast Asian interactions, as explained in Chapter 3.

By the time the abundant Dutch reportage becomes available a century later the situation had already changed substantially. Portuguese ships had grown larger, China-based ships of around 500 tons had dominated China-Southeast Asia trade since the official licensing began in 1567, and Southeast Asian vessels had become numerous but smaller. The first Dutch voyage reported, "the East Indian islands are very rich in ships, but all little vessels, so that the largest junk I have seen would not carry more than forty tons" (Lodewycksz 1598/1915, 132–3). The Portuguese had inflicted some spectacular defeats on the profitable but unwieldy large ships, and made them too risky for local entrepreneurs to continue to invest in. There were still a few large vessels owned by Southeast Asian rulers in the early 1600s, both rice-carrying junks on the major supply routes and some military galleys of huge proportions. But the Dutch warships had even more of an edge in naval warfare than the Portuguese had had a century earlier, and there was a further reduction in the size of Southeast Asian ships by 1650. Apart from a few vessels built to European or Chinese design by some of the strongest kings, Southeast Asian vessels were then seldom of more than 20 tons. Large-scale shipping, as well as the longest-distance routes, had become a matter for Europeans and Chinese, and a diminished number of Indian vessels built to European design.

Linked to these naval setbacks was the destruction of the most important maritime entrepôts in Southeast Asian hands. Three of these occurred in the sixteenth century – Melaka's conquest by the Portuguese in 1511, Brunei's sacking by the Spanish in 1578, and the devastation of Pegu in the 1590s, first by its own disastrous king and then by its neighbors. The first two of these were probably made good by the rise of alternative entrepôts as was the usual Southeast Asian pattern. The destruction of Pegu and the seventeenth-century setbacks that followed were of much greater long-term significance. Tuban, Surabaya, and the other ports of central and east Java were conquered by Sultan Agung in 1625, with the effect that the center of Javanese life moved to the interior. The cosmopolitan coast was so marginalized that it was regarded as the enemy by subsequent Mataram rulers, to be squeezed and hobbled until finally surrendered to the VOC. Javanese commercial life, like that of the Mons after Pegu's destruction, suffered a permanent setback both absolutely and in relation to rival modes of life.

Under the Governorship of Jan Pieterszoon Coen (1618–29), VOC naval power in Asia was purposefully and ruthlessly deployed to establish permanent strategic strongholds and monopolies over the most vital items of trade. It was Southeast Asia's misfortune to provide the headquarters of this efficient Asia-wide operation in Jakarta, renamed Batavia in 1619. The five tiny volcanic islands of Banda, source of all the world's nutmeg and mace and governed by a remarkable oligarchy of traders, were conquered and depopulated in 1621. Slaves were introduced to tend the nutmeg under Dutch and Eurasian plantation-owners.

A military turning point between Asian and European power came in 1629, when coincidentally Aceh attempted to expel the Portuguese from Melaka, and Mataram to expel the Dutch from Batavia. Both were spectacular failures, and the main European enclaves were not seriously threatened by Asian power again. The VOC had also established a dominant position over the erstwhile clove center and sultanate of Ternate in the 1620s, and completed its monopoly of cloves with victories in the Ambon area in the 1650s. But since Makassar remained a powerful free-trading rival to Dutch dominance in eastern Indonesia, as Banten did in the Java Sea area, these now became targets. The VOC was able to wait until internal conflicts made it possible for them to find important local allies, with the result that Makassar fell in a series of battles ending in 1669, and Banten in 1682.

Only Aceh in the west and Ayutthaya in the north remained as great alternative magnets for free trade, and refuges for the mercantile groups expelled by these Dutch conquests. But in mid-century the VOC gradually prised loose from Aceh its lucrative pepper-growing dependencies in Sumatra and its tin-producing colonies in Malaya. Ayutthaya was the last great refuge for Southeast Asian cosmopolitanism and innovation under King Narai (1657–88). He tried in turn to play Muslims, English, and French against the Dutch, but ended by seeming to be so dependent on insensitive French troops that an anti-foreign revolution took place as he lay dying. Both Muslim and European trade largely deserted Ayutthaya, leaving the Dutch and Chinese to contest a much-reduced international trade.

The earliest European sources give witness to a diverse maritime trading world, in which Javanese were the most prominent, but Cham, Makassarese, Bandanese, "Luzons" (from Manila and Brunei), and Mon (from Pegu, coastal Burma) also owned and operated trading ships of over 100 tons, holding their own with those of Gujarat, south India, Bengal, and China. The Javanese and Mons were no longer considered maritime people after the disasters discussed above, however. Many of the indigenous rulers who survived the pressures of the mid-seventeenth century preferred to deal with foreign traders – European, Chinese, and Indian – rather than risk the turbulence of independently wealthy subjects. The indigenous maritime trading groups that best survived into the eighteenth century were Malays (a catch-all term for Malay-speaking Muslims, initially seen as a diaspora from Melaka) and Bugis originating in south Sulawesi. Neither group had a home port of consequence behind them; both were essentially diasporas surviving by their mobility in small vessels of 20–30 tons.

The monopolies and quasi-monopolies established by the VOC over some of Southeast Asia's key products in mid-century certainly affected the regional economy more severely than that of other parts of Asia. The most severe hit was to revenues from Malukan spices – cloves, nutmeg, and mace – which were the easiest to monopolize because production was localized on a few small islands. Pepper was a much larger trade item in quantity though only slightly larger in value in the boom years of the early seventeenth century. The Company could not monopolize it fully, since the English and Portuguese continued to ship smaller quantities to Europe and the Middle East, and the Chinese to East Asia. Nevertheless, the most important Southeast Asian production areas in Sumatra (apart from those tied to the struggling English company post at "Bencoolen" – Bengkulu) and west Java were under Dutch control following the conquest of Banten in 1684.

The effect was to reduce somewhat the prices paid to growers, but more importantly to cut out altogether the numerous traders who had brought the spices to entrepôts around the region, sustaining much of the commercial dynamism of these cities. Prices paid by European buyers at these Southeast Asian entrepôts of course dropped as the VOC-controlled price system replaced the open market. For cloves the estimated average prices paid fell from about a thousand Spanish dollars per ton at the peak period of competition in the 1630s and 1640s, to a fixed 206 dollars once the monopoly was established in 1656. Average pepper prices fluctuated between about 90 and 160 Spanish dollars per ton in 1600–60, but dropped sharply thereafter before stabilizing at the fixed price paid by the Dutch company of 83 dollars (5 reals per pikul; Bulbeck et al. 1998, 58, 84). Quantities of Malukan spices declined, as the higher prices the VOC could impose in Europe discouraged consumers there and drove them to alternative products. The total effect on Southeast Asian trade of the decline in return for the two most valuable exports of the time is estimated in Table 7.1.

The strong VOC stake in the world supply of these items, and of other Southeast Asian products like nutmeg, cinnamon, sandalwood, tin, and sugar, gave the Company enormous leverage also in other aspects of trade, including Southeast Asia's key imports from India (cloth) and Japan (silver, and later copper). The quest for monopoly dragged the Company into huge military expenditures, creating a vicious circle in which high overheads made it increasingly difficult for it to maintain profitability except under monopoly conditions. Southeast Asia's products in the long run suffered in world markets, especially in Europe and Japan, because the Company kept prices high and experimentation with new products minimal. By the eighteenth century the items of greatest interest to world trade were no longer Southeast Asian, but

Table 7.1   Pepper and clove exports by quantity and value at European (Amsterdam) and Southeast Asian (entrepôt) prices, in thousand Spanish dollars.

Decade	Estimated clove exports p.a.			Estimated pepper exports p.a.		
	Tons	Europe value	SEA value	Tons	Europe value	SEA value
1600–09	300	1866	210	4000		600
1630–39	400	1196	400	3800	2005	462
1640–49	308	718	308	3800	1954	602
1650–59	300	855	90	4000	1710	417
1660–69	160	822	33	4900	2286	357
1670–79	136	405	28	6500	1924	417
1680–89	134	389	28	4700	1542	392
1690–99	176	505	36	5300	2082	442

Source: Bulbeck et al. 1998, 58, 86.

had shifted to the cotton cloth of India, the tobacco and sugar of the New World, and the silks, porcelains, and tea of China.

Chinese shippers contributed much to Southeast Asia's trade boom of 1570–1630, as they would again after 1750 (Chapter 9). Their trade was devastated, however, by the crisis which led to the fall of the Ming in 1644, and the brutal methods adopted by the conquering Qing (Manchu) regime in its struggle against the Ming-loyalist Zheng family regime with its power base in Fujianese maritime trade. Chinese vessel arrivals in Manila, officially registered as averaging 34 a year in the 1630s, slumped to five to six a year (most of them Zheng's) for the whole period of the conflict, 1644–83. The Manchus conquered Taiwan in 1683 and lifted their ban on maritime trade in 1684. Chinese arrivals in Manila picked up again, but only to half the level of the boom period. As the winner in the conflicts of the seventeenth century, Batavia suffered less than Manila, and was at or beyond its boom-period levels by 1688.

Southeast Asian-controlled ports were affected in various ways by the China upheaval, and some were able to defy the overall downward trend for a time, as illustrated in shipping records of Manila and Nagasaki (Table 7.2). Vietnamese ports once again profited from China's restrictions on its own traders. During the Ming maritime bans in the fifteenth century, Dai Viet (like Champa and some Tai *muang*) had filled the gap by exporting millions of ceramics around Southeast Asia through its port of Van Don. The Van Don export system appears to have collapsed during Dai Viet's internal conflicts in the early 1500s, along with extensive Viet involvement in foreign trade. "Over the Four Seas, there was utter misery," declared the royal chronicle (cited Whitmore 2011, 114). Tomé Pires (1515/1944, 114) could report that the Viet "are a weak people on the sea" and had little trade except with China.

The conflict and repression on the China coast in the mid-seventeenth century for a time redirected some Chinese ships to Southeast Asian ports, and created an opportunity for Dai Viet to export its silks to Japan to replace the Chinese supply through the new port of Pho Hien. In consequence there was a remarkable late-flowering trade boom in mid-seventeenth-century Dai

Table 7.2 Chinese junks arriving Nagasaki from Southeast Asian ports[1] (in brackets ships arriving Manila; from Chaunu 1960).

Decade	Tongking	Cochin-China	Cambodia	Siam	Patani	Banten	Dutch ports	Total
1651–60	15 (1)	40 (6)	37 (5)	28 (3)	20	1	2	143
1661–70	6 (1)	43 (5)	24 (2)	26 (7)	9		14	122
1671–80	8	(5) 41	(1) 10	(10) 26	9	1	38	133
1681–90	12	25 (1)	9 (1)	31 (7)	9		23	109
1691–1700	6	29 (0)	23 (1)	19 (15)	7	1	18	103
1701–10	3	12	1	11	2		2	31
1711–19	2	5	1	4			1	13
1720–24		4	1	2				7
Total	52	199	106	147	56	3	98	661

Viet (Tongking), bringing in supplies of chiefly Japanese silver many times larger than state revenue from internal taxes. Since this increased trade revenue coincided with disruptive warfare against the southern Viet regime of Cochin-China, and apparent sharp declines in agrarian population and revenue (see below), the effect in changing the orientation of Dai Viet toward a more cosmopolitan outlook was especially marked. After 1684, however, direct China-Japan trade became possible, albeit under the tight controls of the Nagasaki system, and Dai Viet's final maritime moment ended.

Cambodia also did well briefly in the 1690s, after the 1688 revolution in Siam disrupted trade there, but the overall trend was relentlessly down. An increasingly restrictive Nagasaki quota system in principle limited vessels from Southeast Asia to ten a year in 1689 (of which three from Cochin-China) and five in 1715, although Table 7.2 shows there was a lag in implementation. Taken together with Spanish and Dutch data, the Nagasaki figures well reflect the extent to which the leading Mainland ports suffered.

Tempting as it is to seek a single cause in climate, environment, silver, or aggressive Dutch monopolies, none of these will do on their own. While changes in global climate and trade damaged the long-term environment for Southeast Asian commerce, there were numerous specific setbacks that had their own causes, whether or not ultimately linked in complex ways with global phenomena. Individual actors too had a decisive impact on the outcomes, with incompetent or tyrannical rulers bringing ruin on their people as frequently as brilliant ones achieved success.

GLOBAL CLIMATE AND LOCAL CRISES

Progress has been rapid in recent years in the understanding of global climate changes. It has become clear that what is "normal" weather for one generation or even one century may not be normal in the longer life-span of the planet. As shown in Chapter 2, tree rings and stalagmite sequences have confirmed that Mainland Southeast Asia, like China, enjoyed benign conditions for agriculture during the warm medieval climate anomaly between 900 and 1250, and that worsening conditions thereafter contributed to the collapse of the temple-building *nagara* of Pagan and Angkor. Another period of climate amelioration in 1470–1560 allowed for substantial new growth in northern rice-growing societies such as Sukhothai, Chiang Mai, Vientiane, and Dai Viet, though even more so in the new port-states also able to profit from the great rise in seaborne commerce, like Pegu, Ayutthaya, and the new Cambodian capital at Phnom Penh. The Eurasian cooling which set in about 1570, and produced the little ice age in the mid-seventeenth century, then severely disrupted climate, and hence agriculture and population, in the northern part of Southeast Asia as in China. From about 1700, on the other hand, the global climate warmed gradually, though with an acceleration in the twentieth century. Major short-term disruptions to this pattern were caused by volcanic eruptions and solar irregularities.

The temperature swings in the island tropics have been shown to be less than those in the great Eurasian landmass, with only about a 0.6 degree rise in temperatures between the early 1800s and the 1950s, one third the average in temperate zones. The seventeenth-century drop in temperatures should also have been less extreme in maritime Southeast Asia, possibly aiding the rise of its port-polities in the age of commerce at the expense of rice-dependent concentrations in the north. Short-term climatic variations in the Islands caused by volcanic eruptions and by the cyclical El Niño were particularly acute in the seventeenth century.

The Islands were and are the site of the world's most destructive volcanism and tectonic upheavals. Increasingly sophisticated dating techniques, such as ice cores as well as tree rings, have made possible the charting of short-term fluctuations in global climate linked to massive volcanic eruptions which create a dust veil around the planet, cooling temperatures and preventing crops from ripening. The volcanoes of Southeast Asia tend to be both the biggest in explosivity, and the most dangerous for the planet as a whole, since their sulphur-rich dust veil disperses around the whole populated part of the planet whereas northerly and southerly eruptions affect chiefly their own latitudes.

The most extreme years of global cold in the seventeenth century, in 1601–4, 1641–3, 1665–8, 1676, and 1695–9, were probably caused by major eruptions at the beginning of each such period, as of the little ice age as a whole. Although most of the new data has come from the northern hemisphere, the majority of the eruptions big enough to have such effects were located in Southeast Asia's Islands. Like the better-known Tambora and Krakatau in the nineteenth century, the eruptions that affected global climate had their most disastrous effects closer to home in the Islands, both in killing tens of thousands immediately, and in darkening skies and spoiling crops over a much wider area. The first of these global crisis periods, which in Europe and Russia extended throughout 1584–1610 but with a nadir around 1601, has been attributed to two Javanese eruptions uncertainly dated 1586 and 1593. Possibly more important was a massive eruption of Billy Mitchell volcano on Bougainville Island to the north of New Guinea, which has been approximately carbon-dated to 1580 ± 20. In Tongking the years 1586–97 were the worst noted in the annals for crop failures, starvation, and disease, following a similar pattern to Northern Hemisphere crises.

For the Indonesian Archipelago the most useful tree-ring data is still that of Berlage in Java, which shows below-average growth for the whole period 1598–1679 but acutely so in several patches. The first of these was in 1605–16, corresponding with severe droughts in the Indonesian archipelago in 1606–13, and the most notable indigenous record of a famine in the Aceh capital around 1604–5 when "many of the people died" (Raniri 1643/1966, 34). The second was in 1633–8, also coinciding with three of the driest years in the whole 759-year sequence of the recent Viet Nam tree-ring study, in 1633–5 (Buckley et al. 2010). This was presumably the cause of a prolonged drought and crop failure reported for both Siam and Bali in 1633, and a drought in Maluku in 1635. The eruption of Mount Parker in Mindanao in January 1641 spread ash over an area extending to Maluku, Luzon, and Borneo that very likely caused crop failures and famine. The worst period in the Archipelago (but not the

Mainland), both in terms of tree rings and reports of famine, disease, and crop failure, occurred between 1660 and 1665. The cause here is unclear, though a possible culprit is an uncertainly dated eruption of Long Island off the New Guinea coast. In Tongking (and Hainan) the strong El Niño of 1681 brought a terrible drought and crop failure in 1681–2, with so many starving that "bodies covered the roads," as the court chronicle put it. This was followed by an appalling epidemic that killed a third of the population over much of Tongking in 1682–3, and also spread to Cochin-China.

A final geological factor that must be considered in Island Southeast Asia is the record of major earthquakes and tsunamis. Research since the giant earthquake off Northwest Sumatra that produced its deadly 2004 tsunami has established that in addition to the known earthquakes and tsunamis that destroyed Padang in 1697 and 1797, there were major events in the middle of the seventeenth century. The Aceh capital was hit by a tsunami or storm-surge in January 1660, which killed over a thousand people and ended its golden age as a major Indian Ocean port. The historical record on the exposed south coast of Java is very weak, but the most reliably dated Javanese chronicle suggests that a tsunami in 1618 caused sufficient damage to have the Mataram capital moved and the myth launched about the powerful but dangerous queen of the southern ocean (*Ratu Kidul*), who provided power and legitimacy to the kings of Mataram by ritually mating with them.

The end of Manila's golden age was dramatically marked by the earthquake of 1645 that destroyed most of its substantial buildings. This and an earlier quake of 1619 have been estimated to be the most severe (about Magnitude 8) of any earthquakes to strike the Philippines between 1600 and 1900. Dutch Batavia (Jakarta) experienced its most severe earthquake in January 1699. Forty buildings collapsed and almost all houses were damaged. Since known large Java earthquakes have all been centered in the subduction zone off Java's south coast, the damage to population centers in the interior and south must have been greater than in Batavia, especially as it was the uprooted trees that came down from the uplands and blocked the rivers and waterways of the city that caused the most long-term damage.

These climatic and tectonic difficulties seem the likeliest overall explanation for population declines in the mid-seventeenth century, even though civil wars and foreign conquests might appear persuasive in a single location. Reliable population data are scarce, but those we have from Spanish and Dutch censuses of areas they partially controlled show dramatic declines. These amount to a loss of 35% between 1591 and 1655 in the lowland Philippines (Luzon and Visayas), of 17% between 1634 and 1674 in the clove-producing Amboina area (Ambon and Lease), perhaps 37% in the same period in adjacent Seram, about 70% in Ternate over the century ending in 1680, and perhaps a similar catastrophic drop in Minahassa (northeast Sulawesi) between 1644 and 1669. In the Javanese heartland of Mataram there was also a steady downward trend between 1651 and 1755 in the number of households (*cacah*) reported for taxation (Reid 1993, 294–7). Taken overall, this was a dangerous time for agricultural populations dependent on the weather, as well as for the commercial centers facing Dutch monopoly pressures on their trade.

POLITICAL CONSEQUENCES OF THE CRISIS

Taken overall, the seventeenth-century crisis turned many Southeast Asian societies away from reliance on the international market, and reduced the dominance of urban and cosmopolitan factors in them. As the gunpowder states lost the advantages that had propelled them to a brittle prominence – trade wealth, firearms, international allies – they responded in two different ways. In much of the Archipelago, the port-states lost their newly acquired leverage over their hinterlands, with a consequent re-dispersion of power among myriad river-chiefs and lineage units. The memory of founder-kings and conquerors from the age of commerce nevertheless played a role in the growing cultural coherence of such regions. In states which had already developed compact populations in irrigated rice-growing areas, such as Java and several Mainland societies, there was a trend to greater self-sufficiency and internal integration, to some extent making up in their own hinterlands for the losses internationally. In the lowland Philippines a Manila-centered state was created during the age of commerce, which survived the crisis that followed only in a more self-sufficient and Filipinized form. Church, state, and commercial metropolis lost much of their power to transform.

The large Southeast Asian port-cities that dominated the long sixteenth century experienced more than the usual blows in the seventeenth. Cities sacked in earlier times had usually been rebuilt elsewhere, but seventeenth-century setbacks to Asian-ruled cities such as Pegu, Banten, Aceh, Makassar, Brunei, and Patani were of longer-term significance. Euro-Chinese enclaves like Batavia and Manila could fill the role of Asian cities in long-distance trade, but not in cultural and political life. The indigenous population of the Euro-Chinese cities was small, detached from local elites, of generally low status, and in Batavia's case mostly slave or ex-slave. These cities were certainly the site of some remarkable cultural experimentation, but they could not lead the local societies.

In other parts of the world, notably Britain, the Netherlands, and Japan, the seventeenth-century crisis encouraged a trend toward coherent nation-states. It may be, as Lieberman (2003) argues, that the Mainland states – Burma, Siam, and the two Viet Nams – also moved in a different direction from the Islands from this point, developing a more self-contained internal market on the pattern of Tokugawa Japan, and more standardized forms of secular and religious authority. Burma's foreign trade was at considerably lower levels throughout the seventeenth century than in the sixteenth, and in 1632 its capital was re-established as far up the Irrawaddy and away from oceanic trade as it could be, at Ava near modern Mandalay. In Siam and Cochin-China, too, foreign trade played a reduced part in state revenue after the 1680s. Nevertheless, commercialization appears to have continued in all these states internally, increasing social differentiation while making it easier for the crown to build an impersonal revenue base. Whatever stability was reached in these states was fragile, however. In marked contrast with Tokugawa Japan or even Qing China, all the dynasties of mainland Southeast Asia fell in the middle of the eighteenth century. Part of the reason was external and internal warring. A more fundamental problem, however, was the failure to maintain an adequate revenue base once foreign trade ceased to provide its core.

The first of the gunpowder states to collapse was the greatest of them, the empire built by King Bayinnaung of Burma from his commercially successful capital at Pegu. His successor Nandabayin (1581–99) drove the Mon subjects of the capital to rebellion by his demands to sustain the overextended military. This led to further ferocious repression by the desperate ruler, with the ports of Cosmir (Bassein) and Martaban the first to be destroyed. From 1597 the imperial capital was under siege by Nandabayin's many enemies, who completed the destruction of the coastal cities in 1599. A Jesuit source soon after claimed that the whole population had been slaughtered or captured, or had fled, with 240,000 Mons taking refuge in Siam, Laos, and Arakan. "It seems that the whole country is nothing but desert, and that there is nobody left in this kingdom of Pegu" (du Jarric 1608, 626). The Mon merchants were no longer vital participants in the Indian Ocean trade system, except insofar as they could still trade as minorities out of Siam or Arakan. The port of Syriam was initially spared the general destruction. It was governed from 1600 to 1614 by the Portuguese Philip de Brito, initially as a mercenary soldier of the Arakan king, but eventually as ruler of another independent port-state.

The new period of Burma's history (1606–1752) is misleadingly called "Second Toungoo" because later chroniclers sought to stress the continuity from Bayinnaung. It was nevertheless a classic case of the vernacularization described in Chapter 8. Anaukhpetlun (1606–28) began the Bama patronage of the hitherto Mon-sponsored Shwedagon pagoda in Rangoon, and gradually a new port under his control arose around it. A Buddhist reaction enabled him to have de Brito killed in Syriam. He and his brother and successor Thalun (1629–48) were above all concerned to secure the rice-producing power base of the upper Irrawaddy tributaries. They focused attention not on the lost empire but on the Bama irrigated rice-basket near to the new capital at Ava. In this core zone they forced the tributary princely lineages established by Bayinnaung to move to their court, and replaced them in effective control by town governors (*myò-wun*) replaceable by the palace. Spies began to be sent out by the court to ensure their loyalty. A more modest, integrated, and Bama state gradually emerged, and with it a society that can begin to be called Burmese. The overland and river trade to Yunnan became as important as the now-diminished maritime arm. The British and Dutch Companies, now the biggest players in the Indian Ocean trade, lost interest in Burma and closed their offices there in 1657 and 1679, respectively.

Siam profited from the collapse of Pegu and Mon/Burman maritime trade, moving quickly to dominate both sides of the Peninsula through the west coast port of Tennasserim. For most of the century until 1688 Ayutthaya became the biggest entrepôt of Mainland Southeast Asia, attracting Muslim, Chinese, Portuguese, British, and Dutch traders alike.

The seventeenth-century kings who rebuilt Siam after the disaster of Bayinnaung's conquest nevertheless sought the kind of internal absolutism that used the wealth of foreign trade and weapons to crush opposition. The reign of Naresuan the warrior-king (1590–1605) "was the most militant and severe of any which was ever known in Siam … he killed and had killed by law more than 80,000 people … He was the first to make the mandarins come creeping before the king and lie continually with their faces downward … The mandarins lived in great fear of His Majesty" (van Vliet 1640/2005, 229). This form of absolutism in the capital was brought to a peak under Prasat Thong (1629–56) and Narai (1659–88), portrayed by foreign observers as having terrorized the old elite and robbed them of their property while appointing low-born people of ability to official positions. In the manner of other gunpowder rulers with brittle authority, their absolutism was little effective at any distance from the capital, and depended for its success on the wealth generated by foreigners.

These capable kings played the game well and presided over the last of the glittering cosmopolitan courts to fall. The end came only in April 1688, when King Narai's dependence on French soldiers, British port-governors, and his Greek-born minister Phaulkon became too much for his Buddhist subjects. The master of the royal elephants took advantage of anti-foreign sentiment to seize the palace, expel the French, and kill Phaulkon and two potential successors to Narai, who himself died three months later. This coup leader became King Phetracha (1688–1709), under whom foreign trade in all directions was much reduced, though it gradually revived in the eighteenth century as a predominately Chinese affair. Siam too focused on its own internal coherence around a Theravada Buddhist paradigm.

In the Islands, the societies most exposed to the forceful methods of the VOC and its competitors developed an aversion to the export products that seemed to attract both violence and instability. Surviving epic poetry from the pepper-growing areas testifies to this reaction against pepper. It brought wealth but could not replace rice in times of crisis. Greater self-sufficiency seemed desirable to many states, as well as necessary to those who could no longer afford cloth or rice imports.

The gunpowder states that had been the dramatic beneficiaries of the long sixteenth century boom were the most reliant on trade and external support, and therefore the most vulnerable in the crisis. The port-states like Demak, Japara, and Surabaya on the north coast of Java lost their life-blood in the early 1600s when the VOC took over most of the lucrative spice trade from Maluku. This left them vulnerable to dominance by the agricultural interior, and by states for which trade was a minor priority. The great builder of Mataram (with its capital near modern Yogyakarta), Sultan Agung (1613–46), ended the independence of the port-states, conquering one after another until the strongest complex of ports in the Surabaya area fell in 1625. Sultan Agung apparently intended to unite the whole of Java for the first time, but his progress was stopped at Dutch Batavia, which defeated two massive Mataram forces sent against it in 1628 and 1629. Thereafter Agung made a kind of peace with the Dutch, interpreting VOC envoys as tribute-bearers, and professing to be uninterested in their commercial concerns. Instead he patronized a distinctive Javanese court culture, blending some of the cosmopolitan Islam from the port-states he conquered with the Hindu-Buddhist sacred places, the cults of volcano and tsunami, and the agricultural animism of the interior and south (Chapter 8). The political unity of the Javanese-speaking area was of very short duration, as the tyranny and paranoia of Agung's successor Amangkurat I (1646–77) sparked rebellion and Dutch intervention that progressively fragmented Java politically after 1670. The cultural legacy of Sultan Agung's reign was, however, much more durable.

Mataram's rise left Banten as the last independent port in Java, less vulnerable because it was protected from Mataram expansion by Batavia, and faced no interior threat from the scattered Sundanese-speaking population of the west Java uplands. Its trade, moreover, was securely based on its own supplies of pepper, for as long as it could use the support of Muslim, Chinese, English, Portuguese, and Danish traders against the constant threat of Dutch monopoly intentions. In the 1620s and 1630s, Banten was frequently blockaded by the VOC, sharply reducing both pepper exports and food imports, which convinced the once-wealthy city that it needed more self-sufficiency. Under the forceful Sultan Abdulfatah Ageng (1651–82) Banten became the principal resort for all who resisted Dutch monopolies, and an embassy it sent to London in 1682 was funded for a three months' stay by the East India Company, anxious about its exclusion from the pepper-market by the Dutch. Lionized by London Society, the two senior figures in the 30-strong party were received at Windsor by Charles II and knighted as Sir Ahmad and Sir Abdul. This could not prevent internal conflicts and Dutch intervention from defeating Sultan Ageng in a bitter war of 1682–3. Subsequent rulers were "Company's kings", pledged to deliver all their pepper to the VOC at fixed prices. Banten remained distinct from its Sundanese hinterland, Javanese in language but not in politics or religion. Its Islam was oriented more to Mecca than to Mataram.

The other port-states around the Java Sea were all seen as rivals in the spice trade by the VOC, until either forced or coopted into the Company project. Makassar was the greatest of these in the first half of the seventeenth century, expertly playing Portuguese, Dutch, English, and Muslim cards under the guidance of Karaeng Matoaya and his son Pattenggalloang, and keeping its internal coalition intact. When the latter died in 1654, and the impetuous young Sultan Hasanuddin of Goa decided to rule alone without the partnership of a chancellor from Tallo', Makassar suffered from all the problems of a brittle gunpowder state. Rebellions against his authoritarian style broke out in Bone, Mandar, and Buton, enabling the Dutch to attack the capital and take one of its southern approach forts in 1660. One of the Bugis rebel leaders, Arung Palakka, unsuccessful in defending Bone on that occasion, sought help and arms from Batavia. In alliance with the VOC, his Bugis forces were able to defeat a large Makassar force in 1667, first at Buton and then Makassar itself. The sultan was forced to sign the Bongaya Treaty whereby all non-Dutch Europeans had to leave, and Makassar gave up its loophole for the non-Dutch spice trade.

The fall of Banten and Makassar left the VOC as master of the Java Sea by 1685, able to exclude major competitors in the buying of pepper and other tropical produce and thereby to reduce incentives for producers. Dutch expeditions succeeded in destroying Palembang in 1657 and its neighbor Jambi in 1687, in each case tightening its exclusion of other buyers. The Riau Archipelago to the south of Singapore profited from its place on the route to China to accommodate Chinese, English, and Bugis traders through the eighteenth century, though periodically destroyed by Dutch attack or internal conflict. Aceh was the only major Island port not to suffer conquest or destruction by the end of the seventeenth century, and continued to benefit from Indian, Chinese, European, and Bugis trade. Its remarkable experiment with female rule in the period 1641–99 proved successful in maintaining internal order and a port friendly to commerce, but it could no longer defend its more distant possessions. The 1660 flood event (above) did not help. Both the tin of the Peninsula and the pepper of the west Sumatra coast passed out of its control in the 1660s. This diminished the capacity of the queens to control their own hinterland. Their male successors were even less successful in the eighteenth century.

The stage of gunpowder kings of great wealth and brittle power was decisively over. The long eighteenth century would provide opportunities for a greater range of small traders in the economy, and for home-grown leadership in religion, culture, and politics.

NOTE

1   I am grateful to Li Tana and the late Yoneo Ishii for readings of Japanese data compiled by Iwao Seiichi

[8] VERNACULAR IDENTITIES, 1660–1820

EIGHTEENTH-CENTURY CONSOLIDATION

Long-distance trade, universalist religion, foreign borrowing, and gunpowder warfare all began to yield more dangers than opportunities in the seventeenth-century crisis just described. Despite the varied religious and political results, the region as a whole experienced a vernacular response in reaction to the cosmopolitanism of the age of commerce. In the new period, cultural identities consolidated which enable us to speak of Bama, Thai, Vietnamese, Khmer, Acehnese, Bugis, Javanese, and Balinese as coherent identities, more enduring than dynasties that claimed to rule them. If the gunpowder empires had brought together diverse peoples sheltering under a common power center, their successors focused their primary ambitions on religion and culture, seeking to make up as exemplary centers what the gunpowder empires had lost in military power.

The more developed state of Japanese historiography on the self-reliant Edo era after the country's closure (*sakoku*) in the 1630s makes this an interesting model for Southeast Asia's own transition. No Southeast Asian ruler had the power to monopolize violence and exclude foreign influence like the Tokugawa shogunate, but many sought to move in the same vernacular direction. Japan's success was partly theirs, in bridging the gulf between city and hinterland and establishing internal economic, religious, and cultural coherence.

Discussions of Edo society were long dominated in Japan by a neo-Marxist paradigm that labeled it "feudal," and therefore still awaiting its bourgeois revolution. The term "Early Modern" has now become more acceptable a way to link the Edo experience with that of the rest of the world, and the same is true for Southeast Asia. The Early Modern in effect comprised two stages, in both of which the world was unified enough to be affected by new technologies for war and transportation, new foods (see Chapter 10), universal religions, global disease pools, and a recognition that every society was in effect competing against others. But whereas the universal cosmopolis of the long sixteenth

A History of Southeast Asia: Critical Crossroads, First Edition. Anthony Reid.
© 2015 Anthony Reid. Published 2015 by John Wiley & Sons, Ltd.

century was one of frenetic innovation, borrowing, conflict, and competition, in the long eighteenth many Asian societies drew defensive lines against further borrowing, concentrating rather on internal coherence and homogenization. For Asia, therefore, we might usefully subdivide the Early Modern era at some point around 1650 into an earlier cosmopolitan and later consolidating phase.

In the long eighteenth century the societies in question developed literary cultures, unifying religious syntheses, and histories that celebrated the warlike conquerors of the gunpowder age even as the political heritage of absolutism was rejected or lost. Economies became somewhat less dependent on the vagaries of the international market, but more monetized and marketized internally as the cities became more dependent on their internal exchange roles than their international ones. Multi-ethnic slave populations, brought to the prosperous port-cities in their thousands in the age of commerce, were largely integrated into a vernacular idiom. The different political conditions described in Chapter 7, with Mainland and Philippine polities consolidating while Island ones fragmented, should not obscure the vernacular cultural turn that pervaded Southeast Asia and beyond.

RELIGIOUS SYNCRETISM AND LOCALIZATION

The type of polarizing reformism prominent during the age of commerce was periodically revived thereafter until peaking again as the world became more directly unified during the high modernism of the twentieth century. In between these two phases, however, the self-strengthening phase of the Early Modern witnessed some remarkable achievements of synthesis and syncretization, helping to unify societies that had been polarized by external influence. The gunpowder kings (including Spanish governors of Manila) had often enforced universal religion to justify their expansion, but in this second phase religious networks were more autonomous, and rulers needed to honor them in order to share in their charisma.

The survival of Southeast Asian religion, and its understated but effective incorporation into the religious syntheses of the long eighteenth century, has a key gendered dimension. The marginal place of women in all the three scriptural religions that advanced in the age of commerce makes it difficult to understand how such religions could have been accepted in Southeast Asian societies distinguished by the economic autonomy of women and their centrality in ritual life. We know that female shamans were among the strongest defenders of the old religion in the Philippines and other parts of the Island world. But the syntheses that took hold in the longer run allowed women to continue attending to key concerns of healing, childbirth, and agricultural fertility by ritually manipulating spirits. The male specialists of the new religions could be avoided when strict, but asked to add their blessing when accommodating. Female ancestral spirits and rice goddesses remained influential figures, and sometimes the tombs of the wives of Islamic saints received the most offerings from women seeking safe childbirth. When sternly male official Viet Confucianism took over southern areas where the

Cham goddess Po Nagar was previously worshipped, it was obliged to allow Confucianized goddesses to take her place as healer and protector. A British vistor to southern Viet Nam in the early 1800s could still be struck by the number of "priestesses" (spirit-mediums) he encountered.

Since Islam demonstrated the vernacular trend most dramatically, let us begin there.

Islam

The polarization described in Chapter 7 reached a peak in the reign of Sultan Iskandar Thani of Aceh (1636–41). He was a devout Pahang-born Malay prince, brought captive to Aceh after the conquest of his homeland, and married to the daughter of Aceh's tyrannical sun-king, Iskandar Muda. That king had imposed Islam according to his own tastes. He rationalized the law in an Islamic direction so long as it did not interfere with his own absolutism, but in theology favored the mystic monism of Hamzah Fansuri represented at his court by the Sufi master Shamsud-din al-Samatrani (d.1630). Iskandar Thani, however, sought legitimacy through patronizing foreign *ulama* who identified themselves with the universal orthodoxy of the Persian Sunni and Shafi'i theologian al-Ghazali. Chief among them was the prolific Gujarati-born theologian Nuru'd-din ar-Raniri, a stern upholder of what he held to be the literal demands of the *shari'a*. Raniri had tried to make his home in Aceh under the previous sultan, but found him too wedded to his Sufi opponents, the circle of Shamsuddin. He quickly returned after the first Iskandar's death to become the chief religious authority and adviser of the second.

Under Raniri's influence Sultan Iskandar Thani enforced a narrow view of *shari'a* even at the expense of Aceh's internal harmony and cosmopolitan prosperity. Chinese traders were excluded from Aceh because of their pork-eating habits. A Portuguese peace mission was offered the alternative of conversion to Islam or death, resulting in the trampling of several to death by elephants, including the group's French-born priest, Pierre Berthelot, subsequently beatified as martyr by the Catholic Church. The sultan had the books of Hamzah Fansuri and Shamsud-din al-Samatrani burned in front of the great mosque, and invoked the Islamic *murtad* (apostasy) laws to condemn to death those of their disciples who refused to renounce the proscribed views, including the popular Sheikh Jamaluddin.

These divisive interpretations were emphatically rejected after the death of Iskandar Thani in 1641. The commercial elite that dominated the city's commerce had been terrorized by the first Iskandar's absolutism and preference for foreigners, but were shocked when Raniri and the second Iskandar proved both cruel and bad for business. They hoped to correct both excesses by placing a woman on the throne, daughter of one Iskandar and widow of the other, defying Raniri's strictures against female rule. The results were so satisfactory that they enthroned three subsequent women, together covering the period 1641–99. Since they emulated the strategy of other nearby Muslim port-sultanates at the peak of their commercial eminence, notably Patani (from 1564) and the Maldives (fourteenth century), we might ask whether the conventional disbarring of women from exercising religious authority was seen as an advantage for the queens by contrast with the pressures of office Raniri had been able to impose on Iskandar Thani. It may have been seen as a means of effectively legitimating, by default of a sole religious authority, the pluralism that was essential to stable commerce. Under the queens the Chinese returned, a Franciscan mission served the small Christian community, and Aceh became the only Southeast Asian maritime state to survive the VOC and the seventeenth-century crisis with its independence wholly intact.

Hearing of the death of Raniri's protector, a Minangkabau disciple of the executed sheikh, Sayf al-Rijal, returned to Aceh from his studies in Arabia, and bitterly attacked Raniri's views and actions. As Raniri himself put it:

> Sayf al-Rijal … held debates with us over the matters which had been discussed before. We ask: "How could you approve of the people who assert that 'man is Allah and Allah is man'?" He answers: "This is my belief and that of the people of Mecca and Medina." Then his words prevail, and many people return to the wrong belief (Raniri, *Fath al-Mubin*, as translated in Azra 2004, 60–1).

Aceh opinion clearly favored Sayf, and Raniri was forced to flee back to Gujarat in 1643. This opened the way for a new consensus personified in Aceh's most beloved Sufi master, Sheikh Abdul-Rauf al-Singkili (c.1617–84). He had abandoned his native Aceh for Arabia after Raniri's witch-hunt, and used his time there to study both Sufism and law with the most prominent scholars of the day. He returned in 1660 under the first queen, who quickly appointed him the chief religious authority. His own copious writings never condemned either Hamzah Fansuri or Raniri, but sought a synthesis that would reconcile a commitment to *shari'a* with the appreciation of the inner knowledge of the mystics. It was probably he who appealed to one of his teachers in Mecca, the prominent authority Ibrahim al-Kurani, for a ruling as to whether it was legitimate for a sultan to have executed a *wujuddiyah* (monist) Sufi accused of heresy by another *ulama*, when the Sufi in question responded that he could not repent as his argument had not been understood. He received the answer he appears to have hoped for, that such executions were very grave errors, and that a statement that could be interpreted in multiple ways could not be held as evidence of heresy.

Although religious courts continued to function in several port-cities, there is little evidence in Aceh or elsewhere after the 1660s of the harsh application of *shari'a* laws, or of executions on religious grounds. The decline of absolutist port-rulers reduced the coercive power of the state in religious matters, and allowed religious solidarities to center rather in the mystical *tarekat* (Sufi orders), notably the Qadariyyah and Shatariyya. These encouraged an inner piety expressed in ecstatic chanting and rituals at the graves of the great saints and founders of mysticism, particularly the great local sheikhs, Abdul-Rauf in Aceh and Yusuf of Makassar, and the nine *wali* of Java.

In Java the sixteenth century had seen much conflict between coastal and cosmopolitan Muslims and old-school Javanese. A guide to Islamic behavior of that period, probably from Demak, warned against honoring idols, denying one's Islam, or suggesting it made no difference. It condemned new Muslims who killed unbelievers only to take their property rather than for truly religious motives (Drewes 1978, 15, 35–9). In the seventeenth century, by contrast, the coastal centers of international Islam were destroyed or marginalized while a remarkable synthesis of distinctively Javanese Islam was created in the interior by selectively borrowing from the defeated ports. This synthesis became established in the warlike reign of Sultan Agung of Mataram (r.1613–46), who unified the Javanese-speaking area for the first and only time by conquering the coastal Muslim port-states one by one from his then-rustic base in what became Yogyakarta.

Despite the Hindu subject matter of its stories from the Mahabharata and the Ramayana, the Javanese shadow-puppet theater (*wayang kulit*) appears to have developed its modern form in those urban crucibles of Islamic innovation. It may have been a cultural compromise to avoid depicting human forms in deference to Islamic prohibition, but instead show their shadows. As elite patronage of Javanese performance moved to the inland capital of Mataram, the stories of Arjuna and Bima continued to enthral Javanese audiences, and to convey the deeper inner truths for which the world of Islamic legal obligation was the outer shell. Monist philosophers equated the puppeteer and story-teller (*dalang*) with absolute being or God, the puppets as relative being, and the screen as the outer world of essences where formal religion had its place. The screen on which the shadows played thereby represented the hiddenness of the ultimate reality of unity.

It was after the disastrous defeat of Sultan Agung's attack on Dutch Batavia in 1629 that he turned his greatest attention to creating an integrated and self-sufficient culture within his realm. He came to accept the Dutch as coastal tributaries, concerned with the international trade that provided exotic luxuries to his court but no longer of more substantial interest. The sultan brought to his capital the Surabaya prince and exemplary *literatus* Pangeran Pekik, famous for rendering the new Muslim knowledge into elegant Javanese poetry. Agung coopted Pekik's charisma by strategic intermarriages between the two families, and gave him the task of domesticating and Javanizing the most sacred centers of coastal Islam – Ampel, Giri, and Tembayat. A hybrid architectural style was developed for these sacred places and for the royal cemetery Agung built for himself at Imogiri, giving the entrances to the holiest Muslim centers a Balinese external appearance to modern eyes (Figure 8.1). Sultan Agung also authorized a uniquely complex Javanese calendar, incorporating the Islamic cycle of weeks and lunar months into the solar Indian-derived *Saka* calendar. Many former Buddhist retreats (*pesantren*) were Islamized as autonomous centers of study, meditation, and often martial arts, guaranteed immunity from taxes and levies like their Hindu-Buddhist predecessors.

Sultan Agung's post-1629 kingship model, followed according to their lights by his successors, was to focus much of his creative energy on symbolic assertions of his essential role as king-priest (*prabu pandita*). The chronicles show him as a supernatural figure who could magically pray in Mecca every Friday, and patronized the newly Islamized holy hills of Java like Giri and Tembayat.

Figure 8.1 Seventeenth-century grave of a Sufi saint at Tembayat, Central Java. Source: Photograph by the author.

At the same time, however, he could control the spiritual forces of Java through his ritual couplings with the tsunami-inspired Queen of the South Seas (*Ratu Kidul*) and rituals to the spirits of the volcanoes. The older martial traditions described by Portuguese writers were subsumed into an inner mystic quest to control unseen spiritual forces. What Merle Ricklefs (2006) calls the "mystic synthesis" that successfully brought virtually all Javanese into the new religion, still had to survive repeated challenges from a more literal legalistic form, and might not have been able to do so had not the Dutch presence on the coast served to disempower its bearers. Agung's tyrannical successor Amangkurat I notoriously had 5,000 Islamic leaders massacred at his capital to control what he saw as the threat, and other kings only held off the challenge with military help from Batavia.

The Dutch takeover of the high points of commerce had the effect throughout the Archipelago of marginalizing the international Muslims for whom the *shari'a* was a helpful common factor and strengthening a local aristocracy. In south Sulawesi the fall of Makassar to the VOC in 1669 re-established the complex autonomies of the Bugis and Makassarese nobilities, who established their own mystic synthesis. Their lineages continued to be regarded as descended from the upperworld, and surrounded with supernatural mystique. Transsexual *bissus* remained to celebrate their enthronements, weddings, and funerals. While pork was abolished and elaborate death rituals (still present among the upland Toraja) wholly Islamized, other rituals of the kingship, agriculture, and the life-cycle survived with an Islamic addition. In each state a *kadi* and an imam for the state mosque were appointed, though usually these were members of the nobility who could ensure that Islam sustained rather than undermined hierarchy and custom. Like the Javanese kings who managed to claim descent both from the Adam and Abraham of Islamic tradition and from Hindu-Javanese deities, their Bugis counterparts merged the gods of the pre-Islamic La Galigo cycle into Islamic lineages and made the culture hero Sawerigading into a prophet foretelling the Quran. There is an apocryphal story in some Islamic texts that Sheikh Yusuf returned to Makassar to preach a purer Islam, but the rulers were committed to their synthesis in which gambling at cock-fights, drinking, and opium smoking were part of the ritual feasting designed to please the ancestors and ensure their benevolence to the living (Azra 2004, 94).

The eighteenth century was not lacking reformist scholars who promoted the more mainstream Sufi interpretations of al-Ghazali, and criticized cooperation with the Dutch. But as communication between Southeast Asia and the Middle East became more difficult, they were more likely to remain in Arabia seeking to influence events through their writings. The Dutch and English ships that dominated the Indian Ocean long-distance trade in the late seventeenth century had often taken paying passengers on pilgrimage to Mecca, but in 1716 the VOC prohibited its ships from bringing such pilgrims home because they began to fear Mecca-inspired plots against themselves. Abd al Samad of Palembang (c.1704–88) was perhaps the most prominent such scholar, whose writings permeated the Archipelago in the nineteenth century as contacts became easier. In the absence of the gunpowder kings as patrons of an expanding Islam, three overlapping networks provided non-coercive forms of leadership. Firstly, scholars and their students formed a growing interconnected ecumene of literacy in Malay, which in turn helped to build a written corpus of hitherto oral poetry and epic stories. After the Sultanate of Patani was finally crushed by Siam in 1786, Sheikh Da'ud bin 'Abd Allah led an exodus which proved seminal in establishing a network of scholars and their students in the Peninsula and beyond. Secondly, the Sufi orders brought to Southeast Asia in the seventeenth century expanded their scope as they localized in the eighteenth. And finally, Hadhrami Arabs began in the eighteenth century their great emigration to Southeast Asia, marrying locally and mixing trade with Islamic teaching.

Southeast Asia is rightly celebrated for its capacity to retain diversity, in human society as in its flora and fauna. In religious terms, however, this point must be qualified by the "frontier" quality of scriptural religions. Diversity inhered in the myriad ways in which the local was combined with the universal, the highly plural spirit world with revealed scripture. Universal religion itself, however, was strangely uniform. The inherent diversity of Middle Eastern Islam, with its entrenched Sunni and Shi'a sects and its four schools of law, was exported to India but not Southeast Asia. Because Islam played the role of external legitimator of local eminence, it was perceived as singular even when practiced as plural. Shi'ite rituals and texts found their way Below the Winds, but whenever orthodoxy became an issue for states it was purely Sunni with the Shafi'i school of law. The prominence of Arabs from Hadhramaut in mediating Middle Eastern complexities to Southeast Asia may be the key reason for this. In the long term this would hold dangers for the acceptance of diversity. Independent Indonesia officially recognized two Christianities as permissible for its citizens, but only one Islam. Only in the twenty-first century, however, did the quest for universal orthodoxy make this a problem.

Christianity

The Christian communities that had developed under Portuguese auspices in Southeast Asia saw few Catholic priests after the Dutch conquered Melaka in 1641. The first VOC priority was to expel Portuguese and priests from all its conquests around the Archipelago – notably the large communities in Makassar and Ambon (Maluku). Only a tiny Portuguese elite withdrew to Goa or Portugal. Most faced the choice of remaining in Dutch-controlled cities by accepting the Reformed (Calvinist) official faith of the VOC, or moving to Asian-ruled areas such as Siam, Cambodia, Burma, or the southeastern archipelago. The best-known refuge was Ayutthaya (Siam), which became a new center for predominately French missionaries to train Asian priests for East and Southeast Asia (though not the Spanish-exclusive Philippines). In Siam itself, however, there were only about 2,000 Catholics in the 1660s and only a few more in the 1810s, when a more peaceful modern period of expansion began. More influential in the long term were hybrid communities known as Topaz or "black Portuguese" in Flores and Timor. From bases first in Solor, then Larantuka (Flores) and Lifao (Timor), they established local alliances that the Dutch largely ignored because they were almost totally devoid of priests or of Portuguese officialdom. Their lay organization, a *confraria* (brotherhood) devoted to Mary, retained a vernacular Portuguese-Malay synthesis of Catholicism into the era of modern missions in the late nineteenth century.

The Christians of the Philippines, too, were left much more to their own devices after the phenomenal transformation of the first 60 years of mission. This conversion process has been claimed to be the most rapid and profound anywhere in Christian history, partly through the insistence that converts would not be baptized unless they agreed to a subsequent ongoing course of instruction. There was no expansion of the 300 European priests in the islands in the early 1600s despite their vastly extended responsibilities for the mushrooming population for whom they represented both church and state. Rather than moving to the training of a Filipino clergy, the friars exchanged their missionary zeal for a comfortable role as provincial elite, presiding over a calendar of festivals, marriages, and funerals. An elite received some Christian education but the majority expressed their piety primarily through feasts, rituals, dramatizations, and the partial Christianization of the major rites of passage. Religious orders were generally closed to indigenous recruitment, but Filipina women could not be denied their demands for spiritual equality. Two Filipina-led religious communities (*beatarios*) were established in this period by the determination of pious and persistent women, overcoming both racial and gender prejudice to establish the first acknowledged traditions of vernacular and female Christianity. Mother Ignacia del Espíritu Santo established a Community of the Virgin Mary in Manila in 1684 under the wing of sympathetic Jesuits, while two determined sisters from Calumpang in Bulacan, surnamed Talangpaz ("sacred rock") perhaps in evocation of older spirit cults, overcame many setbacks to establish the *Beaterio de San Sebastián de Calumpang* in 1719 under that of Augustinian Recollects.

Even without a significant number of Filipino priests the gospel was vernacularized through extensive translation and printing. Spanish religious texts in translation were the first to be translated, but Filipino delight in oral poetry was extended to the bilingual (*ladino*) poetry of figures like Tomas Pinpin, who was able to publish some of his Tagalog prose and poetry because he worked in the printing house of the Dominicans in the early 1600s. Several Spanish friars were able enough to produce sacred works and dictionaries in Tagalog, Cebuano, and Ilocano, but what the Filipinos loved most were poetry and dramatization of the Christian feasts, especially when written by their own poets. The first poetic rendering of the passion (death and resurrection) of Christ by a Filipino was published in Tagalog in 1704, from the pen of prominent Tagalog layman Gaspar Aquino de Belen. His version was emulated, amended, and enacted in parishes throughout the Philippines thenceforth, generating a vernacular idiom of the Christian experience.

The endemic church-state jockeying for power culminated in the 1760s when a new "enlightened despotism" in Madrid sought to control the clergy in the national interest. The Jesuits were suppressed throughout the empire and consequently expelled from 130 parishes in the Visayas and Mindanao. There was a sudden demand for Filipino diocesan priests answerable to the Manila Archbishop and the king, to replace European friars answering to their order and to the Pope. The result was at last to produce a Filipino clergy, though one trained so hastily that a large cultural gap emerged between them and the Spanish-trained religious orders. An English visitor wrote in the 1820s of "a keen and deadly jealousy … between these [Filipino priests] and the Spanish ecclesiastics, or rather a hatred on one side and a contempt on the other" (cited Schumacher 1979, 213). Filipinos entrusted with parishes tended to abandon the big stone structures the friars had built for their needs in favor of living Filipino style in wood and bamboo houses, less concerned with maintaining celibacy and orthodoxy than their Spanish colleagues but more with their kinship networks. They tended to be less critical of the Filipino sensuality that had shocked the Castilians, or of the universal belief that spirits of the dead needed to be manipulated and assuaged by the living. The healing syntheses that emerged here were made possible by Catholicizing offerings and prayers for the dead, notably at funerals and the annual graveside feasting on

All Saints' Day. This period of explicit vernacularization after 1760 saw a Filipino clergy actively generating a Filipino identity based on what we today call popular religion or folk Catholicism.

Buddhism

Theravada Buddhism was also sustained by a celibate male clergy, but not one that was foreign-born as in the early Catholic Philippines. The key to the long eighteenth century in the Theravada Mainland was the gradual homogenization of monastic rules of ordination and practice, but their separation into distinct Bama, Thai, Lao, and Khmer vernaculars. The rich and powerful monasteries sustained by royal or aristocratic endowment gave way to a more popular pattern of integration with the population. Monks received alms from ordinary villagers as well as town-dwellers and pilgrims, and in return provided not only blessings and key agricultural and life-cycle rituals, but instruction in literacy and Buddhist virtues for young boys temporarily assigned to the monkhood. Burmese monks were especially successful in this role. By 1800 they were estimated to comprise about 2% of the Burmese population, and "there was not any village, however small," which did not have at least one monastery, where all boys at puberty were supposed to spend some time (Sangermano 1833/1966, 113). This practice had produced by the nineteenth century more than 50% male adult literacy in Burmese – perhaps a record for any pre-industrial society.

The Buddhist *sangha* was particularly important in developing a common cultural identity among Lao and Khmer, for whom the long eighteenth century was a time of political fragmentation and foreign intervention from Siam and Cochin-China. King Surinyavongsa had ruled Lanxang (Vientiane, 1637–94) as a remarkable gunpowder king, making his capital the religious and cultural center for the whole middle Mekong basin, but after his death none of the three successor princedoms (Luang Prabang, Vientiane, and Champassak) could dominate the others nor resist pressures from Thai and Viet rulers. Nevertheless, the That Luang temple in Vientiane remained a focus of Lao unity, and the Lao-speaking *sangha* more famous for its wealth, self-indulgence, and arrogance in that earlier era became a popular localized institution. Even after two centuries of Thai rule on the west bank of the Mekong, Lao language and identity remain strong in what is today called Isan (northeast) Thailand. In Cambodia kingship was so contested that the longest-serving ruler (1643–58) of the seventeenth century was a Muslim convert, and his Buddhist successors were beholden to either Ayutthaya or Hue. Khmer identity was largely fashioned in this difficult time by the education and example of Khmer-speaking monks.

Burmese and Thai monarchs did better, largely by an alliance with the *sangha* that made clear that the primary purpose of kingship was to promote the *dharma*, or Buddhist teaching. The "enlightened despot" figure of King Narai in Siam was overthrown and a new line enthroned in 1688 with the support of popular monks outraged at his secularism and friendship with Europeans. Monarchy became more consensual, and less warlike. The Buddhist quality of kingship peaked with the reign of Borommakot (1733–58), who maintained external peace, devoted much of the national resources to temple-building, patronized writers, and became an exemplar even for reformist monks in Sri Lanka, reversing the older pattern of looking there for external legitimacy. Two missions of monks were sent to Sri Lanka in 1753 and 1755, carrying Pali texts and Buddha images, in response to a request from the King of Kandy. Even if internal order and the economy stumbled, he was remembered popularly as a "king who ruled according to the *dharma*" (Thai *thammaracha*) on the model of the Buddhist founder-king, Asoka of India. In Burma, too, at this time rulers sought their legitimacy by upholding the *dharma*, banning the public sale of meat and alcohol, building temples, and patronizing the *sangha* while seeking to unify it under royal control.

Each culture area emerged with its own compromise with the older pattern of spirit worship. The kings of this period did not attack the spirits as some had in the age of commerce, but accommodated them within the Buddhist framework. Thai kings retained Brahmins at court to enhance their supernatural power with Shaivite ritual, but popularly the Hindu deities (beloved in the Thai version of the Ramayana) were incorporated into a Buddhist pantheon. Burmese rulers went further in seeking to nationalize and unify the extraordinary diversity of the spirit world through a state cult of 37 recognized great spirits (*nat*), said to originate, like many traditions, with King Anawrahta of Pagan (1044–77). Though royal rituals propitiating this pantheon may have served unifying purposes, the official cult by no means excluded local spirits. Millions of other *nat* were described in official cosmology, embedded in the rituals of Buddhist monks, or simply honored by a household. Every village had its own guardian *nat* and, as in Siam, every building honored a spirit or collection of spirits. Finally, an elaborate system of omens was incorporated into the synthesis, some based on the calendar and the stars, others relating to bodily particulars. Increasingly systematized as the Burmese and Thai realms became more integrated, these syntheses of universal and vernacular served to unify culture areas according to language.

PERFORMANCE IN PALACE, PAGODA, AND VILLAGE

Dance, music, and drama were central to life and identity Below the Winds. From the depictions of dancers and musicians on the temples of Angkor and Prambanan it is clear that dance provided a link between the world of gods and spirits and the world of men. Everybody knew how to dance, and was expected to do so at sacred festivals, weddings, and funerals. The missionaries described the non-Indic pattern of the Philippines where singing and dancing was the core of every feast and ritual. Elsewhere Indic religious ideas were added, conveying the beloved stories of the Mahabharata, the Ramayana, and the Jataka stories of Buddhism not as literature but as performance. Long after the orthodoxies of Islam, Theravada Buddhism, and Confucianism took hold, these story cycles retained an aura of both sacredness and popular entertainment through their repeated performance on every great occasion.

The age of commerce produced enormous innovation in performance and literature, as in other spheres. Outside observers were intrigued by the diversity of performance and exhausted by its abundance. Because of the cosmopolitan nature of such centers, the gunpowder kings who presided over them pressed each foreign community into service to embellish the theater of state. Europeans were not the most successful in this competition, but they described how they had to participate in royal festivals, dressing up their trumpeters or devising dances as best they could to take part in the processions that went on for weeks to celebrate a royal wedding or other ritual. Foreign styles of performance such as Chinese opera or Javanese *wayang* were appreciated even when their language was not understood.

The spectacles favored by the gunpowder kings were decidedly public, designed as they were to enact and embody a mighty king presiding over a diverse and flourishing capital. Contests, tournaments, and processions were prominent features of the age of commerce, often showing the king himself symbolically prevailing over enemies. There was no doubting the popularity of the various forms, or the competition to draw the biggest crowds, but the diversity of these ports put a premium on spectacle rather than sophistication of language. The passing of that era saw a rapid decline of such spectacles, and a bifurcation of what remained. Court performance became increasingly slow and refined, representing ritually the supernatural power no longer displayed on the battlefield, while popular theater traveled around sacred sites and village markets performing to whoever would pay.

These peripatetic performers, puppeteers, dancers, singers, and reciters were the principal architects of the identities of Bama, Thai, Lao, Khmer, Viet, Javanese, Bugis, Acehnese, Malay, and Tagalog in the long eighteenth century, even if by their nature they did not leave written records as court or religious writers did. All the popular forms of the period were in verse, intended to be recited and memorized. While the Pali, Sanskrit, Old Javanese, or Arabic cosmopolitan languages of the earlier period survived in the philosophical core of the religiously inspired dramas, what made them popular were the quotidian interpellations of clowns, servants, and rustics, who invariably spoke the vernacular to be understood. Love stories also went the rounds in memorized poetic form, often escaping from the religious frame altogether. Only toward the end of the period, in the late eighteenth and early nineteenth centuries, do written versions of these epics appear (earlier in Dai Viet, later in the Islands). Since scholarship inevitably traces the texts, the pale reflection rather than the essence of performance, the central role of performance has been too often overlooked.

Even the texts show a remarkable flowering of vernacular verse forms in the period, generally intended to be performed or chanted rather than read. We might trace to this period the beginnings of a grand tradition of romances, of doomed heroines forced to choose between love and duty; the beginnings of something like national history in the vernacular; and the linking of city and village cultures into national traditions. The growth of literacy through the efforts of Buddhist monks, Islamic *ulama*, and Christian schools, together with the manuscript-collecting habits of nineteenth-century Europeans, may partly account for the emergence of these texts only late in Early Modernity. But there is also a case for dispersion of ideas, most clear in the Vietnamese case.

The Viet literati elite had been schooled in the Chinese classics since the examination system was introduced in the thirteenth century, and by the sixteenth century they wrote much in Chinese prose and verse forms. In the eighteenth, however, there was a remarkable flowering of popular literature in *nom*, a script adapted from Chinese characters to better render the sounds of Vietnamese, and more accessible to women and the non-elite because of both its form and its romantic subject matter. Scholars like Le Quy Don used it to write *phu*, a verse form derived from Chinese Tang-era poetry but expressing the grief and dilemmas of young women facing a loveless marriage. But still more popular was a particularly Viet style of *luc-bat* poetry of alternating six-, seven-, and eight-syllable verses capable of expressing tenderness and melancholy. Some of the authors of this genre were scholar-officials schooled in the Chinese classics, or their family members, who evidently enjoyed relaxing with Chinese popular novels and love stories. One such scholar wrote a "Lament of the Warrior's Bride" (*chinh-phu ngam*) in classical Chinese in the early eighteenth century, but the genre became more popular when rendered into mournful Vietnamese written in *nom*. Rightly famous is that of Doan Thi Diem (1705–48), herself evidently a young bride whose husband went off to wars in China.

> The current runs clear and pure beneath the bridge,
> The grass nearby shoots up, tender and soft.
> You left me behind here, my heart broken.
> If only I could be my foot soldier's horse, my sailor's boat!
> The stream runs on, yet cannot cleanse my sorrow,
> The grass is sweet, yet cannot calm my pain
>
> (trans. Gioseffi 2003).

The greatest achievement of *nom* writing in this or perhaps any period is the *Kim Van Kieu* or "Tale of Kieu," an improved version in Vietnamese verse of a probably seventeenth-century Chinese prose original. It was written by Nguyen Du (1766–1820), also educated in the Chinese classics, whose father had been a minister of the Trinh court, but whose mother earned her living by writing and singing poetry. It is a tragic story of a sweet and loyal woman who chooses duty over love by marrying to save the family from disaster, but is repeatedly betrayed and sold into prostitution, from which she is also repeatedly rescued by lovers. The story was recited all around the country and has been ever since a national icon, memorized by many in its verse form.

Connections with Chinese popular literature may help explain the brilliant zenith of Viet vernacular verse. Elsewhere, too, there were bicultural Sino-Southeast Asians who translated Chinese epics like the "Romance of the Three Kingdoms" into Thai, Javanese, and Malay as well as Vietnamese. Yet the eighteenth-century literary flowering was too widespread to put down to a single influence. Emblematic of Thai performance is the epic verse romance *Khun Chang Khun Phaen*, which began to be recited at the height of the Ayutthaya period, although not beginning to be written down until the nineteenth century. Its origins appear to be earthy and Thai, with little reference to high traditions of Pali. In the eighteenth century its recitation, punctuated by the striking of two wooden sticks (*krap*), became the most popular and widespread genre, usually lasting all night during the post-harvest season of festivals. The two figures of its title, the coarse but devoted Chang and the glamorous but irresponsible Phaen, compete for the affection of the lovely heroine, Wanthong, through wars, rural escapes, royal interventions, and much comedy. It is usually presented in an eight-syllable meter (*klon paet*) reminiscent of some Viet and Chinese analogies, so that some cross-border influences cannot be ruled out. Unlike the virtuous heroines of the Viet equivalents, Wanthong's viewpoint is less well presented, and the story ends with her execution because her wavering caused such chaos (Baker and Pongpaichit 2010).

Such was the eminence of the city of Ayutthaya in the seventeenth century that its styles also influenced Burmese and Khmer performance in the eighteenth. In the Burmese case the Siamese element is clearly datable, since the Burmese conquerors of Ayutthaya in 1767–8 brought home as many artists, writers, performers, and musicians as possible. This helps explain the exceptional burst of innovation and new popular genres in Burmese theater in the late eighteenth century. Drama in Burma had long had a less inhibited *nat pwe* dance ritual designed to call forth the spirits (*nat*), alongside the *zat pwe* more decorously portraying the Jataka (or *zat*) stories. In this period, however, performance escaped these restrictions altogether, and developed the romance-drama themes already popular in Siam, as well as puppet theater, Ramayana stories, and borrowings from the Javanese Panji repertoire through mediation of its Thai equivalent, the *Inao* (Burmese *Eenoun*).

Because the Burmese court played a prominent role in popularizing the new styles, we know the names of many of the official poets and dramatists of the period. Myawadi Mingyi U Sa (1766–1853) adapted the Ramayana into evocative Burmese poetry and song. Many of the poetic innovators at court were women, such as Princess Ching Ming (1738–81) and Mae Khwe (1781–1836), both killed in the fratricidal court wars of the time. They nevertheless left a fine corpus of love poems and appreciations of the changing seasons, with insights into the tastes of the time. We must assume that alongside the writers whose names were preserved by the court was an army of anonymous performers adapting court and folk styles to popular fashions at the fairs and festivals around the country.

In Java the divisive upheavals of the sixteenth-century transition to Islam hardly ceased in the following century. Warfare continued as Sultan Agung sought to subjugate all of the Javanese-speaking area, and as his heirs tried in vain to cling to that inheritance against dynastic rivalries, challenges from Islam, and Dutch intervention. Only in 1757 did peace descend on Java after the VOC had secured its interests on the coast and the warring Javanese princes had agreed to subdivision of what remained. The years following saw a vastly increased literary output conventionally known as the "Surakarta Renaissance" for the more creative of the two surviving royal capitals. It was a renaissance in that *kekawin* poetry of the pre-Muslim period was rediscovered in old collections to form the basis of much new poetry in the revised language and meters of middle Javanese. In reality there was much more writing that was avowedly pursuing Islamic mystical ideas, though this was less interesting to the early

Dutch Javanists. Islamic schools (*pesantren*) were at least as important centers of production and recitation of poetry as the courts, and trained even the most illustrious court authors like Ranggawarsita (1802–73), the famous "last *pujangga*" (official court poet) of Surakarta. The great majority of the Javanese writing preserved is *macapat* verse meant for recitation. The royally inspired collections of written texts should be seen as only the tip of the iceberg of the popular audience for poetry. Many of those deemed formally illiterate might have a highly cultivated sense of the literary canon through performance.

Only Javanese royalty themselves and their official court poets like Ranggawarsita are named, known, and celebrated in modern textbooks. The majority of recitations, and of the textual versions of them, were anonymous because the scribe who wrote them was not usually the real creator, but simply the transcriber (sometimes accurate, sometimes creatively adaptive) of poetry already many times recited. The greatest popularizers of the literary canon, the puppeteer-narrators (*dalang*) and female singers (*sindhen*) of the shadow theater, seldom referred to texts in their night-long recitations, and learned their craft chiefly through memory and a measure of improvization. In addition to the *wayang kulit* repertoire largely taken from the India-derived Mahabharata cycle with the addition of purely Javanese servant-clown-god figures (*punakawan*), the Islam-derived Amir Hamzah cycle was very popular in the form of doll-puppets (*wayang golek*). Texts of *wayang kulit* performances accumulated in library collections only during the nineteenth century, but it is safe to say that in the eighteenth the *wayang* already served to unite the eastern two thirds of Java culturally, however divided politically. "The constant exhibition of these plays in every part of the country … has served to … disseminate a general knowledge of native legendary history" (Raffles 1817/1978 I, 339). The *dalang* of all forms of theater were the most popular teachers of the mystic synthesis, not in competition with the *ulama* of the religious schools but operating in a different spiritual sphere often understood to be both more profound and more Javanese.

In the rest of the Archipelago, where the religious revolution of the age of commerce had introduced first Arabic and then Malay in Arabic script as the language of Islam, the eighteenth century extended the reach of vernaculars as local languages were written down and standardized. Acehnese, for example, was virtually unknown to the many visitors to the Aceh capital in the seventeenth century. Malay was the language of the cosmopolitan capital and the written language of both court and *ulama*. Spoken Acehnese, very distinct in vocabulary and structure, became standardized as the inner oral language of communication with the population of farmers and fishermen through the circulation of reciters and performers at this time. The first evidence is only in the 1660s of a scholar popularizing an Islamic text "in the manner of our recitation," because "so few people know the *Jawi* [Malay] language" (cited Durie 1996, 115). The learning of literacy in Muslim centers like Aceh occurred chiefly in Arabic, as children learned to recite the Quran (though not at first to understand it). If they managed to write as well as read, it would be in Malay, for which an Arabic-derived script had been standardized in the sixteenth century. Once the recitation and memorization of verse in Acehnese became popular, the experiment began of adapting the Arabic script also to write it. The first surviving manuscripts putting Acehnese verse into Arabic script are from the late eighteenth century. They include some extremely popular epics such as the *Hikayat Meukota Alam*, of which there are many manuscripts from diverse parts of the country. In such ways, through public performance, Acehnese became a recognized language and source of identity for a people.

Sundanese (in Java), Minangkabau (Sumatra), Banjarese (Borneo), Sasak (Lombok), and Bima (Sumbawa) were other languages, or dialect ranges, which existed primarily in oral form while serious writing was done in Malay or Javanese. The very identity of Sundanese as opposed to "mountain-Javanese" seemed unclear to the first Dutch scholar who investigated the question in the 1830s. The popularization of poetic forms through frequent recitation, performance, and memorization gradually created literary communities, linked by *ulama* to the broader worlds of Malay, Javanese, or Arabic writing, but conscious of their own distinctiveness. This vernacularization in performance terms preceded the creation of written literatures, which in many cases had to wait until European encouragement in the late nineteenth or early twentieth century. Then it often occurred in romanized form, as was increasingly the case with Sundanese (Indonesia's second-largest vernacular) as it distinguished itself from Javanese and Malay by writing down the oral poetry. Performance, nevertheless, was the key to creating community.

HISTORY, MYTH, AND IDENTITY

The audiences for the poetic epics discussed above heard them as entertainment, as metaphysic, and as sources of wisdom for life. All this constituted a shared identity autonomous of state actors. Yet the more coherent a "national" audience this became, the more necessary it was for kings and their literati to demonstrate their legitimacy within it. All monarchies experienced grave crises in the seventeenth or eighteenth centuries, and yet the cultures in which they operated were now distinct enough to give rise to something more like national kings thereafter. The literary outpouring of the late eighteenth century accompanied the rise of new strong men with few sources of traditional legitimacy. They needed to demonstrate both the optimism of a new start and continuity with the best of the remembered past. The continuities had to be multiple. The new rulers sought not just to imagine a biological link with past dynasties, but evidence that they shared the supernatural powers of the Indic gods and heroes. Furthermore, they now operated in a world of scriptural religions, each of which had its own sacred narrative of linear time. Where the stories of the Mahabharata, Ramayana, Jatakas, Panji, or La Galigo operated in a kind of equidistant but exemplary past, Islam and Christianity brought specific time frames since the divine intervention, and devalued as myth whatever went before. Even Buddhism had its 5,000-year cycle following the Buddha's enlightenment, and gave rise to Pali-influenced chronicles of the progress of the *dharma* and its transplantation into local venues.

These combined imperatives may help explain the puzzle of how national history began to be written in Southeast Asia's eighteenth century. We cannot attribute it to direct foreign influence, even if the skepticism of Islamic or Christian apostles, Chinese traders, or post-Enlightenment Europeans toward the older myths may have influenced some of the new creativity. European nationalist example was undoubtedly critical in recasting histories in a linear direction in the late nineteenth and twentieth centuries, but there is little evidence for it in the eighteenth. Yet there was an undoubted shift toward a vernacular expression of the lineage of a community ruled by dynasties, in prose intended to be preserved, read, and consulted rather than recited.

The first tradition to produce a national history in prose was that of Burma, the one least beholden to any conceivable European, Muslim, or Chinese influence. U Kala's "Great Royal Chronicle" in 21 volumes produced in 1711–24 was revolutionary in writing not just about one hero, dynasty, or sacred place, but about various parts of the by now Bama-speaking lowlands. U Kala was a layman descended from Bama and Shan administrators, but wealthy enough to devote himself to this mammoth task even without explicit support from court or *sangha*. He is thought to have consulted as many as 70 Buddhist or royal texts, and even to have had access to some court documents dating back to the sixteenth century, but also the great Sri Lankan *Mahavamsa* chronicle of Buddhism, and some early Siamese texts. Conscious of the novelty of his "national" enterprise he anticipated criticism from Buddhist scholars, arguing that a better knowledge of the past would demonstrate the impermanence of all things, and thus Buddhist piety. His account of the sixteenth and seventeenth centuries is remarkably accurate and matter-of-fact, even if his tracing of the thread of Buddhist civilization beyond eleventh-century Pagan to the Buddhist center of Thaton (followed by all subsequent Burmese and British historians) has recently been undermined by Michael Aung-Thwin (2005).

Numerous versions of U Kala's text were produced during the last Konbaung or Alaungphaya era (1752–1885), one of which presented itself explicitly as national history – "A New Chronicle of Burma" (*Myanma Yazawinthit*), commissioned by King Bodawpaya (1782–1819) but not accepted by him. Among Vietnamese literati, meanwhile, a similar trend toward secular national history was embodied in the scholar-official Le Quy Don (c.1726–84), who wrote a "Complete History of Dai Viet" (*Dai Viet Thong Su*) in biographical form.

The Siamese capital of Ayutthaya experienced such profound trauma following its destruction by the Burmese in 1767 that a total rethinking of history was understandable. The secularizing reign of King Narai (Chapter 6) had already produced a more secular dynastic history (*phongsawadan*) well aware of Siam's position among its neighbors as well as European, Indian, and Chinese visitors. However, the Buddhist reaction against this cosmopolitanism, followed by the horrors of the 1760s, produced a new beginning. Artists, writers, performers, texts, and sacred images had been carried off by the Burmese, the country fragmented into rival centers, and monks left their monasteries to forage for mere survival. The upstart half-Chinese soldier who restored order and successfully drove out the Burmese, King Taksin (1767–82), had delusions of sanctity that drove him to have flogged 500 monks who refused to prostrate themselves before him, and in effect to divide the *sangha* into warring camps. It was in the aftermath of this "unrighteous" reign that the last of Siam's Buddhist Pali-influenced chronicles (*tamnan*), the so-called "1789 Chronicle," was written. An anti-Taksin monk compiled it as part of an attempt to reunite the *sangha* and convince it that the new king, Rama I (1782–1809), had restored Buddhist rectitude by summoning a Buddhist Council (1788) and building a new capital with many monasteries at Bangkok. The same monkish author himself made the transition to secular history by writing in 1809 a chronicle of the Kings of Ayutthaya and the inauguration of the Bangkok dynasty. In the nineteenth century, Thai historians became increasingly concerned to show the existence of a Thai nation and the legitimacy of its kings through time.

The trauma that overcame Java in the eighteenth century was perhaps more lasting, in that Muslim-inspired resistance against the VOC and its royal Javanese allies was roundly defeated. Purwasastra may have written a realistic if partisan history, the *Babad Balambangan* of 1773–4, because of both the sharp reversal represented by VOC military victories and the awareness of multiple options of understanding it among the many different actors in easternmost Java. In the Javanese royal heartland following its Dutch-enforced division in 1757, writing had to explain how each of the four rival kings remained legitimate and central. One response was to reemphasize the supernatural inner power of slight but elegant heroes of the *wayang* like Arjuna and Yudhisthira, who supernaturally prevail against gross monster figures (*raksasa*) identified with the Dutch. Much of the historical writing continued to show how Islamic piety could be reconciled with a belief in the local spiritual forces of Java. Its far greater abundance and diversity in the eighteenth century was prompted by a wider audience for written Javanese, and effective independence from any one court tradition. The *Babad Ing Sengkala* (dated chronicle) committed to Javanese verse in 1738 showed unprecedented accuracy with its dates. The Dutch presence in nineteenth-century Java nevertheless accentuated the divide between what came to be thought of as Javanese mythic "tradition" on one side and European-style objective history on the other. Ranggawarsita sought to bridge the divide by writing a prose version with dates of Javanese epic and *wayang* poetry in his mid-century "Book of Kings" (*Pustaka Raja*). It was, predictably, neither poetic enough to interest a Javanese audience nor scholarly enough to convince Dutch readers that his dates made sense.

In the world of Malay writing, literature was still less beholden to specific kings and courts. Politically plural even in the age of commerce, that world continued to be held together by its writers, its performers, its religion, and its trade. The role of Malay as trade language became even more important within the Archipelago, now also accommodating Europeans and Chinese in prominent roles. As high literature its scope shrank in the eighteenth century to a few centers around the Malacca Straits. This was also the crucible of European interactions in the early nineteenth century. Munshi Abdullah in Singapore, and the school of Raja Ali Haji in Riau to its south, best represent the ways in which the elegant poetic conventions of Malay letters made the transition to secular definitions of a broader community. Munshi Abdullah, influenced by British officials for whom he acted as Malay writer, wrote straightforward prose accounts of his life and times that identified the Malay rulers as obstacles to the kind of progress the Malays as a people needed to make. Raja Ali Haji's mid-century writings were more influenced by Islamic values and narratives about how princes should behave to avoid conflicts. An heir to the remarkable Bugis input into the Straits area over the previous century, he also saw literature and religion as means to reconcile potentially conflicting ethnic groups and create broader communities.

CONSOLIDATION AND ITS LIMITATIONS

Victor Lieberman has made a strong case for a sustained pattern of integration in Mainland Southeast Asia over the whole period from the fifteenth to the nineteenth centuries (or in some formulations for a millennium), interrupted by dynastic crises which grew shorter with each repetition. "Each of the principal states expanded its territory, centralized its administration, and saw elements of its population adopt more uniform cultural and ethnic identities" (Lieberman 2003, 44). In a healthy corrective to colonial and nationalist presumptions about the decline of "golden era" states to a point of ossified feudal impotence inviting European conquest, he argued that by the early nineteenth century this political consolidation "had yielded an unprecedentedly powerful and extensive formation" (457).

It should be clear from the foregoing that I welcome his demonstration of greater cultural integration in the long eighteenth century, while demurring about the necessary centrality of states. Making the big three (Burma, Siam, Dai Viet) the focus of Mainland history over a millennium makes an important point, but obscures equally illuminating stories regarding crises and changes of direction along the way. The gunpowder states came and went, moving people about and creating urban melting-pots like Ayutthaya, Mrauk-U (Arakan), Pegu, Banten, Aceh, Phnom Penh, and Vientiane. The more peaceful and self-sustaining period that followed consolidated some cultural identities around royal courts as exemplary centers, but had similar effects with cultural identities that had no centralizing states (Karen, Chin, Batak, Minangkabau, Sundanese, Balinese), very weak ones (Khmer, Aceh), a plurality of them (Viet, Malay, Javanese, Shan, and northern Tai), or a state ruled by others (Mon, Tagalog, the Betawi of Batavia, Ambonese). Despite the marginality of enforcing legal institutions or bureaucracies, certain civilities of restrained politeness became characteristic of many of these cultures through media such as theater, dance, and ritual. The counterpoint of this civility was the calculated brutality of the ruffians at its margins, who could achieve remarkable compliance for themselves or their elite patrons through limited displays of force.

The limitations to the process of cultural consolidation even in the eighteenth century were evident by comparison with Europe or China. The hills, forests, and small islands remained untamed until the colonial interventions of around 1900. The majority of lowlanders even in the larger concentrations of settled irrigated-rice agriculture were within two days' walk of the freedom and statelessness of the highlands, and knew they represented an alternative.

[9] EXPANSION OF THE SINICIZED WORLD

I<small>N</small> Chapter 1 we identified the Vietnamese people as one of the major barriers to further expansion southward of the Chinese state and civilization. They controlled the most accessible land route into Southeast Asia, but absorbed enough of the military and bureaucratic lessons of the Chinese model to be able to hold expansionism back. Having learned these valuable lessons, and relearned them forcefully in the fifteenth century, the Viet were able to commence their own expansion south, which eventually brought them to the Gulf of Thailand. Chinese traders, meanwhile, expanded into all the areas of Southeast Asia where Indian and European trade was weakest. The great expansion in China's population in the eighteenth century, and resource hunger, drove Chinese miners and agriculturalists southward, to become the region's largest and most economically dynamic minority.

FIFTEENTH-CENTURY REVOLUTION IN DAI VIET

In replacing an ailing Mongol Empire in China in 1368, the Ming Dynasty inherited some of its predecessor's interest in world empire. A flurry of missions were sent out to Southeast Asia, and assumed gigantic proportions under the Yunglo Emperor (1403–24) in the form of Zheng He's fleets. Gunpowder was one of the assets the Ming were able to use in their confrontations with southerners in this period, and played a particularly prominent role in the Chinese occupation of Dai Viet in 1406–7. Dai Viet itself was known to have used a new type of gun to save itself from what appeared certain defeat by an attacking Cham force in 1390, but the Ming forces ensured their victory by developing for the first time a firearms battalion employing various types of cannon and grenade. These innovations enabled the Chinese to conquer the difficult southern neighbor that had escaped its tutelage five centuries earlier, but not to hold it for long. The Viet proved quick learners as they seized more and more weapons in repeated rebellions. In 1427 the Viet troops of Le Loi

A History of Southeast Asia: Critical Crossroads, First Edition. Anthony Reid.
© 2015 Anthony Reid. Published 2015 by John Wiley & Sons, Ltd.

captured the key remaining Chinese citadel, and a new Chinese emperor was unwilling to continue his predecessor's adventures in the south when faced with serious threats in the north. Dai Viet was again independent, though careful not to alienate the northern dragon by triumphalism. It quickly returned to a familiar deference through the regular tribute missions on which the Ming set great store.

It was, however, a different Dai Viet. Its army became for a time the most effective in Southeast Asia, equipped with firearms and hundreds of galleys each armed with a simple cannon. This enabled Hanoi to expand its sway to the south and west. The Le Dynasty inaugurated by Le Loi also took advantage of the undoubted strengths of the Chinese system of direct bureaucratic control. Its adoption was regularized under the strongest of the Le rulers, Le Thanh Tong (r.1460–97), who had been educated in Confucian orthodoxy in the post-Chinese-occupation palace. The very Confucian literati on whom the Chinese had relied for their administration now became his state ideologists. He did his best to discourage Buddhism and curb the power of its monks, while extending to the provinces the Confucian "Temples of Literature" (*Van Mieu*), the oldest of which at the capital already went back to 1070. He established six ministries on the pattern of the Chinese court, and sought to transfer power outside the capital from hereditary war-leaders to Confucian-trained bureaucrats selected by competitive examination in the Chinese classics. Administrators were appointed by the court and rotated at regular intervals at three levels of provincial administration, the lowest of which (*chau*, or district chiefs) in turn appointed village heads also required to be literate in Chinese. Although Buddhism, spirit cults, kinship networks, and local customs remained popular and periodically challenged Confucian orthodoxy, fifteenth-century Dai Viet marked a Southeast Asian peak of bureaucratic control over an agricultural population. That population doubled or tripled in the fifteenth century to at least three million in Tongking (*Dong Kinh*, the broader Red River delta), as a consequence of enforced peace, favorable climatic conditions, and perhaps new rice strains. The Le kings were able to control this peasantry as other Southeast Asian rulers were not, and to extract enough tax and labor from it to provide for the capital's needs. They thereby became less dependent than their predecessors or rivals on international commerce, and indeed more Confucian in giving it a low status in their official outlook.

Le Thanh Tong's regime could be seen as a revolution as profound as the religious change affecting the rest of Southeast Asia in this and the following centuries. Rather than seeking continuity, Confucian literati of the period excoriated the pre-Ming-occupation regime as thoroughly reprehensible in its personal and public behavior. The Viet victory was justified by its great literati chronicler Nguyen Trai not by rejecting the Chinese model but rather asserting equality with it. "Mountains and Rivers have demarcated the borders. The customs of the North and the South are also different. We find that the Trieu, Dinh, Ly and Tran [dynasties] built our country. Alongside the Han, Tang, Song and Yuan [Dynasties of China], the [Viet] rulers reigned as emperors over their own part." (Trai 1428 in Truong 1967). This Confucian revolution appears also to mark a vital break in the relation between Dai Viet and its neighbors. Where earlier regimes had fought with Champa and exchanged consorts with hill peoples as virtual equals, the fifteenth-century Le court insisted that it was equal to China in virtue and civilization, and thereby contrasted with its non-Sinified neighbors necessarily classified as "barbarian." The literati justified the campaigns that Le Thanh Tong launched against Chams to the south and Tai people to the west in terms of civilized behavior and heaven's mandate. Captured Ming soldiers were settled on the land as model subjects, but captured southerners were required to make more drastic adjustments, adopting the virtues, dress, language, and habits of the *Han,* not of course in its modern Chinese-ethnic sense but as the civilization with which the Le court identified.

VIET EXPANSION, NAM TIEN

Under Le Thanh Tong the Viet held the upper hand against both Chams in the south and Lao-Tai peoples in the western hills. Dai Viet chronicles, confirmed to a degree by Chinese ones, relate that expeditions penetrated as far as the Mekong and extracted booty and tribute from the Lao princedoms. The Muong and Tai peoples up to the watershed between the Tongking Gulf rivers and the Mekong were no longer equals, but tributaries expected to recognize the superior virtue of the lowland civilization. Along the coast Dai Viet used its galleys and artillery to press southward to successive Cham centers. In the fourteenth century, coastal warfare had moved back and forth. Viet galleys reached as far as the Hai Van pass in 1308, but the Cham king Che Bong Na in turn attacked the Viet capital itself on at least three occasions. The expeditions of Le Thanh Tong were of a more permanent kind, designed to settle Han ("civilized" Viet or Chinese) in areas previously Cham, and to force the Cham to adopt similar norms. Champa was even less a united polity in this period than usual, and it is clear that the Dai Viet troops were able to overcome local resistance piecemeal. The lucrative Quang Nam area just beyond the Hai Van Pass was probably secured in a campaign of 1460–1, and the southerly center of Vijaya, in what became Quy Nhon, was taken in 1471.

The fall of Vijaya was a major event in Southeast Asian history. It was mentioned not only in Chinese and Viet chronicles but also in the Melaka annals (*Sejarah Melayu*) because a party of commercially oriented Cham refugees from this disaster played roles as China traders in Melaka and as commercial-military elites in the rise of Aceh in Sumatra. The most striking confirmation of this movement of Chamic peoples is that a hybrid variant of their languages, Acehnese, spread with the Aceh sultanate around the coasts of northern Sumatra to become the largest surviving Chamic language of today. The Cham of the coast had in fact four options, apart from capture or death in battle (some 60,000 were listed as killed in the Viet chronicle): to flee to the nearby hills where there had long been symbiotic relations with forest collectors; to flee further south to the southernmost holdout of a Cham polity (Panduranga) near modern Phan Rang; to join trading partners in Cambodia or the

Malay-speaking world, an option taken by most of the Cham Muslim minority; or to stay and negotiate the pressures to assimilate as "civilized" Viet.

We must assume this last process to have been a long and complex one. Dai Viet fell into disastrous internal conflict in the sixteenth century, which appears to have coincided with a drying-up of the former arteries of trade along the northernmost outlets of the Red River and their replacement by the present main channel much further south. There were frequent famines, and the population appears to have been set back after the surge in the fifteenth century. The Viet state was not again in a position to dictate the terms of Cham or Khmer assimilation until the next great surge of Confucianization in the nineteenth century. Recent revisionist histories have replaced the nationalist narrative of continuously expanding Viet control in favor of a high degree of local agency and variation, and periodic reassertions of a separate polity in the commercially crucial Quang Nam area through most of the sixteenth century. In the longer term, hybrid southern patterns of ritual activity, domestic and gender relations, and music kept Cham influence alive up to the nineteenth century, by which time some of these were reinterpreted as Vietnamese. Further south the Panduranga Cham polity sent tribute to whichever Viet state demanded it, but also pursued its own foreign relations with China, with the Muslim Malay *negeri* to its south, and with the first Portuguese to pass that way, until prevented by tighter Viet control after 1611. The importance of Muslim traders in sustaining Panduranga was reflected in the steady Islamization of its elite, with the king following the traders into the faith in the seventeenth century.

In one sense the *Nam Tien* (lit. South marching) celebrated in nationalist histories represented an historic shift southward of the frontier of the Sinified world of Chinese writing, manners, and political ideals, at the expense of "Indianized" Southeast Asia. In another, however, it helped secure the long-term Southeast Asian identity of the Viet by enmeshing them not only in hybridizations with Cham and Khmer cultures, but also in negotiations with their now multiplied regional neighbors. Until the nineteenth century, indeed, it was far from clear that the long coastline today recognized as Viet Nam could ever be a single country. The eternal preoccupation of the north (Tongking) with its autonomy from and equality with China was a world away from the multiple ethnic, cultural, and political negotiations of the south, which we may begin to call Cochin-China from 1600.

The achievements of the Le Dynasty in the fifteenth century were sufficient to ensure it a nominal and ritual place for the next three centuries. Like Japanese emperors in the same period, however, the Le counterparts were rendered powerless by new forces that valued them only because of their historic eminence in Viet and Chinese eyes. The first such force into the field was the Mac family of military guardians of the weakened court, which claimed the throne in its own name in 1527. This inaugurated one of the most turbulent periods of Dai Viet history, when the population was significantly reduced by incessant warfare and instability. Mac rule was challenged by two military clans from the Thanh Hoa area, the same southern borderland of Tongking that had led resistance against the Chinese. The Nguyen and the Trinh jointly recovered a Le pretender from the Lao hills and fought the Mac in his name. Distrust between the legitimist allies was, however, intensified by the political assassinations of the two leading Nguyen figures, father and son, in separate incidents. Fearing for his safety as the Trinh gained the upper hand, a younger son, Nguyen Hoang, volunteered in 1558 to go to the newly conquered but contested south as Governor of the Quang Nam area in the name of the Le. Concentrating his forces there in relative safety from the fratricidal horrors of the civil war in Tongking, he gradually built up his power. He found abundant local resources to sustain a new state known to Europeans as Cochin-China, and to Vietnamese as *Dang Trong*.

Recent studies have emphasized that Nguyen Hoang by no means built this state in a vacuum. Vietnamese soldiers of or refugees from the various Tongking factions, Cham survivors, and foreign traders had continued to interact in this crucial stage on the route to China throughout the sixteenth century. Up until 1608, Japanese ships had continued to use the term Champa for what was probably the old Cham port and heartland on the Thu Bon River. By the 1620s this port emerges into Vietnamese usage as Hoi An and foreign usage as Faifo, and one assumes the Nguyen had gained control of it. An acute northern observer later noted that this "was a place in which ships gathered since ancient times. Since the Nguyen occupied the area, they gained much from the taxes on the shipping trade" (Le Quy Don 1776/1993, 26). Hoi An quickly became a center of choice for exchanges between Japanese traders (banned from direct access to China) and Chinese. Although drawing some of their power from Vietnamese-style delta agriculture further north in Quang Nam and Thuan Hoa, the Nguyen drew most of their wealth and military *materiel* from this port, in the manner of *negeri* in the Islands.

By 1600 it was becoming clear that Nguyen Hoang had given up ambitions for the center and was seeing himself as an alternative shogun-like lord (*Chua*), whose loyalty to the nominal Le emperors held little meaning as long as they were held hostage by the Trinh. Not until 1624, however, did Hoang's son and successor formally reject a Trinh demand for tax revenues, precipitating a series of seven bitter wars between the two Viet states in the period 1627–72. While vastly outnumbered by Tongking troops, the southerners held their own through superior arms (many from Portuguese sources), organization, and perhaps motivation. Thereafter mutual exhaustion dictated a stalemate that became a permanent walled border to the south of Nghe An (Map 9.1). The following century was one of relative peace, allowing Cochin-China to expand its activities further south. In 1702 its ruler requested China to recognize him as king of Dai Viet, but received the reply that the Le were already so regarded. In practice the Nguyen were independent kings capable of innovative Confucian justifications of their virtue. Nguyen Phuc Khoat (r.1738–65), in particular, called himself not only king but "Grand Mentor," in emulation of one of the virtuous small states admired by Confucius 2,000 years earlier.

Debate will long continue on the extent to which the *Nam Tien* did shift the Indo-Chinese Peninsula in a more Sinified or Confucian direction and transform the lifestyle of the peoples who fell under Viet control. At the level of the literate elite on whose records we largely rely, ideals of correct behavior upheld

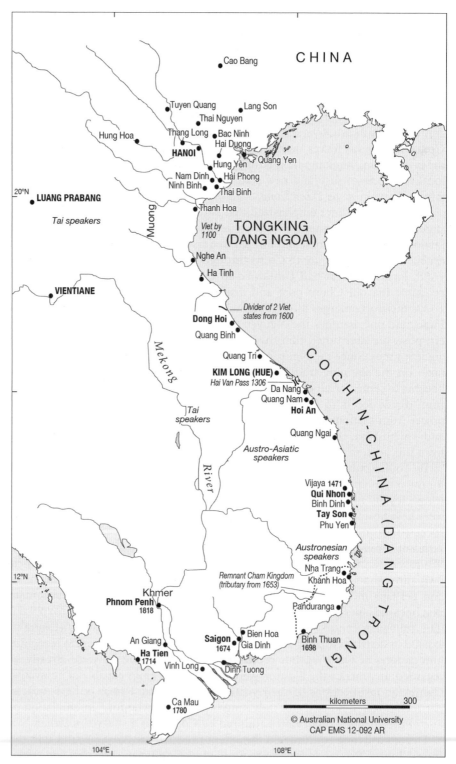

Map 9.1 Viet expansion southward.

by Tang and Song Dynasty writers in China became the standard, by which Southeast Asian practices like eating with the right hand, chewing betel, and dressing in simple wrap-around *sarung* were found wanting. More central is the position of Chinese women, whose bound feet and powerless transfer from control of the father to that of the husband and his family seems the antithesis of the Southeast Asian pattern we have sketched. The Nguyen legal code issued at the height of the late neo-Confucian reaction of the nineteenth century (see below) appeared indeed to seek to impose a replica of late Chinese Qing-Dynasty codes. It was a relief to nationalists when the older Le Code was found to embody more even-handed provisions on matters such as women's inheritance. This was based on older Chinese models before Chinese inheritance had been adjusted by neo-Confucians to exclude female inheritance. Both codes probably encouraged literati families that read them to treat their women in a more Confucian way. But social practice diverged very profoundly from these norms on matters of marriage and inheritance. In the south and in the western hills, nineteenth-century visitors still found women conducting virtually all commercial transactions. Chapter 15 looks more carefully at the ways in which European, Chinese, Islamic, and otherwise "modern" gender relations tended to spread more restrictive female roles downward from the top, as an unfortunate aspect of status systems that privileged the foreign. But Viet interaction with the peoples and environment of the south made it far more difficult for these idealized Confucian models to impose themselves on social realities.

COCHIN-CHINA'S PLURAL SOUTHERN FRONTIER

Tens of thousands of Tongking-born Viet farmers came to the less-populated south in the seventeenth century, as soldiers of the Nguyen, captives and defectors from the Trinh armies, refugees from the incessant fighting in the north, or simply in search of more land. In mid-century over 20,000 captives were settled on land in Phu Yen alone, close to the northern border of the remnant Champa state of Panduranga at modern Phan Rang. In 1693, when the last of a series of Cham rebellions was crushed and Panduranga was reduced to a powerless tributary little different from a province, even that barrier was removed. Where they settled, the Viet adapted local Cham agricultural methods, but also added deltaic techniques of dykes and canals long practiced in Tongking. They did not always directly displace Cham farmers whose agricultural pattern was more dispersed. These pioneer settlers in turn colonized the immensely fertile Mekong delta in the eighteenth century, but there they faced bigger challenges of a landscape that disappeared entirely under water in the flood season. Keeping the family and the essential buffaloes alive through that season required the special skills the Khmer had long developed.

Cochin-China was already a player in the Mekong delta throughout the seventeenth century. Even if Cham, Malay, and Chinese pioneers were all initially more numerous than Viet, the Nguyen armed galleys had a military edge in many of the contests of that turbulent century. In 1616 a Cochin-China princess was married to the Cambodian king who was struggling to keep order on the lower Mekong. This alliance helped Cambodia defeat a Thai intervention in 1619, and probably established a Viet military presence in the capital at Phnom Penh. Cochin-China intervened again in 1658, to help a rebel alliance overthrow the Muslim king of Cambodia, after which the Buddhist replacement was expected to send tribute to Cochin-China. When the fighting with Tongking stopped in the 1670s Cochin-China was freer to pursue an expansionist policy in its open southern frontier, and intervened regularly thereafter in every Cambodian succession dispute. The shape of the future emerged as early as 1674 when Cochin-China supported a second Khmer ruler near modern Saigon, more of a Viet client than his Phnom Penh rival.

Cochin-China's privileged relation with Chinese refugees and settlers was the key to its eventual success in the Mekong delta. The Nguyen rulers in the south were free to accept Chinese rebels and refugees, while Tongking shared a dangerous border with China and had to manage the delicate tributary relations in the name of the captive Le ruler. This became crucial when the Manchus conquered the China heartland in 1644, and struggled to gain control of the troublesome maritime provinces of Fujian and Guangdong with their many overseas connections. In its fight with the Fujian- and Taiwan-based Zheng family, which proclaimed continued loyalty to the Ming but operated an independent maritime empire with hundreds of ships, the Manchus banned seaborne trade altogether and tried to evacuate coastal trading centers. The maritime traders had little choice but to join the Zheng opposition, which itself was finally crushed in 1684, or to seek opportunities overseas. Cochin-China, and the "water frontier" of the Mekong delta and Gulf of Thailand, was a natural destination. By 1700 there were an estimated 30,000 such Ming loyalists in Cochin-China, and "Ming exiles" (*Minh Huong*) later became the standard way of referring to long-settled Chinese.

The balance of power in the Mekong delta area was tipped in 1679 by a well-armed flotilla of such refugees. Some 50 ships and 3,000 Chinese soldiers defecting from the losing battle being fought by the Zheng family in Taiwan arrived in Hoi An. The Nguyen ruler accepted them as civilized fellow *Han* but shrewdly sent them to settle the Saigon area at the northern edge of the Mekong delta. The squabbling Cambodian rulers had no such resources at their disposal, and, in effect, control of the vital maritime entries to the Mekong passed to this group of Chinese. Not until 1732 did a Viet administration in Bien Hoa end the virtual autonomy of their commercial center on the Saigon River, while the Mekong delta proper remained an ungoverned frontier for much longer. The Ming refugees formed a military vanguard for further Chinese and Viet settlers on Khmer territory, built the Saigon area into a major commercial center, and extended the frontier of *Han* civilization. A Vietnamese chronicler noted that after they arrived "the region around Saigon began to be more and more influenced by *Han* customs" (cited Choi 2004, 39). On the other hand, ethnic relations were particularly bitter in this frontier of "much *yang* and not much *yin*" (Trinh 1820, cited Dutton et al. 2012, 269). Catholic missionaries are the best source for outbreaks of appalling violence in which ordinary Khmer and Viet killed each other in their thousands, in 1730–1, 1750–1, and 1769. Chinese in turn were targeted by the Tay Son in 1782 (see below). As a frontier, the Mekong delta saw a great deal of intermarriage of immigrant males with local women, cultural and religious hybridity, and commercial interaction. In the absence of agreed norms of government, however, it also had a frontier fluidity that allowed conflicts to rage unchecked.

Mac Cuu was an enterprising Hainanese who left his native Guangdong as a teenager in the 1670s, and built up a following among fellow-Hainanese, Cantonese, and Teochiu in the frontier area of Cambodia's coast on the Gulf of Thailand. In about 1700 he bought from the Cambodian king the monopoly license to farm gambling revenues in the small port of Ha Tien (Cancao to Europeans), and gradually built it into an autonomous port-state. He and his Sino-Viet son and successor minted their own coins, built temples and fortresses, and sought to uphold there the dress and rituals of the defeated Ming court. The port's success drew repeated attacks from Siam, which led the Macs gradually to seek more protection from Cochin-China. It remained above all a frontier town throughout the eighteenth century, however, profiting from the absence of the suffocating embrace of any major state. It became a second Chinese-dominated but multi-ethnic commercial frontier for expanding *Han* culture. A third was the Bassac River, the southernmost navigable outlet of the Mekong to the sea, and therefore the furthest from the growing control of Cochin-China.

These three centers between them in the 1760s became the dominant hub for Chinese shipping in its expansive phase in Southeast Asia, replacing both Hoi An and Ayutthaya (Siam), and exceeding Batavia or Manila. With Siam on its knees from the Burmese invasion, tin, sappanwood, pepper, and other "Straits produce" from Siam, Cambodia, the Peninsula, and Sumatra was exported through these frontier entrepôts to China. The upheavals of the Tay Son followed by the rise of stronger Mainland states and of Singapore in the nineteenth century put an end to this phase and created other magnets for Chinese. Nevertheless, Chinese remained vital in the economy of this area as pepper and sugar cultivators as well as traders.

THE GREATER VIET NAM OF THE NGUYEN

The independent history of a single Vietnamese state from the Chinese border to the Gulf of Thailand was of short duration, from 1802 to the French seizure of Saigon and the Mekong delta in 1859–61. The remarkable achievement of unifying this improbably long stretch of coastline was not in fact, and arguably could never have been, the result of a relentless "march south" from the historic Dai Viet state in Tongking. Rather it was the messy, multicultural dynamism of the south that managed to march north at the end of the eighteenth century. It was the product of an extended period of warfare, and imposed by one essentially military regime at the expense of another. Nobody can be sure how long the unified state that now called itself Viet Nam could have endured without the French intervention. But the cultural achievements discussed in Chapter 8 had laid the basis for a common sensibility among all who could read *nom* or enjoy the literature of performance in Vietnamese.

The destruction of the two-state model that had endured almost two centuries was brought about by the very success of the Nguyen in riding the commercial expansion of the southern frontier. By 1770 their original cash cow in Hoi An had become moribund, and the center of commercial exchanges had shifted to the Mekong delta area they were in no position to squeeze. The rice surplus on which the Cochin-China capital and army depended was now produced primarily in the commercial south, and had to be paid for by taxing some more vulnerable province. The heaviest burden in fact fell on cash-crop producers in the central highlands, from whom a new challenge suddenly developed. In 1773 a betelnut trader and minor official named Nguyen Nhac led a party of trained malcontents down from these highlands to capture the provincial capital of Quy Nhon. The movement became known by the name of their home village, Tay Son (western mountains). Having succeeded so easily, they quickly spread the movement north and south. As they went they adopted popular symbols of local Cham and highlander identity, as well as the soubriquet "virtuous and charitable thieves" given them by peasants happy to see them attack the unprecedented riches of the then regent and extortionist-in-chief of Cochin-China.

As the Tay Son began to challenge the Cochin-China heartland, Tongking saw its opportunity to attack from the north in 1774. This pincer pressure from north and south forced the Nguyen to abandon their capital by sea, and re-establish their base in the wealthy but turbulent south. The northern forces then advanced against the Tay Son, whose leader Nguyen Nhac cleverly submitted on the understanding that the Tay Son would continue the fight against the Nguyen in the south while the northerners held Phu Xuan and the center. Warfare then continued for a decade between the Nguyen and the Tay Son for control of the flourishing commercial centers of Gia Dinh and Saigon. These changed hands several times before the final victory of the Tay Son in 1785. In the process the Tay Son destroyed most of the Nguyen forces in 1777, killing all members of the ruling family except the 15-year-old prince Nguyen Anh. Although the Tay Son rise had been made possible by the support of Chinese armed brotherhoods (hui), relations worsened to culminate in anti-Chinese pogroms in 1782 when the Tay Son massacred all the Chinese traders they could find after taking Saigon. Victim estimates range from 4,000 to 20,000.

Nguyen Anh's last stand of this phase of the war was virtually a Siamese incursion, as the prince-pretender fled to Bangkok and persuaded the soldier-king Taksin to back his bid to regain power. The first direct Siamese-Vietnamese confrontation ended in a complete victory for the latter, the Tay Son annihilating the Siamese navy of 300 ships in an ambush on an arm of the Mekong in January 1785. The Tay Son were now free to turn their attention north. Nguyen Nhac had already proclaimed himself Emperor in 1778, though symbolically using a former Cham center as his imperial capital rather than Phu Xuan, now occupied by the northerners. Profiting from a succession crisis in Tongking, he sent his brother north with an army that took Phu Xuan in June 1786, and Thang Long (Hanoi) only a month later as the Trinh regime disintegrated. Nguyen Nhac and his two brothers now divided into three the vast territory that had fallen to them, though the northern third was nominally under the authority of a restored Le emperor whose daughter one of the brothers had married. After a second round of fighting over the north, however, the Le emperor appealed for Chinese intervention. A vast Qing (Manchu) army occupied Hanoi in 1788 without resistance, but was expelled only a few months later as a Tay Son army fell on them unawares at midnight during the New Year holidays. Equally impressive was the skill of the second Tay Son brother in having the Chinese court recognize him as legitimate king of all Viet Nam. His Quang Trung Dynasty began to fall apart with his death in 1792, however. Brief, upstart, *ad hoc*, and bloody as it was, the Tay Son irruption of energy was celebrated by many nationalists and Marxists as a liberation, a peasant rebellion, a unifier of the country, and defender against foreign intervention. Its achievement in destroying the old system is more evident than in building the new, but it did begin an important experiment of translating the Chinese classics into *nom* so that examinations could be conducted in the vernacular.

It was Nguyen Anh who reaped the harvest of founding a new dynasty to rule an unprecedentedly large Viet Nam. He did so in a distinctly southern and pluralist way troubling to nationalist narratives. Desperate for allies to retake the very plural south, he reached out to hybrid southerners we might today label Siamese, Malays, Chinese, and Khmers, as well as Dutch, Portuguese, and French. He attempted alliances with Siam, vitiated by conflicts over Cambodia, and France and other European states, interrupted by the French Revolution. One of his most sustained supporters was the French priest Pigneau de Behaine, who befriended the desperate pretender in 1777 and shared his flight around islands in the Gulf of Thailand. He traveled to Pondicherry and France on Nguyen Anh's behalf in 1786–7, and eventually returned without the promised royal support but with a collection of arms, four ships, and about 40 European mercenaries he had enrolled in the cause. Nguyen Anh's other allies had enabled him to retake Saigon in 1788, but the subsequent arrival of Pigneau's men undoubtedly assisted his subsequent strategic advances. Nguyen Anh eventually conquered the Tay Son stronghold of Quy Nhon in 1799, and the other major centers including Thang Long (Hanoi) in a rapid advance in 1802. A British visitor estimated that the king's able deployment of his few European mercenaries helped produce "a more regular and effective military power than probably was ever before formed" in southern Asia (Crawfurd 1828/1967, 509). Even when the standing army was reduced after the conquest from 150,000 men to 50,000, it included 200 60-oared gunboats carrying up to 22 guns each, and 600 smaller armed galleys.

A new Nguyen Dynasty, Viet Nam's last and most ambitious, thus began the mammoth task of seeking to integrate its entire S-shaped domains. Its roots were firmly in the south, and its military strength based on the battle-hardened southern warriors. Nguyen Anh ruled the center directly from his new capital of Hue near that of his ancestors in Phu Xuan, with the reign title Gia Long (1802–20). In the south he installed a governor necessarily tolerant of the Chinese, Christian, Cham, and Khmer diversities through which he had come to power. Only after his son succeeded with the reign name Minh Mang

(1820–41) did sternly assimilationist policies produce a bitter Khmer rebellion in 1833, even sterner repression, and a legacy of ethnic hostility.

In the north the new administration had to rely on the literati elite then enjoying its most creative phase. Some of its greatest works had already been written as the Dai Viet state was disintegrating, but a new dynasty presented the challenge of an empty slate. In effect the Nguyen regime undertook a neo-Confucian redefinition of the state, beginning in Tongking where it had little other basis for legitimacy except that which was offered by its literati collaborators. These scholars had educated the second ruler Minh Mang, who sought in Confucian virtue a solution to the many challenges assailing the country. He attempted to impose this orthodoxy as a cure-all even in advancing the frontier of *Han* civilization at the expense of Cambodia. His neo-traditional reforms had a provisional quality not unlike the equally short-lived French regime that followed. Each was educating its future officials on radically new principles that were nevertheless unable to keep up with the pace of change. The Nguyen attempt at redefinition will be weighed in a broader context in Chapter 11.

THE COMMERCIAL EXPANSION OF A "CHINESE CENTURY," 1740–1840

The Ming loyalist refugees of the seventeenth century had been exceptional in the long story of Chinese emigration. They consciously sought to use their muscle to build Chinese-style polities outside imperial control. The usual economic factors returned once the new Manchu government vanquished its maritime opponents in the 1680s and reopened its ports for business. There was still official hostility to leaving the Middle Kingdom to live abroad, but only a wealthy trader like Chen Ilao of Batavia would attract sufficient attention to be punished in returning to China. His exemplary trial and banishment in 1749 was the last, and five years later the judgement was effectively reversed by a decree that allowed Chinese males (women were still totally banned) to leave and to return with their foreign wealth. The population of the Manchu Empire as a whole grew from about 150 million in 1700 to 400 million in 1850, increasing its contrast with sparsely settled Southeast Asia, whose population was still below 50 million in 1850. The open frontiers of the south beckoned. The period 1740–1840 has been labeled Southeast Asia's "Chinese century" in a corrective to Eurocentric histories, because of the dynamic role of southern Chinese traders, miners, craftsmen, shipbuilders, and agriculturalists in opening up its economic frontiers.

Europeans had contributed substantially to Southeast Asia's age of commerce in the long sixteenth century, but the Dutch and English monopolies had a stultifying effect in the period that followed, reducing incentives for participation in the world economy. The new commercial dynamic evident in the late eighteenth century was carried by actors outside the mercantilist systems of states. Other Asian or Asia-based traders (including British and

French "country traders" with Asian crews and home ports), and, after 1776, Americans from Boston and Salem, played a major part, but Chinese were the prime exemplars of the trend. If Newbold (1839/1971 I, 9) is right in estimating the total Chinese population of Southeast Asia to have risen to "nearly a million" by 1830, then their proportion of the total Southeast Asian population (2–3%) would then have been greater than in later periods, including that of the notorious "coolie trade." The striking feature of this period is that Chinese enterprise focused on frontiers outside strong state control, such as the Mekong delta area just discussed.

In their early expansive phase as Asian trade hubs, Spanish Manila and Dutch Batavia had been the greatest magnets for Chinese traders and craftsmen, but this honeymoon soured as the European establishments felt their comfortable monopolies threatened by more dynamic and hungry Chinese. An anti-Chinese pogrom spectacularly marked the change of mood, though economic changes were more decisive. In 1740 some disgruntled Chinese who had lost their jobs on sugar plantations attacked the outskirts of Batavia, prompting a wave of paranoia among Dutch and other residents. Some 6,000–10,000 Chinese in the city were massacred and their goods seized, disastrously wounding the city's economic lifeblood. The VOC was upset enough over this atrocity to imprison the Governor-General who had presided over it and to send a letter of apology to the Chinese court. The official reaction in Beijing appeared calmer, since the victims were in any case unfilial subjects who should not have left their homes: "Now that the King [Governor-General] of Java repented and wished to reform … the various barbarians in the southern oceans [should] be allowed to trade with us as usual" (cited Blussé 2008, 42). In Manila, pogroms had already occurred in the previous century without upsetting longer-term trade, but in 1755 the Spanish excluded non-Catholic Chinese from the Philippines altogether. A distinct overseas Chinese identity was for the following century less attractive in the Dutch settlements and virtually impossible in the Spanish. Chinese already in the Philippines became Catholic *mestizo* in the second generation, and were increasingly dominant in the economy until in the mid-nineteenth century they merged with the Filipino elite to become the landed aristocracy of the country. Chinese in Java were more inclined to assimilate into the indigenous states through Islamization. China-based traders and new migrants, on the other hand, shifted focus to Asian-ruled ports that became the new hubs of Chinese commerce in the Nanyang.

The long reign of the Qienlong Emperor (1736–95) was a final period of relative order and prosperity in China before its modern decline. It even renewed the policy, not seen since the fifteenth century, of intervention in the succession crises of its southern neighbors. There were short-lived and unsuccessful invasions by land into Burma in 1766 and Tay Son Viet Nam in 1788. Since the restorer of Siamese sovereignty after a Burmese conquest, King Taksin, was initially deemed a "usurper" in Beijing, there was a disruption even to this natural alliance. Exceptionally cordial relations followed these crises, however, as if all parties recognized the need for solidarity against greater threats from the West. Viet Nam and Siam sent missions almost every year from 1788 to 1830, more than at any time since 1460. Even the slave-raiding island *negeri* of Sulu, anxious for commercial relations outside the threatening Spanish embrace, sent seven "tribute" missions through Xiamen in 1727–66, something no Archipelago state had done for two centuries.

Chinese traders and migrants were an essential resource for Siam and many independent *negeri* of the Malay world in this period, providing precious revenue through export duties and opium and gaming monopolies. The heavily armed Ming loyalists of the seventeenth century had been divisively political, and their ambitions had fed directly into those of the turbulent frontier world of the Gulf of Thailand and Mekong delta. Whereas the Cantonese of Ha Tien assisted the rise of the Nguyen, the rival Teochiu of the Chantaburi area provided the initial military muscle for the half-Chinese King Taksin to establish Siam's authority in the same disputed area. By contrast, later Chinese traders and migrants of the eighteenth appeared relatively harmless to Southeast Asian rulers. "The peaceable, unambitious and supple character of the Chinese [junk traders] and the conviction, on the part of the native governments, of their exclusive devotion to commercial pursuits, disarm all jealousy, and make them welcome guests everywhere" (Crawfurd 1820 III, 185).

The junk trade of Bangkok appears to have risen more than tenfold in the century up to the 1820s, most of the increase being under the auspices of the Chakri rulers from 1782. Bangkok was Southeast Asia's principal entrepôt for Chinese shipping at the time John Crawfurd surveyed it in the 1820s, with about 80 sea-going junks based there and another 60 visiting each year from China (Crawfurd 1828/1967, 410–16). Saigon and other ports in the Mekong delta also had an extraordinary growth once Nguyen control became established, although most of the junks based there escaped official Vietnamese control and duties. Both Bangkok and the Mekong delta ports became great centers for Chinese shipbuilding at about half the cost of building in Fujian. The hybrid European-influenced ships of Nguyen Viet Nam quickly became both the most frequent visitors to Singapore on its establishment in 1819, and the most admired by European observers. Although the Vietnamese chronicles give little hint of such maritime dynamic, these neat "Cochin-Chinese" ships became an essential staple in the rise of Singapore in the period 1820–50.

In the Archipelago and Peninsula, too, Chinese demand for tropical products as well as staples such as rice and cotton increased strongly in the latter part of the eighteenth century and the beginning of the nineteenth. The traditional attitude of the Chinese court that China needed nothing from abroad was broken as population increases and crop failures created a demand for the cheaper imported rice of the Chao Phraya and Mekong deltas. As early as 1722 the Imperial court ordered that 18,000 tons of rice be imported from Siam and the taxes on it waived to relieve shortages. Later in the century, rice exports to southern China became a major factor also for southern Viet Nam and Luzon (Chapter 11). But although the rice trade helped change official attitudes, more valuable items such as pepper, sugar, gold, tin, pearls, sea-slugs, sharks fin, birds' nests, and tortoiseshell were more profitable for shippers. Ports outside the European networks proved the more enterprising in meeting this demand in the "Chinese century." Sulu, a sultanate on the small islands between Mindanao and Borneo, was one example of the phenomenon, gathering sea-products to send to China and using this trade wealth also to fund a slave-raiding and marketing system. Trengganu and Kelantan on the Peninsula, the Riau-Lingga archipelago to the south of Singapore, and Brunei and Pontianak in Borneo were other ports which profited from the demand from China and the visits from its junks.

The trade and shipping indices make clear that it was not European stimulus that explains the return of export growth to Southeast Asia in the late eighteenth century after a long stagnation, but the Asian, and particularly Chinese, demand. Even in a European port like Dutch Melaka, Chinese and Malay ship calls more than doubled between 1761 and 1780 to become the dominant traffic of the port, while Dutch declined and only English rose to a comparable degree. The data compiled by Crawfurd show that only about one eighth of Chinese vessels trading to Southeast Asia visited the European ports, a striking contrast with a century or more earlier, when Manila and Batavia alone attracted more than half.

CHINESE ON SOUTHERN ECONOMIC FRONTIERS

The growth of China's economy in the eighteenth century, and the lifting of restrictions on coming and going, stimulated a demand for minerals and tropical products that drove the frontier of Chinese economic activity southward. Colonies of Chinese miners were established in the northern tributaries of Dai Viet and Burma, and in western Borneo, Phuket, Kelantan, and Bangka. Chinese planters established new export industries of pepper in Brunei, Cambodia, and Chantaburi, gambir in Riau and Johor, and sugar in Siam and Cochin-China.

Yunnan was the Chinese mining Eldorado of the eighteenth century, attracting about half a million miners by the century's end. The thirst for silver, copper, lead, iron, and tin did not respect any borders, however. Chinese miners would negotiate with any authority that claimed a share of the profits. Silver was a constant need of China's expanding economy, and the miners followed the seams southward through the stateless highlands between China and Southeast Asia. The Bawdwin and Mawling mines in the northern Shan area tributary to Burma, one of Asia's richest sources of silver and lead, had attracted Chinese miners since 1412, Ming records suggest, but malaria and the rugged terrain had protected it against imperial control. In the eighteenth century production was lifted to meet the Chinese demand, and tens of thousands of Chinese miners worked there. Having defeated four Chinese invasions of the area in the 1760s, the kings of Ava were able to extract a good revenue from the Chinese miners by the 1820s, reported to amount annually to about 160 kg of silver or 1,200 pounds sterling.

In the northern borders of Tongking, notably what is today Thai-Nguyen Province, there was also a great eighteenth-century expansion of copper and silver mining. Despite Dai Viet attempts to restrict them, by mid-century there were upward of 20,000 Cantonese at the Tong-tinh copper mining complex alone. By the 1760s the copper mines of this region were perhaps the largest complex in Southeast Asia, producing over 500 tons per annum and providing half the revenues of the Tongking court.

Tin was an export from the Peninsula to India from at least the fifteenth century. Attempts by the VOC and the rulers of Siam and Aceh to control and monopolize the trade in the seventeenth century forced it to migrate to new areas such as Phuket (Junk Ceylon), where for a time it was freer. The first Chinese involvement in mining the rich lode of the Peninsula may indeed have occurred in Phuket in the early eighteenth century. The systematic exploitation of tin to meet the burgeoning demand of China for the tinfoil burnt as joss paper in offerings to the ancestors, however, began with the introduction of Chinese miners to Bangka in the middle of that century.

The tin of Bangka had apparently been discovered only around 1710 by Muslim Sino-Malays familiar with mines on the Peninsula. In 1722 the VOC tried to monopolize its output through a contract with the Sultan of Palembang. Production by traditional Southeast Asian methods produced a few hundred tons a year until about 1750, when a local Chinese began systematically importing Chinese contract workers from Guangdong with their more sophisticated sluicing techniques. Production increased rapidly, so that deliveries to the VOC averaged 1,562 tons a year by the 1760s. The VOC monopoly was by no means effective, and English, Chinese, and other traders exported the lion's share of the output in the later eighteenth century through independent ports such as Riau, Trengganu, and Ha Tien. By the 1770s about 5,000 tons of Southeast Asian tin a year was being exported to China, mostly from Bangka, making it the leading production center in the world.

At this point there were probably over 6,000 Chinese miners in Bangka, chiefly Hakkas from the Meixian area of Guangdong. They were organized in profit-sharing teams (*kongsi*, pinyin *gongsi*) of about 30 men, often indebted to a Sino-Malay trader in Palembang who provided the capital for their journey to Bangka. This teamwork made possible an altogether larger scale of operation. The ore was extracted to a depth of 10 meters with a chain-pallet pump and smelted with a superior furnace and bellows. Consequently "Banka tin" gained an unrivalled reputation for purity worldwide. Production faltered during the insecurity at the end of the century, but increased again once the Dutch after 1816 decided to rule the island directly and even supervise the importation of Chinese labor. Tin production was again around 3,000 tons a year in the 1830s, when demand was expanding through the rapid European advances in manufacturing tin plate. By the 1850s Southeast Asia was providing most of Europe's tin.

Chinese mining gradually wrought the same transformation on the rich Peninsula tinfields as it had in Bangka, though with many initial setbacks from the lack of security, feuds among miners, and periodic pogroms against them. Clearing the forest and scouring the surface with their tin pits, they created a rugged frontier that attracted others to feed and supply them. The Sultan of Perak experimented with bringing in Chinese miners on the Bangka model in the 1770s, and his Selangor counterpart followed suit in 1815. In Sungei Ujung (modern Seremban area) there were said to be nearly a thousand

Chinese working in 1828 when a massacre ended the experiment. Each time violence broke out new miners were induced to return a few years later. By 1835 the whole Peninsula was estimated to produce 2,050 tons a year, the largest amounts coming from Perak, Sungei Ujung, and Trengganu. The British Straits Settlements (Penang, Melaka, and Singapore) exported 3,750 tons a year of Peninsula tin by mid-century, keeping pace with the Bangka production. The modern tin industries of Malaysia and Indonesia were a creation of the "Chinese century," not the colonial one.

Gold may have been the first Southeast Asian mineral to attract Chinese miners, with some local traditions suggesting the mines at Pulai, in upriver Kelantan on the Peninsula, go back to Ming times (pre-1644). Firm evidence only exists for the eighteenth century, however, when larger-scale sluice mining by experienced Hakka *kongsis* replaced the earlier individual initiatives. These cooperatives, some having secretive Ming-loyalist rituals since the seventeenth century, flourished most remarkably on the west Borneo goldfields where they became little republics. These were ritual brotherhoods in which capital and labor were shared in acknowledged portions. The capitalist who established the mine and funded the importation of workers of course had the largest share, and laborers still indebted for their passage had none, but older workers did share decision-making and often rotated the leadership among themselves. The social cement of the *kongsi* was its temple-like communal hall with the image of a patron deity at its center, where new migrants from China would be ritually initiated. In Borneo these buildings were typically also strongly fortified in keeping with their often-contested political role.

Borneo had long been known as a source of gold as well as diamonds, and the Malay *negeri* of its west coast river-ports had profited by exchanging salt, rice, and opium for whatever was found by upstream Dayak fossickers. Around 1740 or 1750 the rulers of Sambas and Mempawah learned of the more systematic methods of Chinese (mostly Hakka) miners and invited them to start work in the same areas. Some Hakka *kongsis*, perhaps initially financed by established Hokkien traders, began work with their chain-pallet pumps in similar areas the Dayaks had worked. Gradually the *kongsis* became autonomous by forming their own relations with interior Dayaks, farming the surrounding land, and smuggling their gold out through channels not controlled by the rajas. Though their institutions continued in the Borneo forest the familiar temple-centered village and communal life of rural China, they have been celebrated as Asia's first republics, since they levied taxes, controlled land, and made war and peace. The wealthier Chinese were able to "buy" a Dayak wife by adapting local bride-price customs, and to educate the children of such unions to be literate in Chinese. Despite much initial violence, a degree of integration was achieved between Chinese and Dayak societies, and stories were exchanged attributing Dayak origins to ancient Chinese settlers in Borneo.

In 1776–7 two powerful federations of *kongsis* were formed, and constituted the most effective state-like entities of western Borneo. Their conflicts were chiefly with each other, as Luo Fangbo of the Lanfang *kongsi* reached a dominant position in Montrado, hoping even to turn it into another "outer country" (*waifan*) tributary to China. "In pacifying barbarians and routing bandits, three years were spent. Twice new regions were opened and frontiers established" (Luo Fangbo 1780, cited Yuan 2000, 54). The Dutch began attempts to control and tax them in 1818, but achieved little until an aggressive policy broke their armed resistance in the 1850s. As the gold began to be exhausted and the more established Chinese-Dayak families turned their attention to agriculture, the Lanfang *kongsi* was the last to be disbanded, in 1884.

An English visitor to Pontianak in 1811 was told that the Montrado *kongsi* had about 30,000 Hakka miners and associated farmers and craftsmen. He listed about 5,000 more Chinese miners scattered in other river valleys. In Pontianak town itself the 10,000 Chinese were the largest and most productive group. Many Chinese had by then become settled householders with local wives, farming, fishing, or engaging in various trades and crafts for the regional economy. Crawfurd's survey of Chinese shipping about 1820 identified west Borneo as its busiest southern hub, with seven 500-ton junks each year (as against nine to the rest of the Archipelago) visiting the three ports of the goldfields (Pontianak, Mempawa, and Sambas), bringing men and supplies in exchange for gold and other tropical produce (Crawfurd 1820 III, 183).

In addition to mining, commercial agriculture drew thousands of Chinese to Southeast Asia's less populated frontiers in the eighteenth century. Some of this was to supply the immediate needs of trading and mining communities for vegetables and fruit, but most was stimulated by China's growing demand for imports of tropical crops such as sugar, pepper, and gambir. Chinese enterprise began with trading these items to China or Japan, branched into producing them in areas well placed for shipping to China, and sometimes ended by producing for the world market.

Pepper was perhaps the first of the cash crops to attract Chinese cultivators into new areas and technologies. Planting appears to have begun in Brunei where some thousands of Chinese pepper-growers were engaged in the 1760s until driven away by its insecurity. In mid-century there were already Chinese growers of pepper and gambir in Riau, and smaller settlements in Trengganu and elsewhere on the east coast of the Peninsula. The frontier in the eastern Gulf of Thailand provided another base for Chinese cultivation of pepper and sugar. When this production began to succeed, systematic immigration began in the late eighteenth century of Teochiu agriculturalists from the Swatow area, who extended the cultivation of pepper in what is today the coastal border area of Thailand and Cambodia, around Chantaburi. As full-time cultivators of the cash crops, the Chinese developed much more labor-intensive methods of growing pepper with high applications of fertilizer, clean-weeding, and support on cut stakes rather than the live chinkareen trees used in Sumatra. John Crawfurd (1828/1967, 17–18) praised the Chinese who pioneered pepper growing in the British settlement of Penang after 1786 as producing six times as much pepper per hectare as the moribund monopolies under British auspices in Bengkulu. "So neat and perfect a specimen of husbandry nowhere exists in the East as the pepper culture of Penang." These methods eventually stimulated the more intensive modern industry centered in Sarawak and Bangka.

Gambir is an astringent obtained from the gum of a shrub (*Uncaria gambir* or terra Japonica) native to Sumatra. It had long been collected from wild plants and used in Java as an addition to the betel chew. In the later eighteenth century both demand and supply took off, as tanners in China discovered its use as the astringent for tanning leather and batik-producers in Java its value as a dye. The Bugis rulers of the Riau Archipelago contracted with Chinese traders to bring out Chinese laborers on the usual indebted basis to grow gambir as well as pepper in the late 1730s. After Singapore's foundation as a British colony in 1819 the Chinese planters moved there, and to adjacent Johor on the mainland. Johor's emergence as a modern state was largely built by contracting land to Chinese gambir and pepper growers. In the 1830s gambir was introduced to the expanding British leather industry as tannin, which thereafter became the principal source of demand. Britain already imported five million tons of gambir through Singapore in 1839. Much of the thick forest and mangrove of the coastal areas both north and south of Singapore was cleared for the first time by Chinese planters to make way for gambir and pepper cultivation and to provide fuel for the gambir cooking pots.

In the twentieth century, "Chinese" would be redefined as the entrepreneurial minority of Southeast Asia *par excellence*, and their relationship with majority nationalism was fraught by resentment and misunderstanding (Chapter 15). In the pre-nationalist age they must be understood very differently, as Southeast Asia's major source of available skilled labor, and as pioneers of the economic frontiers of its underpopulated "empty center." They were themselves divided by their spoken languages into Hokkiens, Cantonese, Hakka, Teochiu, and Hainanese, though their leaders shared a written language with elites of China and Dai Viet. They married locally, and local languages, as well as *lingua franca* such as Malay and Thai, became their means of communicating with their trade partners and even other Chinese. Like other adventurers from the Indian sub-continent, the Middle East, and Europe, they found many open frontiers in non-colonized Southeast Asia and contributed their share toward its many creative hybridities.

[10] BECOMING A TROPICAL PLANTATION, 1780–1900

In the economically sluggish century before 1760, the VOC sufficiently succeeded in its aim to monopolize key arms of trade to repay its huge outlays in forts and garrisons to protect them. Long before these spice monopolies were broken by the French (1771) and British (1784), however, monopoly conditions had removed all incentives to innovate. The slave-tended nutmeg trees of Banda never recovered from a tsunami that destroyed half of them in 1778. Malukan spices had already become a small part of the VOC system (less than 5% of homeward cargoes), and an insignificant part of Asian or world trade. The growth in long-distance world trade in the eighteenth century was in Indian textiles, Chinese tea and ceramics, West Indian sugar and American tobacco and cotton. Southeast Asia had again become a crossroads rather than a major beneficiary of world trade.

Judging only by the more measurable long-distance trade, the Southeast Asian economies began to grow again in the 1760s, with real dynamism from the 1780s. Much of the growth was generated by Chinese enterprise essentially serving the expanding China market, as described in Chapter 9. Both the junk trade and the Asia-based European "country traders" found Southeast Asia's Asian-ruled ports more attractive in the new quest for products to exchange against Chinese tea and manufactures.

The revolutionary upheavals in Europe and America also shook up the somnolent monopoly systems of the European enclaves in Southeast Asia, and forced some overdue changes. The British occupied Manila in 1762–4, making clear that new types of Asian regional trade had to replace the Manila galleon lifeline to Mexico. The Revolutionary and Napoleonic Wars allowed Britain to occupy Dutch Melaka and Padang (1795), Maluku (1796 and again 1810), and Java itself (1811–16). This British activity in the islands served to increase the opportunities for Asian rulers to throw off monopoly arrangements with the Dutch and Spanish, and to create a freer market in both imports and exports. American vessels, freed by independence from the East India Company's monopolies, became major

A History of Southeast Asia: Critical Crossroads, First Edition. Anthony Reid.
© 2015 Anthony Reid. Published 2015 by John Wiley & Sons, Ltd.

buyers of the pepper and coffee Southeast Asians grew outside the stifling monopoly systems. Southeast Asians rediscovered their entrepreneurial taste for producing for the world market, though now more as individuals than as states.

PEPPER AND COFFEE

The Chinese planters helped bring competition back to the pepper market, but more crucial was the cooperation of enterprising Acehnese and Americans. The western coast of Sumatra was virgin forest land ideal for pepper, probably because it had been exposed to fierce tsunamis every few centuries. After the forest was cleared and burned, pepper vines flourished for several decades under the extensive Sumatran methods, though with diminishing returns as the soil became exhausted. Forced pepper deliveries to the Dutch and British companies were faltering when, in 1787, some officials from British Bengkulu started a private company to contract with independent producers further north. A deal was made with Leube Dapa, the energetic Acehnese ruler of a little river-port, and within a few years this area of what is now southernmost Aceh became the new frontier for pepper-growing. Cultivators were recruited from more settled rice-growing areas of Aceh's north coast and given advances by the entrepreneurial chiefs who opened new river-ports. Fortuitously, enterprising American ship captains discovered this new source of supply in 1793. By 1818 there were 35 ships from Salem and Boston on Aceh's west coast, and they took away most of the harvest of 4,500 tons. French and English country traders soon joined the scramble, some dropping an initial cargo of pepper in British Penang and going back for a second. Throughout the 1820s and 1830s this relatively lawless Aceh frontier produced between 6,000 and 10,000 tons of pepper every year, about half the world's supply.

With a local chief at each small river-port on this exposed coast, competition was robust and conditions were lawless. The Aceh sultanate could neither impose its will nor extract more than a tiny fraction by way of tribute from the competing pepper-rajas. Britain tried to intervene on one side of an Aceh succession dispute in 1819 to establish an alliance with the sultan, while both the United States and France sent gunboats to burn a coastal village as punishment when their nationals were killed in disputes. But neither strategy changed the dynamics of the coast. Both buyers and sellers of pepper preferred dealing with each other directly, with the attendant risks, to buttressing state authority in the area. The profits of the trade appear mostly to have been spent on pilgrimages to Mecca, jewelry, opium, and building fine houses in the more settled Aceh homelands of the planters. Only when the Dutch threatened the southern borders of Aceh territory in 1838 was there a new rallying behind the sultan (Chapter 11). Pepper remained a relatively "free" crop outside state controls for most of the nineteenth century, in contrast to its earlier history.

Coffee was another cash crop well suited to individual enterprise on higher ground previously devoted to shifting agriculture or forest. The coffee tree, native to Ethiopia, had spread around the central Islamic lands in the fifteenth and sixteenth centuries. In 1669 the Turkish ambassador to Paris popularized it as a medicinal drink and by the 1680s cafés were proliferating in France, England, Germany, and Italy. The Dutch Company began by purchasing the beans in Mocha, but when prices were exceptionally high, in 1696, it experimented with planting beans in the environs of Batavia. There was no significant success in these lowlands, and experience would later show that the best results from Arabica coffee were obtained at between 1,000 and 1,700 meters in altitude. Fortuitously, the VOC at the end of the century was beginning to explore the sparsely settled Priangan highlands around modern Bandung in west Java, over which it claimed sovereignty through a Treaty of 1677 with Mataram. In 1707 Governor-General van Hoorn had seedlings distributed to the chiefs in this area, with such brilliant results that by the 1720s west Java eclipsed Mocha to become the main supplier for Europe's burgeoning demand. An average of 1,850 tons of Java coffee a year were delivered to Europe in 1725–39. "Java" became synonymous with coffee. Thereafter, however, Europe's growing coffee demand was met by slave production in the West Indies.

Only after the disruption caused to Atlantic supply by the Revolutionary and Napoleonic wars in Europe did coffee prices rise high enough to stimulate further expansion in Southeast Asia. The same American ships that sought the pepper of Sumatra began buying coffee in Batavia and Padang in the 1790s. The "Priangan-system," whereby coffee quotas at fixed prices were forced on the Sundanese population through chiefs appointed by the Dutch, could not respond as well to this opportunity as free farmers. Minangkabau and Javanese smallholders, who planted coffee on the hillsides above their valley-floor rice paddies, filled about half of Southeast Asian production during the wartime period. The return of Dutch authority and attempts at control after 1824 curbed the Sumatran expansion, but, nevertheless, total Indonesian coffee exports expanded very rapidly up until the 1840s, when it comprised about 60,000 tons a year, over a third of world supplies. By comparison, the high-colonial period that followed was one of stagnation as world leadership passed to other areas such as Brazil.

COMMERCIALIZATION OF STAPLE CROPS

The observable late eighteenth- and early nineteenth-century expansion of trade indicates some more profound changes that would otherwise be difficult to trace. Agriculture was again becoming commercialized, even for staple crops on the valley floors such as rice, cotton, and sugar. Three factors seem to be the most general here: population increase, especially in new frontiers of sedentary agriculture; the spread of Chinese and other entrepreneurs into the agricultural sector; and greater freedom and efficiency in marketing.

Despite the political upheavals that affected Mainland Southeast Asia in the latter part of the eighteenth century, there appears to have been increased population growth, as documented by the new regimes in the early nineteenth century. The same climatic factors that boosted populations in southern China may have been effective further south. In both the Irrawaddy and Mekong deltas there was exceptionally rapid population increase as land-hungry farmers from the crowded northern rice bowls moved to open up newly pacified frontiers in the south. Vietnamese registers showed three times the population in 1847 that they did in 1803, significant even after allowing for under-registration in the earlier period. Land-holdings in these new frontiers were large and surpluses relatively easy to generate. Java's wars finally came to an end at Dutch hands in the Giyanti peace (1755), making possible population increase around 1% a year over the next 80 years. The Philippines population also benefitted from a "colonial peace," rising at similar levels. In the Islands, as in the Mainland, rising population brought intensive irrigated rice cultivation into deltaic and other new areas of relatively high yields.

Much of the production of the new rice frontiers entered the long-distance market, either by going north to feed the capitals of Burma at Ava and of Viet Nam at Hue, or to south China. The Symes mission to Ava in 1795 reported several thousand river boats engaged in taking rice up the Irrawaddy to the capital from the delta. Sugar and cotton production were inherently commercialized since most of the product was exported to China. The advent of Chinese entrepreneurship, labor, and consumption facilitated the new production for the market, whether it went to the cities, the mining communities, or the longer-distance markets in southern China. Chinese merchants also moved into Upper Burma from the 1770s, and there were reportedly 3,000 in Ava alone in 1826. Many focused on cotton production in the dry zone, giving advances to farmers or village headmen to persuade them to plant cotton. In the Philippines, too, the *mestizo* Chinese were reported by 1809 to be advancing money to peasants to secure their rice and sugar crop. In all the core population areas known for intensive agriculture we see a marked increase in the monetization of economies, observable through the mechanism of tax payments in cash.

The relative freedom of trade in the period of revolutionary upheavals in Europe was of course the major external factor that attracted Southeast Asians again into the world market. The success of American free traders helped ensure that the monopolies of the English and Dutch companies did not survive the wartime period, and that Britain's "second empire" in the nineteenth century would be built rather on free trade, opium (see below), and the export of manufactures. The establishment of Penang and, more particularly, Singapore as free trading entrepôts proved a powerful magnet to lure producers into the market. Penang's main trade was in the pepper and betelnut of Aceh, worth over three million dollars in 1858. Singapore quickly became a place where Southeast Asian traders could acquire almost anything they needed in return for their rice, sugar, tin, coffee, or pepper. The Viet Nam emperor Minh Mang, despite his neo-Confucian official preference for self-sufficient agriculture, sent a mission to Singapore in 1825 that opened the door to a flourishing trade exchanging silk, tea, sugar, and rice for cotton cloth, firearms, and opium. At the peak of this trade, in the 1840s, about 150 Euro-Vietnamese hybrid vessels of about 100 tons, known in Singapore as "topes," visited the port each year carrying a trade worth 600,000 Spanish dollars. Siam's trade on Singapore followed a similar pattern, while Bugis and Chinese shippers from around the Archipelago quickly made Singapore the preferred regional entrepôt. Still-independent Bali and Lombok evaded Dutch pressures by shipping their rice to Singapore in exchange for firearms, a trade worth $240,000 at its peak in 1843–4. Overall, Singapore's trade to independent states such as Siam, Viet Nam, Aceh, Asahan, Siak, Trengganu, and the Balinese states doubled or tripled in the period 1825–45, whereas that to European-controlled Java and the Philippines rose only modestly.

Sugar was one of the biggest global growth stories of the eighteenth and early nineteenth centuries, alongside tea, to which English drinkers became equally addicted. England alone imported about 150,000 tonnes a year in 1800, out of a total world production of about 280,000 tons. Because sugar production was labor-intensive, most of the growth occurred under slave conditions in the West Indies. Southeast Asia exported only about 8,000 tons in 1800, though exports rose rapidly as slave production elsewhere faltered. About 44,000 tons per year were exported in the 1830s and 100,000 in the 1840s, by which point it became Southeast Asia's leading export by value.

The earlier history of commercial cane-growing in Southeast Asia had been primarily at the initiative of Chinese, who pioneered production for the China market in the seventeenth century in northern Java, central Siam, and the Quang Nam area of Cochin-China. Typically, a Chinese entrepreneur would find his own Chinese labor for milling, but contract with a local ruler over land and labor for growing the cane. The VOC in Java and Spanish authorities in Luzon had tried to control the industry and channel some of its product to Europe in the eighteenth century, with greatest success in Java during the 1720s and 1730s. The increased demand from China at the end of that century, together with disruptions in Caribbean supply to Europe, provided new stimulus to each sugar frontier. Pampanga in the central Luzon valley, long the rice bowl of the Philippines, began exporting sugar to China in the 1790s and briefly became Asia's biggest sugar exporter in the 1820s. Teochiu Chinese growers in Siam opened a third major frontier of exports on the higher ground of the Chao Phraya valley around 1810, and later extended this in the Southeast of Siam. Sugar became Siam's major export in the 1830s and 1840s, but declined later in the century as domestic consumption took most of the crop and more profitable opportunities opened for exporters in the booming rice trade.

In short, commercialization and world markets returned to playing a major part in Southeast Asian life in the period 1780–1850. This was not a product of the new or high colonialism after 1870, but rather of the liberalization of trade conditions a century earlier.

THE NEW MONOPOLIES: OPIUM AND TOBACCO

The relative success of India-based British traders in this new expansion was inextricably linked to opium. The East India Company succeeded in monopolizing the supply from India in 1773, but its sale to the east remained a quasi-legal undertaking best left to private merchants. Firearms were the other British trade item in demand, and they too were regarded as illegal by established powers. Their quasi-legal status made the trade in opium and firearms dangerous but highly profitable, focusing on markets that were inherently uncontrolled. The rise of British and British-supported state systems in Southeast Asia in the nineteenth century was made possible by these large profits, especially those generated by monopoly opium production.

Poppies can be grown in a great variety of locations, and it was in West Asia that the habit of chewing the opium derived from its seeds began. Though reported much earlier, opium became a major part of medical equipment in both Europe and China by the fifteenth century. It was in eastern Asia that opium began to be smoked in a mixture with tobacco, equally novel an introduction. The mixture was noted in Batavia in 1689. The next step, to dispense with the tobacco altogether by smoking a small drop of a heated syrupy mixture of raw opium and water known as *chandu*, is thought to have been the work of Chinese even though the term is Malay. This made opium consumption both more instantly gratifying and safer than the older practice of ingestion. Sometime in the eighteenth century it began its modern career as a recreational addictive drug, as well as an aid for those enduring heavy labor, arduous travel, or warfare. Controlling the supply to East and Southeast Asia, where it was consumed but not produced, became the new prize of the Asian trade contest.

The VOC had preceded the British in the quest to gain super profits by monopolizing opium supply to any state with which it gained an unequal treaty. Its 1677 treaty with Mataram, which then claimed to rule the Javanese-speaking area of east and central Java, already provided a VOC monopoly on opium supply. The VOC brought an average of 56 tons of opium into Java each year in the eighteenth century, making this one Southeast Asian market where indigenous customers predominated over Chinese. The eighteenth century brought two key advantages to the British: more direct access to the China market through arrangements in Canton from 1716, and a dominant position in Bengal (then including Bihar) after the Battle of Plassey in 1757. Governor Warren Hastings made the purchase of opium a Company monopoly in 1773, and justified this on the grounds that opium was too harmful to be allowed for domestic consumption, but should be controlled for export. Governments in China and parts of Southeast Asia took the same view. By banning cultivation they ensured high prices for the import. The vigorous new dynasties of the Mainland – Burma, Siam, and Viet Nam – all sought to ban opium and keep European traders at arm's length. The struggle around the issue contributed to the downfall of each dynasty except Siam's, which quickly accepted the British model of using the monopoly as a tax on Chinese.

Although strict Muslims and moralists condemned its use in the nineteenth century, there were mystics, aesthetes, and bohemians who applauded its effects. Javanese aristocrats frequently shared an opium pipe as part of important festivals and rituals. The Dutch retained this lucrative monopoly of distribution throughout their dominance in Java, even though they had to buy the opium from the British. Dutch imports for Java rose to 208 tons by 1904, but declined under stricter controls thereafter. There were still more than 100,000 registered smokers in 1929.

In Island Southeast Asia outside Java it was poverty rather than state prohibition that limited consumption to elites in the *negeri*, and to Chinese miners and laborers whom it helped to endure the harsh conditions of the frontier. British country traders and Americans dominated the trade through the Revolutionary and Napoleonic Wars, though progressively losing out in the nineteenth century to Straits-based Chinese vessels. Opium enabled them to buy Southeast Asian tin, pepper, and tropical products valued in Canton in exchange for tea. In the early 1800s, despite repeated imperial bans, China itself became the biggest market. The age-old European "drain" of silver to Asia was now reversed as silver flowed out of China and Southeast Asia to pay for opium and guns. The quantities of opium imported rose ever higher after the East India Company lost its trading monopoly in 1834. From less than 10,000 chests in 1820, India exported over 90,000 at the peak in the 1870s and 1880s, when it was India's most lucrative export with by far the largest profit margin. By then, however, opium was massively produced in China, and its importance in the trade system declined quickly as China became the dominant world producer as well as consumer. Production in Southeast Asia itself was a minor factor among the hill peoples of the north. The colonial powers did everything possible to avoid competition for their highly lucrative importing monopolies. Only in the turbulent 1940s, with the breakdown of monopolies and supplies from India, did the "golden triangle" on the borders with China begin to be a major source.

Opium was in its prime in the nineteenth century as a state revenue earner. Taxing its distribution through a revenue farm allocated to an influential Chinese became a crucial resource of states. Siam, Johor, and British Singapore could not have survived without it. British success in abolishing restrictive levies on trade but instead taxing mostly Chinese consumers through the opium monopoly became a kind of model for Malay states and Siam as well as other colonial regimes. In the second half of the nineteenth century, opium was providing between a quarter and half of the revenues of the more successful port-rulers of the region, and about a sixth that of Netherlands India, through the mechanism of the Chinese revenue farmer.

Revenue farming by contracted agents was a near-universal practice, but it acquired a distinctive form in Southeast Asia through the interaction of Chinese merchants, Dutch Company, and indigenous rulers in the seventeenth century. The VOC, from the outset, had found the commercialism, hierarchy, and unthreatening outsider status of the leading Chinese indispensable. They collected taxes for the VOC on both commercial transactions such as weighing, marketing, and river ferrying, and traditional "vices" including alcohol, opium, and Chinese gambling. Javanese rulers adopted the practice after the Giyanti peace of 1755, and the Sino-Thai regimes in Bangkok, after 1782. Revenue farms concentrated capital in the hands of a handful of wealthy Chinese who became the key mediators between the Chinese community and state power. So central did this institution become in the nineteenth century that the Dutch word for a tax farm (*pacht*) is the source of the modern words for tax in both Indonesian (*pajak*) and Thai (*phaasi*). The battles for control of new frontiers of mining and plantations in the Peninsula and Borneo were often about which Chinese tax-farmer would act on behalf of which ruler.

In Singapore, deprived of revenues from commerce by its free-trade status, the opium farm alone formed about 40% of government revenue for much of the nineteenth century. When a newcomer muscled in at the thrice-yearly auctions, as happened in 1879 with the Governor's support, a major battle ensued as the defeated party tried to destroy the newcomer by smuggling cheaper opium. The stakes were high, since the successful farmer could control many other lines of business. Opium farmers were given legitimacy through Thai, Malay, or Javanese titles and places in the Dutch and British colonial councils. The opium farmers of Singapore usually controlled also the Chinese economy of neighboring Johor and Dutch-ruled Riau, while those in Penang were also involved in monopoly arrangements in Sumatra and the Peninsula. The most spectacular magnate, Thio Thiau Siat (Chang Pi-shih) gained the opium and spirits farm in Aceh after supplying the Dutch military there in the 1870s, and moved into rubber and coffee in east Sumatra, shipping around the Straits with three steamers, and opium and spirits farms in Penang itself (1889) as well as various Sumatran centers. A China-born Hakka, he became Vice-Consul in Penang and Consul-General in Singapore for Beijing in the 1890s, and eventually a major investor in modernizing China itself.

Without direct access to Indian opium, the Philippines did not develop opium as a major revenue source for government. Another narcotic, tobacco, provided the lucrative alternative tax that replaced the defunct exchange role between American silver and Chinese silks. Tobacco had its greatest success in the Philippines, where by the eighteenth century the Filipinos "learned to smoke before they learned to think" according to one Spanish administrator. Another declared that "all over the islands tobacco generally serves as their food and drink … [and] the most effective remedy for the cure of all their deficiencies" (cited de Jesus 1980, 29, 128). The Spanish government, having seen how lucrative a tobacco monopoly could be in Mexico, pressured Manila into developing a similar program to resolve the perennial crisis in its finances. In 1781 Governor José Basco declared all tobacco trade and manufacture a government monopoly, as well as cultivation of the crop in the provinces surrounding Manila. In 1785 the monopoly of cultivation was extended to the unruly and lightly settled Cagayan valley in northern Luzon, which effectively extended the monopoly to the whole island. Despite much initial unrest, the fertile valley became the core of the forced tobacco cultivation system in the nineteenth century, with an influx of growers from Ilocos and Pampanga (Map 10.1).

The manufacture of cigars, cigarettes, and snuff was easier to monopolize, since, in contrast with Mexico, there was an almost blank slate. By 1790 the government had succeeded in forcing all tobacco dealers in Manila to sell to the royal contractor, who then centralized the production of cigarettes in Manila. A factory was built in 1782, and in less than two years was employing 5,000 Filipina women to roll the cigars that in the following century became the trademark of Manila. Even though sales were purely domestic in the first

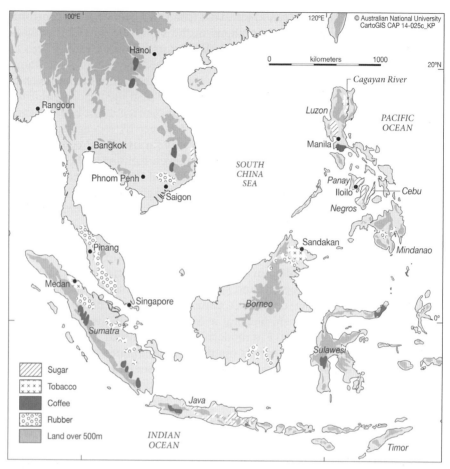

Map 10.1 Export-driven plantation agriculture in the 1920s.

decades of the monopoly, they were large enough to make tobacco the Philippine government's prime source of revenue in the 1790s, with profits averaging 338,000 pesos (Mexican silver dollars) a year. Manila cigars using Cagayan tobacco conquered the world in the following century. The net profits passed 500,000 pesos a year in 1800 and a million by 1840, constituting the principal government revenue until 1870. As the tide turned against government monopolies everywhere, official corruption gave it an odious smell, and sugar became a much more profitable export. The tobacco monopoly was finally abolished in 1882.

Java's Coerced Colonial Agriculture

Java has been labeled the "cradle of colonialism" because of the accident of the VOC headquarters being centered there, but the term more appropriately describes the precocious transformation of the island's economy in the nineteenth century. At the dissolution of the VOC on the last day of the eighteenth century, Batavia was still a declining Euro-Chinese enclave, not unlike a Southeast Asian court held together by marriage networks, a theatrical style of state ritual, and personalistic relations of overlordship with the sultans of Banten to the west, Cirebon to the east, and more tenuously the heirs of the Mataram Dynasty in Yogyakarta and Surakarta. Private estates were distributed to wealthy, often hybridized, Europeans and Chinese in many of the lands closest to Batavia and other Dutch-controlled ports. Within a half-century, however, Java had the tightest system of state control in Southeast Asia, refashioned in the interests of producing a marketable profit through tropical agriculture. A mobile population still able to rely on a diversity of agricultural and forest resources, and very unevenly taxed by various authorities, had been replaced by a system of villages responsible to relatively central control through their appointed headmen. The agents of this change were revolutionary new ideas from Europe, a ruinous war, and a new phase of mercantilism in response to Holland's critically weakened commercial position.

It was Napoleon's brother Louis, as king of the Netherlands, who sent the revolutionary general Herman Willem Daendels out in 1807 to govern Java and rid it of British influence. Contemptuous of the pretensions of foppish monarchs, Daendels began the process of disrupting the old order, starting by abolishing the sultanate of Banten in 1808 (Cirebon would follow at British hands in 1813). Daendels was determined to make Java an efficient military bastion, and forced Javanese convicts and peasants into building the great post road along the north coast of Java, as well as massive public works in Batavia. Thousands died, and the Javanese rulers were sufficiently alarmed to respond warmly to British overtures against him. When Britain took over Java (1811–15), its governor, Thomas Stamford Raffles, proved equally radical a reformer. He sought to abolish forced cultivation and slavery, and to raise revenue through a land tax. This had in the end to be collected on a village basis and required even more compulsion. Since he took the very radical view that all land belonged ultimately to the state, he raised further revenue by selling large holdings as private estates. He cut down the number and privileges of the Javanese elite. On the positive side, he began a system of inoculation against smallpox that eventually contributed to the rapid upturn in Java's population.

Full-scale war came to the Java heartland in 1825, and placed the Dutch for the first time in full control of Java, with the remaining monarchs subordinate both in theory and practice. The innovations of Daendels and then Raffles, followed by the return of an indecisive Dutch regime in 1816, had caused great anxiety in Yogyakarta and Surakarta that the dignity and resources of the kings were endangered, and perhaps their very survival. When a charismatic Yogyakarta prince, Dipanegara, began a revolt that placed the Dutch garrisons under siege, much of the old elite rallied to the cause of restoring a purer kingdom free of barbarous and infidel influence. The Dutch colonial army lost 8,000 of its men and 7,000 of its Javanese allies over the five years of warfare, while Javanese casualties are estimated at about 200,000, or 10% of the affected population. At the end of the Java War, in 1830, Dutch resources were exhausted, but Java lay prostrate and unable to resist a new colonial regime.

Since the more industrialized south of the post-Napoleonic greater Netherlands had just seceded as a newly independent Belgium, Holland was desperate to create a system in Java that could restore the fortunes of the homeland.

The Netherlands returned to its colonial outposts in Southeast Asia after 1816 in a much weaker position than that in which the VOC had originally acquired them. Britain was now the master of the seas, and British cloth manufactures and British-controlled opium were the dominant imports to exchange against tropical produce. Whereas Britain had much to gain from its free-trade ideas, and obliged Holland in the 1824 London Treaty to impose no more than double the duty on British ships and imports that it charged on its own, Holland had every incentive to return to an extreme form of mercantilism. Its ingenious means to achieve this was the Netherlands Trading Company (NHM), known as *Kompeni kecil* (little Company) in the Indies because of its resemblance to the monopolistic VOC. After much dispute with Britain over more blatant violations of the 1824 Treaty, a 12.5% tariff was for the first time imposed on Dutch imports to Java in 1835, so that the British could be charged 25%. This 12.5% was then given to the NHM to help it build and subsidize a viable textile industry in Holland. Under Johannes van den Bosch (Governor-General 1830–3) a system of forced cultivation (*cultuurstelsel*) of export crops, chiefly sugar, coffee, and indigo, was imposed upon Java for delivery to the NHM at artificially low fixed prices. He argued that an allocation of one fifth of their land and labor for this type of taxation was consistent with earlier impositions by their own rulers. The system quickly exceeded the expected profits to the Netherlands, averaging 9.3 million guilders per year in the 1830s and fourteen million in the 1840s, speeding the recovery of the Netherlands. The exports of the then Netherlands Indies (basically Java) increased from thirteen to 74 million guilders in the first ten years of the system, two thirds of it in the hands of the NHM.

Its effect on Java has been much debated. It was the most spectacular example at the time of profitable colonization, and more recently of "drain theory," the exploitation of a periphery by a center, and of Clifford Geertz's (1963) theory that "agricultural involution" could multiply a peasant population without increasing its wealth. In practice even the unprecedentedly pervasive administrative arrangements built up to extract these crops could not control more than a small percentage of all arable land. It did impose sugar and indigo on the best irrigated rice land (*sawah*), rotating these crops with rice in a sequence that often occupied a third of the land time, and as much as a half of the labor time of peasants on it. Coffee was grown permanently on higher land, and occupied as much as 5% of Java's total arable land in 1875. Production of sugar increased 50-fold, to 233,000 tons, by 1876, and coffee eighteenfold, to 91,000 tons, but rice too tripled in production to 2.4 million tons in that period. Population grew rapidly under the stable and hierarchic conditions of the *pax neerlandica* (see Chapter 13), but all the growth was stuffed into the rural sector, where landlessness increased, average land-holding decreased, and the amount of labor extracted per family increased considerably. Peter Boomgaard (1989, 97–9) has shown that although agricultural production per capita did increase throughout the *cultuurstelsel*, income and consumption per capita declined by a third or more between 1815 and 1840, and was still below the 1815 figure in 1880, as the system was beginning to be dismantled under pressure from its many critics. The key problem was that farmers were obliged to devote their land to crops for which they were paid only a fraction (24% in the case of sugar) of their market value, whereas they had previously had some freedom to move between food crops and the market. The hierarchic nature of Javanese society became far more marked, though already notable in the seventeenth century as the rulers and the VOC together squeezed Javanese out of trade and industry. A "dual economy" emerged in which the modern sector was almost exclusively the affair of Europeans and Chinese, and the Javanese were confined to agriculture, with no middle class.

These factors changed little when a harsh time of famine in the late 1840s forced The Hague to examine its conscience about the *cultuurstelsel*, or when a set of new laws in 1870 began what was generously labeled a "liberal" period. In theory this meant that forced labor was dismantled but private European entrepreneurs could acquire land rights which often had the same result. Sugar milling and transportation became the key driver of capitalization of the sector, with the NHM transformed from a monopolistic buyer of crops to a finance house competing with other banks to promote the industry. "Liberalism" in no sense reached the Javanese farmers, for whom sugar cultivation for uneconomic returns remained an obligation even beyond independence in 1945.

PLANTATIONS AND HACIENDAS

The rapid industrialization of Europe and North America in the later nineteenth century created an ever-greater demand for raw materials. The abolition of slavery in the Americas, regular steamer routes, and the opening of the Suez Canal (1869) removed most of the disadvantages Southeast Asia had suffered in supplying it. The capital derived from various forms of nineteenth-century monopolies began to be used to pioneer plantations for tea, coffee, tobacco, sugar, nutmeg, and indigo, and with success came further mobilization of capital from abroad. Marginal land was made available as colonial authority expanded; but labor was the principal constraint. Only in parts of Java and Tongking, where landlessness and poverty had become acute by the late nineteenth century, was it possible to find Southeast Asians willing to work under the regimented conditions of European-owned estates. The rapid expansion of the plantation sector after 1870 would not have been possible without importing labor from one of these places or India and China, under some form of contract with a punitive element.

In contrast to the state-imposed sugar production of nineteenth-century Java, Filipino Chinese *mestizos* were the main providers of capital and enterprise for the Philippine sugar industry. Having relocated from Manila to the Chinese *parian* of Iloilo (on Panay, Visayas) in the eighteenth century, many Chinese integrated through Christianity and hybrid Spanish names and lifestyles into a *mestizo* commercial class there. They sponsored in Iloilo the Philippines' leading textile industry, but as this fell to the pressure of manufactured cloth, they seized the new opportunities that came with Iloilo port opening to international trade in 1855. These Iloilo *mestizo* entrepreneurs began buying land for sugar production in Negros Island, across the strait from Iloilo but still scarcely inhabited with a settled population of less than 36,000 in 1850. Best documented is Eugenio López (1837–1906), who used the capital his family had acquired in trade and textiles to make successive purchases of Negros land amounting to about 4,000 hectares in the period 1864–92, typically from Europeans or church bodies who had acquired titles from the colonial state for very little but been unable to develop them. Like other *mestizo* entrepreneurs, Lopez and his brothers managed to persuade workers from heavily populated Iloilo and Cebu to work the sugar land, often on a seasonal basis when labor was required for cutting, laying the foundation for one of the great landed families that would dominate Philippine politics in the following century. The population of Negros expanded to 104,000 in 1879 and 372,000 in 1887, boosting Philippine sugar production to 75,000 tons in 1870 and 200,000 in 1885 (half that of Java; Map 10.1). This unique domination of the Philippines sugar industry by an indigenous planter class would mean in the longer term that instead of being attacked and marginalized by twentieth-century nationalism, as elsewhere in tropical Asia, the planters became a hereditary upper class who did much to shape both Filipino nationalism and the conservative cast of the modern Philippine state.

In the open frontiers of Indonesia and Malaysia, by contrast, the same period saw Chinese enterprise grow more separate from indigenous landholding. European capital was there more prominent, and its alliance proved lucrative with advancing colonial states on one hand and ambitious port-rajas willing to grant concessions to vast tracts of forest land on the other. The local Chinese who did invest in plantations in Malaya (like Tan Kah Kee) or Sumatra (like Tjong A Fie) tended to do so on the established European-run model. This high colonial pattern of large-scale European-managed estates with migrant labor had begun tentatively with Dutch pioneering of tobacco, tea, and coffee plantations in upland areas of Java, and some problematic British experiments in Penang and adjacent areas of the Peninsula. The great boom, however, began in the coastal plain to the east of Lake Toba, the rich volcanic soil of which had been only lightly exploited by Karo and Toba Bataks for hill rice, pepper, and tobacco. A Dutch tobacco trader, Jacobus Nienhuys, went there as soon as Dutch authorities established relations with the local sultans, initially to buy the local tobacco. The Sultan of Deli proved generous with land concessions, so Nienhuys contracted some Chinese labor from Singapore and grew an initial crop in 1863 which suggested the soil was remarkably suitable. Deli leaf quickly became the preferred wrapper in the world's cigar production, and the forests of east Sumatra were felled and burned to create choice tobacco fields. By 1889 its estates produced 40 million guilders' worth of tobacco, prompting attempts all over the tropical world to replicate this type of plantation agriculture for export. Only in the first year after clearing was the soil judged rich enough for the famous Deli leaf, after which it was left fallow for six years. In the later years, with increased population pressure and better regulation, those deemed the sultan's indigenous subjects were given an allotment of prepared fields to grow food crops in the year following the tobacco harvest and before fallowing.

Labor was initially brought from south China via Singapore and Penang, and from 1888 directly from Swatow (Shantou, eastern Guangdong). Chinese, especially Teochew farmers from the Swatow area, were regarded as more responsive to the cash incentive for high-quality tobacco leaf. Chinese planters and tin-miners in Sumatra and Malaya had their own means to control Chinese labor recruitment to their advantage, but the dominant European plantation mode required cooperation with colonial government to enforce a secure and submissive supply. In east Sumatra, Javanese labor began to be recruited under paternalistic Dutch-colonial auspices in 1887, and by 1900 became the principal labor source, especially in non-tobacco crops such as tea, rubber, and oil palm. Some 30,000 Javanese were even sent to plantations in Dutch Guyana (later Surinam) between 1890 and 1914, as well as to many other economic frontiers in Indonesia. Provision of Javanese labor beyond the Dutch sphere was less successful, though a little occurred for Malaya, North Borneo, French New Caledonia, and even Queensland, Australia, before the white Australia exclusions were enacted. In British Malaya the recruitment of Tamils from south India was regulated under legislation of 1880, and reached its peak in the 1910s when between 50,000 and 80,000 Tamils entered every year to tap and maintain the rubber trees that fueled Malaya's early twentieth-century growth. Such labor migrants, whether in Sumatra, Malaya, or elsewhere, tended to be insulated from others in paternalistic plantation labor barracks, and were less likely than other migrants to rise up the social ladder over the generations. Several million Tamil migrants in Malaya, and Javanese in east Sumatra, remained a relatively disadvantaged proletariat throughout the twentieth century.

MONO-CROP RICE ECONOMIES OF THE MAINLAND DELTAS

While the plantations had a spectacular effect on the environment, turning tropical forests into vast centrally managed gardens, it was the rice trade that directly altered millions of Southeast Asian lives by drawing rice farmers into commercial production for the world. Commercialization of the rice crop took place in many areas for domestic markets, but the vast commercial expansion of the deltas of the Irrawaddy, Chao Phraya, and Mekong Rivers made Southeast Asia the center of the international rice trade (70% of world exports before 1930). The three deltas had remained relatively scarcely populated until 1850. They had been malarial and swampy, unattractive sites for smallholder mixed agriculture, and all had been subject to ruinous warfare over the previous century. They boomed when stable political conditions and government stimulus and infrastructure enabled them to respond to a new international demand for rice from Europe and Asian rice-deficit areas like Malaya, east Sumatra, and Japan. In the process, an exceptional combination developed of smallholder production with mono-crop dependence.

Siam's transformation may be considered the most "natural," without the additional disruption of colonial conquest. The rice export trade became theoretically possible when the Anglo-Siamese Bowring Treaty opened Siam to international trade in 1855, ending the virtual monopoly that Chinese traders had exercised. European investment was on a much smaller scale than in Burma and Viet Nam, though it produced the first steam-driven rice mill in Bangkok in 1858 and dominated rice milling and exports. Neither the state nor foreign investors played as significant a role as in the colonial cases. The digging of canals to facilitate communication in the Chao Phraya delta was the work of Chinese labor and royal or noble initiative, as a way to provide more accessible land to their relatives and dependents. Rice milling and export was initially dominated by Europeans who broke the dominance of the Chinese "merchant lords" (*jao sua*) who had dominated the old China-oriented economy, but by 1890 a new generation of Chinese migrants had taken over both rice collection and milling. Siam's rice export trade looked modest in comparison with its neighbors, but nevertheless grew 25-fold between 1860 and 1930. Holdings were generally smaller, indebtedness and landlessness less salient, and social conflict less pronounced than in the colonial cases. Siam/Thailand was therefore less affected by the crisis of the 1930s depression, and surpassed Indochina to become the world's second exporter in those years.

The star performer was the Irrawaddy delta, annexed by Britain after the second Anglo-Burmese war in 1852. Once the milling and export infrastructure was established, the industry expanded at extraordinary speed. Between 1885 and 1906, the area under rice cultivation in the delta grew eightfold and rice exports twelvefold, making Burma the world's leading rice exporter with over two million tons a year by 1910. The favourable conditions in this open land frontier made it a magnet for landless migrants from Upper Burma and eastern India, who might hope to become independent landowners with a substantial house and disposable income. Much higher wages in all sectors of the economy drew Indians of their own volition into the delta, unlike the controlled estate labor and clerks of Malaya. The population of Lower Burma as a whole grew fourfold in the second half of the nineteenth century, and while most of the increase was ethnically Bama, about 2.6 million Indians had entered by 1937. Indians formed 51% of Rangoon's population by 1901. The wealthiest of them were Chettiar money-lenders, who by 1930 had come to supply about 60% of the agricultural credit in the delta. Burma became the only Southeast Asian "plural society" in which the largest migrant minority was Indian rather than Chinese, and their roles in the economy eventually made them even greater targets of majority nationalism. Conflicts over credit as well as competition for urban laboring jobs would give rise to racial riots in the crisis-ridden 1930s and expulsion in the 1940s (Chapter 17). Once the open land frontier closed in the early 1900s, poor farmers lost their bargaining power, vulnerability to the market increased, and landlessness and landlordism became serious problems.

The Mekong delta was the other spectacular success story, following French annexation of the area in 1862–7. French engineers, like the British in Lower Burma, took pride in opening up new frontiers of agriculture through the building of canals and dykes. The land under rice cultivation increased fourfold and rice exports tenfold in the three decades before 1900. The delta had already been more commercialized than other areas of Viet Nam, but French control exacerbated both commercialization and social conflict between landlord and tenant by auctioning off large tracts of land to French or Vietnamese investors willing to cooperate in the new regime. This became the most polarized of the three rice frontiers, with a quarter of peasants being landless while the richest 2.5% of landholders controlled almost half of the rice land. Far from maximizing communal land and "shared poverty" by extracting surpluses from the village through an increasingly bureaucratized hierarchy as in nineteenth-century Java, southern Viet Nam was a relatively raw example of rapid commercialization, large landholders, and considerable class tension.

PRE-COLONIAL AND COLONIAL GROWTH COMPARED

The spectacular transformation that European colonial capital wrought on Southeast Asian infrastructure in the "high colonial period," 1870–1930, long mesmerized economic historians. The mushrooming of railways, roads, harbors, and port-cities was often seen as the consequence of a new economic dynamism contrasting with the static, chaotic, or unknowable conditions which preceded it. Enough work has now been done on the less accessible statistics of 1780–1850, however, to show that the rate of increase even in export income was in fact greater in that period than under high colonialism, and growth in per capita exports, and indeed incomes, must have been markedly more favorable in the earlier period. The even higher export growth in the region after 1970 leaves the century preceding it looking like an interlude of relatively sluggish growth in exports, and stagnation or decline in per capita incomes, while population grew rapidly.

Taken overall, there is no doubt that the Southeast Asian economies underwent a marked expansion in the late eighteenth and early nineteenth centuries after the consolidations of the previous century. Although some of this was due to the expansion of tobacco, coffee, and sugar cultivation under semi-colonial conditions in the Philippines and Java, the expansion appears to have been faster in that great majority of the region which lay outside effective European control. Chinese miners and cultivators tended to avoid the European colonies after the mid-eighteenth century in favor of the open frontiers and weak polities elsewhere. The world economy again had a stimulating effect on Southeast Asian economies, after the monopoly systems of production established in the seventeenth century had lost their grip. The relative economic freedom and dynamism of the period had its counterpart, however, in instability and piracy. The raiders known as Iranun (Illanun) and Balangingi in the Island world, or as Chinese pirates in the Tongking Gulf, reached a peak of notoriety in this period. The profits of trade, mining, and cash-cropping tended not to accumulate in visible investment in infrastructure or production, but in personal consumption, political conflict, remittances to more stable areas, or at best investment in state-building that ultimately failed. Colonialism, by contrast, provided more stability and infrastructure, and a rapidly increasing population, but less commercial dynamism.

[11] THE LAST STAND OF ASIAN AUTONOMIES, 1820–1910

THE nineteenth century witnessed the last phase of distinctive Southeast Asian societies making their autonomous choices how to deal with the challenges of modernity. Around 1900 the world-system represented by steamships, railways, banks, and telegraph would become inescapable, whether through force of arms, economic pressure, or cultural emulation. The last societies and polities to stand outside that world-system deserve particular interest in our increasingly monochrome world, but until recently they have had a bad press. Colonial writers condemned them for taking the wrong path of isolation and defiance, Marxists for their anachronistic and doomed feudalism, and nationalists for their compromises and weakness. Their final confrontations with expanding European power did not inspire the later nationalists so much as did rediscovered ancient kingdoms or foreign models like Japan and Turkey. Yet their attempts to obtain the secrets of modern technology without losing whatever was deemed their essential ethos are particularly interesting. Defining that essence often led to a radical neo-traditionalism, leading to imaginings of a purer form of alien ideology. This urge for radical renewal in face of the European threats took Confucian, Theravada Buddhist, and Islamic forms, each reaching beyond the immediate past toward some more viable anchor in the storm.

Europe had achieved significant innovations in science, technology, state-forming, and capital accumulation much earlier, but only in the century 1815–1914 were its quarreling states sufficiently accepting of a plural "balance of power" political system to be able to focus on partitioning the rest of the planet according to its dictates. During this remarkable century a handful of European nation-states, joined late in the period by the United States and Japan, succeeded in drawing boundaries throughout the world within which their sovereignty was theoretically absolute (Chapter 12). No sooner had they absorbed French and American revolutionary ideals of popular sovereignty in democratic nation-states than these states paradoxically began declaring

A History of Southeast Asia: Critical Crossroads, First Edition. Anthony Reid.
© 2015 Anthony Reid. Published 2015 by John Wiley & Sons, Ltd.

themselves empires, somehow reconciling Roman and Asian ideas of empire with their hard-won nation-state concepts. International standards began to be developed to regulate this increasingly integrated system, using the fiction that only "civilized" states could claim the equal sovereignty acknowledged by it, and others would have to be subordinated to one of those "civilized" states. The subject of this chapter is the choices made by Southeast Asians, with their radically different political systems, in responding to these revolutionary developments. We will begin with Siam, as the gold standard of success in creating a state sufficiently absolutist internally, and accommodating externally, to pass the test of "civilized" status as defined in Europe. Not without their share of luck in balancing English and French, the Siamese kings gained more than they lost in reinventing themselves as "enlightened" absolute rulers.

SIAM AS "CIVILIZED" SURVIVOR

Siam's success owed something to the totality of the destruction from which it was reborn. The Burmese conquest of 1767 came after 150 years of relative peace and consolidation, but was unprecedented in its sustained attempt to eliminate Siam permanently as a rival in the broader Southeast Asian Peninsula. Everything valuable and movable was carried away, including artists, writers, craftsmen, and some 2,000 members of the royal family; Ayutthaya was reduced to ashes, its people dead or dispersed. Attacks continued against the northern Thai *muang* until 1787, leaving historic centers such as Chiang Mai and Phitsanulok virtually unpopulated. What remained was the favorable port location familiar to Chinese traders, and the religious and performance culture described in Chapter 8.

It was an obscure Sino-Thai newcomer with military talents, Phaya Taksin, who began to reorganize remnants of the old order within months of the sack of Ayutthaya. Profiting from the Chinese commercial boom described in Chapter 10, he mobilized the Teochew pepper- and sugar-growers in the southeast, and Chinese traders looking for a new commercial center in the Gulf, to establish a fortified port at Thonburi, nearer the mouth of the Chao Phraya River than the old Ayutthaya. He was able to defeat the initial Burmese expeditions sent against him, and quickly gathered a sizeable army from those who had fled the disaster. Like Thai kings before and after, his natural alliance was with China, the great threat to both his rivals in Burma and Viet Nam. Despite his lack of dynastic legitimacy and a protest to Beijing from his Cantonese rival in Ha Tien, China eventually recognized Taksin's new port as the continuation of Siam for the controlled tribute trade. Siam as always was a useful ally for China against its troublesome neighbors, Burma and Viet Nam. The new Siam's greatest asset against its rivals through the following half-century was the unqualified welcome it gave to Chinese traders – the preeminent "gateway" strategy described below. Chinese far outnumbered Thais in Thonburi and its successor after 1782, Bangkok (renamed Krungthep or City of Angels), just across the river. Nevertheless, the Sino-Thai (*lukjin*) elite were always ready to assimilate the refinements of the Thai aristocracy, as well as retaining enough Chinese-ness to control the inflow of Chinese labor and enterprise. Taksin and his equally militant successor brought thousands of Mon, Khmer, Bama, Lao, and Malay captives into the depopulated heart of Siam, but Chinese migrants were the most vital economic asset. By the 1820s Bangkok was again by far the dominant Mainland port, and Chinese migrants were entering at the rate of 7,000 a year.

Taksin's vigorous, soldierly style of leadership contrasted greatly with the courtly ways of the old elite, who managed his overthrow and execution in 1782 with the claim that he was insane. Thongduang, scion of one of the surviving Mon families of the old elite, but with a Chinese mother, had joined Taksin's army as a trusted general but was now installed as the new king, Yotfa (or Rama I, 1782–1809). The Bangkok or Chakri Dynasty he established sought to distance itself from Taksin by shifting the capital across the river and doing its utmost to recover the old Ayutthayan traditions. Nevertheless, the military style of government and the Chinese cosmopolitanism of the capital continued. Rama I himself was more Chinese and Mon than Thai in origins, but of an established family with roots in Ayutthaya. His military machine proved highly effective in reconquering key *muang* and *negeri* with long-established distinct histories, which had previously done no more than send occasional tribute to Ayutthaya. The anti-Burmese campaign helped justify these actions, as in the case of Chiang Mai which had been oriented to Burma for over a century, or Nakhon Sithammarat and other Peninsula *negeri* where Thais, Chinese, and even some Malays welcomed Taksin as less destructive than the Burmese.

Beyond the limits of Thai-ness, the goal of Taksin and Yotfa seemed to be to attack ancient but vulnerable neighbors to make up what had been lost to the Burmese in not only population but skills and symbols of Buddhist sovereignty. In 1779 Taksin had sent Thongduang to attack the old Lao capital of Vientiane, on the middle Mekong. He brought back to Bangkok many of its elite (some to provide royal consorts for the upstart new regime), craftsmen, and its most treasured image, the Emerald Buddha, to become the palladium of the Chakri Dynasty. One of the princes who had then been captured, Chou Anuvong, returned to rule Vientiane from 1805 as a tributary of Bangkok. In 1826, however, encouraged by his English and Viet contacts to think he might get support, Anuvong sought to re-establish an independent Lao state. This time the destruction by Bangkok was total. Vientiane was razed to the ground, its population moved across the Mekong to be better controlled, with virtually nothing remaining when the French decided in the 1890s to make it the capital of a reinvented Laos. Anuvong naturally became the hero of later Lao nationalism and source of continuing discord with Thailand.

Taksin and Yotfa similarly took advantage of Viet distraction during the Tay Son interlude to capture key Khmer human resources. Cambodia was attacked in 1782, 1784, and 1794, when the western provinces including the symbolically important Angkor ruins were placed under direct Thai rule. In Phnom Penh, Cambodian kings continued to try to balance Thai and Viet claims to supremacy until the 1830s, when both the giants seemed to conclude they would rather obliterate the Khmer altogether. The 1833 army that Bangkok sent to Cambodia was instructed "to carry off Khmer families to be resettled in Thai territory, do not leave any behind. It would be good to treat Cambodia as we did Vientiane" (cited Baker and Phongpaichit 2009, 28–9). In practice, similar tactics by Viet Nam proved more successful from the 1840s.

The uncompromising nature of the early Bangkok regime was also evident in the south. The army sent to destroy Burmese military forces in the Peninsula proceeded in 1785 to besiege the Malay-ruled *negeri* of Patani, which had as ever been slow to accept the new Thai regime as a legitimate overlord. After a year's resistance the city fell, and many of its inhabitants were massacred or (if young and female) carried off to Bangkok. In 1791, Bangkok divided the former Patani *negeri* into seven districts all under the Sino-Thai ruler of Songkhla to its north. Enough population nevertheless returned to Patani to earn it an even more savage destruction in 1832, some 5,000 survivors being taken as slaves to Bangkok. In between these two punishments it was the turn, in 1821, of Kedah, a significant tin-exporting *negeri* which had hoped for protection by ceding to Britain its offshore island of Penang in 1786. Although judiciously sending tribute to Bangkok and even chastising neighboring Perak on its behalf, the sultan baulked at a summons to go to Bangkok in person. A Thai expedition devastated and subdivided the state, with thousands taken captive to Bangkok. The British gave the sultan asylum in Penang but did nothing to discourage the Siamese.

Bangkok was not yet in a position to rule this expanded territory, but its determination to destroy possible rivals permanently was new. At first it used force for want of other forms of leverage, but by the settled 1820s the court elite was aware of the changed world of national competition. The first British official mission, in 1822, was surprised how knowledgeable the Thai ministers were about British power. One pointedly questioned the envoy why, if as committed to peace as he claimed, Britain maintained such a large navy. The Siamese were anxious to ensure that there were no rivals in a position to invite these powerful foreigners in to defend them. Although the British in turn were scandalized by the high opinion Siamese had of themselves, the cosmopolitanism of the city was in fact producing a society very well aware of social and cultural difference, as displayed realistically in the temple murals of the period. Since they were already markedly dependent on Chinese imports and enterprise, it was not a great step to accepting a European presence. The most important advocates of an opening to westerners were gathered around Prince Mongkut, who had withdrawn to a monastery to be safe from his older but less legitimate brother reigning as Rama III (1824–51).

Mongkut used his time in the monastery well, in the words of his friend the Catholic Bishop, "to devote himself patiently to the study of Sanskrit, Pali, history, religion, geography, physics and chemistry, astronomy, and finally the English language" (Pallegoix 1854/1969 I, 101). At his brother's death, his succession was peacefully organized by his circle of reformers, and the transformation of Siam began. Whereas his predecessor had placed great store in the Chinese connection, the mission Mongkut sent to China to announce his accession turned out to be Siam's last. The envoys witnessed the disruption of China by the Taiping rebellion and its humbling by Britain in the opium wars.

Imperial officials told them they could not enter the palace like European envoys because "you are envoys from small countries … Only envoys from big countries such as Britain and France can be given an audience in the palace." The envoys reported that on their way home the Governor of Hong Kong, John Bowring, explained to them the new principle of sovereign equality. Siam's status was the same "as that of Britain, France and the United States. You should not go to pay tribute to China any more" (cited Masuda 2004, 37). Mongkut was impressed, and invited Bowring to come to Bangkok to negotiate Siam's place in this new order. He subsequently declared the "shameful" practice of sending tribute abolished, although no formal relationship of equality would be established in its place until 1975.

The Bowring Treaty of 1855 was a victory for Mongkut's reforming party, formalizing the end of royal monopolies, equal treatment of European and Chinese vessels, a switch to revenue farms such as opium as the source of the government's budget, and extraterritorial rights for resident Europeans including the influential British Consul. The European idea of mutually agreed boundaries between sovereign territories was in principle accepted, with Siam agreeing that its sovereign claims ended with British territory in Lower Burma to its west and Penang and Perak in the south. In 1857 Mongkut sent 27 people to Britain to study its technology and institutions, and upon their return began to hire westerners as advisers for the more technical departments. He famously invited Anna Leonowens to educate his sons in English. Internally, however, he returned to an older Ayutthaya pattern of leverage over the extremely diverse territory he claimed through patronage of the Buddhist *sangha*, personal ties with entrenched hereditary rulers and nobles, and a more hierarchic status ladder than had been the style of the early Bangkok warrior kings.

One of the great advantages of Siam as against its neighbors in this dangerous period was the relatively smooth succession of able princes. Ex-monk Mongkut had begun propagating only in his forties, but nevertheless produced 82 children from 35 mothers, and their relative youth made it easier to mold them in the new bicultural direction. These princes directed Siam through its vital modernization. Prince Chulalongkorn, who ruled for 42 years (1868–1910) as Rama V, and his key reforming minister and half-brother Prince Damrong, deftly managed the transition to absolutism within while balancing the quarreling Europeans without. Chulalongkorn's first foreign experiences as a fifteen-year-old king were devised by the British to take advantage of his English, exposing him not to Europe but to the colonial conditions of Singapore, Java, and India. The more Britain and France advanced on his borders, however, the more Chulalongkorn appreciated the need to embrace the monarchs of Prussia and Russia, both readier to sympathize with old-fashioned hierarchies and to accept him as an equal than were the two colonial powers. In 1891 he sent Damrong to Singapore to escort the Russian crown prince to a magnificent reception in Bangkok, and the following year sent him off to St Petersburg to consolidate this relationship. When the Tsarevitch acceded as Tsar Nicholas II he proved happy to embrace Chulalongkorn as a "brother king," and to provide him with an exceptionally warm welcome in St Petersburg in 1897.

Such attempts to balance the European powers proved fatal in the Burma and Aceh cases below, which underlines both the skill with which Chulalongkorn managed it and the importance of Siam's buffer location between French and British. But the internal revolution was more fundamental, establishing for the first time the kind of control of population demanded by modern states. The young Chulalongkorn first attacked the power of the provincial elite by phasing out slavery from 1874, and then that of the great households of the capital by transferring the tax farms that sustained them to direct control by one of his half-brothers. Starting with Chiang Mai, the king took advantage of his privileged relations with foreign concession-hunters to take over the revenues of vital logging and mining resources, sending half-brothers as royal commissioners to the key *muang*. On the model of British colonial officers in India, Burma, or Malaya, his agents gradually took control of the economic levers of power as the hereditary incumbents aged and died. They were initially his royal half-brothers and later his own western-educated sons and the products of the western-style schools for aristocrats established in the capital Prince Damrong invented a new Interior Ministry in 1893, establishing a salaried bureaucracy throughout the country. Over a hundred European "advisers" were in place by 1900, half of them British, both to disarm western criticism and provide models for modernity. The revolts that local interests managed to promote against these policies, often in religious or millenarian terms, were put down by a new, royally led, European-trained professional army, just as in the colonial neighbors.

All of these revolutionary changes were justified in the name of the need to be "civilized" – one of the few English words rendered directly into Thai, as *siwilai*. In place of Asian criteria of legitimacy in a hierarchy of polities came a new measure imposed by powerful and prestigious westerners, by which the Thai royal elite needed to position itself. To mix successfully in the dominant social circles even of Bangkok, let alone Singapore, London, and St Petersburg, the Thai elite had to stop chewing betel, blackening their teeth, and cropping their hair in a "brush" form, and adopt some of the dress styles of Europe. Having to deal so much with Europeans who refused the practice, it was prudent for the king to abolish the requirement of his subjects to prostrate themselves and avert their eyes in his presence. Chulalongkorn reinvented kingship as a public spectacle, driving his automobile around Bangkok and having himself represented in images such as the equestrian statue modeled on that of Louis XIV at Versailles. Slavery, corvée, and polygamy were more difficult obstacles to *siwilai* status, but gradually they too were abandoned, the last only in the following reign.

There were clear limits to western borrowing, however. Unlike many of its neighbors Siam emphatically rejected missionary ideas that *siwilai* had anything to do with Christianity. Once the foreign-educated elite had purged Buddhism of popular magical elements, they were convinced that Buddhism was a more rational religion. Chulalongkorn also ruled out any democratic element in the *siwilai* formula, insisting to younger royal reformers that Siam had no constitution because "it is understood that the king has absolute power," and the people "believe that the king more than anybody else practices justice and loves the people" (Rama V 1888, cited Murashima 1988, 85–6).

In the short run, it also proved more acceptable to Europeans to deal with a stable hierarchic polity than a contested one.

KONBAUNG BURMA – A DOOMED MODERNIZATION

Turning from the Chao Phraya to the equally Theravada Buddhist Irrawaddy valley, one immediately notes the different balance between upriver and delta. Bama kings, we saw in Chapter 8, withdrew their capital from the ethnically mixed, commercially connected but vulnerable delta in the seventeenth century, to build a more culturally coherent identity around the key rice baskets of Upper Burma – what we may call a "heartland" strategy. From there they periodically subdued and devastated the troublesome coastal zone. Siam, with the advantage of its commercial connection with an unthreatening China, was able not only to retain control of the Chao Phraya outlet to the sea, but eventually to gain the upper hand from there in rivalry with the many upriver *muang* of the Thai-speaking world. The geography of the Chao Phraya watershed permitted an alternative "gateway" strategy, shared with many Malay *negeri*, which made possible the transition from Chinese to Europeans as the principal external partners. By contrast, the Bama kings, like their Viet and Javanese counterparts, gained advantages of cultural coherence through their "heartland" strategy, but lost control of the most commercial and cosmopolitan coastal regions piecemeal to the Europeans.

The collapse of Bama kingship in the 1740s was the first of the Mainland's eighteenth-century crises, and its militarist re-emergence was also the first of the three modern transformations. The Konbaung Dynasty's founder, Alaungpaya (1752–60), and his sons and brothers, culminating in Bodawpaya (1782–1819), galvanized and reorganized the Bama heartland after its invasion by Mon, Shan, and Manipur forces, and used its demographic advantage to punish the Mons ferociously. They were in control of the ports of the delta by 1757, and systematically required arms of all incoming ships until an estimated 60% of the large Burma army had flintlocks. By reorganizing society on a new military basis, the Konbaung armies were able to devastate Siam but also those who resisted in the Mon country of Lower Burma and in Arakan, Manipur (in modern India), among the *muang* of Shan, Lao, and Kachin territories in the north and east, and even into what is modern Yunnan province of China. Conflicts with the other rising military powers of the period, British India and Manchu China, were inevitable. The Burmese armies managed to defeat four increasingly massive Chinese invasions in the 1760s. The mountainous frontier areas had remained tense until in 1790 local authorities restored diplomatic relations by misleading both Ava and Beijing courts into believing their demands had been met. British India proved more problematic, especially after 1813 when the king decreed an invasion of India to restore Buddhism to its homeland. The army obliged in 1817 by entering the Bhramaputra valley in Assam.

The unprecedented degree of control and even cultural integration over this vast region was achieved by military means, supplying manpower to the central zone with tens of thousands of captive slaves, and terrorizing those who thought of resisting. John Crawfurd admired the body of laws assembled by scholars but seldom referred to, and the capacity of people of low birth to rise to administrative and military eminence. The system of government around the king was unusually despotic, yet many of his orders were disregarded once outside the capital. A succession of rebellions by Mons, Arakanese, and Manipuris kept the troops busy, and led to appeals to Calcutta for intervention. Frustrations on both sides led to the outbreak, in March 1824, of the bitterest of Britain's colonial wars. The Burmese troops, unaccustomed to defeat, put up a vigorous fight for two years, leading to 15,000 deaths on the British side and many more on the Burmese. Only with the formidable Burmese commander Bandula killed, the British force advancing up the Irrawaddy, and the pride of Burma's river-fleet demolished by one of the first steamships ever used in warfare, the *Diana*, did the Burmese sue for peace in 1826. In the resulting treaty, the Burmese agreed to cede their claims over Manipur, Assam, and the coastal dependencies of Arakan and Tenasserim, while the British agreed to withdraw from Rangoon and the Irrawaddy delta after an indemnity had been paid.

A consequence was that a more manageable kingdom remained as the signatory of the Anglo-Burmese treaty. The areas under direct control of the court at Ava were far more populous, homogeneous, and proudly conscious of being Bama than any population at the disposal of Thai kings. Burmese scholars also became aware of European knowledge, and a few, like Bodawpaya's son Prince Mekkaya, learned English and translated geographical and other texts into Burmese. But the attempt to reinvent Burma as a tightly ruled modern nation-state had to await another setback and the assumption of power by a new generation. A second Anglo-Burmese war lost Rangoon and other ports to another British offensive in 1852, but led to no Burmese readiness to sue for peace until Prince Mindon wrested control of the capital from his half-brother. Mindon reigned from 1853 until his death in 1878, and sought energetically to transform his realm into an absolute monarchy that would be strong and "civilized" enough to survive, as Chulalongkorn would later manage to do in Siam. As king he was even more Anglophile and determined to avoid war than his Siamese counterpart. The first British mission to deal extensively with him declared him the first king in recent Burmese history to be

> just and mild in temper, easy of access … heartily desirous that his subjects shall not be oppressed … The people speak in terms of admiration of his good qualities, and uniformly, and with apparent sincerity, declare that they never had a king so just and beneficent (Yule 1858/1968, 193–4).

King Mindon moved his capital to nearby Mandalay to signify a new start (Figure 11.1). He sought to acquire western knowledge by sending about 70 elite children to schools in France (especially St Cyr military academy), England, and India, and funding an English-language school in Mandalay from 1870 run by missionary John Marks. He put his younger brother, soul

Figure 11.1 King Mindon's capital at Amerapura, as sketched by a member of Henry Yule's British mission in 1855. A section of the palace and a revered white elephant. Source: Yule 1858/1968.

mate, and heir, Prince Kanaung, in charge of military modernization, until Kanaung was assassinated in 1866 by two of his own sons embittered not to have been named to succeed. In the optimistic first phase of the reign, Kanaung sponsored many modern factories, to produce rifles, ammunition, coins, lacquer, sugar, and cotton cloth, though most proved more valuable as symbols than as economic assets. French and Italian officers were brought in to help reorganize the military. A flotilla of steamships was acquired to patrol the Irrawaddy. More critical were his attempts to rule rather than preside over the diverse patchwork of local magnates. Mindon steadily expanded the authority of a salaried judiciary against that of local bosses. He replaced appanages with salaries for military and civilian officers, and adopted from British-ruled Lower Burma the institution of township officers (*myo-ok*) as salaried royal agents of the crown. He attempted to systematize the revenue system, collecting a kind of property tax from every village in accordance with wealth, to replace the contributions from local magnates (*myo-thugyi*).

Even in the Bama areas close to the Irrawaddy, however, these reforms were very partially successful by comparison with the (somewhat later) reforms of Chulalongkorn. The key difference was the perennial shortage of money in Mindon's court, giving him little bargaining power against local power-holders. A rice surplus could no longer be extracted from the expanding frontier of the delta, so rice supplies had to be bought on the market. The squeezing of the remaining peasantry was limited not only by Mindon's milder nature, but by the British-ruled open frontier in the south beckoning discontented or landless farmers. Mindon was deprived of port revenues by the loss of the coast to Britain, of the major state monopolies by treaty with the British, and of the enormously lucrative vice taxes on the Chinese by the very different nature of Buddhist kingship on the Irrawaddy. It so abhorred opium, gambling, and alcohol that it could not countenance licensing it. Only the growing exports of cotton, teak timber, and gems provided an easily taxable resource.

Culturally also Mandalay sought to define itself in neo-traditional terms, as a virtuous exemplary center not only for Buddhists in Burma but worldwide. The new capital was built with its complement of monasteries and temples, and great store was placed on further embellishment of the Shwedagon pagoda in the now-British territory of Rangoon. Nearly half of Mindon's decrees were concerned with ceremonies either at the court or among the chief nobles, and his public ritual activity took up much of his time and resources. Most ambitious was the holding of a Fourth Buddhist Council in 1871, theoretically a global phenomenon reprising the work of councils 2,000 years earlier to recite and purify the canon of Buddhist texts. In practice, it targeted those influenced by Burma's style of Theravada Buddhism, now extending well beyond the reach of its kings. The whole of the Tipitaka was inscribed in stone in one of Mandalay's temples. A kind of high fundamentalism was evident in stricter rules for the *sangha*, the banning of animal slaughter, and the creation of vast national parks where no animals could be killed or captured. Like many of his subjects, Mindon was seeking a purer Buddhist ground on which to stand against the swirling challenges of the time, but he was in a weaker position than his Thai counterpart in imposing one version on all the options struggling to be heard.

Outside the Bama areas along the Irrawaddy, the Shan, Kachin, and Karen had a different quality of loyalty to the monarchy. Bama identity had been greatly strengthened by the great flowering of written and performance literature on the one hand (Chapter 8), and by the conflicts with the British on the other. Neither factor bound other ethno-linguistic groups, in the habit of paying only an annual tribute to the extent that the kings were strong enough to insist upon it, or their trade with the capital required it. Among the major causes of eventual war with the British were conflicts over the teak and other resources of these border areas, where the ideas of the commercial community in Rangoon and those of the Burmese court were very far apart. The hereditary rulers (*sawbwa*) of Shan *muang* valued their personal relations with the king, placing their daughters as his minor wives. That this practice was dropped by Mindon's successor, Thibaw, contributed to their alienation, and rebellion.

The first act in the drama that began with King Mindon's death in 1878 seemed an emulation of the young Chulalongkorn's ascent in Siam a decade earlier. The reformist party, led by the Chief Minister, Kinwun Mingyi, a westernizer convinced by his European travels in 1871 of the need for change, ensured the succession of a pliable young prince. He arranged for the twenty-year-old King Thibaw to travel to Europe to convince himself of the task ahead. The reformists eased power away from the remaining old guard of royals and nobles, and set in train further reforms that would centralize power in the hands not of the king but of the key reformist ministers themselves. The second act, in February 1879, was melodrama calculated to convince the critical audience in Rangoon, Bangkok, Calcutta, and London that oriental despotism was implacably alive. The ambitious young queen, Supalayat, and her mother orchestrated a coup that executed all the royals deemed a threat to Thibaw and his queen. Forty of Mindon's 110 children, and many of his wives and retainers, died in two days of bloodletting. Power shifted to the young royal couple and their royalist allies in the military. The British Resident and much of the European community evacuated among rumors that the Indian Army would place some more "civilized" refugee prince on the throne.

Although Thibaw never recovered from the image problem this created, the British attack did not come until 1885. Thibaw's reign continued as a kind of compromise between a pious king and his extravagant wife on the one hand, both determined on royal prerogatives, and reforming ministers anxious to follow the Thai example. The government was undoubtedly much less competent and less popular than Mindon's, but it can be argued that it had so much weaker a hand than its Thai counterpart that no wisdom could have saved it. Increasingly, the economy became tied to that of British Burma in the south, as the China trade was disrupted by rebellions first in Yunnan and then in the Shan area. This meant that British planners could justifiably argue that royal instability was itself the greatest threat to the stumbling economy, as both people and capital fled at each crisis. The government's debts increased, banditry became rife, and the rebellion of the Shans was soon joined by rebellions much closer to home in the Sagaing hills across the river from the capital. Ultimately, the fall of the Konbaung Dynasty owed more to its lack of real administrative authority than to despotism, oriental or otherwise. Yet the pride of a conquering people continued to make deference to British India unpalatable.

The British takeover was made more certain by the desperate attempts of Mandalay to find friends elsewhere to balance Britain. A Burmese mission to Paris in early 1885 signed a treaty of friendship with France, which had newly extended its Indochina territory to the Burmese boundary at the Mekong. The mission reportedly also negotiated with commercial interests for a Hanoi-Mandalay railway and a Franco-Burmese bank. Britain was alarmed, and sent an avenging force up the Irrawaddy at the end of 1885 with instructions to occupy Mandalay and dethrone Thibaw. After two battles along the way, the Burmese government surrendered upon the fleet's arrival at the capital. Thibaw and his wife were immediately sent into exile in India.

The Chief Minister, Kinwun Mingyi, made the case for a constitutional monarchy under British protection, whereby ministers like himself would administer the country in consultation with a British Resident. Many British policy-makers would have preferred such an arrangement, but their opponents won the day by pointing to the collapse of the authority of the governing system. Although the Shan area under its many *sawbwa* was governed indirectly in relative peace, the British found that the section of the elite in Mandalay prepared to cooperate with them had no real leverage in the Bama heartland itself. The generation of reform had undermined traditional lines of patronage without creating a modern bureaucracy. Having decided to rule directly, the British had to bring in a far bigger force than in the original invasion, some

40,000 men, to suppress an insurgent countryside, part patriotic and part bandit. The task took at least two years, and created a new and very different Burma governed centrally from Rangoon. The symbolic role of Bama kings in patronizing the *sangha* and providing a glittering exemplary center of performance was at an end.

HIGH CONFUCIAN FUNDAMENTALISM – NGUYEN VIET NAM

We saw in Chapter 9 that the unifier of Viet Nam in 1802, Gia Long, had been the most successful of the Mainland conquerors in absorbing Napoleonic-era advances in warfare to build a modern military machine. His own regime successfully brought together an improbable polity exhausted by war and held together by his military force. While the Nguyen lineage carried weight in his capital at Hue, the demographic core of the new polity in Tongking was a conquered country with no love for its new rulers. The quest for legitimacy there led Gia Long to its cadre of literati, who seized the opportunity to try to create a virtuous state more genuinely Confucian than the giant to the north, deemed badly compromised by its Manchu conquerors. They reached back not simply to the Ming, which provided the model of dress and court ceremony (Figure 11.2), but to the pre-Buddhist Han and beyond for models. The Confucian classic, "The Great Learning," probably written before the third century BC, was reprinted in Hanoi in 1809 and made the basis for the examination of all future officials. Over the following ten years Phan Huy Chu compiled the 49 volumes of his "Classified Survey of the Institutions of Successive Courts," which ranks as perhaps the greatest achievement of Southeast Asian rationalized statecraft, defining the objective principles on which all states should be judged. This world-view was far removed from a Christian or Buddhist dualism between the mundane and the cosmic worlds. The cultivation of the moral self, the family, and the state according to fixed moral principles was the only way to a righteous and peaceful world.

Phan Huy Chu's monumental work was presented to Gia Long's son ruling as Minh Mang (1820–41), who had himself been carefully educated by the literati of the new court in Hue. He was unusually intelligent and erudite in the classics, but had none of the practical military savvy of his father. His reign marked a peak of Confucian high fundamentalism, with a new capital built at Hue on the model of Ming-era Beijing. He traveled to Hanoi to be inducted by an Imperial Chinese envoy, and renamed the country Great South (*Dai Nam*) in an ambitious bid to place the virtue of his regime beyond ethnicity or territory. The quest for legitimacy through Confucian virtue, however, distanced his government further from a diverse population, particularly in the south. In marked contrast to other Southeast Asian rulers, religion had virtually no part in his program for uniting the kingdom. Crawfurd (1828/1967, 500) was

Figure 11.2 The Nguyen emperor Minh Mang (r.1820–41), as sketched by a member of John Crawfurd's British mission in 1827. Source: Crawfurd 1828/1967.

struck at the very peripheral place of Buddhism in Minh Mang's domains, receiving "no support from the civil power," and at the lack of religious devotion except in connection with ancestors. Although Viet Nam of this period had the most sophisticated civilian and military bureaucracy in the region, its lack of the religious sentiment that bound other Southeast Asians to each other and to their religious and secular elites rendered it probably the most brittle of the three Mainland polities.

Minh Mang's hostility to Christianity was particularly virulent, presumably because it seemed with European backing the most overt threat to his new order. In two decrees of 1825–6 he banned all missionaries from working in Viet Nam and commanded any who were there to come to Hue and work on translating European books. In 1833, once their protector Le Van Duyet was dead, he demanded that all churches be destroyed and all Christians renounce their religion by trampling on a crucifix, on pain of death. The worst violence against them occurred, however, in the period 1837–41 when the king associated them with rebellion in the south. Unsatisfied with earlier results, he then declared,

> Previously, we strictly established regulations banning [Christianity]; we burned its books, destroyed its residences, and chased people away so that they no longer could gather together. ... We killed stubborn [adherents] and released those who repented ... All those who have not previously abandoned the religion must now appear at the provincial capital to confess the truth, and they will be ordered to step repeatedly on the cross" (Minh Mang in Dutton et al. 2012, 327–8).

Le Van Duyet had been the most successful general of Nguyen Anh in his defeat of the Tay Son, rewarded by being made Viceroy of the South. Although he had opposed Minh Mang's accession, the new king had to work with him to have any leverage in the south. Duyet was appreciative of the role of the Europeans in making the Nguyen victory possible, and continued to work with foreign traders, Christians, Chinese, and other locals able to operate in the plural world of the delta. He was also responsible for extending his and the Emperor's sway into the Khmer heartland around Phnom Penh, keeping troops there to dominate the Cambodian King. However, after Duyet's death, in 1832, Minh Mang moved quickly to reverse his policies, emphasizing that only *Han* customs, dress, and ritual were valid and should be maintained. Direct rule of Cambodia was attempted. Ten educational officers were sent to Khmer areas in 1835 to teach *Han* ways. "Force the sons of Khmer people to go to officials in charge of education ... to learn Chinese characters," he commanded. "Forbid them from going to their own monks to learn. Whoever learns Chinese characters will be appointed head of the village" (cited Choi 2004, 138). Viet settlements should be moved into such areas to provide an example. "Barbarians ... in remote and mountainous places" should also be instructed in correct ways, for "they are my people too. Therefore, we have to teach them everything from the way of cultivation, to language and clothes. Let them gradually forget barbarian habits and let them be affected by the *Han* way" (cited Choi 2004, 142).

Rebellion in the delta began in 1833 and kept the region in turmoil for two years. It was led by Le Van Duyet's adoptive son, outraged by the way Minh Mang had ordered the desecration of his patron's tomb. The rebellion was supported by many Chinese, Christians, and other southerners dismayed at the reversal of his Duyet's policies. Duyet would remain a focus of controversy, generally hailed as a hero by southerners who rebuilt his Saigon tomb, and condemned or ignored by the communists. There was no such ambivalence in Cambodia, where revolt also began in 1840 after the Vietnamese removed the last symbol of Khmer autonomy, a young queen. Minh Mang's successor, Thieu-Tri (r.1841–7), withdrew the Viet garrison from Phnom Penh amidst deep ethnic bitterness. In the ongoing contest to impose alien rule on the Khmers, Viet Nam had won many of the battles but repeatedly lost the peace across perhaps the widest cultural gap in the region, between Confucian and Theravada ideas. Conflict continued until 1847, when Cambodia enjoyed its own last moment of relative autonomy as the reforming King Ang Duang (1848–60) managed the delicate balance between his Thai suzerain and an exhausted but still dangerous Viet Nam. His son Norodom had little choice other than to accept a French Protectorate.

Ever since losing the contest with the British over India in the eighteenth century, ambitious French governments had dreamed of finding some alternative base in Asia. Pigneau de Behaine's intervention to help Gia Long, followed by Minh Mang's persecution of French missionaries, turned the attention of Napoleon III to Viet Nam. An indecisive attack near the capital in 1858 was followed by the occupation of the less defended and more restive Saigon area the following year. By 1867 this had expanded to a colony renamed Cochin-China, and a protectorate over the struggling Cambodian kingdom. The succession crisis in 1847 led to another convinced Confucian scholar succeeding as Tu Duc (1847–83), but having to campaign against even more rebellions including that of his older brother. Rather than seeking alternative European support against the French like other embattled kings, Tu Duc alienated them all by continued persecution of Christians. He preferred to turn for help to the Black Flag bandit group and to his acknowledged suzerain in China. The Chinese intervention he invited, in 1882–5, was also the desperate last attempt by a collapsing Imperial China to convert its ramshackle "tribute" system into modern sovereignty.

After Tu Duc's death the court was plunged into internal vendettas and bitterness from which it was only rescued by a French protectorate over the much reduced and poorest middle section of the country, renamed Annam, from 1885. The most effective resistance came from northern literati faithful to a cultural system that mandated loyalty even to emperors who seemed to have betrayed everything they held dear. Several committed suicide rather than submit to the barbarians. The commander of the Hanoi citadel penned an elegant farewell:

> Responsible for the death of the citadel and devoid of any hope of recovering it, I feel the death sentence too mild a punishment for my misdeeds. ... My only recourse is to imitate [Tang Dynasty Chinese general] Zhang Xun by ending my life in order to honour the great responsibilities entrusted to me" (Hoang Du 1882, cited Dutton et al. 2012, 339).

"PROTECTED" NEGERI

Plurality and mediation were the essence of the Malay-speaking *negeri* that arose at each of the significant river-ports of Sumatra, the Peninsula, and Borneo. One *negeri* might, through hard or soft power, succeed in exacting a kind of tribute or deference from others, but never in absorbing them. Each pursued its own "gateway" strategy in mediating between upriver farmers or foragers and the broader world of oceanic trade. Accommodating international traders was not only necessary but the *raison d'être* of the polity.

Indians, Arabs, and Bugis were co-opted not only as port and Islamic officials but also as rulers. European, Chinese, or upland individuals were blocked from this route unless they adopted Islam, but the nineteenth-century *negeri* needed these communities above all to continue their mediating role. In return for the financial levies and gifts the traders provided, the *negeri* offered legitimacy and access to the puzzling interior world of diverse languages and cultures.

The squabbling European companies and their successors wanted above all to exclude their competitors. The Netherlands Indian government had less military and economic muscle than the former VOC in a world now dominated by British and Chinese trade, and its efforts to pressure the *negeri* into signing exclusive treaties proceeded slowly. Faced with Dutch gunboats, most rajas would sign the treaty, but would equally trade with British, Chinese, and American vessels once the guns had departed. There was usually at least one *negeri* in the Straits area attracting a large share of trade despite Dutch efforts. Riau (on the island of Bintan south of Singapore) did this before being punished by a VOC fleet in 1784, while Siak and Palembang in Sumatra, and Trengganu and Kedah on the Peninsula had their moments during the commercial boom that followed.

Eighteenth-century Palembang controlled the tin of Bangka and a substantial riverine hinterland, and developed a significant Islamic literary culture. The decline of VOC naval hegemony after 1760, however, left it exposed first to Ilanun piracy, and then to Anglo-Dutch conflict. After a decade of civil war with British and Dutch supporting alternate sides, the Dutch sent an expedition to capture the place in 1821, and finally abolished the sultanate altogether after further conflict in 1825. A similar measure was taken in 1860 in Banjarmasin, the only Borneo *negeri* with a significant Islamized hinterland. Removal of the symbolic mediation of a raja only intensified a four-year resistance to Dutch attempts to regain their foothold there (1859–63). As in Palembang, Sufi brotherhoods (*tarekat*) were strengthened by the struggle against infidel meddling. They proved more effective in galvanizing and extending the Muslim population, but also more divisive in consolidating its borders against non-Muslim highlanders.

The other river-mouth rajas of Borneo, eastern Sumatra, and the Peninsula had no such Islamized agricultural population to fall back on, and proved ideal partners for the expanding naval and commercial power of Dutch and British governments. The most remarkable success here was Johor, reinvented as a Malay *negeri* after the British established their base in Singapore in 1819. Stamford Raffles initially sought legitimacy for his acquisition of the island (in the teeth of Dutch opposition) through agreements with a local vassal of Riau, the Temenggung of Johor, and the brother of the Dutch-allied Riau sultan, to whom he accorded a pension and recognition as Sultan of Johor. Anglo-Dutch *realpolitik* established that Singapore could remain British, but the legitimacy of all the Malay actors became highly contested. The Temenggung line was the more active in acquiring Chinese and British allies, and in 1855 it was recognized by the British as ruling Johor.

From his growing capital just across the causeway from Singapore, Temenggung Abu Bakar (1862–95) played his diplomatic cards expertly enough for a British Governor to declare him "in his habits and tastes ... an English Gentleman ... and the only Rajah ... who rules in accordance with the practice of civilized nations" (Ord 1973, cited Trocki 2007, 155).

Enjoying a growing income from land concessions to Chinese planters, he matched an extravagant European lifestyle with a key role as intermediary between Malay courts, British power, and Chinese entrepreneurship. On his five tours of Europe he balanced visits to Britain's Queen Victoria and successive Ottoman sultans in Istanbul, the two modern monarchies from which he sought "civilized" and Islamic legitimacy, respectively. Eventually both recognized him as sultan, and the Queen gave him a knighthood. He rivaled Chulalongkorn in his visits to other European courts. His marriages were even more cosmopolitan, including a high-born Malay, a Chinese, a Eurasian (daughter of Mads Lange of Bali), and an Ottoman Circassian. Before his death he decreed a European-style but absolutist constitution as well as an Islamic law code modeled on the Ottoman one, in the hope of securing Johor's autonomy after his death. Although deferring to British needs and employing Europeans liberally, he was the only Malay ruler to have so long avoided being placed under the watchful eye of a British, Dutch, or Siamese Resident.

"Protection" proved a more efficient outcome than direct European rule for both the *negeri* of the Peninsula and the *muang* on the Mekong. Britain was primarily concerned with India and the Malacca Straits route to China, making the Straits Settlements of Penang, Melaka, and Singapore vital but the adjacent *negeri* of interest only incidentally provided the costs were minimal. The diverse Peninsula rulers were molded into the modern pattern of nine "Malay states," eventually homogenized as sultans enjoying much larger and more secure incomes but restricted by British Residents to focusing on land issues and Islam. For its part France was concerned with Viet Nam, Siam, and alternative routes to China, and the Mekong *muang* were explored initially as part of the latter. King Norodom of Cambodia signed treaties with France in 1867 and 1888, which rescued him from Siamese absorption but surrendered effective control to French officials with many subordinate Vietnamese. Of the numerous Lao *muang* only Luang Prabang had its capital on the east bank of the Mekong that became French after 1893. Its king, Unkham, had even less chance of survival under the rising Siamese pressure of the 1880s, but he also became a protected king under the French. His territory was much extended and his palace and income at last secure while effective control of the economy passed to alien hands. The most sympathetic British and French officials felt genuine affection for these colorful royal courts and their charming rural subjects, but did not imagine them as potential nation-states. Gradually the idea of "protection" ceased to be against Siam or some other foreign power, but against the kind of modernity represented by more aggressively commercial minorities, Chinese, Indian, and Vietnamese. This perceived threat would ensure that monarchy continued to be important in the transition to independence (Chapter 17).

MUSLIM ALTERNATIVES IN SUMATRA

Those in the Archipelago who declined *negeri* accommodation of European norms found a range of alternatives in the Islamic world. The economic expansion after 1780 brought new opportunities for travel, new religious schools and more questioning of older localism and synthesis. Former gunpowder empires were no longer in a position to enforce the compromises of official faith, which were increasingly challenged by reformist *tarekat* and returning pilgrims from Mecca. Nowhere was the conflict sharper than in the Minangkabau highlands of central Sumatra, where kings were only symbolic and matrilineal inheritance an affront to trade-enriched male hajis returning from the pilgrimage. Three such became persuaded in Arabia by the violent and uncompromising fundamentalism of the Wahhabis, who conquered Mecca in 1803 and destroyed the sacred tombs and relics they deemed idolatrous. In the following years the "Padri," as they became known, dressed like Wahhabis and created separate communities where their pure version of Quranic morality could be applied. As they gained strength they waged a violent campaign against traditional feasting with alcohol and cock-fighting, against matriliny and female autonomy, and against elite defenders of the old order. The killing began out of arguments over property inheritance, as Padri leader Tuanku nan Renceh killed his maternal aunt. It climaxed with the spectacular massacre of the nominal rulers of Minangkabau at Pagarruyung in 1815.

The traditionalist party appealed for assistance to the Dutch when they returned to Padang in 1821 after the British interregnum. After ending the challenge of another Muslim rebel in Java, Dipanegara, in 1830, more substantial Dutch forces gained the upper hand. They established a system of forts throughout Minangkabau by 1833. A remarkable transformation then occurred, whereby Padri leader Tuanku Imam Bonjol appears to have made peace with the traditionalists, agreed that true Islam and Minangkabau custom could co-exist, and even returned some of the property he had plundered. His violent men were now redirected to the non-Muslim Batak areas to the north, where they introduced the new doctrines by force to the southern Bataks (who as Muslims came to prefer the term Mandailing). This campaign among the Bataks generated enough plunder to sustain Padri strongholds in the Minangkabau heartland, where the war became a more conservative resistance and guerrilla war against the Dutch intrusion. Imam Bonjol's turnaround may have been shrewd *realpolitik*, but for himself and the faithful he had a principled explanation, set out in his later memoirs. In 1832, already on the back foot, he had sent four men to Mecca to learn more of the "true law of Allah." They returned with the news that the Wahhabis were totally defeated and discredited in the holy places. Their plundering of pilgrimage sites had brought a backlash through the Turkish-Egyptian reconquest of 1812. Mecca and Medina were back under Ottoman control. The property the Padris had plundered in the name of religious purity was no longer justified. Tensions between *adat* (custom) and *agama* (religion) would remain in colonial-era Minangkabau, and the questioning

of both laid a foundation for one of Indonesia's most successful modernizations through education.

The Dutch advances in the Minangkabau area were of great concern in
Aceh, Indonesia's strongest sultanate and the only one still fully independent
in the nineteenth century. Aceh's "last stand" bears interesting comparison
with those of the Mainland. Aceh depended on trade like the Malay *negeri*, but
like Viet Nam possessed an unwieldy long coastline of many potential ports.
Neither "gateway" nor "heartland" strategy were possible. A common Acehnese
culture had developed in the eighteenth century, but there was always tension
between this and the cosmopolitanism of the ports. The great expansion of
pepper-growing after 1790 had strengthened the minor rajas (later known as
uleebalang) against the sultan. After 1850 the most prosperous were in a new
eastern pepper-frontier accessible to Penang traders. The sultan's attempts to
use Europeans and Eurasians to strengthen his navy to impose a customs
regime along the coast were never very successful, and in mid-century the
sultan appeared more of a symbol and referee, enjoying some tribute payments
from the flourishing *uleebalang*, and using personal connections with the richest of them to advance his cause with others. Thus he was able to assemble a
fleet of 200 small vessels to assert Aceh's authority on the Malay rulers of east
Sumatra, in 1854, for the first time in two centuries.

Which way would Aceh turn for inspiration as the Dutch advanced on the
west coast in the 1830s and later the east coast in the 1860s? French and
Italian traders proposed their respective countries, but a passive Ottoman
Turkey had much more allure. The idea of renewing the sixteenth-century
alliance with the Turkish sultan began around 1838 as a vigorous new sultan,
Ala'ad-din Mansur Shah (r.1838–70), responded to the loss of Aceh's
southernmost districts to the Dutch. Despite Turkey's nineteenth-century
weakness, its attractions were that it had charge of the holy places of the
Hejaz, and could claim a universal Caliphate evoking past Muslim power.
The growing Arab minority in Southeast Asia could claim it as their "civilized"
passport to equality with Europeans. Aceh's ancient label as "the verandah
of Mecca" was revitalized with steam navigation in the mid-nineteenth
century, as many Archipelago pilgrims used that departure point to escape
Dutch controls and charges. Finally, any non-Muslim potential "protector"
evoked visceral hostilities that went back to Aceh's sixteenth-century anti-
Portuguese origins, whereas *Rum* (Istanbul) was remembered as the protector
that had sent the large cannon that still remained. Like its Vietnamese
counterpart, the Acehnese elite looked for salvation to the remembered,
idealized exemplar of a familiar civilization, however decadent, rather than
to a bullying alien one.

Aceh dispatched an envoy in February 1849 with letters to both the
President of France (from whom a beautiful but bland letter had been
recently received) and to the Ottoman Sultan Mejid I. Both rulers were
flattered by such distant deference, and provided funding for the envoy to
travel on from Cairo to Paris and Istanbul, respectively. The envoy had no
doubt that Turkey was the best chance, and sent only one of his entourage

to Paris, where he was feted but not given any concrete support. The Ottoman relationship was far more intense. The Aceh letter insisted that the sixteenth-century acceptance of Turkish suzerainty (Chapter 5) was still valid, so that Acehnese "have truly been the born slaves of Your [Ottoman] Majesty from ancient times to the present day." The Ottoman sultan in February 1852 approved expenses to send the envoy back to Aceh together with an appropriate Ottoman official who could report back, though there appears to have been no follow-up.

Sultan Ibrahim in Aceh, however, was sufficiently encouraged to send 10,000 Spanish dollars to help Turkey in the Crimean war in 1853, and received in return an Ottoman sword and decoration he made a point of wearing when receiving Dutch envoys in 1855. The next to appeal to this ancient link was a talented Hadhrami *sayyid*, Habib Abd'ur-rahman az-Zahir, who had fallen out with Sultan Ibrahim after four remarkable years accumulating influence as imam of Aceh's great mosque, which he had rebuilt. In 1868 he carried an appeal for Turkish help as far as Mecca. The idea of universal Ottoman protectorate was exciting to endangered Muslims but acutely embarrassing for the powerless Istanbul court. In southern Sumatra the young Sultan Taha of Jambi had, in 1855, already refused to declare his allegiance to the Dutch sovereign and instead attempted to have Jambi declared Turkish territory. His rebellion continued for a decade. Turkey responded to Abd'ur-rahman and the Acehnese with sweet words, as they had to Taha, while telling the Dutch that these appeals were rejected.

Once Holland removed, through the 1871 Sumatra Treaty (Chapter 12), the obstacle of Britain's guarantee of Acehnese independence, the war-clouds quickly gathered. Abd'ur-rahman, who had meanwhile become guardian and prime minister for the new sultan, Mahmud (1870–4), departed again in early 1873 to appeal to Turkey. In his absence less skillful hands continued the desperate search for foreign protector, but their attempts to sign a treaty with the United States only provided the trigger for a Dutch invasion. The Netherlands took the unusual step of a formal declaration of war against Aceh intended to keep out third parties, and launched a rushed and disastrous naval expedition against its capital in three weeks of April 1873. The Dutch defeat then left seven months for frenzied war preparations and diplomacy on both sides. Abd'ur-rahman gained the purely symbolic victory of persuading the Turkish government to offer its mediation to the parties. Holland's humiliation, however, required an avenging victory, and the largest-ever fleet was assembled to carry 10,000 men to invade again in November. After three months of cautious campaigning and an outbreak of cholera that killed the young sultan and thousands of others, the Dutch commander took over the deserted and pestilential citadel in January 1874. He abruptly declared Aceh part of Netherlands India with the sultanate abolished, ending what little chance there was of a "protected" *negeri*. Acehnese kept a guerrilla war going for 40 years, united in resistance to the Dutch as they had never been in support for the sultan. Leadership of the resistance became gradually more Islamic as it became more hopeless. A more normal colonial regime only emerged in the 1920s by supporting the territorial aristocracy of *uleebalang* against this resistance party, at the cost of leaving Aceh the most polarized of provinces at the end of the Dutch regime.

BALI APOCALYPSE

The last stand of Bali and adjacent Lombok was perhaps the most poignant. Having fiercely resisted both Muslims and Europeans since the sixteenth century, Balinese had developed a culture proud of its Hindu-Javanese origins and a military organization effective enough to conquer and control the eastern salient of Java for over a century and neighboring Lombok from 1750 onward. Yet military success never changed the state-averse pluralism that Bali retained from older times. Its rajas were many, but their status rivalry was expressed not in seeking to absorb each other militarily but in outdoing each other in spectacular displays of religious ritual requiring thousands of participants. The common purpose demanded by the irrigation of elaborate rice terraces was achieved not by "Asiatic" despots but by irrigation associations (*subak*) in each run-off area held together by essentially ritual means. The island was united by complex economic, ritual, and kinship systems. This strength in plurality would endure through the nineteenth century.

That century began badly when the eruption of Sumbawa's Tambora volcano in 1815 darkened the skies of Bali and Lombok and deposited a thick layer of ash on their rice fields. Tens of thousands died of hunger as harvests were meagre for the next four years. The effect was worsened by a severe earthquake in November 1815 which caused the crater lake of Mount Pangilingan to burst its banks, destroying seventeen villages in north Bali and killing an estimated 10,000 people. Only after fifteen years of misery did the ecological curse turn to a blessing as the nutrients in the ash were absorbed to fertilize the soils. The years 1830–50 were a period of bounty as Bali and Lombok each exported some 20,000 tons of rice a year, chiefly to Java and Singapore. Balinese themselves took little part in the trade, but rival rajas would gain revenue by leasing the right to operate their ports to some non-Balinese port official (*bandar*) – Chinese, European, or Bugis. At first carried out in small Bugis vessels, the booming trade to Singapore attracted the interest of Europeans, including the Dane Mads Lange in Kuta (south Bali, 1839–56) and the Englishman George Pocock King in Ampenan (west Lombok, 1834–49). Both were successful mediators fluent in Balinese, and models for Conrad's later *Lord Jim* figure. Lange famously entertained visitors by playing his violin in a quartet with his Danish relatives. He built the first modern road in Bali and managed a well regulated port.

The advent of steamers in mid-century demanded a technological leap this low level of economic activity could not make. The Dutch invaded northern Bali and gradually brought the rajas of Buleleng and Karangasem under their control in 1846–50. Singaraja, on the north coast, was developed as their port for the steamer routes. South Bali ceased its modest steps toward modernity with the collapse of trade, but retained what Geertz (1980, 16) called

> an acrobat's pyramid of "kingdoms" of varying degrees of substantial autonomy and effective power ... based ... primarily on ceremony and prestige ... the more fragile and tenuous in actual political dominance and subordination the higher up one went.

Because their status was perceived to be based on their godlike-ness, defeat and humiliation in war represented a metaphysical crisis, resolved only by suicide. This was expected by Balinese whenever conflicts were pushed to the limit, but was incomprehensible to the Dutch armies that finally confronted the remaining defiant rajas. First to fall, in 1894, was the only one capable of mounting serious resistance, the Balinese court that ruled the whole of Muslim-majority Lombok in an unusually hierarchic, colonial way. In 1906–8 it was the turn of the rajas of south Bali – Badung, Tabanan, and Klungkung.

Figure 11.3 The Badung *puputan* of 1906, as dramatized in *Le Petit Journal* of Paris. Source: *Le Petit Journal*, Paris, 1906.

When its time came, the leading members of each court processed out as if in a trance, dressed in white, demanding that the Dutch troops kill them; if that failed, they stabbed themselves and one another in a ritual suicide.

These "closures" (*puputan*) were at once a dramatic last stand of an old order, gaining headlines in Europe (Figure 11.3), and an acceptance that a new order must have been divinely ordained. Bali was transformed within a decade from a savage and haughty site of traditional resistance to a famously peaceful and artistic tourist attraction – a transformation that had taken three centuries in Java.

MOBILE "BIG MEN" IN THE EASTERN ISLANDS

Between Borneo, Mindanao, and New Guinea lies a maritime world of thousands of islands (many actively volcanic) affording many hiding places but very few naturally dominant harbors or river-mouths. Its marginality after the decline of the spice trade in the late eighteenth century allowed the region unusual fluidity. The importance of the trade in clove and nutmeg had brought Portuguese and Dutch to the region, and by 1670 Makassar (the largest single port), Ternate, Ambon, and Banda were firmly under VOC control. A handful of other polities – Brunei, Sulu, Magindanao, and Tidore – had used Islam and the anti-Iberian cause to seek to overcome the intense local pluralisms and reciprocities that had previously been the basis of integration. Even these self-declared sultanates were in reality plural federations and alliances, while dozens of other power centers came and went with the vagaries of trade and warfare. The Spanish and Dutch made treaties with various rulers and occasionally sought to enforce them, but with decreasing effectiveness from the 1760s. The British became the strongest naval power of the region, while Chinese and Bugis traders shared most of its trade. Bureaucratic power was at a minimum, and charismatic "big men" could accumulate armed followers through activities regarded by settled societies as raiding, piracy, and slave-trading. Besides preying on rivals, however, these groups protected the trade of ports that supported them. Arung Bakung, a Bugis who fled Bone after a dispute in 1816, operated with a growing band of followers first in the island of Muna, then in Kendari until 1842, using his alliances and the threat or reality of violence to protect traders and fishermen in each of these places in turn. Once these ports became prosperous enough to invite attack by other raiders, as happened in turn to Tembuku, Kendari, Toli-Toli, and Banggai in the east Sulawesi region, the armed bands would move on.

The Sulu archipelago between Mindanao and Borneo particularly profited from the expansion of Chinese trade, which used it as a suitable base of minimal European control, to purchase the sea-cucumbers (*trepang*), mother-of-pearl, tortoiseshell, birds' nests, and other sea and forest produce for which there was a growing market in China. As its trade expanded so did the Sulu elite's hunger for slaves and captives, both to manifest their wealth and to collect and process the needed trade goods. A pattern of financing Illanun (Iranun) and Balangingi peoples to raid settled coastal communities for slaves had begun before 1600. More than 25,000 Christian Filipinos were reported to have been taken by 1635. This scourge intensified after 1770, with some estimates as high as 2,000–3,000 a year being seized in the coastal Philippines and as far afield as Sumatra for sale in Sulu and ultimately the Dutch settlements of Makassar and Batavia. The population distribution in the Visayas and other coastal areas was affected by the intensity of raiding, with increasing numbers taking shelter in those Spanish settlements capable of protecting them. The religious polarization of 1570–1600 appears to have provided an initial impetus for this pattern, but subsequently it was driven more by profit. Filipinos kept alive the fear of Muslim raiders combined with Spanish memories of much older struggles to produce a caricature of the "Moro" enemy in performance and poetry.

Only in 1848 did the acquisition of steamships enable the Spanish to get the upper hand militarily over this threat, with the main Balangingi stronghold captured and destroyed. The Spanish were becoming alarmed at the tendency of other imperial powers to see the Sulu area as independent. A French party in 1845 signed a treaty with Sulu for the cession of Basilan Island and an American did the same in 1865 to legitimate the cession of northern Borneo. The Spanish steamships finally conquered the Sulu capital at Jolo after a fierce campaign in 1876. As in Aceh, however, a highly decentralized and embittered polity proved extremely difficult to pacify, and a spirit of Islamic martyrdom inspired regular suicidal individual attacks up to the end of the Spanish regime in 1898.

The island of Mindanao was large enough for its major river to support both the "gateway" sultanate of Magindanao (later Cotabatu) at the mouth of the Pulangi River, and the polity of Buayan at an upstream river junction out of reach of Spanish steamers. The former had flourished in the age of commerce, enjoying Dutch and Muslim help against the Spanish, but had become dependent on Spanish support in the eighteenth century. Buayan in the 1860s was able to deploy a "heartland" strategy to become the last independent sultanate of the Philippines. The prince, Datu Utto, did not succeed his father officially as sultan, allowing his uncle to occupy that more vulnerable interface with the Spanish. Nevertheless, he accumulated more power than any of his royal predecessors, by strategic marriage alliances and the control of an alternative land route to the coast, along which slaves and forest products could be exchanged for "smuggled" firearms. Just as in Aceh, a fundamentally fragmented region could be united only in an Islamically inspired holy war (Arabic *jihad* or Malay *perang sabil*) against Spanish control.

Among the many other "big men" who achieved a brief personal eminence in this fluid world was Nuku of Tidore, always the alternative and rival of the adjacent volcanic island and clove capital of Ternate. In 1780 Nuku left Tidore in protest against the tighter Dutch regime imposed on the sultanate, and began to gather supporters in the outer islands of Maluku and Papua by the usual methods of charisma, alliances, and raiding. His resources in playing this role were much enhanced when, in 1795, English traders began to trade with him, supplying guns and cloth for his network in exchange for the cloves and nutmeg he could extract from a collapsing Dutch monopoly. Two years later he was able to take control of his Tidore homeland, and in 1801 he allied with a British force in conquering the Dutch fort on Ternate. Recognized as Sultan of Tidore and an ally rather than a vassal by the British, he appears to have dreamed of a neo-traditional polity in Maluku that could restore some of the ancient balance between four island groupings and reject the novel hegemony of Ternate and the Europeans. He has been rediscovered recently as an Indonesian national hero, but to his followers and immediate successors he was more appropriately known as the "Blessed Lord" (*Tuan Berkat*) who could rise to remarkable eminence through the good fortune of his alliances.

These smaller eastern islands remained as resistant to state control as the highlands of the larger ones. Mobile, maritime peoples could always find another island refuge whenever state levies and impositions became bothersome in their existing one. Some such centers remain today, free of all taxes and duties. The pioneer of evolutionary theory Alfred Russell Wallace spent fascinated months in the small-island port of Dobo in the Aru Archipelago in 1857, and marveled how its extraordinarily diverse inhabitants

> live here without the shadow of a government, with no police, no courts, and no lawyers; yet they do not cut each other's throats, do not plunder each other day and night, do not fall into the anarchy such a state of things might be supposed to lead to. … Trade is the magic that keeps all at peace, and unites these discordant elements into a well-behaved community (Wallace 1869, 215–6).

THE LAST STATE EVADERS

Highlanders typically clung even more fiercely to their autonomy because they had chosen it. After experience with predatory states and the global religions that justified them, they had rejected both in favor of a freer, more mobile lifestyle. Wider integrations occurred, as ever, through trade, kinship, ritual, and performance, but were not formalized through written histories or literatures. Whereas lowland sedentary populations could all be expected to speak and perhaps read some variant of one of the widespread languages associated with scriptural religion – Bama, Thai, Vietnamese, Javanese, or Malay – linguistic diversity remained intense in the unincorporated highlands. While the language of their village might be unique, highlanders could perforce also speak the languages of neighbors or the lingua franca at ever-broader circles of trade, migration, warfare, or feasting. Political integration was what they had chosen to avoid. They united only when under military threat, and then usually behind a charismatic millenarian figure.

Movement was common from one language group to another, and between the free hills and the more secure lifestyle and larger socio-linguistic units of the valleys. In many cases, involuntary incorporation through slaving raids also occurred. Edmund Leach observed in Upper Burma that "the hill people who are neighbours to the Shans are astonishingly varied in their culture; the Shans … are astonishingly uniform." He concluded that the Shan had retained a stable pattern through their river-irrigation economic niche and shared written and religious culture with other *muang*, even while constantly incorporating refugees from the highly varied hills (Leach 1959, 40). In benign times, politically and environmentally, the lowland populations grew very quickly by these means, but in crises that crippled agriculture and spread famine and disease, the highlanders survived better.

The coming of global orthodoxies – Islam and Christianity but to an extent also Theravada Buddhism and Confucian/Han identity – had ensured that religion would be part of the distinctiveness of highlanders. As described in Chapter 5, the animist "Southeast Asian religion" that continued there was local, intensely varied, and experimental, in that every ritual practice and practitioner was constantly judged by the results they appeared to deliver. In the nineteenth century, when the astonishing new powers of industrialization began to be felt, millenarian saviors flourished. Karen hopes of a "Karen King" who would restore the primacy of Karens over their lowland neighbors and inaugurate a time of happiness and equality, were especially prominent at the time American Baptist missionaries arrived to record them in mid-century. European adventurers could appear briefly to be "stranger-kings" who might make the new power accessible to highlanders. The Roman traveler Elio Modigliani was hailed as Raja Rum, the great ruler of the west, when he toured the independent Batak areas near Sumatra's Lake Toba in 1890. His visit was the springboard for the millenarian Parmalim movement, which incorporated some elements of Christianity and Islam into a novel neo-traditional Batak religion. Ex-legionnaire Marie-Charles de Mayréna (1842–90) in 1888 used letters from the French Resident and the influence of Catholic missionary Fr Guerlach among the Bahnar to briefly create a comic-opera "kingdom of the Sedangs," complete with flags, stamps, and titles. For the Bahnars and other Chamic peoples around modern Kon Tum, he appeared to offer a direct route to modern autonomy without having to become Vietnamese.

In a few cases, the growing crisis of identity for the highlanders helped Christian missionaries – typically Protestant evangelicals newly energized by the unification of the world. Long-standing Catholic missions in Burma and the Viet area had already gone to the highlands in the mid-nineteenth century, in part as a refuge against persecution in the lowlands. But the best of the German and American Protestants had absorbed Herderian ideas about the primacy of language in a people's identity, and approached highlanders with less lowland baggage. Their profound innovation was to offer hill peoples the book many felt they had lost to their lowland neighbors. Highland languages were romanized and printed for the first time by missionary presses, often thereby stabilizing and standardizing what had been vast dialectical variation. The two great successes of the 1860–1910 period, and indeed of Protestant missionary history worldwide, were those of American Baptists among the Karen of the Burma/Siam frontier, and of German Rhenische Mission Lutherans among the Toba Batak of Sumatra. In both cases it helped that missionaries were not of the same nationality as the threatening colonial power, and began their work in advance of colonial control. Their task was facilitated by the conviction of highlanders that their identity was defined by not being incorporated into lowland religion and identity. The missionaries devoted their early intellectual resources to rendering the bible into vernaculars which were thereby rendered standard. A Sgaw Karen Bible was published in 1853 and a Kachin New Testament in 1911, while a Toba Batak New Testament was published in Batak (Indic-derived) characters in 1876 and in romanized form in 1885. Millenarian expectations focused on certain missionaries were quickly disappointed. Except in certain cases where the old order was in crisis, the huge cultural gulf to married European missionaries (inevitably implicated in the colonial caste system, however personally critical of it) was a major obstacle to expansion. A tiny but well-educated highland Christian minority was disproportionately important everywhere in the nationalist transition to independence, but the most expansive time for highland and small-island Christianity would come after independence and local leadership of the churches.

One of the key changes of the short high colonial period after 1890 was in ending the autonomy of these most determined state-evaders. Incorporation was both possible and necessary to the high colonial states because of their radical new idea, discussed in Chapter 12, that sovereignty had to be uniform and total up to the internationally agreed borders. Some unlucky highlanders found their land had been leased to European estates by a river-mouth "gateway" *negeri*. This happened to the Karo Batak of east Sumatra at the hands of the sultans of Deli and Langkat, when they suddenly had to defend their territory against European-led armies in the "Batak War" of 1872. Military columns were sent into the highlands in the years after 1880, to subdue defiant millenarian leaders such as the Toba Batak priest-king Singamangaradja XII (killed in 1883). With the exception of already Islamized uplands like the Gayo plateau in the interior of Aceh, however, there were few murderous pitched battles in the highlands. Colonial governments were often welcomed as referees and peacemakers, and made rapid progress in ending petty warfare, raiding, and head-hunting. Slavery was phased out much more slowly, replaced by other forms of patronage. But full and effective incorporation into the new polities, economies, and ideologies was not a priority for governments and proceeded very slowly except where it was assisted by networks of mission schools. In some cultural respects the trend toward assimilation into lowland culture was reversed, as it became clear that there were other routes to modernity and affluence. The new colonial overlord states were frequently seen as protectors and referees by the highlanders, who saw less reason than ever to adopt sedentary lowland ways.

[12] MAKING STATES, 1824–1940

EUROPEAN NATIONALISMS AND DEMARCATIONS

In 1810 Southeast Asia was still a fluid region of religio-cultural exemplary centers but no fixed boundaries except that which separated Dai Viet and China. Rulers made competing claims to supernatural eminence, but their power to control events or exploit populations diminished rapidly with distance from their courts. Such rulers were more comfortable with relations of deference than of equality, and skillful diplomacy sought to keep the more powerful at bay by sending them tokens of honor, without sacrificing status or autonomy at home.

A century later the map of the region was in multiple blocks of color divided by fixed international borders. It had been incorporated into a world system of theoretical equality between sovereign states. Essentially this was a product of intensely competitive European nationalisms, which fought each other fiercely until 1815, but thereafter tended to divert their rivalries into competitive expansion abroad. The lesson of these intra-European conflicts was the so-called Westphalia system, requiring recognition of fundamental equality between sovereign entities. It therefore needed to establish the boundaries between one sovereignty and another. Because we live in the world this system created, it is difficult to appreciate quite how revolutionary a notion it was in Asia.

Even before they had reached Asia by sea, Spain and Portugal had signed the Treaty of Tordesillas (1494), demarcating their respective ambitions beyond Europe by a straight-line meridian in the Atlantic. This was later argued to imply a Pacific anti-meridian allotting most of Asia to Portugal. The VOC, after 1600, rejected these claims, but shared the Iberian preoccupation with excluding other Europeans. They alternated wars and treaties with England and Spain, and in 1667 obtained British agreement to stay away from spice-producing Maluku in return for the abandonment of all Dutch rights over New Amsterdam (New York) and New England. After each major war, lines were redrawn in Asia that were designed to exclude other Europeans without necessarily implying anything about who governed the Asian populations. Treaties with Asian rulers were also designed above all to prevent them trading with Europeans other than themselves – usually in vain.

A History of Southeast Asia: Critical Crossroads, First Edition. Anthony Reid.
© 2015 Anthony Reid. Published 2015 by John Wiley & Sons, Ltd.

The nineteenth century was a different matter, with a modern understanding of sovereignty and fixed boundaries being extended to the whole map of Asia. No sooner had the British annexed Arakan and Tenasserim to make Siam their neighbor, than envoy Henry Burney explained to the Thai court (1826),

> the advantage of having regular boundaries established as soon as possible between the Siamese dominions and our conquests on the coasts of Tenasserim. … I added that the English earnestly desire to live in the vicinity of the Siamese as good friends and neighbours, and not in the same unsettled and unsocial terms as the Burmese had done; that for this reason we are anxious to have the boundary and rights of each party fixed, so as to prevent all chance of mistake or dispute between our subordinate officers (Burney 1971 I, 85–6).

This fixation for clarifying boundaries long preceded any idea that the Europeans might be building states in Southeast Asia, but the long-term implications of the process were immense.

FROM MANY TO TWO POLITIES IN NUSANTARA

The lower Peninsula and the Archipelago stretching from Sumatra to Timor and Maluku comprised at once the more politically fragmented and the more culturally coherent half of Southeast Asia. The Java Sea formed a mediterranean world of natural interaction, while the Malacca and Singapore Straits were an equally natural hub region because of their essential role in world commerce. Malay as the language and Islam the religion of commerce spread out from the Straits area to the ports around the Java Sea to give a certain coherence to what was known to Europeans as the "Eastern" or "Indian Archipelago," and for English writers eventually as "the Malay World." *Nusantara* (the islands between) has sometimes been deployed as a needed indigenous term. The spices of Maluku ensured that the sphere of constant maritime interaction would extend to that eastern frontier, but not beyond. Within that world was a cornucopia of polities and peoples. The names of the two eventual states into which the twentieth century divided it, Malaysia and Indonesia, both began as artifical scholarly abstractions for the whole.

The boundaries were negotiated in the nineteenth century between the British, as the dominant regional power, and the Dutch, as a much weakened ally. The Netherlands Indies government nevertheless proved a jealous heir to all the treaties the VOC had signed with gateway rulers around *Nusantara* to exclude outsiders. The Napoleonic wars had completed the collapse of Dutch commercial hegemony and produced a temporary British occupation of Dutch posts that some would have liked to make permanent. Stamford Raffles, the young and visionary British Governor of Java, was convinced of Britain's destiny in the region, claiming the VOC had brought only misery through its monopolies. But post-war British diplomacy decreed that there should be a strong and expanded Netherlands in Europe, including modern Belgium, as a buffer against France. The 1814 Anglo-Dutch Treaty provided that Holland's Southeast Asian possessions were to be restored. A disappointed

Raffles was made Governor of the somnolent British pepper post at Bengkulu on the earthquake-exposed southwest coast of Sumatra. He did his utmost to ensure British influence continued, especially in the vital Malacca and Singapore Straits.

As an eager student of Malay, he knew the importance and the independence of Aceh at the northern end of the Straits. He signed a treaty in 1819 promising mutual support with the contestant to its throne he considered legitimate, Sultan Johor al-Alam. He also knew that the Melaka chronicle he labeled "the Malay Annals," told a story of ancient Singapore as the capital of a maritime polity that connected the Malay lineage of Melaka with much older Sriwijaya (Palembang). He may not have known that the maze of shoals and islands to the south of Singapore rendered the shipping pathway closest to the island as the safest way through this vital choke point of world commerce. His questionable treaties with Malay chiefs there (Chapter 11) enraged the Dutch, who had reclaimed their post in Melaka and considered Singapore part of "their" region. But the Dutch missed their chance to remove the British post, which quickly proved too valuable to be given up. Acrimonious exchanges led inevitably to another colonial line of demarcation.

This was agreed in the Anglo-Dutch London Treaty of 1824, the fundamental charter for the two eventual states. It determined that the great thoroughfare of the Malacca and Singapore Straits would become also a boundary. Dutch Melaka was exchanged for British Bengkulu, Britain agreed to make no further settlement in Sumatra nor conclude treaties "with any Native Prince, Chief or State therein," and the Dutch agreed the same for the Peninsula. Britain was thus confirmed in possession of the islands of Singapore and Penang and the small ex-Dutch territory around Melaka, which collectively became the Straits Settlements. Raffles' 1819 Treaty with Aceh was incompatible with the treaty, and in a confidential exchange of notes Britain promised to modify that treaty to meaninglessness, and Holland undertook to try to arrange that Aceh, "without losing anything of its independence," would be a more secure area for commerce. Neither agreement was carried out, although all parties eventually became aware that Aceh was in a kind of limbo where both its dominant trading partner (the British Straits Settlements) and its chief military threat were forbidden by treaty from interfering.

Dutch leaders hoped the 1824 Treaty would gain them British support in gradually expanding their sway throughout the Archipelago, but there were disputes almost from day one. Holland was determined to industrialize, and to use its Asian possessions as a market for its otherwise struggling textile factories. The Dutch Indies discriminated prohibitively against British textiles and other manufactures, and the Straits merchants therefore protested every extension of Dutch control that would close off their natural markets in Sumatra, Borneo, and elsewhere. These protests slowed the Dutch advance in the middle of the century, and obliged them to operate a more open economy in Sumatra than they did in Java.

The growing intensity of commercial competition around the Malacca Straits convinced Britain that a Dutch Sumatra was better than any other option, and so in 1871 supplemented the 1824 Treaty with a Sumatra Treaty. This allowed the Dutch free reign in Sumatra in exchange for further guarantees of free trade. Eighteen months later the Netherlands had rushed into a disastrous war against Aceh, while the British had an Ashanti War on their hands at the Dutch fort of Elmirah in modern Ghana (West Africa), transferred to Britain as a kind of (unacknowledged) compensation for Aceh. The harvest of *realpolitik* was bitter.

Britain valued the Peninsula itself initially only for its strategic ports. In the 1870s, however, the Straits commercial lobby, the attractions of the tin trade, and the divisiveness of Malay and Chinese politics combined to propel Britain to "protect" one Malay *negeri* after another. The first four (Perak, Negri Sembilan, Selangor, and Pahang) then accepted a British Resident whose advice must be followed in "all matters except those pertaining to the religion and customs of the Malays." A generous annual allowance reconciled most of the rulers (who soon became sultans) to this arrangement. By regional standards only limited force was required to compel their dissatisfied rivals. Although in some senses still sovereign, these *negeri* were "federated" into a state-like entity called the Federated Malay States in 1896, with its capital in Kuala Lumpur. The northerly *negeri* of Kedah, Perlis, Kelantan, and Trengganu, already beginning to be modernized under Siamese auspices before they came under British "protection" in 1909, had the wit to follow Johor's example in remaining out of this federation, adding five more "unfederated states" of uncertain sovereignty.

The greatest Dutch fear on their side of the 1824 line was that European adventurers or local rajas desperate for foreign allies would bring a third European player into the Archipelago. There were plenty of both in the nineteenth century, but James Brooke was the only European adventurer to succeed in founding his own dynasty. His vital assets were his choice of the northern coast of Borneo, outside the core "Dutch lake" of the Java Sea, and the indulgence toward him of Britain. Armed only with one gunboat bought with a £30,000 inheritance, Brooke was able to tip the balance in local conflicts in the Sarawak River area, and have himself appointed representative of the Sultan of Brunei there in 1841. He played the role of referee between rival upriver Dayaks, coastal Malay traders, and Chinese miners expertly enough to stay in charge, styling himself *Raja Sarawak* in the style of a gateway *negeri*. Fortunately for him, London was particularly frustrated at Dutch exclusionary policies in the 1840s. Britain made him its Agent to the Brunei sultanate in 1844, and ocasionally supported him militarily on the pretext of anti-piracy measures, and formalized recognition by appointing a Consul to his Sarawak *raj* in 1863 and establishing a protectorate over it in 1888. Brooke's nephew Raja Charles (r.1868–1917) extended Sarawak to its modern shape and had it accepted as a "civilized" but exotic state. He played a role that was part hard-working official and part charismatic and colorful sultan like his Malay counterpart in Johor. Sarawak thereby extended the Anglo-Dutch "line" to the east, and created its first land frontier.

The northern quarter of Borneo was even more thinly peopled and stateless, so that adventurers had to apply to sultans in Brunei or Sulu for the fig-leafs of respectability for their intervention. The Brunei *negeri* itself was slow to modernize or ally with influential Britons to extend its sway, and found itself the smallest of the three Borneo entities eventually "protected" by Britain in 1888.

It was a North Borneo Chartered Company that eventually achieved British recognition for bringing "civilization" to that quarter, with more commerce and less romance than Sarawak. The rise of Germany and rush to harden boundaries against it led to the Madrid Protocol of 1885, in which Spain was recognized in its possession of the troublesome Sulu Archipelago, in return for yielding to Britain all possible Spanish claims in Borneo. The entire area on the British side of the line was thereby filled with asymmetric anomolies under a loose British umbrella. They had in common Malay and English as the two lingua franca, the Straits dollar as a currency, a metropolitan hub in Singapore, and a diverse Chinese community on which the economies largely rested. A group of Foochow (Fuzhou) Christian agriculturalists largely built Sarawak's second city of Sibu, while Hakka plantation workers were recruited by the struggling tobacco estates of North Borneo. High colonialism did not make this mosaic look much like a single state.

Dutch efforts were much more purposeful, despite very slender resources. Brooke and his emulators forced them to focus on the river-mouths of the remainder of Borneo, trying to tie each *negeri* into a system of treaties, and where possible to explore the river basins in the hope of heading off European speculators for mineral wealth. By 1889 the Dutch were ready to seek a physical demarcation of an effective Anglo-Dutch border, through a boundary commission that laid down the eventual frontiers of Indonesia and Malaysia. The Natuna and Anambas archipelagoes beween the Peninsula and Borneo were "north of the Singapore Straits," the clause used to justify Sarawak escaping the Dutch embrace. Since speculators and adventurers had passed them by, however, they were allowed to fall on the Dutch side on the basis of faint connections with the former Riau sultanate. The 2,000-km land border in Borneo was agreed, in the subsequent formal Anglo-Dutch Treaty of 1891, to follow the watershed between the mighty river systems whose mouths each side claimed to control. It would be another two decades before this boundary could be surveyed, and much longer before most of the inhabitants came to know which side they were on.

The turn of the twentieth century marked a more abrupt shift in the Archipelago world than elsewhere, when Netherlands India effectively became a state – the future Indonesia. It was the draining wound of their long-running war in Aceh that convinced Dutch policy-makers that only the direct application of superior force made many of the islanders cooperative, and that indirect attempts to work through rajas would not suffice to develop the economy nor to fulfill the *mission civilisatrice*. The two men credited with bringing the Aceh war to an end by this application of unrelenting force, General J.B. van Heutsz and Islamologist Christiaan Snouck Hurgronje, applied the lessons to the rest of the Indies when appointed in 1904 as Governor-General and Islamic advisor, respectively. Mobile military columns, mostly Indonesian in personnel, pursued and crushed resistance throughout the vast area on the

Dutch side of the line. All the *uleebalang* in Aceh, and most of the *negeri* elsewhere, were obliged to sign a Short Declaration, to the effect that their territory formed part of Netherlands India and they would obey all its instructions. A well-trained core of Dutch colonial administrators, the *Binnenlandse Bestuur*, could be placed anywhere in the Archipelago, and became the professional iron frame to rule what was still an immensely colorful diversity of peoples and institutions.

The factors that create cultural commonalities in *Nusantara* quickly diminish as one proceeds east through Wallacia, the zone of deep ocean troughs between the tectonic plates of Sundaland (as far east as Borneo and Bali) and Gondwanaland (Australia and New Guinea). The spice trade had created some very plural *negeri* in Maluku, notably the balanced moieties of Ternate and Tidore, but further east there were not even the beginnings of state-like hierarchies with which outsiders could negotiate. These most problematic of Indonesia's frontiers were therefore decided by the imperial fixing of demarcations in unknown territories, with no reference whatever to conditions on the ground or the wishes of the inhabitants. Those wishes, it is clear, were predominately to be left alone. They had successfully resisted state organization for centuries, and would continue to do so.

The less difficult Dutch line was that with the Portuguese. The VOC had captured all the major Portuguese forts in the seventeenth century, and suppressed Catholicism in the populations around them. In the south-eastern corner of the Archipelago, however, a hybrid Catholic population hung on, known to others as "black Portuguese" or Topasses (from Malay *topi*, hat) from their pride in wearing European-style hats. From their main base in Larantuka (eastern Flores), they formed sufficient alliances throughout Timor to dominate its sandalwood exports for two centuries. The VOC established a fort at Kupang (western Timor) in 1653, and the Portuguese authorities of Macao one at Dili (eastern Timor) in 1769. Neither could control the Topasses, although they gave lip service to their Portuguese-ness. It was predictably governments in Europe that felt the need and the right to negotiate fixed borders. In the 1850s Portugal surrendered all claims outside the territories of their principal allies in eastern and central Timor, but negotiations continued until the 1914 judgement of the international Permanent Court of Arbitration arrived at the modern boundary cutting Timor in half, with the East and the Oecussi enclave in north-western Timor judged as Portuguese. Despite all the blood shed in 1975–99 to remove it, this remains the boundary between the modern states of Indonesia and Timor Leste.

New Guinea was partitioned even further in advance of any knowledge of the areas or peoples in question. Anglo-Dutch rivalry was again the driving force, but without the high stakes that Singapore introduced into the westerly frontiers, both sides were shadow-boxing about imaginary empires. Since 1660 the VOC had claimed a right to exclude Europeans from territories as far east as New Guinea, on the basis of Tidore's pattern of slave-raiding and bird-of-paradise-trading there. But competitive flag-waving only came to the region in the climate of wrestling over the 1824 partition of *Nusantara*, and uncertainty about its eastern extension. The British made three tragic attempts to build a second Singapore in northern Australia in 1824–9, and the Dutch responded with a settlement on New Guinea's south coast in 1828–35. Both ventures proved unhealthy, uneconomic, and unwanted by the state-evading inhabitants, in predictable contrast to the reception Singapore received from trading networks further west. But they served their principal purpose, of strengthening British claims to the whole of Australia, and Dutch ones to the Island of New Guinea as far east as its 141-degree meridian, mentioned in earlier Dutch documents as the limit of Tidore's conceivable commercial reach.

So things remained until the scramble for the last remaining patches of stateless territory occasioned by Germany's rapid rise in the 1880s. Bismarck's policy was to support and protect chartered companies, one of which was the Deutsche Neuguinea-Compagnie. This raised the German flag to the northeast of Holland's maximalist meridian in 1884, naming the islands the Bismarck Archipelago and the mainland opposite, Kaiser Wilhelmsland. Britain was less concerned than its colonists in Australia. Queensland had attempted to pre-empt German action by annexing the southern coast in 1883, and succeeded in winning British support to do so in 1885. Thus was agreed a three-way partition of the Island, with all parties accepting, with minor refinements, the 141-degree meridian as the eastern boundary of Netherlands India. Only the newcomer Germans were ambitious colonizers, encouraging missions and forcing reluctant islanders to work on estates near the coast. Since they lost that territory to Australia in 1914 as an early skirmish of the World War, the island's interior was left largely to its own devices until World War II saw it become a battleground. In the long run this arbitrarily declared line would become the frontier not only between Indonesia and Papua New Guinea (independent since 1975), but between Asia and Oceania. Only in the 1960s did most inhabitants of the western side encounter the forces that had begun to create a nation in the rest of the Archipelago, which they had many reasons to reject. As in the cases that follow, maximalist pre-emptive claims by the imperialists stored up problems for those seeking to build nation-states in the same space.

MAXIMAL BURMA, VIABLE SIAM

In the Mainland the boundary-drawing of the nineteenth century confronted also Siam and China, each with its quite different concept of the world order, with the new European idea of sovereignty. Following Burney's initial attempt above, Britain constantly pressured Siamese authorities to negotiate an exact boundary on the ground, but met with incomprehension. The polity consisted of a center and its tributaries, and the former could not be expected to know the detailed geography of the latter. Moreover, as one Siamese official pointed out, "the boundaries between the Siamese and Burmese consisted of a tract of Mountains and forest … which could not be said to belong to either nation" (cited Winichakul 1994, 64). When the Siamese needed British goodwill they urged them to make their own line and just tell Bangkok about it; on two occasions they gave them more than had been asked as a sign of magnanimity. Only after Mongkut's accession in 1851 did the king himself understand the British obsession with a fixed line through the mountains, and sought to educate his officials about it. His son Chulalongkorn finally felt obliged to hire an English surveyor in 1881 to create a Thai capacity for mapping. Before this the Siamese never made an issue of exactly where the British chose to draw lines in the mountains, generally following the watershed between rivers flowing into the Gulf of Thailand and those into the Bay of Bengal.

This had the effect of dividing the stateless and diverse Karen population, which had inhabited the mountainous border zone, between British (the majority) and Siamese sovereignty. One of the few common features of what became Karen identity was resistance to Bama coercion, especially as remembered during "the Alaungphaya hunger" following that king's devastation of Lower Burma in the 1750s. The British wars against Burma therefore enjoyed support from many Karen, especially those who by 1886 had come to see themselves as a distinct and coherent people through Christian schools and the missionary-developed literature in Sgaw Karen. The new kind of (British) state that appeared to act as referee among Karen as well as between Karen and Bama was therefore welcome, as the assimilative civilization of the lowlands had not been. While assimilation to lowland Bama-style Buddhism continued to occur, the separate destiny of a Karen people was already canonized by one English author in *The Loyal Karens of Burma* (Smeaton 1887), a pamphlet that established a stereotype.

The British encountered the northern hill peoples only after the conquest of Mandalay in 1886. In claiming to rule vast uplands as successors to Burma's tributary relations, they approached them initially through Burmese eyes, and named them with Bama names – Shan, Chin, and Kachin. The Tai-speaking *muang* sending occasional tribute to Mandalay had called themselves Tai, as had other Tai-speaking groups in the upper Chao Phraya and Mekong. Their hereditary leaders had an ambivalent role as tributaries of Burmese kings, who called them *sawbwa*, but also as representatives to the outside of their own villagers, who called them *saopha*. The British also needed to distinguish "Burmese Shans" from Tai-speakers in Siam and in China, and to cultivate the *sawbwa* as the entry point of outsiders into their society. Theravada Buddhism and irrigated rice-growing created points of Shan cooperation with lowland Bama, but language and remembered history kept them separate enough to be so acknowledged by the British, who gradually positioned themselves as umbrella and referee between and within ethnicities. In hills of the north, on the other hand, they met conditions not dissimilar to those of the Karen. Chin and Kachin, too, were stateless and diverse peoples whose common identity derived largely from their resistance to religious and state incorporation by lowlanders. They could accept a distant imperial state that put them on the same level as the Bama, even if it imposed restrictions on violence and arbitrarily separated them from trading partners across the new border. From the 1890s they proved receptive to Christianity and to recruitment as soldiers and policemen, serving with distinction in World War I.

The British constructed Burma as Southeast Asia's second-largest state by asserting their absolute (in the modern sense) sovereignty over this vast space between India, China, and a more narrowly defined Siam. They followed watersheds where possible in defining borders, and thereby extended state space into distant mountains that it would never have occurred to Southeast Asian monarchs to covet. On the other side of the mountains lay India (easily managed by the same surveyors) and China, which had its own unique understanding of states and their boundaries, discussed below.

The drumbeat beneath the drawing of the map of the modern Mainland in the nineteenth century was Anglo-French rivalry. The British had come to regard India as their fortress, inadequately protected by the Himalayas. Their fixed policy was to keep the areas beyond its borders in the hands of weak or friendly occupants, but to aggressively prevent influence from rivals – France especially, Russia, or later Germany. King Thibaw had to be defeated rather than ignored because he seemed to be succeeding in attracting French interest. The French were equally determined to make good their loss of territory in India by acquiring strongholds that could ensure access to China and a position as near as possible to equality with Britain in Asia. Having found it in Viet Nam, too far from India for British resistance to be more than nominal, the contest was on for each to maximize their imagined borders in order to exclude the other, except insofar as a truly viable buffer intervened.

Siam succeeded in being that buffer through the skill we noted in Chapter 11, foregoing expansionary dreams in return for security in the core area. For most of the century the Siamese had reason for gratitude that Britain had eliminated the Burma threat and secured the western frontier. The French were a different matter, not only reinventing Viet ambitions in Cambodia but conceiving the Mekong as a kind of French highway to China. The Khmer King Norodom may have hoped to continue the delicate balancing between Bangkok and Saigon, but reluctantly accepted a French protectorate in 1863 that would ultimately sever the Thai connection. Siam in turn was persuaded to accept this move through a Franco-Siamese Treaty of 1867 that allowed Siamese sovereignty over Battambang and Siemreap, including the symbolically important remains of Angkor. Cambodian monarchy survived as part of a paternalistic package that reinforced Khmer hierarchies while expecting others to develop the modern economy.

The Mekong route was explored in a well-documented expedition of 1866–8, which had to haul its boats laboriously around the Khone rapids that had always formed the barricade for upriver autonomy. The Mekong route was not viable for shipping. Nevertheless, the river, with its lower reaches now in French hands, became a crucial card in the broader rivalry with Britain. The *muang* on its eastern side, moreover, had to be controlled to prevent them becoming a refuge for Viet opponents. The Tai-speaking *muang* in the upper Mekong had sent tributary deference when necessary to Mandalay, Hanoi, Luang Prabang, Bangkok, and Chinese officials in Yunnan, but jealously guarded their autonomy and their commercial mediation between these lowlands. Siam's claim on the upper Mekong had been vigorously asserted by the conquests of 1779 and 1826 that left Vientiane an empty ruin. In a foreshadowing of the racial ideology that would blossom in the next century, King

Chulalongkorn claimed in 1885 that "the Thai, the Lao, and the Shan all consider themselves peoples of the same race/nation [*chat*]. They all respect me as their supreme sovereign, the protector of their well-being" (cited Winichakul 1994, 101–2). He was emboldened by the conviction that the Lao would forget their traditional antagonism to the Thai when faced with the greater alien-ness of the French. In a conscious attempt to pre-empt French utilization of Hanoi's tributary relationships, Bangkok sent two military expeditions to the upper Mekong in the 1880s, and focused its mapping and administrative reforms there to simulate modern sovereignty. Eventually sheer force settled the matter.

Siam's slight advantage in getting troops to the disputed areas first was trumped by France's greater naval power. The tension culminated in 1893, when after a clash over an uninhabited sandbar in the upper Mekong, French gunboats entered the Chao Phraya River to force Chulalongkorn to agree to further concessions. The official British view in India had been that Chinese and Siamese claims should be maximized so as to provide a buffer between British and French borders. But London declined the Siamese request to guarantee her integrity against the French, and warned Siam to accept French demands up to the Mekong. Britain once again perceived a waterway as a conveniently "natural" boundary. In the vital crunch it supported Siam's essential viability as a buffer, but would not be drawn into conflict with France over the peripheries. Out of this saga came a reborn Laos, championed by the explorer August Pavie as another form of "protectorate" over colorful kings and submissive peasants. But while Vientiane was rebuilt as a Lao capital, the majority of Lao, who now lived on the west side of the Mekong, were firmly guided to become Northeastern (*Isan*) Thai.

This French assertiveness proved a blessing for Siam, in facilitating its difficult reinvention as a compact modern nation-state. It was the greater diffidence of the British in the Peninsula that bequeathed a major problem. The southern frontier of Siam incorporated former Malay and Muslim tributaries who proved impossible to assimilate in the same way as Theravada Buddhists. The present Thailand-Malaysia border was secured in 1909, following a period of better Anglo-French relations when the two powers were able to agree on recognizing each other's ambitions in the disputed areas. In 1902 Britain negotiated a pragmatic compromise over the Malay states still tributary to Siam, whereby Siamese sovereignty would be confirmed provided a British official was appointed Resident to advise the sultan. Despite hopes in Patani and Singapore, Patani no longer had a sultan and was not covered in this hybrid arrangement. We should now spell it Pattani in acknowledgement of its definitive, if often embittered, incorporation into Siam/Thailand. In 1909 the hybrid arrangement ended and Kelantan, Trengganu, Kedah, and Perlis became British-protected sultanates. At the same time, in return for concessions over the upper Mekong and its former extraterritorial rights, France gained control for Cambodia of Battambang and Siemreap. Its scholars immediately took up the paternalistic task of restoring the temples of the "lost civilization" of Angkor.

WESTPHALIA AND THE MIDDLE KINGDOM

At the other extreme from the stateless highlanders, the Chinese world-empire was also confronted by the new doctrine of equal but absolute sovereignty. What little remained of the "tribute" system had lost its economic rationale for Southeast Asians once China was opened to trade in the nineteenth century. As we saw (Chapter 11), the last non-contiguous state to send "tribute" was Siam in 1852, announcing Mongkut's accession. China modernized its diplomacy in the last decades of the Qing to deal with European states on a basis of equality, but could not bring itself to do the same for former tributaries. In the 1890s Britain considered bringing China into a club of states to guarantee Siam's independence, but could not do so as long as Siam-China relations were in ambivalent suspension (as they remained). Among the powers, Britain was the most interested in propping up the Manchus, as a further buffer against Russia and other parties, so that it did nothing to support the many Muslim and other anti-Qing rebels in south-western China. The conquest of Mandalay in 1885 presented the British with an exceptionally complex border problem.

The importance of overland trade between Upper Burma and Yunnan had obliged the traders to find some way to restore relations after China's disastrous adventure in Burma in the 1760s. A peace was negotiated in 1769, but only by producing very different documents to satisfy each of the proud courts involved. The Chinese record specifies the sending of tribute by Burma, but the Burmese kings agreed only to "good-will missions" every ten years. When no tribute mission from Burma appeared, the Qing closed the border until 1787, when Yunnanese traders desperate to restore their business sent a bogus but highly respectful "Chinese" mission to the Burmese capital. Since China appeared to have taken the first step toward an equal relationship, Burma felt able to resume missions to Yunnan on what it understood to be an equal basis. The last ones took place in 1843, 1853, and 1874.

This miscommunication was replayed during the British expedition against Mandalay in 1885. The Chinese Foreign Minister cabled London to claim sovereignty over Burma on the basis of tribute, and to threaten intervention. British authorities in Burma and India culled Burmese documents to assert that the Burmese missions were between equals, while China and the British Sinologists quoted Chinese documents for the reverse. London compromised by signing a treaty with Beijing in July 1886, which in return for Chinese recognition of British sovereignty in Burma conceded that since "it has been the practice of Burmah to send decennial Missions to present articles of local produce, England agrees that the highest authority in Burmah shall send the customary decennial Missions, the members of the Missions to be of Burmese race" (cited Myoe, unpublished, 3). No mission was ever sent, as the Qing Empire began its disintegration. Demarcating a border in the stateless highlands over which neither Burma nor China had had effective rule would have been a herculean task even with stable conditions in China. It was only in conditions of war against Japan that Britain and the nationalist government in Chongqing (Chungking) agreed to the arrangements of a League of Nations-mandated boundary commission in 1941.

While modernizing Siamese and Burmese courts saw the "tribute" system as no longer appropriate, Viet Nam's Emperor Tu-Duc (1848–83) sought to reinvent the relationship as a lesser evil than the French. He appealed to China first to help him suppress the Chinese rebel bands moving into the border hills. This enabled the Qing government to tell the French, in 1880, that it was Viet Nam's suzerain and had fulfilled its commitments to Tu Duc as a dependent king. France nevertheless brushed aside Chinese protests when it began the conquest of Tongking in 1882. Beijing responded robustly by sending troops across the border from Yunnan, leading to repeated clashes with French troops which escalated into a Franco-Chinese war in 1885. In the Treaty of Tientsin (June 1885) which ended it, China agreed to withdraw its troops from Viet Nam, and to respect all treaties made between France and the Vietnamese ruler (including the French protectorate). The asymmetric view from the Middle Kingdom was quaintly honored with the words "In those things which concern the relationships between China and Annam, it is intended that they will be of a nature such as not to affront the dignity of the Chinese Empire." Ironically, as the "Chinese world order" theory died, the only Southeast Asian ruler who appeared to support Beijing's view of it was that of Viet Nam, the state that had most tenaciously fought for a thousand years for autonomy and equality.

BUILDING STATE INFRASTRUCTURES

European imperial rule over Southeast Asia was of very short duration, roughly 1880–1940. Economically it was a depressingly static period (Chapter 13), and nationalist history-writing sought to marginalize or demonize it. Yet its impact was profound precisely because it brought the region into a new world order of theoretically equal and absolute sovereignty, which subsequent nationalists wholeheartedly embraced. The transformation was achieved by the globalized nationalism of the European imperial states, which ensured that most of the resources of the region would go into constructing state infrastructure that carried the new order into the furthest corners of arbitrarily drawn maps.

Among the most ardent imperial expansionists of the nineteenth century were those who sought protection for building just such an infrastructure of telegraph lines and railways. The telegraph made high imperialism and the new global order possible through unprecedentedly rapid communication around the world. Southeast Asia's first telegraph cable linked Batavia (Jakarta) with Buitenzorg (Bogor) in 1856, and other local lines followed in Siam and Burma. At the beginning of 1872, only seven years after the first transatlantic cable, a telegraph line was opened that connected Penang, Singapore, and Saigon with India, Japan, and Europe. After the opening of the Suez Canal in 1869, steamship travel from Europe to Southeast Asia was cut by more than half, and each European maritime country developed its shipping link. The newly invented telephone was demonstrated in Singapore in 1878, and was also operating in three cities of Java by 1884. These links enabled resident colonial elites to be much more British, Dutch, and French than was possible at the beginning of the century.

The effect of these technological revolutions coinciding with the high colonial era was to divide Southeast Asia into British, Dutch, French, and Spanish/American blocks. As the dominant shipping and manufacturing power until the advent of the Germans at the end of the century, Britain had an interest in low tariffs. It encouraged Singapore to be the natural hub of regional shipping. France and the Netherlands had the opposite interest, to use their populous eastern colonies as captive markets for their manufactures. French textile manufacturers secured the incorporation of Indochina into the French tariff system in 1887, which became even more protectionist after 1892. Whereas Viet Nam and Cambodia had obtained their manufactured imports overwhelmingly from China, Singapore, and Bangkok until the 1860s, 30% of Indochina's imports came from France in the 1910s, 40% in the 1920s, and half in the 1930s. While consumers had to pay around 15% more for their clothes and other manufactures than if they had imported from neighbors, France was rescued from a large balance of payments deficit by its export surplus with Indochina. The Netherlands was equally determined to use its colony as a captive market for its otherwise weakly placed domestic textile industry (Chapter 10). The Philippines, tied to the giant US market after 1909 by the Payne-Aldrich law for zero tariffs between them, had 62% of its imports and 70% of its exports with the United States by 1920.

The prominence of Singapore and Penang in the shipping of the Archipelago was a particular problem for Dutch attempts to create a state in the Islands, as it would later be for Indonesian ones. British and other international lines made Singapore rather than Batavia (as in VOC days) the crucial entrepôt of the Straits area, while the local routes were dominated by smaller Straits Chinese steamers. Only in 1888 was the Royal Packet Company (KPM) assembled with enough Dutch government and corporate support to act as an effective instrument of state integration. In 1891 it used nationalistic arguments to wrest the mail contract from the British-owned NISM. As Dutch control of the Archipelago advanced, the Straits Chinese advantage of closeness to local rulers was replaced by a Dutch advantage of cozy supply arrangements with government and estates. The KPM effectively forced out British competition by 1900, and was saved from the rising challenge of the German fleet by its confiscation during World War I. The Dutch Parliament granted the KPM large subsidies and a monopoly of all government mails and business in order to ensure a pan-Archipelago network centered at last in Java rather than Singapore. Its most difficult opponent to subdue was the "mosquito fleet" of small Chinese-owned steamers mostly operating from Singapore, visiting small harbors with a low cost structure and evading Dutch customs when it could. Having failed to defeat them, the KPM adopted a strategy that turned rivals into vassals by buying out the Singapore-based ones and encouraging Indies-based Chinese firms to operate as feeders to KPM lines. Its 137 ships (1929) tied the Indies together with fixed schedules for passengers and freight, facilitated by massive government investment in infrastructure to enable large steamers to unload cargo directly in new ports at Tanjung Priok (for Batavia, 1886), Surabaya (1917), Makassar (hub for the east, 1917) and Belawan (for the plantation area around Medan, 1920). Vertically integrating as many operations as possible, the KPM also developed the colony's largest coalmine in eastern Borneo to supply its fuel. Economically speaking, it was a classic colonial monopoly. It built technological modernity within a static hierarchy that suppressed rather than stimulated local entrepreneurship, but it did wonders to create a state.

Hong Kong around 1900 had assumed a similar role for the Philippines as Singapore for the Indies, linking the islands to regular steamer routes. The American administration after 1900 directed major investment into building deep-water docks at Manila so that major shipping lines could load directly there. With a much tighter Archipelago the success could be more complete, and by 1930 Manila was so dominant a hub that it accounted for 80% of all Philippine customs receipts. Coastal trade in the central and southern Philippines was dominated by Cebu and Iloilo (Panay). They developed a network of steam lines around Mindanao and Sulu, carrying Visayan workers to extend the frontiers of settled agriculture and of state-incorporated Christians into what had been the lightly populated domain of largely unincorporated, culturally diverse Muslims and animists. The commercial orientation of the southernmost Muslim centers to the Muslim Archipelago was effectively ended.

Java and Luzon played a somewhat similar role within the two colonies, with a developed and integrated infrastructure that could provide the kernel for still highly plural archipelagos. Daendels' post road from Batavia to Surabaya in Java was unique in nineteenth-century Southeast Asia, delivering express despatches along its 800 km within five days by 1830. Corvée labor was extensively used also to build and maintain a series of feeder roads along this artery, linking all Java's main cities by all-weather roads for carts and carriages on the eve of the railway revolution. This began in the 1860s with three lines from interior centers to the ports of Batavia, Semarang, and Surabaya. In the 1890s these were linked by two east-west railway routes to give Java the region's most effectively integrated economy. Luzon was about twenty years behind, with a post road begun in the 1830s and the *Camino Real* linking Manila along the northern Ilocos coast with the fertile Cagayan Valley. The Spanish opened a railway from Manila through the central valley to Dagupan in 1892. This suffered much during the upheavals of 1896–1902, but was eventually extended down the Bikul Peninsula under the Americans. As in Java, the railways were able to replace the river waterways as they became impassable through deforestation and silting. Unlike the waterways, however, they were a state-operated hierarchic monopoly, not unlike the KPM.

In the Mainland the railways introduced very different integrations than had been possible with the river traffic of the past. British Burma had the most navigable of the region's rivers, and the 270 steamers of the Irrawaddy Flotilla Company, reputedly the world's largest inland fleet by the 1920s, made it railway-like in speed, efficiency, and British-topped hierarchy. But the non-Bama regions beyond this central artery could only have equal access to the Rangoon-centered modern economy as an ambitious railway system was built, beginning in the 1870s. Soon Rangoon was linked not only with newly conquered Mandalay (1889) but with Myitkina in Kachin country (1899), Lashio among the Shan (1903), and southerly Moulmein (1929), a center for Mon and Karen.

This pattern was still more striking in Siam, where the busy traffic of the Chao Phraya in central Siam did nothing to incorporate the Lao of the north-east, whose natural artery was the Mekong, now dominated by the French. Strategic reasons predominated in building the first lines into the north-eastern watershed of the Mekong at Nakon Ratchasima (1896, extended to Khon Kaeng 1937) and toward Siam's remaining Khmer provinces before these were lost and the railway stopped at Chachoengsao (1907). The northern line to Uttaradit (1909) and Chiang Mai (1921) was also begun for military purposes, and was far from covering costs initially. The southern route down the Peninsula reached Surat Thani by 1915 and the border three years later, hoping to direct southern commerce to Bangkok and away from the British ports. As a vital arm of the state, the railways were primarily managed by German technicians, presumed to have fewer political interests than British and French, and they were protected from competition from road development with its democratic possibilities. In consequence, Siamese in the 1930s had slightly better access to rail per head of population than their neighbors, but only a sixth of the road coverage of Burma and Indochina.

Indochina's transport integration was boldly envisaged in the 1890s but faced the daunting task of traversing countless flood-prone rivers to connect even the two main population centers. The 1,800 kilometers of the *Transindochinois* was built in sections, using large government subsidies and levies of Vietnamese labor before the two population centers around Hanoi and Saigon were finally linked in 1936. Although ruinously expensive and never as effective for carrying freight as the shipping links, the railway was popular with Vietnamese who made up 90% of the passengers. The fact that it united them, but notably failed to link Cambodia and Laos, undoubtedly contributed to the conceptual unification of a national rather than imperial space, as well as the movement within it of students, journalists, activists, and revolutionaries.

With the exceptions of Siam and Java, railways were less effective than roads became in the 1920s in integrating economies. The logistic difficulties of mountains, rivers, and jungles were too great. The Americans in the Philippines led the way in creating an effective national road network in the 1920s, but the French also built one of Asia's best road systems. Accomplishing in the 1930s what the railways could not, this linked the five administrative sections of Indochina by 38,000 km of paved roads, some sealed in asphalt but most paved with stone. Three east-west corridors linked the upper Mekong to the coast, and tied Laos in the first half of the twentieth century more effectively to Viet Nam than to its natural partner in Siam. In the Islands outside Java and Luzon, railways had been significant only in Sumatra, with three distinct networks linking the ports of Belawan, Padang, and Palembang to their hinterlands. Road networks, however, did finally integrate such large and diverse islands as Sumatra and Mindanao in the 1930s, and opened south Bali to a growing tourist traffic from Singaraja in the north.

Financial infrastructure was no less critical. Southeast Asia had been a silver zone since the sixteenth century, and Spanish and Mexican dollars continued to be acceptable everywhere through the nineteenth, supplemented locally by a variety of copper and zinc base coins. The new states were not at first strong enough to discard this pattern, but produced their own versions of the Spanish dollar – the Straits dollar in the Peninsula, the *rijksdaalder* in the Indies, gradually replaced by the guilder, the *piastre* in Indochina, the *peso* in the Philippines, and the *baht* in Siam. Paper money was introduced in the early 1900s, with the usual national distinctiveness. It was shifted to the gold standard in one country after another, pegged to the metropolitan country, and forced into use in many areas by the requirement that taxes be paid in it. New banking systems and tax regimes were introduced, all having the effect of tying the economies more closely together and to the metropolitan country, and less to their neighbors.

Finally, distinct language regimes linked the elites of different regions within the newly established boundaries. Portuguese, Malay, Arabic, English, and Chinese (especially as spoken in Hokkien dialect) had acted as *lingua franca* for different groups across the region and beyond it, but in the twentieth century distinct fault lines developed between English, French, Spanish (surviving in the Philippines until World War II), Thai, and Dutch zones. The higher levels of education, administration, the judiciary, and business were conducted in these languages. For wider communication, Malay remained a very important *lingua franca* in *Nusantara* (British and Dutch). Vietnamese in Indochina and Bama in Burma were also standardized for use in lower schools and administration. The romanization of both Malay (from Arabic script) and Vietnamese (from Chinese) had begun pragmatically much earlier to help traders, missionaries, and later colonial administrators make themselves understood. In the twentieth century, however, these romanized languages were taught widely in primary schools, and became powerful tools for intellectuals and nationalists to mediate their forms of modernity into a national linguistic space.

How Many States in Indochina?

The borders drawn between competing European nationalisms would quickly be endorsed by nationalists as the boundaries of their own destined space. The infrastructure of modern statehood ensured that modern nation-states would have exactly the boundaries of colonial state-building projects. Only French Indochina did not become one single state, but three. Both the French and the anti-French nationalists wavered on what it was they sought to construct in the new space, depending on what they identified as the chief threat. Despite the division of French Imperial space into five constitutionally separate units (Tongking, Annam, Cochin-China, Cambodia, and Laos), and three protected monarchs, the space was governed centrally by French officials as a new zone of absolute sovereignty. One official insisted in response to de Mayréna's quixotic "kingdom of the Sedangs," "The political map of Indochina contains no blanks ... leaving no room for independent tribes" (Résident-supérieur Rheinart 1888, cited Salemink 2003, 52). The bureaucracy of this entity was French above and Vietnamese below; its infrastructure was centered around the hubs of Hanoi-Haiphong and Saigon; its schools, culminating in the "Indochinese" Hanoi University, brought all peoples of the colony together through the medium of French. Most of the same factors that gave rise to a maximalist Burma and Indonesia, in other words, applied also in Indochina.

Anxiety about Chulalongkorn's attempts to mobilize a greater Tai unity led some French officials to toy with fostering a greater Viet identity (labeled "Annamese" in the colonial era), maximizing the Nguyen legacy. Vietnamese nationalists educated with ideas of a broader destiny frequently saw their task as liberating all Indochina from the French, particularly if they were among the 10,000 Vietnamese living in Vientiane in 1937 (outnumbering Lao there) or the 140,000 living in Cambodia. In 1929 it was an Indochinese Communist Party (ICP) that was formed to be the vanguard of this revolution.

Emotionally, the tide was turned by the passionately ethno-nationalist Vietnamese Nationalist Party (*Viet Nam Quoc Dan Dang*), formed a year earlier. It sought to popularize the term Viet Nam, little used since the early nineteenth century, in place of Annam, which was increasingly invalidated by its use by the French for the Protectorate in the center, and before that by China to imply submission. Its leader Nguyen Thai Hoc demanded that patriots violently sacrifice themselves in the name of this concept. He showed the way immediately before his public execution in 1930 by shouting dramatically "*Viet Nam van tue* (Long live Viet Nam)." Although Ho Chi Minh was among those influenced by these events toward a more ethnically defined nationalism, the younger communists, supported by the Soviet and French parties, continued to press for an Indochinese vision well into the 1950s. Fundamentally, however, even the ICP was always too Vietnamese to recommend itself to Lao and Khmer elites, whose own nationalism tended to contain a good deal of anti-Viet ethnic sentiment.

ETHNIC CONSTRUCTION IN THE NEW SOVEREIGN SPACES

The revolutionary concept of sovereign space, within which all were, in principle, subject to the same law, would transform Asia in the twentieth century. With the exception of lowland Filipinos and Javanese, most Southeast Asians encountered the idea of the modern state relatively late in its career, when in the late nineteenth century it already had long abandoned the natural hierarchies and personal charisma of the *ancien régime*. The European colonial officials who spread the new state idea around were sustained by extraordinary confidence in their project of liberating Asians from traditional constraints on trade and industry, and in the superiority of their technology and rationality. Even when they appeared to defer to local custom, religion, and hierarchy, they had so much more in common with each other than with the people they ruled over that they generated a highly centralized and uniform mode of operation among themselves, beneath a façade of respect for local tradition.

This revolution brought perhaps the greatest changes to stateless and highland people who had previously known states as harbor gateways and periodic predators, to be conciliated with tribute when necessary, assimilated to when advantageous, and avoided otherwise. As we have seen, such people were extremely plural and mobile, multilingual and able to adopt whatever local identities they found themselves in. The colonial umbrella placed them unambiguously within newly absolute borders with "no blanks," but also offered the possibility of their becoming politically equal to the lowland incorporated populations, or even privileged, on certain conditions. These included generating elites with a certain level of education, and defining themselves and their languages as units large enough to be comprehensible to the colonial states and the outside world more generally. The state apparatus of administrative units, educational languages, textbooks, censuses, and maps gradually brought about a kind of "ethnogenesis," whereby each colonial space recognized a certain manageable number of standardized ethnicities.

Although it is often said that Siam in this period was reinvented in the image of its colonized neighbors, in this respect it was distinctive. The Thai Buddhist identity of its royal elite was explicitly the norm for a modernized state, and others should, and with some (Muslim) exceptions could, assimilate to that norm. Because the only route to elite status was education in Thai, even the Lao/Isan, who were as numerous as the central Thai, learned a second identity as simply Thai. When nationalism arrived in the early twentieth century, initially at royal inspiration, it was under the slogan "nation/race, religion, monarchy" (chat, sasana, pramakakasat), all of which were Thai and Buddhist. Though colonial rivalries had ensured that Siam had the fewest minority problems, it also made the fewest concessions to them.

In Burma and Indochina the Bama and Viet, respectively, were demographically and historically dominant, but the colonial state ensured that minorities were documented, classified, and to some extent homogenized as ethnicities distinct from the lowland majority. The enormous diversity of Burma was simplified into the eight "big races" – Bama, Mon, Shan, Karen, Kayah, Kachin, Chin, and Rakhine (Arakan) – even though colonial censuses acknowledged as many as 40 dialect sub-groups of Chin alone. The military government of 1988 tried to repudiate a century of consolidation by proclaiming the unity of "135 national races of Myanmar," but it was too late. Though their map-makers and census-takers were baffled by the internal diversity of every group, British planners were clear about the line between lowland Buddhists (Bama, most Mon and Rakhine) whom they held to have been integrated into the Burmese kingdom, and the "excluded areas" under direct British control in the 1922 and 1935 Constitutions (Map 12.1). These excluded or scheduled areas, representing 47% of Burma's area and 16% of its population, became a laboratory for anthropologists and missionaries. Helped by a growing body of written literature, they gradually developed elites who saw themselves as speaking for the "big races." Political state-building, therefore, would necessarily be of a federal type which acknowledged these separate identities.

Neither process, separation or remolding into larger blocks, was as developed in French Indochina. Early French policies were markedly influenced by lowland presumptions, shared by Catholic missionaries who came to the highlands with their Viet flock, that highlanders were savages who needed to be educated up to the Viet level. Initially, today's Central Highlands were, in the

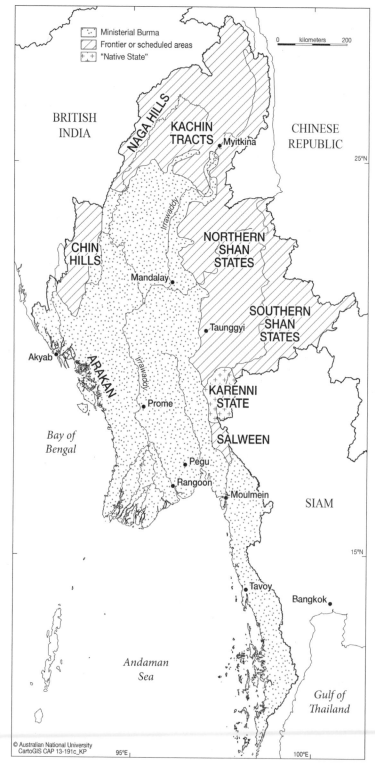

Map 12.1 The two Burmas: nationalist and "scheduled," 1930s.

east, administered by the mandarins of Annam, who channeled their forest products to the market, and in the west, regarded as part of Laos. Paul Doumer's energetic centralization of Indochina administration resulted by 1907, however, in three new highland provinces (Pleiku, Darlac, and Haut-Donnai) including former Laos highlands, envisaged as being in practice under French control albeit nominally in the Annam protectorate. Léopold Sabatier became a paternalistic advocate for the separate identity of the Montagnards he administered in Darlac (Ban Me Thuot) from 1913 to 1927, and encouraged education in romanized Rhadé rather than Vietnamese. The battle he waged to stop French rubber interests and Viet colonists from entering the Highlands was lost with his departure, however. The unincorporated highlanders remained, in French eyes, all Montagnards, a slight advance on the Viet characterization as *Moi* (savages), while scholarship divided them into a mosaic of diversity. The 13% of the Viet Nam population that was officially considered "national minorities" in the 1980s was divided into 48 groups, even the largest of which was less than 2% of the population, and unable to bargain over the definition of state.

The Islands' states were constructed as two trade empires, in which Batavia and Manila were initially commercial hubs not dependent on any particular hinterland. Even when, in the eighteenth/nineteenth centuries, Dutch and Spanish built their alternative economic bases in Java and Luzon, respectively, no one ethno-linguistic group had any special place. Indigenous inhabitants were all "Indians" (*Indiërs* and *Indios*, respectively) or natives. To the colonizers the vital distinctions appeared to be between these indigenous peoples on the one hand, and Europeans and Chinese merchants on the other. There was therefore an inherent equality at the base of the pyramid between the different ethnicities that constructed themselves under the colonial umbrella. Legal equality led to imaginings of community, expressed in Malay and Dutch in the Indies, and in Spanish and, later, English in the Philippines. Ethno-nationalism naturally appeared, particularly among Javanese and Tagalogs, but was no match for a common anti-imperial nationalism (Chapter 15). That nationalism had to be named neutrally, and once "Indian" was felt to be unsatisfactory, Indonesian and Filipino were settled upon as artificial alternatives.

In the Philippines, unincorporated highlanders and southern Muslims were outside the negotiations over national identity. In the Indies, however, highlanders who had rejected incorporation into the Islamic gunpowder empires of the sixteenth and seventeenth centuries found they could enter the new twentieth century umbrella state as equals with their former adversaries, once they had defined themselves in broad enough terms to be legible by that state. Minangkabau and Mandailing Muslims in Sumatra, and Minahassan Christians in Sulawesi, were sufficiently ahead educationally to be over-represented in the emergent educated class of functionaries, teachers, and nationalist intellectuals. Late-arriving Balinese, Bataks (northern Sumatra), Torajans (Sulawesi), and Dayaks (Borneo) eventually also found their way to the same status as Javanese in the Dutch census as a *landaard* (inaccurately translated officially as race) and in Indonesian usage as a *suku* (group or component).

The British parts of *Nusantara* remained awkwardly diverse. In Sarawak and North Borneo, the colonial regimes had treated the key religio-linguistic groups, including Chinese, as equally necessary parts of an undeveloped polity. The Peninsula was a mosaic comprising three cosmopolitan colonies where "natives" (Asians) were roughly equal under the law, and nine protected sultanates defining themselves increasingly as "Malay." Never conceived as a single state, this complex of twelve diverse pieces nevertheless had enough in common (English and Malay *lingua franca*, British institutions, acknowledged pluralism, however differently) eventually to become one in 1963. The tensions between a more Mainland-like ethnic primacy and a more Island-like cosmopolitanism provided an uncomfortable dynamic that nevertheless gave birth to Southeast Asia's two most prosperous and orderly states, Malaysia and Singapore.

STATES, NOT NATIONS

This extraordinary burst of state-making, concentrated in a mere half-century (1890–1940), was made possible by the equally extraordinary self-confidence of its European agents that it was necessary, justified, and progressive. The changes they introduced made the new structures effective but not owned; familiar but not loved; understood but not empathized with. They had been able to establish states of an exceptional degree of pragmatic centralism dressed in symbolic diversity, precisely because the steel structure of European officialdom was divorced from social realities and cultural norms on the ground. The creation of some kind of empathetic nation within each of these structural frames would be accomplished by the nationalists of the mid-twentieth century (Chapters 15 and 19). This transformation from an alien, resented, and artificial structure to a passionately felt nation required what I have called "alchemy" of a very high order (Reid 2010). The revolutionaries who brought it about would prove even more astonishingly self-confident, in the face of much greater barriers and costs, than their colonial predecessors.

[13] POPULATION, PEASANTIZATION, AND POVERTY, 1830–1940

MORE PEOPLE

Up until the early nineteenth century Southeast Asia remained very lightly populated by world standards, considering its mild climate, high rainfall, and reasonable soils. Its then roughly 32 million people represented a little over 3% of the world's population, but this rose rapidly to over 5% in 1900 and 8.3% by 2012. Around 2000 it passed the population of Europe, of which it was only a sixth in 1800, while narrowing the gap to China and India. The puzzling thing for demographic historians is that this take-off in population was well under way in the 1830s, and already exceeded the nineteenth-century growth of Europe, which had been considered the leader in the "demographic transition" developing societies experienced. Poor and traditional societies were thought to have both high birth rates and high death rates. During the transition to greater affluence, death rates fell through better nutrition (especially), more sanitary and peaceful conditions, and better disease control, whereas birth rates took some time to respond by also dropping to a kind of equilibrium. During the transition, therefore, populations grew rapidly. Europe's rapid growth in the nineteenth century could be explained this way, but not Southeast Asia's even more rapid growth. Levels of income and welfare rose scarcely at all in most of Southeast Asia until the 1970s. The scientific control of disease certainly played a part in twentieth-century survival rates here as elsewhere, but it is difficult to show such effects in the nineteenth.

Java had probably the highest nineteenth-century growth, which Peter Boomgaard (1989, 166, 202) calculated as 1.4% per year over the century, but much less in the early decades and at a world-leading 2.21% a year for the period 1840–80. Fortunately, Java is also the best documented and the most analyzed case, though controversy continues about the causes of this rise. It is difficult to ignore the establishment of a kind of "colonial peace" as one factor, after one period of ruinous warfare ended in 1755 (Giyanti peace) and another in 1830 (Java War). Earlier than elsewhere an absolutist regime took control

A History of Southeast Asia: Critical Crossroads, First Edition. Anthony Reid.
© 2015 Anthony Reid. Published 2015 by John Wiley & Sons, Ltd.

that was dedicated to stability, order, and a state monopoly of violence. It markedly reduced opportunities for individual initiative and mobility, but did create the kind of security likely to have raised birth rates as well as lowering death rates. Smallpox inoculation campaigns had a major effect in reducing mortality from this source to almost nothing by 1880, whereas it had been a major killer at the beginning of the century. It is now possible to add a third factor, that the period between 1830 and 1880 was mild in terms of natural disasters. The appalling eruption of Mount Tambora in 1815 certainly reduced population in its east vicinity (Chapter 11), while in the 1820s other eruptions as well as the Java War in Java continued to devastate agriculture. It seems likely, however, that the period of gradually warming temperatures, and no super-eruptions except Krakatau (1883), made the whole period 1830–2000 relatively benign from a long-term Java perspective. As suggested earlier, such a conclusion would imply that there had been other periods of rapid population growth in Java's past, interrupted by dramatic declines as a result of tectonic events.

There were three other areas of rapid nineteenth-century growth, above 1% a year. The Philippines can be explained by factors similar to Java's, growing fourfold in the century (compared with Java's almost sixfold) to an 1898 population of almost eight million, followed by five years of war, disease, and population loss. On the other hand, the exceptional population growth of the lower Peninsula that became Malaya, and the Mekong delta area, are explained by high immigration levels to the two great economic frontiers of the region. The century also saw populations more than double in Burma, Siam, and Viet Nam, with most of the growth in the southern deltas. Relatively stable political conditions seem the most obvious explanation, particularly by contrast with the devastation that wars had wrought in the eighteenth.

Stateless hill peoples appear not to have shared at all in this population rise, though less is known about them. Those only recently or partially incorporated into states at the time of twentieth-century colonial censuses still had exceptionally low birth rates, whether in Upland Luzon, Sumatra, Borneo, Sulawesi, Sumba, or the jungles of the Peninsula. It appears that those who were incorporated into a new and more sedentary lifestyle through either Christianity or Islam typically had much higher birth rates. The earliest reports on pre-Christian Filipinas noted they "dislike to give birth many times ... saying that in having many children they are like pigs," and used various means to procure abortions (Dasmariñas 1590/1958, 413). By contrast, Christianized Filipinas already had high fertility by the eighteenth century. Recently Christianized highland populations in Sumatra and Sulawesi had exceptionally large families in the 1930s, reporting seven or eight children per woman. The fertility of highland women had been kept low by the hard work and high mobility imposed by foraging or shifting cultivation, especially when exposed to raiding and head-hunting. Christianity as taught by Victorian-era missionaries, and Islam as understood by Arab and Indian teachers, both favored a much more domestic, house-bound role for married women, so that ideology often reinforced the social changes favored by state incorporation. In short, the rapid growth of lowlands population in the nineteenth

Table 13.1   Southeast Asia population estimates, in millions, 1900–2000.[a]

Country	1900	1950	Annual % growth 1900–1950	2000	Annual % growth 1950–2000
Burma	10.5	18.5	*1.1*	43.5	*1.7*
Thailand	7.3	19.1	*1.9*	61.2	*2.4*
Laos	0.7	1.8	*1.9*	5.6	*2.3*
Cambodia	1.5	4.5	*2.2*	10.6	*1.7*
Viet Nam	13.5	28.7	*1.5*	78.8	*2.0*
Malaysia	3.2	6.3	*1.4*	22.3	*2.6*
Singapore	0.2	1.0	*3.3*	4.0	*2.8*
Brunei	0.02	0.05	*1.8*	0.3	*3.6*
Indonesia	40.2	83.4	*1.5*	205.1	*1.8*
Philippines	7.6	20.3	*2.0*	76.1	*2.7*
Total	84.7	183.7	*1.56*	507.5	*2.06*

[a]The 2014 Burma census, the first since 1983, revealed several million fewer people than had been anticipated, requiring a downward revision of the hitherto established 2000 figure for Burma.

and twentieth centuries marginalized the remaining animists and mobile shifting cultivators not only by incorporating many of them, but also by outbreeding them.

Mortality fell throughout the region through the twentieth century while fertility only began to decline in the 1970s. Population growth was therefore at a peak everywhere, slowed but not reversed by the political disasters of 1942–80. Life expectancy was probably already less than Europe's 40–50 in the late nineteenth century, and the gap widened in the impoverished first half of the twentieth, before closing again after 1970. As more children survived, family sizes initially grew and population soared, before a sharp decline in fertility began to set in from the 1970s (Chapter 18). As Table 13.1 shows, populations more than doubled in the first half of the century and almost tripled in the second half. Burma was consistently the slowest growing, as a result of malnutrition and instability, but also of a high degree of female economic and personal autonomy, leading to a higher proportion of never-married women than elsewhere in Asia. The slower decline in the Philippine birth rate than elsewhere saw its population rise to become second-largest in the region soon after 2000.

INVOLUTION AND PEASANTIZATION

The short explanation of the difference between Southeast Asian economies and more successful ones in the period of very high population growth was that the latter absorbed their additional labor force in industry and urbanism, and Southeast Asia stuffed all the extra people into agriculture. In much of the region this was achieved by extending the area of irrigated agriculture, notably in the three deltas of the southern Mainland, discussed in Chapter 10. In many other areas extensive swidden agriculture was transformed into intensive *sawah* (bunded, flooded *padi* fields), with much encouragement from government. Some gains were thereby made in productivity per hectare, but productivity per person remained stable or, at worst, declined. Clifford Geertz (1963, 70) labeled the process of keeping all the increased population on the land as "agricultural involution," with "the Dutch growing in wealth and the Javanese in numbers."

This was true also of the rice bowls of Tongking, Upper Burma, Bali, and elsewhere, but Java became an extreme case through the Dutch forced "cultivation system," which directed any available surplus into production of export crops in the period 1830–70. Because Java was seen as a model colony seemingly combining profitability with harmonious development, it was also exemplary. Population was concentrated in the carefully irrigated sugar areas, which were intensively cultivated to produce both sugar for monopolistic export and rice for subsistence. Nineteenth-century Java has also been the area most studied and debated, ever since famine and "declining welfare" forced themselves on Dutch attention in the 1840s and again around 1900. A summary of the abundant evidence advanced is that Javanese had significantly less *sawah* per head in 1880 than in 1815. Because they had been forced by hunger to grow less-preferred maize and cassava on ever more marginal non-irrigated land, the dry-land crop area per head remained about the same. Any productivity increase was in export crops for which the profit went elsewhere. Javanese farmers had less income per labor input in 1880 than in 1815, and consumed less even in calorie terms, though this was very much worse in terms of the quality of diet due to growing dependence on cassava.

The Java model of forcing farmers into peasants by requiring intensive production of cash crops at low monopoly prices was extended to some other areas, including previously lightly populated west Java and west Sumatra. Landlessness also produced a surplus labor force in Java as in Tongking by the 1880s, which was taken up as a resource not by industry but by European estates planting tobacco, tea, and later, rubber and oil palm on upland slopes. In the delta areas of the Mainland an open frontier had kept conditions for rice farmers relatively favorable in the 1880s and 1890s, but as this frontier closed, similar conditions of land hunger and intensification developed there. Even in British Malaya, whose open frontier and healthy economy had drawn enterprising migrants from south Thailand, Sumatra, and southern Borneo, their initial attempts to become commercial farmers were discouraged. A Malay Reservations Enactment of 1913 forbade the alienation of land to a "non-Malay," seeking to absorb even Muslim newcomers into a protected peasantry insulated from commercialization. Given the relative success of immigrant Chinese and Indians in the commercial sector, the instincts of colonial governments everywhere were to inhibit the commercialization of farming and the emergence of a politically dangerous class rendered landless by indebtedness and commercialized agriculture. There was little alternative to fragmentation, also encouraged by Southeast Asian bilateral kinship systems favoring relatively equal inheritance between children. Already by the early 1900s Southeast Asia's farmers had become "truly and deeply 'peasantized'" (Elson 1997, 120).

The commercial enterprise of free farmers had been replaced by a struggle to simply survive.

The static character of this involution is demonstrated by the lack of urbanization even as the population mushroomed. Southeast Asia was among the more urbanized parts of the world in the sixteenth and seventeenth centuries, as the commercial boom drew both local and distant migrants into the great entrepôts. The Euro-Chinese cities that subsequently dominated the long-distance trade were much smaller than their Asian predecessors. During the "vernacularization" of the long eighteenth century (Chapter 8) the indigenous capitals remained large: Bangkok still had about 10% of the population of Siam in 1909, and Amarapura 13% that of Burma proper in 1802. The Euro-Chinese port-cities, however, were initially little dependent on their hinterlands, and even when they became so they discouraged immigration from the countryside by strict land controls and their distinctly alien character. There was little of the informal sector and the slums that filled the cities immediately after independence. As usual Java showed the trend earliest, with its urban population (towns over 20,000) no more than 3% of the population in 1890, where it had been 6.7% in 1815. The last independent capital of Burma, Mandalay, declined even in absolute terms, from 170,000 in 1891 to 135,000 in 1931, while the urban proportion of Burma's total population dropped from 12.4% to 10.4%.

Of the eleven Southeast Asian cities with more than 100,000 population in 1910, seven were colonially created port-centers with European direction and a Chinese (or, in Rangoon's case, Indian) commercial and laboring class, and minimal indigenous participation. Mandalay, Hanoi, and Surakarta (Java) were old royal capitals the centrality of which was in decline, and only Bangkok played both roles, as "gateway" and also cultural capital. The former royal capitals retained some lightly modernized traditional manufactures such as batik in Java and lacquer in Hanoi, but labor-absorbing modern industry was virtually absent until some tentative beginnings to counter the Japanese challenge in the 1930s. In the high colonial era Southeast Asia became one of the world's least urbanized areas. Several centuries of de-urbanization only began to be reversed in the 1920s. The biggest cities of the 1930s were the colonial-era port-capitals. Batavia/Jakarta, Manila, Singapore, Rangoon, and Bangkok in that rank order had all grown to between 400,000 and 550,000, foreshadowing their post-war "primate" mega-city role through the expanding roles of government, transportation, and services.

The "peasantization" of the core population areas of Southeast Asia produced not only involution for survival with very small-scale production, but a hierarchic and static social order. The colonial regimes of the twentieth century were protective rather than transformative, aiming to preserve peace, orderliness, and if possible, welfare. The British and Dutch in *Nusantara*, and the French in much of Indochina, believed "protection" meant preserving the deference of a peasantry to aristocratic rulers in a form often romanticized as organic, traditional, and precious. Even though the devastating colonial wars in Java (1825–30), Burma (1824–6), Minangkabau (1830–8), Aceh (1973–3) and Tongking (1883–6) required the reinvention of indigenous hierarchy from among those who would cooperate, hierarchy itself was held to be traditional. Disturbing it was breaking faith with the colonial mandate. There were radical modernizers among the European elite, but many of those who best knew and loved the culture they encountered adopted a highly protective attitude toward it. "Let us not destroy anything of the ancient Asian edifice ... So that, in a century, France does not have to face reproach for having destroyed, under a pitiless centralization, the originalities of this faraway country ... Let us leave this garden as we found it ... Let us preserve the gentle poetry of Annam" (Pierre Pasquier 1907, cited Brocheux and Hémery 2009, 109). The Philippines and Burma were more profoundly removed from any organic social hierarchy by the nature of their colonization, but indirect rule always had a conservative bias. As the colonial system was collapsing, one of its most acute observers noted that "an organic autonomous society maintains order ... in virtue of its inherent vitality, but a dependency is kept alive, as it were, by artificial respiration" (Furnivall 1948, 8). The hierarchic indigenous order of aristocrats and peasants was kept in place no longer by its own dynamic, but by a rusting European steel frame.

DUAL ECONOMY AND THE ABSENT BOURGEOISIE

The counterpart to this process of peasantization was the absence of an indigenous middle class, setting Southeast Asia's transition to modernity apart from the norm, and particularly from both South and East Asia. The pattern whereby outsiders occupied commercial roles, it must be said, had begun to form well before the high colonial era. Foreign traders and sojourners were always a feature of the Southeast Asian crossroads. If the age of commerce had fostered gunpowder port-states that incorporated outsiders, the vernacular societies of the long eighteenth century had again preferred to emphasize internal coherence against the foreign. Ever since the legalization of Chinese overseas trade in 1567 there had been distinct Chinatowns (*kampung Cina*, or *parian*) in every maritime city. They were economically and culturally self-sufficient and yet vital for supplying the larger society. As noted in Chapter 9, a "Chinese century" of commercial expansion had preceded the great European forward movement, and in gateway states, both Malay and Tai, had already established interdependence between indigenous port-rulers and Chinese economic actors.

As explained in Chapter 6, the earliest Spanish and Dutch enclaves were also dependent on the economic activity of Chinese, but kept them separate in a different way. The early Spanish acted much like Asian rulers in allowing Chinese to move into the governing apparatus only if they adopted the key markers of local identity – in their case Christianity and Spanish language and dress. This created an intermediary *mestizo* category that ultimately merged with the local elite to become in the nineteenth century Southeast Asia's most influential middle class. The Dutch and British, however, acknowledged no such intermediate status for the localized *peranakan* Chinese, but legally classified them as simply Chinese, unless by Islamization they could opt for indigenous status. Dutch law created absolute barriers in the nineteenth century between three categories: European, "Foreign Oriental" (mostly Chinese), and "Native." Each had their own courts and administrative arrangements. Only in 1920 did it become possible for individuals to cross these lines by applying for a change of status, but none of the reformist attempts to obliterate the distinction in the 1920s and 1930s was successful. An association of land with the indigenous population, and of trade, finance, and the modern economy with foreigners, was evident everywhere, but sanctified by law in the Dutch Indies. The economically dominant "Chinese" figures of the late colonial period were as culturally "Indonesian" as anybody, despite the legal and census category they shared with newcomer sojourners. They spoke Indonesian (Malay) and Dutch rather than local languages or Chinese, they were born in the ethnically mixed cities of the colony, and they identified with the Netherlands Indies as a whole rather than with a local ethno-nationalism. This was in marked contrast to European business leadership, strongly oriented to a Dutch or German fatherland. The Sino-Indonesian business elite, like its equivalents in the Philippines and Siam/Thailand who more readily assimilated to the majority, invested much in Indonesia and little in China.

The influx of Chinese labor was at a peak throughout the period 1870–1925, with several hundred thousand migrating each year. Where the long-established elites had been chiefly Hokkien-speakers from Fujian, Cantonese became the largest group of this new wave because of the Hong Kong-Singapore shipping nexus. The much greater ease of return than was previously possible, and the tiny number of female Chinese migrants until the 1920s, meant that the settled population of Chinese grew more slowly, and actually declined as a percentage of total population in Siam, Java, and the Philippines. The huge growth of Chinese population occurred in the hitherto lightly populated areas surrounding Singapore. Malaya (including Singapore) had little over 100,000 Chinese residents in 1860, but 2.1 million in 1930. The relative dominance of *totok* (newcomers) in the period, together with a wave of Chinese nationalism and support for the new Chinese Republic in 1911, created a measure of resinification, with Chinese schools being established everywhere to educate a new generation in a language (Mandarin Chinese) their parents had never known. This occurred at just the moment when the Chinese commercial minorities had escaped from the constraints imposed on them by the older systems of "protective" passes and monopolistic revenue farmers to join a twentieth-century state system as a potential middle class.

The social hierarchies of the high colonial period have parallels with the theory of the status gap, developed primarily to explain how an "outsider" Jewish entrepreneurial minority became necessary in eastern Europe to bridge the social gulf between aristocrats and peasants. Arguably this gap was even wider in the colonial situation, making the Chinese role (supplemented in Burma and Malaya by Indians, and in Laos and Cambodia by Vietnamese) even more prominent and indispensable. As twentieth-century conditions took them out of the ghettos and into productive roles in rice-milling, sugar-processing, distribution, and manufacture, they came more frequently into competition with weaker indigenous entrepreneurs, and became the resented "other" of indigenous movements rather than their leaders. While anti-Chinese riots began to afflict Siam, Indochina, the Philippines, and Indonesia from about 1910, some of the worst such violence occurred in Burma against Indian domination of the modern economy and government.

By the 1930s the gulf between the shared poverty of the peasant mass and the modern economy had become painfully obvious. The laissez-faire capitalism of the early twentieth century encouraged employers to use immigrant labor because it was easier and cheaper. Government policies after 1900 focused whatever protective and welfarist measures there were on the indigenous population, allowing market forces in the immigrant-dominated sectors to maximize profit more brutally than they could under the mixed systems of Europe. Dutch economist J.H. Boeke (1953) contrasted the modern with the indigenous economy, which he believed could not respond to the same economic stimuli because of a moral economy that bound members of a village together in shared poverty. J.S. Furnivall was more inclined to blame colonial policies themselves, especially in Java, for producing a rural society incapable of responding to capitalism effectively. "The [Dutch] Government has employed 'gentle pressure' [*perintah halus*] to protect the village community against dissolution, and to promote welfare; yet 'gentle pressure' may be debilitating rather than a stimulant, making the patient less able ... to stand alone" (Furnivall 1948, 271).

Boeke's dichotomy became known as a Dutch school of "dual economy" theory, which had its parallels elsewhere. Furnivall promoted the influential idea of a "plural society" created by a heartless capitalism, where none of the separate racial groups had effective social will or constraints, and collectively met only in the market. In Indochina the 1930s witnessed the *politique du paysannat* (peasantry policy), officially acknowledging that something had to be done to improve "the fate of the peasant masses, which are the most numerous and the most empoverished ... all other needs must give way to this" (Governor Brevié, 1930, cited Brocheux and Hémery 2009, 277). This late-colonial reaction against the value of liberal economic theory in poor countries, together with a strong dose of Marxism and the experience of war, laid the intellectual foundations for much more robust government intervention in the 1950s, discussed as "high modernism" in Chapter 19. In the many-sided crisis of the 1930s, however, such ideas made little headway against colonial instincts to conserve and protect the endangered harmony of villages imagined as traditional.

SUBORDINATING WOMEN

The well-publicized images of the Javanese aristocratic daughter Kartini learning liberation from her Dutch correspondent and of the "English governess" Anna Leonowens, tutor to King Mongkut's children, defending his daughters against a cruel oppression, began a discourse of "female liberation" as a modern western import. Conservative Southeast Asian men certainly took this theme up in the twentieth century in an attempt to control women and resist new trends. The reality of the high colonial period was, however, closer to the reverse. Up until the nineteenth century the great majority of Southeast Asian women had more latitude and agency than their European (or Chinese or Indian) counterparts, and played economic roles equivalent to (though different from) those of men. Only in the royal and noble households did men strictly control women's reproductive power or practice polygyny. It is true, however, that theater and ritual gave high status to exemplary men, whether kings or religious sages, and established a restrained, elegant style of speech and manner which was necessary for the exercise of that status. Men and even women in Java would grant men higher status and expect them to behave in the appropriate manner, in a low, even voice that would eschew contradiction, bargaining, or certainly anger. Women could also use this register and occupy high status positions, but were far freer to adopt a diverse range of language and behavior in order to achieve their (or their family's) objectives. Not unnaturally, therefore, women in Southeast Asia, managed their own and the household's money and engaged in the business of marketing, buying, and selling.

We cannot know whether or how a different, less masculine, form of modernity would have arisen if the modern absolutist state had not been imposed at European hands. Foreign, patriarchal models of behavior were, of course, influential long before high colonialism made them absolutely inescapable. The scriptural religions gave religious leadership and literacy in its sacred languages exclusively to men. Yet the old ways survived in the "vernacular" phase. There was little change to the patterns of sexual and gender relations for the non-elite, of female dominance and autonomy in the marketplace and many other productive fields, and of ever more prominent female writers. By contrast, the state structures and modern state-related economy that developed from the late nineteenth century were exclusively male projects, whether in the hands of European colonial officials in administration, Chinese, Indian, and Arab males in the economy, or a royal Thai elite in Siam.

Up through the early nineteenth century, European sources are unanimous in judging the women of Southeast Asia as more effective than men in dealing with practical matters and money. Both European and Chinese men found their sexual partners extremely helpful in their business as well as their homes. We might instance the situation in Cochin-China, where Crawfurd found women performing many of the tasks reserved for men in Europe or India, partly because their men were required to serve the ruler in the newly militarized Nguyen order of Viet Nam. "They plough, harrow, reap, carry heavy burdens, are shopkeepers, brokers, and money-changers. In most of these cases they are considered not only more expert and intelligent than the men, but what is more extraordinary, and what I have never heard of in any other country, their labour is generally of equal value" in terms of pay (Crawfurd 1828/1967, 522–3). In Java, Raffles (1817/1978 I, 353) noted: "It is usual for the husband to entrust his pecuniary affairs entirely to his wife. The women alone attend the markets, and conduct all the business of buying and selling. It is proverbial to say the Javanese men are fools in money concerns."

As communication improved after 1870, European and Chinese women joined their men in the region, and clubs and institutions of expatriate life developed. Elite European and Chinese men lost contact with local women. They looked to men to staff the new structures of a modern state. The government positions on offer were prestigious and hierarchic, and therefore seen even in local society as the business of men, but this shift only strengthened the perception that traditional societies were incapable of operating the modern economy. Even in Siam, where the reforms of King Chulalongkorn and Prince Damrong built a western-style bureaucracy, this was staffed entirely by well-born men as both domestic military precedents and the European model dictated. Since entrepreneurship had never been among the skills developed by such men, they left modern business to the Chinese and only domestic business to their wives.

The earliest large-scale manufactures in Southeast Asia did in fact mobilize the productive tradition of its women, as in the Philippine tobacco industry described in Chapter 10, and the tobacco and *batik* factories of nineteenth-century Java. The European ideal that women should not work outside the house at all, particularly prevalent in Britain and the Netherlands, interacted explicitly with Southeast Asian patterns in a debate in the all-male Indies assembly (*Volksraad*) in the 1920s. The Netherlands in 1922 had signed one of the first attempts to regulate labor globally, an ILO convention banning "the weaker sex" from paid work at night. Resistance to the impracticality of this reform by employers in the Indies sparked enquiries that showed that the majority of the labor input in agriculture on Java was still by women. Although the western-run sugar and other plantations routinely sought male staff and supervisors, even there around a third of the labor was done by women. The 1930 census ignored "unpaid" labor in agriculture, but still found that women formed 43.5% of the paid workforce in Java, as against 22.5% in the Netherlands (Locher-Scholten 2000, 52–60). Many male reformers sought a modernity that would restrict married women to the home, as in Europe, and to some extent they succeeded. Between the 1930 and 1961 censuses the proportion of adult women in Java listed as employed dropped from 36.6% to 30.7%, and the proportion of those in manufacturing collapsed, from 27.7% to 8.7% (Booth 1998, 68).

A remarkable Philippine textile industry developed in Iloilo (Panay) in the century before 1860, through an alliance of Chinese-*mestizo* males and their Filipina partners rather than by the state. At its peak in the 1850s this involved about 60,000 women of the port and its surrounding hinterland (about half the adult female population of the province), weaving local cotton and pineapple fibre, as well as abaca thread from Bikul and silk from China, on rudimentary bamboo looms. This was supplying much of the population of the Philippines with its cloth, but also contributing over a million Mexican dollars' worth of export income for the country in the early 1860s, when shortage of cotton in the US Civil War held back the competition from Manchester. By 1870, however, this thriving industry was virtually wiped out by cheaper British machine-made cloth replicating the popular Filipino patterns. A male-run sugar industry took over the export economy, and women had to work in domestic situations if at all. "Women weavers fell from the status of independent producers to unpaid workers in the family or paid workers who had neither control of the proceeds of their labour nor command over the production process. In this sense, women's economic position declined absolutely and in relation to men" (Eviota 1992, 59).

A similar story was repeated everywhere, usually with even less attempt than in Iloilo to modernize and commercialize in competition with imports. Imported manufactured cloth dominated everywhere by the 1870s, and penetrated into the furthest highlands and islands as colonial control made access easier at the end of the century. The other specifically female productions of the region – ceramics, basketwork, and medicinal herbs – were similarly replaced by imported manufactures. British officials, dismayed by female control of rice land in Negri Sembilan (Malaya), and the consequent lack of interest by males in agricultural improvement, entrusted males with coffee land to reverse this pattern. Peasantization drew women out of specialist manufacture and into the agricultural sector where they shared the burden with men of producing export crops under foreign control for survival. Philippine censuses showed 71% of women engaged in agriculture in 1938 where there had been 51% in 1902. When they joined the European-managed modern economy they were invariably paid less than men on the European model – on average only 60% in agriculture and 40% or less in factories and offices. This was a marked contrast with the old order (in northern Siam) where female slaves had been priced much higher than men because they were better workers.

Socially the urban fashions were set by Europeans in this high colonial period. Southeast Asian male elites were first to adopt the bourgeois habits of late nineteenth-century Europeans. Traditionalists found justification for the constraints these manners imposed on women in the demure demeanor of the ideal princess of Southeast Asian theater; religious reformers in the neo-traditional puritanism of foreign Islamic, Christian, or Confucian ideals. Upward mobility in the modern lifestyle, even more than in Victorian England and Holland, was seen to involve women withdrawing from the public and commercial spheres to play decorous roles as upholders of an imagined pure "national" essence of impractical modest dress, large hierarchic families, handicraft, and domesticity. The more the Filipino *ilustrados* (enlightened ones) of the 1880s, pioneers of Southeast Asian male modernity, enjoyed the demi-monde of the ladies of Paris and Madrid, the more they adopted a *haut bourgeois* ideal for their sisters in the Philippines. In editing Morga's description of the pre-Spanish Philippines, nationalist hero José Rizal defended the loyalty and virtue of womanhood and glossed over all Morga's evidence of female desire and freedom. He wrote home to tell his sisters to emulate German women, who "are home-loving, and they study cooking with as much diligence as they do music and drawing" (Rizal 1886, cited Reyes 2008, 239). One Filipina analyst judged that all this pressure succeeded to the extent of transforming "the lively sexual assertiveness of Filipino women into a more prudish, cautious image of womanhood" (Eviota 1992, 60). In the process, the European picture of Southeast Asian womanhood also changed, from that of the hardworking economic actor in the early 1800s to the exotically submissive feminine a century later.

Some of the modernizing legislation on names, marriage, and inheritance explicitly required a shift to patriarchy, notably where Asian men themselves were in a position to impose it – in Japan and Siam. Meiji Japan in 1875 required all males to adopt surnames that their wives and children were obliged to follow, and narrowed inheritance to this same male surname line. In 1913 King Vajiravudh also imposed surnames in Siam, claiming that this would make Thais "civilized," and promote "the maintenance of family tradition … as an incentive to everyone to uphold not only personal honour but the honour of the family as well" (King Vajiravudh 1914, cited Reid 2009, 31). In an otherwise surname-free region (except for Vietnamese on the Chinese model), the only colonial government to require a shift to male-inherited surnames was the Philippines, in 1849, in an explicit attempt to strengthen family control over its members across time. Both Siamese and Philippine changes succeeded in creating powerful patriarchal families across the generations, largely because the introduction of surnames coincided with the merging of wealthy Chinese-*mestizo* families into the local elite, adopting local names to become the Thai and Filipino corporate "big families," where there had been none before.

The nineteenth-century European ideal of permanent monogamy altered the general pattern of Southeast Asian marriage chiefly in its disapproval of divorce, especially female-initiated, and its domesticizing of a subordinate wife. Polygamy was one of the pretexts Europeans used for not granting "civilized" status to Asian societies and for demanding extraterritoriality in them, but in reality it was restricted to a tiny minority of royals and rich Chinese and Arabs. Southeast Asian kings had taken women from varied communities into their palace to cement alliances. For the Chakri kings of Siam, however, an abundance of wives and children became an obsession, both signifying royal potency and facilitating royal monopoly of all high offices in partnership with the Europeans and Chinese. The first five Chakri monarchs sired a total of 324 children through 176 mothers, but the two reformers, Mongkut and Chulalongkorn, were the champions with 60 and 153 wives, respectively. Each designated a clear heir along the lines of European kings (avoiding the fratricide of the past) but used their brothers and sons to staff all crucial positions in the cabinet, diplomacy, and the army. This unique royal dominance of the "modernity" project ended abruptly with the next king, Vajiravudh, thought to have been homosexual, who took only four wives late in life in a vain attempt to produce a male heir. Nevertheless, Siam was unable to legislate against polygamy until 1935 after the absolute monarchy was abolished, despite the acknowledged cost to its "civilized" status.

SHARED POVERTY AND HEALTH CRISES

"Shared poverty" was Clifford Geertz's apt description of the condition of the majority of lowland Southeast Asians in the high colonial era. Population increased rapidly because modern transportation networks, better communication, and a modicum of welfare eased the effects of disastrous years, while natural disasters were less severe. Indebtedness and dependence was a more likely outcome of a bad harvest than starvation and death. On the other hand, the chances of escaping poverty into the more dynamic part of the economy steadily diminished. As agricultural frontiers closed, the bargaining power of peasants became ever less. The social variegation of Javanese villages had come to be between the "just enoughs" (*cukupan*) and the "not quite enoughs" (*kekurangan*). The absence of risk-taking and the tendency to share good fortune with neighbors through sponsoring feasts were rational group responses to the very small margins above survival on which people operated. The continued high birth rates until economies began to lift in the 1970s were also conditioned by the lack of other safety nets than children for people as they aged.

Before this era of population and infrastructural growth, smallpox, as well as water-borne diseases such as cholera, were reported periodically to have carried off large proportions of urban populations, as noted in Chapter 7. Remote highland communities were even more savagely affected by a first exposure to smallpox, though most of that story will never be known. In the nineteenth century smallpox became less terrifying through vaccination and becoming endemic rather than epidemic. Cholera replaced it as the scourge of the century. In its first rage through Southeast Asia in 1820–1 it is estimated to have caused 125,000 extra deaths in Java, and about 30,000 in each of the cities of Bangkok, Saigon, and Hue. The total deaths in Viet Nam were counted officially at over 200,000, though the number may have been twice as great. The next great attack was in the middle of the century, a time when Russia and much of the world was affected. Java underwent a many-sided crisis of disease and famine in the early 1850s that together accounted for 600,000 extra deaths. The Viet Nam royal chronicle gives the most dramatic figure, claiming that cholera killed 600,000 people in 1849–50 in the central part of the kingdom around Hue. This could well have been a quarter of the population.

Cholera was also the grim companion of nineteenth-century wars, typically beginning among the unsanitary conditions of military camps and besieged forts, and spreading quickly through a population often weakened by other effects of war. The first officially reported cholera in Burma broke out among the British troops attacking Prome in the war of 1824–6, and then devastated the Burmese population of the city. The 200,000 extra deaths attributed to the Java War (1825–30) were also largely the effect of disease. When the hastily assembled Dutch troops attacked Aceh in November 1873, cholera claimed 1,300 of their men by April 1874, ten times the deaths from war itself. The disease immediately spread to wreak havoc among the Acehnese defenders. The central Aceh river valley was largely depopulated after the campaigns of 1873–8, so that total Acehnese deaths from disease may have exceeded 100,000. Again, during the third Anglo-Burmese War in 1885, cholera was a factor, and represented 7–9% of all deaths recorded in Burma through 1876–91.

The last crisis of the sort was that of the Philippines in its heroic moment of revolution and war from 1896. The fall of world sugar prices and some poor harvests were already making things difficult in the 1890s. The revolt of Bonifacio and Aguinaldo against Spain in 1896, the American invasion to oust the Spanish two years later, and above all the American campaign of savage repression against the Filipino revolutionary nationalists in the subsequent four years brought a crisis of disease and deprivation, most acute in southern Luzon. Despite the otherwise high (1.5% a year) growth rate of the Philippines that should have produced an extra 600,000 people, the census of 1903 reported 200,000 fewer than that of 1898. Deaths from cholera alone in 1902–3 were estimated at 110,000. There was a substantial loss of cultivated area, and at the nadir a rice crop that reached only a quarter of its pre-war levels.

This type of demographic crisis was common in the old order, but diminished as the stable, indeed static, conditions of colonial shared poverty spread around the region. The crisis mortality of epidemics and disasters may have contributed about 10% of total mortality in the nineteenth century, but progressively less in the twentieth despite the inroads of the 1918 influenza pandemic. Improvements in countering acute famine and disease with better infrastructure were, however, balanced by the increasing misery of the densest rural populations, and their simple inability to buy food. Death rates declined rather little despite much better control of diseases. By the 1930s Java and Tongking were facing a crisis of nutrition, where despite all the ingenuity of consuming less preferred marginal crops, there simply was not enough to go around. Studies in 1928, certainly a happier time than the following decade, showed 219 kg rice equivalent available per person per year in Indochina, but only 211 kg in Tongking, whereas the minimum should have been 220–70 kg (Brocheux and Hémery 2009, 265–6). How close peasants were to the border-line was revealed in a number of household studies in the late 1930s, showing the poorer majority spending 60% or more of their income on food in Cochin-China and Ilocos (Luzon), 71–3% in Java, and 79% in Tongking (Booth 2007, 136). Conditions certainly worsened during the economically harsh 1930s and politically disastrous 1940s. In the early 1960s over 60% of Java's rural population was below a poverty line then established as 240 kg of rice equivalent a year. On average, Southeast Asians appear to have survived infancy better but to have been less well nourished in the 1930s than they had been a century or even two centuries earlier. The physical size of Javanese has been estimated as at its nadir in 1870–1910, about 2 cm less than it had been around 1850 and 6 cm less than it became by 2000 (Baten et al. 2013).

It must be said that neither enterprise nor opportunity was lacking in some frontiers with more abundant land. The rubber boom of the 1920s, in particular, brought relative prosperity to about 800,000 smallholder farmers in the Peninsula, Sumatra, Borneo, and Sulawesi. Indigenous smallholders (as against western-managed estates) held 57% of rubber land in Netherlands India, 40% in British Malaya, and 96% in Sarawak. Unprecedented numbers of *Jawi* (Southeast Asian Muslims) could afford to make the pilgrimage to Mecca. An average 32,800 a year did so in 1923–30 through official Netherlands Indies channels alone, constituting more than a third of the world total in these years. Once a road was opened into the cool and fertile highlands in Sumatra, Karo-Batak farmers switched to vegetables to supply the lucrative markets of Medan and Singapore. The most successful Southeast Asian economies of the time, Malaya (led by Singapore) and the Philippines, in the 1920s had overall

GDP per capita rates analogous to many East European and Latin American countries and double those of China and India.

When Chinese Southeast Asians are acknowledged as the entrepreneurial middle class, potential leaders of some future take-off, there are many spectacular individual success stories. Semarang-born Oei Tiong Ham (1866–1924) was perhaps the richest man in Southeast Asia when he died leaving an estate of 200 million guilders. He had exported sugar and other tropical products, imported opium very lucratively, and built a bank and steamship concern. Rangoon-born Aw Boon Haw (1882–1954) developed his Tiger Balm patent medicine into a worldwide enterprise, and used the profits to establish a stable of Chinese newspapers in Southeast Asia and Hong Kong. Bangkok-born Chin Sophonpanich (Tan Piak Chin, 1910–88) was one of many who scaled his activities up a notch to fill the gap left by western institutions during the Japanese occupation, establishing the very successful Bangkok Bank in 1944 and later expanding into agri-business. These examples could be endlessly multiplied. But the fatal divide of dual society thinking was sufficiently internalized by Southeast Asians to make the gulf seem unbridgeable at the end of the colonial era. Shared poverty ideologies inclined majority nationalists to target such tycoons as part of the capitalist class-race enemy, and many of the tycoons themselves directed their patriotism to China rather than to the countries of their belonging.

★★★★★

Looked at overall, the high colonial era created the infrastructures for ten states in Southeast Asia, and for a sophisticated system of export agriculture. But by discouraging labor-intensive manufacture, hardening economic dividing lines into racial ones, and monopolizing the state-related utilities in European hands, this phase of European rule produced stagnant economies which trapped most of the indigenous rural majority into a culture of poverty.

[14] Consuming Modernity, 1850–2000

Housing for a Fragile Environment

Southeast Asia's warm and humid environment was responsible for some broad common features of diet and lifestyle, which continued to distinguish the region even as it embraced new possibilities from elsewhere. The mild climate and the abundance of water, wood, bamboo, and palm in most places made for relatively light buildings easily assembled and demolished. Frequent flooding, the proximity of jungle wildlife, and the mosquitoes dictated that most domestic buildings were erected on poles, allowing refuse to fall down below and maintaining the domestic space above as a shoeless clean area. Even palaces were overwhelmingly of wood, bamboo, and thatch, although on a grander scale. Only Hindu and Buddhist temples were of stone, brick, and mortar on modified Indic models, since merit accrued to their builders and rebuilders regardless of the earthquake damage that was certain in most areas. Mosques or monasteries, on the other hand, built for people rather than gods, were of wood and thatch.

By the sixteenth century, Tongking, Java, and Bali had departed from the Southeast Asian pattern to build their houses on the ground with some use of brick or stone foundations. These populous pockets first felt the scarcity of wood as the forest frontier was rolled back and ceramic kilns, metalworking, and domestic cooking required ever more wood as fuel. Chinese and European merchants had always feared to store their cloth and other trade goods in fire-vulnerable wooden buildings, and their cities encouraged a more dense building pattern in brick or stone. The Manila Chinese were manufacturing bricks and tiles locally as early as the 1580s, and the other Euro-Chinese cities were not far behind. Some rulers then followed this example, using European architects as early as the seventeenth century to build some solid buildings as exotic showpieces or armories. There was a reward in security from fire and attack, but a major cost in both earthquake damage and unsanitary heat and congestion. After Manila, in 1645, and Batavia, in 1699, suffered terrible

A History of Southeast Asia: Critical Crossroads, First Edition. Anthony Reid.
© 2015 Anthony Reid. Published 2015 by John Wiley & Sons, Ltd.

earthquake damage, there was more experimentation even in the cities with hybridized styles of building.

This process extended in the eighteenth and nineteenth centuries to all urban centers and the major irrigated rice bowls. The supporting poles grew shorter in the denser valley-floor settlements of the Bama, Thai, Minangkabau, and Tagalog. In the Philippines a hybrid style developed with a masonry lower floor and a light, wooden upper level. The onset of cement in the late nineteenth century encouraged bathrooms and kitchens to be built on the ground even in an otherwise elevated timber house. The Manila earthquakes of 1863 and 1880 damaged the lower portions even of houses built with unusual thickness, leading to a Filipino urban standard that supported the upper house on a wooden frame and used brickwork only as an outer shell.

For most rural agriculturalists housing remained essentially impermanent well into the nineteenth century – easily built and easily rebuilt after fire, war, or natural disaster. Split-bamboo was preferred for walls, so that the laborious sawing of timber for planks was largely limited to boat builders and the finer palaces. The retreat of the forests with population pressure, however, made this pattern increasingly difficult to sustain in the late nineteenth and twentieth centuries. For the scattered populations of most areas in earlier times wood had no cost except the goodwill of neighbors to help cut and haul it for the house-posts. As dense settlements of irrigated rice and sugar spread in the nineteenth century, while shifting cultivators had to cut the secondary forest ever more frequently, good timber had to be bought. The central valley of Luzon and the islands of Panay and Negros were largely deforested by the expansion of sugar and tobacco by 1900. Gradually, therefore, the poor built closer to the ground and with flimsier fast-growing material such as bamboo, and the new corrugated iron or zinc roofing.

The twentieth century witnessed the first evidence of rat-borne plague in the Islands, with a major epidemic in East Java in 1913–14 and periodic attacks thereafter. This induced the Dutch government to begin a radical rebuilding program, enforcing the replacement of rat-friendly bamboo and thatch with solid materials and a tiled roof. Over two million houses were built or modernized in the Indies by 1940, giving Java villages their current neat look. The new model houses were also smoke-free with separate kitchens, though unfortunately this had the effect of driving overall mortality up as malaria-bearing mosquitos were able to invade the homes. Cement and zinc gradually transformed the housing of more affluent villagers as the century wore on.

The rapidity of urbanization since the 1940s saw a deterioration of building standards, as access to affordable timber and bamboo declined and crowded makeshift slums developed in such giant cities as Manila, Jakarta, Bangkok, and Saigon. The urban opportunities for education, informal-sector employment, and modern glamor outweighed the undoubted loss of housing comfort as the poor moved to the cities. For all their disproportionate share of national wealth, these hastily built coastal conurbations were vulnerable to floods, typhoons, earthquakes, and tsunamis, as if the lessons of earlier generations had been forgotten . The disasters came with unprecedented frequency and magnitude as the twenty-first century began (Chapter 18). The rush to develop new cities and nations in the twentieth century left little attention for the fragile environment and traditional means of building to resist earthquake and flood.

THE EVOLUTION OF FOODS

The Columbian exchange should in the Pacific be named the Magellan exchange, in that the crucial new crops from the Americas – maize, tobacco, chili, papaya – entered Asia through the route opened up by the Spanish between Mexico and Manila. Irrigated rice complexes had developed sufficient surpluses by then to supply the large trading cities and spice-exporting regions. When the seventeenth century crisis forced them toward greater self-sufficiency, the New World crops were fortunately available to assist. By the mid-seventeenth century maize was being planted in many hillier or drier regions of Southeast Asia as a supplement or replacement for rice. In the eastern Archipelago, especially those places hitherto dependent on imported rice or on sago, maize became a primary staple in the eighteenth century. One index of Java's growing impoverishment was the increasing acreage devoted to maize, from 18% of non-irrigated agricultural land in 1815 to 36% in 1880 and 50% in 1910. Although rice was always preferred, maize (like tapioca) kept people alive, with about the same number of calories produced per hectare of land as rice, but with much less labor and without the need for irrigation.

Visitors from temperate climates were usually enthusiastic about the abundance of fruits of Southeast Asia, the mango, durian, mangosteen, rambutan, and jackfruit being long established and a pleasant surprise to visitors, while there was also no shortage of citrus options. Papaya, pineapple, and soursop made their entry from the Americas in the seventeenth century, papaya being the quickest to establish itself within the staple diet through its hardiness and the portability of its seeds. Widely available coconuts and other fruits of the palm provided vital additional calories and nutrients and enriched local cuisines. In a few areas of the eastern islands they became the primary source of food. Essentially grown as a standby by householders, fruits were not commercialized into large-scale production until the twentieth century.

Vegetables had been less developed until the settlement of Chinese increased the range, with items such as kangkong and spinach entering the local cuisine. Soybeans were also introduced from China by the sixteenth century, and in the form of both soy sauce and soybean cakes (*tofu*) took a place in the diet of many Southeast Asians. The most remarkable adaptation occurred in Java by the eighteenth century, to turn soy by fermentation into chewy compact cakes (*tempe*), which had some of the functions of meat in both food and protein content.

The commercialization of rice production in the Mainland deltas from the late nineteenth century provided the means to sustain the plantation sector, as well as city-dwellers, military personnel, and miners. Rice was a complete food capable of long storage, and thus ideal for such purposes. The plantation and mining areas of Malaya, Bangka, and East Sumatra became, with the cities, the great importers of commercial rice. This expansion of the trade in steam-milled rice produced an epidemic of beriberi in such areas, with 30,000 a year estimated to be dying from it in Malaya alone around 1900. It was research on this problem, begun by Christiaan Eijkman in Java in the 1890s, which established that unhusked rice protected against the disease, whereas a dependence on milled and polished rice exposed people to it. This discovery was followed by further research in Malaya and the Philippines that succeeded, in the 1930s, in isolating the chemical thiamine as the active protective element. Beriberi was gradually contained, and the contribution of these discoveries to the development of vitamin theory led to a Nobel Prize for Eijkman in 1929.

The commercialization of rice production and export in the Mainland deltas also had the effect of lowering its price relative to cloth and other consumption goods. Where there was abundant land farmers might switch their efforts to rubber or coffee and do well in good years. In the lowland rice bowls of Java, Viet Nam, and Burma, however, the return on their crop was ever more marginal and debt became a critical problem. In the 1930s the shift was evident to less preferred foods for survival, such as tapioca, taro, and sago. The Japanese occupation of 1942–5 marked the nadir of this mid-twentieth century crisis (Chapter 17). The spiciness of many Southeast Asian diets, not mentioned by earlier observers, appears to have been a response to this impoverishment. Meat, fish, eggs, and vegetables increasingly became luxuries, and only the spicy pickled sauces made the essential starch palatable.

FISH, SALT, AND MEAT

As explained in Chapter 1, Buddhism and Islam changed meat-eating habits. Though domesticated in Southeast Asia thousands of years ago, probably the first important meat source to be so, pigs retreated as Islamic and Theravada norms took greater hold. Pork remained nationally popular only in Viet Nam and the Philippines, together accounting for 60% of Southeast Asia's pig population of some 60 million in recent years. Elsewhere it was associated especially with Chinese, Balinese, and the hill peoples who rejected the scriptural religions. Chickens and ducks, on the other hand, became the major meat resource in most of the region. Whereas the sight of chickens running freely around a village house was once universal and is still very common, the expansion of battery hen farming in the late twentieth century provided most of Southeast Asia's 1,500 million chickens in 2002, over half of them in Indonesia.

Until this recent expansion of the chicken population and the return of greater affluence from the 1970s, meat was a negligible factor in the nutrition of all but the elite. Rice itself provided most of the proteins, but the share of animal proteins in most diets was overwhelmingly derived from the ubiquitous waters of the region – freshwater rivers and ponds in the interior, especially of the Mainland, and the seas and estuaries in the coasts and islands. The shallow waters of the Sunda shelf, stretching all the way from Bali to the Gulf of Tongking, formed one of the world's most abundant fisheries, while the great river systems of the Mainland, including the extraordinary bounty of the Tonle Sap river system, made fishing a universal skill. Crawfurd

(1820 I, 195) was convinced "There is no art which they have indeed carried to such perfection."

Fresh fish was consumed by those who caught it, but it decayed so quickly in the tropics that it was a minor factor in consumption. Most fish was immediately dried in the sun, with salt added where possible, or else pickled in salt until it produced a spicy fermented paste. The pickled prawn, squid, or fish paste known as *belacan* in Malay, *ngapi* in Bama, or *nuoc mam* in Vietnamese was a key feature of the Southeast Asian diet, making rice or other starches palatable even when nothing else was available. The largest item of exchange in the markets was, however, dried fish, since it could be stored and carried into the interior.

Fishing as an industry was limited by the availability of salt, which was most cheaply produced only in coastal areas where there was a marked dry season and flat, non-porous land adjacent to the sea that could be flooded with sea water to form salt pans. These conditions were best met on the north coasts of eastern Java and Madura, the northern shore of the Gulfs of Thailand and Martaban, Pangasinan in Luzon, the southern coast of Sulawesi, and the central (formerly Cham) coast of today's Viet Nam. Key fishing grounds around the Malacca Straits and the Tonle Sap had to import their salt, from East Java or the Gulf of Siam. Salt was, however, a tempting source of tax revenue for governments, and the Dutch monopoly of it in nineteenth-century Java hurt the industry to an extent that provided a limitation to Java's own fisheries. The Straits area then began to source its salt primarily from Siam, and later even from the Red Sea.

In the high colonial period of peasantization (Chapter 13), fish consumption per capita probably declined for the rural majority without direct access to the sea. While populations increased greatly, inland waterways were impoverished by deforestation and pollution, in some areas poisoned by the residues from tin mining or sugar milling. If, as Butcher (2004, 70) concludes, per capita consumption of aquatic products as a whole increased very slightly between the 1870s and 1930s, that growth would have occurred in the wealthier Euro-Chinese cities that could afford the prices of commercial fisheries. Chinese-led commercialization did expand production of dried and even ice-cooled fish in a number of key areas, while the new transport networks facilitated distribution. But production methods changed little from the time-honored methods of nets and fish-traps.

From the 1850s, Chinese fishermen opened a number of commercial fisheries on both sides of the Malacca Straits, with close-packed houses over the water in villages such as Bagan Siapiapi, Kuala Kurau, Pangkor, and Pulau Ketam. Singapore and Penang became the commercial hubs through which dried fish was distributed to other cities and towns. At its peak, in 1904, Bagan Siapapi, on the prolific estuary of Sumatra's Rokan River, exported 26,000 tons of dried fish and 2,700 tons of *belacan*. As its salt supply became a constraint, more of the catch was put into the less salt-demanding *belacan*, exports of which reached 10,000 tons in 1909. Siam, with better supplies of salt, was the other area where certain coastal fisheries became commercialized enough to supply fish to Malaya, Singapore, and beyond. The Tonle Sap and other fresh-water fisheries, on the other hand, expanded by traditional means to provide the minimum of fish products to a growing Mainland population.

Technical improvements were minimal during this period for the great majority of fishermen, with the result that catches in Burma actually declined throughout the high colonial period. Southeast Asia by the 1930s was a net importer of fish, primarily in the form of American tinned sardines everywhere, and Indian fish imported to Burma. Colonial experiments with trawling were half-hearted and too costly, but Japanese fishermen began trawling in Philippine waters successfully around 1900. By 1931, 70 Japanese diesel trawlers were registered with the Manila authorities, and supplied a good proportion of the Philippine market. Okinawans specializing in catching deep-water fusiliers (*Caesionidae*) also moved into Southeast Asia in the 1920s, using divers to position their large nets and chase the fish into it. By the 1930s these teams of motorized fishermen based in Southeast Asia accounted for about a third of the fish unloaded commercially in Singapore and a quarter in Batavia.

In short, the high colonial period witnessed a dismal failure of mechanization or planning in Southeast Asia's rich fisheries, partly because poverty kept fish prices too low to attract investment. The rural population probably consumed a little less fish on average during this period, and markedly less during the disastrous 1940s. In 1961 such naturally well-endowed countries as Indonesia, Thailand, and Cambodia produced less than 10 kg per capita of fish per year. The rural poor consumed a small fraction of this amount, mainly in the form of a tiny garnish of *belacan*.

The post-war conversion of Southeast Asian fishing fleets to motorized trawlers with synthetic nets and ice, or later refrigeration, began in the Philippines in the 1950s, Thailand with a great rush in the early 1960s, and the rest of the region progressively thereafter. Fish catches more than tripled to six million tons between 1960 and 1980, with Thailand in the lead, and the region became a major net exporter to Japan, Hong Kong, and beyond. Fish consumption per capita roughly doubled in Indonesia between 1960 and 1996 and increased by more than that in Thailand. But from the 1980s the pressure on fish stocks was palpable, and increasing investment no longer gave comparable increase in yields. Each country in turn declared a 200-mile exclusion zone off its shores in 1977–80. Indonesia and Burma, having the weakest fishing fleets of their own in relation to their maritime zones, led the unequal struggle to exclude or license foreign trawlers. As fish stocks of many varieties plummeted, there was a massive shift into aquaculture, particularly of shrimps. Consumption levels increased with prosperity more generally. But for the small independent fishermen who lined the region's coasts life had become increasingly hard and dangerous, as they were forced to travel ever further in search of the elusive catches.

STIMULANTS AND DRINKS

Water was the main drink for pre-modern Southeast Asians, piped in bamboo from mountain streams in the highlands. Lowlands and cities were less fortunate, getting whatever water they could from springs or wells, and letting river-water stand for weeks until de-silted. Such water was perfumed with lemon or spices. Young coconuts could become a vital resource when clean water was not available, as on boats or in a crisis such as a flood. In northern Burma and Viet Nam there are ancient traditions of tea growing and drinking, but diasporic Chinese habits of tea drinking with boiled water did most to reduce the dangers of dirty water in crowded cities. It was reported of the Siamese capital in the seventeenth century, and of Java in the early nineteenth, that the upper classes had learned to boil their water, whether or not in the form of tea, and advised Europeans to do the same if they wished to avoid disease. Southeast Asia was one of the places in which Europeans first encountered the healthy Chinese habit of tea drinking in the seventeenth century, most languages adopting its Malay name (*teh*) derived from the Hokkien dialect of Chinese traders. Commercial growing of teas for the by then insatiable European markets began in hill districts of Java in the early nineteenth century, later transforming upland forests also in Viet Nam, Burma, and Malaya. By the early twentieth century weak green tea was beginning to replace water as the common drink.

Before and outside the scriptural religions, alcohol was an indispensable part of feasts, but not of everyday consumption. This was most commonly in the form of toddy, fermented from the juice of one of the many available species of palm. The new religions disapproved of the whole practice of farewelling the dead through all-night feasting, drinking, and dancing, and this type of indulgence was by the nineteenth century only to be found in the unincorporated highlands. By comparison with Europeans, or even with the Chinese who ran the urban drinking houses for *arak* (distilled spirits), Southeast Asians became a notably sober people. The drunken European was a standard caricature of popular theater in the nineteenth and twentieth centuries.

The great social facilitator and relaxant was not alcohol but a quid of chewed betel. Of its three essential ingredients to produce the active alkaloids, the leaf of the betel vine (*Piper betle*) was widely grown in household gardens, and consumed fresh. The nut or seed of the *Areca catechu* palm was dried and traded over large distances from the coastal areas where it was grown. Aceh exported it on a substantial scale to India throughout the nineteenth and early twentieth century. The third ingredient was lime, obtained from shells in coastal areas and limestone outcrops in the highlands. Most parts of the region, therefore, had adopted by the sixteenth century the habit of mixing betel in this way, chewing it frequently, and offering it to guests as the standard euphoric stimulant. A set for storing and preparing betel was an essential item of every household, and a servant to carry it a necessary part of elite rituals and social interaction. The complementarity of the "heating" areca nut and the "cooling" betel leaf held erotic implications, manifest in courting rituals, when a woman's delicate folding of the quid for a man was a prelude to engagement or to love.

Tobacco was one of the most eagerly adopted introductions from the Americas, both directly from Mexico to Manila and through Europe. Some smoked it in pipes as the Europeans did, but more did so as a smoked cheroot in the seventeenth century, put together from locally grown tobacco and wrapped in a leaf of maize or palm. The great Viet encyclopaedist Le Quy Don condemned it as an evil barbarian introduction, in contrast to civilized tea, but complained that "officials, ordinary people, wives, and unmarried girls" even went without food in their passion to smoke it, despite a ban by the Dai Viet court (cited Woodside 1997, 258). Tobacco was seen as having relaxing effects similar to betel but more powerful. Beginning in the eighteenth century it was added in small amounts to the betel quid and chewed as a more economical means of gaining a stronger effect.

If betel was the great facilitator of male-female relations, the twentieth century cigarette became in its place one of the key modern markers of the gender boundary. The increasing power of modern fashions rendered betel chewing increasingly unacceptable. European males in Asia had abandoned the habit before 1800 in favor of the cigars being produced in Manila. By 1900 Europeans saw spitting betel-juice in a public place as the epitome of the dirty native habits of the East, their prejudices bolstered by the new bacteriological theories. The Asian elites who dealt extensively with Europeans quickly sensed this scorn and adopted instead the European fashion of handing around Manila cigars. Manila cigarettes became fashionable among Southeast Asian elites in the 1850s, swiftly following the new European fashion, and their affordability made it possible for the new urbanites to smoke them. Modern schooling became coterminous with the abandonment of betel chewing on a mass level. So eager was the Thai nationalist dictatorship of Phibun Songkhram to enforce "civilized" modernity that it declared the chewing of betel illegal in 1940.

Apart from the chic cigars and cigarettes of Manila, designed for export, there was much local production of home-made cigarettes with an image almost as rustic as betel itself. The Malay term was simply "bundle" (*bungkus*), since all kinds of aromatic or sweet additives could be put in the maize-leaf wrapper along with tobacco, not unlike the betel quid itself. These became commercialized in Java from the 1880s, once the Sino-Javanese entrepreneurs of Kudus began to open small factories employing local women using hand-operated rollers. This production for the market used a formula of ingredients in which cloves played the major part alongside tobacco. The way they crackled when smoked caused them to be called *kretek*, onomatopoeically. These were cheap and popular, but not at first seen as modern. Only after British American Tobacco (BAT) opened a cigarette factory in Cirebon in 1924 did the Kudus manufacturers modernize their production in competition. They produced a trimmer cigarette and advertised it as modern, with the result that output increased tenfold in the 1920s. In 1939 the *kretek* industry was already a Java manufacturing success story, producing about ten billion cigarettes a year and employing 80,000 women to roll them. In the 1970s production expanded and became more mechanized, and by 2000 Indonesia was producing 200 billion *kretek* cigarettes a year as against 25 billion of "white" or international style cigarettes. The importance of this lobby and source of tax revenue helps explain why Indonesia remains one of the few countries not to have signed the World Health Organization convention to limit smoking.

BAT brought modern cigarette production to most of the region in the 1920s and 1930s. In Thailand the nationalist government established a revenue-earning tobacco production monopoly in 1939, initially in partnership with BAT. For Viet Nam and Burma, state tobacco monopolies in the post-war era also became important sources of revenue.

Betel use was dying altogether for men by the 1950s and women by the 1980s. Its role in rituals of courtship, marriage, birth, and death continued only in symbolic form. In many rituals cigarettes were substituted as a gift to guests or to the spirits. The shift was a revolution in gender relations. The incidence of Southeast Asian male smoking has become among the highest in the world, from Indonesia's 61% down to Burma at 40%. Women smokers were, however, among the lowest proportion in the world (Indonesia 5%, Thailand 3%, Viet Nam 1.5%), except in the Philippines (10%) and Burma (8%) where female smoking had a long history. Whereas betel chewing had long provided protection against many forms of bacteria and parasites, tobacco has had very negative effects on male health, and more so in its *kretek* form. This item of overwhelmingly male expenditure, moreover, consumed around 5% of Indonesian household budgets in surveys of the 1970s and 1980s, more than the expenditure on medical and educational expenses combined.

The twentieth century universalized coffee drinking as another primarily male substitute for betel chewing. The coffee shop became a ubiquitous place in every village for males to gather, smoke, and sometimes also drink coffee, milo, or something stronger and eat snacks. In Malaysia and Singapore the mixed clientele gave rise to the hybrid term *kopitiam*, combining the Malay for coffee with the Hokkien Chinese for shop. Bottled drinks (including bottled tea) were seldom part of the coffee shop menu before the war, but became widespread from the 1960s.

CLOTH AND CLOTHING

Chapter 6 showed how beautiful Indian cloths in the form of wrap-around *sarung*, scarves, and wall hangings became the item of conspicuous consumption par excellence of the age of commerce. Southeast Asian imports of Indian cloth rose to a peak of 1.7 million "pieces" (averaging about 11 square meters each) in the period 1620–50. The period of consolidation that followed drastically reduced the demand for Indian-made cloth. Southeast Asians turned again to their own resources, with some centers of large-scale production for the market adapting the favored Indian patterns. Javanese batik and south Sulawesi checked patterns began to be traded as far as Siam, Cambodia, and Lower Burma, where local production was less competitive in price.

As East India Company monopolies withered, India-based private traders, both Tamil Muslim (Chulia) and European, continued to supply Indian cotton cloth affordably to the western ports of Southeast Asia such as Aceh, Phuket, Mergui, Rangoon, and after 1786, British Penang. Neither traders nor Southeast Asian consumers were quick to make the transition to the much cheaper British manufactured cloth that became available in the 1790s. But the British occupation of Dutch possessions in 1811–16, followed by the founding of Singapore (1819) enabled British cloth to replace Indian imports in British-controlled areas. Even the *batik* industry of Java switched to the use of machine-made white cloth on which to draw their wax-resist patterns. Singapore became the chief distribution point for a host of small Chinese, Bugis, Malay, and Vietnamese boats to pick up factory-made European cloth, sales of which rose from 245,000 Spanish dollars' worth in 1828–9 to four million dollars' worth in 1865–6. Indian cloth rapidly fell out of the trade after 1840, and constituted only 2.5% of Southeast Asian imports by 1865. Almost none of the British cloth went to Dutch ports in Java and elsewhere because of prohibitive tariffs in favor of boosting Dutch industry, but Siam and Viet Nam became the largest importers of the cloth through Singapore.

By mid-century cheap manufactured European cloth was replacing not only imported Indian but also locally produced cloth. In the first half of the following century this imported cloth was more dominant than it had ever been in clothing Southeast Asians, and was again the major item of importation. Fluctuations in the level of imports began to be used as a measure of welfare, and the fact that far less was imported in the 1930s depression years than in the 1920s (about half in Burma's case) was taken to imply a marked drop in welfare. The 1940s were even more critical, reducing many to wearing old rags, skimpier clothing, and gunnysack material for want of cloth. Once again there was a reversion to local production and replanting of cotton. Factory production began very modestly in some areas in the 1930s, while others rediscovered ancient spinning and weaving methods.

Dress styles had become more ethnically standardized in the eighteenth century after the wild experimentation of the age of commerce (Chapter 6). The extensive mixing between foreign men and local women produced some common ground of acceptable dress, whereby both men and women would wear a long *sarung*-like wrap-around in the house, although men might wear trousers in the office or marketplace. Southeast Asian men frequently wore a dark jacket and ethnically differentiated headdress with their *sarung* for more formal occasions, or a collarless shirt for everyday.

Pre-twentieth century Vietnamese and Filipinos had been the most fully dressed in western eyes, using locally produced silk and cotton cloth. Both Vietnamese realms maintained the old Ming style of Chinese dress and long hair, distinguishing them from Manchu-ruled Chinese with their pigtails. Both sexes wore loose trousers down to the ankles and one or more loose tunics down to the knees. Garments were commonly of silk for the upper classes but cotton for the poor. Not until the 1920s was the ensemble refitted with tight-fitting tucks to become the female national dress, *ao dai*. Lowland Filipinos also incorporated their Spanish fashions from the seventeenth century into more distinctive hybrid styles in the eighteenth. The male shirt began its evolution to the modern embroidered *barong Tagalog* not tucked in, and at first collarless. For women the skirts (*terno*) became fuller, the sleeves of the blouse (*camisa*) shorter and more starched in what eventually became the character-istic butterfly style, while the scarf (*panuela*) became ever more decorative and highly starched.

As undergarments were introduced in the late nineteenth century, fashion-able Burmese as well as Archipelago women initially revealed them beneath the sheer upper garment. Because it was more comfortable than European or Chinese female fashions in the tropics, the *sarung-kebaya* became a cosmopolitan urban dress, and even the European women who began to come to Southeast Asia in greater numbers in the 1870s were instructed how to purchase and wear them. Around 1900, however, the more numerous women born in Europe or China (the *totok*, in Chinese-derived Malay usage) began to distance themselves from the "native" in dress, and to be influenced by global fashions. *Sarung-kebaya* was first restricted to morning wear or when receiving lady friends, but by 1920 it was definitely out for Europeans or those who sought to emulate them. Chinese had more choices, between local, Chinese, and European styles, with Paris and Shanghai increasingly setting the pattern for the modern woman. Eurasians and Christians were among the first to follow the trend to more European styles of dress, and western-educated young men and women were not far behind.

Modern Dress and Identity

The globalization of dress fashions in the twentieth century was the most visible marker of the end of autonomy discussed in Chapter 11. Before 1900 the few elite Asians who dressed like Europeans stood out as anomalies; by 1960 it was survivals of locally particular dress in urban settings that seemed anomalous and in need of explanation. Nothing better than dress expresses the tortured conflict between desires to emulate the modern status of the European and to reject his alien arrogance. Each time and place revealed different nuances in the nature and outcome of this conflict. There were dramatic moments of overturning tradition or asserting neo-tradition, but the overall current was irresistible in the direction of globalized modernity.

Status hierarchies were everywhere expressed in dress, but these differences had seemed relatively minor to Europeans in Southeast Asia. In particular, male and female dress and hairstyles had seemed disturbingly similar, whether it was the "masculine" short brush look of Thai women or the "feminine" long locks of Bama, Javanese, and Viet men. Palace sumptuary codes and hierarchies became stricter as the courts became defensive, but did not extend to whole societies as they had in Europe. It was the Europeans in Asia who became obsessive about dress codes as ideas of racial hierarchy took hold. Experimentation and hybridity was no longer acceptable to the Europeans who set the tone from 1900, so that men and increasingly women should dress as they did in Europe. The British officials, accustomed to wearing shoes as a mark of identity wherever they went in India, seemed willing to risk war or rebellion in Burma rather than remove their shoes in palace and pagoda.

"Protected" royals in the colonial context tended to insist on distinctive dress styles held to be traditional among their own subjects, since it imposed a pattern of deference in walking, crouching, and speaking which was seen to be under attack elsewhere. In Siam, however, the determination of successive rulers to achieve "civilized" status in the eyes of the powerful Europeans drove the most explicit and orderly westernization. King Mongkut (1851–68) already required those attending court to wear shirts, and began the habit of wearing a military uniform in emulation of the most powerful of his European visitors. His successor Chulalongkorn wore immaculate European dress on his travels in the 1890s (Figure 14.1), and full dress uniform for his public representation at home in statues and portraits. Government officials, the epitome of the thrust to modernity, wore a white uniform. A hybrid style of *sarung*-like cloth tucked in such a way as to resemble knee-length pantaloons was fashionable into the twentieth century, but increasingly was replaced by western trousers for the intelligentsia and fashionable urbanites, Chinese and Thai. At a popular level, a decree had to be issued in 1899 imposing fines for women who did not cover their breasts and men who did not wear the *sarung* down to knee length during the visit of Prince Heinrich of Prussia to Bangkok.

The imposition of global modernity reached its peak after the absolute monarchy was overthrown in 1932, and particularly under the wartime dictatorship of Marshall Phibun Songkhram (1938–44). Decrees of 1941 insisted that Thais must be dressed properly when in public to uphold the civilized status of the country. This meant European dress or the approved hybrid style of national dress. Women were not excluded, and a "Miss Thailand" competition was officially encouraged in which from 1941 only European dress should be worn, complete with gloves, hats, and high-heeled shoes. Ahead of the rest of the region, Thailand appeared to have made its choice.

The same desire to claim the modern, civilized, and free status of elite Europeans weighed even more heavily on the racialized status hierarchies of the colonies. Men who dressed, acted, and spoke like Europeans were more likely to be treated respectfully and feel the equal of their masters, so nationalists became the foremost westernizers. In Indonesia a radical young Soewardi Soerjaningrat (1914, 267) had marveled how "a slavish attitude and manners, yes even opinions, change into ways which are unforced, free … through the

Figure 14.1 King Chulalongkorn of Siam, pictured with eleven of his 33 sons at Eton College, England, 1907. Source © Photos 12 / Alamy.

change of clothes." Filipino politicians of the 1920s discarded Spanish or local styles for a dark jacket, the *americana*, once they had to deal with Americans. Those engaged in revolution, whether in 1890s Philippines or the 1940s elsewhere, were particularly eager to embrace European military or civil dress.

Burma proved the exception to this westernizing pattern, perhaps initially because of the influence of Gandhi's ideas during its administrative incorporation into British India until 1935. The first generation of English-educated nationalists in the YMBA of the 1920s did adopt western dress as a mark of equality. Their more radical successors of the 1930s, however, who adopted the respectful term of address to Europeans, *Thakin*, as their own badge of equality, preferred a Burmese style of *pinni* (jacket) and *longyi* (*sarung*-like wrap-around, with an opening at the front). Post-war politicians, concerned to assert Bama distinctiveness, were more concerned than elsewhere with uniformity of dress. U Nu already emphasized national dress as the "very backbone" of "the culture of the race or nation" in 1951 (cited Edwards 2007, 133). The advent of military rule in 1962 brought to a new level the enforcing of a dress code centered on the *longyi*, which had the probably intended effect of making trousers, the symbol of assertive male modernity, the prerogative of the ruling military alone.

The same nationalist men who embraced modernity in dress often preferred the presumed delicacy and deference of traditional dress in women. Another struggle between equality and identity took place here, the battle lines being drawn differently. The first women to achieve high levels of education or political office adopted modern western dress, like Sundanese lawyer Maria Ulfah Santoso (1911–88) or Filipina pediatrician Fe del Mundo (1911–2011) – the first woman (accidentally) admitted to Harvard Medical School. The wives of political leaders were more likely to appear in a distinctive Asian style, however modernized. Once the revolutions were over, a "national" style of female dress became established in the 1960s and 1970s in each of the new countries. For men too there were experiments with adding a "national" touch to a fundamentally modern/universal dress, beginning with the Indonesian headdress. Javanese might combine their *blangkon* in batik cloth with a European suit, while Sukarno popularized a black fez (*pici*) as a unifying symbol for all Indonesian men.

The antithesis of modernizing nationalist dress was the undress of those most recently incorporated into the world system through colonialism. For lowlanders in the early 1900s, the wearing of a simple loin-cloth or *sarung* without clothing the upper body became the preeminent sign of savage and marginal status. As education spread to the highlands, particularly if at missionary hands, cheap manufactured shirts were accepted as the price of acceptance in the broader society. The cultural conservatism of late colonialism, however, allowed this relative undress to survive, notably in the "cultural museum" of Bali and in Rajah Brooke's Sarawak. Nationalism was more confident of its mission to civilize, and these pockets disappeared quickly after 1945. Yet there is evidence at least from the Luzon Cordillera that highlanders understood and used their undress as one of the weapons against incorporation, even against President Marcos in the 1970s.

Southeast Asia's dress, like its politics, emphatically joined the new international pattern during the middle third of the twentieth century. Once the diverse local patterns of dress had gone, however, and the struggle for equal dignity won, elites made a return to local color from the 1970s and 1980s. Batik shirts became pervasive on even formal occasions in Indonesia and Malaysia, as did the *barong Tagalog* in the Philippines. The graceful *ao dai*, shunned by revolutionary North Viet Nam during the war, made a great comeback thereafter beginning with the tourist trade. Weddings in particular became occasions for experimenting with modern adaptations of traditional wear, where competitive ethnic pride could be displayed within accepted national and international parameters. This kind of sartorial display became a feature of the many international summits held in the region, each country feeling obliged to produce its "national" dress at its turn as host.

PERFORMANCE, FROM FESTIVAL TO FILM

Public performance, we have seen in earlier chapters, was the Southeast Asian social activity par excellence, playing the cohesive role for palace, temple, and village occupied by the written word in China and parts of Europe. Print had little impact in popular culture until the twentieth century, and we should look rather to the world of theater, recitation, procession, and display for the transmission of shared knowledge and values. Patronizing such spectacles had been a central concern of palaces until they made their own exit in the nineteenth century, or withdrew to less central "cultural capitals" like Hue, Luang Prabang, Yogyakarta, and Surakarta. In rural areas the festivals, pilgrimage sites, and larger weddings and funerals provided the patronage to sustain both peripatetic full-time performers and villagers who would turn their hand to the arts in the post-harvest dry season. The traditions of theater, dance, puppetry, and recitation continued and developed, even though peasantization and poverty reduced the scale of such patronage.

Meanwhile, a different cultural space developed in the polyglot coastal cities, where quite new forms developed out of cultural interaction and technical innovation. The years around 1900 seem again to have been decisive in creating indigenous or hybrid majorities in most of these cities, who became not only consumers but sponsors and creators of new forms of performance. Public urban spaces had long been the venue for Chinese opera at big Chinese festivals and weddings. In the eighteenth and nineteenth centuries they were sometimes rendered in Malay or Thai and included local-born female singers, many of them not Chinese by any definition. Nevertheless, Chinese opera changed little in form and content no matter how hybrid the audiences. Like European theater, it became more *totok* (China-born or pure) in the late nineteenth century as steamships allowed troupes from south China to try their luck among the wealthy Chinese diaspora. The Vietnamese variant (*Hat tuong* or *hat boi*) made the transition to a kind of secular national theater in the nineteenth century, as King Tu Duc (1847–83) had theaters built for it in the central region he best controlled.

In contrast to the open-air style of most Southeast Asian performance, European theater developed in enclosed theaters with paying patrons in the nineteenth century port-capitals, the new bourgeois model. The British and French colonial authorities invested much in theaters both as solidarity-makers for the colonial elite and symbols of the *mission civilisatrice*. Raffles already had a theater opened in Batavia during his governorship there, and Singapore in turn had its early venues. Singapore's classical Town Hall was built in the 1850s to accommodate performances, which moved to the Victoria Theatre in 1901. The Opera Houses of Saigon (1901) and Hanoi (1910) were (and are) the grandest buildings of the two cities, able to accommodate 1,800 and 900 people respectively. Private initiative was more important in Dutch and Spanish colonies. Handsome neo-classical theaters (*schouwburg*) were erected in Batavia (1821), opening with a local production of Shakespeare's *Othello*, and in Surabaya (1854). In Manila a circus-like wooden building was upgraded to become first the Teatro Nacional in 1890, and then the Manila Grand Opera House under the Americans in time to receive a touring Italian opera troupe in 1902.

With the advent of regular steam-shipping routes, international touring companies and performers became ever more frequent. Some would stop only with the steamers at Rangoon, Singapore, Batavia, and Surabaya on their way to Australia, or at Singapore and Saigon on their way to Hong Kong and Japan. Others toured the provincial centers, spending weeks or months in the region before moving on. It may have been touring French players who so popularized the term *comédie* for indoor paying theater that it passed into urban Malay. The *schouwburg* of Batavia and other centers became known as the *gedung komedi* (theater house), while *komedi* tents and arenas sprouted throughout the Archipelago covering every type of show. Opera may have been the most prestigious, but Russian circuses, Indian magicians, American vaudeville, Chinese jugglers, and Japanese acrobats were more popular in urban societies of diverse languages and tastes.

A bewildering variety of shows passed through the urban space of Southeast Asia around the turn of the century, offering precious opportunities for its plural populations to wonder and laugh at each other. "*Komedi* culture was transregional, brash, and unapologetically oriented to all that was ephemeral and novel. It was the culture of the [urban] masses, volatile and sensitive to public taste and opinion" (Cohen 2006, 21). It also had profound effects on older and purer theatrical traditions. Dance drama performed by human actors was best able to adapt to polyglot urban audiences, especially when the role of clowns was extended to provide slapstick interludes making playful use of different languages. The Bama *zat pwe*, Khmer *lakhon khol*, Thai *lakhon nai*, Vietnamese *hat boi*, East Java *ludruk*, and palace-derived central Java *wayang wong* all responded to the demands of urban audiences for more spectacular effects and costumes, male and female actor/dancers, comedic interludes that crossed cultures, and an often boisterous paying public inside an enclosed theater rather than court or festival patronage. The most phenomenal success attended new commercial romance genres born of the early twentieth century, using an innovative mix of themes – Vietnamese *cai luong* (literally "reformed theatre," mostly derived from *hat boi*), Thai *likay*, a popularized court drama, and Javanese *ketoprak*, a hybrid form with dance, spoken Javanese dialogue and western instruments as well as gamelan. In the 1920s, Viet Nam and Siam were each supporting several hundred professional troupes and Java about 500. Local Sino-Southeast Asian mediation was often essential in providing the capital and commercial know-how to support the innovative methods of indigenous actors and directors.

The period also gave rise to hybrid genres more influenced by foreign example and local demand than by traditional proprieties. Parsi troupes, having already developed hybridized popular forms in India, were also a hit in the cities of Southeast Asia in the 1870s and 1880s. It was in Penang that local Indian and Arab entrepreneurs sought to replicate their style in Malay, though adding actresses rather than the all-male Indian style. One leading group established in 1885 was named Indra Bangsawan after its most popular Malay tale, and the term *bangsawan* stuck for this genre. It developed a novel degree of professionalism and stagecraft, touring the cities of British Malaya and Netherlands India with large troupes, Indian-style musicians, elaborate costumes, and stage props. In contrast with its high Malay language and Indian inspiration, *komedi stambul* developed first in Surabaya with low Malay for its even more polyglot audience and European musical and theater models. Its early repertoire was taken from the Arabian Nights stories of Baghdad, which may account for the exotically Turkish-flavored name. A company of that name was formed in 1891 with primarily Eurasian actors initially, but Chinese capital and management. The dominating figures were the high-school-educated actor, director, and talented composer Auguste Mahieu (1865–1903) and the multilingual impresario Yap Gwan Thay. Mahieu went on to direct a number of companies, touring Java, Sumatra, and Malaya with a variety of musical romances. This genre of theater had many emulators over three decades, and prepared multilingual audiences for the advent of film. It well represented the excitement and scandal of crossing boundaries of race, gender, and class as these were becoming harder and more contested.

The European model was most influential in the Philippines, where Christian festivals were enlivened by popular vernacular theater, including Moro-Moro romances (also called *komedya*) climaxing with battles between Christians and Muslims, and the passion of Christ (*pasyon* or *sinakulo*) during Holy Week before Easter. A secular romantic light opera, *zarzuela*, was popularized in Spain in the 1850s and spread quickly to Manila. It was an immediate hit with music-loving Filipinos and companies were formed throughout the provinces. The same creative moment around 1900 that saw the creation of other popular stage genres in the region also witnessed the vernacularization of zarzuela into *sarsuela*, musical romances that also experimented with contemporary themes including the revolution against Spain. Severino Reyes (1861–1942) in 1902 founded the most successful of the many professional companies that flourished in the new century, the *Gran Compania de Zarzuela Tagala*. Among its first hits was "Not Wounded" (*Walang Sugat*) about heroic guerrilla fighters and their loves.

All these popular new forms flourished in the first decades of the twentieth century, and faded before the onslaught of film in the 1930s. Even though steadily losing this battle, live theater held on in rural areas. James Brandon (1967, 172–3) could still document over 1,100 professional theater troupes in Southeast Asia in the 1960s, twenty times the density to population of the United States. All combined music with the dancing and dialogue of actors or puppets, but in a bewildering variety of forms. Performance, more than the written word, continued to create common meanings and values in this transition to commercial modernity.

The earliest experimental cinema spread quickly along the steamer routes of Asia within a few years of 1895, when the Lumière Brothers showed the first commercial films in Paris. Short documentaries were shown in Manila, Singapore, Batavia, and Bangkok as early as 1897, and quickly fitted in to the *komedi* niche of commercial popular entertainment. The first short films, including clips shot locally as early as 1898 in Manila, were typically shown as part of a more extensive vaudeville routine. The first dedicated cinemas were opened in the Philippines in Manila (1900) and Cebu (1902), then in Singapore and Bangkok (1904), initially focusing on French productions. Japan was the quickest Asian society to take up the new medium, and its entrepreneurs were exciting Southeast Asian audiences in the early 1900s with depictions of their country's modernity and military successes against the Russians.

Manila, with its greater affluence and links to Hollywood, led the move to local production. Edward Gross, an American married to *sarsuela* star Titar Molina, devised the first locally produced film in 1912 on the life of nationalist hero José Rizal. His firm followed this up by other nationalist-themed films and adaptations of popular *sarsuelas*, before selling their equipment in 1917 to the first Filipino film-makers, the brothers Nepomuceno. Even in the silent era they sought to adapt the Tagalog *sarsuela* to the screen, with live singers accompanying the action on the screen. In 1932 Manila studios produced a total of 23 Tagalog silent movies of this sort, often intertitled in English and Spanish as well, while Cebu produced a few in Cebuano. Intertitled Bama, Thai, and Malay (Indonesian) language films had their first successful features in *Myitta Ne Thuya* (Love and Liquor, 1920), *Nangsao Suwan* (Miss Heaven, 1923), and *Loetoeng Kasaroeng* (1926), respectively. All required cosmopolitan resources, as well as audiences, but had such an electric effect that local firms mushroomed thereafter.

The silent era marked the first stage of vernacularizing the new medium and thereby expanding enormously its appeal. Every Southeast Asian town had its cinema venue, usually owned by Sino-Southeast Asian entrepreneurs. Much larger than the professional live theaters that preceded them, they also provided venues for other public activities such as nationalist politics. The cinemas cut across race, class, and gender, mixing more expensive chairs with the cheap benches that allowed the urban poor a little escape. In Bangkok they were alleged to be associated with dalliance and prostitution. Despite the popularity of local products, the main fare of cinema audiences was Indian, Chinese, and especially Hollywood romances. So subversive of colonial hierarchies were the latter seen to be that censorship of foreign films was introduced to the Dutch Indies in 1926 and the Philippines in 1929. An article in the London *Times* complained that Hollywood movies now reached the great Asian masses, revealing "scenes of crime and depravity ... as faithful representations of the ordinary life of the white man in his own country. The pictures of amorous passages ... give him a deplorable impression of this morality" (cited Sen 1994, 14). For the first time, indeed, global audiences were consuming the same mass culture, emanating from a novel world where romance was for all and status was determined by looks, talent, and money rather than birth or education.

The domination of Hollywood was greatly increased by the advent of sound movies around 1930. The level of technology and capital required was beyond the resources of local studios, most of which collapsed or merged in this depression era. The first Bama feature of the talkie era was made in Bombay, and the Vietnamese equivalent in Hong Kong. Led again by Manila, however, local studios with larger capital were churning out dozens of vernacular talkies by the end of the 1930s in each of the urban *lingua franca* in process of becoming national languages. While the intertitles of the silent era could be written in several languages and understood in the viewer's own dialect, sound film required actors to speak in the most commercially viable common languages, thereby greatly spreading their reach. Urban Malay spread and standardized with the movies (and newspapers), in step with the Indonesian nationalist movement, as did Tagalog in the Philippines. As screen idols spoke, so did their young audiences. In this way the talkies were complicit with nationalism in rendering popular culture less cosmopolitan, less local, and more national.

Distribution networks had been dominated by Chinese business since the early days. The most successful of them, the Shaw Brothers, opened an office in Singapore in 1924 and began acquiring or building theaters throughout the Peninsula, as well as in Bangkok, Saigon, and Batavia. By 1940 they owned or operated 69 such venues in British Malaya alone, as well as seven amusement parks featuring various live performers including *bangsawan* troupes. Initially their primary expertise was in distributing Shanghai-made Chinese silent movies, though of course they showed also Hollywood and Indian films to multilingual audiences. In 1932 they made the transition to sound film production with a western-dress modern Cantonese opera, *Baijin long* (white golden dragon), also a hit with Cantonese audiences in Malaya. This success led to a hundred more Cantonese films in the next decade. In 1939 they established Malay Film Productions in Singapore, which produced eight Malay-language talkies based on the *bangsawan* tradition before the war. The heyday of the studio, and of Malay film, came after the war, with a peak production of thirteen Malay films in 1952. Many of them starred Penang-born Acehnese heartthrob P. Ramlee, and had India-born directors and local Chinese cameramen. The gradual decline thereafter involved conflicts that would end by sending Malay, Chinese (increasingly in Mandarin), and English films in different directions.

The beginning of Indonesian language talkies in the 1930s was also cosmopolitan, as the Wong Brothers produced the first Jakarta-based action film based in part on local theater traditions. Chinese-managed local industry mushroomed, producing 41 talkies in 1941. A minor player in this flowering was the government's small unit (ANIF), but it planted important seeds, notably with the hit movie *Terang Bulan* (Full Moon). The Japanese military administration of 1942–5 expanded this unit into a powerful instrument of propaganda while suppressing all independent film-making. Having excluded Dutch and Chinese and introduced Indonesians to heroic nationalist imagery, the unit helped provide independent Indonesia with both an institution helpful to its government, and a broader taste for nationalist themes. Sino-Indonesian companies, however, again initially dominated the massive expansion of commercial films in the 1950s.

By the end of the 1950s, film dominated the popular culture of the region's expanding cities, with 676 cinemas registered in the Philippines, 655 in Indonesia, and 264 in Thailand (Brandon 1967, 305). In the Philippines and Malaysia this was the end of live popular performance, but elsewhere it continued to be a vital factor in rural areas, helping to keep alive many local languages and traditions. Centralized systems of universal schooling, however, followed by the extension of television into rural areas in the 1980s, eventually brought about the death or museumization of the cornucopia of live popular theater, and the birth of new national cultures – or more realistically, national versions of global culture.

[15] PROGRESS AND MODERNITY, 1900–1940

F<small>ULL</small> modernity, as opposed to the Early Modernity discussed in chapters 5 and 8, came late to the region, with a rush of new factors before and after 1900. The twentieth was Asia's century of modernity, culminating in an astonishing revolutionary embrace of what in Chapter 19 I call "high modernity," between 1945 and 1980. Its beginnings around 1900 found expression in the replacement of despair at the failure of the old order with hope at the possibilities of the new. A belief in progress was the vital ingredient of this new hope. It spread around the region with modern-style education, starting in the Philippines in the last decades of the nineteenth century. The fruits of the industrial revolution – telegraph, trains, steamships, electricity, canned goods, and newspapers – carried a message more powerful than propaganda that a new era had begun. Full or high modernity involved a conviction that rapid progress was possible and desirable if government and institutions were organized rationally, scientifically, and purposefully

These technical accomplishments at the same time broadened the gulf between Europeans and Asians. They convinced the former that their civilization was the only humane and progressive one, which should therefore be the sole inspiration of the modern state. The exceptional moment of European confidence between 1870 and 1914 also generated the realization that imperial structures were in fact states, which therefore had to assume responsibility for their subjects. The colonial governing structures of the twentieth century typically became more rational, secular, centralized, and professional than those of European and American states themselves, freed as they were from historical anomalies and democratic constraints. Colorful and cultivated royal courts appeared to survive and flourish through indirect rule, but these were removed from the modern technocratic power structure (except in Siam/Thailand), which saw them as irritating if decorative anachronisms especially when they attempted to do anything. Nationalists found them indefensible. The majority of rural people probably continued to see the state as something to be evaded or even replaced by some imagined religious or royalist past.

A History of Southeast Asia: Critical Crossroads, First Edition. Anthony Reid.
© 2015 Anthony Reid. Published 2015 by John Wiley & Sons, Ltd.

A vital and growing educated minority, however, quickly perceived the advantages of the new centrally controlled states, and began to hope to capture them from arrogant alien rulers, rather than seeking to return to an older order.

FROM DESPAIR TO HOPE

For many Southeast Asian elites the late nineteenth century had seemed a time of gathering darkness as the values by which they lived were defeated, demoralized, or abandoned. Many had grasped at neo-traditionalism or even millenarianism as battles were lost and treasured civilizations appeared unable to cope with the unprecedented challenge from the West. Rural revolts were common as prophets arose claiming to have found the key to western power without abandoning the old value systems. Muslims in Aceh, Sulu, and elsewhere sought martyrdom through frenzied suicidal attacks on the new order. What transformed this dark mood was not military force but the hope of a new generation that modernity could be theirs.

The highly westernized generation which came to maturity in the Philippines in the 1870s and 1880s were precociously early in their Spanish-style education and in their embrace of this type of modernity. Some were educated for the priesthood in Manila, while the sons of the landed elite could pay for a classical education at the Dominican or Jesuit universities. These elites rejoiced when a liberal governor was appointed to the Philippines after the Spanish revolution of 1868, promising to establish racial (though certainly not gender) equality in access to church and state positions. Among his enthusiastic supporters were the local-born secular priests, such as the well-educated José Burgos, resentful of the wealth, hypocrisy, and perceived arrogance of the Spanish-born friars. A conservative reaction in Spain sent a repressive governor out to reverse these changes, who ruthlessly targeted the more outspoken of the secular priests. Fr Burgos and two colleagues were publicly executed on imagined charges in 1872. This event radicalized a whole generation of educated youth. José Rizal (1861–96) declared he would have become a Jesuit but for this savage defense of Spanish and friar privilege, but instead chose the path of anti-friar writing and political liberalism. The privileged sons who could afford it made their way to Europe for further study and political mobilization, finding allies there in liberal, masonic, and scholarly circles. In exile these *ilustrados* (enlightened ones) laid the basis for the first inclusive Southeast Asian nationalism, expressed in Spanish and aimed at making the colony into an independent republic with a European-style liberal constitution. They did not intend revolution, but were pushed into it during the Spanish-American War in 1896 by the working-class *Katipunan* of Andrés Bonifacio, more Tagalog and millenarian in style. By forging evidence of *ilustrado* support for his insurrection he provoked the desperate Spanish regime into executing Rizal. This drove the educated elite to take over Bonifacio's insurrection, turning it into the liberal, Masonic, and Spanish-speaking Malolos Republic of 1899–1901. Only American intervention destroyed it through a mixture of bloody repression and cooption.

So westernized did these Filipino pioneers seem that they were less of a model for the rest of Southeast Asia than Japan, with its stunning naval victories over Russia at Tsushima and Port Arthur in 1904–5. This success amidst a series of Asian military failures appeared to demonstrate that pride could be restored and the Europeans reduced to size, but only by adopting modern technology and state organization. Phan Boi Chau (1867–1940), a talented Vietnamese literatus well-trained in the Chinese classics, at first responded to the French conquest like most of his literati peers by plotting to restore the monarchy and its neo-Confucian ideas. As he recalled from prison in 1914, however, the Japanese victory

> had a tremendous impact upon us. For it was like a new and strange world opening up … In the … nineteenth century, even though the universe was shaken by American winds and European rains, our country was still in a period of dreaming in a deep sleep … Even well-known people from the higher classes like myself were like frogs at the bottom of a well … going round and round in circles of literary knowledge, examinations, and Chinese studies … If we had not been awakened by the guns at Port Arthur, perhaps we should not yet know that there were other foreign countries besides [China and] France (Phan 1914, 10).

He therefore made his way to Japan to look for inspiration and modern weapons, engaging in written conversations in Chinese characters with Japanese and Chinese reformists and pan-Asianists there. The embattled Filipino Republic of Aguinaldo had already sent Mariano Ponce (1863–1918) to be its representative in Japan, who had had a little more success gaining support for a shipment of arms.

The early twentieth-century pioneers who first perceived the allure of progress and modernity agreed that changing education was the key to it. How could one master the new technological marvels if education was still restricted to the Chinese, Arabic, or Pali classics of centuries past? About 200,000 Vietnamese students were still being educated in Chinese in 1906, when 6,000 of them took the examination to become mandarins. But so little use was this education for modern employment that the examinations were abandoned in 1919. Romanized Vietnamese (*quoc ngu*) was the language of the new government schools from 1906, and it soon made the effort of learning Chinese characters appear misplaced. In the Islands, romanized Malay was embraced as a vital key to modernity, also giving readier access to European languages and to printing. The Roman script had been used to print Malay and Vietnamese for Christian purposes since the seventeenth century, but had had little appeal to non-Christians until the spread of newspapers in the late nineteenth century. Romanized Malay newspapers began in the cities of Java and Malaya in the 1860s, typically edited by Eurasians but owned by Sino-Southeast Asians. Increased numbers of Sino-Indonesians (*peranakan*) became involved in the Malay-language press at the end of the century as editors, authors, owners, and subscribers. Around 1905 the Minangkabau Abdul Rivai (1871–1937) and the Javanese aristocrat Tirto Adhi Soerjo (1880–1918) pioneered journalism in romanized Malay among indigenous communities, laying the foundations for a clamorous Indonesian press by 1918.

The question of "progress" (*kemajuan*) first appeared in these newspapers in the 1880s but became a dominant theme after 1900 for the growing clientele of indigenous readers. Progress meant the pursuit of education, technology, and the cultural accoutrements of "civilization" as exemplified by the European elite. Increasingly, Chinese, Javanese, Sundanese, and Malays saw themselves engaged in a kind of competition for survival through modernization. The modernizers identified themselves as *kaum muda* (the young group), a term that spread around Malay readers of all ethnic groups in the first decade of the new century. Even among the religiously educated who preferred to read their newspapers in *Jawi* (Arabic-scripted Malay), *kaum muda* became a powerful signifier that modernization was essential.

Among *Nusantara* Muslims the *kaum muda* supported a new type of religious school incorporating western classroom methods and secular subjects, and tended to reject the worship of saints and other mystic rituals in favor of a rationalized return to the sources in the manner of Egyptian modernizers like Muhammad Abduh. In 1912 Ahmad Dahlan (1868–1923) established in Yogyakarta a movement for such reformers, Muhammadiyah, which quickly became the most influential indigenous organization in Indonesia, without real parallels elsewhere in the Muslim world. Dahlan had already made his name for pointing out that the mosque of Yogyakarta was not correctly oriented to Mecca, and would attack many other local usages that made Islam harder to defend to the competitive moderns. Muhammadiyah became the greatest single builder of new schools after government itself, but also a polarizer of Javanese society. It called into question the fundamental compromise of Sultan Agung. The place of Hindu mythology in the beloved *wayang kulit* was no longer secure. Muhammadiyah was enthusiastically received in the Sumatran highlands (Minangkabau and Mandailing), which had a longer experience both of Islamic modernism and western education. After Dahlan's death the organization was led primarily by Sumatrans and western-educated urbanites, less tolerant of Java's "mystic synthesis."

While the religious syncretism of the vernacular period had been local and hierarchic, modern religious reformism was inherently universal. Muhammadiyah's critique of the religious status quo appeared to equalize all those who could read the Quran and Hadith and express their thoughts in the lingua franca of romanized Malay. The first and most profound polarization of the modern age was not between nationalism and its opponents, but between a new universalism in religion that embraced key aspects of modernity and expressed itself in the lingua franca, and the many local religious idioms that had consolidated in the previous period. The reaction to Muhammadiyah was rural and vernacular, and of course found its strongest expression in Javanese. Kiai Hasjim Asjari (1871–1947) came from a line of *ulama* leading a traditional religious school in Jombang, East Java. Like Dahlan he went to Mecca in the late nineteenth century, studying with the same Sumatran teacher as Dahlan at a slightly later time. Yet the kind of reformism he espoused remained Javanese and mystic, maintaining respect for the spiritual world of the *wayang*, and for pious practices such as pilgrimage and meditation at holy graves. In 1926 he coordinated an organization of *ulama* to defend the time-honored practices of

Javanese Islam, as well as the Shafi'i school of law, against Muhammadiyah criticism. This Nahdlatul Ulama (NU) became by 1940 the largest religious movement in Indonesia or indeed the Muslim world, establishing with Muhammadiyah an enduring organizational dualism in Indonesian Islam.

Among the rural majority who did not experience western-style education various kinds of millenarianism arose to offer a way out of the crisis. The messianic Maitreya Buddha figure in the Mainland, and the Mahdi of Islamic prophecy in the Islands, joined a plethora of invulnerable and magic-working figures who emerged to lead their people into a new age of plenty. In the late nineteenth century, British, Thai, Viet, and later, French expansion overrode ancient lineages and sacralities, threatening especially the age-old autonomy of highlanders. In the Mekong delta a Vietnamese soldier unreconciled to the French advance made common cause with a Khmer holy man Pou Komboto to keep the border area in turmoil from the 1860s to the 1880s. Rebel holy men like U Parama, U Ottama, and U Kelatha mobilized thousands of men to defy government troops in Upper Burma in the 1880s. Ong Kaeo brought most of the southern Lao highlands into rebellion against both Thai and French authority in 1901–2. In *Nusantara* it was the Qadiriyya and Naqshabandiyya Sufi orders that mobilized peasants into millenarian hopes, among which the 1888 Cilegon rebellion in Banten most worried colonial authorities. In the Philippines, as Reynaldo Ileto (1979) showed, the popular success of the liberal *ilustrado* revolution of 1896 rested on Christian-based religious longings, the identification of Rizal's execution with the passion of Christ, and a host of magic-wielding rural holy men. The times provoked a sense of crisis as well as hope for radical change, but this was far from a coherent program for revolution.

That modern concept, the violent overturning of the political order, became known at the opposite end of the social spectrum, among the most urban, western-educated, and cosmopolitan. It was the Chinese diaspora who first became familiar with the concept of revolution through the Chinese Revolutionary League, established by Sun Yat Sen in 1905 with the aim of turning the world's oldest and grandest monarchy into a Chinese Republic. Sun shuttled between his main base in Tokyo and the wealthy Chinese communities of Southeast Asia throughout the years 1905–9, raising funds for his newspapers and mobilization. Most Sino-Southeast Asians preferred the more moderate reformism of Kang Youwei and the Singaporean Lim Boon Keng (1869–1957), but Sun's success in toppling the Manchu Dynasty and proclaiming China a republic in 1911 sent a wave of excitement through the diaspora. Even many of the *peranakan* much closer culturally to Southeast Asia than to China were seduced into redefining themselves as "modern" republican Chinese. On the eve of the emergence of indigenous nationalisms, they were powerfully tugged in another direction more concerned to demand equality with Europeans than with "natives."

The revolutionary wave in Europe in 1917–19 had a profound impact on majority sentiment, particularly in Java and Viet Nam. The First World War (1914–18) not only ended with the toppling of Russian, German, and Austrian monarchies, it also was a turning point in left-wing European attitudes to colonialism. While moderate socialists reacted to capitalism's unexpected strength and democratic reformism since Marx's prophecies by embracing a parliamentary road and supporting the national colonial projects, the radicals led by Lenin developed the thesis that capitalism had only survived so long by its desperate acquisition of colonies to exploit. For the new Soviet Union and the Communist International (Comintern) it sponsored, Asia was an important field of action, and the destruction of colonialism justified as a step toward the eventual socialist triumph. On this basis Dutch socialists embraced Tjipto Mangunkusumo (1886–1943) and Soewardi Soerjaningrat (later Ki Hadjar Dewantoro, 1889–1959) when exiled in 1913 for their political activity in Java, and the young Ho Chi Minh (1890–1969) made such common cause with French radical socialists as to join them in forming the French Communist Party in 1920. The Comintern became in the 1920s an unprecedented promoter of the revolutionary idea in Asia.

The first revolutionary socialists in Southeast Asia were Europeans, even further removed in spirit from popular longings than the Chinese revolutionaries. Hendricus Sneevliet (1883–1942) was a passionate, idealistic socialist when his radicalism lost him his job as organizer of the Dutch railway union in 1912. He moved to the Indies and quickly became the leader of the radicals within the (chiefly Dutch) social democratic and union movements there. Convinced that socialism must be given indigenous roots, he helped found the first "native" (chiefly Javanese) branch in 1917 and the first Indonesian-language socialist newspapers. *Suara Rakyat* ("Voice of the People," 1918) would remain the theoretical journal of Indonesian communism. His most charismatic convert, Semaun (1899–1971), was a second-generation railway employee and teenage firebrand when he became the leader of the first stage of Indonesian communism. His key strategy, encouraged by Sneevliet and later influencing the Comintern's "bloc within" strategy, was to penetrate the largest mass organization of the day and push it in a radical, revolutionary direction.

That organization was Sarekat Islam, established in one of the Javanese royal centers, Surakarta, in 1911–12. It began as a commercial association, in reaction against Chinese revolutionary enthusiasm and the competition between Sino-Indonesians and Javanese Muslims for control of the batik textile industry there. During the economically difficult war years it became a catch-all inspiration for every aspiration for change, from modernizing Javanese religious practice to combating Dutch, Chinese, and aristocratic arrogance; from local grievances to millenarian hopes. In its heyday from 1916 to 1920 it claimed millions of members, some of whom looked to its leader, minor aristocrat, journalist, and reformist Muslim H.O.S. Tjokroaminoto (1882–1934) as the righteous king (*ratu adil*) of Javanese messianic prophecy. Semaun proved a persuasive voice within Sarekat Islam for the view that the only way for that movement to retain its mass following was to highlight the impoverishment of the peasant masses and propose radical reforms. "Islamic socialism" seemed no contradiction in this heady period, and Islamic leaders like Haji Misbach were among the most radical revolutionary voices. One claimed "the Prophet Mohammad was the man who removed all inequality between the sexes, did away with the difference between ruler and subject, between rank and class ... the socialist par excellence" (Hasan Ali Surati, 1916, cited McVey 1965, 364–5). Only after the climax of 1918–19, when Sarekat Islam's radicals inspired strikes in the cities and violent resistance to government labor and rice requisitions in the countryside, was there a conservative reaction that divided religion from socialism. Sarekat Islam expelled its revolutionary members, and quickly lost its mass rural following.

The Russian revolution of November 1917 and the revolutionary wave engulfing Germany and Austria the following year had contributed to that climax. The Soviet Union, and to some extent China, now replaced Japan as the source of inspiration, and occasional support, for revolutionary change. Asia's first and for some time largest communist party, the PKI, was formed in May 1920, mobilizing those socialists committed to revolution and the Soviet-backed Comintern. The initials first represented Perserikatan Kommunist di India (Communist Association of the Indies); the modern Partai Komunis Indonesia came in 1924. Semaun was president and the more educated minor aristocrat Raden Darsono Notosudirdjo (1893–1976) vice-president, succeeding to the leadership on Semaun's departure for Europe. In Europe the early communists met other Southeast Asians such as the future Ho Chi Minh, and debated the merits of internationalism or nationalism, bourgeois or proletarian revolution. These pioneer Asian communists were highly cosmopolitan, with Semaun, Sneevliet, Darsono, Netherlands-educated Tan Malaka (1897–1949), and Ho Chi Minh (1890–1969) all spending time in Moscow and playing significant roles in Comintern affairs.

For a few years the PKI's readiness to encourage diverse movements allowed many to dream of a rapid overthrow of the colonial government. The more populist leaders who dominated when the intellectuals were exiled found themselves under pressure to follow words with action. Tan Malaka warned that they were playing with uncontrollable fire, "where capital is concentrated, well-organised and protected ... and where on the other hand the people are still completely superstitious" (cited McVey 1965, 318). Disaster followed swiftly after these leaders decided for revolution at a meeting in Prambanan on Christmas Day of 1925. The only serious acts of violence that resulted were anti-Dutch revolts in Islamic strongholds Banten and Minangkabau, driven by the millenarian hopes of rural Muslims. The government banned the PKI and its activists were rounded up, interned, or exiled through 1926 and 1927.

Some of the exiles went to neighboring Malaya, where they had disappointing results among Muslim Malay farmers. The strength of Malayan communism had been Chinese, with the Chinese Party (CCP, formed 1921) sending agents to agitate for support and funds. In 1928 they formed a Nanyang (Southeast Asia) Provisional Committee of the CCP, though also reaching out to some local Javanese and Malays inspired by the Indonesian revolutionaries. In a visionary move strongly supported by Comintern agent Ho Chi Minh, a Communist Party of Malaya (rather than China) was established in April 1930. Even if most of its leaders spoke only Chinese dialects and were forced to operate clandestinely, it was the first party to commit to the idea of a Malayan polity. The same year saw clandestine formation of a Philippine and an Indochinese Communist Party (ICP), all influenced by the Comintern's abandonment of a "bloc within" strategy in favor of distinct communist leadership. "Indochina," like "Malaya," was a term favored by the Comintern as against the dangerous ethnic nationalism of "Viet Nam," Ho Chi Minh's original preference.

The first phase of revolutionary dreams was largely ended by 1927. Only in Indonesia were communists organized early enough to catch the naïve seduction of modernity as a world made anew. During this period from 1905 to 1926 a rainbow of radical views could enchant because very few had an adequate modern education, and the indigenous bourgeoisie was particularly thin. Pioneer intellectual Marxists argued that the Southeast Asian colonies could aim directly for socialist revolution without industrialization, because even more than in Russia, India, and China, capitalism was alien and colonial, and Javanese or Burmese needed little persuading that it was evil. The 1917 Sarekat Islam Conference compromised with the strong Marxist bloc within by condemning "sinful capitalism," meaning European and Chinese capital rather than that of the struggling Muslim entrepreneurs whose support the movement needed. Colonial governments were, moreover, themselves swept by waves of reformism or even revolution, and hard lines had not yet been drawn between Marxism, religion, and nationalism. The particular attraction of Marxism was in giving an intellectually respectable substance to the hope of change, and the longing for escape from desperate poverty and humiliation.

EDUCATION AND A NEW ELITE

European governments had in the nineteenth century extended their home education to the colonies primarily to educate their own sons. At secondary and tertiary levels, Spanish-, Dutch-, French-, and English-medium schools, respectively, were simply expanded to cope with ever-greater proportions of Asian students. There was an almost unbridgeable gap between this model and older patterns of purely religious instruction in Arabic (for Muslims) or Pali (for Buddhists), or the education in written Chinese available to a few Vietnamese and diasporic Chinese. A fundamentally new elite class was produced in the western schools, and since they were the ones with access to progress, modernity, and employment, they looked with incomprehension and disdain on the older forms of education.

Christians had the advantage of a narrower gap between the older religious education and a modern secular one. The nineteenth-century Philippines, indeed, offered educational opportunities not far behind those of Spain. In 1876 there were reported to be 385,000 boys and girls attending basic primary schools in the country, while the higher education mandated after 1865 under the supervision of the Dominican Santo Tomas University had established 185 high schools instructing in Spanish and Latin. Between 1861 and 1898 over 40,000 students of every race attended the Dominican university, Southeast Asia's first by 300 years. The great majority studied secular subjects – law, medicine, and philosophy. Even the dropouts found work teaching in private schools. This system provided the foundation of a middle class, including the *ilustrado* elite and the leadership of the Independent Republic that confronted the American takeover of the country in 1900. This exceptional inheritance ensured that the US administration had also to invest heavily in education, in 1908 founding the English-speaking and secular University of the Philippines. This continued the Philippine lead in modern education, with over 10,000 students attending universities in 1938, against 800 at the University of Hanoi, and only 128 Indonesians studying in the country. Rangoon University was the other prestigious center of education, after absorbing the Baptist Judson College in 1920. The royal foundation of Chulalongkorn University in Bangkok (1917) made it the only Southeast Asian university to teach in the vernacular before 1945.

With the exception of the Philippines, the colonial-era governments appear by hindsight to have been derelict in providing education well below the standards of successful twentieth-century states. Of course, they never shared the aim of nationalist governments, whether in Europe or Asia, to use education for the mass socialization of a population into national norms. Only in the early 1900s did they begin to accept that they were the governments of modern states, with some responsibility to provide popular education to indigenous subjects. There remained much unease about too much and too alien an education producing only misfits and malcontents. The indigenous population, now overwhelmingly peasants, should be kept contentedly on the land. The subjects of protected Malay, Khmer, and Lao monarchs were particularly likely to be encouraged into vernacular religious schools that led nowhere, such as the hundreds of "Reformed Pagoda Schools" in Cambodia and Laos. The senior British officer in the Federated Malay States argued in 1919, "It will not only be a disaster to, but a violation of the whole spirit and tradition of, the Malay race if the result of our vernacular education is to lure the whole of the youth from the kampung to the town" (cited Roff 1967, 138). Many Muslim and Buddhist communities were themselves initially reluctant to embrace what western-style education there was, for fear of their children being Christianized or alienated from parents and community.

A few fortunate individuals in the 1890s and early 1900s negotiated these pressures through exceptional wealth, the patronage of a European, or even a scholarship, to study at the highest levels of the European systems in Asia, and even at universities in Europe. These proved difficult to fit into the strict racial hierarchy of late colonial society. After a little experimentation in the early 1900s, appropriately university-trained Southeast Asians were discouraged or forbidden from entering the elite European administrative corps (British Indian or Malayan Civil Service, Dutch *Binnenlands Bestuur*), but rather directed to a parallel indigenous corps with more status than power. Some of them, like Tjipto Mangunkusumo (1886–1943) in Java or Nguyen Van Vinh (1882–1936) in Viet Nam, became passionate advocates for replacing the old civilization and language altogether by western ones. Others, like Tjipto's initial comrade Ki Hadjar Dewantoro or the Singaporean Lim Boon Keng, sought to rediscover their lost heritage (Javanese and Chinese, respectively) in very selective modernized form. The general elite acceptance of modernity as an aspiration by 1920, and the rapid success of some educated role models, transformed the early reluctance into a hunger for modern education in the 1920s and 1930s.

Sino-Southeast Asians proved early enthusiasts for modern-style education. They inherited the traditional respect for learning of Chinese civilization, but also possessed the wealth, communal organization, and urban location, to do something about it. Independent of colonial or Thai authorities they built Chinese-language schools throughout Southeast Asia, to ensure that some of their sons were Chinese-literate, whatever their mother dialect. The Chinese revolution and the wave of overseas Chinese nationalism that followed transformed these schools into an increasingly modern but China-oriented school system, importing the textbooks of the Republic. By 1938 there were 91,500 students in such schools in Malaya, far outweighing the 27,000 Chinese attending government and English-language schools. Malaya was the extreme case of modern Chinese schools "resinifying" Sino-Southeast Asian communities, but a substantial minority everywhere had a modern, Chinese-nationalist education by the 1930s. In Indonesia the Confucian revivalist Tiong Hoa Hwe Koan was already established in 1900 to recover knowledge of and pride in China, and by the 1930s was educating almost half of the 98,000 Sino-Indonesians reckoned to be in school in 1936. The Dutch in reaction established specifically "Dutch-Chinese schools" from 1908, the only government to make such specific provision. The great demand for European-language education was elsewhere met primarily by mission schools, such as the impressive networks erected by the Catholics everywhere, the Methodists in Malaya, Sarawak, and north Sumatra, American Presbyterians in Siam, and Baptists in Burma. By these various means those of Chinese backgrounds became Southeast Asia's best-educated communities (after Europeans), though profoundly split between those educated in Chinese and those in the prestige languages – English, Dutch, French, or Thai.

The example of the Chinese (and of the educationally dominant Indians in Burma and Vietnamese in Cambodia) was an additional goad to the majority communities. Indigenous spokesmen everywhere clamored for more and better education, and began to emulate the Chinese in setting up their own schools outside the government system. School-leavers not absorbed into the bureaucracy often did become critics of the system, as conservatives had feared, but they also found poorly paid employment as teachers in the proliferating "wild" or national schools, and as writers for nationalist newspapers. Many of the new schools were religious, as both traditional Quranic schools and Buddhist pagoda schools responded to the demand for more modern education. Indonesia's Muhammadiyah established one of the region's most effective school networks, but it had many imitators among less radical Islamic reformers who nevertheless sought to make their students employable in the cities by teaching Dutch, romanized Malay, and other modern subjects. Soewardi Soerjaningrat, renaming himself Ki Hadjar Dewantoro, founded an independent school system in Yogyakarta in 1922, Taman Siswa (Garden of Students), in an idealistic spirit of training students to be "free body and soul" (*merdeka lahir batin*) rather than slavish imitators of western knowledge and hierarchies. In Burma the enthusiastic mobilization of the 1920 university strike (below) expressed itself in the commitment to build a complete system up to university level free of government control.

At the end of the colonial period, in 1940, Southeast Asians were still poorly educated by world and especially East Asian standards, with the exception of Filipinos, Thais, and Sino-Southeast Asians. Educational enrolments as a proportion of total population were an impressive 11.5% in the Philippines and 10.7% in Thailand, but only 5.4% in Burma, 4% in Indonesia, and 2.5% in Indochina (Booth 2007, 138). Modern schools had not lifted literacy rates significantly over the pre-colonial systems. What they had done was to create a new, restless elite with a privileged relation to colonial modernity through their education. Typically detached from traditional cultures, they eagerly devoured debates on how to create new national ones. These debates were conducted chiefly in newspapers, in the colonial language but increasingly vigorously in national vernaculars that dominated newspaper consumption by the 1920s. The recorded circulation of Bama-language newspapers was already 70,000 in 1921 and several times that in the 1930s. Romanization made newspapers even more accessible in the Philippines, Viet Nam, and Indonesia, each of which had several hundred thousand consumers of nationalist-inclined newspapers in the 1930s.

Although education in the high colonial period presented critical dilemmas between the European, Chinese, or national languages, it narrowed the contest drastically to those at the colony-wide or national level. The new education developed to a very slight degree in the hundreds of local vernaculars, so that modernity appeared to represent only a choice between French, Chinese, or *quoc-ngu*; Dutch, Arabic, or romanized Malay; English, Pali, or Bama; English or Tagalog. The holdouts were in the linguistically diverse islands. Javanese and Cebuano (or Visayan) were substantial enough to be taught at primary level, while missionaries promoted romanized Toba Batak in Sumatra, Iban, and Kadazan (Dusun) in Borneo, to emphasize the distinction from Muslim-colored Malay. Sgaw Karen, the missionaries' choice of Christian lingua franca for the diverse Karen, on the other hand, was endowed with an alphabet derived from that of Bama. Of languages not regarded as "national," only Cebuano and Javanese made the transition to printed newspapers in the 1920s and 1930s, which in turn encouraged the emergence of modern literatures. European-language education was the best path to employment, and the developing national languages to journalism and political engagement. Local vernaculars were all too weakly modernized to withstand the onslaught of nationalism in the 1940s and 1950s. Javanese, by far the oldest, richest, and numerically strongest of the languages that failed to gain national status, was also burdened by a hierarchic system of language levels which the more radical intellectuals were convinced was incompatible with the modernity they sought. After the trauma of the 1940s, there would be only one language left viable as print expressions of national modernity in each of Indonesia, Viet Nam, Thailand, Burma, Cambodia, and Laos. The new media of expression and education would steadily unify the ways this language was spoken. The basis was laid for a nationalism based on imperial borders.

VICTORY OF THE NATIONAL IDEA IN THE 1930s

The growing educated urban constituency produced a hothouse of contradictory ideas in the second decade of the century, sharing only a conviction that change was necessary and possible to compete effectively in the race for modernity. Up until 1918 the speed of events often justified the hopes of change, with new associations and publications springing up and governments experimenting with representative bodies. The Philippines, by far the most advanced, was in the 1916 Jones Act given an elected bicameral legislature, an independent judiciary, and the promise of independence. Burma advanced through its involvement in Indian constitutional progress, and a system of "dyarchy" was implemented in 1923 whereby two Burmese elected members of the Legislative Council became ministers responsible for such areas as education, agriculture, and health. In Indonesia, experiment with elected city councils since 1903 was extended to the national level in the multi-racial Peoples' Council (*Volksraad*) elected from a tiny elite constituency. This first met in 1918 amidst revolutionary hopes for its rapid assumption of increased authority. In Indochina, Albert Sarraut, Governor-General for most of the period 1912–19, talked of self-rule and emancipation.

The earliest associations advocating colony-wide political and social progress appealed to an elite comfortable in the colonial language, with disproportionate representation of the better-educated minorities. Indonesia had by far the largest settled European and Eurasian community, one of whom demanded, in 1912, "*Indië* for us, the *blijvers* [stayers, as opposed to transient migrants], domiciled Europeans, Indos [Eurasians] and Indonesians, who have the primal right of birth" (Douwes Dekker, cited Furnivall 1939, 244). As with communism, the nationalism of colonial boundaries began with those closest to colonial ideas. The most heroic new imagining, that of a nation embracing the whole Dutch colony, began with the Eurasian E.F.E. Douwes Dekker (1879–1950), and the two Javanese intellectuals who joined him in founding the Indische Party in 1912, Soewardi Soerjaningrat and Tjipto Mangunkusumo. Tjipto declared (in Dutch) that the party's goal of one Indies nation would require "all the people of the Indian Archipelago … to set aside what is peculiar to them, just as the Friesians have to do to be part of the Dutch political unity" (cited Elson 2008, 16). In exile they joined the students in Holland who popularized the neologism "Indonesia" (islands of India), previously used only in European linguistic circles. By 1920 the term had become accepted by activists in Europe as a necessary advance from the established but ambiguous "Indian" (*Indiër*), even if its linguistic origins might have implied a step back from including Chinese and Eurasian *blijvers* in the imagined community. Despite their even more European origins with King Philip II, *Filipinas* (anglicized as the Philippines) and Filipino had already been agreed as the comparable national terms in the 1890s – the earliest and most stable of Southeast Asian national identities.

In the Mainland, by contrast, the names and memories of former kingdoms seemed so "natural" a basis for identity to majority communities, yet so threatening to minority ones, that a secular identification with colonial boundaries per se was even slower to emerge. The most passionate anti-colonial movements in Viet Nam and Burma in the early twentieth century were still inspired by that memory. An ethnically neutral colony-based view of identity was slower to emerge than in the Islands. It appeared in the multi-ethnic high schools and universities schools, among Marxists and other internationalists, and sometimes in colonial legislatures.

Those who sought to mobilize a larger indigenous constituency had to do so on the basis of religion, as did the Marxists within Sarekat Islam. When distinguishing themselves from the alien colonial rulers, most of the *Nusantara* population saw themselves as Muslim (*wong slam* in Javanese), however nominal their religious practice may have been. In Burma too, the prominence of the monks (*pongyi*) as social leaders in the countryside, competition and resentment against Indian migrants, and the explosive issue of shoes in temples, ensured that Buddhism would be the marker for mobilization. Some highly educated Bama founded in 1906 a Young Men's Buddhist Association (YMBA), modeled on its Christian equivalent and dedicated to educated lay-led reform of Buddhist society. Motivated by a popular campaign to enjoy the same political advances being legislated for India, and to end the practice of Europeans wearing their shoes into temples, it merged into a more populist General Council of Buddhist Associations (GCBA) in 1919. Its leaders already demanded that Burma should be administratively separated from India, but at the same time they resented being left behind the relatively advanced democratic reforms proposed for India in 1919. Support from educated young Christians during the university strike movement of 1920 against the restrictive nature of Burma's first university persuaded the GCBA to change the "Buddhist" of its name to "Burmese." Nevertheless, it was *pongyis* who led the most populist and widespread uprisings. An earlier wave of unrest in the 1920s was influenced by the much-traveled Arakanese monk U Ottama (1880–1939), who studied in Calcutta, affiliated with the Indian National Congress, and represented it at Sun Yat-sen's 1925 funeral. Although personally an advocate of non-violence, his blunt calls for the British to leave Burma raised the political temperature and earned him several periods in prison. Far more alarming to the British was the millenarian/nationalist rebellion initiated in 1930–1 by Hsaya San (1876–1931), discussed below.

The optimistic phase of multiple possibilities passed in the 1920s, as revolutionary violence provoked government repression, and the colonial establishment grew fearful of popular demands. Soviet patronage of revolutionary movements also collapsed, as Stalin became obsessed with his own and the Soviet Union's survival, and the Comintern became a mere instrument of his cynical foreign policy. The revolutionary communists of Indonesia were the first to be crippled by government repression after the PKI uprisings in 1926–7. Some 13,000 of its supporters were arrested, and 1,300 of them confined in internal exile at Boven Digul, in the swamplands of Southeast Papua. It was the turn of Viet Nam's communists in 1930. Soon after the ICP's formation it was caught up in a revolutionary wave of strikes and peasant protests which it had difficulty controlling. Its modest success in organizing peasant soviets in the Nghe An/Ha Tinh area of central Viet Nam was enough to convince the

French that it was truly dangerous, and the crackdown of executions and imprisonment was harsh.

The tradition of Viet ethno-nationalism had been prone to violence since the royalist resistance of Phan Boi Chau and others at the beginning of the century. In 1927 Nguyen Thai Hoc (1902–30) formed an explicitly republican and nationalist party on the model of the Kuo Min Tang (KMT) in China – the Viet Nam Quoc Dan Dang (VNQDD). This began a program of mobilization and subversion aimed at ending French rule. Arrests of key leaders in 1929 drove the remainder toward more desperate preparations among Vietnamese soldiers garrisoned in Tongking. In February 1930 a mutiny killed some French officers and Vietnamese notables and briefly took control of Yen Bay garrison before other troops restored order. The French reaction was ferocious, the criminal commission sentencing 80 to death (though only thirteen, including the VNQDD leaders, were executed after a vigorous campaign in France against the severity), 102 to forced labor for life, and 243 to deportation.

Burma suffered the same bitter memory of a humiliated monarchy, and the same intense pressure on farmers as landlessness and commercialization drove living standards down even as a large share of the rice crop was exported. The Hsaya San rebellion, not coordinated by a revolutionary party and therefore harder to decapitate, also climaxed in revolutionary violence in 1930–1. In the 1920s the GCBA gradually embraced the idea that the primary issue was the colonial bond itself with its burdens of taxation and racial humiliation. It opposed cooperating with British official structures, but successfully developed its own rural nationalist (*wun-tha-nú*) associations, which stressed village grievances such as taxation and obligatory services. Hsaya San, a charismatic monk from the Moulmein area, rose quickly through this organization to be appointed a delegate to national conferences, and in 1928 to head the nationwide GCBA enquiry into rural taxes. The GCBA leadership in Rangoon could not deliver on any of the hopes this rural mobilization aroused. Instead millenarian longings focused on Hsaya San himself, as a miracle-working superior being (*weik-za*) and future king. A movement began in December 1930 against the village headmen who had been the local focus of tax grievances. Over the next year almost 300 headmen were attacked by the rebels and 38 of them killed. British retaliation was even fiercer than that of the French. Some 1,300 rebels were killed in action, Hsaya San and 125 others were tried and hanged, and 1,389 others imprisoned or deported.

The lessons of the wave of violence would govern the superficially calmer 1930s. Colonial authorities concluded that overt demands for independence were potentially revolutionary and should be suppressed through an elaborate security apparatus. The key to stability was to keep educated urbanites insulated from the rural mass, to break any possible link between rational modern organization and rural yearnings for change. For those who dreamed of independence, it became clearer that it would not be obtained without education, careful political training, and foreign assistance. But the violence of the 1920s had shown that anti-imperial nationalism could be a unifying basis for struggle, in a way that religious or class-based movements could not.

Globally, the most notorious of twentieth-century nationalisms were the exclusive ethnic variants, especially when combined with state nationalism as in Europe in the 1930s and 1940s and again in the 1990s. Asians were of course also attracted to ethnic nationalism, but under the conditions of the 1930s and 1940s it was a secular anti-imperial nationalism that triumphed in Indonesia and the Philippines, and blended with ethnic nationalisms on the Mainland. Its key features were the adoption of the boundaries of the multi-ethnic empire as its sacred space, and the reversal of the imperial racial hierarchy within it. The undifferentiated "natives", whom imperialism had placed humiliatingly on the bottom of that hierarchy, could thereby be imagined as one. Europeans were firmly excluded from this imagined community, while the intermediary entrepreneurial classes, Indians in Burma, Vietnamese in Cambodia, and Chinese everywhere, had to earn their inclusion against a popular mood of resentment. Anti-imperial nationalism also had a radically modernizing agenda centered on providing the imagined mega-community with a national language and education system, ending traditional monarchies and particularities, and breaking the economic bonds of dependency on the industrialized imperial power.

The Philippines was well ahead of its neighbors in adopting this type of nationalism, which had already triumphed there conceptually during its struggle to proclaim and defend an independent Philippine Republic in the 1890s. That revolution's symbolic achievements – imperial boundaries as sacred territory, Rizal as national hero, and the agreed aim of building a modern nation-state to take over the colonial structures – were already in place in the 1930s, precociously being transformed into the official nationalism of schools, textbooks, and state rituals. Politicians competed at three-yearly elections to demand yet fuller and faster independence, but to arouse populist enthusiasm they also flirted with anti-Chinese resentment over the shares of the economic pie. The contemporary Philippine problems of family and patronage politics were already in evidence. The masters of this game, Spanish-descended but revolutionary lawyer Manuel Quezón (1878–1944) and Cebu Chinese *mestizo* sugar magnate Sergio Osmeña (1878–1961), competed robustly but reconciled in time for Quezón to become the first elected President of the Philippine Commonwealth in 1935 with Osmeña as his vice-presidential running mate. They won overwhelmingly on the Nacionalista Party ticket, with 68% of the vote in 1935 and nearly 80% in 1941. Their planning for the promised independence in 1946 included the agreement to make Tagalog the national language, to be taught compulsorily in schools from 1941 after the preparation of an official dictionary and grammar.

Constitutional arrangements were secular, with American-style separation of church and state, but this was not enough to reassure the fragmented Muslims of the south to embrace the nationalism of the majority Christian lowlanders. While some participated in the Constitutional Convention and electoral politics, many were alienated by Quezón's promotion of the southward migration of majority Christians. "The so-called Moro problem is a thing of the past," he declared. "The time has come when we should systematically proceed with and bring about the colonization and economic development of

Mindanao" (Quezón 1936). The Muslims had not joined the defining nationalist moment of 1896–1900, and their memories were of a separate series of sacrificial "holy wars" against American intrusion in 1902–13. There were demonstrations in Mindanao in the 1930s against incorporation into an independent Philippines, storing up problems for the future.

Indonesia's defining nationalist moment would come in the 1940s, but the groundwork was laid by the urban and student politics of the 1930s. The first explicitly Indonesia-nationalist *Partai Nasional Indonesia* (PNI) was founded in 1927 by Javanese-Balinese Bandung-trained architect Sukarno (1901–70). The first of his many marriages was at age nineteen to the daughter of Sarekat Islam leader Tjokroaminoto, with whom he boarded as a student in Surabaya. He shared his father-in-law's faith in charismatic oratory to generate unity, and tirelessly preached the unity of *sini* (here) against *sana* (there). By 1927 the repression of the radical left and the reactionary turn in the colonial administration had convinced many that the colonial bond was the ultimate problem. Sukarno joined a nationalist trend to non-cooperation in the powerless Dutch representative assemblies and sought a platform on which Muslims, Marxists, and others could unite. Parties that had sought reform across the racial divide of Eurasians, Chinese, and Indonesians, on the other hand, collapsed in the *Volksraad* elections of 1931. The gulf had become unbridgeable. Deprived of its capacity to agitate among the masses, the urban political elite had less interest or need for older cultural symbols, and could follow the lead of students in elite schools whose separate language traditions seemed less important than their unity against the *sana*. A student-dominated Youth Congress of 1928, with representatives from earlier-formed regional movements such as "Young Java," "Young Sumatra," and "Young Batak," declared that all delegates had "only one fatherland, Indonesia; ... only one *bangsa* [race or nation], *bangsa* Indonesia; ... only one language, the Indonesian language." This dramatically optimistic "Youth Oath" would be sacralized later as the charter of anti-imperial nationalism, and the de-legitimizing of the ethnic nationalisms that had preceded it.

Soon after establishing his PNI, Sukarno managed to engineer a federation of all the nationally based political parties. In 1929 he was arrested, but his well-publicized "Indonesia accuses" defense speech of 1930 gave him still more popularity, and he gained early release from prison at the end of 1931. The banned PNI had meanwhile been replaced by Partindo, of which he assumed the leadership on his release, but also by a "new PNI" led by Holland-trained Minangkabau intellectuals Mohammad Hatta (1902–80) and Sutan Sjahrir (1909–66), convinced that only a better-trained cadre organization would survive Dutch repression. By 1934 all these key non-cooperating leaders were sentenced to internal exile in eastern Indonesia. Cooperation seemed the only option for reaching the masses, and was also encouraged by the Soviet-influenced left. One of the Moscow-based Javanese communists, Musso (1897–1948) brought the new Soviet line of a common front against fascism to Indonesia in 1935. His most spectacular convert to a loose underground communist network, it later appeared, was Amir Sjarifuddin (1907–48), a brilliant Medan-born Batak lawyer and Christian convert, who became Sukarno's nearest rival for fiery oratory. He led a Marxist-influenced but cooperative Gerindo party from 1937. By 1940 the main political parties were all Indonesian in spirit. Far more numerous than their members was the readership of Indonesian-language newspapers, alienated by colonial arrogance and conservatism, and impatient for change.

Siam became Thailand as part of its own nationalist revolution of the 1930s, seeking to define nation or race (*chat*) rather than king as the focus of loyalty. This idea developed as a counterpoint to the royal nationalism of three Chakri kings. Chulalongkorn (r.1868–1910) had built an absolutist modern state, but expected his English-educated homosexual son to adopt a constitution and parliament. Instead, Vajiravudh (r.1910–25) used the symbols of nationalism – a red-white-blue flag to represent his slogan of nation (blood), Buddhism, and king, and Europe-inspired tirades against Chinese as "the Jews of the East" – to combat and censor the growing tide of criticism. According to his brother and successor Prajadhipok (r.1920–35) "the court was heartily detested and in the later years [of Vajiravudh] was on the verge of being ridiculed" (Prajadhipok 1926, cited Handley 2006, 41). But the princes who monopolized his cabinet stymied Prajadhipok's belated attempts at constitutional reform and left no alternative than force to bring the polity up with the times. On 24 June 1932 a small People's Party, established in Paris five years earlier by European-educated intellectuals and young military officers, bloodlessly arrested key members of the royal family and announced the end of the absolute monarchy in the name of "the people." The move was popular in the capital, but royalist officers mobilized up-country troops under the king's cousin, Prince Boworadet, in a failed counter-coup of October 1933. The king left for Europe three months later, and monarchy was absent and nominal for the next twelve years.

The People's Party government that followed introduced even less electoral democracy than most of its colonial counterparts. Power remained within the two wings of the People's Party, the civilians led by French-educated political economist Pridi Banomyong (1900–83) and the military led by French-trained artilleryman Phibun Songkhram (1897–1964). Both sought to use nationalism to build a strong and modernized state, but with different emphases. Pridi promoted a state-led economy, the abolition of unequal treaties with European states, expanded education culminating in the progressive Thammasat University he founded in 1934, and the replacement of the king by the new constitution as the focus of loyalty. Phibun, Minister of Defense from 1934 and stronger with each royalist plot he defeated, insisted on expanding the military, doubling its size in four years. He made talented writer and publicist Luang Wichit Wathakan his mouthpiece to promote ethnic nationalism, increasingly attracted to the fascist model of 1930s Japan, Italy, and Germany. Luang Wichit's glorification of the past achievements and military heroes of the Thai "race" shifted popular consciousness away from an exclusive focus on monarchy, but became more extreme with rising world tensions, particularly once Phibun became Prime Minister in 1938. A boycott of Japanese goods by Chinese shopkeepers following Japan's invasion of northern China in 1937 provoked heightened measures against Chinese schools, newspapers, and businesses. Luang Wichit denounced Chinese as even worse than Europe's Jews, since they sent their profits to a Chinese homeland. A publicity campaign began in 1939 to recover "lost territories" from the colonials. Phibun changed the country's name to Thailand in June 1939 to emphasize its racial character, and decreed that language, dress, food, and culture must all be modernized to a single "civilized" identity. Muslim, Chinese, and Christian schools were closed or obliged to adopt the national language and syllabus, while Malays, Laos, Chinese, and other minorities were expected to redefine as Thais. Muslim resistance in the south gained momentum.

Elsewhere in the Mainland anti-imperial nationalism contended with and sometimes blended with this ethnic nationalism. In Burma the rapid advance toward elected government inadvertently encouraged ethnic tension, since each politician gained election by appealing to his own ethnically defined constituency. The constitution of 1935, after separation from India, made cabinet responsible to a Parliament elected from 132 constituencies, of which 92 were "general," and effectively Bama-dominated, while twelve were Karen and eight Indian, both groups being relatively educated and dispersed among the lowlands. The uplands of the north and east were declared "scheduled areas" whose peoples were thought unready and unwilling to join a Bama-dominated polity. The Shan *sawbwas* (chiefs), a small Karen highland state, and the Kachin, Chin, Naga, and smaller groups retained much of their traditional autonomy under the direct authority of the Governor (Map 12.1). The leading Bama politicians were committed to the boundaries of British Burma and outdid each other in criticizing British rule and Indian immigration, but had little incentive to work out linguistic, religious, or political common ground with the minorities.

The radical young students at Rangoon University who staged a student strike in 1936 were more secular and socialist, impatient with the elected politicians' compromises. Their attacks on the "imperialist" university management gained some traction across ethnic boundaries, but they had even less experience than their elders at practical political accommodation with minorities. Post-war premiers Aung San (1915–47) and U Nu (1907–95) both shot to prominence when expelled from the university in 1936 as outspoken strike leaders. Their generation of Bama students, uncompromised by practical policy issues, united under the self-designation of *Thakin* (Lord) as rightful lords of the country. Despite Burma's relatively rapid progress toward electoral self-government, they proved the most radically alienated Southeast Asian youth elites of the period. Thirty of the Thakins, including post-war leaders Aung San and Ne Win (1910–2002), left Burma in 1940 to be trained by the Japanese military to fight the British.

Anti-imperial nationalism at the level of French Indochina was the most difficult goal, because of the imbalance in education between Vietnamese, Khmer, and Lao, and the memories all three of them had of their glorious but conflicted royal pasts. The sole university, in Hanoi, had only eighteen Cambodian and twelve Lao students in its last year of operation (1944) before being closed by the Japanese, as against 837 Vietnamese and 346 French. Indochinese organizations, including the French bureaucracy and the communist party (ICP), had only token Khmer and Lao membership as against dynamic Vietnamese networks everywhere. On the other hand, French scholarship as well as romantic imaginings had focused more on "protected" Cambodia and Laos than on the "difficult" Vietnamese. The star project of the Ecole Française d'Extrême-Orient (EFEO) was to restore the wonderful monuments of Angkor, as they later also did to the symbols of Vientiane's former centrality – the That Luang and Phra Keo temples. Pride in these newly prominent monuments, along with Buddhism, formed the basis of nationalist stirrings of Khmer and Lao in the 1930s. Both were of the ethnic type, and at a popular level more directed against Vietnamese domination than French. When a Lao committee of the ICP was formed in 1934, only one non-Vietnamese local could be found to join it.

The debates that did develop in the 1930s about political emancipation of Indochina were in practice between Vietnamese and French. The dominance of ethnic Viet in cities and French-medium schools throughout Indochina made it easier for both cooperative constitutionalists and Marxists to conflate Vietnamese past and Indochinese future, much as Nguyen Ai Quoc (later Ho Chi Minh) did in claiming his demands were from "the people of the former Annamese Empire, today French Indochina" (Nguyen 1919, cited Goscha 1995, 47). This stoked a debate between Viet and Indochina identity similar to the contemporary one between Javanese and Indonesian, but it was ultimately resolved the opposite way. Marxists were much the likeliest to anchor their identity in a secular future rather than a monarchic past, and both the pro-Moscow ICP and their rival Troskyists supported the Indochina idea well into the 1940s. The strongest Trotskyist base in Southeast Asia was in the French colony of Cochin-China, where they won the 1939 election to the Colonial Council of Cochin-China, criticizing the ICP for its flirting with rural mille-narianism in 1930, its compromises with bourgeois nationalism, and its parroting of Moscow's changes of direction. The advent of a Popular Front Government in France in 1936, with a Socialist Minister of Colonies, together with Moscow's anti-fascist turn, nevertheless encouraged both Marxist factions to join the Constitutionalists in championing an Indochina Congress in 1936–7 to advocate progress toward full statehood for the whole French terri-tory. This phase might be compared with the Soetardjo petition submitted to the Indies Parliament (*Volksraad*) in 1936, also uniting many ideological strands behind a relatively moderate petition for advance of the colonial unit toward self-government. The rejection of both initiatives by French and Dutch governments served to entrench anti-imperial nationalism as the obvious basis for a common platform.

Ethnic nationalism remained far more persuasive to Khmer and Lao, most of whom in the turmoil of the 1940s would reject the ideal of Indochina unity led by Vietnamese. Malayan communists had a similar commitment to the colonial territory, and eagerness to find Malay and indigenous (*orang asli*) members, both as tokens of credibility and for strategic reasons when they moved from urban origins to rural "liberated areas." But the subjects of Malay kings, like those of Khmer and Lao ones, had been conditioned to feel that they needed "protection" for the preservation of their way of life against dynamic immigrants. This imbalance in the plural societies created by the contradiction between colonial development and "protection" policies in the three areas would ensure that Malay and Khmer ethnic nationalism would continue to bedevil territorially based and inclusive nationalisms.

NEGOTIATING THE MALENESS OF MODERNITY

To this point women have scarcely appeared in the way self-consciously "modern" Southeast Asians sought to remake their societies. Since, as Chapter 13 showed, modernity arrived in exclusively male and patriarchal (European, Chinese, and Arab) dress, which intersected badly with "the only region of the world as we know it which features such androgynous or at least sex-similar systems" (King and Wilder 2003, 265), it is disappointing to find so little explicit female contestation of it. Men readily embraced not only the government positions made available exclusively to them, but also the modern spheres of journalism and political association. Women appear to have conceded these to be part of a male sphere of public discourse, status, and hierarchy. Formal ideology, especially as associated with the male-centric scriptural religions, was itself in the male domain, so that women tended to evade ideology rather than contest it. It was not so much that modernity usurped their roles in the economy (though this happened too as production was mechanized in textiles and agriculture), as that industrialization, bureaucratization, and the spread of foreign ideologies expanded the "male" spheres of life in unprecedented ways. Foreign models of religion (first and foremost), healing and medicine, production, the organization of knowledge, and even business came to resemble the hierarchic and status-filled world of male politics.

The image of the upwardly mobile family presented in the 1920s and 1930s was one in which the wife and mother was not in the workforce at all. Male-written manuals for domestic behavior, such as "Husband and Wife" (*Soeami-Isteri*, eight times reprinted by the Indies government publishing office, 1921–41; Hadler 2008, 79–81), emphasized that girls should be educated, as the European model decreed, but only in an elementary school close to home so that they could be prepared for a domestic life of keeping a clean and regulated household. David Marr (1981, 206–14) describes 25 such books written in *quoc-ngu* in the 1920s, almost all retaining Confucianism's "three submissions" of women to father, husband, and eldest son in succession, but within a context of a "modern" nuclear household. The radical transformation of the family required by urban modernity proved a great opportunity for puritanical religious reformers to emphasize female pre-marital virginity, submissiveness, and domesticity as if they had been normative. In Europe, too, nineteenth-century industrialization and urbanization had called forth revivalist religion in a puritan and patriarchal form. The real and imagined dangers of urban anonymity and industrial mixing required strict new codes for separating upwardly mobile respectability from the urban flotsam. Salvation depended now on individual morality which showed itself in frugal habits, hard work, and the exaltation of the nuclear family over which a breadwinner father presided. Respectable women were unprecedentedly constrained in dress, deportment, and domesticity.

The few young Southeast Asian women who did persevere to western-style education beyond puberty would often find themselves living away from home and in male-majority schools, mixed in both gender and race. This kind of adolescent mixing was indeed different, though in reality more controlled, than that which occurred in every rural market or festival. The novel image of "modern" youth free to mix, much stimulated by Hollywood films, did indeed create a false dichotomy in the minds of both progressives and conservatives between modern freedom and traditional constraint. When articulate elites took up the "women's question," therefore, it was on westernized assumptions about the "emancipated woman" of the 1920s and 1930s. Indigenous male literature eroticized the tempting female European or Chinese "other" much as European literature fantasized the oriental feminine. Debate pitted neo-traditional males championing novel concepts of male supremacy and female domesticity, dependence, and subservience as understood through textual Buddhism, Islam, Confucianism, and Christianity, against westernizing men and women who saw female emancipation in largely middle-class western terms.

The women's movements of the colonial era, particularly as reconstructed in the subsequent official-nationalist narrative, appear a disappointing handmaid of male initiatives. The realm of modern political associations had already been conceded to men, as an extension of their traditional preoccupations with status and public talking. The biggest female movements were women's wings of religious organizations like Muhammadiyah, Sarekat Islam, and the YMBA. Their pronouncements represented "quite strongly entrenched western bourgeois notions of femininity ... that had little basis in the lives of most Indonesian women" (Blackburn 2004, 19). In the 1920s such movements aligned themselves generally with the nationalist trend, to the point of muting their pursuit of specific advances for women. The banning of polygamy was an issue on which European reformers and women's organizations could agree, and the revolutionaries finally achieved it in Siam/Thailand as part of their anti-monarchy agenda. But even though it was only a tiny Muslim elite that indulged the practice in Indonesia, the women's movements ducked the opportunity to support such a law in 1937 on the grounds that a Dutch-dominated government should not meddle with Indonesian marriage customs. Semi-legendary warrior women from the less patriarchal remote past, like the Trung sisters of Viet memory, sexually ambiguous Srikandi of the Javanese *wayang* tradition, and the romantic heroines of Luang Wichit Wathakan's historical plays, were recycled only to show that women, too, could sacrifice for the nation.

The progress that did occur in bringing greater equality for women within this political realm were often the work of male liberals, European or Asian, rather than the indigenous women's movement. The dyarchy reforms of India were extended to Burma in 1923, with the addition of equal female suffrage in deference to the more balanced traditions of Burma than India. They could vote, on a restricted property qualification, but not stand for election. That further step was strongly debated by the men elected to the Legislative Council, with neo-traditionalists claiming that Buddhism insisted on female inferiority, and that equality was a western idea. Elected Filipino male politicians also devoted much heat to debating female suffrage. Quezón eventually insisted that the women themselves should decide the issue in a plebiscite. Half a million women took part in 1937, opting ten to one in favor of having the vote. In Indonesia the men of the *Volksraad* narrowly defeated the government's proposal for equal female suffrage in 1925, ethnic Indonesians voting 9–8 against, but passed the measure in 1937. The various transitions to nation-statehood in the 1940s and 1950s gave power temporarily to radical modernizers, and there was little further controversy about women getting the same political rights as men.

This record could be read to mean that Southeast Asia's historic gender balance was forgotten in the rush to embrace a pre-1914 western image of modernity with all its profound patriarchy, so that a return to greater balance in a modern urban context had to play catch-up with post-modern progress in the West. Neo-traditional religious reformers, and at times even authoritarian post-war governments, were ready enough to condemn sexual liberation as an unwanted western import. Does the region's remarkable heritage of relative gender balance and flexibility suggest anything by way of a less patriarchal model of modernity? The answer must be yes, though neither well-meaning reformers nor the ever more influential religious neo-traditionalists are much inclined to celebrate it.

Firstly, despite a century of tutelage in modern western ideas of fixed and binary sexuality, the new anthropology of gender recognizes the widespread survival in Southeast Asia of flexible and heterogeneous sexual identities strikingly at odds with older western norms. Colonial regimes criminalized homosexuality, but could never enforce this in indigenous societies that continued to accommodate European and Chinese refugees from sterner systems. Wazir Jahan Karim (1995, 35–7) insists that Southeast Asian bilateral descent still involves a preference for kinship terminology based on age rather than gender in everyday social relations. Male and female are free to explore and exploit their complementary sexuality, but also to transgress these through "the fluidity of sexual boundaries" and the acceptance of an "intersexual third dimension of behaviour." While gender theorists describe the readiness of Southeast Asian women to concede status superiority to men, especially in the realms of formal religion and politics, this relative freedom from status concerns still allows women more latitude in everyday business matters. Moreover, the resilience of custom (Malay *adat*) and folk animism in everyday life renders it "the constant 'equaliser' or 'moderator' for women" against neo-traditional religion and normative ideology (Karim 1995, 44).

Moreover, as noted in Chapter 13, Southeast Asian women did make the transition to industrial wage labor more willingly and successfully than European women, or Southeast Asian men, even if colonial capitalism insisted on paying them much less than men. The most "indigenous" manufactures of the colonial era, cigarettes and textiles, overwhelmingly employed women, and even European-run enterprises did so on a much larger scale than in Europe. The older male labor system of the region had been based on vertical ties of patronage and bondage. Free male wage labor was slow to emerge except among Chinese and Indian migrants, so that employers even into the 1920s complained of the stereotyped "lazy native," and the need to create bonds of indebtedness as an incentive to work. "Eating wages" (*makan gaji*, in Malay) for an impersonal or foreign boss was still a last resort of indignity for many Southeast Asian men into the 1970s. Women had always been freer of these status inhibitions, and readier to do what was necessary to feed the family. When large-scale manufacture for the world market again became a major feature of Southeast Asian economies, in the 1970s, it was a largely female workforce that made this possible in electronics, textiles, footwear, and food processing, as it had earlier in textiles and tobacco.

The gender pattern also permitted women more labor mobility than was the case in other industrializing situations, even if this was concentrated in the informal sector and largely invisible to governments. Filipino migration to Manila was already predominantly female in the mid-nineteenth century, when employment in the women-dominant cigar factories was a major draw. Male migration prevailed during the revolutionary period of the 1890s and early 1900s, but a balanced pattern re-established itself in the 1920s and 1930s, to be again replaced by the female-dominant post-war pattern. The Ilocos coast, to the north of Manila, was already a notable stand-out in the nineteenth century for the readiness of its women to postpone or forego marriage in order to seek economic autonomy and support for their families in the city. The abolition of slavery in Siam in 1905, later than elsewhere, ended one form of female urban migration but opened up a more free and commercial recruitment for the urban service sector.

The lop-sided male majority among Chinese, Indian, and European migrants to the cities created a demand for sexual and domestic services, covering the whole range from prostitution to stable marriage. Commercial prostitution flourished everywhere to serve this urban imbalance, but Bangkok and Rangoon were noted as especially freewheeling centers. Poor rural Thai and Bama women could hope to make some money when young without necessarily sacrificing the chance for a respectable family life back in the village. Bangkok was reported to have 20,000 prostitutes already in the 1920s (rising to about 200,000 in 2000), serving principally a resident clientele (Barmé 2002, 82). This was the high-risk edge of a much broader pattern of vigorous female participation in the commercial urban economy. From the 1970s, it had its extension in the massive international movement of female migrant workers out of the Philippines (the world leader), Thailand, Indonesia, and Burma, serving Asia and the world in the domestic, health, tourist, and entertainment sectors. Southeast Asian gender flexibility appears to have made it easier for women to leave children in the charge of stay-at-home males, who could assume nurturing roles without stigma.

Politically, the revolutions of the 1940s offered unprecedented opportunities for change. Vietnamese communists, like their Chinese counterparts, demonstrated their reversal of Confucianism by recruiting women into revolutionary violence, warfare, and leadership. Revolutionary bodies in their heroic early stage included women, like Maria Ulfah Santoso and S.K. Trimurti in the second and third Indonesian revolutionary cabinets, or Nguyen Thi Binh (b.1927), Foreign Minister of the provisional communist South Vietnamese government from 1969 and a prominent figure at the Paris peace accords of 1973. The authoritarian phase that followed tended to retreat to tokenism, but there could be no going back on the principle of equality in law and politics. The election of Philippines Presidents Cory Aquino (1986) and Gloria Macapagal-Arroyo (2004), and Indonesia's Megawati Sukarnoputri (2001), and the anti-establishment election victories of Aung San Syu Kyi in Burma (1990) and Yingluck Shinawatra in Thailand (2011) all owed something to a more aggressive male relative being *hors de combat*, but undoubtedly something also to a particular style of female charisma attractive to the region's voters.

Taken overall, Southeast Asians have so far managed the transition from rural peasant poverty to urban modernity with many fewer constraints on female employment and economic autonomy than in nineteenth-century Europe or other comparable transitions in twentieth-century Asia. In a 2013 ranking of gender equality in terms of economic, political, and educational access and health status, the Philippines was rated fourth out of 136 countries, behind only the Scandinavians, and in a class otherwise occupied only by very wealthy (or in the case of Cuba, very revolutionary) countries (World Economic Forum 2013). Nevertheless, the confident male ideology of puritanical piety, rationality, and suspicion of women outside the home that accompanied the urban transition in England, France, and Holland (but faded there after 1914) is still an aspect of modernity in rapidly urbanizing Southeast Asia (Chapter 19). The high female participation rates in the workforce in Thailand, Laos, and Viet Nam appear to have dropped as they grew more prosperous between 1990 and 2010. Neo-traditional Islam has imposed certain forms of puritan dress and behavior on the model of respectability for upwardly mobile urban women. While in some respects this has echoes of Victorian England, Southeast Asia's contemporary women have long since arrived at a far more satisfactory place than that analogy would suggest, close to equality with men in education, the professions, and business, and with crucial roles as breadwinners and heads of households.

[16] *MID-TWENTIETH-CENTURY CRISIS, 1930–1954*

FOR Asia in general, but Southeast Asia in particular, the middle decades of the twentieth century were an astonishing time of crisis and transformation. Some return of economic growth and political influence to Asia would have taken place under almost any circumstances, and more rapidly without the destructive violence of mid-century. The political changes, however, transforming multi-ethnic empires into populist nation-states, were telescoped together by the Pacific War. Not only did the European empires end at Japanese hands in three dramatic months of 1941–2; the war's sudden end in August 1945 also created an unexpected revolutionary opportunity that ensured the transition to nationhood would be both violent and radical, marking a dramatic rupture and rejection of pre-war patterns.

Out of this crisis came the new world order of theoretically equal sovereignty among actual or potential nation-states. Whereas South Asia (together with Malaysia and the Philippines in Southeast Asia) moved to independence through negotiation, compromise, and the recognition of minority interests (albeit with the accompanying murderous violence of partition), in eastern Asia Japan's rapid conquest and sudden surrender provided the opportunity for revolution. Armed, mobilized, and traumatized populations would fight their way to victory or defeat, and the victors typically sought no compromise with the defeated. The 1940s became the furnace in which new identities and ideals were forged.

ECONOMIC CRISIS

The middle decades of the twentieth century were not only revolutionary in politics, but also a terrible nadir in the struggle for survival of the majority of Southeast Asians. The region was transformed from a frontier of tropical agriculture producing for the markets of Europe and America, importing much of its wage labor from China and India, to an impoverished but expectant

A History of Southeast Asia: Critical Crossroads, First Edition. Anthony Reid.

maelstrom of millenarian and nationalist hopes. Malaya and the Philippines recovered quickly from the disaster of war and occupation in the 1940s, but the remainder of Southeast Asia's new or reinvented countries embarked on their revolutionary agenda of nation-building in a context of poverty exacerbated by economic nationalism and instability.

The distorted colonial economies had reached their peak in the 1920s, exporting vast amounts of sugar, rubber, oil, tin, rice, and tropical specialties through preferential tariffs to their respective metropoles. The collapse in prices for export products during the world depression of 1929–34 marked the end of this distortion. Indonesian sugar, the staple of the Dutch regime, represented about a fifth of world sugar exports at over two million tons a year in the 1920s, but dropped to only 60% of that in the 1930s and 10% in the 1940s. The attempts of the local sugar industry to make up for export losses in the 1930s by persuading Indonesians to consume its white refined product were so successful that the country became a major sugar importer by the 1960s. The European-run plantation economy in rubber, oil-palm, coffee, and tobacco was devastated by the collapse of international prices for these commodities, but local smallholders made up much of the ground the plantations were forced to abandon. The smallholders typically grew perennial cash crops on hill slopes as a supplement to their subsistence food crops on the irrigated valley floor, and had negligible losses since they only harvested when prices were adequate. In the *Nusantara* area about a million smallholders were cultivating rubber alone by the late 1930s. Small farmers often profited from the switch to greater economic self-sufficiency the depression enforced. But it was the beginning of the end of the distorted pattern tying Southeast Asia to distant markets and suppliers in Europe. Japan produced textiles far more cheaply than Europe in the 1930s, and despite discriminatory tariffs it began to restore a more natural pattern of intra-Asian trade.

Hundreds of thousands of Chinese and Indian laborers entered the region every year between 1860 and 1929, with the flow peaking in the 1920s. Singapore and Malaya represented the extreme cases, with 72% and 44%, respectively, of their population recorded as foreign-born in the census of 1921, but southern Thailand and the Burma delta were not far behind. The Great Depression marked the end of this phase of mass immigration, and a partial reversal as more migrants returned to India and China than arrived. The Thai nationalists after 1932 made the ending of Chinese immigration one of their policies, while the colonial regimes introduced new restrictions on the inflow as problems multiplied. Yet the Chinese share of the population continued to rise slightly more rapidly than the overall population, as the local populations became more stable and gender-balanced, with higher than average birth rates. About 3.8 million people were classified as Chinese in 1931 in Malaysia/Singapore, Indonesia, and Thailand combined, but 9.1 million in 1960.

Indian and Chinese nationalism claimed more and more converts among the immigrant communities in the 1930s, rendering them more resented by indigenous nationalists and more problematic for governments. In Rangoon the Indian dock-workers went on strike in May 1931 in protest against

Table 16.1 GDP per capita by country, 1913–1980, in 1990 Geary-Khamis dollars.

	1913	1938	1950	1970	1980
China	552	562	448	783	1067
India	673	668	619	868	938
Indonesia	892	1175	840	1194	1870
Philippines	1015	1522	1070	1764	2376
Thailand	841	826	817	1694	2554
Burma	685	740	396	642	823
Malaysia	920	1361	1559	2079	3657
Singapore	1367	2070	2219	4439	9058

Source: Maddison 2006, supplemented for 1913 by 2014 consultation of Maddison project data base, http://www.ggdc.net/maddison/maddison-project/home.htm.

Gandhi's arrest, and when Bama workers were hired to replace them the resulting mob violence left 120 dead, mostly Indians. The Hsaya San rebellion also produced much anti-Indian and anti-Chinese violence, frequently led by extremist monks. As the Japanese began their invasion of British Burma at the end of 1941, Indians clamored to leave in fear of violent popular resentment. For most there was no option but to walk. About half a million made it across the border into India, but thousands died in terrible privations along the way.

Table 16.1 shows that the economic recovery in the late 1930s, aided by cheaper consumer goods from Japan, left most of Southeast Asia fractionally better off before the Second World War than the first. Even though the whole high colonial period looks very sluggish by comparison with post-1970 growth, Southeast Asian economies remained in better shape than those of India and China. The 1940s, however, were economically even more disastrous for the Southeast than for Asia as a whole, as war, Japanese occupation (1942–5) and revolution left most countries poorer than they had ever been at the moment their independence was recognized in the period 1947–54. According to Angus Maddison's figures (Table 16.1), Indonesia, Thailand, and Burma (like China and India) were poorer in 1950 than they had been in 1913. The anaemic growth of the late colonial era had been wiped out by the disasters of the 1940s.

The Japanese occupation was ruinous for the export economies. Starting with Indochina under its nominal Vichy-French government from 1940, the Japanese prohibited trade with free China and confiscated the Chinese companies engaged in it. They declared monopolies of vital supplies for Japan and its military forces. By 1943, however, Japanese shipping had suffered so much from Allied attacks that it could no longer import the oil, coal, tin, rubber, and rice for which it had invaded in 1941. In 1944–5 Japanese military governments imposed a policy of maximum self-sufficiency in each district (*shu*), and massive requisitions at low prices to support military and urban needs. The food situation became critical in 1944 when drought, and in Viet Nam an exceptionally destructive typhoon, accentuated these maldistribution problems. Though statistics were unreliable and often politicized, there were about 1.5 million extra deaths in Viet Nam and 2.45 million in Java in this grim period. A proportion of the Java figure were forced laborers sent to build railways and airfields under appalling conditions, but glamorized by Sukarno as "volunteers" (*romusha*) for the anti-Allied cause. Military action itself killed fewer Southeast Asians than famine. Only Burma (where about 250,000 were killed) and the Philippines (over a million) were seriously fought over as the Allies counter-attacked. About 100,000 perished in the February 1945 battle for Manila, virtually destroyed by American bombardment (Figure 16.1).

Total rice production recovered to pre-war levels in the Philippines and Thailand by 1949, and in southern Viet Nam and Java by 1960, though Burma would never recover its status as a major rice-exporter. Given the rapid postwar increase in population, feeding Southeast Asia was a critical problem until the green revolution of the 1970s. Wars, rebellions and social conflict, population growth, economic nationalism, and the flight of capital ensured that Indonesia, Viet Nam, Cambodia, and Burma grew even poorer in the 1960s. Only the Asian countries that were neither "liberated" nor revolutionary did well, notably Japan as the first miracle economy of Asia. Contrary to nationalist hopes, Europe rather than Asia forged ahead after the destruction of the

Figure 16.1 The Destruction of Manila in the US reconquest, February 1945. Source: Topfoto.

colonial economic system. The gap between a rich West and the independent but poor countries of Asia was wider in 1970 than ever before.

JAPANESE OCCUPATION

As the first of Asia's economies to master the formula of state-led industrial growth, Japan spearheaded the end of the colonial order, which was already on the defensive against nationalism and communism. Japan followed the European model of exchanging its cheap manufactures for the raw materials of Southeast Asia, but was inhibited by colonial monopolies and tariffs from lucrative trade with the region. In 1940 the United States, Britain, and the Netherlands placed embargoes on strategic exports to Japan in reaction to its moves in Indochina, including blocking its vital oil supply in 1941. These moves apparently convinced the Japanese military that they had only a narrow window to achieve their goals in the south before the oil ran out, prompting the reckless gamble of attacking Pearl Harbor. It thereby dragged the United States into a war that ended with American military hegemony in Asia. The unexpected ease and popularity of their initial victories in Southeast Asia made the Japanese military lose sight of whatever negotiated exit strategy it had entertained there. The whole region would be administered in the interests of Japan's total war effort, with some areas, such as eastern Indonesia and Singapore, marked for permanent Japanese control.

Japan's war of expansion had effectively begun in 1931 with its invasion of Manchuria, followed by all-out war with China from 1937. It was the war in China that brought Japanese troops to Southeast Asia in 1940, intervening at the border crossings of the French railways from Hanoi into China. Once the Netherlands and France fell to German aggression in May and June 1940, European vulnerability in Southeast Asia was clear. The French colonial forces in Indochina, nominally under the pro-German Vichy government, skirmished with Japanese troops at the border but had little choice other than to agree to the stationing of first 6,000, then 40,000, and finally 140,000 Japanese troops in Indochina in stages of 1940–1. The French authorities remained in control until the Japanese suddenly took over on March 9, 1945, worried by the collapse of the Vichy regime in France and military threats from the Allies. The Japanese therefore had only five months to mobilize an anti-western nationalism there.

During the height of Japanese power in Southeast Asia, Indochina resembled Thailand in Japanese eyes, as two dependent client states allowed to govern themselves as long as Japanese strategic and economic aims were served. Between them, however, Japan made its preference clear after the aggressive nationalist premier Phibun Songkhram took advantage of the fall of France to invade French Indochina in December 1940, gaining some advantage on land as against serious losses at sea. Japan intervened to mediate a peace in which the French were obliged to surrender territory on the west bank of the Mekong, an internal propaganda victory which Field Marshall Phibun commemorated in a very prominent "Victory Monument" in Bangkok. After Japan conquered Burma and Malaya, and Thailand declared war on

Britain and the United States (January 25, 1942), Phibun was further rewarded by a visit of Japanese premier Tojo to Bangkok in 1943. He there announced the transfer to Thailand of the four northern Malay states formerly under Thai suzerainty, and the easternmost Shan states of Burma (Map 16.1). The nationalist dreams of a greater Thailand seemed to be within reach.

British, Dutch, and US colonial possessions were attacked as soon as Japan joined the war on the side of the Axis with the bombing of Pearl Harbor (December 8, 1941, or December 7 in Asia). Within two days the Japanese had sunk the two battleships representing British naval power in the region, disabled American air power in Manila, obtained the surrender of Thai troops and an alliance with Thailand, and taken Kota Bahru in northeast Malaya. The Japanese entered Manila without a fight on January 2. They took the supposed British stronghold of Singapore on February 15, Java and the Indies on March 12. Burma was occupied from south to north in March, and the American holdout at Bataan in the Philippines finally surrendered on May 8. General MacArthur left Bataan before the surrender and established the headquarters of what became the Southwest Pacific Command in Australia, launching the counter-attack that brought him back to the Philippines in October 1944. The British began fighting their way into Burma from India at about the same time, but the involvement of the United States in the Pacific War was essential to its emergence as the dominant military power in eastern Asia after the war.

The rapid Japanese advance of 1941–2 was welcomed by far more Southeast Asians than opposed it. Millennial expectations were initially high, as one participant remembered: "Burma would at last be free ... The Japanese were arriving as friends ... they were ready to die for Burma ... a Burman prince rode in the Japanese vanguard" (Nu 1975, 102). A few actively sought ways to assist the Japanese militarily, notably Aung San's Thakins in Burma, the Cao Dai religious movement in the Mekong delta, and the Islamic PUSA movement in Aceh. Even they were soon disillusioned by Japanese military cruelty and arrogance. The active opponents of the Japanese were few but important – communists, socialists, and a tiny liberal elite ideologically opposed to the Japanese military as fascists; Chinese nationalists already mobilized to support the Kuomintang against Japanese aggression; and educated Filipinos who did have a stake in the independent Philippine Commonwealth already promised for 1946. These groups supported a guerrilla resistance in the highlands of the Philippines, Malaya, and northern Viet Nam – the latter two predominately communist. In the two most exposed Japanese fronts in the Philippines and Burma, coincidentally also the most advanced toward democracy, the Japanese were obliged to make greater concessions to residents less convinced of their eventual victory.

The replacement of colonial administrations by Japanese military ones marked a dramatic turning point for Southeast Asia. The status of European government, law, and manners was abruptly punctured by European failure on the battlefield. The lesson was driven home by the dramatic public removal of colonial monuments (such as that to Jan Pieterszoon Coen in the heart of Batavia, renamed Jakarta), street and city names, and symbols. An alternative model of modernity arrived that paid not even lip service to democracy, but stressed rather discipline, a nationalist spirit, and unity between ruler and

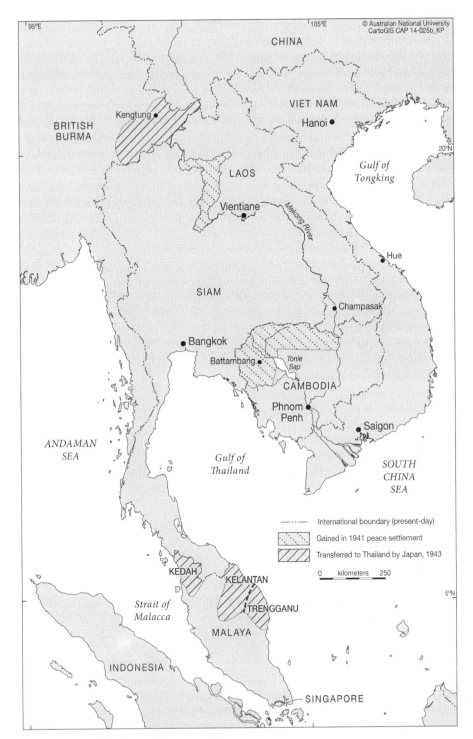

Map 16.1 Thailand's wartime expansion.

ruled. The strong position of government-linked European and Chinese firms in the economy was quickly dismantled, to the advantage in the first instance of government-linked Japanese firms. But the controlled nature of the wartime economies gave new opportunities also to hungry newcomer business, both Chinese and indigenous, ready to risk smuggling essential goods by a mixture of bribery and stealth. The "Euro-Chinese" cities were nationalized by the influx of the indigenous majorities to staff government, business, and propaganda roles, in much greater numbers than the departing Europeans. The Japanese government downgraded the prestige of European languages in favor of Japanese and the new, modernizing national languages. For Dutch, in particular, the Japanese had no use at all. They banned its public use, and since Japanese could in no way take its place, Indonesian (romanized and modernized Malay) had rapidly to be promoted in government, education, and popular culture.

The sudden change of overlord risked raising the political stakes dangerously. The assassination of "collaborators" by guerrilla movements, and Japanese execution of those denounced to them as pro-Allied, embittered the normal process of elite competition. Ethnic tensions were sharpened between majority communities generally welcoming the Japanese, and minority communities fearing them. In the *sook ching* (purification by elimination) massacre in Singapore, the Japanese executed about 10,000 "anti-Japanese" activists identified by hooded informers once the whole male Chinese population was assembled. In west Borneo the Japanese also rounded up hundreds of leading figures, including the ruling sultans, Chinese, and others, for execution in 1943 on allegations of an anti-Japanese plot. In northern Sumatra activists opposed to the local rulers the Dutch had "protected" denounced them to the Japanese, and were in turn denounced by their intended victims, causing the execution and imprisonment of many. In the Philippines political assassinations followed pre-war factional lines more clearly than the collaboration-resistance logic used to justify them.

Yet taken overall, the rough arbitrariness of inexperienced Japanese powerholders had a unifying effect in establishing an indigenous moral community that far outweighed the divisiveness of their initial actions. Traditional monarchs, European-trained bureaucrats, fiery nationalists, and religious leaders had all to find a way to survive as mediators between unpredictable Japanese and suffering masses; all were humiliatingly made to sing the Japanese propaganda tune; all became to some extent complicit in the perilous privileges enjoyed by all elites at a time of suffering for the majority. When it came time, in 1945, to face the return of Europeans, who had brought quite different agendas from their P.O.W. camps or exile, there was more elite solidarity than score-settling on the part of Southeast Asians. Killings were worst in the vacuum after the Japanese surrender where communities had been unusually polarized, as on racial lines in Malaya and Burma and class ones in Sumatra. The fact that the Europeans and some of their closest collaborators had been excluded, by flight or imprisonment, from the dramatic events of 1942–5, and were targets of the nationalist propaganda of those years, contributed further to their exclusion from the national communities as they were imagined after the war.

Initial hopes that Japan supported independence for Southeast Asians were abruptly and often violently crushed in 1942. As the Japanese strategic position worsened, however, concessions had to be made to at least match the cautious steps and promises of the colonial powers. In the Philippines a preparatory commission opted to replace Quezón's Commonwealth with the symbolism of the revolutionary Republic of 1898, the ageing Aguinaldo on hand to again raise its flag. José P. Laurel (1891–1959), Yale PhD and former Secretary of the Interior and Justice of the Supreme Court, known as a critic of the United States with sympathies for Japan, in October 1943 assumed the position of President of a nominally independent "Second Philippine Republic." It was a single-party state with a slogan of "one flag, one nation, one language [Tagalog]." As elsewhere, the politicians who had evacuated with the Americans fared worse in subsequent elections than those who had collaborated. Manuel Roxas (1892–1948), another prominent lawyer and legislator who served in the Laurel government, defeated Osmena in the Presidential election of 1946, and Laurel himself only narrowly lost an unusually flawed election in 1949.

In Burma the "30 Comrades" who had joined the Japanese invasion force and formed the Burma Independence Army (BIA) were initially given responsibility to organize civil government. These young activists proved too divisive and were replaced in mid-1942 by the established political elite. Ba Maw (1893–1977), a Bama Catholic with a French PhD on Buddhism, a lawyer gaining prominence by defending the firebrand Buddhist monk Hsaya San, and first premier of British Burma (1937–9), was one of the richly ambivalent figures prominent in this period of transition to independence. Although the most prominent Bama politician of the day, he was in prison at the Japanese invasion for having opposed the participation of Britain and Burma in the Pacific War. The Japanese released him to become Chief Administrator in August 1942, to chair its constituent assembly, and eventually become Prime Minister (with the old royal title *Adipadi*) in August 1943. Aung San, the 28-year-old Thakin and BIA leader, became his Defense Minister, while the BIA, 50,000 strong by then, became the Burma National Army (BNA or *Bama Tatmadaw*) and underwent extensive Japanese training. This nominally independent *Bama* was also a one-party state heavily controlled by Japan. Like the British-sponsored self-government that preceded it, *Bama* included only the Bama and Buddhist lowlands and coastal areas, granting autonomy to Shan rulers and the Karen state as had the British. Since the BIA was almost entirely ethnic Bama, whereas the British had trained Karen and other minority soldiers, Karen resistance to the BIA deteriorated into mutual village-burning and interethnic killings, leaving a lasting legacy of bitterness.

Ba Maw, President Laurel, and a Thai representative (Phibun pointedly did not attend) all flew to Tokyo in November 1943, along with Japanese clients in China, Manchukuo, and Indian National Army leader Bose, symbolizing the Greater East Asia Co-prosperity Sphere of independent states with Japan as "nucleus" (Figure 16.2). Army headquarters refused to add token representatives from Indonesia and Malaya, despite the propaganda setback this represented, having quietly annexed these areas to the Japanese Empire in May. In a muddled compromise between military hardliners and civilian and navy

Figure 16.2 The Greater East Asia Co-prosperity sphere leaders' conference in Tokyo, November 5–6, 1943. Participants left to right: Dr Ba Maw (Burma), Zhang Jinghui (Manchukuo), Wang Jingwei (China), Hideki Tōjō (Japan), Wan Waithayakon (Thailand), José P. Laurel (Philippines), Subhas Chandra Bose (India). Source: Wikipedia, http://en.wikipedia.org/wiki/Greater_East_Asia_Co-Prosperity_Sphere#mediaviewer/File:Greater_East_Asia_Conference.JPG.

leaders concerned with Japan's long-term standing in the islands, Sukarno, Hatta, and the Muslim leader Ki Bagus Hadikusumo were invited to tour Japan for two weeks immediately following the conference. Hatta believed the *Kenpeitai* (the dreaded military intelligence) had plans to eliminate or exile him in Japan, irritated at his insistence on Indonesian unity and independence, but that an award from the Emperor protected him. Nevertheless, the following year was very dark for the cooperating Indonesian nationalists, with nothing to show for their humiliation and the misery of their people. Only in September 1944 did an increasingly desperate Japanese government make a commitment to "independence in the future" for "the East Indies" – intended to include at least Java and Sumatra.

Sukarno's emotive rhetoric of anti-western unity and his relatively uncritical acceptance of their war aims were particularly valuable to the Japanese. Released from internal exile in Bengkulu, he headed a succession of organizations intended to unify Java in the Japanese cause. His justification for the many compromises he made was positioning himself as unrivalled popular leader and symbol of unity. "I addressed 50,000 at one meeting, 100,000 at another. Sukarno's face, not just his name, penetrated the Archipelago. I have the Japanese to thank for that" (Sukarno 1965, 179). Only Java was in fact allowed to see Sukarno's face until April 1945, when the navy (but not the Army in Sumatra) allowed him to visit three eastern cities. Indonesia had been divided between the 25th Army in Sumatra (initially joined to Malaya and administered from Singapore as Japan's "nuclear region"), the 16th in Java, and the navy in eastern Indonesia. Only Java was envisaged for Indonesian political participation, since the remaining islands and Malaya were the real objects of Japanese colonization. Yet the very lack of political concessions outside Java, and the ban on travel between the islands, had the paradoxical effect of making Java much more central to the transition to independence than it could have been under freer conditions. In Sumatra the 25th Army permitted no political/ propaganda bodies beyond the Residency level (roughly today's provinces) until forced by Tokyo to begin preparations for independence in March 1945. They did, however, from November 1944 permit the powerful symbols of an Indonesian future – the red-white flag and the anthem Indonesia Raya – while still banning contact with Java.

The preparations for Japanese-sponsored "independence," which would become the basis of the Republic proclaimed at the Japanese surrender, were almost exclusively made in Java. The expected Sumatran delegates were not permitted to attend the Body to Investigate Indonesian Independence that met in Jakarta from May 28 to July 17, 1945. The "1945 Constitution" it prepared was therefore little troubled by minority interests. Only two delegates, born outside Java, were recorded as preferring a federal system to Sukarno's vision of unity. The constitution was drafted by law professor Soepomo on "integralist" principles akin to fascism, and gave the executive President extensive powers to appoint and dismiss ministers and veto any legislation proposed by an ill-defined representative council. Sukarno answered a critic of this vagueness with the words, "What embodies the sovereignty of the people is the president, not the representative assembly" (Yamin 1954 I, 263). Liberal and socialist ideas were muffled by the Japanese military context of the meeting, and Sukarno's leadership was reinforced by the delegates' knowledge that he bore the greatest risks in the high-wire act between the Japanese and a populace increasingly embittered against them.

Only in the desperate last stage after the bomb on Hiroshima did the Japanese fly three delegates from Sumatra and two from Makassar to join an independence preparatory committee. This first met on August 16, the day after the Emperor's radio broadcast announcing the Japanese surrender. Sukarno, Hatta, and Leiden-trained lawyer Achmad Soebardjo (1896–1978), a crucial link with the Japanese navy representative in Jakarta, Admiral Maeda, had planned to get Japanese approval for an independence proclamation in time to present it to the preparatory committee meeting. But Sukarno and Hatta had been kidnapped by angry revolutionaries determined to have independence proclaimed on their own terms rather than as a gift of Japan. Admiral Maeda, with some of his aides close to the nationalists, helped defuse this crisis by bringing Sukarno, Hatta, and their youthful captors back to his house (the former British consulate) in Jakarta to hammer out a proclamation under his personal protection. Intense debate between "cooperating" and revolutionary nationalists on one side and Japanese army and navy figures on the other produced the needed compromise by dawn on August 17. The proclamation voiced no heroics or ideals. Sukarno and Hatta read out two terse sentences: "We the Indonesian people hereby declare Indonesia's independence. Matters concerning the transfer of power and other matters will be executed in an orderly manner and in the shortest possible time."

Alone of the Southeast Asian nationalists cooperating with the Japanese, Sukarno and Hatta could thereby transition uninterruptedly to post-war leadership as President and Vice-President of the Republic, with Soebardjo as initial Foreign Minister. Their advantage was the absence of "anti-fascist" alternatives, with no effective guerrilla movement resisting the Japanese. Monarchies generally survived the change, including those of Cambodia and Laos, "independent" under the Japanese since March (see Chapter 17). By contrast the "independent" Prime Ministers, José Laurel (in April 1945) and Ba Maw (August), fled to Japan as their power was undermined by local guer-rillas and Allied counter-attacks. In Malaya, Ibrahim Yaacob (1911–79) was the Malay radical chosen to head Japanese propaganda and military mobiliza-tion, but had no chance of imagining himself a national leader once the Japanese had handed Malaya's four northern states to Thailand. Chinese were the largest group (47.7%) of what remained as *Malai* under the Japanese, and Tokyo even considered in 1945 incorporating it into Japan's Chinese client state. In the desperate days of August, incorporation into Indonesia seemed the only viable choice for Japanese clients, however, especially after Java's inde-pendence investigation committee had voted for a "Greater Indonesia" includ-ing British and Portuguese-ruled parts of *Nusantara*. As the local advocate of this idea, Ibrahim Yaacob fled to Jakarta after the Japanese surrender, where he became a protégé of Sukarno and a member of the Indonesian Parliament.

The most striking difference between Japanese regimes and their predeces-sors in Southeast Asia was the former's provisional, emergency character, making mobilization for the final struggle take precedence over the stability and order of other colonial regimes. It had been a preoccupation of European colonial governments in the 1930s to deprive nationalist leaders of access to a mass base, and to keep religious leaders out of politics altogether. The Japanese, by contrast, favored mass rallies, public rituals, and the maximal use of the media for anti-western and pro-Japanese propaganda. Japanese training of local armies began in 1943, and became critical in Indonesia and Burma as the professional core of later national armies. Some 40,000 soldiers in Java and 30,000 in Sumatra underwent its stern discipline and emphasis on *seishin* (spirit, resonating with Indonesian *semangat*) as the key element of Asia's supe-riority over the West. The Japanese-trained young officers of the generation of later military dictators, Suharto in Indonesia and Ne Win in Burma, were less technically competent than their European-trained counterparts, often from Christian or other minorities, but they had absorbed essential elements of melodramatic public ritual on one hand and brutal control of dissidents on the other. Similar numbers of paramilitary auxiliaries were prepared to oppose the expected Allied counter-attacks, with even heavier doses of *seishin* and less discipline.

In Java, Muslim leaders were preferred for the most senior positions (*daid-ancho*, or battalion commander). Among these it was a Muhammadiyah schoolteacher, Sudirman (1912–50), who would be elected by his peers as Army Commander-in-Chief in November 1945. Muhammadiyah, Nahdatul

Ulama and other Muslim organizations were obliged to join a single Muslim propaganda organization under the name Masjumi. It also acquired a paramilitary wing, the *Hizbullah* (Army of God), some 50,000 strong in Java by the war's end, which would provide some of the most fanatic opponents of the Allied reoccupation, and problems for post-1950 Jakarta governments. In the Mekong delta the Japanese also encouraged the militarization of the anti-French Cao Dai syncretic religious movement, as a potential anti-Allied force.

The Japanese military model of national mobilization had some resonance everywhere, but its strongest legacies were in Indonesia and Burma, where those most influenced by it remained in government and formed the new national armies. The Japanese wartime neighborhood associations (*tonari gumi*, later known as *rukun tetangga* in Indonesia) were extended throughout the region as a key means of social control. A neighborhood of between ten and twenty households became the base unit for rationing resources, mobilizing manpower and crops, and for propaganda, civil defense, and crime control. After independence both Indonesian and Burmese military-dominated governments continued this system of obligatory labor for public projects, though dressing it as a harmonious national tradition of mutual assistance (*gotong royong* in Indonesian). Women were also mobilized, though without significant empowerment. Occupation authorities suppressed all women's (and other) organizations and established a single obligatory women's movement (*Fujinkai*), headed in each locality by the wives of the ranking government officials. This again had some influence on later authoritarian attempts to control and domesticate women nationally through such organizations as Indonesia's *Dharma Wanita* (Women's Duty) and Malaysia's *Kaum Ibu UMNO* (UMNO women's or mother's group).

Throughout the region, the last months of the Pacific War were a time of frenzied mobilization amidst increasing desperation of an impoverished and exploited population. Paramilitary and religious groups absorbed the anti-western propaganda, but were increasingly ready to turn their zeal equally against the Japanese or against their own cooperating elites through whom labor and rice exactions were mediated. Revolts against the Japanese gathered pace, not only in upland areas they never fully controlled but also among the favored military trainees given the most intense Japanese training. The youth generation most vigorously mobilized by Japanese trainers was increasingly alienated from the compromises of its seniors, and demanded action from whoever could lead.

1945 – THE REVOLUTIONARY MOMENT

The Emperor's August 15 broadcast of Japan's unexpected surrender threw a match into the revolutionary tinderbox of 1945. In the cities of Java/Sumatra, Indochina, and Malaya there had been little sign of Allied counter-attack, and the unexpectedness of the surrender left Japan's clients demoralized and its opponents off-guard. Manila and Rangoon (along with Balikpapan and Tarakan in Borneo) had by then already fallen to the Allies amidst massive

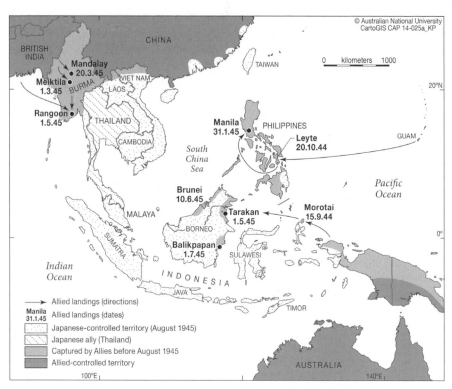

Map 16.2 Allied and Japanese control at the August 1945 surrender.

destruction, Japanese structures in the Philippines and Burma had already collapsed, and the scramble for leadership in the new order begun (Map 16.2). The two portentous declarations of independence occurred in Jakarta for Indonesia (as we have seen) on August 17, and in Hanoi for Viet Nam (*not* Indochina) on September 2 (Figure 16.3). Allied troops, caught unprepared, arrived to take control from the defeated Japanese only later. Some Nationalist Chinese troops, to whom northern Indochina had been assigned, reached Hanoi on September 9, while British troops reached Saigon on September 12, Jakarta on September 30, Medan and Padang (Sumatra) not until October 10, and Surabaya and Palembang on October 25. The French also managed to regain control of the Cambodian "independent" monarchy in October, arresting the leading Khmer nationalist allied with Japan, Viet Nam-born and Paris-educated Son Ngoc Thanh (1908–77), Prime Minister under King Norodom Sihanouk since early August. There was a power vacuum of varying length during which the Japanese troops on the ground were more likely to sympathize with assertions of independence than with returning colonials.

Communist parties were the obvious candidates to lead revolutions in 1945, though only Ho Chi Minh's ICP did so. The parties aligned with Moscow had long histories of revolutionary organization, they had been the most consistent and effective fighters against Japanese occupation, and the USSR, China, and other friends among the victorious Allies seemed likely to support them. Their

(a)

(b)

Figure 16.3 The independence proclamations of 1945: (a) Sukarno (reading) and Hatta proclaim Indonesia's independence in Admiral Maeda's house, Jakarta, August 17, 1945; (b) Ho Chi Minh declares independence in Hanoi, with armed guards prepared for trouble, September 2, 1945. Both scenes were much used and doctored as the proclamations became mythologized in subsequent years. Sources: a) Wikipedia, http://commons.wikimedia.org/wiki/File:Indonesia_declaration_of_independence_17_August_1945.jpg; b) David Marr.

international links, however, were a source of weakness as well as strength. Since Moscow had launched its common front against fascism in 1935, realizing that aggressive Nazi Germany and militarist Japan were more dangerous to the USSR than the colonial powers, communist parties in Asia had become more moderate but lost the support of militant nationalists. Sino-Southeast Asian communists were strengthened in their struggle to support China against

Japan, but some of the Indonesians and Vietnamese who had devoured Marxism as a fast route to revolution shifted their support to anti-Moscow Trotskyists or national communists like Tan Malaka. The Nazi-Soviet non-aggression pact of 1939 had reversed this Moscow line and created lasting distrust of it among nationalists with European experience, like Hatta and Ba Maw. Finally, the German invasion of Russia in June 1941 reversed the line again, and encouraged communists everywhere to engage in anti-fascist united fronts.

In their last months the British, Dutch, and American authorities had released communists, and other convinced anti-fascists like Hatta and Sjahrir, from prison, and discussed with them strategies of resistance. In Surabaya a Dutch intelligence official entrusted lawyer, socialist (later acknowledging himself a covert communist), and Christian convert Amir Sjarifuddin (1907–48) with 25,000 guilders to organize underground resistance. Amir was seized by the Kenpeitai in 1943 and would have been swiftly executed but for Sukarno's intervention, but after the surrender he was firmly "anti-fascist" and thus accepting of the Allied return. In Malaya the war transformed the Chinese-Malayan Left from the greatest threat to the British into their most promising ally. Both communist and KMT Chinese were legalized and mobilized in the defense of Malaya, while pro-Japanese Malay supporters of Ibrahim Yaacob were arrested. British intelligence gave communist cadres some military training, arms, and radios so as to sustain a guerrilla resistance from Malaya's abundant jungles throughout the war, under the structure of the Malayan People's Anti-Japanese Army (MPAJA).

This overwhelmingly Chinese force, supplied in 1944–5 by British air drops, succeeded in killing at least 600 Japanese soldiers (by Japanese count) and 2,000 predominately Malay policemen. At the Japanese surrender it moved to take control of all centers outside the main cities, executing a number of Malay officials and policemen as enemy collaborators. The Chinese-Malay racial tension these events produced, obstructing MPAJA contacts with elite Malays, was one of the factors that inhibited the Malayan Communist Party (MCP) from declaring Malayan independence in 1945. Through the crucial months of power vacuum they were still treating the British as their allies and the Malay establishment as part of the fascist enemy, joining victory parades in London and Singapore and receiving British medals. Finally, their leader Lai Teck (1901–47) appears to have been a triple agent, working ingeniously with British and Japanese intelligence. Only in March 1947 was he exposed and executed by the party, and replaced by Chin Peng (born Ong Boon Hua, 1924–2013), who would remain its Secretary-General virtually until death. Relations with the British worsened as the MCP demanded independence, opposed the Federation of Malaya constitutional proposals, and launched a wave of labor strikes. Between March and June 1948 the Party shifted to a strategy of armed struggle, which conformed to the new Soviet "two-camp" doctrine that communist parties must lead progressive forces in confrontation with capitalism and imperialism. The MCP fought a long insurgent war from the Malayan jungles and bases among Chinese rural communities, but it was too late for them to capture the chaotic nationalist moment. The British and their aristocratic Malay partners were already established in government, with enough wealthy Chinese support to continue the plural society. The booming rubber and tin industries were too important for Britain to surrender lightly. Malaya became one of the hottest fronts of the Cold War, but by the time sovereignty was transferred to an independent Federation of Malaya in 1957, the communist threat was contained to a few hundred jungle guerrillas.

Elsewhere, too, the communists emerged from the war taking a firmer anti-fascist than anti-colonial line, and thereby lost the chance to use their anti-Japanese credentials to lead a broader nationalist armed struggle, as in Viet Nam or China. The Hukbalahap communist front in the Philippines had taken a leading part in the anti-Japanese resistance, but entered democratic politics when the Americans returned. Two of the communist leaders, Luis Taruc and Jesus Lava, were elected to the first national congress in 1946. When their election was disallowed on shaky grounds by the establishment, they prepared for armed insurrection in their heartland among the Pampanga peasants of central Luzon. The exceptionally unequal distribution of land, wealth, and power in the Philippines gave them strong support among the landless majority. By 1948, when both were outlawed, the revived Hukbalahap militia was thought to have thousands of members, and the communist front organization, National Peasants' Union, hundreds of thousands. Their rebellion was only gradually curbed through the determination of Ramon Magsaysay (1907–57), also a successful anti-Japanese guerrilla leader with some understanding of the peasant discontents behind their rebellion, as Secretary of Defense from 1951 and President from December 1953.

The Burmese Communist Party under Thakin Soe (1906–89) also made great gains from its anti-fascist stance throughout the war. As the young Thakins who had initially welcomed the Japanese grew disillusioned and turned to opposition, the communists were in a position to guide a common resistance front. Aung San, while still Defense Minister in the pro-Japanese government, had begun plans to revolt at the end of 1943, sending some of his key men to India to contact the British. In 1944 he briefly joined the communist party (before quarreling with Thakin Soe), and federated his political followers into a communist-led front organization, the Anti-Fascist People's Freedom League (AFPFL). Although Aung San's BNA was the strongest fighting force in this front, acknowledged as a partner by the British forces which took Rangoon on May 3, 1945, it was the AFPFL structure which began taking over government in Burma in the wake of the Japanese retreat and eventual surrender.

The communists weakened their central position in the AFPFL by a split in March 1946, when Thakin Soe quarreled with more moderate communists returning from India, and left to form his own insurgent "Red Flag" Communist Party. The mainstream Burmese Party remained loyal to the Soviet common front line, supporting the government even when expelled from the AFPFL in November 1946. The Party moved to armed struggle only in March 1948 as the Soviet line changed, denouncing the AFPFL "bourgeois nationalists" and the "sham independence" they had achieved. The embattled prime minister at the time believed that "the Communists, by placing their faith in Stalin [and the two-camp doctrine] forfeited … the almost certain prospect of winning power from the AFPFL in the next … election" (Nu 1975, 193). The rest of

Figure 16.4 Aung San and family in 1947, shortly before his assassination. The later illness and death of his widow Daw Khin Kyi (left) in 1989 brought daughter Suu Kyi (here center as a two-year-old) back from Oxford to Rangoon and a meteoric but unexpected political career. Source: © Kyodo News/AP/Press Association.

the Marxist-inclined AFPFL managed to retain a sufficiently unified stance toward immediate independence outside the British Commonwealth to give the British no choice but to accept Aung San's demand for a clear majority in the Executive Council in September 1946. Aung San and several colleagues were assassinated during a cabinet session of July 18, 1947, removing the nearest Burma had to a unifying symbolic figure (Figure 16.4). Nevertheless, sovereignty was swiftly transferred by the British, in January 1948, to a government headed by Aung San's AFPFL deputy, (Thakin) U Nu.

Having had its revolutionary break with the past in 1932, Thailand alone was in no revolutionary mood at the Japanese surrender. Leftist intellectual Pridi Banomyong (Figure 16.5) had made contacts with the British since early 1944 even from within Phibun's government, putting himself at the head of an alternative pro-Allied government. In July 1944 Phibun was ousted by the Assembly in favor of one of his ministers, civilian Khuang Aphaiwong, and Pridi became sole regent for the absent king. Khuang resigned at the Japanese surrender, and Pridi invited Seni Pramoj (1905–97), pre-war ambassador to the United States and leader of the Free Thai movement there, to become Prime Minister. It was the British Air Force that represented the Allies in Bangkok from September 9, but Seni's American contacts were critical in moderating British demands for reparations – notably in the form of rice exports to feed its starving subjects in Malaya, Borneo, and Rangoon. Pridi had

Figure 16.5 Pridi Banomyong as Thai Prime Minister in 1946. Source: AFP/Getty Images.

already agreed to return the British territories gained from Japan. Seni readily dismantled the worst authoritarian excesses of Phibun, notably in its repression of Muslim, Christian, and Chinese minorities, and legalized the very weak communist party in deference to the USSR. Giving up the coveted gains from France was more difficult. Bangkok reluctantly permitted their reoccupation by France in December 1946, though the official acceptance of this loss by the National Assembly took two more years. Although Pridi was sympathetic to the revolutionary cause in Indochina and elsewhere, communism as such remained in Thailand an almost exclusively Chinese affair, looking for guidance to the Chinese rather than the Soviet party.

Only in Indochina did a communist party take the lead in declaring and defending independence, ignoring the then Soviet line that had inhibited others. The revolutionaries in the former French territories had the unique advantage of borders with a sympathetic China and a temporarily (1945–7) sympathetic Thailand, but the disadvantage of a colonial power which had not yet made its adjustment to a post-war world of independent nation-states.

Smarting from humiliations in Europe, France had announced its intention to reconstitute an Indochinese Federation within the French Union. But by September 1945, when British and French troops began to arrive, Ho Chi Minh had already proclaimed Viet Nam's independence on September 2 to an enthusiastic populace, and his Vietminh controlled most of Tongking, with networks throughout Indochina. Ho showed great agility in putting together his fronts, and disguising the role in them of the disciplined Indochinese Communist Party. The party was even dissolved in November 1945 in favor of a Marxist study group, though the army remained under the firm control of communist intellectual Vo Nguyen Giap (1911–2013).

The Vietminh had been formed by Ho in southern China in 1941 as a front for the independence of Viet Nam, but could achieve little inside the country until late 1944. Giap then led about 40 men across the border to begin creating liberated zones and capturing arms and men from the French. They grew much stronger after the Japanese took over from the French in March 1945, and were supplied and trained against the Japanese by the US military. The KMT authorities in Guangxi Province allowed Ho to establish a multi-party Vietnamese provisional government to further weaken the Japanese, even though their sympathies were with the non-communist nationalists. Ho continued the work of coalition-building from Giap's guerrilla zone. At the Japanese surrender he moved much more quickly than did the Chinese authorities to set up a government. Giap's troops, only a few hundred strong, reached Hanoi on August 28, enabling Ho to declare the independence of the Democratic Republic of Viet Nam (DRV) on September 2. This was followed by a welter of decrees and mobilizations designed to give substance to a bold new republic with broad appeal. Bao Dai had already agreed to transfer his authority as "independent" Emperor under Japan to Ho's provisional government, in return for a role as Supreme Advisor. A cabinet was announced with a number of non-communist ministers, and Ho was able to capture the euphoria of the moment.

Problems arose with the arrival of Chinese troops in the north, but more so when British troops reached Saigon and quickly moved to transfer authority to French representatives. The Chinese occupied major buildings and looted many resources, but allowed the DRV to function and the Vietminh to build up its forces, while favoring the nationalist group whenever possible. In the chaotic south, however, the Vietminh was less well placed than a number of other radical forces, trained by either French or Japanese, less willing to compromise with the Allies than the communists in the north. Refusing to acknowledge the DRV committee in Saigon, British General Gracey instead rearmed French troops imprisoned by the Japanese, who inflamed resentment when they aggressively took control of key buildings in the spirit of the old regime. Undisciplined Vietnamese countered with a reign of terror on September 24, killing over a hundred French civilians. This convinced doubters in Paris, London, and Saigon that the Allies had to regain control of the city by force, using Japanese soldiers to do so.

The French took control of the strategic core of the former colony of Cochin-China within the next few months. The DRV in the north seemed responsible and moderate by comparison with contending nationalists in the south, and reached agreement with France on March 6 that French troops could return to Haiphong and Hanoi in place of the Chinese, while France would recognize the DRV as "a free state … forming part of the Indochinese federation and the French Union." All Ho's skill could not overcome the multiplying conflicts on the ground, however. After fierce fighting in Haiphong and Hanoi the Vietminh withdrew from the cities in November 1946 and began its guerrilla strategy. The war with France would last until 1954, when as a result of multilateral talks in Geneva with China playing a moderating role, France agreed to evacuate the north and the Vietminh the south. Common elections were agreed to be the route to eventual reunification, but were never held. Viet Nam reached formal independence as two rival countries, the communist-led DRV ruling north of the 17th parallel and an essentially anticommunist Republic of Viet Nam to its south. The events of 1945–6, however, had been critical in establishing Ho Chi Minh and his DRV as the most plausible embodiments of Vietnamese nationalism.

Communist party structures were weak in Indonesia since the suppression of 1926–7, though Marxist ideas were widespread. The best-known "antifascist" politician was Amir Sjarifuddin, still in a Japanese prison when he was named Minister of Information in the first cabinet of the Indonesian Republic on September 4, in an attempt to balance its otherwise Japanesecooperator elite composition. The leaders most attractive to the impatient mood of mobilized youth in the capital were two contrasting Minangkabaus. Sutan Sjahrir, Hatta's pre-war socialist colleague, had agreed with Hatta to play a non-cooperator role during the Occupation and maintain contacts with dissidents. He became central in August as mediator between revolutionary youth and the older Japanese protégés. National communist Tan Malaka had the most developed strategy for revolution, having written "Towards the Indonesian Republic" (in Dutch, 1925), and "Mass Action" (in Indonesian, c.1926), and established a Partai Republik Indonesia (PARI) in exile. His experience in Russia, China (especially), and the Philippines was comparable with Ho Chi Minh's, and he returned to Indonesia in 1942 to plan revolution, but remained in hiding until the Japanese surrender. He would have been the most plausible "revolutionary President," but lacked Ho's pragmatic approach to the incoming Allies. Critically, Sukarno demonstrated in August and September that he was indispensable as a recognizable figure for a diverse and desperate population, and the only one capable of controlling the passions aroused.

The Republic managed its own internal transition to a form that might be acceptable to the British who landed in Jakarta on September 30, amid Dutch calls for Sukarno to be tried as a war criminal. Sukarno took a back seat in the following weeks, while Vice-President Hatta issued a number of decrees establishing a parliamentary system, in which transitional authority would be largely in the hands of the parliament's "working committee" hand-picked by Sjahrir and Amir. Sjahrir became Prime Minister and Foreign Minister on November 14, responsible to parliament rather than the President, and Amir Sjarifuddin occupied the other key ministries of Defense and Interior. A multi-party system replaced Sukarno's attempt to build a single state party (also favored by Tan Malaka), largely as a pragmatic means to channel the energies of armed groups of young pro- and anti-Japanese nationalists, Muslims, and communists. Amir's and Sjahrir's diverse supporters united in a pro-government Socialist Party, which together with the Communist Party led by returning exiles was the most reliable support of the government for the next two years. Amir, the government's most persuasive and popular asset, sought to build a national army responsible to the government. It struggled to curb the violent demands of armed groups for "popular sovereignty" (*kedaulatan rakyat*), at the expense of power-holders, traditional rulers, village heads, Chinese, and anybody who could be accused of partiality to the Dutch. Since General Sudirman and the Japanese-trained backbone of the military resented his accusations of fascist collaboration, however, the most reliably pro-government military leaders were Amir's Dutch-trained fellow-Batak Colonels, T.B. Simatupang, who became Chief of Staff, and A.H. Nasution (1918–2000), commander of the elite Siliwangi Division in West Java.

The Sjahrir/Amir cabinets' negotiations with the Dutch paralleled those of Ho with the French, both parties agreeing under some British and American pressure to a federal structure for Indonesia in which the Republic would be one unit covering most of Java and Sumatra. When the Dutch attacked the most profitable parts of those two islands in July 1947, Australia's Labor government referred the matter to the United Nations, leading to the United States having a vital role through the UN in the eventual compromises of 1949. This diplomacy was increasingly unpopular internally, however, with Tan Malaka and other opponents of the Socialists demanding "100 percent freedom." Sjahrir was forced to resign when even the Leftists withdrew their support, and Amir Sjarifuddin, who replaced him in July 1947, was in turn forced to resign in January 1948. The crisis enabled Sukarno to appoint a "Presidential cabinet" with Hatta as Prime Minister and more conservative Masjumi support, and the Marxists moved into increasingly radical opposition. Peasants and workers were mobilized to turn a political revolution into a socio-economic one, with a growing wave of strikes and unilateral land distributions to poor peasants. This was already polarizing Java dangerously along the cleavage which would dominate the next two decades, pitting poor peasants of syncretic Javanist beliefs against landholders linked with Islamic networks. The return of Musso from Moscow in August 1948 brought Soviet endorsement of a new line whereby "a single party of the working class" must lead the revolution from below, drawing a sharp line against "bourgeois" nationalists. Amir Sjarifuddin and other prominent leaders of the Socialist and Labor Parties, demoralized and radicalized by opposition, fell into line by joining the PKI. This was now led by Musso, who invited other parties to join a communist-led national front openly modeled on the way the Czech communists had come to power the previous February. Hatta, the Muslims, and much of the Japanese-trained army officer corps were not impressed.

Military rivalries provoked a showdown, as government forces led by Nasution's Siliwangi Division traded arrests, killings, and denunciations with the forces loyal to Amir Sjarifuddin. After the Siliwangi took control of turbulent Surakarta, pro-PKI forces took over Madiun (East Java) on September 18, 1948, declaring that a National Front government had begun there. Sukarno forced the issue in a blistering attack asking Indonesians to choose between himself and Musso. Musso obliged next day by denouncing Sukarno and Hatta as "slaves of Japan and America," former *romusha*-dealers and Quislings. The hard Soviet line, borne by the communist least aware of Indonesian realities, thereby sealed the PKI's fate, as even many of its own soldiers were disinclined to fight explicitly against Sukarno and Hatta. The Siliwangi Division and its allies moved with a purposefulness never shown against the Dutch. Some 35,000 communist supporters were arrested, and the leaders executed or hunted down and shot, including Amir Sjarifuddin and Musso. The bloodletting in Javanese villages embittered the growing cleavage between Muslim and Javanist, rich and poor. The PKI survived in Sumatra and the Dutch-occupied zones, but was set back by several years in its Javanese heartland. Nevertheless, in the 1950s it would again become Indonesia's largest and most disciplined party, under the youthful leaders first advanced by Musso, D.N. Aidit (1923–65), Njoto, and M.H. Lukman.

The Dutch were planning a final military attack on the Republic in late 1948, expecting to find it mired in internal conflict and confusion sure to aid an eventual communist victory. Instead, when the second Dutch offensive against the Republic came on December 19, 1948, they appeared to be attacking and imprisoning a leadership with the most effective anti-communist credentials in Asia. Sukarno, Hatta, and their cabinet chose to be arrested by the Dutch rather than chance their survival among more heroic but quarrelsome Republican forces, which sustained an effective guerrilla struggle in Java and parts of Sumatra. Washington, impressed at the Sukarno-Hatta success in contrast to communist advances in China, Indochina, and Malaya, pressured the Netherlands to restore the previous status quo, returning the Republican leadership to its capital in Yogyakarta. This diplomatic victory through the United Nations secured anti-communist leadership of the eventual Indonesian government, to which sovereignty was transferred by the Dutch on January 1, 1950. One revolutionary process had lurched first left, and then right.

INDEPENDENCE – REVOLUTIONARY OR NEGOTIATED?

Indonesia and Viet Nam emerged from the turbulent 1940s with a political leadership that was revolutionary, in the sense of declaring a clean break with the past for which it was prepared to fight. When Sukarno and Hatta became President and Vice-President of the Indonesian Republic, and Ho Chi Minh of the DRV, their legitimacy was based not on links with the past, but on having struggled successfully for a new beginning. The Burmese group of young Thakins transformed into the AFPFL, led by Aung San, U Nu, and Ne Win, had not declared their independence until it was transferred by Britain in 1947, but having fought militarily against the British in 1941–2, and then against the Japanese in 1944–5, they had also broken violently with the legitimacy of the past. All three leaderships staked their claim to represent "the people" on the charismatic popularity needed to control an armed and insurgent population, roughly confirmed in ad hoc elections (Republican Java-Sumatra and Viet Nam in 1945–6, Burma in 1947), and on a strong vision of a united future that could justify the sacrifices of struggle. This contrasts markedly with Malaya, British Borneo, and the Philippines, where the pre-war legal order was effectively re-established, military units mobilized under the Japanese were disarmed and discredited, and the structure of independence was negotiated between the varied stakeholders. In Thailand, too, the constitutional structures in place since the 1930s were liberalized but not overturned, so that stability was quickly restored. Investors focused on these three countries during the globally prosperous 1950s, and their economies rapidly surpassed pre-war levels (Table 16.1 above).

Of course the colonial powers had no intention of abandoning the diversity of clients they had built up in Indochina, Indonesia, and Burma to the victors of the revolutionary process. They sought to transfer power to federal structures in which minority interests and investors were safeguarded through elaborate constitutional provisions. In Indochina, we noted, the French sought to contain the revolutionary Viet Nam of the Vietminh within an Indochina Federation inside the French Union. Dutch strategist H.J. van Mook (1894–1965), faced with much greater ethno-linguistic diversity, developed a more complex plan to devolve authority to large federal units (already foreshadowed in 1938) of Sumatra, Borneo, and "the Great East," to balance and contain Java where the Republic was deemed strongest. In reality Sumatrans were almost equally committed to the idea of unity with Yogyakarta, even if their revolutions had been autonomous affairs. Only the State of East Sumatra (NST), erected in the rich plantation area around Medan conquered by Dutch forces in 1947, had much popular support among the victims of an unusually violent "social revolution" against the sultans in March 1946. In most of Borneo and Sulawesi, pro-Republican sentiment was strong among the majority Muslim population, and had to be suppressed with unusual violence by colonial troops in South Sulawesi. The only effective state was erected in the Great East at a conference of 70 delegates elected by regional (and generally aristocratic) councils or appointed by the Dutch, in December 1946. It adopted the name "State of East Indonesia," the Indonesian language, and "Indonesia Raya" anthem under pressure from below, and exchanged missions with the Yogyakarta government in 1948. Its government resigned in protest at the Dutch military action of December 1948 against the Republic, as did the federal state erected in Dutch-controlled West Java, named Pasundan in the hope of mobilizing the ethnic pride of the Sundanese-speaking third of Java.

In the negotiations leading to the transfer of sovereignty on December 27, 1949, to a Federal Indonesian Republic (RIS) with a democratic and federal constitution, the six states and assorted federations and "neo-lands" of Dutch-controlled territory (Map 16.3) showed their strong commitment to the idea

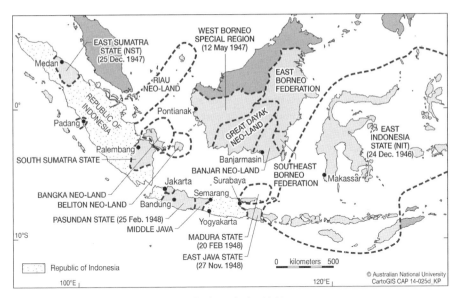

Map 16.3 Federal and Republican Indonesia in 1948.

of Indonesia. They accepted the Republic's flag, anthem, and language, and before the transfer they also accepted Sukarno as non-executive President of the federal Republic, with the right to appoint its Prime Minister; he named Hatta. They even fought successfully against a constitutional provision to allow any state the right to secede, and unsuccessfully for the inclusion of Dutch New Guinea in the RIS. The political leadership in the federal areas was strongly committed, however, to constitutional guarantees of a loose federation, with an upper chamber representing its constituting states equally. In the first six months these hopes were dashed, as one federal state after another imploded. The taint of being Dutch "puppets" (however unfair) prevented serious resistance to the clamor for total identification with the unitary republic of Sukarno and Hatta. Militarily the federal states had no way to protect themselves against armed bands claiming the mantle of unitarism or Islam except by calling on either the former colonial soldiers or units who held the moral high ground of having fought for independence. Attempts to use colonial soldiers quickly backfired in allegations of treachery. The West Java state (Pasundan) and the West Kalimantan state headed by Pontianak Sultan Hamid II were both compromised by a military coup attempt in Bandung in late January. The East Indonesian NIT, representing the remoter islands with most to lose from unitarism, was the last to fall, as a military attempt by ex-colonial soldiers to stop the arrival of Yogyakarta troops backfired in April 1950. This again gave the unitarists the moral high ground, the NIT unraveled, and its leading Christian figure, conservative Ambonese Dr Soumokil, fled to Ambon with many ex-colonial soldiers to declare independence for the Republic of South Maluku (RMS). All the federal units were dissolved into the unitary Republic in time for the fifth anniversary of the independence proclamation of August 17, 1945, confirming that moment, rather than the negotiations of 1949, as the mythic foundation of the nation-state. The world's most ambitious experiment in unitary government over hundreds of ethno-linguistic groups had begun.

In tackling this challenge, however, Indonesia (and the Philippines) had an advantage over the three big Mainland states in having no "core" ethnic-ity tending to confuse its own identity and interests with those of the plural nation-state. Javanese were less than half of Indonesians, and their name and language had not become the nation's. Bama were not only two thirds of the Burma population, but also overwhelmingly dominated the nationalist movement represented by the Thakins, the BIA and the AFPFL, which had effectively forced the British to transfer power. Initially it appeared that the Shan, Chin, and Kachin "scheduled areas" of the north and east would be content to defer to nationalist Rangoon as they had to British Rangoon in return for retaining traditional autonomies. The office of President rotated among ethnicities in the 1950s, the first three being Shan, Bama, and Karen. In the first chaotic years of independence when it appeared the government might fall to communist and Karen dissidents, U Nu attributed its survival partly to the consistent support of the Shan, Chin, Kachin, and Kayah states and their military forces. The overwhelming demographic and symbolic primacy of the Bama area meant this could never be true federalism, how-ever, and it never reassured the Karen, whose anxieties could not be allayed within the small Karenni state. Most Karen villages were scattered through Lower Burma, where many had suffered violence from Bama nationalism in 1942. In effect Britain transferred sovereignty in January 1948 with Karen demands unsatisfied, but referred to a commission to define the size and status of a Karen state on the Thai border and a possible Karen-Mon state in Tenasserim. One British historian defines Britain's departure as a story of "betrayal, incompetence and ignominy," though conceding that the impa-tient AFPFL, demanding immediate independence and always fearful of being outflanked by the communists, gave them little alternative (Christie 1996, 79). The strongest Karen card after the withdrawal of the British was their central role in the infant Burmese national army, but in the growing tension of 1948 between the separatist-inclined Karen National Union and the various Bama armed militants, Karen soldiers began defecting. The Karen rebellion proper began in January 1949, and has proved the most intractable of Burma's many problems.

Burma thus inherited the worst of both worlds. Revolution against British and Japanese had undermined and discredited the legality of the *ancien régime* and mobilized an insurgent armed population with a diversity of goals; but the assassination of Aung San had removed the figure capable of inheriting the supernatural charisma of a successful break with the past. Its structure was federal, but the very low participation of non-Bama in the anti-British struggle confirmed the fear of Karen and Shan that they would never gain true sym-bolic or practical equality with Bama in the state. In particular, the army, led from 1949 by Ne Win, one of the "30 Thakins" who had traveled to Japan, was reconstructed as a predominately Bama institution, purged of the Karen officers, and strongly committed to a unitary vision.

The euphoria of the revolutionary moment in Viet Nam, Indonesia, and Burma particularly affected the young. "Everywhere it was young people who took the initiative, speaking directly, ignoring taboos, refusing to worry about personal safety, exuding confidence. Alongside the iconoclasm and bravado there was a longing ... to find new order ... Youthful heroics and the wish for order came together in the rush to join militia units, where inventiveness and bravado counted for more than social origin, schooling, or wealth" (Marr 2013, 2–3). Arrogant European claims to technical superiority, and Japanese to spiritual superiority, seemed joyfully overturned by the ability of Southeast Asians to do the job themselves, however creatively improvised. The "1945 generation" who experienced these things would never forget the mood, nor imagine sacrificing it for the pedestrian pleasures of young Malaysians or Filipinos, who in turn envied them their "real" revolutions. In the long term, moreover, the very destructiveness of the revolutionary process, and the ability of the winners to impose a single view of heroic national history in schools, would create the most well-defined national moral communities (Chapter 18).

Malaya/Malaysia and Singapore form the non-revolutionary control case where the pre-war legal order was restored, and the shape of independence only gradually negotiated between the colonial power and the varied stakeholders. The process was unheroically peaceful, except on the side of the defeated communist insurgency, leaving many Malaysians feeling that their nationhood was somehow incomplete. In the long term, moreover, the elaborate compromises made between the different states (especially different in Borneo) and the center, and between Malays, Chinese, Indians, and indigenous Borneans, have failed to produce a single idea of the nation. Sukarno's relentless insistence that "There is no *bangsa* [race or nation] Kalimantan, there is no *bangsa* Minangkabau, there is no *bangsa* Java, Bali, Lombok, Sulawesi or any such. We are all *bangsa* Indonesia" (Sukarno, 1949, cited Omar 1993, 209) eventually succeeded, though least satisfactorily with those of Chinese, Eurasian, or Papuan descent. Dr Mahathir's tentative 1991 project to work toward a single "*bangsa* Malaysia" notably failed. As in France as compared with Britain, the outcome of revolution was not so much liberty, equality, and fraternity as a unitary sense of the nation.

The debit side of the revolutionary ledger is, however, much longer. Economically, Malaysia and Singapore parted company with Indonesia only after 1945, and began their ascent toward First World, or at least middle-income, status. Indonesia remained mired in poverty until the 1980s, and Burma, and Indochina still longer. As infrastructure deteriorated in Indonesia and Burma, Singapore and Penang became more essential entrepôts than they had ever been, and Indonesia even lost control over much of its internal maritime communications. The rule of law, a competent bureaucracy, and stable civilian governments responsible to parliaments survived in Malaysia/Singapore, whereas military rule, corruption, and arbitrary dictatorship became common in the post-revolutionary countries. Above all, the habit of political violence that began in the revolution could not readily be undone. Not only the external fight against colonial or Cold War interventions, but above all the internal contests for power, caused hundreds of thousands of casualties in the post-revolutionary countries over the period 1945–80. The revolutionary assertion of a single nationhood did not end the struggles, but rather increased their intensity by implying a single satisfactory outcome.

[17] *The Military, Monarchy, and Marx: The Authoritarian Turn, 1950–1998*

T HE first generation of revolutionary nationalists had more difficulty occupying the legal-bureaucratic space of the colonial states than the
charismatic space in people's hearts. The first symbolic leaders of the
upheavals that delivered proudly independent and assertive states – Aung
San, Ho Chi Minh, Sihanouk, Sukarno, Phibun Songkhram, Tunku Abdul
Rahman – achieved an almost supernatural aura from their identification
with racial/national liberation, though some of their henchmen also spilled
considerable blood to achieve that result. Their successors invariably
imposed more of an iron hand; particularly so in the post-revolutionary
regimes that enforced a single definition of the fruits of revolution. The shift
to military rule in the 1960s was frequently justified in terms the Japanese
military had taught, that liberal democracy was inherently weak, divisive,
and unsuited to Asia, and that unity against foreign threats was the supreme
goal. Where monarchy made a kind of comeback it was seen sometimes as
revalidating endangered identities, sometimes as a gentler means than the
military one of maintaining the legitimacy and charisma of the fragile new
state. Even as democracy returned after the Cold War, the Thai and Brunei
monarchies, and communist parties in Viet Nam and Laos, provided surprisingly enduring bulwarks for those who feared its rise.

Democracy's Brief Springtime

The young idealists who powered the revolutionary tide of the late 1940s had
little doubt that popular sovereignty and democracy were the goal and destiny
of the vast new nation-states they sought to create. Fascist ideas of single-party
integralism had been popular earlier, but were discredited by the defeat of

A History of Southeast Asia: Critical Crossroads, First Edition. Anthony Reid.
© 2015 Anthony Reid. Published 2015 by John Wiley & Sons, Ltd.

Japan and the other Axis powers. Even amidst the desperate if euphoric first months when the survival of the newly proclaimed states was in grave doubt, Republican Indonesia, Viet Nam, and Burma held makeshift elections. For all its shortcomings, David Marr (2013, 52) points out that the Vietminh effort "proved to be the fairest election the DRV/SRV has experienced to the present day."

In post-revolutionary Burma and Indonesia, the extraordinary diversity of armed groups and competing visions – religious, Marxist, ethnic – made democracy both necessary and unworkable. As Hatta pointed out in attempting to deal with the problem, "National Revolution stimulates and embraces elements that cannot distinguish means from ends, reality from an ideal, who believe that every change has to be by revolution" (Hatta 1954 IV, 171). Democracy was seen as the only way to incorporate contradictory visions within a single state, and to establish which had electoral strength. But convincing those with armed followings to wait for and then abide by the results of elections was a tall order. Those who had grasped the executive authority from the departing colonials proved unwilling to surrender it to the ballot box. The Vietminh allowed no challenge to its leadership of the revolution, and even the more plural and parliamentary AFPFL only prevailed in its 1956 election by using the military to engineer the right vote.

Indonesia was the only Southeast Asian country to make a habit of changing governments in response to parliamentary shifts. There the 1950 negotiated constitution had continued the de facto separation of the revolutionary period between the presidency (Sukarno and Hatta) and an executive cabinet responsible to parliament. Prime Ministers and their cabinets changed, if anything too frequently, with ten cabinets under five Prime Ministers of the embattled Republic of 1945–9, and ten more under nine Prime Ministers in the remainder of the parliamentary democracy period to 1959. With Sukarno (Java-Bali), and Hatta (Minangkabau), until his resignation in despair in 1956, remaining as its symbolic embodiments, the nation appeared strengthened rather than disrupted by these changes of cabinet. The first (and last until the new century) fully democratic elections in 1955 drew 39 million enthusiastic Indonesians to the polls, a turnout of 92%. The nationalist party (PNI, 22% of votes) and Islamic reformists (Masjumi, 21%) did well as expected, but socialists and others were destroyed, while votes from the Javanese rural heartland enabled two newcomers to join what became the "big four" parties – the NU traditionalist Muslims (18%) and the communist PKI (16%). It had been hoped that the election would somehow deliver on the high but contradictory expectations that independence had brought. It appeared to do the opposite, increasing the dismay of the political elite at the rise of the non-elite NU and PKI, and the polarization between the increasingly vociferous PKI, indulged by the President, and anti-communist elements such as Masjumi and the military.

The dissident armed groups did not wait to test their strength at elections. Communist and Karen rebels made survival difficult for the AFPFL Burma government, and did not participate in the 1950, 1956, and 1960 elections. In Indonesia the communists after their 1948 disaster took a legal and parliamentary path, but those who believed their revolutionary struggle had been for an Islamic, or a loosely federal, state declined to surrender their arms to a centralized secular order. The Ambonese separatism of the South Maluku Republic was relatively quickly if bloodily suppressed in 1950, but the Islamic rebellions were more tenacious, since militants were already hardened to a guerrilla existence in Dutch-occupied areas. S.M. Kartosuwirjo (1905–62) had established the Darul Islam (DI) guerrilla force in West Java in 1948, and in August 1949 declared a separate Islamic State – Negara Islam Indonesia. In January 1952 this was joined by the charismatic South Sulawesi guerrilla leader Kahar Muzakar (1921–65), and in 1953 by the now-disgruntled leader of Aceh's exemplary resistance to the Dutch in 1945–9, Mohammad Daud Beureu'eh (1899–1987). The parliamentary governments, fortunate in avoiding Burma's problem of long land borders to sustain its rebels, countered all these movements comparatively successfully through a mixture of negotiation and brutal repression by its increasingly effective army.

Malaya (1955) and Singapore (1955 and 1959) established through elections under colonial auspices the leadership that would inherit the charisma coming with independence – Kedah prince Tunku Abdul Rahman (1903–90) and Cambridge-trained lawyer Lee Kuan Yew (b.1923), who led Malaya/ Malaysia until 1970 and Singapore until 1990, respectively. Neither country has abolished parliament and regular elections since, though ensuring against changes of government through control of the media, juggling the voting system, and either co-opting opponents or crushing them judicially. In the mid-1950s Thailand had a brief experiment with democracy, a freer press, and an election in 1957, though quickly reversed by another military coup. Even in embattled Indochina the 1950s were the time of democratic optimism. The 1954 Geneva agreements specified that the two Vietnamese states (together), Cambodia, and Laos would have elections to determine all the disputed issues. South Viet Nam declined to take part in the joint election, but did hold its own parliamentary election in 1955 without any significant parties being allowed to organize. Laos and Cambodia had already had French-supervised elections in 1946–7 and 1951, delivering support to nationalists pressing for rapid independence and a neutralist line toward Vietnamese communism. In Laos, the neutralist Paris-educated prince Souvanna Phouma (1901–84) was again returned as premier in 1955 having already won the 1951 election. In Cambodia, King Sihanouk was more strongly placed (see below), and increasingly hostile to nationalists and leftists such as the Japanese-era Prime Minister Son Ngoc Thanh whom he saw as opponents of the monarchy. Most had chosen or been forced to flee to Viet Nam or the border area in the early 1950s, and Sihanouk used his position to propel himself into the position which constitutional democracy should have occupied.

The 1950s experiments in democracy, for which only the Philippines had been adequately prepared, look reasonably successful in relation to the magnitude of the task, and by comparison with what came before or after. They managed to keep extremely fragile and unlikely new states intact, gained rapid international legitimacy and support, developed radically new education systems around a newly defined national identity, and even delivered significant economic growth. Yet having promised so much more than the now reviled colonial systems, they could deliver much less of stability and physical security. The results of elections seemed pedestrian, corrupt, and parochial by contrast with the heady, emotive leadership of the transition to independence. Only the communists appeared able to persuade mass voters to choose a coherent political platform, and their success alarmed religious and economic elites. Those marginalized by elections began again to voice ideas about the unsuitability of liberal democracy for their local conditions. Some of those who believed they had an entitlement to rule would welcome these discontents as a chance to act.

GUNS INHERIT THE REVOLUTIONS

The forces with enough internal discipline and external ruthlessness to overcome rivals and impose their own vision as the national one were best placed to inherit the revolutions. The military and the communists were not always the two toughest competitors on the ground, but the Cold War made it difficult for other players with more comprehensive or pluralist visions to survive. In this context what seems surprising is how long it took the communists (in Viet Nam, Laos, and Cambodia) or the military to achieve that dominance. Democracy endured for a decade not just because it was the global gold stand-ard, but because the intense pluralities in each country could not be contained in any other ring.

The other factor, however, was the unpreparedness of either communists or soldiers to take over at a national level. Unlike the communist party of China, those of Southeast Asia had been crushed by colonials or Japanese since 1926, and had at most a few years of experience since regrouping. The people with the guns were extraordinarily divided, and mostly in their twenties, with negligible strategic or technical training. Only Thailand had a long tradition of a national army, which had already inherited the 1932 revolution when Field Marshall Phibun Songkhram became the increasingly authoritarian Prime Minister in 1938. As noted in the previous chapter, he was eased out in the necessarily anti-fascist atmosphere of 1945, but returned to the Prime Ministership in another military coup in November 1947. The intervening period of Pridi's dominance had been one of Thailand's most liberal, when a fully elected legislature was finally inaugurated, and laws were passed against military involvement in politics. Pridi even made peace with the royalists and invited King Ananda Mahidol to return for his twentieth birthday. When the king was mysteriously killed, however, the royalists and militarists found a pretext to unite in support of a coup, manufacturing some rumours that Pridi was responsible for regicide.

Thailand's was the only army at this stage with enough centralization and technical competence to become the backbone of state government. By doing so it established a model for those that would follow, making military rule appear respectable and even desirable in the growing Cold War confrontation with communism. Washington had declined to embrace Phibun after his 1947 coup, but began to fund Thailand as a strategic Asian ally immediately after the communist victory in China. At the outbreak of the Korean War in 1950, Phibun's government was the first in Asia to offer military support to the United States, and was rewarded with further military aid. The army was thereby emboldened to dispense with its uncomfortable royalist allies and take over government in the 1951 coup. It cemented its strong relationship with Washington by cracking down on the remaining liberals and leftists in Thailand's public sphere. For Phibun the alliance was needed not against the negligible communist party, but as internal legitimation, and strengthening against traditional rivals Viet Nam and Burma. However, US military aid to the army, and CIA support for the police, strengthened these two rival networks of patronage to the extent of undermining Phibun's control. He responded with another round of liberalization, ensuring that his allies won a flawed election in 1957. The army, now led by Field Marshall Sarit Thannarat (1908–63) and General Thanom Kittikachorn (1911–2004), shifted to a more blatant military dictatorship in two coups of 1957 and 1958. Sarit ruled as Prime Minister until his death, and Thanom thereafter until the pro-democracy movement of 1973. Wholly Thai-educated, these generals were unapologetic in declaring democracy unsuited to Thailand, preferring an imagined harmonious order under the old monarchy. During America's Indochina wars, Thailand became its essential base for bombing raids, vital supplies, Thai troops deployed in Viet Nam and Laos, and a congenial rest and recreation center for its troops. Military-backed "development" was touted as the only viable model for growth short of communism.

Burma's determined policy of neutrality in the Cold War did not prevent its becoming the second of Southeast Asia's military dictatorships, in 1962. Like Indonesia's, Burma's armed force, the *Tatmadaw*, believed itself an heir to the revolutionary struggle against Japanese and British, essential to the survival of the state. Its units were more accustomed to sustaining themselves by rent-seeking in legal and illegal business than to control by civilian paymasters. By 1956 it had achieved a unified command of the three services under General Ne Win, fellow-Thakin of Aung San and U Nu. The civilian politicians, by contrast, had been in disarray since Aung San's assassination in 1947, with the ruling AFPFL appearing an ever more dysfunctional and corrupt coalition, up to its eventual split in 1958. Under pressure from Ne Win, Prime Minister U Nu then agreed to hand authority to a caretaker government led by Ne Win and the *Tatmadaw*, simply to deal with the temporary crisis in six months. Ne Win had this period extended until elections in 1960, but meanwhile gave an appearance of purposefulness in cleaning up Rangoon, fighting the communists, controlling prices, and replacing discredited politicians and Shan and Karen traditional chiefs.

U Nu's faction of the AFPFL won the 1960 election easily, helped by the aura of Aung San and Nu, the promise of making Buddhism the state religion, and some strong-arming from the military. The last Nu government appeared more chaotic and incompetent than ever, as his divisive push for a Buddhist Burma took most of his interest. The *Tatmadaw*, committed to a centralized revolutionary vision, was particularly disturbed by U Nu's attempt to accommodate the Shan *sawbwas*, whom Ne Win's first stage in power had pushed side, and who now threatened departure from the Burma Union unless there was a transition to federalism. Ne Win launched his military coup on March 2, 1962, arresting the cabinet and dismissing the Parliament. Declaring that parliamentary democracy had been proven unsuitable to Burma, the *Tatmadaw* proclaimed its own "Burmese Way to Socialism," which would have a single state party, nationalization of all key sectors of the economy, and state control of land, but would be superior to Marxism-Leninism in representing all of Burmese society, not only workers and peasants. Though beginning with some high-sounding reversal of Nu's policies on Buddhism, the press, and minority relations, it quickly moved to monopolistic total control of the press, and crackdowns on any expressions of opposition. Whatever claims it had to revolutionary legitimacy were lost in May 1962, when troops invaded Rangoon university to suppress political activity, and in the ensuing melee killed over a hundred students and blew up the Student Union building, hallowed site of the nationalist movement of the 1930s. The *Tatmadaw* established Southeast Asia's most enduring and uncompromising military dictatorship, in the name of the Revolutionary Council (from 1962), the Burma Socialist Program Party state party (BSPP, progressively from 1971), and the State Law and Order Restoration Council (SLORC) after a brief democratic experiment in 1988. These governments responded to the Cold War with a neutrality that involved drastically reducing foreign engagement, training, and assistance, and securing their long endangered boundary with China by carefully avoiding public disagreements with Beijing.

Indonesia's armed forces (ABRI) had similar revolutionary habits of engagement in the country's political and economic life, but none of the taste or opportunity for isolationism. In 1950 it also lacked any leader of comparable political stature to Ne Win. The choice of the Japanese-trained officers for leadership, General Sudirman, had died in 1950. The young Dutch-trained colonels to whom the Jakarta government gave the task of building a disciplined modern force, Nasution and Simatupang, were sacrificed after the October 1952 affair, an abortive army attempt to prevent political interference in its affairs by abolishing Parliament. Nasution was brought back as Chief of Staff of ABRI in late 1955, after a series of crises had consolidated army support behind him. Jakarta could not, however, control its colonels in command of wealthy districts outside Java, who resented the growing pressure for military and economic centralization that threatened their soldiers' livelihood from semi-legal "informal" trade to Singapore, Malaya, and the Philippines. They also distrusted the growing power of the Java-based PKI after the 1955 election, and Sukarno's desire to include the communists in government. The growing polarization marked by the resignation in December 1956 of Vice-President Hatta, Sumatran, anti-communist, and pragmatist, also propelled the dissident colonels toward open rebellion.

A state of emergency, proclaimed in 1957 to deal with this regional threat and with the confiscation of Dutch assets under nationalist and communist pressure, legalized and extended the power of the military in every region. ABRI moved quickly to take over Dutch plantations and businesses, and to prevent the PKI doing so through its militant unions. These assets ensured that the military would be able to sustain itself independent of the civilian government, and that the officer corps had a major interest in the continuation of emergency conditions that justified this privileged position. When the dissident colonels allied with some Masjumi and socialist politicians to proclaim an alternative "Revolutionary Government of Indonesia" (PRRI) in 1958, Sukarno and Nasution moved decisively to use Java troops to crush the rebel units in Sumatra and North Sulawesi. Although elite officers and politicians were treated mildly, dismissed or exiled rather than executed, some 35,000 men died on both sides of the battlefield. The Army extended its role in political and economic matters, particularly in the ex-rebel provinces of Sumatra and Sulawesi occupied by Javanese units. It became more centralized, more ready to use violence domestically, and more Javanese (about 80% of the top officer corps by 1970), as officers from Sumatra and Sulawesi were dismissed or marginalized.

Through these crises, between the declaration of martial law in 1957 and the return to the authoritarian 1945 Constitution in 1959, the army grew steadily more powerful at the center as well as in the regions. Sukarno also grew more powerful with each crisis, preaching revolutionary unity as against the divisiveness of parliamentary democracy. When the Constituent Assembly declined his proposal to reinstate the emergency 1945 Constitution he summarily dismissed that Assembly and proclaimed that constitution on his own authority, making the cabinet responsible only to himself. His attacks on the parliamentary system were designed to appeal to the armed forces as well as the communists. "The instruments of state power must be completely weaned from liberalism, now that they are in the shade of the flag of the 1945 Constitution. They must now become instruments of the Revolution again" (Sukarno 1959, cited Feith and Castles 1970, 107). ABRI's centrality in the system of "Guided Democracy" Sukarno inaugurated was demonstrated when the military filled one third of cabinet positions, including Nasution as Defense Minister, and many governorships.

Military power was allowed to override constitutional propriety by the continuing state of emergency, justified by an aggressive campaign to force the Dutch to yield West New Guinea (later renamed West Irian, Irian Jaya, and West Papua in turn) to Indonesia. The campaign ruptured all relations with the Netherlands and culminated in armed infiltration. Encouraged by the United States, the Netherlands decided in 1962 it had more to lose by resisting this pressure than by abandoning the Papuans in its care, and agreed to a UN-supervised transfer of power to Indonesia. The military, Sukarno, and the PKI had all benefited from this campaign, and found another reason to maintain emergency government by "confronting" the formation of Malaysia in 1963 (see below). Neither British nor Malaysian government were likely to concede as the Dutch had done, however. International opinion roundly condemned Indonesia's "crush Malaysia" campaign, leading Sukarno to take Indonesia out of the United Nations in January 1965 and increasingly to align with China. The PKI was the most vociferous supporter of crushing Malaysia, able to mobilize mass demonstrations in favor of Sukarno and against Malaysia and the British (Figure 17.1). It sought to have "volunteers" armed and trained

Figure 17.1 Anti-Malaysia demonstration, Jakarta, 1963. Demonstrators are standing on the roof of the British Ambassador's car, having pushed it out of the Embassy grounds. Source: AP/Topfoto.co.uk.

for the struggle, outside the control of the army command. Despite rivalry between the blunt Defense Minister Nasution and the more pliable Javanese General Achmad Yani who had replaced him as Chief of Staff, the army leadership again saw the PKI as its primary enemy and secretly maintained contacts with the United States and Malaysia. Polarization was also rising again in the countryside, where the PKI mobilized landless peasants to insist on the implementation of a land reform already agreed by Parliament, to the extent of unilaterally occupying the land of richer peasants. Muslim (chiefly NU) youth were mobilized to oppose such actions, and bloody clashes became increasingly frequent through 1965.

In an atmosphere of economic collapse, exaggerated revolutionary rhetoric, and rumors of coups after Sukarno had a sudden bout of illness on August 4, a coup did take place against the army leadership on the night of September 30, 1965. Achmad Yani and five of his general staff were captured and killed, while Nasution managed to escape by scaling the wall of his neighbor. The coup was the work of a Revolutionary Council led by Lt Col Untung, an officer of Sukarno's palace guard, seemingly aimed at obtaining the support of air force, navy, and police as well as disgruntled lower ranks in the army against a "Council of Generals" who were "power-crazy, neglecting the welfare of their troops, living in luxury over the sufferings of their troops," according to Untung's first announcement, as well as in league with the CIA. Untung was clearly a Sukarnoist, and probably believed that Sukarno wanted to find a way around his "disloyal" generals. The action appeared to have implicit support from the air force commander Omar Dhani and the PKI leader D.N. Aidit, both of whom were at the Halim airport where the coup group gathered, and who issued generally supportive but uninvolved statements during the following day. Sukarno himself also went to Halim believing the action was to protect him, though he avoided any public endorsement before news of the bungled murders and of the army's recovery made that unwise.

Major General Suharto (1921–2008) was the most striking omission from Untung's targets, as commander of the Jakarta-based army strategic reserve (KOSTRAD), often deputizing for Yani. There were several reasons the plotters assumed he was a loyal Sukarnoist, not opposed to the President's move to the left: he had in 1948 been sent by General Sudirman to mediate with the communists involved in the Madiun uprising (rather than confronting them); he had a grievance against Nasution, who had relieved him of the Central Java command in 1959 on the grounds of his raising funds by dubious dealings; he had been a patron of Untung in Central Java, and later in the command to "liberate" New Guinea, and had attended Untung's wedding; he was close to another key plotter, Colonel Latief, who visited him at his son's bedside in hospital on the evening of the coup (and was never put on trial for his role, suggesting the danger of implicating Suharto); and he was a reserved Javanese not given to outspoken comment. If they expected him to support the move, however, the plotters were badly mistaken. He moved early on the morning of October 1 to have his KOSTRAD troops take over the radio station and the central Merdeka square from the coup group, and by evening could announce on the radio that he had taken command of the army, and that together with the navy and air force they were determined to crush the "30th September movement" and protect Sukarno from it.

Once Suharto's forces had captured the coup base at Halim airport the next day and found the bodies of the murdered generals, Suharto began a campaign to destroy the PKI under the thin legal veil of Presidential authority to "restore order." Army agents encouraged Muslim and Catholic youth groups best known for opposing the PKI advance to form an "Action Front" against the coup. As word spread that the army was on their side, anti-communist demonstrations quickly followed, leading to the burning of the PKI headquarters in Jakarta on October 8, later emulated elsewhere. Despite constant appeals by Sukarno for a political compromise, the army seized and summarily executed all the communist leaders they could find. Aidit and cabinet minister Njoto were killed in November. Only a handful of PKI leaders, and Untung himself, were kept alive for subsequent public military trial. Sukarno's charisma alone was not enough to counter the military without the PKI to represent mass support. Although maneuvering constantly to defend the PKI and maintain a cabinet loyal to him, he was finally forced to capitulate on March 11, 1966, when troops surrounded the palace during a cabinet meeting, in an atmosphere of unprecedented demonstrations against the President. Sukarno signed a letter instructing Suharto "to take all measures considered necessary to guarantee security, calm and stability of the government and the revolution." Suharto now used this cover of Presidential authority to ban the (already-destroyed) communist party, arrest the Leftist or Sukarnoist members of cabinet, and reshuffle military appointments to support the anti-communist stance. Carefully avoiding any direct criticism of Sukarno, Suharto did not replace him as "Acting President" until a year later, resisting many harsher voices demanding his impeachment for participation in the 1965 coup (Figure 17.2). It was a military coup by instalments, but a carefully camouflaged one.

It was also far more – a massive bloodletting that ended the conflicting revolutionary dreams, and established a state with an iron fist. Mass killing of not only cadres but entire families of PKI sympathizers began in October in Aceh, where the party had represented a significant voice for unpopular Jakarta policies of secularism and centralization. In Central Java, where the PKI was strongest, the tough anti-communist Colonel Sarwo Edhie quickly trained and armed members of anti-communist Muslim groups to do the work of rounding up and killing PKI activists. The pattern was repeated in East Java, where the NU youth group Ansor did most of the killing. But even without the Muslim factor, in Bali, sufficient tension had arisen over the PKI challenge to village hierarchies that pro-nationalist youth felt entitled to slaughter thousands of their rivals. The best argument against the army's well-publicized and later enforced interpretation that the PKI was responsible

Figure 17.2 President Sukarno and General Suharto in February 1967. Source: Associated Press/Topfoto.

for the September 30 coup was the complete communist unpreparedness for an armed struggle of any kind. The Party's link to the military coup plotters through a suspected double-agent called Sjam was known to very few PKI leaders, and even they had no control over the likes of Untung. Nevertheless, the whole left wing of Indonesian politics, which had appeared to be rising unstoppably in influence, was ruthlessly crushed. How many died cannot be known, though a figure of a half-million has become widely accepted. Half or more of the total died in East Java, though the highest proportion to population was probably in Bali, and every province had its victims. A larger number were imprisoned and subject to interrogation and torture, and even after release were denied state employment and voting rights. About 12,000 were sent to a penal colony in underdeveloped Buru Island (Maluku) until its closure in 1979.

Suharto remained in power until 1998, and gradually relied less on terror and more on legal and bureaucratic means of control. His regime turned the economy around and allowed it to grow at a pace unknown since records began. It created a "one plus" party system of which Sukarno had only dreamed, whereby a favored government party, Golkar, guaranteed safe parliamentary majorities and the return of bureaucratic hierarchies undermined since 1942. Indonesia swiftly made peace with Malaysia and Singapore, rejoined the United Nations, and became a reliable member of international organizations. Internally it imposed a single, centralized education system and syllabus, defining the fruit of the revolution as being a unitary state coinciding with the boundaries of Netherlands India. Liberal parliamentary democracy and federalism remained condemned, as under Sukarno's Guided Democracy, but Suharto was able to ensure that rival ideas were not heard, where Sukarno could only keep them in unstable balance. These changes came with an appalling cost in lives and liberties, but they delivered a unified nation-state.

Viet Nam, Cambodia, and Laos were never models of democratic governance, but it was significant of the times that there, too, there was a phase of military coups and rule by the gun. General Duong Van Minh took power in South Viet Nam in November 1963, in a coup at least condoned by the American protector. Although the coup was discredited from the outset by the murder of the incumbent president, Ngo Dinh Diem (1901–63), military governments succeeded one another thereafter until the fall of the regime to the communist DRV in 1975, having little but force and US backing to sustain them. In Cambodia military commander Lon Nol seized power from King Sihanouk during his absence in Paris in 1970, complaining that his neutralism allowed too much latitude to North Vietnamese forces in the east. He ruled as President until this country too was taken over by communist forces five years later. The Royal Lao Army, in contrast to its Pathet Lao enemy, paid little heed to the civilian government of Prince Souvanna Phouma in the 1960s. The commanders of each district became in effect warlords controlling the local economies including the drug trade on one hand, and accepting US military support directly on the other.

Why were the 1960s so congenial to military rule? The superficial answer is the Cold War – the United States sought dependably anti-communist allies at a peak moment of communist success. The country cases show, however, that the American role was marginal to the political dynamic, usually limited to a quiet nod that support would not be withdrawn if the military took power. Fundamentally, the revolutionary process had aroused passions about national sovereignty that were a poor fit with existing political communities. No less than the whole of the arbitrarily defined imperial spaces could satisfy as the goal of national struggle, but only force, and perhaps not even force, could control the diverse demands aroused in that space. Some influential political scientists of the time went further, arguing that in the conditions of the new countries only the military had the "strong leadership backed by organizational structure and by moral authority" to act as effective agents of state-building and modernization (Pauker 1959, 343; also Johnson 1962). But the military record in government was generally worse than that of the civilians who preceded, with only the Indonesian case having much on the positive side of the ledger.

DICTATORSHIP PHILIPPINE STYLE

Even Southeast Asia's most robust parliamentary democracy had its authoritarian moment in the 1970s. The Philippines had had an educated middle class since the 1870s, its revolutionary moment of self-definition in the 1890s, and a free press and American-style electoral democracy since the 1920s, which regularly threw out incumbents in a tradition of rivalry among the great propertied families. The constitution limited the President to two terms, but none had won a second election until Ferdinand Marcos (1917–89) came to the Presidency in 1965. With his beauty queen wife Imelda he promoted a populist personality cult like no other, and claimed to be changing the old elite family politics by bypassing Congress to borrow money for major public works and expansion of the military. The Cold War indulgence of military dictators was a factor in his rise, since he had earned Washington's approval by controversially sending Philippine military engineers to support the US fight in Viet Nam in 1966. As if on cue, a communist threat emerged soon after his big-spending success in the 1969 election, in the form of a Mao-inspired and reconstituted Communist Party of the Philippines. In 1972 the Moro National Liberation Front began a rebellion in the Muslim south.

This radicalized atmosphere was Marcos' justification for declaring martial law in 1972. Claiming the need and opportunity to surpass the "familiar and mediocre past," he ruled by decree, imprisoned vocal opponents such as Senator Benigno ("Ninoy") Aquino (1932–83), confiscated many assets of the old elite, suspended Congress, and installed military officers, technocrats, and his own favorites in key positions. A constitutional convention was persuaded to write a new constitution, allowing Marcos to continue in power beyond his term in 1973. The armed forces were kept on side by a tripling of their budget and manpower between 1972 and 1976 and a centralization of the command structure. Military aid flowed generously from the United States. Many

Philippine intellectuals began to think that the communists had a point in targeting the "neo-colonial" US alliance as the problem.

While Marcos' "New Society" emulated some of the rhetoric, the electoral and legal coercion, and the extrajudicial killings of Suharto's "New Order," he notably failed to match Indonesia's 7% annual growth rates. Indeed it was under martial law that the Philippines began its late twentieth-century pattern of economic underperformance and stagnation. The populist support that had flowed from his attack on the ruling oligarchy eroded in face of the rising burden of debt from his projects, and the corruption (increasingly public in the 1980s) that outrageously enriched his own family and his close cronies. Controlled elections (boycotted by the opposition) were reintroduced for Congress in 1978 and for President in 1981, after martial law had been lifted prior to a first visit by the Pope to this most Catholic of Asian countries. As an ailing Marcos increasingly appeared to lose control to his flamboyant wife and military favorites, his leading critic, Ninoy Aquino, was assassinated very publicly at the Manila airport on his return from American exile in 1983. This extraordinary blunder turned the world as well as the Philippines against Marcos. He attempted to stem the tide of protest with a snap election for February 1986, in which Aquino's modest widow, Corazon ("Cory"; 1933–2009), bravely led the opposition. As usual it was declared a Marcos victory, but the energized people of Manila, the Catholic Church and the commander of the Philippine Constabulary, Fidel Ramos, all believed it was stolen and that Marcos had to go. Two weeks later "People Power" propelled Marcos and his wife to exile in Hawaii and Cory Aquino into Malacañang Palace as Southeast Asia's first female head of state and government. Her key ally in that vital uprising, General Fidel Ramos, succeeded her in 1992. Between them they re-established a democratic constitution, less corrupt administration, civil liberties, and the return to modest economic growth. It was also a return to politics as usual, as the dominant families quickly resumed their pattern of control of the legislature.

REMAKING "PROTECTED" MONARCHIES

In Chapter 11 we noted how those monarchical systems closest to modernizing into states – Burma, Viet Nam, Aceh, and the Balinese rajas – were those hardest for expanding European empires to deal with in the nineteenth century, resulting in their eventual brutal conquest. Those Malay, Tai, and Khmer monarchs accustomed to drawing their revenue essentially from entrepreneurial foreigners, and to sending deferential tribute where necessary to stronger trading partners, found the transition to colonial rule much gentler and less disruptive. Their weakness in legal-bureaucratic terms was their strength. In 1945 they were still clinging to fragile thrones, endangered by their collaboration with the Japanese on the one hand, and Marxist-influenced demands for the end of "feudalism" on the other. Their survival in the Malay world, Thailand, and Cambodia is one of the surprises of the mid-century crisis. It owes much to the quest of conservatives for a barrier against the unknown perils of populism and Marxism, but perhaps more to the simple immensity of the challenge of turning multi-ethnic and cosmopolitan imperial space into a nation-state. In the absence of political community, charisma was a precious commodity.

The Japanese occupation of Southeast Asia (Chapter 16) was a shock for both rajas and their opponents. In principle the Japanese had no time for divided or qualified sovereignty, and favored the slogan of the Meiji restoration – *hanseki hokan* (all domains yield to one sovereignty). In practice they naturally worked with any influential figures who professed to support their aims, and that of course included many rajas. But the very fact of one sudden and radical change of regime in 1942 and another in 1945 encouraged the hopes of all who opposed the status quo, and thereby turned rivalries and personal conflicts into deadly choices. In Langkat (East Sumatra) the Japanese were met with slogans demanding the end of monarchy. Where royal families were deeply split by succession disputes, the Japanese advent offered a chance for changing the incumbent, risking reversal and further embitterment when the Japanese departed. In Laos the readiness of one prince to embrace the doomed Vichy regime, and his rival to embrace the Japanese who ruled directly for less than a year, bedevilled subsequent royal politics. In Selangor (Malaya) the Japanese replaced the sultan by his more popular brother, whom the British in turn arrested and exiled in 1945. Everywhere the charisma of royalty was profoundly damaged by the way Japanese officers disregarded the formal status of nominal kings, obliging them to share the propaganda spotlight with nationalist politicians who despised them, and even to give a public example of "voluntary labor" for the Japanese cause. Only a few of the youngest western-educated rulers, notably Norodom Sihanouk in Cambodia and Sultan Hamengkubuwono IX (1922–88) in Yogyakarta, could adapt to the populist style expected by the Japanese, but this served them well in facing the trials of nationalism to follow.

The sudden Japanese surrender in 1945 created further crisis, particularly where the colonial regime could not re-establish itself. Several of the rulers were too quick to make public their eagerness for the restoration of the old regime, and too slow to look for protection from the nationalists. In East Sumatra a radical alliance of Marxists, nationalists, and ethnic rivals attacked the palaces of the once-wealthy Malay rajas in March 1946, killing hundreds of aristocrats and capturing the rest in what was dubbed a "social revolution" in the name of popular sovereignty. In Yogyakarta, by contrast, Hamengkubuwono astutely invited the Republican government to transfer its capital to his, away from Dutch control in Jakarta, establishing thereby a solid alliance with nationalism. By contrast, his perennial royal rivals in Surakarta focused the animosity of the radicals, and suffered another "social revolution" in July 1946. The Republic took a firm stand against the remaining monarchies with the sole exception of Yogyakarta. Once it assumed responsibility from the Dutch for the whole Archipelago with its many and varied rulers, these were eased out of power without serious violence in the 1950s. The most influential of them, in Sulawesi and the other eastern islands, made the transition by becoming the first of the Republic's district officials (*bupati*). The prevailing rhetoric in Indonesia, as in

Indochina, was to regard "feudalism" as akin to colonialism in symbolizing a vanished and despised era.

The British returned to the Peninsula in August 1945 with a new plan to make the messy mix of colonies and protected sultanates acquired over 260 years into a potential national unit, the Malayan Union. All the races living there would have an equal stake as citizens, but Singapore would be separated as an Anglo-Chinese commercial hub and military base. This new "Malayan" identity could only be achieved if the sultans agreed to surrender their nominal sovereignty, a task made much easier by their vulnerability as collaborators with the Japanese enemy. Sir Harold MacMichael achieved this task in October 1945, reversing the pre-war alliance with the Malay elite in recognition of Chinese sacrifice during the war. In Sarawak a similar cession of sovereignty was enforced, from the Brooke family rulers to the British crown, resulting in an increasingly violent anti-cession movement culminating in the murder of the second colonial governor in 1949. In Malaya, too, outrage gradually spread among a hitherto quiescent Malay population against the loss of Malay sovereignty, but more emotively against the plan's acceptance of the majority of the large and energetic Chinese population as equal citizens.

The better-educated aristocrats of the nine Malay states became mobilized in an unprecedented series of national-level meetings, culminating in the formation of a United Malays National Organization (UMNO) in March 1946. Though dedicated to opposing the Union and restoring pre-war Malay sovereignty and privilege, its very existence showed that everything had changed. In standing up to the sultans, and forcing them, unprecedentedly, to boycott the ceremony installing the first governor of the Malayan Union in April, UMNO shifted the object of protection and loyalty from the sultans to the race – the *bangsa Melayu* (Malay race or nation). This was explicitly opposed to the vision of a multi-racial citizenship and eventual identity as *bangsa Malayan*, a term UMNO leaders denounced as an incongruous British creation supported only by non-Malays. Thus was born the most enduring of Southeast Asian's ethno-nationalisms, sustained by its most enduring ruling party, UMNO.

The British felt obliged to yield, since the Malay opposition to the Union had been so apparently united, while potential supporters of it were divided between the strong but increasingly anti-British communists, anti-establishment Malays attracted to the "Greater Indonesia" idea, Chinese and Indian nationalists, and English-educated "Straits Chinese" opposed to separating Penang from Singapore. UMNO and the rulers now demanded an exclusively "Malay" federation of states in which non-Malays were tolerated but had no political rights. In Anglo-Malay negotiations for a new compromise, Malay representatives insisted on retaining "Malay" as the only valid nationality, whereas they "took the strongest objection to being called or referred to as Malayans" (Report of Constitutional Working Committee, 1946, cited Omar 1993, 107). The name of the new country, inaugurated in 1948, became Federation of Malaya in English, but *Persekutuan Tanah Melayu* (Federation of Malay Lands) in Malay. Nominal sovereignty was returned to each of the nine sultans, though now as explicitly constitutional monarchs obliged to accept federal and state legislation.

This was no recipe for a viable independent state, toward which the British were obliged to move in their competition with the MCP insurgents. The UMNO leader (and Johor Chief Minister), Dato Onn bin Jaafar (1895–1962), was leaned on by the British to find common ground with the Chinese and Indian leadership in the hope of emerging as leader of an independent Malaya. He eventually agreed to concede Federation citizenship to non-Malays, but when he sought to turn UMNO into an inclusive party for all races he was rejected by its members. In 1951 he left the party to form a multi-racial Independence of Malaya Party, which was heavily defeated at the first election in 1955 despite British support. Leadership of the transition to independence passed instead to an Alliance Party made up of three racially exclusive parties – UMNO, the Malayan Chinese Association, and the Malayan Indian Congress.

The constitution negotiated for the independence of the Federation of Malaya in August 1957 was a unique hybrid. So central to Malay ethno-nationalism had the sovereignty of the sultans become that the Federation was constitutionally required to "guarantee the sovereignty of the Malay sultans in their respective states." Since most matters fell under federal jurisdiction, how-ever, the sultans were still left only with land, local government, and Islam, and even here had to follow the advice of a chief minister responsible to a state parliament. The head of state of the federation was elected for a five-year term by the nine sultans from among themselves, and named Yang di Pertuan Agung, like the long-established elective king of the "nine states" of Negri Sembilan.

The contradiction between Malay and English names of the state was finally resolved when the scholarly neologism "Malaysia" was adopted for the broader federation embracing Sarawak and Sabah (North Borneo). Malaysia was rushed into being in 1962–3 because of the danger of pro-communists coming to power through elections in Singapore. Aided by the British, who imprisoned the popular Chinese leftists who had brought him to power, Lee Kuan Yew managed to sell the idea of Malaysia as the only acceptable route to independ-ence. Sarawak and Sabah were brought on board by the distribution of timber contracts to key ethnic leaders, disproportionately large representation in the Malaysian parliament, control of their own immigration, and a ten-year guarantee of English as their state language. Like Penang and Melaka, their heads of state were governors appointed by the Yang di Pertuan Agung, so that they had no say in choosing the federal head of state. The Malaya constitution was simply amended by act of parliament to add these new states, and the unique features of Malay-style federalism remained. Lee Kuan Yew's aggressive championing of a "Malaysian Malaysia" of equal rights for all quickly aroused a Malay nationalist reaction, leading to Singapore's expulsion and independ-ence on August 9, 1965.

Many in the Borneo territories would come to feel that their hasty merger with an already-established Malaya left them at a permanent disadvantage in modernizing on their own terms. The alternative plan favored by many British officials and Indonesian-influenced Muslim politicians was that the two colonies and the British-protected sultanate of Brunei should first establish their own constitutional federation, and then negotiate merger on the basis of equality with Malaya. This idea was not helped, particularly in the eyes of

Brunei's Sultan Omar Ali Saifuddin (1914–86, r.1950–67), by being championed by A.M. Azahari (1928–2002). He had returned to Brunei in 1952 from Java, where the Japanese had sent him for training, and three years later established the Brunei People's Party (PRB), British Borneo's first. It campaigned in Brunei and London for a constitutional monarchy with a fully elected legislature, and gained popularity by attacking British, and later Malayan, arrogance. When the British and the hitherto theoretically absolute sultan eventually agreed on a constitution with a part-elected legislature, Azahari's party won all sixteen of its elected seats in September 1962.

The rapid moves to bring all three Borneo territories into Malaysia were attacked by Azahari as a neo-colonial plot to retain British influence, while the sultan worried that he was being rushed into union with states far less Malay-dominated and royalist than his own. PRB could not have been ignored, but the party destroyed itself in a rebellion in December 1962, with some support from Indonesia and Chinese communists in Sarawak. Since Brunei had at the time no army, and the rebels succeeded in taking over most of the police stations (and capturing dozens of Europeans), they may have hoped that a mixture of force and diplomacy would eliminate the colonial presence as in Azahari's model, the Indonesian revolution. The British however despatched enough troops from Singapore, Sarawak, and nearby Labuan to retake control in three days. The sultan broadcast his condemnation. Azahari was at the time safely in Manila, and eventually took refuge in Jakarta, while many of his supporters preferred Malaysia.

Although the revolt increased the pressure for accepting Malaysia on security grounds, it also left the sultan as the sole voice for Brunei after its elected representatives were arrested or fled. He stubbornly resisted the pressure to join, anxious to safeguard the oil revenues which had transformed Brunei from the poorest to the richest Malay state during his reign, and perhaps to resist Malaysia's electoral democracy. He preferred the status quo of British protection, but now from a position of vastly greater strength. Britain had already agreed to self-government in 1959, but the constitutional side of the bargain had collapsed. The sultan was in effect the government, and proved stubbornly adept at resisting British pressure to return to a constitutional path. Omar Ali Saifuddin resigned in favor of his son Sultan Bolkiah in 1967, but continued to advise him to distrust the electoral process that had opened the way to Indonesian and Malaysian sympathizers. Singapore, the other awkward residue from the Malaysia push, became a vital supporter of Brunei in its resistance to Malaysian-backed democratization, providing infrastructure and a currency. Britain's democratic resolve weakened before Brunei's value as an oil and gas exporter, and the international environment became less hostile in the 1970s. Anxious to withdraw from colonial entanglements, Britain allowed, indeed insisted, that Brunei become independent in 1984 as Southeast Asia's smallest and richest country, and its only absolute monarchy.

Malay monarchy, touted by its defenders as the indispensable essence of Malayness, appeared to experience the full spectrum of possibilities. Brunei celebrated its difference as a completely palace-centered polity, with more than enough oil revenue to make life comfortable for its Brunei subjects and to import Malaysian Chinese and Filipinos to do most of the work. Its ideology, an emulation of the Thai model, was "Malayness, Islam, monarchy" (*Melayu, Islam, Beraja*). Indonesia, by contrast, had almost totally rid itself of monarchy in the revolutionary 1940s and 1950s, and even the exception, Sultan Hamengkubuwono IX in Yogyakarta, declared that his kingdom would end with his death. But that did not happen in the very different climate under Suharto, whom the sultan helped legitimate as his first economic minister and then Vice-President (1973–8). His successors as sultan remained unelected rulers of Yogyakarta even in an increasingly democratic era. Throughout the Archipelago, the descendants of rulers used first Suharto's hierarchic authoritarianism, and then the post-1998 devolution of power to districts, to make a comeback as political and cultural leaders.

In Malaysia the incongruous privileges of the rulers continued through independence and democracy. Only Dr Mahathir, Prime Minister from 1981 to 2003, felt strong enough to curb these privileges. He had the constitution changed in 1983 to oblige the rulers to sign any bill presented by federal or state parliament within 30 days; and in 1993 to remove judicial immunity and other perks of office. Control of the press enabled him to reveal a flood of royal scandals at the right moment to shame the rulers into complying. Yet because Malay nationalism found much of its legitimacy in the idea of historic Malay sovereignty and "protected" privilege, the sultans frequently bounced back. Opposition leader Karpal Singh was convicted of sedition in 2014 for having questioned the Sultan of Perak's controversial appointment of an UMNO Chief Minister without a parliamentary vote of no confidence in his opposition predecessor. Whereas revolutions in the Philippines (earlier), Indonesia, and Viet Nam had sacralized the nation, its heroes, and symbols, as a new form of charismatic legitimacy, the other countries found it difficult to manage without monarchy.

TWILIGHT OF THE INDOCHINA KINGS

Although their historic domains fitted better the boundaries of nationalist aspirations, the kings of Indochina came to a more pathetic end. Emperor Bao Dai (1913–97) had already achieved the long-cherished goal of uniting the three French territories of Tongking, Annam, and Cochin-China into a nominally independent Vietnamese kingdom, under Japanese auspices in 1945. Ho Chi Minh acknowledged his symbolic power by incorporating him as "advisor" in the Vietminh government of September 1945. But when he took refuge in Hong Kong the following year and gradually became the focus of anti-communist nationalist hopes, the communists systematically vilified him. In April 1949 the French lured him back on terms similar to those of Japan – head of state of a nominally independent, united Viet Nam. His government achieved many hard-won concessions and transfers of practical authority, but too many French officials were anxious about their own pride and dignity after the war to allow Bao Dai the major symbolic victories that would enable him to rival Ho in charisma. After the 1954 Geneva agreements he remained as head of state of South Viet Nam only for a year. His stern Prime Minister, Ngo Dinh Diem, wanting no division of his authority, then manipulated a referendum to replace him by a Diem Presidency. The scion of the once-mighty Nguyen Dynasty retired to a relaxed lifestyle in Monaco.

Only one of the many Lao *muang*, Luang Prabang, had a continuous history through the nineteenth-century partition into Siamese and French territories. Its French-protected ruler, the ailing King SisavongVong (b.1885, r.1904–59), was, like Bao Dai, called first by the Japanese in April 1945, then by the French a year later, to represent as king a whole new nation-state. He, however, was resolutely pro-French, and wanted nothing to do with Lao attempts to make their independence real after the Japanese surrender. Most of the leading French-educated nationalists came from the second great family of Luang Prabang, that of the *uparit* or viceroy. Its forceful Prince Phetsarath (1890–1959), the leading Lao figure under France, Prime Minister under the Japanese and leader of the Lao Issarak ("Free Lao") nationalist movement, declared in September 1945 that Laos remained independent and that its treaties with France were invalidated by France's failure to protect the country. When the king repudiated all this and tried to dismiss Phetsarath, the Prince convened an assembly to dethrone him. Laos retained this fragile independence until April 1946, in a delicate military balance between the KMT Chinese army theoretically representing the Allies, and questionable pro-Vietminh allies among the urban Vietnamese population. When the French then reoccupied the cities, Phetsarath and the whole Lao Issarak government fled to Thailand, and from there organized a modest resistance.

SisavongVong again became king of the whole of Laos as an "autonomous state" in the French Union, but by continuing to live in Luang Prabang he never became an effective symbol of national unity. France was obliged by international pressure and conflict with the Vietminh to make the independence of Laos more meaningful. In 1949 the Lao Issarak leaders returned and took part in the transfer of most authority from France to the royal government. Following elections, a fully independent government was established in 1953. The United States would be its most important supporter thereafter, making Laos per capita the largest global recipient of US aid, but also of US bombing designed to destroyVietminh bases and supply lines in eastern Laos. The key political players were two more French-educated princes of the Luang Prabang *Uparit* family – Phetsarath's younger brother Souvanna Phouma (1901–84), Francophile, with a French wife and an inclusive neutralist approach, and his half-brother (from a commoner mother) Souphanouvong (1909–95), who had a Vietnamese wife and had been the Lao Issarak link to the Vietminh and the military support it rendered. The former was most frequently Prime Minister of Laos, only briefly succeeding in building broader coalitions among the great lowland Lao (Lao Lum) families, whose rivalries were the main obsession of the political process. The latter had presided since 1950 over an insurgent Vietminh-influenced "Free Lao Front," whose communist-dominated revolutionary government became known as Pathet Lao ("The land of the Lao"). Because it was forced to rely on highland minorities who collectively outnumbered the Lao Lum, the Pathet Lao was unprecedentedly inclusive of them in its organization. Their support, together with tough Leninist organization and much North Vietnamese assistance, ensured their 1975 victory in the tragic polarization of the Cold War. Both King Sisavang Vatthana (who had succeeded his father in 1959) and Souvanna Phouma stayed in Laos, giving the communist government an initial veneer of legality amid short-lived hopes of reconciliation and peace. Six months later the Pathet Lao organized a more orthodox communist government, and the king was persuaded to abdicate. In March 1976, he and all his family were taken to one of many notorious "re-education camps" near the Vietnamese border, where they died obscurely some years later in conditions that remain unclear.

Miraculously, King Norodom Sihanouk (1922–2012) survived. His royalist Cambodia was the epitome of the modernized Southeast Asian theater state, in which the king was always the star though the sets kept changing, his supporters represented as adoring and his critics evil and treacherous. Other monarchs, and even such flamboyant dictators as Sukarno and Marcos, may well have envied his success in rejecting a constitutional role, manipulating elections, and protecting the rich but hierarchic culture of the court as the essence of the nation, while preserving his country amidst the dangers of the Cold War. Yet in throwing the monarchy into politics, his long career established a pattern from which the Khmer would suffer terribly, even after his death in 2012. He emphasized the uniqueness of the ancient Khmer race and his own ability to represent its "little people," and rejected any concept of legitimate opposition or criticism.

There was a similar cast of characters in the 1940s to that in Laos, of royalist king and nationalist prime minister being nominally independent under the Japanese, and then jockeying to regain that power under the French. But while King Sihanouk had a more central role than his ageing counterpart in Luang Prabang, the nationalist Son Ngoc Thanh failed to grasp the opportunities of French withdrawal in 1952–3. Instead he left the capital to begin an anti-French insurgency. It was to Sihanouk as king that the French in 1953 handed their remaining powers, notably over the military and foreign affairs. He not only positioned himself as the liberator from colonialism, but appeared to have his anti-colonial cake and eat it, strutting the non-aligned stage in Bandung, befriending China and North Viet Nam, yet having France supply his military training and schoolteachers, and the United States generous amounts of aid. At this moment of euphoria he established a "People's Socialist Community" (*Sangkhum Reastr Niyum*) as a state movement that could sweep away conventional competitive politics. He resigned as king so as to head it, and then entrusted notoriously violent supporters to manage the 1955 election in its favor. This crippled the parliamentary system, and ensured that the national assembly comprised exclusively members of the *Sangkhum*. Although styling himself only Prince, he had himself declared head of state for life in 1963.

Sihanouk's balancing act could not ultimately survive the advance of the Vietminh and the polarization of Indochina during the Viet Nam War. The Vietminh-backed guerrilla resistance attracted nationalists who saw no other option, but the Khmer communists were inevitably the only organization that mattered within this resistance. Sihanouk himself damaged the economy by a wave of nationalization and the rejection of US aid in 1963, the latter particularly irritating the army. Despite having allied with China and North Viet Nam in 1965 and allowed Vietminh bases in the northeast, his government was nevertheless undermined by the communists. A civil war began in 1967 as unrest grew in the east and Sihanouk encouraged draconian military action against it. When even Sihanouk's most trusted supporter, the military commander Lon Nol, changed sides, the Assembly removed him as head of state. Sihanouk was then in China, and in horror at this affront accepted Zhou Enlai's proposal in effect to join the communist side of the civil war to overthrow his usurpers. At home the Cambodian army had to fight an unequal battle to try to expel the Vietminh from Cambodia, while in revenge for its setbacks it allowed Khmer civilians to slaughter Vietnamese in and around the capital. American support for Lon Nol did nothing to slow the military regime's rapid collapse. Sihanouk's willingness to travel to communist-held areas in 1973 for photo opportunities with his lifelong enemies may have improved the image of the chauvinist thugs who led the Khmer communists. In 1975 the latter prevailed amidst the US debacle, and Cambodia was plunged into unparalleled misery.

Despite the pathos of Sihanouk's last decades, as a virtual prisoner in 1975–8 of the appalling Khmer Rouge government he had helped to power, and as an indulged but powerless guest of China and North Korea thereafter, he was again proclaimed king in 1993 by the pro-Vietnamese Hun Sen government. His last abdication and withdrawal to Pyongyang and Beijing occurred amidst illness and powerlessness in 2004. Yet Cambodia remained a kingdom, with one of his many sons on the throne, even though it was the Hun Sen regime that wielded almost absolute power.

Reinventing a Thai Dhammaraja

The Thai monarchy's reinvention after the mid-century crisis was ultimately the most complete, paradoxically because the royalists began in such a hopeless position that they played their hand with cautiously incremental skill. Since the 1932 coup the kings had been in powerless exile, and competition had been chiefly between two French-educated anti-royalist strong men – Marshal Phibun Songkhram and socialist intellectual Pridi. It was Pridi who first opened the door for a comeback after 1945 to gain royalist help against his military and fascist rivals. Soon after the return to Bangkok in 1946 of the two young brothers, King Ananda and Bhumibol, however, Ananda was found dead in the palace from a single shot from his pistol. This disaster could well have ended the monarchy if its cause were announced as suicide or accident or argument in the family. The cause of death was instead initially hushed up, and later turned to advantage by royalists led by the influential Prince Dhani Nivas, who fostered fantastic rumors that Pridi himself was involved in a murder plot. This helped consolidate an alliance between the royalists and Marshall Phibun, who seized power again in a 1947 coup, and through his 1949 constitution returned many royal privileges taken away in 1932. Eighteen-year-old

Bhumibol Adulyadej (b.1928, Cambridge, Massachusets) seemed crushed, and was quickly returned to Switzerland. He only occupied the throne in Bangkok from 1951.

Phibun used the royalists only so long as he needed them, and confined the young king to ceremonial duties in the capital. He took patronage of the Buddhist *sangha* away from the palace by returning the top jobs in its administration to the Mahayanikai order the revolutionaries had favored since 1932, rather than the royalist-favored Thammayut monks who had resumed authority in the anti-Phibun moment of 1944. He sought to celebrate the 2,500-year anniversary of Buddhism in 1957 as a state rather than royal event, symbolizing reconciliation with republican Burma by inviting its devout premier U Nu to join him in presiding over the extensive ceremonies at Ayutthaya. The lesser role allotted to the king reportedly offended the palace, and Bhumibol boycotted the key event. A few months later General Sarit, previously considered an uncouth and corrupt playboy, gained royal approval for his coup against Phibun. This inaugurated a new phase of unconstitutional authoritarianism publicly justified by restoring royal honor and centrality. The symbols of the 1932 revolution could be removed with the exile of its main defender, the national day was shifted to the king's birthday, and control of the Buddhist *sangha* returned to the Thammayut. In the intense Cold War context, the United States welcomed the monarchy's rise as a more acceptable face for corrupt military dictatorship, and encouraged Bhumibol's interest in touring the countryside and sponsoring rural development projects.

The following decade of dictatorship and crude Americanization of Bangkok certainly polarized society and encouraged clandestine leftist activity, but it also enhanced the king's popularity as a symbol of Thai-ness, of decorum, and of concern for his subjects. When in 1973 opposition to the generals boiled over in massive student-led demonstrations demanding a constitution, and the military responding by firing on the crowd and killing 77, the king emerged as a savior of the nation. He demanded that the key generals go into exile, and appointed a civilian prime minister to bring in at last a constitution. The following three years were heady, exciting, but turbulent. Many schools contended to redefine the nation as the Americans abandoned the war in Indochina and scaled down support for the Thai military. With tensions mounting, right-wing paramilitaries and the CIA- and palace-linked Border Patrol Police surrounded the student stronghold of Thammasat University on October 6, 1976, and conducted a gruesome massacre of students darkly etched in national memory. The king endorsed a military takeover and the installation of his favorite general, an anti-communist cold warrior, as prime minister. It appeared that student radicalism had convinced Bhumibol that popular democracy could not be trusted to safeguard the monarchy. The new generation of advisers around him were uniformly conservative, convinced that the country could only be harmonious under a hierarchic order of virtue with the king at its apex, and the military as its guarantor.

The most important of these trusted advisors came to be the relatively clean and astute General Prem Tinsulanond (b.1920), successively army commander (1978), Prime Minister (1980), influential member of the King's Privy

Council when he stepped out of overt politics in 1988, and head of that council in 1998. The alliance between Prem and the palace delivered a "safe" constitution with an appointed senate, and an expanded role for the monarch. The king became champion of rural development designed to undermine communist appeal, star of a series of theatrical celebrations of royal anniversaries, and a pure and virtuous Buddhist king, a *dhammaraja*. Stability returned with regular elections, and the economy boomed, also in provincial centers where agri-business and manufacturing developed. The governments after Prem's relied more on increasingly powerful business interests outside Bangkok, and eased the military out of many of its lucrative fiefdoms, prompting another military coup in February 1992, a popular pro-democracy reaction, and another royal intervention in May 1992 to require both military and populist leaders to stop the ensuing violence. This setback appeared to mark a terminal decline in the dominance of the military in Thai politics. Its hold over cabinet and boardrooms collapsed, its share of the budget dropped (from 22% in 1985 to 6% in 2006), and its *raison d'être* was undermined as Burma and Viet Nam became business opportunities rather than enemies.

The winner in the shifts of power in the 1990s, however, proved to be Thai telecommunications billionaire Thaksin Shinawatra (b.1949), whose parties won unprecedented majorities in elections in 2001, 2005, 2007, and 2011 by implementing policies genuinely helpful to the rural majority, but also by a slick use of the media, money politics, and a popular but extra-legal war on drugs in 2003. Opponents of this novel populism and power concentration in non-military hands had little left to fall back on except the charisma of the king. General Prem and his military supporters were concerned at Thaksin's attempts (partly blocked by the king) to gain control of military appointments; the ageing king by Thaksin's popularity and aggressively polarizing style. When another palace-supported military coup in 2006 failed to stop Thaksin's electoral successes, his opponents took to the streets in the royal color, yellow, and demanded a new way of governing that would keep established hierarchies immune from electoral outcomes. The monarchy was most dangerously politicized by a vastly expanded use of the *lèse majesté* laws, already tightened in the 1976 lurch to the right, to prevent any discussion of the monarchy's role or of the military coups it had supported. Although the king himself declared in 2005 that he did not want to be above criticism, prosecutions for *lèse majesté* increased tenfold in the poisonous atmosphere that followed the 2006 coup, increasingly deployed to silence critics. In June 2014, when military coups were decidedly out of global fashion, Thailand experienced a particularly draconian one. This time the military appeared to gain much establishment and Bangkok middle-class support by promising to eliminate forever the possibility that an electoral majority could overturn their dominance. While at one time a force for stability and moderation, the monarchy had become a key ingredient in Thailand's disastrous twenty-first-century blind alley.

Monarchy remains a major factor in Thai society and governance, as also in Brunei, Malaysia, and Cambodia in different ways, commanding a charismatic sphere beyond constitutionalism and democracy. It represents not only a link with a vanished past, but a symbol of the right of a few people to rule over many that was strongly challenged by "popular sovereignty" in the 1940s. Those revolutionary memories, along with globalization, education, and post-Cold War democratization, make thrones ever more vulnerable as long as uncertainty remains about their place in a democracy. Even among those elites seeking legitimation to reject majority rule, some Muslims found a globalized scriptural fundamentalism more persuasive than monarchy (Chapter 19).

COMMUNIST AUTHORITARIANISM

Viet Nam's democratic springtime was the least developed of any. While Saigon had a robust pattern of plural politics since the 1930s, there was no such tradition in the north. The clandestine habit of communist cells to judge "enemies" and dispose of them covertly militated against judicial autonomy or political give and take from the beginning. Yet the communists' minority position, and their need for both internal and external allies in the overarching goals of independence and unity, had created some tolerance of diversity. Only in 1949 did the communist victory in China, and western support for the Bao Dai government, convince Ho Chi Minh to align clearly with the Soviet bloc. Ho traveled to Beijing and Moscow in January 1950, learned that Stalin had agreed to Chinese leadership of the Asian revolutions, and negotiated the terms on which China would assist the DRV to defeat France. The price included acceptance of the Chinese line on the importance of absolute communist domination of government and army, and of an aggressive policy of land reform designed to destroy the landlord class (Figure 17.3). The Indochinese Communist Party, which had officially dissolved itself in 1945, was formally re-established as the Viet Nam Workers' Party in 1951, and a campaign of terror against landlords began in 1953. Although the numbers executed in the years 1953–6 are highly controversial (from 8,000 to 500,000 have been estimated by opposite sides of the spectrum), it was certainly enough to persuade wealthy farmers who could do so to flee to the south in 1954.

During a moment of openness in late 1956, the Party conceded that "grave mistakes" had been committed during the agrarian reform. Truong Chinh, principal author of this "leftist deviation" was publicly demoted. In apparent emulation of Mao's "hundred flowers movement," following Khrushchev's denunciation of Stalin, Hanoi intellectuals were at the same time permitted to publish a few issues of two critical journals, "Literary Selections" and "Humanities," pleading for freedom of artistic expression. These were closed down at the end of 1956, a campaign of denunciation by harder-line Marxist-Leninists ensued, and in the first months of 1958 the critics were humiliated and forced to recant. Like the Confucian scholars who had provided embellishment and legitimacy for the pre-colonial monarchy, the role of intellectuals could only be to serve the state absolutely.

At the time of the triumph of communist parties in Saigon, Phnom Penh, and Vientiane in 1975, there was a diversity of intellectual tendencies in all three countries eager to see the end of war and US intervention, and hopeful for a new era of honesty and reconstruction. Theirs was the cruellest deception.

Figure 17.3 Chinese Prime Minister Zhou Enlai visits North Viet Nam President Ho Chi Minh in Hanoi, 1960. Zhou had played a key role in the Geneva peace talks of 1954, dividing Viet Nam at the 17th parallel. Source: Three Lions/Hulton Archive/ Getty Images.

The pro-communist southerners who had fought the southern regime were pushed aside as the northern army and Party took over the south. "Third force" neutralists, intellectuals, and artists were (again) imprisoned, their books banned. Truong Chinh, bouncing back as second in the Party hierarchy, inaugurated a program to eliminate all differences between north and south, and guided a new constitution for the united country declaring that "The Communist Party of Viet Nam … armed with Marxism-Leninism, is the only force leading state and society" (1979 Constitution, cited Jamieson 1993, 361). More than a million of South Viet Nam's twenty million people were sent to a gulag of "re-education" prison camps, while about two million managed to flee the country, typically in small boats, over the next two decades.

The Pathet Lao depended heavily on Vietnamese communists for guidance, and followed their example of "re-education" camps where more than 10,000 of the old elite were imprisoned for ten to fifteen years. Flight across the Mekong to Thailand was easier than elsewhere, and about 10% of the total population of Laos, including most of the educated elite, took this option in the first five brutal years of Pathet Lao rule. Nevertheless, it could be said that although both Lao and Vietnamese communists followed the example of China in eliminating "class enemies," neither suffered the Maoist extremes of political purges and massive sacrifice of their own peasant populations. The Khmer communist leader Pol Pot (1925–98), by contrast, exceeded Mao in his careless cruelty.

The Cambodian regime of 1975–8 was the work of Indochina's weakest communist party, seething with racial resentment of its Vietnamese protectors as well as of the aristocratic or non-Khmer elites of Cambodia. Its primitive version of Maoist class war was to empty the cities, which it lacked the sophistication to control, and to eliminate not only those with privilege and property but also those with skills, education, or entrepreneurship. The 65,000 Cambodian Buddhist monks, who had for centuries provided much of Cambodia's social cohesion, were killed, disrobed, exiled, or pressured to abandon the monastery for survival. While perhaps 100,000 of the Cambodian elite were deliberately killed during this short period, many times that number, a fifth to a quarter of the total population of eight million, died through brutality, starvation, disease, and neglect. Another quarter managed to flee as refugees. This was the most catastrophic of the communist utopian experiments in Asia.

The brave new world of popular sovereignty could not deliver the social equality it promised. As Hannah Arendt (1968, 78) pointed out, removing traditional justifications for inequality of condition created the cruellest twentieth-century conflicts between classes and peoples in the quest for a new basis of order. Southeast Asia's sudden embrace of this aspect of modernity in the 1940s began a very violent period, out of which those who controlled the guns, whether communist or anti-communist military, necessarily emerged the victors. Where monarchies survived, patently denying this equality of condition, the worst extremes of violence were postponed (in Cambodia) or even perhaps avoided.

The end of the Cold War removed what international support and credibility there had been for military or communist rule, and rendered monarchic powers still more anachronistic. Ideological gaps narrowed to something like the humdrum consensus of established states. The reassuring banality of electoral changes of government became gradually accepted, first in the Philippines, after 1998 in Indonesia, and more problematically in Thailand. Even the stubborn military dictatorship of Burma began in 2010 a transition that appeared likely to give an eventual electoral victory to its democratic opponents. Elsewhere parties entrenched in power since independence showed little sign of relaxing their grip upon it, yet affluence and education multiplied the number of contestants demanding a say at local and national levels. Gradually and incompletely, the political tensions that arose in 1945 were being defused.

[18] THE COMMERCIAL TURNAROUND, 1965–

ECONOMIC GROWTH AT LAST

Lee Kuan Yew simplified his formula for success with the Singapore economy to two pieces of advice given him by his economic advisor Albert Winsemius in 1961: "First, to eliminate the communists who made any economic progress impossible; second, not to remove the statue of Stamford Raffles" (Lee 2000, 66–7). This was a crude version of the sober dictum of Sutan Sjahrir (1968, 31) at the height of the revolutionary enthusiasm of 1945: "So long as the world we live in is dominated by capital we are forced to make sure that we do not earn the enmity of capitalism." Most revolutionary leaders of the 1940s had believed the opposite, that Southeast Asian poverty resulted from the sinister control of foreign capital, and that the newly liberated states must nationalize the strategic levers, repudiate foreign debts, and plan for domestically led industrialization. In practice neither formula could be put to the test by early Southeast Asian independent governments torn by internal conflict, external intervention, rent seeking, and capital flight. Although Malaya and the Philippines rebounded fastest from the war by returning to pre-war structures, these economies looked "neo-colonial" to their revolutionary neighbors. Through the 1960s, the apparent discipline of many communist parties, and the stage-managed "success" of communist China in mobilizing a population to industrialize and end poverty, gave socialist central planning and self-sufficiency wide appeal in Southeast Asia and beyond. Sukarno and Sihanouk appeared convinced.

A few months of 1965, however, put some important levers in the hands of the Winsemius view. Singapore's emprisoning of the charismatic Leftists followed by separation from Malaysia, and Indonesia's savage turning against its communists, gave leadership in these two contrasted countries to ruthless anti-communists with enough hard-headed pragmatism to link their survival to the need for economic growth. Having benefited from draconian measures against the Left, both leaders had exceptional powers

A History of Southeast Asia: Critical Crossroads, First Edition. Anthony Reid.
© 2015 Anthony Reid. Published 2015 by John Wiley & Sons, Ltd.

to determine the allocation of internal resources and to keep wages lean and competitive.

Lee Kuan Yew, despite having won elections on an anti-colonial platform, became convinced that the salvation of Singapore in a hostile environment was "to leap-frog the region, as the Israelis had done," by attracting investment from the First World and disrupting as little as possible of the stability implied by colonial symbols like the Raffles statue (Lee 2000, 75). Singapore already had advantages in the most sophisticated infrastructure, highest incomes and most entrepreneurial traditions of the region, its port facilities essential even to its resentful neighbors. This role recovered quickly as Suharto called off Indonesian "Confrontation" of Malaysia-Singapore (Chapter 20), and it continued to contribute much to Singapore's growth. The new element was Singapore's successful wooing of multinational corporations, first American, later Japanese, to make Singapore their base for labor-intensive manufacture and Asian distribution. Unlike other development stories, Singapore wasted little time with import-substitution, but moved aggressively into manufacture for export, particularly in the rapidly growing fields of electronics and office equipment. By the 1980s it was the world's largest exporter of Winchester disk drives. By the early 1970s manufacturing had become the leading sector of the economy. Overall the Singapore economy grew by a world-leading 10.3% between 1966 and 1980, and a still healthy 7.2% in the 1980s. On a per capita basis incomes were comparable with southern Europe by 1990, and among the highest in the world in the following century.

Of course this first Southeast Asian success story was part of a much larger reordering of global commerce in the 1960s and 1970s, which finally brought real growth to the poorer countries of Asia (though notably not tropical Africa) and reversed their centuries-long decline relative to Europe and America. Wealthy countries had enjoyed a post-war trade boom from 1950 to the oil shock of 1973, encouraged by a progressive lowering of trade barriers through GATT. Although the prices of its raw materials (except oil) and tropical crops continued a long-term relative decline, Southeast Asia became a major actor in the emergence of a new global economy of production. Manufacturers began moving their production centers to wherever they could find favorable political and legal conditions and lower prices for labor, land, and resources. The other Southeast Asian economies were able to profit from the massive expansion in global exchange, later than Japan and the first four "Asian tigers" (South Korea, Taiwan, Hong Kong, and Singapore), but ahead of China and India.

Malaysia was, after Singapore, the best-placed Southeast Asian economy to exploit these conditions, with the next best infrastructure and rule of law, per capita incomes, and entrepreneurial export orientation. From 1970 the Malaysian government vigorously encouraged investment in export-oriented manufacture, leading to an annual growth of 25% in manufactured exports throughout the 1970s. Industry had been only 6% of the Malaysian economy in 1960, but was 20% by 1980. Real GDP grew at 8% a year through the 1970s, and continued at more than 6% up to the financial crisis of 1998, lifting Malaysia comfortably into the middle-income category with little remaining poverty. Electrical and electronic goods led this expansion, and factories sprouted around all the cities of the western communications corridor of Peninsular Malaysia. The bulk of the 1.3 million factory workers by 1990 were young Malay women, the first generation since the peasantization phase of the nineteenth century to return to the commercial export economy.

Thailand, Indonesia, and the Philippines, with their vast and growing peasant populations, represented a completely different challenge. Thailand was the strongest performer among them, averaging about 7% per annum growth as it transformed per capita GDP from US$100 in 1961 to US$2,750 in 1995. It gained something from US aid and was among the first destinations of Japanese and US foreign investment, notably in textile production and agri-business. Perhaps Thailand's greatest economic advantage, however, was the absence of that barrier between entrepreneurial Chinese and subsistence indigenous economies that bedeviled its neighbors. Chinese male immigrants had routinely married Thais, their descendants becoming bilingual Sino-Thai (*lukjin*) in one or two generations and Thais thereafter, adopting Thai names and Buddhist practices. Like the Chinese *mestizos* of the Philippines a century earlier (Chapter 10), the *lukjin* became an entrepreneurial middle class that moved purposefully into manufacturing, agri-business, and banking in the 1960s. The "big five" *lukjin* families that had dominated the export of rice since the 1920s were replaced a generation later by diversified conglomerates, such as that of the Sophanpanich (Tan) family controlling the Bangkok Bank and many related enterprises, or the telecommunications empire of Thaksin Shinawatra, later Prime Minister (2001–6).

The Philippines had recovered strongly from the war to be again one of Asia's wealthiest countries in the 1950s, and had a marked lead in education. Its progress in the following period looked modest by comparison with its stellar neighbors, however, particularly in the 1980s. In per capita income it was passed by Thailand in the 1970s and challenged even by Indonesia in the 1990s. The Philippines was the least able to curb population growth (see below), and its political mix of robust democracy, vested interests, and nationalist resentments also prevented its exploiting the global division of labor as effectively as some neighbors.

Indonesia's was the most dramatic turnaround, from a 1965 situation in which inflation was over 2,000% a year, foreign debt was unmanageable, and mass starvation threatened. Suharto appeared the opposite of Sukarno in his rural roots, modest education, and quiet (but ruthless) manner. He badly needed the legitimacy of an improved economy and was willing to listen to sensible advice about it. This came from a remarkable group of economists, most of them students first of Professor Sumitro Djojohadikusumo (rehabilitated in 1967 after being exiled for his role in the PRRI rebellion) at the University of Indonesia, and then of the University of California at Berkeley on a Ford Foundation program. These "technocrats," sometimes called the "Berkeley mafia," convinced the military whom they already knew from teaching courses at the Staff College to commit to an ambitious program in October 1966. The exchange rate was made realistic, subsidies cut, inflation and debt brought under control (with help from Western donors and the IMF), and resources devoted to expanding agriculture and developing import-substituting investment. Foreign investment in oil and gas was relatively easy to achieve, and provided about a third of all government revenue up to the APEC oil price rises of 1973, and almost half for the remainder of the 1970s. By directing much of this to improving agricultural and transport infrastructure, Indonesia enjoyed unprecedented growth in excess of 7% a year for the whole period 1966–81. Having been one of the world's poorest countries in 1965, Indonesia ended this phase of rapid growth at the threshold of the World Bank's "lower middle income" category, with acute poverty reduced from near 60% to 35% of an increasing population.

MORE RICE, FEWER BABIES

The leaders of the 1950s had focused most attention on taking charge of the cities, and using what resources were available to build and staff the institutions and symbols of statehood there. Agricultural infrastructure tended to go backward, and neglect of the sector forced Indonesia, Malaysia, the Philippines, and even Viet Nam to devote scarce resources to importing rice on an increasing scale. Indonesia's rice production declined by 13.6% between 1960 and 1964, even while its population was growing at 3% a year. The replacement of the western-educated intellectuals of the first generation by such homespun leaders as Generals Sarit and Suharto, for all their repressiveness, may have increased the willingness to listen to schemes to help the rural areas they came from. The key change, however, was the technological improvement in varieties of rice and other crops, often labeled the "green revolution" in the 1960s to 1980s. The Ford and Rockefeller Foundations collaborated with the Philippine government to establish in 1961 the International Rice Research Institute at the University of the Philippines agricultural campus at Los Baños. New, highly productive varieties became available from 1966, able to deliver three or four times the product per hectare, with more intensive methods of irrigation and fertilization.

Indonesia, the Philippines, Thailand, and Malaysia were among the first countries in the world to benefit, thanks to their openness to US and World Bank programs and to governments with a desperate need for results. Until the 1960s they had appeared to be part of a more general Malthusian crisis in Asia, whereby population was relentlessly increasing at a faster rate than food production while industrial growth occurred only in the rich world. This pattern was reversed in the next two decades. In Southeast Asia as a whole, cereal production increased from 33.8 million to 73.6 million metric tonnes between 1970 and 1995. Indonesia achieved its goal of self-sufficiency in rice production in 1984, while the Philippines closed the gap for its more rapidly rising population.

This transition accompanied, and to some extent required, a profound transformation of the peasant production pattern established in the high colonial period. The colonial-era myth of a self-sufficient agricultural village as the bedrock of Southeast Asian identities was overthrown in what Elson (1997) called "the end of the peasantry." Agriculture was revolutionized by a commercial and mechanized pattern of ploughing, harvesting, and rice-milling, spurred by government credit and marketing schemes. Where the rice plant had been considered to be animated by a supernatural life-spirit, only to be harvested stalk by stalk by local women wielding a small finger-knife (*ani-ani*), the fast-growing, short-stemmed varieties were seen as a commercial resource that could be harvested with sickles by contracted male outsiders. Roads, electrical grids, and telecommunications were extended into rural areas, while the massive import of affordable Japanese motorcycles revolutionized communications even along footpaths impassable by horse- or ox-carts. Motorcycle use took off in Indonesia and Thailand in the 1980s. In the 2000s even cheaper Chinese motorcycles flooded into Viet Nam, Laos, and Burma. By 2010 Indonesia, Thailand, and Viet Nam were the world's three largest motorcycle markets after China and India, and there was one motorcycle for every four to six people. Education and employment in the cities drew young people away from the farm, but in former rice-bowl areas of central Thailand, Java, and the central Luzon plain diversified employment also came to villages. Agriculture occupied less than half the labor force of all non-socialist Southeast Asia by the 1990s, and even rural villages frequently drew most of their income from off-farm employment.

The surprise reversal of the gloomy 1960s assessments of Southeast Asia's economy had its counterpart in population forecasts. Post-war independence initially seemed only to increase fertility, threatening the ability even to feed the extra mouths. Southeast Asia as a whole had in 1965–70 a total fertility rate (TFR) of 6.06 children born to every woman, when the population growth rates were about 2.5% a year. The wealthiest countries, Singapore (3.65) and Malaysia, predictably had the lowest TFR, but war-torn Viet Nam was paradoxically the highest, at 7.38. Birth rates began to go down in one country after another, beginning with the wealthy cities, as infant mortality dropped and expectations of survival and education changed. Singapore's TFR dropped below the 2.1 replacement level in the 1970s, followed by Thailand, Viet Nam, and Burma in succession. These four countries by 2005–10 had a Northeast Asian pattern of extremely low TFR rates of 1.25, 1.63, 1.89, and 2.08, respectively, while Southeast Asia as a whole was at a moderate 2.26. Increasingly, universal education for women and later ages of marriage were part of the explanation for this classic demographic transition, with lowered birth rates following lowered death rates after an interval in which population grew rapidly. In cities such as Bangkok and Singapore, where 15% and 14%, respectively, of women (2005) reached menopause without marrying or giving birth, there is the added Northeast Asian factor of female education and careers outpacing any updating of the traditional deference expected of wives and daughters-in-law.

As noted in Chapter 13 (Table 13.1) populations continued to grow rapidly as the post-war bulge moved through the generations. Fertility was still very high in Timor Leste (TFR 6.53) after its 2002 independence, while the birth rate among Filipinos and Malaysian Muslims dropped less rapidly than elsewhere for complex reasons of which religion was only part. Less populated Laos and recently traumatized Cambodia also had above average fertility.

These differentials in birth rates were to some extent offset by high migration from poorer countries to richer ones, to fill roles as manual and construction workers, domestic help, and agricultural pioneers. Singapore had the highest population growth despite the lowest birth rate by encouraging educated migrants from Malaysia (especially disaffected ethnic Chinese and Indians), India, and China, and strictly controlled contract workers from Thailand, Bangladesh, the Philippines, and Indonesia. Thailand welcomed economic and political refugees from Burma, Laos, and Cambodia, more than a million in total by the 1990s. About two million Indonesians were in West Malaysia and Sabah, both as legal contract workers and illegals arriving by boat and melding into the Malay population. As poorly educated but traditionally minded men failed to find marriage partners in Singapore, Taiwan, South Korea, and Japan, an international marriage market developed in the 1990s bringing in wives from Viet Nam and the Philippines.

OPENING THE COMMAND ECONOMIES

Communism won the Indochina wars in 1975, but in economic terms decisively lost the peace. Up until that point it was not difficult to argue that the socialist planned economies were delivering a better life to their non-elite peasantry than their capitalist neighbors, that only decades of warfare were holding them back from growth, and that state-led industrialization might make Viet Nam the sort of military power in Asia that the Soviet Union had become in Europe in the 1930s. Statistical comparisons were impossible given the very different accounting methods of the socialist economies from what became in the 1990s the global norm of national income accounting. The strategy and determination that made military success possible nevertheless suggested that communist governments would be able to bury their neighbors industrially. Yet within a decade all four of the socialist experiments (including idiosyncratic Burma) were seen to have failed, their chronic poverty an inescapable contrast to their booming capitalist neighbors. Reforms were then introduced to bring these economies gradually back to the market-driven world.

The first surprise was the intensity of conflicts within the socialist bloc. Pol Pot's hyper-communism in Cambodia was driven by a chauvinism that provoked a Vietnamese invasion in 1978 to replace that murderous regime by a pro-Vietnamese communist one. Since China considered Cambodia an ally in its struggle against the Soviet Union, it in turn invaded the border areas of Viet Nam early in 1979. Although the Sino-Viet Nam war changed little on the ground, it completely ended Chinese aid, which had been critical to North Viet Nam's survival and military effectiveness, and even its food supply, before the 1975 reunification. This war intensified what had already become a stalling of Viet Nam's economy in the years 1977–80, when per capita incomes declined.

Secondly, Viet Nam was poorly suited to implement a Soviet-type emphasis on heavy industry. What little industry existed in the north in 1954 was reduced by US bombing and the evacuation of targets in the cities, so that by 1975

North Viet Nam was a country of poor peasants. Capital, entrepreneurship, and urban labor had long been concentrated in the Saigon area, but the years after its conquest by the North were marked by harsh repression and desperate flight rather than development. The few available resources were wasted in building industrial capacity for which there was little market. Agricultural policy in the south was another disaster, less brutal than the northern collectivization of the 1950s, but more ruinous of production. Whereas the Mekong delta rice bowl was expected to be the salvation of the north, collectivization so reduced output that Viet Nam had to import substantial food in 1977–80 from the Soviet Union. Destitution, and the stubborn resistance of farmers in southern Viet Nam and even more in Laos, meant that collectivization had to be progressively abandoned from 1979, with a key step in 1981 when individual farmers were allotted plots of land on contract. This relaxation began the recovery of agricultural production and staved off starvation, though it was not until the 1990s, and the benefit of green revolution technologies, that Viet Nam returned to its pre-war role as a major rice exporter.

This modest success strengthened the arguments for more radical reform, as did the obvious need for "catch-up" with Viet Nam's more successful neighbors, now including China under the Deng Xiaoping reforms. In 1986 the sixth congress of the Communist Party endorsed the so-called "new change" (*doi moi*) program, legitimating a succession of market-friendly liberalizations not only in Viet Nam but also in its then client states of Laos and Cambodia. Crucially, a foreign investment law was adopted in 1987 that enabled Viet Nam to use its exceptionally low wages to attract export-oriented industry. Textile and footwear factories began to sprout around Saigon and Hanoi. The result was that Viet Nam's economy began to grow rapidly, and that of Laos more hesitantly, from a very low base at least twenty years behind Thailand, Indonesia, and the Philippines (Table 16.1).

Had all the suffering of the war for socialism been a tragic mistake? The regimes firmly in place have certainly not said so. Officially the doctrine was that socialism must be postponed until the capitalist phase has been more successfully passed. As this future grew ever more distant and implausible, the more influential private belief became rather similar to that of Singapore's ruling party – that a unified, meritocratic, authoritarian ruling party can better deliver welfare for the majority than the messy democracies, ideological battlegrounds, and rampant consumerism of neighbors. There is some support for this in social indicators such as education, health, and life expectancy, where Viet Nam performed better than its lowly economic ranking (see below). The same, surprisingly, seems true for Cambodia, rising from the ashes of the terrible 1970s. A client of Viet Nam from 1978 until United Nations intervention in 1991, Cambodia became thereafter a nominal democracy, forcefully ruled by ex-communist strongman Hun Sen (b.1952). Its relative success in growth and welfare in this period, notably by contrast with Burma, was due more to its unusual openness to international investment and aid projects than to coherent planning.

It is even harder to find positives in "the Burmese way to socialism," save that it managed the longest of Southeast Asia's China borders without becoming a Cold War battleground. This was the ideological justification for Ne Win's military dictatorship (1962–88), nominally incorporating elements of Buddhism's "middle way" in total military domination of the economy. Existing firms were taken over by rent-seeking generals, and further foreign investment and even foreign travel permission were restricted to a paranoid degree. The economy was in the worst state of any by 1988, when Ne Win was overthrown by his generals and an initially more liberal junta with the acronym SLORC took over. By holding an election in 1990, spectacularly losing it to the charismatic Suu Kyi (b.1945), daughter of independence hero Aung San, and then ignoring the results and harshly repressing the victors, SLORC became even more isolated by embargoes on trade and aid. China, which successive regimes had been careful not to confront openly, became the junta's favored supporter and foreign investor, further fueling resentment in the country. Increasingly desperate after 2000 to find a formula to remain in power but grow the economy, the military began to allow foreign investment, notably to exploit its abundant oil and forestry resources. Finally, after 2011 it liberalized politically under General Thein Sein, allowing Suu Kyi to return to electoral politics and thereby escaping the international embargoes that had kept it down. After a lost half-century of impoverishment, Burma's economy began to improve in the late 1990s but still had a huge economic gap to bridge with its neighbors.

GAINS AND LOSSES

Overall, it is impossible to avoid the conclusion that the period since the 1970s has been the best of modern times for Southeast Asia's inhabitants, though only since the 1980s in Indochina and 1990s in Burma. The wealthiest countries and individuals now have a first-world lifestyle, and the population as a whole lives better than South Asians, though they have been surpassed by East Asians (Table 18.1). They are living longer, healthier lives than ever before, have greater food security, better education, and more access to reliable information. They know this, and share an optimism about progress that is harder to find in the rich countries that began their economic growth a couple of centuries ago.

There are, however, many negative features of the globalization and consumerism that have progressively taken over the region. Growing wealth in general was accompanied by growing inequality. The richest countries, Singapore, Malaysia, and Thailand, had greater inequality, measured by Gini coefficients of 48.1, 46.2, and 40.0, respectively, in the period 2008–10.[1] Even while more and more were brought out of statistical poverty and malnutrition, their sense of relative deprivation may have grown through exposure to consumer products and resentment of the rich. Among countries with adequate data, inequality was more marked in some times and places than one would expect from relative income levels. Suharto's Indonesia was surprisingly the most effective at keeping inequality low at a Gini of around 34 while incomes rose rapidly. The lowest 40% of the population even increased their share of national income from

Table 18.1 GDP per capita by country, 1970–2010, decennial averages.

	1970–79	1980–89	1990–99	2000–09
Brunei	7,484	18,111	14,854	24,240
Singapore	2,280	6,998	19,883	29,114
Malaysia	839	2,026	3,711	5,506
Thailand	353	864	2,175	2,789
Philippines	346	635	920	1,256
Indonesia	234	590	918	1,425
Burma	124	154	155	256
Viet Nam	90	131	247	654
Cambodia	85	114	240	473
Laos	63	151	283	514

Source: United Nations Database.

19.6% to 20.9% in the decade 1976–87 (Rigg 2003, 106). The introduction of a robust democracy in 1998 in the context of the Asian financial crisis set back all incomes briefly. The new de-centered growth of the twenty-first century appears to have facilitated rising inequality. Greater regional autonomy under democratization only worsened the relative poverty of eastern Indonesia, remote from industrial centers and markets. Nevertheless, Indonesian development remained fairer than that of its market-driven neighbors.

Military-dominated Thailand was the worst example of unequal development as the new wealth concentrated around Bangkok and some commercial and tourist centers in the south. Its Gini coefficient rose from 43 to 54 between 1975 and 1992, while the share of the lowest 40% in national income shrank steadily from 16.5% in 1962 to 11% in 1992. In Thailand's case, the more democratic politics in 1997–2006 coincided with, and perhaps caused in the case of the Thaksin governments of 2001–6, a much-needed turnaround in inequality, as development and welfare finally spread to the chronically poor northeast and north of the country. The weak Philippine state, much derided by its own feisty activists as ineffective and patrimonial, produced less growth but less inequality than this Thailand extreme, its lowest 40% always earning 12–15% of the national income. Its relatively modest growth between 1961 and 2009 coincided with a slight decline in its initially high Gini coefficient, from 49 to 45.

Did Viet Nam's strong communist state manage its catch-up development more equitably? Comparable figures only became available in the 1990s, and suggest, on the contrary, that the initial phase of marketization benefited privileged sectors and produced unusually high inequality. The earliest Gini coefficient of 45 for 1993 suggests inequality almost as bad as fifteen times richer Malaysia. Compared with post-communist Russia and China this nevertheless looks moderate, and the next two decades saw it come down to a more normal level of inequality for its income, approaching that of Indonesia. The incidence of serious poverty (income below US$1.25 per day at PPP) in the population reduced even more impressively to only fourteen million people in 2012, a proportion no higher than that of richer Indonesia and the Philippines.

If there is an argument for communist effectiveness, however, it lies rather in the ability of the state to lift some measures of social welfare not monetized in the same way. A strong and confident government insisted that everyone go to school, take their vaccinations, and accept the state's modernization of childbirth practices, hygiene, and female participation in the workforce. Female participation in the once-communist Indochina states, but also Burma, was well above world norms, at 80% or above in the period 1990–2010. Viet Nam (but not Laos) did better than Indonesia and the Philippines at lowering infant mortality, reducing child malnutrition, and distributing contraceptives. In consequence of such measures, life expectancy of Vietnamese was already in 1980 the highest in Southeast Asia except for super-rich Singapore and Brunei, and it remained that way during *doi moi* (Table 18.2).

This type of international data is collected on a country basis, and reveals interesting comparisons on the relative effectiveness of governments at stimulating growth and distributing its benefits. But more striking than the contrast between countries is the way Southeast Asia as a whole has been transformed since the 1960s. The new commercialization plugged everyone into patterns of consumption, leisure, and communication that began earlier in Singapore, Malaysia, and Thailand, and only reached Burma in the twenty-first century. There is a remarkable commonality in the way the changes have widened opportunities and separated generations. The move to the cities was only part of the story, though it transformed the region from one of the world's least urbanized in the 1960s to nearly 50% urban in 2010, with Manila, Bangkok, Jakarta, and Saigon among the world's mega-cities of beyond ten million. Every family was engaged in the city through its studying children, its migrant workers, and the programs beamed on television, radio, and social media. Prosperous rural villages were engaged in production for the market through extensive networks of outsourcing; less prosperous ones were denuded of young people as they moved to opportunities in the city. Air-conditioned shopping malls became the new leisure centers.

Table 18.2 Female life expectancy by country, 1980–2010. Note that male life expectancy is on average five years less.

	1980	1990	2000	2010
Singapore	75	78	80	84
Brunei	73	76	78	80
Viet Nam	72	75	78	80
Malaysia	70	73	75	77
Thailand	67	74	75	77
Philippines	65	68	70	72
Indonesia	60	65	69	72
Burma	57	61	64	67
Laos	50	55	63	68
Cambodia	33	57	65	73

Source: World Bank 2014.

This commercialization has also linked Southeast Asians to the world as never before. As of old they travel to Mecca, India, Rome, and Palestine on pilgrimages, and jumbo jets increased their numbers tenfold to almost a million pilgrims each year. But this flow was dwarfed by the millions traveling to the regional shopping and entertainments hubs – Singapore, Hong Kong, Bangkok, and Kuala Lumpur – as well as to study or holiday in Australia, Europe, China, and North America. In the twenty-first century, annual outgoing tourists from Singapore and Malaysia were more numerous than their populations, while around six million each departed from Indonesia and Thailand.

Southeast Asia itself entered the international tourist market in the 1960s, stimulated by the spending of American servicemen on rest and recreation leave in Bangkok. Singapore and Bangkok became the two key transit airports of the region as mass travel took off. Indonesia's second international gateway was opened in Bali in 1968 and quickly became the leading one for tourists. One center after another developed its formula of cultural exoticism, night life, and tropical beach resorts – Pattaya and Phuket in Thailand, Kuta and Sanur in Bali, Pangkor and Langkawi in Malaysia. Thailand never relinquished its lead in attracting long-distance tourists, with a total of 11.6 million visitors in 2011 and 26.7 million in 2013, 70% of them from outside Southeast Asia. Singapore was next with its pattern of short stopovers between Europe and Australia as well as providing a service and shopping center for the region. Malaysia and Indonesia (primarily Bali) also earned significant revenue from tourism, and in the 1990s peace finally enabled Viet Nam and Cambodia (with its spectacular Angkor ruins) to join the chase for tourist dollars. Southeast Asia as a whole welcomed 43 million outsiders in 2011, while 37 million more visited one another's countries within the region. The pioneering 1970s and 1980s were dominated by Europeans, Japanese, and Australians, but by 2012 China was much the largest single source, supplying 10% of external tourists.

The prominence of sexual tourism and prostitution in Southeast Asia is the most controversial feature of the commercial turnaround and its tourist face. Colonial governments had regulated prostitution in the interests of their soldiers, and allowed Japanese and later Chinese prostitutes to immigrate to serve the bigger urban centers. Independent Southeast Asian governments, by contrast, all regarded prostitution as illegal, and elite public disapproval was high, notably in Muslim countries. Yet tourists were attracted to Bangkok, Saigon, Manila, and later Phnom Penh for their sexual services, which were publicly on display in various forms.

The economic autonomy but lower status of women, discussed in Chapter 15, help explain the distinctiveness of the Southeast Asian commercial sex industry. Prostitution was already noted in the Siamese capital in the seventeenth century, but the preferred means of dealing with abundant male traders in the ports had been through temporary marriage, profitable and without stigma for both sides (Chapters 1 and 6). This older pattern of serial monogamy, with relatively easy divorce, was adapted in the commercialized late twentieth century to a kind of "contract marriage" (*kawin kontrak*, in Indonesian), to cater for miners or estate laborers on contracts far from home.

A form of "Islamic prostitution" even developed on the edge of Arab tourism in Java, using a legal Saudi concept of "traveler's marriage" (*misyar*) to distort an older Southeast Asian habit.

Theoretically monogamous European men, however, needed their guiltier sex to be quick and discreet, and the twentieth-century adoption of urban modernity Asianized the institution of commercial prostitution. Its rewards rose with every influx of well-paid transient men – soldiers and sailors, but also local truck-drivers. The relative affluence of American soldiers during their long engagement with Indochina and the Philippines gave a boost to the sex trade around US bases and in the recreation centers of Bangkok and Manila. When the bases closed, in Indochina in 1975 and Subic Bay with the Mount Pinatubo eruption of 1992, sex tourism provided a new market with high profit margins. Recent studies have shown that the majority of sex workers in both Thailand and the Philippines enter the trade because it offers the highest returns for limited education. They typically support families, either parental or their own, to break out of desperate poverty. Villages in north-eastern Thailand known for sending many girls to the Bangkok sex trade are well provided with new modern houses and ornate Buddhist temples.

Thailand's pragmatic approach to female and male prostitution made it a leader both in experiencing an epidemic of HIV/AIDS and in combating it through safer practice. Over 580,000 Thais died of the epidemic between 1984, when it was first reported, and 2008. The best-known campaigner for safe sex, Mechai Viravaidya, known as "Mr Condom" for his flamboyant style of offering contraceptives to all, was appointed Minister for Tourism and AIDS Prevention (1991–2), helping Thailand turn the corner toward reducing the incidence of the disease. In Cambodia a high 2% of the population, mostly women connected with the sex trade, were reported to be carrying HIV/AIDS in 1998, sparking a campaign that lowered incidence after 2003. Elsewhere statistics were less reliable, and reported deaths much lower. Indonesia began addressing its problem in 1994, but incidence appeared to increase after 2000, partly through unprotected sex in Papua. In the cities of Indonesia, Malaysia, Myanmar, and Viet Nam, HIV/AIDS came after 2000 to be seen as a problem primarily associated with intravenous drug use.

DARKER COSTS – ENVIRONMENTAL DEGRADATION AND CORRUPTION

The commercial turnaround profoundly and rapidly changed the mind-set of Southeast Asians, who became part of a consumption-driven world. In a region previously noted for the world's greatest biodiversity one must ask how far such commercial expansion was sustainable or prudent when accompanied by rapid population increase. The literature is replete with gloomy predictions of imminent collapse of fish stocks, water supplies, agriculture, and biodiversity. The reduction of the forests that still covered about 75% of Southeast Asia in

1870 was the most visible loss. From then until the 1960s the retreat of the forests was relentless but gradual, resulting from the expansion of the agricultural frontier at the hands of an expanding population and the planting of tropical export crops such as coffee, pepper, tobacco, tea, and, after 1900, rubber and oil palm.

Timber exports had been limited to the prized teak of Burma, Siam, and Java until the 1920s, when other hardwoods began to be exported, especially from the Philippines. Colonial governments boldly declared that forested land belonged to the state, ignoring both the complex arrangements they knew from Europe and the even more complex hunting, gathering, and shifting cultivation practices in Southeast Asia. They established forestry departments, first in Burma (1856) and Java (1869, after earlier short-lived experiments), and began introducing German "scientific" foresters to plan the classification and replanting of lucrative teak forests in the manner of an orderly plantation. They established an important precedent in creating some protected, as well as productive, forests. These were initially for scientific purposes but increasingly also to ensure the survival of endangered fauna – rhinoceros, orang-utan, elephants, and tigers. Their most important legacy was, however, the negative one, of claiming the right of the state to allocate logging licenses over vast territories to timber companies.

The serious assault on Southeast Asia's old-growth forests of dipterocarps (tall straight hardwoods) took off in the 1960s. The process had begun earlier in the Philippines, with exports initially to the United States, but the vast expanding needs of Japan's post-war boom quickly took over as the engine of destruction. Having encouraged its farmers to plant timber to meet the needs for reconstruction, Japan soon found it cheaper to use Southeast Asian hardwoods and leave its own forests intact. The loggers moved from the Philippines to new frontiers in Thailand, Borneo, Sumatra, and eventually eastern Indonesia and New Guinea. Indonesia alone increased its annual log production more than tenfold between 1960 and 1995, from 4 million to over 40 million cubic meters. Undisturbed forest cover dropped to 20% by 2000 in the Philippines and Thailand, having been 45% and 55%, respectively, in 1960. Log production declined in these countries and in Indonesia in the 1980s, chiefly because the most accessible forests had gone, but also because of government restrictions designed either to preserve what remained, or in Indonesia's case to boost employment by permitting export only of processed timber – plywood, pulp, and paper. The loggers responded by moving to new frontiers in Burma, Laos, Cambodia, and New Guinea, often ignoring government restrictions and bribing local power-holders.

The revenues helped fuel the early stages of economic growth, less through the taxes going to government budgets than the rents that enabled power-holders and their business cronies to build corporate empires in transportation, processing, and the oil-palm, rubber, coffee, and other plantations that replaced many of the forests. By 2010 Indonesia and Malaysia, which together produced 85% of the world's palm oil, had 7.7 million and 5.2 million hectares, respectively, planted in oil palm, increasing at about 7% a year. The advancing frontier of smallholder agriculture also accounted for much of the forest loss, while the brackish waters of coastal mangrove forests were lost to commercial prawn farms. Little more than a tenth of the area felled appears to have been reforested with a view to sustainable logging.

Arguably this transformation of the Southeast Asian landscape, though now in the global spotlight because of its damaging effect on carbon emissions, is little different from the domestication of land for farming and pasture already wrought on temperate forests from England to Australia over the past few centuries. Yet the pace of destruction of tropical rain forest raises some particular concerns. Firstly, the planet's remaining biodiversity owes a disproportionate debt to Southeast Asia's humid tropics, including to those of its humans who have somehow maintained a hunter-gatherer lifestyle dependent on the forest. The effect of deforestation in high-rainfall tropical areas affects the local climate and environment even more than the global. Average temperature rises of several degrees over the past two decades have been noted in inland cities such as Bandung and Chiang Mai. Once-navigable rivers have silted up, and flooding becomes more frequent as run-off is not absorbed. Burning for dry-season forest clearance in Sumatra and Borneo has since the 1980s produced periodic acute air pollution throughout the equatorial region, with damaging peaks affecting health also in Malaysia and Singapore in 1997, 2006, 2009, and 2013.

The rapid growth of the region's coastal cities since 1945 exposed ever-larger numbers to flooding and storm surges in one of the planet's most dangerous seascapes. The giant Swiss reinsurer Swiss Re in 2013 put Jakarta and Manila among the five most endangered cities in the world in terms of numbers at risk. The coastlines most exposed to tectonic tsunamis on the western and southern boundaries of the Sunda shelf, and to typhoons on the eastern coasts of the Philippines, had been avoided by pre-colonial settlers but now support large cities such as Padang, Cilacap, and Davao. Millions were therefore made homeless by such disasters as the December 2004 tsunami that killed about 230,000 people in coastal cities like Banda Aceh (Sumatra) and Phuket (south Thailand). Typhoons killed a thousand or more in the Philippines in each of the years 2004, 2006, 2011, and 2012, and over 6,000 when Typhoon Haiyuan devastated the central Philippines in November 2013. Cyclone Nargis in the Irrawaddy delta in 2008 killed 138,000 and made millions homeless. Southeast Asia's biggest cities are sinking at an alarming rate as a result of overbuilding and the extraction of the water table below, factors even more drastic than sea-level rise through global warming. Since 2000, Jakarta, the most imperiled, has been calculated to be sinking at 5 cm a year, and Bangkok and Saigon at more than 2 cm. Siltation and the asphalting of surfaces contributed further to turning annual floods into major disasters. The Jakarta floods of 2007 and January 2013 affected tens of thousands of homes. The flooding that submerged Bangkok and all the deltaic areas of Indochina in 2011 was rated by Swiss Re as the most destructive of property of any freshwater flood in human history, with US$47 billion in losses and over fifteen million people affected.

These environmental costs of rapid development would not have been easy to resolve in well-regulated polities, but were intensified by the flouting of planning regulations by developers and business tycoons with access to national or local power-holders. Corruption, in the sense of distorting the application of neutral law for private gain, was practiced for much higher stakes as the economies took off. Opinion polls put corruption top of popular concerns wherever democratic conditions allowed such views to be expressed. As this book has emphasized, authority in pre-colonial Southeast Asia was personal and charismatic, and a patron's symbiotic relation with his clients was his most precious asset. Foreign traders learned that in most ports judicious gifts were more effective than observation of law in doing business. The legal-bureaucratic state arrived unusually late, and then was in alien, colonial hands that limited its internalization. Where revolutions overthrew the legitimacy of colonial law, personal authority and charisma became still more important. Suharto's Indonesia, the communist countries, and Burma routinely resorted to extra-judicial state terror and torture. Suharto was perhaps the only leader to admit these tactics, explaining that when criminals and state enemies were arbitrarily shot, the bodies would be left where they fell as "shock therapy, so that people would understand that criminal actions would still be combatted and overcome" (Suharto 1989, cited Elson 2001, 237). Only in Singapore and Malaysia were colonial legal-bureaucratic values relatively smoothly domesticated into the independent states. Elsewhere military hierarchies and Leninist parties sought to replicate the centralized discipline of former colonial officials, but only Singapore's People's Action Party maintained that tight discipline in the face of a booming economy.

Independence hugely inflated the bureaucracies of the new states, as nationalists sought their rewards in prestigious government office. Increasingly poorly paid and motivated, local officials could only maintain their status and livelihoods by requiring bribes for the routine licenses and approvals they issued. The fact that in Indonesia, the Philippines, and Malaysia entrepreneurship was largely in the hands of politically marginalized "Chinese" created a vicious circle of discrimination, bribery, and flouting of the law. At the top of the hierarchy dictators like Suharto in Indonesia, Marcos in the Philippines, and Sarit in Thailand increasingly surrounded themselves with Sino-Southeast Asian cronies who could provide the non-budgeted extra income both to support pet projects and to enrich the dictators and their families. The egregious corruption that transformed them and their relatives into increasingly parasitic billionaires turned public opinion eventually against each of them, making it unlikely that such figures could arise in the twenty-first century.

Corruption is impossible to measure, and the attempts to do so by Transparency International since 1995 have had to rely only on the perceptions of international business as to how far corruption discouraged investment. Not surprisingly, the rankings for transparency given to Southeast Asian countries reflected their wealth and sophistication, with Singapore always in the top five of global rankings, followed by Malaysia and Thailand in the upper-middle and lower-middle, respectively. Indonesia was judged the most corrupt of the 41 states assessed in the first survey of 1995, but gradually improved to about two-thirds of the way down the list by 2010. The (ex-) communist countries fared a little better than their poverty would have suggested when first assessed, but by 2010 they were ranked below Indonesia near the bottom of the league, while Burma was at the very bottom. However flawed, these rankings do provide a corrective to the perceptions of citizens themselves, who tended to be most outraged at the corruption of their leaders when more democratic conditions allowed civil society and the press to expose it. The rankings of Transparency International showed that, on the contrary, Thailand, Indonesia, and even Burma were internationally perceived as less corrupt when they democratized. Thailand dropped again in the rankings after the military coup of 2006, until in 2013 it was below the Philippines, which appeared to be on the way back up after a ranking below Indonesia in 2010 (Transparency International 2014).

Singapore is rightly proud of its excellent reputation for doing business, always ranked far ahead of any other Asian country and matched only by Scandinavians at the top of such league tables. Its formula of paying the political, bureaucratic, and judicial elite the highest salaries in the world and expecting them to adhere to a high standard of probity and loyalty in return, combined with stern corporal and capital punishment of offenders, worked well in delivering a reliable implementation of the national laws. It could not be replicated in larger countries with inherently more dispersed power, nor in democracies with a critical press that would make such high salaries politically untenable. The Singapore model was in fact less attractive to its neighbors than to authoritarian regimes in China and Viet Nam, seeming to offer economic success, social stability, and international respectability with a high concentration of power in a few hands. The democracies suffered a new form of corruption in the form of money politics, whereby politicians could only get elected by distributing rewards that were paid for by vested interests that needed their support. Like much low-level corruption, this at least had the advantage of distributing some of the new wealth to the poor, as Thaksin proved adept at doing in Thailand. More damaging was the chronic inability of Southeast Asia's "soft states" to implement laws on environmental protection, rational planning, and health and safety because of a prevailing culture of patronage and corruption. While this rightly enraged Southeast Asian reformers, outside observers perceived a marked growth in accountability as power was diffused away from the center through the democratization that followed the Asian financial crisis of 1997, and the rise of increasingly sophisticated critical voices in civil society and the social media.

Most Southeast Asians would agree that the economic gains of this period outweighed its costs. The economic growth that came to Southeast Asia after 1970 was the first time since the sixteenth century that the regional economy not only equalled but outperformed the global norm and closed the gap with earlier-developing industrial countries of the north. It gave the lie to the gloomy analyses of the colonial period that the tropical regions were doomed to shared poverty and Malthusian crisis. The optimism of the nationalist modernizers was at last justified by results. Not surprisingly, the lifting of vast populations out of rural poverty and into expanding globally connected cities had also profound effects on religious and cultural modes of thinking, discussed in Chapter 19.

NOTE

1   Figures on inequality are assiduously recorded by the World Bank, but the coverage is incomplete either because data is simply lacking, as in Burma and Laos, or because it is obscured by a nervous government, as in Singapore. They must be treated with caution. Gini coefficients are measured on a scale 0–100, where 0 would be absolute equality.

[19] *Making Nations, Making Minorities, 1945–*

The High Modernist Moment, 1945–1980

The period of "liberation" from the power inequalities of the imperial age, from the independence declarations of 1945 to the end of the Viet Nam War in 1975, was a remarkable stage in history, usually described through the way the "Cold War" was tragically fought out on Southeast Asian soil. These wars cost millions of lives and bitterly divided the region, though over issues that turned out not to be the crucial ones. In the longer term the period may rather be seen as a miracle of nation-building in which the modern nation-state ideal won a resounding triumph everywhere. The heroic declarations of 1945 could not mask the tenuous fragility of governments with few resources seeking to impose themselves on illiterate and impoverished populations of great diversity. It is difficult to see their first stage as a success either in the violence they deployed or tolerated or the meagre economic results they achieved. Yet in cultural terms this period delivered a truly profound transformation in which diverse peoples began to see themselves not only as Indonesians, Filipinos, Vietnamese, and so forth, but as committed to transformative progress through education to modernity. Paradoxically, the period of liberation from European power structures marked an unprecedented embrace of modern European cultural and political norms. It marked probably the most dramatic iconoclasm toward Asian traditional cultures of any period in history.

The mind-set that pervaded both camps of the Cold War has been described as "high modernist" by James Scott (1998, 4). It was a robust, often extreme, version of modern rational state planning, exuding "self-confidence about scientific and technical progress, the expansion of production, the growing satisfaction of human needs, the mastery of nature (including human nature), and, above all, the rational design of social order commensurate with the scientific understanding of natural laws." These ideas, of course, began in the European Enlightenment and the French Revolution, creatively universalized by communist and socialist movements, but their most extreme manifestations occurred in

A History of Southeast Asia: Critical Crossroads, First Edition. Anthony Reid.
© 2015 Anthony Reid. Published 2015 by John Wiley & Sons, Ltd.

Asia in this period. They are remembered chiefly as negatives – the appalling social and cultural destructiveness of Pol Pot's Cambodia, or Mao's China in the Great Leap Forward and the Cultural Revolution. Yet high modernism was equally evident in the education programs, media control, and five-year plans of anti-communist and military regimes determined to build a new national man. Its successes can be seen in the universal education of girls even in Confucian-influenced Viet Nam, and in the architecture of Lee Kuan Yew's Singapore. In the 1970s and 1980s the majority of Singaporeans were relocated from villages, shop-houses, and squatter settlements to high-rise government-built apartments, owned by their occupants through compulsory contributions to a Central Provident Fund, which also gave Singapore a high savings rate rising to 25% of wages. Lee boldly insisted that each new apartment block would be racially integrated, with quotas fixed in 1989 at 25% Malay and 13% Indian (Chinese being under-represented because more were wealthy enough to buy privately). The social and physical landscape was completely transformed. The state acquired land at below-market rates to accommodate an ever larger population in modern skyscrapers, allowing space in the world's most crowded country for parks and even forests (Figure 19.1).

The generation of nationalists who came to power in most of Southeast Asia in the late 1940s were an exceptional intellectual elite. They were western-educated within colonial regimes that were self-justifying in terms of rational modernity, but which systematically humiliated them, contradicting that rationality through a racial hierarchy that kept real power in the hands of

Figure 19.1 1980s Singapore. The new high-rise apartments and offices ousting the older shop-houses. Source: Topfoto/ImageWorks.

Europeans of similar education to themselves. Late colonialism's pseudo-deference to puppet aristocrats of education inferior to or more traditional than their own convinced them that the decorative royal traditions of their societies were "feudal" anachronisms. In their hearts these intellectuals were nationalists, but their heads were widely persuaded by a greater or lesser degree of Marxist internationalism. In the form in which they devoured it in the 1920s and 1930s, Marxism offered a rational and modern set of arguments why imperialism was doomed along with capitalism, and why the future belonged to a revolutionary vanguard of people like themselves.

The reactionary nature of both Dutch and French colonial regimes in the 1930s convinced many that independence could only come by violent revolution. Although this was a minority view even among nationalist intellectuals at the time, the astonishing revolutionary opportunity provided by the sudden Japanese surrender of August 1945 seemed to justify those who held it. Revolution appeared a more rational, even scientific, way to describe the process of decolonization and state-forming. It proposed that serious progress to modernity could only be achieved by a radical rejection of the validity of existing structures, not through negotiated inclusions. Revolution meant, as a younger Ho Chi Minh put it, "to destroy the old and build the new" (Ho 1926, cited Taylor and Whitmore 1995, 212). The otherwise demoralizing violence and conflict in the process could be explained and justified as "revolution" against traditional elites, colonial influences, and other relics of a reviled past.

Sukarno, President of Indonesia from 1945 to 1966, had a particular love affair with this revolutionary version of high modernism, even though, like Ho, his practical politics were designed for inclusiveness. His extensive 1956 travel to West and East climaxed with the orchestrated enthusiasm of his reception in China, where 300,000 people were assembled along the triumphal way from the airport to Beijing shouting *Hidup Bung Karno* (long live brother Karno). Sukarno was overwhelmed not only by the apparent achievements of China's revolution, but with its "fervent hearts and burning spirit (*semangat*)." He attributed both to strong leadership and revolutionary commitment. Immediately on his return he began his campaign to "bury" the political parties of liberal democracy, and build a socio-democracy or "guided democracy" as he perceived China's, with himself as the dominant "mouthpiece of the Indonesian revolution" (Liu 2011, 217–26). He took an increasingly millenarian tone even as the economy deteriorated, insisting that "Revolution is to 'build tomorrow and to reject yesterday.'" Indonesia was not alone. "It has never before happened that the history of man has gone through such a revolution as the present one – so strong and so tremendous, so wide-sweeping and universal, a Revolution of Humanity which surges, flashes and thunders simultaneously in almost every corner of the earth" (Sukarno 1960, in Feith and Castles 1970, 111–15).

Equally profound in the devaluing of Asia's past was the borrowing from European Marxism of the concept of "feudalism" as a discredited stage of history. Marxists succeeded in so popularizing the twin targets of revolution as feudalism and colonialism that the varied array of kings, raja, *sawbwa*, and *datu* of indigenous hierarchies stood condemned, along with conservative attitudes and structures deemed to be hangovers of that past. For most leftist intellectuals the pre-colonial past was as unacceptable a model as the colonial past. Tan Malaka (1926, cited Ali 1963, 145) claimed that "The true Indonesian nation does not yet have a history of its own except one of slavery." The mistier past of the classic temple-builders uncovered by European orientalists seemed more attractive, because disconnected from any present reality. Cambodia put Angkor Wat on the national flag. With the notable exceptions of royalist Thais, and Filipinos fascinated by the Rizal revolutionary generation of 1896, modern history was deemed only relevant as a source of potential anti-colonial heroes.

Since late colonialism had exoticized the charming distinctiveness of Southeast Asian dress, and royal courts, schools, hotels, and shipping lines imposed it in modernized form, nationalist high modernism embraced the presumed no-nonsense equality of western dress (Chapter 14). What had been the minority choice of self-conscious modernizers became under nationalist rule an indispensable means of rejecting the past. The presumed rational modernity of the military made uniforms especially popular, with the fashion set at the top by Sukarno, Ho Chi Minh, and even King Sihanouk.

The few opportunities the impoverished high modern phase offered for monumental buildings were seized to create symbols of universal modernity rather than Asian distinctiveness. The US$300 million agreed in 1957 as Japanese war reparation to Indonesia went largely on four large modern hotels, and other tall modern buildings intended to demonstrate the new country's equal place in the modern world. The most powerful symbolic expressions of the nation, the Ho Chi Minh mausoleum in Hanoi (1973–5) or the National Monument in Jakarta (1961–75), were emulations of Lenin's tomb and the Washington Monument, respectively, even if Sukarno saw his monument as a *lingga* to match the female *yoni* of its base. The very pluralism of every country's traditions reinforced the need to build the new modern identities on neutral, cosmopolitan ground.

Religion, the primary maker of Southeast Asian community, took a back seat to nationalism and modernity in this period. Religious leaders were largely persuaded that building the new nation must take priority, and those who were unconvinced found themselves side-lined as divisive. Cambodia's Khmer Rouge regime of 1975–8 was extreme by any standards, defrocking all Buddhist monks and demolishing the Phnom Penh cathedral brick by brick. But everywhere communist parties of the period sought to end the role of religion in education, to discourage donations to religious institutions, and to attack religious justifications for hierarchy. The more profound effect of high modernist attacks on "feudal superstition," however, was to provoke a religious reaction in more rational, modernized forms. The modern and universal was privileged against the traditional and local. Cold War conditions encouraged the kinds of religious leadership that would stand up to communism with an alternative globalism, like Ngo Dinh Diem's Catholicism or Mohammad Natsir's Saudi-influenced reformist Islam, not the local syncretist traditions.

High modernism lost conviction in the 1970s, and by the 1980s the post-revolutionary generation of power-holders were all feeling the need to buttress their legitimacy by claims to local and religious distinctiveness. Disillusion was bound to follow revolutionary expectations, but was speeded by the excesses of Pol Pot and by the wars of 1978 between Khmer, Vietnamese, and Chinese communists. Chinese embassies and misguided China-loyalists felt obliged to display the arrogant silliness of the Cultural Revolution in 1967, alienating even the ever-careful government of Burma.

In turning violently against Marxist ideology in 1965, the Indonesian military was particularly in need of new sources of legitimacy. There a kind of "battle of the kitsch" began with a giant theme park in Jakarta, "Mini-Indonesia," sponsored by Suharto's wife in 1972 to represent the quintessential cultures of each region. Housing and dress were the chief battlegrounds, as each ethnic lobby group advanced its sanitized and simplified symbolic representation. Provincial museums and other public buildings in the 1980s became sites of contestation between ethnic and regional lobbies advancing their respective simplifications. Opulent weddings revived long-neglected styles of formal dress. Such contests were now empty of political meaning. Because they were formulaic revivals of lost lifestyles they demonstrated the victory of the national idiom within which each was deployed. The summit meetings associated with ASEAN and other regional forums (Chapter 20) brought this bland cultural symbolism to the international arena, as even the once-communist states were obliged to generate their counterpart to the batik shirt. Tourism played its part in cultural commodification. Having banned the elegant female *ao-dao* after conquering the South in 1975, Hanoi brought it back after *Doi Moi* (1986), first for airline and hotel staff and cultural representatives abroad.

Viet Nam, Laos, and Cambodia freed their Buddhist and Christian communities to restore and patronize temples and shrines, and even sought legitimacy like kings of old by publicly making gifts to the monks on festival occasions. In 1991 the Laos regime replaced the communist hammer and sickle in the center of the national symbol on every document with the beloved ancient That Luang temple of Vientiane. Having dethroned their own king in 1975, they permitted Thailand's royalty to make frequent popular visits in the 1990s. The legitimacy-poor generals of SLORC in the 1990s ignored independence hero Aung San (father of opposition leader Suu Kyi) and cloaked themselves in the mantle of past kings like the conqueror Bayinnaung. They began building a new capital in 2002 and named it Naypyidaw, "royal city of the sun." The high modernist moment had certainly passed, but it had achieved fundamental changes.

EDUCATION AND NATIONAL IDENTITY

The great success of this modernist phase was in expanding education, and with it literacy in the national language and the national idea. The national elites of all contending ideologies agreed that this was the new state's first task, and both sides of the Cold War were eager to provide assistance. Those who had resisted modern education at colonial hands because it smelt of Christianity and foreign bullying embraced it enthusiastically as the new agent of nation-building. Southeast Asia was ahead of India, China, and the Muslim world, especially in educating girls, and the revolutionary countries had literacy and school participation rates above the norm for their relative poverty. Thailand, the Philippines, Viet Nam, and Singapore had passed 80% adult literacy by 1980, and Indonesia, Malaysia, and Burma by 1990. Indonesia had 954 secondary schools and four universities in 1950, but 4,600 and 135 a decade later. Southeast Asia as a whole roughly doubled the years at school of its populations in the period 1950–75. By the 1980s it was only the old who were illiterate or without schooling. Education was one of the great drivers of urbanization, as secondary education took young people away from the village, often never to return to farming.

This rapid expansion of schools was overwhelmingly in the national languages. Only English was a post-war competitor, as the Philippines, Malaysia, Singapore, and Burma maintained the colonial language in higher education for global purposes. French had survived in the minimal higher education provided in the Laos and Cambodia capitals until 1975, but had no role in the communist countries thereafter. The Indonesian rejection of Dutch in 1942 was the most complete, and even the universities banned its use when Indonesia broke relations with the Netherlands in 1956. Uncertainty about which alternative to adopt kept English well entrenched as language of instruction throughout the school systems of Singapore and the Philippines, but Malaysia and Burma phased it out. Their universities were the last to begin the transition to Malay and Bama in 1969 and 1965, respectively, though with various subsequent attempts to recover the international lost ground. By contrast with other parts of the post-colonial world, national languages triumphed quickly and relatively completely in Southeast Asia.

Developing new modern literatures, and new vocabularies for science, technology, and higher education, in these languages absorbed the energies of intellectual elites in the 1940s through to the 1960s. They achieved marvels of creativity in drawing not only on the colonial languages in which they had been educated, but on Sanskrit, Arabic, or (in Viet Nam) Chinese roots to develop the new concepts. Only Thai had previously been used at university level and developed a corpus of textbooks. The national languages all had a history of popular literature developed in the newspapers and "dime novels" of the 1920s and 1930s, but modernity called for a canon of classic works that could be taught in the classroom, and serious writers who could join the international writers' conferences sponsored by both camps in the Cold War. High modernity was an exciting time for writers, though it proved also a dangerous one as official ideologies changed. Leading liberal writers like Mochtar Lubis and the supporters of the "universal humanist" Cultural Manifesto of 1963 were banned and imprisoned under Indonesia's Guided Democracy of 1958–65. Their opponents in the Marxist cultural organization LEKRA suffered a worse fate under Suharto, Pramoedya Ananta Toer spending fourteen years in internal exile in Buru. In Viet Nam, writers who had sided with the Viet Minh were nevertheless banned and denounced in the 1956–8 crackdown (Chapter 17). Those who had chosen the other side experienced a worse fate after 1975, spending a decade or more in the "re-education" gulag.

Amidst this heady contestation over new national cultures, little thought was spared for the fundamental losers of the process, the hundreds of indigenous languages. In the 1930s it was still an open question which of Southeast Asia's vernaculars would successfully make the transition to modern print cultures. Newspapers in Javanese, Sundanese, Batak, Cebuano, and Karen, as well as Chinese, had made their appearance in the 1920s, and brought a flowering of printed novels and poetry as well as journalistic reportage. Primary schooling, and the production of school textbooks, had begun in these and other languages. From the turbulent 1940s onward, however, all available resources for cultural development focused on the task of building the national languages. In Burma (after 1962), Thailand, Viet Nam, and Indonesia teaching was in principle only in the national language, and textbooks and examinations were prepared only in those, even if vernaculars were often used orally by teachers in the lower-level classrooms.

Broadcasting technologies vastly increased the range, penetration, and popularity of these national languages. The revolutionary regimes all went to great lengths to control both radio and television, and to use them to extend the national language and the government's propaganda into every village. The governments of Burma (after 1962), Malaysia, Singapore and the communist regimes of Indochina were the most relentless in ensuring that there was a single voice on the airwaves, and monopolized both radio and television in the high modern phase. The new television technology proved a powerful new tool easiest for authoritarian governments initially to control. The pioneers, however, were free-wheeling capitalist Thailand and the Philippines in 1955 and 1953, respectively, the latter being among the first in Asia to manufacture TV sets locally. Both continued an unusually free competition of private commercial stations. Everywhere else authoritarian governments ensured their own control of the powerful new medium from the outset. Indonesia, Malaysia, and Singapore introduced television as a government monopoly in 1962–3, South Viet Nam and Cambodia in 1966, North Viet Nam in 1970 with Cuban assistance, and finally Burma in 1980. Indonesia was a pioneer in extending the reach of its Indonesian-only state television into the remotest islands by satellite in 1976. The Suharto government made it a priority to ensure that each village head had a TV receiver and a diesel generator to power it. Papuan highlanders and remote Borneo longhouse dwellers gathered around the sets in the evenings, fascinated by the images of Jakarta life and the accompanying national language they may never have heard before. The government station (TVRI) retained the monopoly until 1989. The private stations that flourished thereafter proved equally Jakarta-centered and monolingual in Indonesian even if, like the private stations of Bangkok, this monolingualism was now driven largely by advertising revenue. Television may have done more even than education to associate the national languages firmly with progress and modernity.

Revolutionary Indonesia and Viet Nam were exceptionally successful in "rejecting yesterday" in its varied linguistic forms, as their romanized national languages cut them off from pre-colonial pasts, while the collapse of Dutch and rapid decline of French helped further alienate youngsters from the colonial period. Malay, the basis of modern Indonesian, had been recorded as the first language of barely 2% of the Indonesian population in the 1930 census, though the written language and *lingua franca* of many more. By the 1980 census Indonesian was used in the home by 12% of the population, but 36% of city-dwellers and a very large proportion of younger age-groups. As Indonesian became the language of modernity, education, and urban life, the loss of the Archipelago's rich literary cultures in Javanese, Balinese, Sundanese, Bugis, and Makassarese was extremely rapid. Viet Nam had arguably had the richest of the region's pre-colonial literary traditions, and by abandoning the scripts of its expression, the written Chinese of the scholars, and the popular *nom* of vernacular literature, in favor of romanized *quoc ngu*, its rupture with the past was most severe. Romanization in both cases nevertheless helped "build tomorrow" in making literacy universal, uniform, and relatively egalitarian, and in narrowing the gap to world literatures. The success of these two languages in building a national idiom in both educated and popular idioms was nothing short of phenomenal.

The utility of English in the post-war world created a different scenario in the non-revolutionary Philippines and Malaysia/Singapore. National languages were certainly pushed by the nationalists, but those who preferred other language options could shelter behind a strategy of continuing to use English as the *lingua franca* that brought separate linguistic communities together. The Philippine Commonwealth in 1940 had mandated the development of a national language based on Tagalog, the language of the Manila area. Renamed Pilipino in 1959 and Filipino in 1973, this encountered significant opposition from speakers of major languages such as Cebuano and Hiligaynon (Ilonggo) in the Visayas and Ilocano and Kapampangan in Luzon, each with its own romanized literature since Spanish times. The 1973 Constitution compromised by making English and Filipino equally official and requiring the development of a bilingual education policy using both languages in schools. Filipino alone was declared the national language amid the nationalist enthusiasm of the Manila-based "People Power" movement that overthrew Marcos in 1986, but debate did not stop. In 2006, in the era of globalization, a "return to English" bill was passed requiring that English again be the medium of instruction.

In Malaysia and Singapore it was Mandarin Chinese rather than vernacular instruction that provided the major challenge to building national languages and identities. Chinese communities throughout Southeast Asia had built a formidable education system in the twentieth century. By the 1930s Chinese-language schools were educating about 30,000 students in Indonesia, 25,000 in Malaya, and 8,000 in Thailand. The China-nationalist enthusiasm of the first decades of the century was a major motive for the modern school movement. Textbooks were invariably those of the Republican government in China, and teachers were frequently themselves China-educated nationalists.

The Singapore pineapple and rubber magnate Tan Kah Kee (1874–1961), while giving generously also to English-medium schools, sought to make China the natural pinnacle for *Nanyang* Chinese education. His biggest single donation went to establish Xiamen (Amoy) University in his Fujian birthplace in 1919, and he installed as its president the first Chinese-Singaporean to win a Queen's Scholarship to Britain, Dr Lim Boon Keng (1869–1957). Even laissez-faire colonial governments had become concerned at the China-nationalist orientation of the syllabus as communist sympathies spread, but for the nation-building Southeast Asian nationalists this became a critical issue.

Post-1932 Thailand was the first to tackle it, by insisting from 1933 that those teaching in all schools should have a minimal competence in Thai, and that Chinese should be taught only as a foreign language. Chinese school enrolments dropped markedly in an atmosphere of bitter recriminations, but grew again as practical compromises were worked out. The Japanese surrender in 1945, however, brought an explosion of Chinese nationalist enthusiasm, and by 1948 Chinese school enrolments had reached 175,000. In that year the Phibun dictatorship began a relentless campaign to curb Chinese schools, and to Thai-ify those that remained. Despite initial protests, this onslaught, together with the expansion of Thai-language education and the closing off of China through the communist victory of 1949, effectively ended the attractiveness of Chinese education for Sino-Thais.

Indonesia experienced the same surge of Chinese nationalist education after 1945, but differed in recognizing the People's Republic (PRC) from 1950. This made it easier during the authoritarian turn in 1957 to close all schools sympathetic to Taiwan. That in turn left the remaining Chinese schools, still educating over 100,000, exposed to the anti-communist hysteria of 1965. All were closed, and in an extreme overreaction all import of Chinese printed material was banned. The adoption of Indonesian names was encouraged, and all public manifestations of Chinese-ness such as shop-signs and festivals were banned. The Suharto policies did indeed Indonesianize the population culturally, but unfortunately also appeared to legitimate anti-Chinese prejudice in the bureaucracy and to divert anti-capitalist frustration into Sinophobic violence. Chinese schools in Indochina were also caught in Cold War nation-building contests. South Viet Nam followed the Thai example of Vietnamizing its Chinese schools and enforcing Vietnamese names in the 1950s, and all remaining schools were closed with the communist takeover in 1975. The few Chinese schools in the north were permitted to continue in deference to communist brotherhood, but when this turned bitter with China's invasion in 1978 this privilege became a curse and the majority of Chinese left the country.

Malaysia and Singapore had much the highest proportions of Chinese-speakers at independence, and a highly developed school system that had largely succeeded in resinifying the hybrid local-born Chinese communities, in contrast to neighboring experience. At its apex was Nanyang University in Singapore, brought into being in 1956 by the frustration of Chinese school-leavers at the closing of access to universities in the PRC after 1949, and by a surge of popular enthusiasm that had millionaire tycoons as well as trishaw-drivers and bar hostesses donating to this symbol of Chinese-language dignity at the heart of Southeast Asia. Although primarily a Chinese-Singaporean creation, it taught also Indonesian and English and attracted Chinese-educated students from a much wider region. It represented a pinnacle of Sinophone Southeast Asian identity and literary creativity. Frustration remained among its graduates, however, as the Lee Kuan Yew government favored English as a common language. Under the government's policy of universal bilingualism between English and "mother-tongue" (Chinese, Malay, or Tamil), parents opted overwhelmingly for the better English of traditionally English-medium schools. The Chinese-medium ones that had taken 45% of Chinese students a decade earlier dropped to 11% in 1978. Nanyang University, also in trouble for the radicalism of its students, was forced to merge in 1980 with its English-medium rival to become the National University of Singapore in purely English medium.

Like the Singaporean, the Malaysian government insisted on a common syllabus for all its schools, whether teaching in English, Malay, Chinese, or Tamil. From 1961 it required secondary schools to teach and examine only in English or Malay to obtain government funding. Privately-funded "Independent Chinese Schools" (ICS) could continue, but rapidly lost enrolment as long as higher educational opportunities were available in English. After the embitter-ing experience of race riots in May 1969, and the more rigorous imposition thereafter of Malay as sole medium of the whole national system, the ICS experienced a remarkable revival from 1973. Chinese teachers mobilized effectively to raise private funds from the community, and to organize a sepa-rate examination system which would give access to Chinese-medium (in Taiwan) and English-medium universities overseas. Gross post-1969 discrimi-nation against Chinese in admission to Malaysia's Malay-medium universities ensured that the education system failed as a unifying device, even if it did ensure that all citizens had a workable knowledge of Malay. The ICS system became a kind of alternative stream for those who either fared badly in Malay examinations or simply saw the independents as a better route to the overseas qualification they needed to survive. Non-Muslim indigenous Borneans were also attracted to them because of disenchantment with the increasingly Muslim-colored national system, so that a disproportionate number of Malaysia's independent Chinese high schools (23 out of 60) were in Sarawak and Sabah in 2010.

By the 1980s, with the exceptions noted for English and Chinese, high modernism had succeeded in making the eight national languages virtually the sole means of written expression. The hundreds of other languages were well on the way to becoming purely oral mediums where they were not also fossilized literary remnants for academic study. Just because the vernaculars thereby ceased to be a serious threat to national unity, they experienced some-thing of a revival thereafter. New technologies helped, in the first place with music. Cassettes and DVDs, followed later by miraculous electronic devices, made the private recording and reproducing of music exceedingly cheap, undercutting the domination of national television. By 1997 Indonesia had

217 registered private radio stations, many of them specializing in "Pop Batak," "Keroncong Sunda," or "Musik Minahasa." The operators of mini-buses in Jakarta, Bangkok, and Manila would often regale their clients with their favorite ethnic repertoire from the provinces – often Batak, Isan, and Cebuano, respectively.

The universalizing of education in the national language also rendered it mundane and taken for granted, no longer a privileged route to modernity. Direct access to English became by the 1990s the perceived route to both modernity and employment. Calls also began to be made for reviving education in vernaculars without necessarily appearing in conflict with the already-established national language. In chiefly Malay-educated East Malaysia the largest indigenous languages, Iban in Sarawak and Kadazan/Dusun in Sabah, were in the 1990s permitted to take their place alongside Malay, Chinese, and Tamil as legitimate media for primary instruction, even though they were still in the controversial process of standardization as written languages. The Philippines took another linguistic turn in 2009 when the legislature decreed the introduction of one of twelve "mother tongues" in each of the country's primary schools, adducing a global educationist consensus that literacy is best learned in the mother tongue. Learned discussions were held, invariably in the national language or English, as to how to standardize local vernaculars and prepare textbooks and dictionaries in them. The churches often joined or even led this rediscovery of local idioms, following international trends in favor of inculturation and multiculturalism, once older associations of local music and arts with spirit-cults were forgotten.

Javanese, the world's largest non-official language with some 75 million speakers, even underwent a minor resurgence of vernacular publication with rising prosperity in the 1980s. George Quinn (1992, 39) estimated there might then still have been 140,000 readers of reinvented Javanese weekly magazines, with their diet of popular stories and serialized novels. These, however, could only decline as their older and predominately rural readers died out. Very few of the independence generation could read any of the old scripts, except the Arabic-derived Malay script some learned in religious schools. The reaction to Suharto's extreme centralization in Indonesia that returned administrative autonomy to provinces and districts after 1998 had a minimal effect in reviving vernacular education. Local cultural enthusiasms were restricted to rediscovering and recording idioms already rendered harmlessly decorative, private, and oral.

PURITAN GLOBALISM

Foreign visitors were often dismayed at the speed with which the old Southeast Asian order of tolerance and diversity was overturned in the high modernist era. Southeast Asians, however, offered little resistance, and widely welcomed the public sanitization of culture as asserting an equal dignity with their former European masters. This section argues that the various surges of puritan conformity that affected much of Asia, both in the authoritarian phase and afterward, were inherent to the process of urban modernization, tied to the need for both external, global validation and individual moral responsibility.

The first phase was distinctly high modernist, as newly powerful revolutionaries condemned public phenomena that embarrassed them in western eyes. Female dress was an immediate target, with the bare breasts of Bali, Borneo, and upland societies disappearing very quickly from public view. The vernacular religious practice which had accommodated spirits and magical healers (Chapter 8) was again marginalized in favor of modernity and sanitized out of public performance, ritual, and literature. Rejecting the US "Imperialist" side of the Cold War included banning its "decadent" culture, whether in Hollywood movies or French novels. The long sufferings of communist parties in the underground before 1945 had involved such sacrifice of private sexual and domestic life that cadres acquired a habit of practical asceticism, and felt entitled to impose puritanical discipline more widely once in power. Because the rich urban elite could be easily portrayed as foreign, its "bourgeois decadence" could more readily be condemned by the new rulers, anti-communist Lee Kuan Yew and Ngo Dinh Diem as well as communist Ho Chi Minh and Pol Pot. Neil Jamieson (1993) defines this phase in terms of a Vietnamese cosmology, as the temporary dominance of male, orthodox, and hierarchic *yang* and a marginalizing of its necessary balance in empathetic and accommodating female *yin*.

The more important long-term shift, however, occurred as the states lost their will or capacity to further modernize and sanitize culture. From the 1980s the rise of puritanism was driven from below by the newly urban and educated middle class and was typically opposed to the perceived corruption of the state. As noted in Chapter 18, the process of urbanization and commercialization was extremely rapid after 1970, particularly for the indigenous and Muslim population that had been overwhelmingly rural in the colonial era. In particular the parallel between the Muslim half of Southeast Asia in the period 1970–2010 and Protestant England of the Victorian era is instructive.

The urban population of England and Wales had increased from 2.3 million to 20 million between 1801 and 1891, by which date England was 72% urban. Southeast Asia, by contrast, was still only 13.6% urban overall in 1950, and most indigenous communities below 10%. Indonesia was still only 15% urban in 1971, but 50% in 2010. Malaysia was 28% urban in 1970, when Malays were only a little over a quarter of the urban total. By 2000 Malaysia was 62% urban and Malays were almost half of that vastly increased total. These newly urban Muslims needed a wholly new form of "modern" religious mentality, just as did the upwardly mobile newly urban puritans of Victorian England. They were no longer served by the rural cycle of religious festivals, agricultural and life-cycle rituals, and established hierarchies. They needed a more abstract and rationalized faith, both individual in focus and national/global in reach, which could provide meaning, discipline, respectability, and moral equality before God in the dangerously competitive conditions of the city.

From the vantage point of western post-modernity, it appears that the modernity of Europe in the century before 1914 (and of Southeast Asia a century later) was accompanied by a particular kind of public piety – ascetic and puritan in sexual morality; patriarchal in the home, where respectable married women should focus; hard-working, frugal, and disciplined in the essentially male workplace; optimistically committed to the city, to progress, rationality, and technology; and appealing beyond established religious hierarchies and compromises to the original scripture as legitimation. The religious face of this modernity was a quest for personal, individual salvation through a direct relation with God. This showed itself in frugal habits, hard work, and the exaltation of the nuclear family where a breadwinner father presided and respectable women were confined to very active child-bearing and nurturing as well as church and charitable activity. The muscular Christianity of Victorian England expressed itself in campaigns against alcohol, prostitution, and gambling at home, and a missionary movement abroad confidently spreading a gospel of modern, rational, and moralistic religion.

Islam, perhaps even more than Christianity, was long familiar with waves of puritanical reformism of this type. We noted how in the sixteenth century and again in the early nineteenth commercialized elites with international connections had been the bearers of a radical puritanism fiercely intolerant of Southeast Asian compromise (Chapters 5 and 11). Even during the high colonial period of increasingly peasantized Muslim societies, the growth of pilgrimage to Mecca and of new Islamic school systems created a novel political polarity between a self-consciously Muslim identity and the secular mainstream, whether colonial or nationalist. The Japanese occupation had politicized the Muslim-educated minority, mobilizing it to play a distinctive role in fighting the Allied return. The western-educated leaders of both Indonesia and Malaysia were firmly committed to a secular state with religious freedom, but the large minority educated in Arabic never abandoned the idea that a righteous struggle (*jihad*) could only be for an Islamic state. Islamic militias fought some of the bloodiest battles against the Allied return to Indonesia, and some continued this armed resistance to the firmly secular Indonesian government under the banner of an Indonesian Islamic State, or *Darul Islam* ("house of Islam," the traditional name for parts of the world under legitimate Islamic rule). Most of the *ulama*, however, preferred to form Islamic parties with more limited electoral goals. In Malaysia they formed the opposition Pan-Malayan Islamic Party (PAS from 1973), which already gained 20% of the national vote at Malaya's 1959 election and secured long-term control of the rural state of Kelantan.

By the 1970s, when the surge to the cities took off, Muslim armed insurgency in Indonesia had been crushed and the secular state tolerant of minorities seemed secure. Suharto's quest for an organic state devoid of political conflict climaxed with 1985 legislation that forced all mass organizations to have only one basis – *Pancasila*. These "five principles" had been Sukarno's syncretizing formula of 1945, reemphasized under Guided Democracy and enforced as dogma by Suharto's terror-backed regime. It sidestepped the religious problem by making monotheism the first principle, applied in the anti-communist hysteria of 1965–6 to mean that every citizen was obliged to subscribe to one of five official religions: Islam, Catholic or

Protestant Christianity, Hinduism, or Buddhism. Pancasila became the weapon against the military's two chief enemies, atheistic communism on the left and demands for an Islamic state on the right. In requiring even Islamic movements to agree that their basis was something other than Islam, the 1985 law aroused predictable opposition, including a bomb attack on the greatest of Indonesia's monuments, the Buddhist Borobudur. It was a high-water mark of Muslim alienation from the political process. For some prominent Muslim thinkers such as Nurcholish Majid and Abdurrahman Wahid (1940–2009, elected Indonesian President 1999–2001) this depoliticization of Islam was a welcome opportunity to turn away from the fruitless quest for a utopian Islamic state. Under a slogan "Islam yes; Islamic Party no," Nurcholish advocated an Islam that embraced the plural modern world by emphasizing its essentially transcendent and moral role in improving the individual. In the 1990s Indonesia seemed the hope of liberal Muslims throughout the world.

There was, however, a much harder undercurrent of political Islam throughout the region, drawing sustenance from connections with Saudi Arabia, Pakistan, and the Muslim Brotherhood in Egypt. Among its intellectual leaders was Mohammad Natsir (1908–93), the Dutch-educated and puritanical leader of Indonesia's first Muslim party, Masjumi, and Prime Minister in 1950–1. Disappointed by the failure of Indonesia's leaders to support the imposition of Islamic laws, and of Indonesians to vote for Muslim parties, he founded the Indonesian Council for Islamic Proselytism (*Dakwah*) in 1967, concluding that the first priority was to Islamize Indonesian society. He quickly became the leading channel for Saudi salafist ideas into Indonesia, through the Saudi-funded Muslim World League and its many scholarships for study in the Wahhabi kingdom. His movement helped position a moralist and legalist version of Islam, free of its local compromises, as an attractive channel of youth resistance to Suharto in the 1980s and 1990s. The liberalism of Nurcholis Majid was demonized by the organization's journal in 1992, linking him darkly to Zionist plots against Islam. *Dakwah* study groups became influential in secular universities. They popularized the militant pietist ideas of Sayyid Qutb, executed in Cairo in 1966 and a later inspiration for the Muslim Brotherhood and Saudi-backed militant Sunni activists worldwide. Many secular-educated students welcomed these ideas as a means to preserve personal moral integrity in the seductive urban consumerist world to which they had newly arrived, though Muslim-educated youth associated with Indonesia's two mainstream Muslim movements – NU and Muhammadiyah – were less impressed.

Only a few thousand Southeast Asians, many linked to older insurgent Islamic movements, were sufficiently radicalized by these ideas to go and join the Taliban fight against the Soviets in Afghanistan in the 1980s, or later insurgencies. The more important transition that took place in the later years of Suharto in Indonesia and Mahathir in Malaysia was the embrace of a specifically Islamic understanding of modernity, in which young women and men could engage in universities, factories, and urban shopping malls with the defensive armor of individual morality and communal reassertion of identity as Muslims. The struggle was no longer of the nation against imperialism, but of global Islam against imagined Jewish, Christian, or American conspiracies against it. The most widespread symbol of the shift was in the dress of young urban women, which underwent a complete transformation within twenty years. The covering of the hair with a veil (Arabic *hijab*, Indonesian *jilbab*, Malay *tudung*) became so popular with the upwardly mobile newly urbanized young women that Indonesia was obliged to drop its opposition to it in government offices in 1991. The many studies devoted to the phenomenon show most women negotiating this transition confidently, with little sense of conflict between the desires for Islamic piety and stylish modernity.

The resort to violent *jihad* against the perceived enemies of this revived vision of Islam was restricted to a tiny minority, though they became more influential once the authoritarian hands of Suharto in Indonesia and Mahathir in Malaysia were removed in 1998 and 2003, respectively. Militant Muslims fought Christians for control of plural districts in eastern Indonesia to which power was devolved after 1998. The Islamic Defenders' Front established a kind of protection racket out of raiding profitable nightclubs and gambling dens and threatening others. Galvanized by the attack on the World Trade Center in 2001, extremists of the al-Qaeda-affiliated Jemaah Islamiyah attempted numerous bombings of targets associated with foreigners, succeeding most dramatically when suicide bombers killed 202 revelers, mostly foreigners, in the nightclub hub of Bali in October 2002. It was easier for Indonesian and Malaysian governments to pursue and convict the killers than to combat the polarizing mind-set giving rise to this extremism. There were few powerful internal Muslim voices willing to oppose it directly after the deaths of Nurcholish and Wahid. On the contrary, Indonesia's officially recognized Council of Ulama in 2005 condemned liberalism and pluralism as forbidden by Islam, while Malaysia's ruling UMNO party was dragged by its extremist wing into adopting positions increasingly hostile to the freedom of religion promised in the constitution.

In the more open-ended political contests of the twenty-first century, the implementation of *shari'a* as God's law has again become a refuge for those unable to accept the verdict of the ballot box. Having flirted earlier with ideas for belatedly reintroducing constitutional rule to Brunei, Sultan Bolkiah decided instead to remain absolutist. He announced in 2013 that a strict, Saudi-like version of *shari'a* would be introduced, with no concessions for non-Muslims. Internal criticisms of the royal decision would be regarded as treasonous. In Malaysia the ruling coalition's loss of the popular vote in the 2013 election increased calls for redefining Islam as the non-negotiable center of the state. In Indonesia the decentralization after 1998 enabled Aceh province and a number of districts to implement varied systems of Islamic law locally. In the four national and local electoral contests since 1998, however, parties that explicitly espoused implementing *shari'a* as their policy progressively lost their share of the vote, declining to below 20% in 2014. The shift since the 1980s to more public expressions of Islamic piety had been profound, but this was not inhibiting traditionally strong female participation in the workforce and the public square.

JOINING AN INTEGRATED BUT PLURAL WORLD

The remarkable intensification of globalization since the end of the Cold War in 1991 and the spread of new communications technologies had multiple effects on the relations between citizens and their states. Universal national-style education and the strengthened authority of global-level ideologies, described above, continued to undermine the local and the vernacular. Reformist pressures operated overwhelmingly at the level of the nation-state, demanding more efficient and honest administration internally and more robust defense of national dignity externally. The most remote corners of the region, hitherto insulated from change by inaccessibility, were reached by the new media. The time-honored idea of self-sufficient village communities and authentically untouched tribal ones appeared totally discredited and absurd in the twenty-first century.

Yet globalization also pluralized the idea of the nation in novel ways, and provided new tools for the hitherto voiceless. Except where Chinese cultural influence was profound (Viet Nam and the Chinese diaspora), Southeast Asia had been a relatively oral region, underachieving in the usual measures of print culture and the reading habit. It took to the new electronic media, however, with an enthusiasm that suggested closing that gap to the East Asian cultures. As long as communication was dependent on government-monopoly telephone or telegraph systems and reliable electricity supply, it remained an elite privilege. Knowledge spread largely through government-controlled channels – television, radio, and print media. Computers brought access to the Internet in the 1990s and vastly greater individual choice over where to seek knowledge. Although ownership of a computer was beyond the reach of all but a wealthy elite, Internet cafes sprouted in small towns across most of the region where ordinary youth cut their teeth on the new media by renting time.

The statistics on Internet access initially followed those on relative wealth. In 2000 Singapore and Malaysia were far ahead with 36% and 21% access, respectively, with Brunei, Thailand, and the Philippines in single digits and others minimal. Isolated and impoverished Burma (still only 1.1% access in 2012), Laos, and Cambodia remained below Asian averages, but the other countries were all well ahead of South Asia, or developing world averages. Internet access reached 40% in Viet Nam in 2012, compared with 36% in the Philippines, 27% in Thailand, and 15% in Indonesia (World Bank 2014). Only China expanded faster, with 42% access by 2012. The standout trailblazer was Dr Mahathir's Malaysia, which launched its Multimedia Super Corridor between Kuala Lumpur and its airport in 1996. This was designed to become a Malaysian silicon valley, attracting high-tech companies and promoting free and high-speed access as a means to catapult the country into First World status. Although these lofty ambitions faltered in the face of the Asian Financial Crisis of 1998 and Mahathir's political excesses, the push did make Internet access more widely available, reaching nearly half the population by 2005 and two thirds by 2012, not far behind Singapore and other developed countries. Because Mahathir also promised that the Internet would be free from censorship, in dramatic contrast with the government-owned print media and television, Malaysia developed an exceptionally vibrant online and interactive press. Journalists frustrated by a decade of increasingly tight control of the media and its one-sided treatment of Mahathir's fall-out with former deputy Anwar Ibrahim, launched in 1999 the online newspaper *Malaysiakini*, setting a new standard for journalistic probity and openness.

This expanded connectedness, giving Internet access to roughly one in three Southeast Asians by 2012, was carried after 2000 by the extraordinary expansion of mobile phones (Table 19.1). Introduced in the 1990s as the showpiece of the minority who could afford it, these had become virtually universal in the region by 2012. They became ever cheaper to own and to operate, as Korean, Chinese, and local companies entered the market to undercut the Japanese and European pioneers. They did not depend on an electricity supply or fixed network, and enabled even remote rural producers to gauge prices, market their goods, and purchase supplies without leaving home. As tools for development they were revolutionary, at last reversing some of the acute disadvantages rural-dwellers had suffered in every other technological advance. Because of its relative openness to international competition, Southeast Asia was well ahead of global norms in this phenomenal transition, outdistancing both China and India. That all countries except Laos and Burma had more mobile phones than people by 2012 is a testament to the fierce competition between providers, and the readiness of Southeast Asians to use different mobile phones and networks for different purposes.

Table 19.1 Mobile phone use in Southeast Asia, 2000–2012. Mobile cellular subscriptions per 100 people, with India and China as comparison.

	2000	2005	2009	2012
Singapore	70	98	139	152
Viet Nam	1	11	111	148
Malaysia	22	76	108	141
Cambodia	1	8	44	129
Thailand	5	46	100	127
Brunei	29	63	105	114
Indonesia	2	21	69	114
Philippines	8	41	82	107
Laos	0	11	52	65
Burma	0	0	1	10
India	0	8	44	77
China	7	30	55	81

Source: World Bank 2014.

This appears especially true of Viet Nam and Cambodia, both with far more phones than their relative poverty would suggest. One reason may have been the prominence in both countries of Viet Nam's army-owned provider Viettel, which pushed for maximum coverage at minimum cost. Despite its cheapness, it was perceived as slower in Internet access than its rivals, but also subject to Viet Nam's tight control of the expression of dissident views on the Internet.

It is too early to be able to assess the full effects of this cellular revolution on social interaction, culture, welfare, and political life. It appears to have begun narrowing the distance not only between urban and rural, global and local, but also between rich and poor, more and less educated, high and low status, even perhaps male and female. It has alarmed parents and governments by the speed at which information spreads, including pornography, revelations about corruption, mobilization for demonstrations, and rumors of all kinds. The elaborate system of pronouns by which Southeast Asians placed themselves in relations of status with others, already challenged intellectually by the political revolutions, was further challenged practically by the demands of terse text messages and abbreviations. The cornucopia of material available on the Internet and on social media sites in English and the national languages made access to these languages even more vital, but each network of interaction developed its own language hybrid, where words in English, national language, vernacular, or urban argot were selected for punch and brevity rather than linguistic purity.

As mobile phones spread everywhere, the minimal cost of establishing both local and global information networks contributed to a proliferation of Non-Government Organizations (NGOs). Democratization in the Philippines (1986), Indonesia (1998), Burma (2009), and elsewhere also helped – Indonesia's registered NGOs increased from 10,000 before democratization in 1996 to 70,000 in 2000. The "People Power" overthrow of President Marcos (1986) made the Philippines a path-breaker for NGO action on democracy, peace, the environment, and development. After Cambodia opened to the world through United Nations intervention in 1992–3, it became dependent on international NGOs for every kind of welfare activity. With 3,500 registered NGOs (2012) this small country soon had the highest per capita coverage in the world. The global spread of multinational corporations since the 1970s was followed by the internationalization of their NGO critics, seeking to investigate and combat on the ground the environmental impact of international miners and oil-palm companies, the working conditions in factories, and the returns to poor producers. Western governments learned to allocate their aid where possible to domestic NGOs to avoid government corruption. For better or worse, Southeast Asian governments ceased to be the bottleneck through which international ideas and aid flowed into the region. Irritatingly for many locals, the agenda of the NGO world was often also set by western concern for democracy, female empowerment, human rights, and the environment, and western multinational companies were attacked more robustly than domestic exploiters. Abuses occurred. Yet the biggest and best of international NGOs took pains to localize their staff and indigenize their operations, changing in the process the balance of power between civil society and government.

Pluralizing the idea of the nation became possible toward the end of the twentieth century because the centralizing nation-builders had done their job. The twin pressures of nationalist schools and global corporate technology finally realized the unfinished projects of universalism, whether by scriptural religion to extend the reach of correct belief and ritual behavior, or of late imperialism to extend that of "civilized" modern states. James Scott (2009, 282) calls this twentieth-century incorporation of Southeast Asian stateless highlanders "the world's last great enclosure." The hill-dwellers whose ancestors fought for centuries to evade the hierarchic "civilized" order of the lowlands were now selling their forest products and accessing their favorite songs by texting in the national language. Their sanitized picturesque dress and rituals had become of special interest to both international tourists and national image-makers.

The pattern of ineluctable state advance into the hills punctuated by millenarian rebellions of wonder-working holy men had been overwhelmed in mid-century by global struggles. The highlands and jungles became strategic areas in the Pacific War for guerrillas fighting Japanese control, in the Cold War for communist guerrillas and their opponents (1948–75), and for all kinds of movements of resistance to the new national states. Allied agents armed and empowered highland minorities in the process of incorporation, even permitting a revival of older head-hunting practices against the Japanese in the Luzon Cordillera and in Sarawak (Borneo). The large and warlike minority known as Miao in southwest China but Hmong in the Indochina highlands were armed by the United States to fight the communists in Viet Nam and Laos, at terrible cost to themselves in lives lost, displacement of some 200,000 to the United States and Thailand, and retribution after the communist victory in 1975. The longer-term effect of this mobilization, however, was to force governments to find some place for the uplanders in the national project. During the insurgency in Malaya the communists moved first to use *Orang Asal* (people of the origin) to replace pejorative terms such as *Sakai* (associated with slaves) for forest-dwelling stateless peoples. Forced to respond in kind, the government adopted *Orang Asli* (Original People), and established a Department of Orang Asli Affairs in 1954, which endured despite various attempts to convert and incorporate these diverse groups totalling some 90,000 people (2000) as Malays.

In the longer wars over Indochina both sides worked hard to understand and classify minorities and gain their support to control the mountain areas. The DRV strategy was to woo them for the war effort through a "unity in autonomy" strategy, while seeking their long-term development and integration. With the communist victories of 1975 the Soviet model of "nationalities" was pursued through a system of classification that led in 1979 to the definition of 54 nationalities including the Kinh (Viet) majority, equal in theory but all subject to relentless pressure to join the "scientific" advance toward a single modern citizenship. Between 1960 and 1992, over five million lowland Viet were moved to "New Economic Zones" in the highlands, while the forest cover was removed through logging and agricultural expansion. Resistance was expressed in various ways, one of which was the spread of highland Christianity, both Evangelical and Catholic, despite the opposition of authorities, partly as an alternative modernity and site of resistance to the state. With development in the 1990s came tourists, both domestic and local, giving commercial value and international connections to the colorful exoticism of the highlands. Sa Pa and Dalat, former French hill retreats in the northwest and center, respectively, became tourist centers with theme parks and museums devoted to the minorities. As in Indonesia, Thailand, and East Malaysia over a longer period, the architecture, dance, dress, and rituals of once-stateless upland peoples have been rescued from apparently terminal decline, though only at the cost of commodification.

Along with most forms of protest, indigenous movements became globalized in the late twentieth century. The United Nations set up a Working Group on Indigenous Populations in 1982, the work of which was triumphantly concluded when an overwhelming majority of the General Assembly supported the UN Declaration on the Rights of Indigenous Peoples in 2007. The campaign was stimulated by movements of Arctic and indigenous peoples in rich countries – Scandinavia, North America, and Australia/New Zealand – but Southeast Asian governments soon found themselves placed in an awkward position by their support for it. The rapid advances of state power, national/global culture, and forest felling sparked widespread support in the international NGO movement for those marginalized or threatened with absorption by the process. Non-sedentary forest-dwellers whose habitat was being destroyed by forest felling and dam construction were supported not only by anthropologists but also by international environmentalists. The UN, the United States, and other governments began reporting on breaches of indigenous rights as an aspect of human rights, and local NGOs supporting such rights could obtain international funding.

These most marginalized groups had the best claim to oppressed status and distinctive culture based on non-incorporation, high illiteracy, miserable health and welfare, and in some cases distinctive language and appearance. Rich in indigenous legitimacy, and therefore threatening to the privileges majorities such as Malaysia's Malays arrogated to themselves, they were nevertheless small in number and miniscule in educated leadership. The indigenous movement, however, began to attract a much larger constituency of peoples who felt that immigration and development were making them disadvantaged minorities in their own state. This was strongly felt by many Kadazan and Dusun in Malaysian Borneo, outnumbered by Muslim immigrants from Peninsular Malaysia, the Southern Philippines, and Indonesia, and left behind in the growing affluence of Malaysia. They formed an Indigenous Peoples' Network of Malaysia together with the Centre for Orang Asli Concerns in the Peninsula, to join the global movement (Lasimbang and Nicholas 2007). The Philippines accommodated the same trend with the passing of an Indigenous Peoples' Rights Act in 1997, which established a National Commission of Indigenous Peoples charged with safeguarding these peoples and surveying, approving, and protecting their "ancestral lands." The highlanders not incorporated into Catholicism and the Philippine state at the time of the American arrival in

1898 were generally accepted as "indigenous," even though historical and linguistic evidence does not support any greater indigeneity for most of them than for lowlanders.

In Indonesia, Viet Nam, and Burma claims to superior indigeneity were even more problematic. Nevertheless, a subtle shift was everywhere apparent in the balance of power and legitimacy between center and periphery. As infrastructure reached the highlanders and gave them education, they acquired key weapons to reclaim rights lost to the high modernist nation. Where democratization was added to the mix in Thailand and Indonesia, some long-suppressed minorities could no longer be ignored. Thaksin's electoral victories in 2001 and 2005 revealed that the one third of the Thai population that was essentially Lao-speaking and forever disadvantaged in the northeast could use its education, growing economic strength, and electoral weight to its own advantage. The "yellow-shirt" reaction that brought government into crisis thereafter could be seen as the desperate resistance of a Bangkok, central Thai and "Upper South" establishment against the rising power and impatience of the northeast and north.

The most striking reversal occurred when Indonesia's Parliament passed a radical regional autonomy law in 1999, in the full flush of reaction against the ruthless centralism and autocracy of Suharto, overthrown the year before. The Parliament transferred a wide range of legislative powers to elected local parliaments at the level of Indonesia's 26 provinces (33 by 2009) and at the lower level of its 266 districts and cities (484 by 2009). Both executives and legislatures were to be directly elected for these levels at five-yearly intervals, and entrusted with a greatly expanded range of state revenues. The immediate effects appeared mostly negative, as inexperienced politicians competed for the new perquisites of local office and the punitive hand of the military was relaxed. Corruption took flagrant new forms, violence broke out between Muslims and Christians (Maluku and Sulawesi) or immigrant and indigenous ethnic groups (Maluku and Borneo), and separatist hopes peaked in Aceh, Papua, and East Timor (the only province allowed to progress through a referendum and UN intervention to independence, in 1999). Some thousands of people were killed in the period 1998–2002, and over a million displaced. There was talk of a "failing state." Yet by the time of the successful second election in 2004 stability had returned, and both democratization and decentralization appeared to have been achieved with much less disruption than comparable processes in Yugoslavia and the Soviet Union. Much expenditure was wasted at local levels through rampant corruption and mismanagement and the multiplication of provinces and districts. Yet each election produced more political leaders with a populist touch, more local journalists willing to expose corruption, and more money politics that directed immediate gratification to poor voters. Although a few districts did seek to implement divisive Islamic laws and anti-minority policies, the overall effect of electoral contests in the localities was to disarm extremism and encourage politicians to form alliances across ethnic and religious boundaries.

This decentralizing context made it easier for Jakarta to make essential concessions to its most rebellious peripheral provinces. East Timor, we noted, was let go in a climate of terrible military violence and bitterness. Following the tsunami of 2004 which killed 170,000 of its people, Aceh became the subject of peace talks in Helsinki which agreed to a package of unprecedented self-government within Indonesia, allowing former rebels to take charge of the province through elections in 2006. Muslim separatist rebellion in the southern Philippines was also accommodated through much-contested autonomy arrangements, complicated by the Christian migrant majority in Mindanao and robust Filipino traditions of democracy and constitutionalism. An Autonomous Region in Muslim Mindanao (ARMM) was established in 1989 when four provinces in western Mindanao and the Sulu chain of islands voted for it. It was ineffective in ending either insurgency or poverty among a very divided population, and was replaced in 2014 by another deal negotiated with different rebels for the autonomy of "Bangsamoro." These debates fed into a push for federalism for the whole country. A 2008 proposal supported by the President suggested Bangsomoro as one of twelve autonomous federal states. Thailand, on the other hand, proved resistant to solving its own violent insurgency in the Muslim south through the kind of autonomy that might prove infectious in a highly Bangkok-centered political system.

Established Sino-Southeast Asian minorities also appeared less of a "problem" for nationalists in the new century. Despite their strength in the economies, they had become less significant demographically and more integrated culturally. Chinese minorities led the downward trend of birth rates after 1980, as well as being the most inclined to migrate out – to China or Europe in the 1940s and 1950s, to Singapore, Australia, and North America thereafter. Prosperous Singapore alone counted 250,000 ethnic Chinese from Malaysia and 22,000 from Indonesia at its 2000 census. Many simply changed identity as they intermarried. Malaysia's census counted only 24.6% Chinese in 2010, compared with 34% in 1970. Indonesia's first census to measure ethnicity, in 2000, surprised all by finding only 1.1% declaring as Chinese. The massive flight from Viet Nam in 1975–80 reduced the Hoa (Chinese) minority there from about 2.6% to 1% of the population. The suppression of Chinese schools and cultural expression, most extreme in military-ruled Indonesia and Burma, and the ASEAN countries' break in relations with Mao's China, had made the national languages universal among Sino-Southeast Asians while Chinese language was of diminishing utility. Later, China's opening and economic rise in the 1990s ensured that it became the leading trade partner of Southeast Asia and a significant investor. "Chinese-ness" largely ceased to be seen as a challenge to Southeast Asian nationalisms, especially as rediscovered by the local-born majority who had no ties to the People's Republic. It could be part of a chic new cosmopolitanism. After its last and most shocking round of anti-Chinese rioting that accompanied Suharto's fall in 1998, Indonesia reversed its draconian measures against Chinese cultural expressions and allowed the language to be taught.

As had happened in the late nineteenth century, the advent of a new wave of China-born migrants and visitors made most of the local-born feel more Southeast Asian, even if some were able to exploit new economic opportunities as brokers with China. China's rise and perceived bullying on border issues created anxiety and resentment, but the protests were now anti-China, not anti-Chinese. The exception was Burma, with the longest and most porous China border. After anti-Chinese riots (1967) and military repression had reduced the Chinese minority to a quarter million in 1983, a new wave of business migrants from Yunnan responded to the opportunities of Burma's gradual economic liberalization. By 2008 there were estimated to be 2.5 million new migrants, and they quickly dominated the new opportunities for business and investment, especially in Mandalay and the north. The combination of powerful neighbor and its resented emigrants produced a palpable reaction that may be a harbinger of wider future problems.

★★★★★

The astonishing pace of change since 1950 finally succeeded in producing nations to more or less match the states that had been fashioned a century earlier at colonial hands. By the twenty-first century even the most remote Southeast Asians were entangled in the national languages, education systems, dominant religions, and political cultures of the nation-states. These engagements had provided a window to broader global entanglements – consumerist, cultural, and religious. The transformation had revealed to some that they had become "minorities" in the new nation-states, defined by their religion, language, or lifestyle as having a less direct and privileged relation to the nation-state than others. For many these minority identities nested comfortably within a national and a global-religious identity; for others there was tension, alienation, and perceived discrimination – notably for non-Muslims and less orthodox Muslims in the Muslim majority countries, for Muslim minorities elsewhere, and for Papuans, highlanders, and others who felt they were losing control of their own place.

[20] THE SOUTHEAST ASIAN REGION IN THE WORLD

THE term "Southeast Asia" is a twentieth-century invention, and its regional organization, ASEAN, has embraced the whole space only since 1999. While this might suggest the growing coherence of a politically fragmented region, in many respects the opposite is the case. Historians are more inclined to write of the region as a whole the more remote the period they deal with. The growing importance of states and scriptural religions in Southeast Asian lives over the last two centuries has created some profound cleavages.

At the beginning of the nineteenth century Southeast Asia still appeared to outsiders as a coherent whole. John Crawfurd's qualifications as a regional observer enabled him to write that the various peoples of the tropics between India and China

> differ widely from those adjacent to them in physical form, in the structure of their language, in manners, institutions and religion, [but] agree with one another in so remarkable a manner in all these characters, that I am disposed to consider them entitled to be looked upon as a distinct and peculiar form of the human race." (Crawfurd 1828/1967, 310)

A century later this no longer seemed the case. Imperialism had divided the region into British, Dutch, Spanish/American, and French spheres of education and idioms of modernization, linguistic scholarship had revealed it to be one of the world's most diverse regions in speech, and nationalism was beginning to convince Europeans, Chinese, Filipinos, Thais, and others (in roughly that order) of their distinct national destinies. The following (twentieth) century divided the region bitterly along the battlefront of the Cold War, while a global jihadist trend convinced a small but divisive minority of Muslims that they should no longer tolerate the pluralities of the region. Crawfurd's listing of religion among the commonalities seemed bizarre to those far removed from the village world of spirits, mediums, and healers. The urban, commercial, and communications revolutions rendered Southeast Asia's distinct pattern of rice

A History of Southeast Asia: Critical Crossroads, First Edition. Anthony Reid.
© 2015 Anthony Reid. Published 2015 by John Wiley & Sons, Ltd.

agriculture, fisheries, and material culture only a memory, while its cities looked much like the rest of the post-modern world.

Even more potentially dangerous to any sense of commonality was the divergence between Southeast Asia's rich and poor. Lee Kuan Yew took pride in having converted Singapore to a First World country, with one of the highest per capita GDPs in the world, 35 times that of Laos and Burma (2013). With its people educated bilingually in English and "mother tongue," which for three-quarters of the population was held to mean Mandarin Chinese, Singapore was in many ways less Southeast Asian in 2010 than it had been a century earlier when it had a Malay *lingua franca* and village lifestyle. Yet the resentment that Jakarta and Kuala Lumpur in particular had felt since colonial times toward the rich Island Republic, through which much of their trade passed both legally and illegally, was markedly eased by ASEAN, but still more by the commercial turn. In an ever more economically integrated world, Singapore positioned itself as an essential regional asset for financial, technical, communications, education, and medical services. The frustration of nationalist planners at the leakage to Singapore of smuggled exports was gradually overcome by the region's manifest need for a global port. Containerization and the vast expansion of trade it heralded from the 1970s made Singapore more essential than ever as a trans-shipping center. In fact the regional integration of Southeast Asian economies around the twin hubs of Singapore and Bangkok can be seen as an aspect of the global integration taking place everywhere.

THE REGIONAL IDEA

Conceptually, Southeast Asia became more distinct as it became detached from its neighbors. It had long been a region in the eyes of these neighbors themselves, as *Nanyang* (South Seas) to the Chinese, *Suwarnadwipa* (Goldland) to the Indians, or *Jawa* to the Arabs. But Europeans long thought of all tropical Asia as "India," the source of the fabled spices that had propelled them outward in the first place. Since it was clearly very different from Hindu India, for centuries it was "Further" or "Ultra-Gangetic" India. The islands became the Indian Archipelago, later Latinized as Insulinde, but increasingly also distinguished as Dutch (as opposed to British) India. The first important Anglophone journal on the region was the Singapore-based *Journal of the Indian Archipelago and Eastern Asia* (1847–62), while Moor (1837) and Crawfurd (1856) devoted their surveys to "the Indian Archipelago and Adjacent Countries." "Indochina" was another way of defining the region in terms of its giant neighbors, first proposed by scholars at the beginning of the nineteenth century, but rendered too specific by the French adoption of the term for their colonies in 1886.

It was German-language scholarship that in the 1890s began using "Southeast Asia" (*Südostasien*) as a purely geographical expression free of these problems, initially for the region of dispersion of Dongson bronze drums. By the 1930s it had become more widespread, and was adopted by the

New York-based Institute of Pacific Relations, which commissioned a number of important books on the region. The Japanese invasion gave the term a more obvious political character in 1941, and the British force assembled in Sri Lanka to reconquer the region was called the Southeast Asia Command (SEAC). The question of a name appeared resolved in the post-war world, even if Southeast Asia then seemed a region of conflict rather than coherence.

Lord Louis Mountbatten's SEAC, relying on chiefly Indian troops for its reoccupation of the region in 1945, can be considered the last effective projection of influence from India to Southeast Asia. Nehru's independent India notably failed to continue the millennial pattern, while China's civil war, revolution, and communist isolation delayed its return to a position of influence. It was on the Left that enthusiasm for a separate Southeast Asian solidarity was first manifest. Aung San in Burma and Ho Chi Minh in Indochina were already calling for a specifically Southeast Asian regional grouping in 1946. They tended to look to Pridi's leftist government in Thailand as its obvious leader, since it alone was in unquestioned command of its national space. The few years between the Japanese surrender and the arrival of the Cold War offered a rare opportunity for Asian self-discovery.

Pandit Nehru was by far the best-placed Asian leader to create and lead a broader Asian solidarity movement as India moved confidently to independence in 1947. In March 1947 he hosted an Inter-Asian Conference in New Delhi, personally inviting Ho Chi Minh to send a DRV delegation, and sending a plane to Jakarta for Sjahrir to represent the other embattled republic, Indonesia. As he rightly declared in opening the conference, "Asia is again finding herself … One of the notable consequences of the European domination of Asia has been the isolation of the countries of Asia from one another." Malaya was able to send twelve delegates from its quarreling parties, some of whom supported the pleas of Indochina and Indonesia delegates for more than words of support for the anti-colonial struggles. Nehru, however, was firmly opposed to expanding the armed conflict and bluntly refused DRV requests for arms. This disappointment, together with the manifest conflicts in the big countries, with India's Muslim League and China's Communist Party boycotting the meeting, convinced many of the delegates from Indochina, Burma, Thailand, Malaya, Indonesia, and the Philippines that they would be better off with their own grouping free of bigger powers. Saigon communist leader Tran Van Giau (1947), in a subsequent letter to the *Bangkok Post*, envisaged a kind of Southeast Asian political union as the only means to overcome their balkanization and "strengthen our right to be masters in our own land" (Goscha 1999).

The communist rebellions in Malaya, the Philippines, Burma, and Indonesia in 1948 brought the Cold War brutally to Southeast Asia and killed these early dreams. The DRV needed the support of communist China to survive militarily and economically, while the other national movements needed to distance themselves from communism to gain the western trust they needed for independence. Pridi's support for Southeast Asia's revolutionary struggles was unpopular with the military who overthrew him in November 1947 (Chapter 17). As a bulwark against the advance of China's communist model, the United States enrolled the Philippines, Thailand, and six powers external to the region in the Southeast Asia Treaty Organization (SEATO) in 1954. This was hardly a regional organization, and its role in legitimating the involvement of SEATO members in the Indochina wars served more to divide than unite.

Indonesia's Sukarno was more interested in ideological solidarity beyond the region, first through the Afro-Asian Conference he hosted in Bandung in 1955 on a non-aligned basis. This signalled China's re-entry to Asian diplomacy, as Zhou Enlai's apparent moderation and readiness to encourage Sino-Southeast Asians to embrace the nationality of their host countries upstaged Nehru, who had been expected to lead. Sukarno himself became a highly divisive figure as he moved closer to China, confronting Malaysia in 1963, withdrawing from the United Nations in 1964, and establishing what he called the New Emerging Forces or the "Jakarta-Phnom Penh-Beijing-Hanoi-Pyongyang axis" in opposition to the UN.

Meanwhile, a network of regional cultural and sporting organizations gradually evolved in non-communist Southeast Asia, while the DRV participated in Soviet-sponsored events. The Southeast Asian cultural festival in Singapore attracted Indonesian and Burmese performers as well as the usual non-communist states during a calm before the Confrontation storm in 1963. It reasserted some long-neglected similarities of dance and theater forms among the countries of the region, and led to many further exchanges. A separate sporting body took the form of the Southeast Asian Peninsula Games, first held in Bangkok in 1959, to allow Thailand, Burma, Cambodia, Laos, Malaya, Singapore, and South Viet Nam to compete every two years with better hope of medals than at the four-yearly Olympic and Asian Games. One of the Games' most popular innovations was the addition of one genuinely Southeast Asian sport known as *sepak raga* in Malay and *takraw* in Thai. Though it began as an amusement to keep a rattan ball in the air as long as possible without use of the hands, it was modernized into a volleyball-like competitive sport with three men on either side of a net, and given the hybrid name *sepak takraw* for international purposes. After the communist victories of 1975 the games became a distinctly non-communist grouping, renamed the Southeast Asian Games and embracing Indonesia, the Philippines, and Brunei in place of Viet Nam, Cambodia, and Laos. Cambodia rejoined, however, in 1983, and Laos and Viet Nam in 1989, making this the most popular, if rowdily partisan, celebration of Southeast Asian interaction.

Malaysia and Singapore had a long tradition as commercial hubs around which the region's trade and communications revolved. Too plural themselves to be unqualified nationalists, they were the most consistent boosters of the regional concept, even if their vulnerability first to communist insurrection and then Indonesia's Confrontation made them cling to British and Australian protection. Already in 1959, the then Malayan Prime Minister sought to persuade a lukewarm Thailand and the Philippines to join an Association of South-East Asia (ASA), realized in 1961. Negotiations to forestall Indonesian and Philippine opposition to Malaysia in 1963 produced a very short-lived tripartite "Maphilindo," evoking an old dream of some Filipino nationalists for "Malay" racial unity. Hostilities peaked during Indonesia's Confrontation of

Malaysia (1963–6), and it was negotiations to end this, brokered by Thailand, which produced the ASEAN idea. Suharto's military regime now shared the fear of its neighbors about rising communist power, though rejecting external military alliances, and therefore Indonesia became a crucial convert to regionalism. Newly independent Singapore pressed its case to join what was first envisaged as the three ASA members plus Indonesia, allowing five countries to hammer out the Association of Southeast Asian Nations (ASEAN) in August 1967 (Figure 20.1).

Initially involving little more than annual meetings to build trust, ASEAN became more important as the British withdrew from Singapore (1971) and the Americans from Indochina (1975), allowing communism to triumph there. Viet Nam's invasion of Cambodia in 1978 and takeover from the appalling Pol Pot regime was worrying particularly to Singapore, as a possible precedent for eliminating inconvenient small states by force. ASEAN lobbied to keep Cambodia's UN seat in the hands of an unlikely anti-Viet Nam coalition and to encourage eventual UN mediation of a settlement, elections, and Viet Nam's withdrawal in 1989. An ASEAN secretariat was established in Jakarta in 1976, Brunei was added in 1984, and in 1992 members agreed to an ASEAN Free Trade Area, obliging members to charge no more than 5% tariff on goods originating in another ASEAN country. In the 1990s ASEAN adopted a strategy similar to the European Union's, of expanding to include former enemies, though without Europe's democratic admission standards. ASEAN adopted a policy of engagement with Burma's military dictatorship rather than supporting the western-led sanctions that appeared only to force Burma into the arms of China. After its economic opening through *doi moi*, Viet Nam was the first of the blatantly authoritarian countries to join ASEAN in 1995, having already negotiated with it over Cambodia. With that precedent Laos and Burma were permitted to join in 1997 despite little evidence of improvement in their human rights record. Cambodia should have joined then but was delayed until 1999 because of Hun Sen's provocative coup against the democratically elected government.

At the end of the century the whole of Southeast Asia had at last a vehicle for moderating differences and promoting integration, even if the Asian Financial Crisis (1997–8) created a mood more of cynicism than celebration. Cynicism seemed justified by ASEAN's inability to deal with the internal crises and human rights abuses of its members, to resolve border disputes, or to present a united front on bigger global issues. Yet by any standard except that of the European Union it proved a successful regional organization. It developed means for very different regimes to meet regularly on a basis of equality and growing trust, to avoid armed conflict, and to move gradually toward integration in trade and other spheres. Explosive border conflicts between Thailand and Cambodia, Malaysia and Singapore, and Malaysia and Indonesia were referred satisfactorily to the International Court of Justice. Some insiders gave the credit to the "ASEAN way" of informal sing-alongs, golf courses, and colorful shirts, attempting to work chiefly by consensus. A more important advantage over other regional organizations was the balance between its members, with smaller Singapore, Malaysia, and Brunei making

(a)

(b)

Figure 20.1 a) The five original members of ASEAN at Foreign Ministers' signing meeting Bangkok, August 1967. From left: Narciso Ramos (Philippines), Adam Malik (Indonesia), Thanat Khoman (Thailand), Abdul Razak (Malaysia), Sinnapah Rajaratnam (Singapore); b) Southeast Asia's warring countries at last united in ASEAN, minus Cambodia. The 1997 Kuala Lumpur summit. Source: © Bernama/AP/Press Association.

up in wealth and infrastructural capacity what they lacked in size. The giant of the group, Indonesia, was, under Suharto and his elected successors, pragmatically interested in development rather than dominance, and was among the world's lowest military spenders in relation to GDP. Tiny Singapore was much the biggest arms buyer. No country was in a position to bully, nor to offer military assistance to embattled neighbors.

Another helpful factor was the acceptance of English from the outset as the sole working language of the grouping, sparing it the symbolic battles of other parts of the world. Since the national languages of Indonesia, Malaysia, Brunei, and nominally even Singapore were slightly different modernizations of the same (Malay) language, this was the only possible internal rival. In the early days of rediscovering each other in the ASEAN context, Malaysia and Indonesia did try to standardize their languages with a view to giving them a larger role in the world. They agreed to introduce a common spelling system in 1972, which for example replaced the *ch* sound of English/Malaysian and the *tj* of Dutch/Indonesian orthography with the letter *c*. Differences, however, persisted and even widened, with Malaysian more inclined to borrow from Arabic and Indonesian from western and local languages. English had the merit of neutrality, so that no party had to defer to others. It also helped ASEAN play an ever-larger role as host to broader Asian forums. In 1993 the annual ASEAN meeting agreed to sponsor an ASEAN regional forum, which gradually became the major regular meeting for the Asian region, with America and Europe also attending. From 1997 ASEAN +3 provided a valuable forum for fractious China, Japan, and Korea to meet annually in a broader ASEAN-hosted context where many financial, trade, security, environmental, and other problems could be addressed.

ASEAN also had profited from some trends not really of its making. It proved well placed to ride the post-Cold War pattern of global integration, and the rise of English as a global language. The return of constitutional civilian government in Burma in 2010, and of Aung San Suu Kyi to its parliament, turned Burma from an embarrassment to something that could be claimed as an achievement for regionalism. Above all, the rising strength and assertiveness of China created a common problem for the region and a strong incentive to resist pressures through greater cohesiveness. As China developed a strong naval power in the twenty-first century and began to use it to expand its claims to the whole of the South China Sea, the Philippines and Viet Nam both came into physical conflict with Chinese naval activity near their shores. Malaysia, Indonesia, and Brunei also have Exclusive Economic Zones that conflict with China's unexplained "nine-dot-line" that appears to include virtually all the maritime space. Burma's anxiety about Chinese dominance was a factor in its military rulers' opening toward ASEAN and the West. Although ASEAN's members diverged widely about how to deal with the northern giant that was also their major trade partner, all could see the advantage of a common front.

GLOBAL COMPARISONS

Southeast Asia in 1941 began a period of four decades in which it was of central strategic interest to the world as a battleground of how the colonial system would end. First the Japanese, then the communists, made it the major region of challenge to western dominance, where the Cold War was at its hottest. Since relative peace and global integration returned to the region, how does it compare to others in the world? It started its economic take-off before China and India, and while surpassed by China after 2000, it retained a more balanced pattern, less vulnerable to ageing, credit, and environmental crises. Most of its countries had climbed up to the third quartile of the global wealth rankings by 2010, though with super-rich Singapore and Brunei, as well as

Malaysia and Thailand, in the top half. It is undoubtedly a star among the tropical areas historically less given to capital accumulation.

It has retained, or rather regained, its historical character as a crossroads, relatively open to trade, migration, and ideas. Sriwijaya, Champa, Melaka, Manila, Batavia/Jakarta, Bangkok, and Singapore all had their turns at preeminence in the seaborne trade of Asia, but the hubs and routes were always multiple and competitive, and many cities lived primarily by trade. High colonialism certainly diminished this pattern in the nineteenth and twentieth centuries, as populations were peasantized and much regional trade redirected to supplying Europe with tropical commodities. Nationalism in turn had a half-century of experimenting with autarchy to different degrees, including self-defeating attempts to curb or even expel its productive cosmopolitan minorities. As a result Singapore and Bangkok, the two cities most friendly to such minorities, became the only global hubs during the commercial turnaround, disproportionately well-endowed with capital, expertise, and global connectivity. The communist countries and Myanmar were the most resistant to the return of foreign capital and entrepreneurship, as indeed they had been at earlier times, but from the 1990s they competed all the more vigorously for it. The triumph of the mobile phone, the shopping mall, and global consumer trends appeared secure in the new millennium.

Throughout this long story it has been easy to picture Southeast Asia, indeed, as primarily a consumer rather than a producer of global trends. What surprised Janet Abu-Lughod (1989, 296) about its past, that "a region that for so long occupied the position of cross-waterway of the world should have had so little to say for itself," appeared to be still true in this era of integration. Khmer architecture, Javanese music, and Balinese dance were discovered by Europe in the nineteenth century, but only Southeast Asian food has so far been carried triumphantly around the world by its own people. In winning such recognition as Nobel Prizes, Olympic medals, and civilizational landmarks it has performed below what its size would warrant. The long years of conflict and repression, the flight of much of its outstanding minority talent, and linguistic obstacles are all part of the explanation for this. But it must also be conceded that Southeast Asian societies, in marked contrast with those of Northeast Asia, have valued oral more than written communication, performance more than literary entertainment, and harmony more than competition.

Their post-colonial education systems were developed quickly, valuing quantity more than quality and discipline. With the exception of Singapore and Viet Nam with their Northeast Asian features, Southeast Asia performed disappointingly in international student assessments, with Indonesia near the bottom of PISA tables for mathematics, science, and reading. Total new book publications were well below the level of Europe or Northeast Asia, though comparable with South Asia. The picture was more dire in international scholarly publications. Singapore was again up with the best at about 1,000 a year per million people in the period 2002–8, while Indonesia was near the bottom and the Philippines and Viet Nam also below ten per million. Even in publishing internationally about their own country, the larger Southeast Asian states had little to say for themselves, Indonesia and the Philippines being the source of less than 20% of the articles on themselves (Guggenheim 2012). It is not in these areas that one looks for Southeast Asian leadership.

In the Preface I suggested three reasons Southeast Asia and its history were critical – environment, gender, and low states. The dramatic changes of the twentieth century rendered these factors no less relevant. The exceptional biodiversity of the region has been diminished by deforestation, but remains a resource for the world. Southeast Asia's vulnerability to environmental disaster appears more acute than ever, as global warming and the subsidence of mega-cities like Bangkok and Jakarta made floods, typhoons, and tsunamis threatening to ever more people. The 2004 tsunami that devastated Aceh and damaged coastal areas around the Indian Ocean, the world's worst that we know of, underlined the exceptional tectonic dangers of this most populous section of the "ring of fire." It also prompted an unprecedented global effort to assist in the recovery of these areas, a critical learning experience for our global future. When volcanic eruptions recur on the scale of Tambora 200 years ago, much more global resourcefulness will be called for.

As I argued in Chapters 15 and 19, urban and industrial modernity powerfully affected the gender pattern, introducing an urban dichotomy between male work-place and female home-place. Neo-traditional religious puritanism sought to make contemporary Southeast Asian women appear in some respects more constrained than their western sisters. Yet Southeast Asia's experience of this modern urban transition from a relatively gender-balanced starting point is an important model for a world seeking to reinvent its gender relations in post-industrial ways. Women moved relatively smoothly from rural to urban work, often leaving home to do so. There was little overt confrontation on gender issues, in part because of the high values placed on harmony and on acceptance of the different but complementary roles of male and female. Nevertheless, women continued to participate vigorously in the workforce even as they modernized, and remained in control of their own and much of the family assets.

There is little doubt that the low state role in Southeast Asian lives has contributed to the low profile of the region in the world. The region's new states (always excluding Singapore) have appeared unable to deliver what they promised through international agreements or domestic legislation. Gunnar Myrdal (1968) attempted to define the problem through his influential notion of the "soft state," unwilling or unable to be punitive against those deemed part of the national moral community. Others saw the return of "patrimonial," "personalist," "patron-client," or "network" features deemed characteristic of precolonial political systems in the region. Personal charisma or military arbitrariness often took the place occupied by institutional strength and legal discipline in twentieth-century European states.

Past attempts to analyze the "problem" were generally in response to crisis, when particular states dramatically failed the tests of order, democratic accountability, or a reliable climate for investment and growth. The period, since 1980, of relative peace, high growth, and the partial return of democracy is often understood to be simply catching up with the strong states of the West, implicitly taken to be the norm. It is appropriate to ask, however, whether the "softness" of Southeast Asia's states is part of a distinctive political pattern that has inherited some positive as well as negative elements from its past. This book has sought to demonstrate that the adjustment to a world-system based on the absolute sovereignty and coherence of nation-states was a huge challenge for Southeast Asian societies with no experience of state absolutism except the brief colonial one, rejected as alien in the 1940s. The "soft" uncertainties of the following attempts at nation-building probably accentuated the terrible conflicts and foreign interventions of the Cold War. Yet the states survived, and in effect invented an increasingly stable layer of nationhood on top of the immense diversity of society. In comparison with other such transitions in world history this was a success, embracing pluralism as Europe and Northeast Asia did not in their nationalist phase, yet escaping acute poverty and oppression as South Asia did not. The comparisons with either China's strong but not accountable state, or India's democratic state still unable to emancipate lower castes and women, make the Southeast Asian transitions an important third way.

The twenty-first century of global economic integration caused all states to lose their real or imagined autonomy. All were required to deal with increasing cultural pluralism internally as well as in their foreign entanglements. The inescapable pluralism of all Southeast Asian societies has never gone away even in the age of nationalism. They have demonstrated that profound conflicts, even those involving massive killings, can be overcome without effective legal systems to punish the guilty and exonerate the innocent. Although state law remains little trusted and weakly imposed, social cohesion is maintained by the high value placed on civility and harmony in personal interactions and public life, as well as by shared religious cultures and new national myths. The attachment to consensus rather than majority rule has been abused by dictators, but remains a feature of public life in a very plural region. Electoral politics have necessarily institutionalized a pattern of negotiation and coalition-building. In a world in need of new ways of combining cultural pluralism with human rights and government accountability, this experience demands attention.

REFERENCES

Abu-Lughod, Janet L. 1989. *Before European Hegemony. The World System A.D. 1250–1350.* New York: OUP.

Acabado, Stephen. 2009. "A Bayesian Approach to Dating Agricultural Terraces: A Case from the Philippines." *Antiquity* 83, 801–14.

Albuquerque, Braz de. 1557/1880. *The Commentaries of the Great Alfonso Dalboquerque,* trans. W. de Gray Birch, Vol. III. London: Hakluyt Society, 1880.

Ali, R. Moh. 1963. *Pengantar Ilmu Sedjarah Indonesia.* Jakarta: Bhatara.

Arendt, Hannah. 1968. *Antisemitism.* San Diego: Harcourt Brace Jovanovich.

Aung-Thwin, Michael. 1985. *Pagan: The Origins of Modern Burma.* Honolulu: University of Hawaii Press.

Aung-Thwin, Michael. 2005. *The Mists of Ramañña: The Legend That Was Lower Burma.* Honolulu: University of Hawaii Press.

Azra, Azyumardi. 2004. *The Origins of Islamic Reformism in Southeast Asia: Networks of Malay-Indonesian and Middle Eastern "Ulama" in the Seventeenth and Eighteenth Centuries.* Sydney: Allen & Unwin.

Baker, Chris and Pasuk Phongpaichit. 2009. *A History of Thailand,* 2nd edn. Cambridge: Cambridge University Press.

Baker, Chris and Pasuk Pongpaichit, eds. 2010. *The Tale of Khun Chang Khun Phaen.* Chiang Mai: Silkworm Books.

Barmé, Scot. 2002. *Woman, Man, Bangkok: Love, Sex, and Popular Culture in Thailand.* Lanham, MD: Rowman & Littlefield.

Baten, Jörg, Mojgan Stegl, and Pierre van der Eng. 2013. "The Biological Standard of Living and Body Height in Colonial and Post-colonial Indonesia, 1770–2000." *Journal of Bioeconomics,* doi 10.1007/s10818-012-9144-2.

Beaulieu, Augustin de. 1622/1996. *Mémoires d'un voyage aux Indes Orientales, 1619–1622,* ed. Denys Lombard, 1996. Paris: EFEO.

Bellwood, Peter. 2005. *First Farmers: The Origins of Agricultural Societies.* Oxford: Blackwell.

Blackburn, Susan. 2004. *Women and the State in Modern Indonesia.* Cambridge: Cambridge University Press.

Blair, E.H. and J.A. Robertson, eds. 1903–9. *The Philippine Islands, 1493–1898,* 55 vols. Cleveland: Arthur H. Clark.

A History of Southeast Asia: Critical Crossroads, First Edition. Anthony Reid.
© 2015 Anthony Reid. Published 2015 by John Wiley & Sons, Ltd.

Blussé, Leonard. 2008. *Visible Cities: Canton, Nagasaki and Batavia and the Coming of the Americans.* Cambridge, MA: Harvard University Press.

Blust, Robert. 1995. "The Prehistory of the Austronesian-Speaking Peoples: A View from Language," *Journal of World Prehistory* 9:4, 453–510.

Boomgaard, Peter. 1989. *Children of the Colonial State: Population Growth and Economic Development in Java, 1795–1880.* Amsterdam: Free University Press.

Booth, Anne. 1998. *The Indonesian Economy in the Nineteenth and Twentieth Centuries: A History of Missed Opportunities.* Basingstoke: Macmillan.

Booth, Anne. 2007. *Colonial Legacies: Economic and Social Development in East and Southeast Asia.* Honolulu: University of Hawaii Press.

Braginski, Vladimir. 2004. *The Heritage of Traditional Malay Literature: A Historical Survey of Genres, Writings and Literary Views.* Leiden: KITLV Press.

Brandon, James. 1967. *Theatre in Southeast Asia.* Cambridge, MA: Harvard University Press.

Brocheux, Pierre and Daniel Hémery. 2009. *Indochina: An Ambiguous Colonization, 1858–1954.* Berkeley: University of California Press.

Buckley, Brendan M., et al. 2010. "Climate as a Contributing Factor in the Demise of Angkor, Cambodia," *Proceedings of the National Academy of Science* 107:15, 6748–52.

Bulbeck, David, Anthony Reid, Lay-Cheng Tan, and Yiqi Wu. 1998. *Southeast Asian Exports since the Fourteenth Century: Cloves, Pepper, Coffee, and Sugar.* Singapore: ISEAS.

Burney, Henry. 1971. *The Burney Papers,* 5 vols. Bangkok: Vajiranana National Library, 1910–14. Reprinted 1971. Gregg International.

Butcher, John. 2004. *The Closing of the Frontier: A History of the Marine Fisheries of Southeast Asia, c. 1850–2000.* Singapore: ISEAS.

Chaunu, Pierre. 1960. *Les Philippines et le Pacifique des Ibériques (XVIe, XVIIe, XVIIIe siècles). Introduction méthodologique et indices d'activité.* Paris: S.E.V.P.E.N.

Chirino, Pedro. 1604/1969. *Relación de las Islas Filipinas: The Philippines in 1600,* trans Ramón Echevarria. Manila: Historical Conservation Society.

Choi Byung Wook. 2004. *Southern Vietnam under the Reign of Minh Mang (1820–1841): Central Policies and Local Response.* Ithaca: Cornell University Southeast Asia Program.

Christie, C.J. 1996. *A Modern History of Southeast Asia: Decolonization, Nationaism and Separatism.* London: I.B. Tauris.

Coedès, George. 1968. *The Indianized States of Southeast Asia,* trans. Susan Brown Cowing, ed. Walter F. Vella. Honolulu: East-West Center Press.

Coen, J.P. *Jan Pieterszoon Coen: bescheiden omtrent zijn bedrijf in Indie,* ed. H.T. Colenbrander, 4 vols. 1919–22. The Hague: Nijhoff.

Cohen, Matthew. 2006. *The Komedie Stamboel: Popular Theater in Colonial Indonesia, 1891–1903.* Athens, OH: Ohio University Press.

Crawfurd, John. 1820. *History of the Indian Archipelago,* 3 vols. Edinburgh: A. Constable.

Crawfurd, John. 1828/1967. *Journal of an Embassy to the Courts of Siam and Cochin China.* Reprinted 1967. Kuala Lumpur: Oxford University Press.

Crawfurd, John. 1856. *A Descriptive Dictionary of the Indian Islands and Adjacent Countries.* London: Bradbury and Evans.

Cruz, Gaspar da. 1569/1953. "Treatise in which the Things of China are Related." Translated in ed. Charles Boxer, *South China in the Sixteenth Century.* Cambridge: Hakluyt Society, 45–239.

Da Shan 1699/1993. "Hai Wai Ji Shi" [Record of Countries Overseas]. Translated in eds. Li Tana and Anthony Reid, *Southern Vietnam under the Nguyên. Documents on the Economic History of Cochinchina (Dang Trong), 1602–1777.* Singapore: ISEAS, 55–9.

Dasmariñas, Gomez Perez 1590/1958. "The Manners, Customs and Beliefs of the Philippine Inhabitants of Long Ago," [Boxer Codex] trans. C. Quirino and M. Garcia, *The Philippines Journal of Science* 87, iv (1958), 389–445.

Drewes, G.W.J., ed. 1978. *An Early Javanese Code of Muslim Ethics.* The Hague: Nijhoff.

Drewes, G.W.J., ed. 1980. *Two Acehnese Poems.* The Hague, Nijhoff for KITLV.

Durie, Mark. 1996. "Framing the Acehnese Text: Language Choice and Discourse Structures in Aceh." *Oceanic Linguistics* 35:1 (June), 113–37.

Dutton, George, Jane Werner, and John Whitmore, eds. 2012. *Sources of Vietnamese Tradition.* New York: Columbia University Press.

Edwards, Penny. 2007. "'Dressed in a Little Brief Authority': Clothing the Body Politic in Burma." In eds. Mina Roces and Louise Edwards, *The Politics of Dress in Asia and the Americas.* Brighton: Sussex Academic Press, 121–38.

Elson, R.E. 1997. *The End of the Peasantry in Southeast Asia: A Social and Economic HISTORY of peasant Livelihood, 1800–1990s.* Basingstoke: Macmillan.

Elson, R.E. 2001. *Suharto: A Political Biography.* Cambridge: Cambridge University Press.

Elson, R.E. 2008. *The Idea of Indonesia: A History.* Cambridge: Cambridge University Press.

Elvin, Mark. 1973. *The Pattern of the Chinese Past. A Social and Economic Interpretation.* Stanford: Stanford University Press.

Eviota, Elizabeth Uy. 1992. *The Political Economy of Gender: Women and the Sexual Division of Labour in the Philippines.* London: Zed Books.

Fansuri, Hamzah, 1986. *The Poems of Hamzah Fansuri*, eds. G.W.J. Drewes and Lode Brakel. Dordrecht: Foris for KITLV.

Feith, Herbert and Lance Castles. 1970. *Indonesian Political Thinking 1945–1965.* Ithaca: Cornell University Press.

Frederici, Cesare. 1581. "The voyage and travell of M. Caesar Fredericke, Marchant of Venice, into the East India, and beyond the Indies," trans. T. Hickocke, 1907. In ed. Richard Hakluyt, *The Principal Navigations, Voyages, Traffiques, and Discoveries of the English Nation,* Vol. III, Everyman's Edition. London: J.M. Dent, 198–269.

Furnivall, J.S. 1939. *Netherlands India: A Study of a Plural Economy.* Cambridge: Cambridge University Press.

Furnivall, J.S. 1948. *Colonial Policy and Practice. A Comparative Study of Burma and Netherlands India.* Cambridge: Cambridge University Press.

Galvão, Antonio. 1544. *A Treatise on the Moluccas (c.1544), Probably the Preliminary Version of Antonio Galvão's Lost* História das Molucas, trans. Hubert Jacobs, 1971. Rome: Jesuit Historical Institute.

Geertz, Clifford. 1963. *Agricultural Involution: The Processes of Ecological Change in Indonesia.* Berkeley: University of California Press.

Geertz, Clifford. 1980. *Negara: The Theatre State in Nineteenth-Century Bali.* Princeton: Princeton University Press.

Gioseffi, Daniela, ed. 2003. *Women on War: An Anthology of Women's Writings from Antiquity to the Present.* New York: The Feminist Press, CUNY Graduate Center.

Goens, Rijklof van. 1656/1956. *De vijf gezantschapsreizen van Rijklof van Goens naar het hof van Mataram, 1648–1654,* ed. H.J. de Graaf. The Hague: Nijhoff for Linschoten-Vereeniging.

Goscha, Christopher. 1995. *Vietnam or Indochina: Contesting Concepts of Space in Vietnamese Nationalism, 1887–1954.* Copenhagen: Nordic Institute of Asian Studies.

Goscha, Christopher. 1999. *Thailand and the Southeast Asian Networks of the Vietnamese Revolution, 1885–1954.* London: Curzon.

Guggenheim, Scott. 2012. "Indonesia's Quiet Springtime: Knowledge, Policy and Reform." In ed. Anthony Reid, *Indonesia Rising: The Repositioning of Asia's Third Giant*. Singapore: ISEAS.

Hadler, Jeffrey. 2008. *Muslims and Matriarchs: Cultural Resilience in Minangkabau through Jihad and Colonialism*. Ithaca, NY: Cornell University Press.

Hall, D.G.E. 1968. *A History of South-East Asia*, 3rd edn. London: Macmillan.

Hamilton, Alexander. 1727/1930. *A New Account of the East Indies*, Vol. II. Reprinted Edinburgh: John Mosman, 1930.

Handley, Paul. 2006. *The King Never Smiles: A Biography of Thailand's Bhumibol Adulyadej*. New Haven: Yale University Press.

Hatta, Mohammad. 1953–4. *Kumpulan Karangan*, 4 vols. Jakarta: Balai Buku Indonesia.

Hikayat Dewa Mandu: Epopée Malaise. 1980. Ed. H. Chambert-Loir. Paris: EFEO.

Ibrahim, ibn Muhammad. 1688/1972. *The Ship of Sulaiman*, trans. from the Persian by J. O' Kane. London: Routledge and Kegan Paul, 1972.

Ileto, Reynaldo. 1979. *Pasyon and Revolution: Popular Movements in the Philippines, 1840–1910*. Quezon City: Ateneo de Manila University Press.

Jamieson, Neil. 1993. *Understanding Vietnam*. Berkeley: University of California Press.

Jarric, Pierre du. 1608. *Histoire des choses plus memorable advenues tant ez Indes Orientales, que autres pais de la decouverte des Portugais*, Vol. I. Bordeaux: Millanges.

Jesus, E.C. de. 1980. *The Tobacco Monopoly in the Philippines: Bureaucratic Enterprise and Social Change, 1766–1880*. Quezon City: Ateneo de Manila University Press.

Johnson, J.J. ed. 1962. *The Role of the Military in Underdeveloped Countries*. Princeton: Princeton University Press.

Karim, Wazir Jahan. 1995. "Bilateralism and Gender in Southeast Asia." In ed. Wazir Jahan Karim, *"Male" and "Female" in Developing Southeast Asia*. Oxford: Berg Publishers, 35–74.

King, Victor and William Wilder. 2003. *The Modern Anthropology of South-East Asia: An Introduction*. London: Routledge.

Kobata, Atsushi and Mitsugo Matsuda. 1969. *Ryukyuan Relations with Korea and South Sea Countries*. Kyoto: Atsushi Kobata.

La Loubère, Simon de. 1691/1969. *A New Historical Relation of the Kingdom of Siam*. London, 1691. Reprinted Kuala Lumpur: OUP, 1969.

Laarhoven, Ruurdje. 1994. "*The Power of Cloth: The Textile Trade of the Dutch East India Company (VOC) 1600–1780*." Ph.D. dissertation, ANU.

Lasimbang, Jannie, and Colin Nicholas. 2007. "Malaysia: The Changing Status of Indigenous and Statutory Systems on Natural Resource Management." In ed. Helen Leake, *Bridging the Gap: Policies and Practices on Indigenous Peoples' Natural Resource Management in Asia*. Bangkok: UNDP, 175–234.

Le Blanc, Marcel. 1692. *Histoire de la revolution du roiaume de Siam, arrivé en l'année 1688*. Lyon: Horace Moulin.

Le Quy Don. 1776/1993. *Phu Bien Tap Luc* [1776], as translated in eds. Li Tana and Anthony Reid, *Southern Vietnam under the Nguyen: Documents on the Economic History of Cochin-China (Dang Trong), 1602–1777*. Singapore: ISEAS, 1993.

Leach, E.R. 1959. *Political Systems of Highland Burma: A Study of Kachin Social Structure*. Reprinted 2004. Oxford: Berg.

Lee Kuan Yew. 2000. *From Third World to First: The Singapore Story: 1965–2000*. Singapore: Times Editions.

Liaw Yock Fang. 1976. *Undang-undang Melaka: The Laws of Melaka*. The Hague, Nijhoff for KITLV.

Lieberman, Victor. 1995. "An Age of Commerce in Southeast Asia? Problems of Regional Coherence: A Review Article," *Journal of Asian Studies* 54:3, 796–807.

Lieberman, Victor. 2003. *Strange Parallels: Southeast Asia in Global Context, c. 800–1830, Vol. I: Integration on the Mainland.* Cambridge: Cambridge University Press.

Lieberman, Victor. 2009. *Strange Parallels: Southeast Asia in Global Context, c. 800–1830, Vol. II; Mainland Mirrors: Europe, Japan, China, South Asia and the Islands.* Cambridge: Cambridge University Press.

Liu Hong. 2011. *China and the Shaping of Indonesia 1949–1965.* Singapore: National University of Singapore Press.

Loarca, Miguel de. 1582. "*Relation of the Filipinas Islands*" In Blair and Robertson, eds., 1903–9, Vol. 5, 34–167.

Locher-Scholten, Elsbeth. 2000. *Women and the Colonial State: Essays on Gender and Modernity in the Netherlands Indies, 1900–1942.* Amsterdam: Amsterdam University Press.

Lodewycksz, Willem. 1598/1915. "D'eerste Boeck: Historie van Indien vaer inne verhaelt is de avontueren die de Hollandtsche schepen bejeghent zijn." In eds. G.P. Rouffaer and J.W. Ijzerman, *De eerste schipvaart der Nederlanders naar Oost-Indië onder Cornelis de Houtman 1595–1597*, Vol. I, 1915. The Hague: Nijhoff for Linschoten-Vereniging.

Ma Huan. 1433/1970. *Ying Yai Sheng-lan: "The Overall Survey of the Ocean's Shores,"* trans. J.V.G. Mills. Cambridge: Hakluyt Society, 1970. Reprinted Bangkok: White Lotus Press, 1997.

Maddison, Angus. 2006. *The World Economy: A Millenial Perspective.* Paris: OECD.

Magalhães-Godinho, Vitorino. 1969. *L'économie de l'empire portugais aux XVe et XVIe siècles.* Paris S.E.V.P.E.N.

Maier, Henk. 2004. *We Are Playing Relatives: A Survey of Malay Writing.* Leiden: KITLV Press.

Marr, David. 1981. *Vietnamese Tradition on Trial, 1920–1945.* Berkeley: University of California Press.

Marr, David. 2013. *Vietnam: State, War and Revolution (1945–1946).* Berkeley: University of California Press.

Marsden, William. 1811. *The History of Sumatra*, 3rd revised edn. London, 1811. Reprinted Kuala Lumpur: OUP, 1966.

Masuda, Erika. 2004. "The Last Siamese Tributary Missions to China, 1851–1854 and the 'Rejected' Value of *Chim Kong.*" In eds. Wang Gungwu and Ng Chin-keong, *Maritime China in Transition 1750–1850.* Wiesbaden: Horowitz.

McNeill, William. 1982. *The Pursuit of Power: Technology, Armed Force, and Society since A.D. 1000.* Chicago: University of Chicago Press.

McVey, Ruth T. 1965. *The Rise of Indonesian Communism.* Ithaca: Cornell University Press.

Minter, Tessa. 2010. *The Agta of the Northern Sierra Madre: Livelihood Strategies and Resilience among Philippine Hunter-Gatherers.* Published dissertation, University of Leiden.

Montesano, Michael and Patrick Jory, eds. 2008. *Thai South and Malay North: Ethnic Interactions on a Plural Peninsula.* Singapore: NUS Press.

Moor, J.H. 1837. *Notices of the Indian Archipelago, and Adjacent Countries: Being a Collection of Papers relating to Borneo, Celebes, Bali, Java, Sumatra, Nias, the Philippine Islands, Sulu, Siam, Cochin China, Malayan Peninsula, etc.* Singapore: n.p.

Morga, Antonio de. 1609/1971. *Sucesos de las Islas Filipinas*, trans. J.S. Cummins. Cambridge: Hakluyt Society, 1971.

Murashima, Eiji. 1988. "The Origin of Modern Official State Ideology in Thailand." *JSEAS* 19:1, 80–96.

Myrdal, Gunnar. 1968. *Asian Drama. An Inquiry into the Poverty of Nations*, 3 vols. New York: Pantheon.

427

Neck, Jacob van. 1604/1980. "Journal van Jacob van Neck." In eds. H.A. van Foreest and A. de Booy, *De vierde schipvaart der Nederlanders naar Oost-Indie onder Jacob Wilkens en Jacob van Neck (1599–1604)*, Vol. I. The Hague: Linschoten-Vereeniging.

Newbold, T.J. 1839. *British Settlements in the Straits of Malacca*, 2 vols. London: John Murray. Reprinted Kuala Lumpur: OUP, 1971.

Nguyen Trai. 1428/1967. "Proclamation of Victory over Wu [China]," trans. Truong Buu Lam, 1967. *Patterns of Vietnamese Response to Foreign Intervention 1858–1900*. New Haven: Yale University Southeast Asia Studies, 55–62.

Nu, U. 1975. *U Nu: Saturday's Son*. New Haven: Yale University Press.

Omar, Arifin. 1993. Bangsa Melayu. *Malay Concepts of Democracy and Community, 1945–1950*. Kuala Lumpur: Oxford University Press.

Pallegoix, Mgr. 1854. *Description du Royaume Thai ou Siam*, 2 vols. Photographic reprint, 1969. Paris: Gregg International.

Parlindungan, Mangaradja. 1964. *Pongkinangolngolan Sinambela gelar Tuanku Rao: Terror Agama Islam Mazhab Hambali di Tanah Batak 1816–1833*. Jakarta: Penerbit Tandjung Harapan. Appendix 31 of this book, purporting to be a reading of Chinese materials by Dutch official Poortman 50 years earlier, was translated and analyzed by H.J. de Graaf and Th.G.Th. Pigeaud in ed. M.C. Ricklefs, *Chinese Muslims in Java in the 15th and 16th Centuries*. Melbourne: Monash University Southeast Asia Monographs, 1984.

Parker, Geoffrey. 2013. *Global Crisis: War, Climate Change and Catastrophe in the Seventeenth Century*. New Haven, Yale University Press.

Parker, Geoffrey and Lesley Smith, eds. 1978. *The General Crisis of the Seventeenth Century*. London, Routledge. The second edition (1997) includes Southeast Asia.

Pauker, Guy. 1959. "Southeast Asia as a Problem Area in the Next Decade," *World Politics* 6.

Phan Boi Chau. 1914. "Prison Notes." In ed. David Marr, *Reflections from Captivity*. Athens: Ohio University Press, 1978.

Pinto, Fernão Mendes. 1578/1989. *The Travels of Mendes Pinto*, trans. Rebecca Catz. Chicago: University of Chicago Press.

Pires, Tomé. 1515/1944. *The Suma Oriental of Tomé Pires*, trans. Armando Cortesão. London: Hakluyt Society.

Pollock, Sheldon. 2006. *The Language of the Gods in the World of Men: Sanskrit, Culture and Power in Premodern India*. Berkeley: University of California Press.

Pomeranz, Kenneth. 2000. *The Great Divergence: China, Europe, and the Making of the Modern World Economy*. Princeton: Princeton University Press.

Quezón, Manuel. 1936. "*Second State of the Nation Address*." 16 June 1936, http://www.gov.ph/1936/06/16/manuel-l-quezon-second-state-of-the-nation-address-june-16-1936 (accessed November 8, 2014).

Quinn, George. 1992. *The Novel in Javanese: Aspects of its Social and Literary Character*. Leiden: KITLV Press.

Raffles, Thomas Stamford. 1817/1978. *The History of Java*, 2 vols. London: John Murray. Reprinted Kuala Lumpur: Oxford University Press, 1978.

Raniri, Nuru'd-din ar-. 1643/1966. *Bustanu's-Salatin, Bab II, Fasal 13*, ed. T. Iskandar, 1966. Kuala Lumpur: Dewan Bahasa dan Pustaka.

Reid, Anthony. 1988. *Southeast Asia in the Age of Commerce*. Vol I: *The Lands Below the Winds*. New Haven: Yale University Press.

Reid, Anthony. 1990. "The 'Seventeenth Century Crisis' as an Approach to Southeast Asian History," *Modern Asian Studies* 24:4, 639–59.

Reid, Anthony. 1993. *Southeast Asia in the Age of Commerce, 1450–1680*. Vol. 2: *Expansion and Crisis*. New Haven: Yale University Press.

Reid, Anthony. 1999. *Charting the Shape of Early Modern Southeast Asia*. Chiang Mai: Silkworm Books.

Reid, Anthony. 2009. "Family Names in Southeast Asian History." In eds. Zheng Yangwen and Charles Macdonald, *Personal Names in Asia: History, Culture and Identity*. Singapore: NUS Press, 21–36.

Reid, Anthony. 2010. *Imperial Alchemy: Nationalism and Political Identity in Southeast Asia*. Cambridge: Cambridge University Press.

Renfrew, Colin. 1987. *Archaeology and Language – The Puzzle of Indo-European Origins*. London: Jonathan Cape.

Reyes, Raquel. 2008. *Love, Passion and Patriotism: Sexuality and the Philippine Propaganda Movement, 1882–1892*. Singapore: NUS Press.

Rhodes, Alexandre de. [1653], as translated in Solange Herz, *Rhodes of Vietnam: The Travels and Missions of Father Alexander de Rhodes in China and Other Kingdoms of the Orient*. Westminster, MD: Newman Press, 1966.

Ricklefs, M.C. 2006. *Mystic Synthesis in Java: A History of Islamization from the Fourteenth to the Early Nineteenth Centuries*. Norwalk, CT: EastBridge.

Rigg, Jonathan. 2003. *Southeast Asia: The Human Landscape of Modernization and Development*, 2nd edn. London: Routledge.

Robson, Stuart, trans. 1995. *Déśawarnana (Nāgarakṛtāgama) by Mpu Prapañca*. Leiden: KITLV Press.

Roff, W.R. 1967. *The Origins of Malay Nationalism*. New Haven: Yale University Press.

Salemink, Oscar. 2003. *The Ethnography of Vietnam's Central Highlanders: A Historical Contextualization, 1850–1990*. London: Routledge Curzon.

Sangermano, Vincentius. 1833/1966. *A Description of the Burmese Empire*, trans. William Tandy. Rome, 1833. Reprinted London: Susil Gupta, 1966.

Santoso, Soewito. 1975. *Sutasoma, a Study in Old Javanese Wajrayana*. New Delhi: International Academy of Indian Culture.

Sargent, Matthew. 2013. "Global Trade and Local Knowledge: Gathering Natural Knowledge in Seventeenth-Century Indonesia". In eds. Tara Alberts and D.R.M. Irving, *Intercultural Exchange in Southeast Asia: History and Society in the Early Modern World*. London: I.B. Tauris.

Schumacher, Frank. 1979. *Readings in Philippine Church History*. Quezon City: Loyola School of Theology, Ateneo de Manila University Press.

Scott, Edmund. 1606/1943. "An exact discourse of the Subtitles, Fashions, Pollicies, Religion, and Ceremonies of the East Indians, as well Chyneses as Javans, there abiding and dwelling." In ed. Sir William Foster, *The Voyage of Henry Middleton to the Moluccas*. London: Hakluyt Society.

Scott, James C. 1998. *Seeing Like a State: How Certain Schemes to Improve the Human Condition Have Failed*. New Haven: Yale University Press.

Scott, James C. 2009. *The Art of Not Being Governed: An Anarchist History of Upland Southeast Asia*. New Haven: Yale University Press.

Sen, Krishna. 1994. *Indonesian Cinema: Framing the New Order*. London: Zed Books.

Sejarah Goa. n.d., ed. G.J. Wolhoff and Abdurrahim. Makassar: Jajasan Kebujaan Sulawesi Selatan dan Tenggara [1968?].

Sejarah Melayu. 1612/1938. Ed. R.O. Winstedt, *JMBRAS* 16, iii, 42–226, trans. C.C. Brown, 1952, *JMBRAS* 25, ii-iii.

Sjahrir, Sutan. 1968. *Our Struggle*, trans. B.R.O'G. Anderson. Ithaca: Cornell University Modern Indonesia Program.

Smeaton, Donald. 1887. *The Loyal Karens of Burma*. London: Kegan Paul, Trench & Co.

Soewardi Soerjaningrat. 1914. "Onze Nationale Kleeding," reproduced in *Karja K. H. Dewantara*, Vol IIA. Jogjakarta: Persatuan Taman Siswa, 1967.

Stapel, F.W. 1922. *Het Bongaais verdrag.* Leiden: Rijsuniversiteit.

Sukarno. 1965. *Sukarno. An Autobiography, as Told to Cindy Adams.* Indianapolis: Bobs-Merrill.

Tan Malaka. 1925. *Naar de "Republiek-Indonesia."* Canton: n.p.

Tan Malaka. 1926/2000. *Massa Aksi.* Reprinted 2000. Jakarta: Teplok Press.

Taylor, K.W. and John K. Whitmore. 1995. *Essays into Vietnamese Pasts.* Ithaca: Cornell University Southeast Asia Program.

Transparency International. 2014. http://www.transparency.org/research/cpi (last accessed November 14, 2014).

Trocki, Carl. 2007. *Prince of Pirates: The Temenggongs and the Development of Johor and Singapore, 1784–1885,* 2nd edn. Singapore: NUS Press.

Truong Buu Lam. 1967. *Patterns of Vietnamese Response to Foreign Intervention 1858–1900.* New Haven: Yale University Southeast Asia Studies.

Vliet, Jeremias van. 1640/2005. *Van Vliet's Siam,* eds. Chris Baker, Dhiravat na Pombejra, Alfons van der Kraan, and David Wyatt. Chiang Mai: Silkworm Books.

Wallace, Alfred Russell. 1869. *The Malay Archipelago.* New York: Harper.

Waterson, Roxana. 1997. "The Contested Landscapes of Myth and History in Tana Toraja." In ed. James Fox, *The Poetic Power of Place: Comparative Perspectives on Austronesian Ideas of Locality.* Canberra: ANU E Press, 63–88.

Whitmore, John. 2011. *"Van Don, the 'Mac Gap' and the end of the Jiaozhi Ocean System: Trade and State in Dai Viet, Circa 1450–1550."* In Cooke, et al. 2011: 101–16.

Winichakul, Thongchai. 1994. *Siam Mapped: A History of the Geo-Body of a Nation.* Honolulu: University of Hawaii Press.

Wolters, O.W. 1999. *History, Culture and Region in Southeast Asian Perspectives.* Revised edn. Ithaca: Cornell University Southeast Asia Program.

Woodside, Alexander. 1997. "The Relationship between Political Theory and Economic Growth in Vietnam, 1750–1840." In ed. Anthony Reid, *The Last Stand of Asian Autonomies: Responses to Modernity in the Diverse States of Southeast Asia and Korea, 1750–1900.* Basingstoke: Macmillan, 245–68.

World Bank. 2014. World Bank Open Data. http://data.worldbank.org. (accessed 2014).

World Economic Forum. 2013. *The Global Gender Gap Report 2013.* Geneva: World Economic Forum. http://www3.weforum.org/docs/WEF_GenderGap_Report_2013.pdf (accessed November 8, 2014).

Wyatt, David K. 1982. *Thailand: A Short History.* New Haven: Yale University Press.

Yamin, Muhammad. 1954. *Naskah-Persiapan Undang-undang Dasar 1945,* 3 vols. Jakarta: Yayasan Prapanca.

Yang, Bin. 2010. "The Zhang on Southern Chinese Frontiers: Disease-Construction, Environmental Changes, and Imperial Colonization." *Bulletin of the History of Medicine* 84: 2.

Yuan Bingling. 2000. *Chinese Democracies: A Study of the Kongsis of West Borneo (1776–1884).* Leiden: Universiteit Leiden CNWS.

Yule, Henry. 1858. *A Narrative of the Mission to the Court of Ava in 1855,* [1858] New edn, ed. Hugh Tinker. Kuala Lumpur: Oxford University Press, 1968.

Zaide, Gregoria F. 1990. *Documentary Sources of Philippine History,* Vol. I. Metro Manila: National Book Store. The instructions to Legazpi by the Royal Audiencia of Mexico, September 1, 1564, 397–410.

Zhou Daguan. 1297/2007. *A Record of Cambodia: The Land and its People,* trans. Peter Harris. Chiang Mai: Silkworm Books.

FURTHER READING

GENERAL SOUTHEAST ASIA HISTORIES

Dutton, George, ed. 2014. *Voices of Southeast Asia: Essential Readings from Antiquity to the Present*. Armonk, NY: M.E. Sharpe.
Lieberman, Victor. 2003–9. *Strange Parallels: Southeast Asia in Global Context, c. 800–1830*. 2 vols. Cambridge: Cambridge University Press.
Owen, Norman, ed. *The Emergence of Modern Southeast Asia: A New History*. Honolulu: University of Hawaii Press.
Scott, James. 2009. *The Art of Not Being Governed: An Anarchist History of Upland Southeast Asia*. New Haven: Yale University Press.
Tarling, Nicholas, ed. 1992. *The Cambridge History of Southeast Asia*. 2 vols. Cambridge: Cambridge University Press.
Tarling, Nicholas. 2001. *Southeast Asia: A Modern History*. Oxford: Oxford University Press.

COUNTRY HISTORIES

Baker, Chris and Pasuk Phongpaichit. 2009. *A History of Thailand*, 2nd edn. Cambridge: Cambridge University Press.
Chandler, David. 2007. *A History of Cambodia*. 4th edn. Boulder, CO: Westview.
Charney, Michael. 2009. *A History of Modern Burma*. Cambridge: Cambridge University Press.
Corpuz, O.D. 2007. *The Roots of the Filipino Nation*. Honolulu: University of Hawaii Press.
Dutton, George, Jane Werner, and John Whitmore, eds. 2012. *Sources of Vietnamese Tradition*. New York: Columbia University Press.
Evans, Grant. 2002. *A Short History of Laos: The Land in Between*. Sydney: Allen & Unwin.
Jamieson, Neil. 1993. *Understanding Vietnam*. Berkeley: University of California Press.
Ricklefs, M.C. 1993. *A History of Modern Indonesia since c. 1300*. 2nd ed. Basingstoke: Macmillan.

A History of Southeast Asia: Critical Crossroads, First Edition. Anthony Reid.
© 2015 Anthony Reid. Published 2015 by John Wiley & Sons, Ltd.

Stuart-Fox, Martin. 1997. *A History of Laos*. Cambridge: Cambridge University Press.

Taylor, Keith. 2013. *A History of the Vietnamese*. Cambridge: Cambridge University Press.

Thant Myint-U. 2006. *The River of Lost Footsteps: Histories of Burma*. New York: Farrer, Straus & Giroux.

Wyatt, David. 1982. *Thailand: A Short History*. New Haven: Yale University Press.

CHAPTERS 1–2: BEGINNINGS

Aung-Thwin, Michael. 1985. *Pagan: The Origins of Modern Burma*. Honolulu: University of Hawaii Press.

Bellwood, Peter. 1997. *Prehistory of the Indo-Malaysian Archipelago*. Honolulu: University of Hawaii Press.

Boomgaard, Peter. 2007. *Southeast Asia: An Environmental History*. Santa Barbara, CA: ABC-Clio.

Coedès, George. 1968. *The Indianized States of Southeast Asia*, trans. Susan Cowing. Honolulu: East-West Center Press.

Gesick, Lorraine, ed. 1983. *Centers, Symbols and Hierarchies: Essays on the Classical States of Southeast Asia*. New Haven: Yale University Southeast Asia Studies.

Ishii Yoneo, ed. 1978. *Thailand: A Rice-Growing Society*, trans. Peter Hawkes and Stephanie Hawkes. Honolulu: University of Hawaii Press.

Higham, Charles. 1989. *The Archaeology of Mainland Southeast Asia*. Cambridge: Cambridge University Press.

Higham, Charles. 1996. *The Bronze Age of Southeast Asia*. Cambridge: Cambridge University Press.

Lombard, Denys. 1990. *Le carrefour javanais. Essai d'histoire globale*. 3 vols. Paris: Editions de l'Ecole des Hautes Etudes en Sciences Sociales.

Pollock, Sheldon. 2006. *The Language of the Gods in the World of Men: Sanskrit, Culture and Power in Premodern India*. Berkeley: University of California Press.

CHAPTERS 3–6: EARLY MODERN TRADE, RELIGION, HYBRIDITIES

Andaya, Barbara. 2006. *The Flaming Womb. Repositioning Women in Early Modern Southeast Asia*. Honolulu: University of Hawaii Press.

Bulbeck, David, Anthony Reid, Lay-Cheng Tan, and Yiqi Wu. 1998. *Southeast Asian Exports since the Fourteenth Century: Cloves, Pepper, Coffee, and Sugar*. Singapore: ISEAS.

Chaunu, Pierre. 1960. *Les Philippines et le Pacifique des Ibériques (XVIe, XVIIe, XVIIIe siècles). Introduction methodologique et indices d'activité*. Paris: S.E.V.P.E.N.

Reid, Anthony. 1988–93. *Southeast Asia in the Age of Commerce*. 2 vols. New Haven: Yale University Press.

Ricci, Ronit. 2011. *Islam Translated*. Chicago: University of Chicago Press.

Wade, Geoffrey. 2009. *China and Southeast Asia: Routledge Library on Southeast Asia*, 6 vols. London/New York: Routledge.

Wade, Geoffrey and Sun Laichen, eds. 2010. *Southeast Asia in the Fifteenth Century: The China Factor*. Singapore: NUS Press.

CHAPTERS 7–8: SEVENTEENTH/EIGHTEENTH CENTURIES

Azra, Azyumardi. 2004. *The Origins of Islamic Reformism in Southeast Asia: Networks of Malay-Indonesian and Middle Eastern 'Ulama' in the Seventeenth and Eighteenth Centuries.* Sydney: Allen & Unwin.

Laarhoven, Ruurdje. 1994. *"The Power of Cloth: The textile trade of the Dutch East India Company (VOC) 1600–1780".* Ph.D. dissertation, ANU.

Parker, Geoffrey. 2013. *Global Crisis: War, Climate Change and Catastrophe in the Seventeenth Century.* New Haven: Yale University Press.

Phelan, J.L. 1959. *The Hispanization of the Philippines. Spanish Aims and Filipino Responses 1565–1700.* Madison: University of Wisconsin Press.

Raben, Remco. 1996. *"Batavia and Colombo: The Ethnic and Spatial Order of Two Colonial Cities, 1600–1800."* Ph.D. dissertation, Leiden University.

Reid, Anthony and David Marr, eds. 1979. *Perceptions of the Past in Southeast Asia.* Singapore: Heinemann.

CHAPTERS 9–11: PRE-COLONIAL POLITIES

Cooke, Nola, Li Tana, and A. Anderson, eds. 2011. *The Tongking Gulf through History.* Philadelphia: University of Pennsylvania Press.

Dutton, George. 2006. *The Tây Sơn Uprising: Society and Rebellion in Eighteenth-Century Vietnam.* Honolulu: University of Hawaii Press.

Heidhues, Mary Somers. 2003. *Golddiggers, Farmers and Traders in the "Chinese Districts" of West Kalimantan, Indonesia.* Ithaca: Cornell University Southeast Asia Program.

Reid, Anthony, ed. 1996. *Sojourners and Settlers: Histories of Southeast Asia and the Chinese.* Honolulu: University of Hawaii Press.

Reid, Anthony, ed. 1997. *The Last Stand of Asian Autonomies: Responses to Modernity in the Diverse States of Southeast Asia and Korea, 1750–1900.* Basingstoke: Macmillan.

Thant, Myint-U. 2001. *The Making of Modern Burma.* Cambridge: Cambridge University Press.

Tran, Nhung Tuyet and Anthony Reid, eds. 2006. *Viet Nam: Borderless Histories.* Madison: University of Wisconsin Press.

Warren, James. 1981. *The Sulu Zone, 1768–1898: The Dynamics of External Trade, Slavery, and Ethnicity.* Singapore: NUS Press.

Woodside, Alexander. 1971. *Vietnam and the Chinese Model: A Comparative Study of Nguyen and Ch'ing Civil Government in the First Half of the Nineteenth Century.* Cambridge, MA: Harvard University Press.

CHAPTERS 12–13: ECONOMIC AND POLITICAL CHANGES, EIGHTEENTH TO TWENTIETH CENTURIES

Boomgaard, Peter. 1989. *Children of the Colonial State: Population Growth and Economic Development in Java, 1795–1880.* Amsterdam: Free University Press.

Brocheux, Pierre and Daniel Hémery. 2009. *Indochina: An Ambiguous Colonization, 1858–1954,* trans. Ly Lan Dill-Klein. Berkeley: University of California Press.

Butcher, John and Howard Dick, eds. 1993. *The Rise and Fall of Revenue Farming: Business Elites and the Emergence of the Modern State in Southeast Asia*. Basingstoke: Macmillan.

Chirot, Daniel and Anthony Reid. 1997. *Essential Outsiders: Chinese and Jews in the Modern Transformation of Southeast Asia and Central Europe*. Seattle: University of Washington Press.

Corpuz, O.D. 1997. *An Economic History of the Philippines*. Quezon City: University of the Philippines Press.

Cribb, Robert, ed. 1994. *The Late Colonial State in Indonesia: Political and Economic Foundations of the Netherlands Indies 1880–1942*. Leiden: KITLV Press

Dick, Howard and Peter Rimmer. 2003. *Cities, Transport and Communications: The Integration of Southeast Asia since 1850*. London: Palgrave Macmillan.

Elson, R.E. 1997. *The End of the Peasantry in Southeast Asia: A Social and Economic History of Peasant Livelihood, 1800–1990s*. Basingstoke: Macmillan.

Furnivall, J.S. 1948. *Colonial Policy and Practice. A Comparative Study of Burma and Netherlands India*. Cambridge: Cambridge University Press.

Goscha, Christopher. 1995. *Vietnam or Indochina? Contesting Concepts of Space in Vietnamese Nationalism, 1887–1954*. Copenhagen: NIAS Books.

McCoy, Alfred and Ed. de Jesus, eds. *Philippine Social History: Global Trade and Local Transformations*. Sydney: Allen & Unwin.

McGee, T.G. 1967. *The Southeast Asian City*. London: G. Bell.

Myoe, Maung Aung. Unpublished. "The Peacock and the Dragon: Myanmar's Relations with China in the Monarchical Era." Singapore: unpublished.

Owen, Norman, ed. 1987. *Death and Disease in Southeast Asia: Explorations in Social, Medical and Demographic History*. Singapore: Oxford University Press.

Trocki, Carl. 1999. *Opium, Empire and the Global Political Economy: A Study of the Asian Opium Trade 1750–1950*. Abingdon: Routledge.

Wong Lin Ken. 1960. "The Trade of Singapore 1819–69," *JMBRAS* 33, part iv.

CHAPTERS 14–15: TWENTIETH-CENTURY MODERNITY

Brandon, James. 1967. *Theatre in Southeast Asia*. Cambridge, MA: Harvard University Press.

Ikeya, Chie. 2011. *Refiguring Women, Colonialism and Modernity in Burma*. Honolulu: University of Hawaii Press.

Marr, David. 1981. *Vietnamese Tradition on Trial, 1920–1945*. Berkeley: University of California Press.

Reid, Anthony. 2010. *Imperial Alchemy: Nationalism and Political Identity in Southeast Asia*. Cambridge: Cambridge University Press.

Reyes, Raquel. 2008. *Love, Passion and Patriotism: Sexuality and the Philippine Propaganda Movement, 1882–1892*. Singapore: NUS Press.

Schulte Nordholt, Henk, ed. 1997. *Outward Appearances: Dressing State and Society in Indonesia*. Leiden: KITLV Press.

Tønnesson, Stein and Hans Antlöv. 1996. *Asian Forms of the Nation*. London: Curzon.

CHAPTERS 16–20: POST-COLONIAL TRANSFORMATION

Abdullah, Taufik. 2009. *Indonesia: Towards Democracy*. Singapore: ISEAS.

Anderson, Benedict. 1998. *The Spectre of Comparisons: Nationalism, Southeast Asia, and the World*. London: Verso.

Benjamin, Geoffrey and Cynthia Chou. 2002. *Tribal Communities in the Malay World: Historical, Cultural and Social Perspectives*. Singapore: ISEAS.

Bertrand, Jacques. 2013. *Political Change in Southeast Asia*. Cambridge: Cambridge University Press.

Cheah Boon Kheng. 2002. *Malaysia: The Making of a Nation*. Singapore: ISEAS.

Christie, Clive. 2000. *A Modern History of Southeast Asia: Decolonization, Nationalism and Separatism*. London: I.B. Tauris.

Crouch, Harold. 1988. *The Army and Politics in Indonesia*. Revised edn. Ithaca: Cornell University Press.

Drabble, John. 2000. *An Economic History of Malaysia, c.1800–1990: The Transition to Modern Economic Growth*. Basingstoke: Macmillan.

Feith, Herbert and Lance Castles. 1970. *Indonesian Political Thinking, 1945–1965*. Ithaca: Cornell University Press.

Goscha, Christopher. 1999. *Thailand and the Southeast Asian Networks of the Vietnamese Revolution, 1885–1954*. London: Curzon.

Handley, Paul. 2006. *The King Never Smiles. A Biography of Thailand's Bhumibol Adulyadej*. New Haven: Yale University Press.

Hefner, Robert. 2000. *Civil Islam: Muslims and Democratization in Indonesia*. Princeton: Princeton University Press.

Hill, Hal. 2010. *The Indonesian Economy*. 2nd edn. Cambridge: Cambridge University Press.

Huff, W.G. 2000. *The Economic Growth of Singapore: Trade and Development in the Twentieth Century*. Cambridge: Cambridge University Press.

Laothamatas, Anek, ed. 1997. *Democratization in Southeast and East Asia*. Singapore: ISEAS.

Lindsay, J. and Liem, M., eds. 2011. *Heirs to World Culture: Being Indonesian 1950–1965*. Leiden: KITLV Press.

McCoy, Alfred, ed. 1980. *Southeast Asia under Japanese Occupation*. New Haven: Yale University Southeast Asia Studies.

McCoy, Alfred, ed. 1993. *An Anarchy of Families: State and Family in the Philippines*. Madison: University of Wisconsin Press.

Osborne, Milton. 1994. *Sihanouk: Prince of Light, Prince of Darkness*. Sydney: Allen & Unwin.

Pan, Lynn, ed. 1998. *The Encyclopedia of the Chinese Overseas*. Singapore: Archipelago Press.

Reid, Anthony. 1974. *The Indonesian National Revolution, 1945–1950*. Hawthorn, Vic: Longmans Australia.

Reid, Anthony, ed. 1996. *Sojourners and Settlers: Histories of Southeast Asia and the Chinese*. Sydney: Allen & Unwin.

Reynolds, Craig. 2006. *Seditious Histories: Contesting Thai and Southeast Asian Pasts*. Seattle: University of Washington Press.

Rigg, Jonathan. 2003. *Southeast Asia: The Human Landscape of Modernization and Development*. 2nd edn. London: Routledge.

Rosaldo, Renato. 1980. *Ilongot Headhunting, 1883–1974: A Study in Society and History*. Stanford: Stanford University Press.

Skinner, G. William. 1957. *Chinese Society in Thailand: An Analytical History*. Ithaca: Cornell University Press.

Suehiro Akira. 1989. *Capital Accumulation in Thailand, 1855–1985*. Tokyo: Centre for East Asian Cultural Studies.

INDEX

Abd al Samad of
  Palembang 163
Abduh, Muhammad 298
Abdul Razak, Tun 418
Abdulfatah Ageng,
  Sultan 155
Abdul Rahman, Tunku 347,
  349
Abdul-Rauf al-Singkili,
  Sheikh 160
Abdul Rivai 297
Abd'ur-rahman az-Zahir,
  Habib 232
Abu Abd Allah Mas'ud
  al-Jawi 102
Abu Bakar, Temenggung
  (later Sultan) 229
Aceh 72, 76, 82, 82, 106–9,
  113–14, 152, 175,
  197, 200, 242–3
  1819 Treaty 242, 243
  disease and mortality 273
  Dutch war against 231–3,
    243
  gunpowder empire 10, 87
  Islam in 108–9, 111,
    113–4, 116–7, 159–60
  literacy 171–2
  queens of 89, 159–60
  rice agriculture 15
  sultanate of 88, 108–9,
    159–60
  trade in 146, 156

urban population 10, 83–4
written scholarship in 134
Acehnese 157, 171–2, 179
Adam Malik 418
Adityavarman 46–7, 53
Aetas of the Mount
  Pinatubo 6
Age of Commerce 69, 74–6
agriculture
  as basis of state and
    society 16–18
  commercialization
    of 198–200, 207–11
  crop failures 8
  cultivation system
    (Java) 206–7
  delta 3–4
  female labor in xviii, 271
  green revolution 376–7
  Khmer 41
  peasantization 204–7,
    263–6
  spread of 8–9, 10–13
  see also crops; meat, rice,
    and under individual
    crops and livestock
Agtas of Northeast Luzon 6,
  8, 12
Aguinaldo, Emilio 273
Agung, Sultan of
  Mataram 88, 105,
  110, 145, 154–5, 161,
  162, 170

Ahom in Assam, rice
  growing 14
Aidit, D.N. 340, 355
Airlangga, King 43
Ala'ud-din Ri'ayat Syah
  al-Kahar, Sultan of
  Aceh 108
Alaungpaya, King 219
Albuquerque, Afonso
  de 120, 127, 134
al-Hallaj, Mansur 103
Ali Akbar: "Book of
  Cathay"
  (*Hitayname*)
  133
Ali Haji, Raja 174
Alor 33
Amangkurat I, King 155,
  162
Ambon 73, 120, 235, 164
  missionaries in 111
Ambonese 175
Amerapura 85, 221
Amir Sjarifuddin 310, 334,
  339, 340, 341
Ampel 161
Ananda Mahidol, King
  of Thailand 350,
  367
Anaukhpetlun, King of
  Burma 153
Anawrahta, King of
  Pagan 42, 99, 167

A History of Southeast Asia: Critical Crossroads, First Edition. Anthony Reid.
© 2015 Anthony Reid. Published 2015 by John Wiley & Sons, Ltd.

FOR MY LOVELY SON LOUIS
WHO GAVE RISE TO THIS BOOK
AND THE CONTENT WITHIN

SINCE 2016

TRD **EVERYDAY** MRK

Baby Food

200

DELICIOUS, NUTRITIOUS AND
SIMPLE BABY FOOD RECIPES THAT YOU CAN
USE EVERYDAY TO KEEP YOUR LITTLE ONE
HAPPY AND HEALTHY!

SOPHIA HAMILTON

LASSELLE PRESS CO

ISBN: 978-1-911364-01-6

Contents

Happy & Healthy
everyday!

What can you expect from
making Everyday Baby Food...

Happy & Healthy

As a new Mom or Dad or a soon-to-be Mom or Dad, there are so many decisions to make for this new little person you are bringing into the world.

For one so precious as your baby, you only want the best for them. There are so many questions you probably have: what kind of diapers should I get? Should we breast-feed or use formula? What is the best way to feed them? How shall I decorate their nursery? The list goes on and on and with so many choices to make, deciding what's best can be so confusing.

If you've purchased this book you're probably thinking about making your baby's food when he or she is ready to eat.

When you make your own baby food, you know exactly what is going into your little one's diet. Yes, you can read the ingredients label on jarred food and get an idea of what's inside but as a mother, I was always concerned about recalls I had heard of and certain things finding their way into my son's food that just didn't belong there! My son is the most important thing in the world to me and I was determined to keep him safe and give him the best nutrition possible. To me this meant taking the time to make his food from scratch and storing it properly to keep him safe. Saying this, every parent has to make the choices that they feel are best for their little one but hopefully this book will give you the right guidance and advice in order for you to consider making your own baby food and ensure you feel confident in making the first steps.

The recipes in this book are designed to take the least amount of time possible, and I will provide safe storage solutions to help you plan and prepare food beforehand. Every choice you make as a parent is a tough decision and I don't want you to feel that if making your baby's food all the time isn't something you can accomplish, that you need to be ashamed of this. Do I recommend it? Of course but why not give it a go and see if it is something that you can achieve, even if just for half of your baby's meals and then build it up should you wish? There are many advantages to making your child's food and it can be a truly rewarding process, knowing that you're giving them the best possible food.

This book contains everything you need to get started. I will go into more depth about the advantages to making your baby's food, explain the advantages of using organic ingredients as well as the best methods for cooking your little one's meals. We will go over foods that are particularly good for your baby, talk about some ingredients that you should avoid using too much of as well as discuss when to start introducing solid foods to your little one's diet.

I will cover food safety and how to store your food as freshly as possible including freezing and thawing methods as well as providing you with 200 recipes for your baby, starting from smooth baby food, to chunky baby food and then solid; this will take you from infancy and right through toddlerhood and is a recipe book that you can return to time and time again! I have even provided a list of ingredients along with their nutritional benefits, so once you've made your way through all 200 recipes, you can start getting creative and mix and match to create your own baby food recipes.

So let's bounce on in to this book together and get started. I hope that, like me, you will be proud of your efforts, knowing that your choices are the best ones for your bundle of joy.

I wish you luck throughout your parenthood journey and hopefully I can help you make your family's food adventures that much easier with this guide.

chapter one

Fresh is BEST

Everything you need to know about homemade baby food!

What are the advantages of making my own baby food?

When you prepare your baby food yourself there are so many aspects that you are in control of, giving them the best possible start in life. You get to choose all the ingredients and therefore you know that everything is fresh and healthy. You also know that there are no contaminates like those that can make their way into the shop-bought stuff.

Furthermore, you will actually save money by preparing your own baby food! You could save up to $40 a month by pre-preparing and buying fresh foods, rather than individual jars. Every company has to make a profit and I would rather that extra money go towards a healthy selection of fresh fruit and vegetables for Louis or a little something extra to treat him!

Although some commercial baby food brands fortify their food with vitamins such as Vitamin C, there are plenty of natural foods that contain this vitamin as well as others, so this should not be a worry for you. In fact, preparing foods freshly has more nutritional benefit than any prepackaged food. You could talk to your pediatrician if you are concerned that your baby is not getting the right balance of vitamins but the chart included later on illustrates the nutritional benefits of an array of fresh foods to help you ensure you're giving your son or daughter a varied diet. Babies only need about 40 to 50 milligrams of Vitamin C in their diet and they easily get this from breast milk or formula.

One of the ways that companies prepare their food is by heating it at a super high heat in order to kill bacteria and allowing the food to be preserved in sealed containers for a longer shelf life. Unfortunately with this they are breaking down a lot of the vitamins and minerals as well as fibre. Further to this, the food becomes concentrated. Although it may be made purely from fruit or vegetables, it's cooked down, becoming a concentrated version of the food, most of the time mixed with water to rehydrate it. This more condensed form also causes a concentration of nutrients – this seems like it would be a good choice over homemade baby food but take a look at the following example to compare a shop bought baby food jar with its homemade equivalent.

Let's say we mash up about 70 grams of natural banana to feed to our baby, as that's about the same amount, on average, of a serving of baby food. About 70 grams of banana has 8.7 grams of sugar, under a milligram of sodium and about 1.8 grams of fiber. Now let's look at a popular brand to see the difference, it contains less than one gram of fiber, 13 grams of sugar and 5 milligrams of sodium. So, there is less fiber in the packaged variety, something that is good for your baby's digestion. As well as this there is more sugar and salt - essentially two ingredients you should try to keep to a minimum in your little one's diet.

Overall, you can be confident in the knowledge that making your own baby food is beneficial to both you and your baby! By using fresh foods you are able to tailor make your baby's diet, providing them with vitamins and nutrients and introducing them to a variety of different foods and ingredients. Many say that by doing this, your baby is more likely to grow up enjoying new foods and are less fussy eaters than those who stuck to a limited diet in infancy. You never know, it might even encourage you and the family to eat fresh and healthily, benefiting you all along the way!

How much salt and sugar should I use in my baby's food?

As a general rule you typically hear no salt and no sugar before one year of age. The reasoning behind this is that babies typically get their daily requirements from breast milk or formula, which is minuscule - they only need about 0.4 grams of sodium for example. When a baby gets more salt than this amount it can be taxing on their tiny kidneys. Sugar, and I don't mean sweet food, but the white processed sugar, should also be kept to a bare minimum if not none at all. This sugar can be bad for a few reasons; the way most sugar is processed requires the use of chemicals which can be harmful, it can also cause decay in their newly forming teeth as well as potentially depress the immune system when eaten in excessive amounts. But this should not be a worry at all if you are preparing all of your own food from fresh and not including extra sugar!

What about organic?

Another choice you can make as a parent when making your own baby food is to go organic. If you are going to make your own baby food, it is great if you can use as many organic ingredients as you can. In order for a food to be considered organic it can only use a limited amount of pesticides or none at all during the growing/production process. This lack of chemicals on your little one's food exposes them to fewer chemicals and irritants. It gives them healthier more natural food but if you can't afford to go organic all the time, ensure you wash your fruit and vegetables before cooking and look out for the 'clean' fruits and vegetables that are not laced with pesticides and GM's. Additionally be aware of the 'toxic' fruits and vegetables that are better to buy organic as current research suggests.

Happy and Healthy Every Day Baby Fruit and Vegetables

This list provides you with a selection of fruits and vegetables that are better for baby and you in terms of pesticide levels and toxins. Select from these if you're not deciding to go organic:

Onions	Mangoes
Sweet corn	Eggplant
Pineapples	Kiwi
Avocado	Domestic cantaloupe
Cabbage	Sweet potatoes
Sweet peas	Grapefruit
Asparagus	Watermelon

The Worst Offenders

These are the top of the list of 'baddies' in terms of the contamination levels of pesticides. If you're not buying organic then these are best avoided where possible. Again, if you do buy these non-organic I would always recommend thoroughly washing before eating.

Apples	Grapes
Celery	Spinach
Sweet bell peppers	Lettuce
Peaches	Cucumbers
Strawberries	Domestic blueberries
Imported nectarines	Potatoes

What are the baby super foods?

Ensuring your baby is the happiest and healthiest he or she can be will be easy when you decide to make your own baby food and focus on using good quality ingredients; these are the top baby superfoods which you should aim to include in your baby's diet from the appropriate age range.

Baby SUPERFOODS

BLUEBERRIES!
CONTAINS FLAVONOIDS, & ANTIOXIDANTS WHICH ARE GOOD FOR BRAIN, EYES AND URINARY TRACT

Dark green leafy vegetables!
CONTAINS IRON AND FOLATE

Lentils!
PACKED FULL OF PROTEIN AND FIBRE

MANDARIN ORANGES!
GREAT SOURCE OF VITAMIN C AND ANTIOXIDANTS – BE AWARE THAT CITRUS IS ONE OF THE FOODS THAT MAY NOT BE RECOMMENDED BEFORE 6 MONTHS OF AGE DUE TO ALLERGY LEVELS.

RED MEAT!
PACKED FULL OF ZINC AND IRON

Prunes!
CAN AID IN DIGESTION AND HELP UNDO ANY CONSTIPATION YOUR BABY MIGHT BE EXPERIENCING

Sweet potato!
CONTAINS PHYTO-NUTRIENTS AND IS HIGH IN VITAMINS A AND C

Avocados!
FULL OF HEALTHY FATS – GREAT FOR BRAIN HEALTH

Coconut!
CONTAINS MEDIUM CHAIN FATTY ACIDS WHICH HELP BOOST THE IMMUNE SYSTEM, IMPROVE DIGESTION, AND BALANCE THE BLOOD SUGAR.

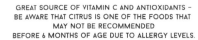
BEANS!
10 TIMES THE AMOUNT OF ANTIOXIDANTS AS ORANGES. HIGH IN FIBER, IRON, PROTEIN AND VITAMIN B. (SOAK THEM OVERNIGHT TO REDUCE COOKING TIME).

Broccoli!
AN EXCELLENT SOURCE OF FIBER, FOLATE AND CALCIUM

QUINOA!

HIGH IN LYSINE – GOOD FOR TISSUE GROWTH AND REPAIR. ALSO FIBEROUS AND HIGH IN MANGANESE, MAGNESIUM & IRON. IT IS ALSO GLUTEN FREE!

Common Allergenic Foods and Foods to Avoid Before Certain Ages:

• No Honey before 1 year of age! Honey can contain botulism spores, which babies below a year might not be able to fight off yet. Now this rarely causes severe reactions in babies however it can be fatal so always wait until 12 months to feed your baby honey and speak with your pediatrician if you're concerned.

• Hold off on chunky foods until your baby is able to chew (you can work up to this gradually through the recommended recipes in each section).

• Shop bought juices are usually packed with sugar and sweeteners – it's better to make your own purees and only use no extra-sugar juices when necessary.

• Whole milk (cows' milk) – advice on this is to hold off from giving your baby whole milk until 12 months, however this is due to the concern that parents will replace breast milk/formula with whole milk, which would not provide their baby with enough nutritious value. Whole milk is fine to give to your baby in the form of homemade or natural yogurt (pg. 76). Due to the fact that yogurt is active, the proteins become easier for your baby to digest. Again this is down to your discretion and your pediatrician's advice.

• Citrus fruits – the acidity levels of citrus can disagree with many babies and cause rashes or stomach upsets; they are not typically allergenic but best avoided for the first year.

• Raw strawberries, raspberries and blackberries are to be avoided before 10-12 months and reactions should be closely monitored.

• Peanuts and Shellfish - highly allergenic foods. Usually recommended to wait until over 1 year old but there are conflicting views on this subject.

• Tree nuts such as walnuts or almonds can cause allergic reactions in babies – there are extremely varied recommendations on when it is safe to introduce tree nuts to your baby and this includes between 1 year and 3 years. As with peanuts, if there are known allergies in the family or your baby has other allergies, it is always better to be more cautious with tree nuts. If unsure, consult your pediatrician.

Allergies?

Some pediatricians may recommend you try feeding your baby one food at a time for about a week so you can monitor a potential allergic reaction to certain foods. Some may even tell you to avoid giving any peanut products in the early stages, due to the high rate of allergic reactions to this particular item. Then again, there are some pediatricians who will advise the exact opposite, encouraging you to feed your baby a variety of foods at all times, as well as peanut products from an early age in order to get them used to different types of food.

There is research that suggests peanut allergies are due to parents withholding nuts from children for too long, meaning that they then have a reaction to an item they haven't been exposed to before. In other countries where peanut products are fed regularly there is believed to be a correlation between that and lower levels of the allergy in their children. If you are concerned with allergies you will want to keep an eye out when your little one eats shell fish, strawberries, any nut, fish, milk and citrus on top of the common peanut as these particular foods are known to cause allergic reactions in many people.

I adopted the approach of introducing new foods one at a time and keeping a close eye on my son for 4-5 days afterwards to ensure that any reactions could be picked up on immediately, thus knowing what the trigger was. Luckily my son has had no allergic reactions so far and is growing into a healthy chubby little thing but I would advise you talk to your pediatrician as well as your family members to help you make the right choice for your son or daughter.

It can be a worrying time introducing new foods to someone so small and so precious but my research as a Mom has given me these findings:

Allergy Reaction Signs To Watch Out For

- Swelling of the face, tongue and lips (or either or) – any swelling of these areas is likely to indicate an allergic reaction.

- Rash or reddish skin – your baby may develop various rashes when growing and this may not necessarily indicate an allergic reaction. For example nappy rashes. Monitor your baby and consult a professional if unsure.

- Hives or welts (a sudden covering of raised red or white bumps or circles on the skin) - These will likely be itchy for baby and even sore; they will probably be different sizes and found almost any where on your baby's body.

- Being sick or experiencing diarrhea.

- Coughing or wheezing can be a sign of an allergic reaction but other causes such as illness or colds need to be considered too.

- Difficulty breathing can be a more serious symptom of an allergic reaction and needs immediate emergency attention, as does loss of consciousness.

chapter two

TOOLS

OF THE

Trade

What you'll need to get started!

Baby Food Safety Tips

First let's go over some safety tips to keep your little one as safe as possible:

1. Always consult your pediatrician with any questions or concerns, as you are getting ready to journey into the world of solid food with your little one.

2. Make sure everything you feed is appropriate for your little one's age. You don't want to give them food they aren't ready to chew yet and risk choking.

3. When heating anything you should test it yourself to avoid any burns. Mix well to avoid any hot spots.

4. Cook all meat thoroughly until it is piping hot throughout.

5. Don't feed any solid foods until at least 4 months of age; babies' systems aren't equipped to handle solids before that age.

6. Scoop your portion of baby food into a different feeding bowl before serving and throw away any left over after feeding. Once touched by enzymes from your baby's mouth the food will begin to break down and is unfit for storage.

7. Keep food cold after it's made to stop the growth of bacteria.

8. Discard opened containers after 24 hours.

9. Use refrigerated foods within 3 days of making or thawing.

Cooking Equipment You'll Need

- A pot or steamer to steam and cook food
- A blender or food processor
- A food storage system that is air tight –Tupperware is fine or use glass jars
- Ice cube tray
- Timer or a phone with a timer
- Strainer
- Vegetable peeler

These are the essentials to preparing your own baby food that you may not already have. Consider checking out second hand stores or asking friends and family with grown up children who may consider donating you theirs if you need to save some money!

You really only need some simple equipment to get yourself started making your own homemade baby food. I used a baby food making and storage system, which I got as a gift at my baby shower and absolutely loved it. But had it not been given to me as a gift I probably wouldn't have been able to afford one. As a parent you have to weigh price versus effective-ness and decide if it's something that is worth the investment. I mostly steamed my food, which you don't really need a fancy baby food system for. Besides the simple cooking and blending process you simply need a way to store the extra food. Easy!

Top tip when blending: Add a little water, breast milk or formula to your steamed food as you blend; your mixture can become very dry and hard for the blender to work with as well as for your baby to eat. So by adding a little water, formula or breast milk you can moisten your mixture and make it more digestible for your baby.

Let's talk a little about some of the systems out there, designed to make your own food preparation easier and faster. They are certainly something to consider but can get pricy so you have to use your judgment on what is best for your family. Systems like the baby bullet that come with the blender and blades, allow you to blend everything from fruits and vegetables to grains with the milling blade. It also comes with a storage system and a book on basic recipes. Systems like the Baby Bullet and others can give you all the tools you need to safely make and store your own baby food but you can also get creative and use a basic blender and Tupperware as a storage solution along with The Everyday Baby Food Cookbook. Yes, those fancy systems can help simplify and streamline things but they aren't necessary so don't think you need to break the bank to give your baby homemade and healthy food.

Top tip for storage: A great way to freeze baby food into little baby servings is to use an ice cube tray. You can freeze the food and once thoroughly frozen you can place in a Tupperware container or zip lock bag to protect from freezer burn. You can also get tiny Tupperware containers; they may be a little larger then a typical serving for your little one but you can always place half in a bowl and save the other half for the next day as long as you use it within 72 hours of defrosting.

chapter three

EVERYDAY *Baby Food*
COOKING
101

How to ensure you're feeding your
baby homemade food everyday...

Every Day Baby Food Cooking 101

The secret to ensuring your baby has healthy food to keep them happy, fulfilled and growing every day is...batch cooking! Get yourself prepared and save time and stress in the long run. This chapter will provide you with information, advice and hints and tips on the most effective methods of cooking, storing and serving food in large quantities. The recipes you will come across later in the book have been created with batch cooking in mind – making one tiny meal at a time just seems silly to me!

Batch cooking makes life easier

Batch cooking can be a lifesaver as well as a time and energy saver. One sweet potato can make quite a few servings of food after you cook and blend it down. Freezing some of what you have made will allow you to thaw and use it later on when you're pushed for time – batch cooking also means that you don't have to serve your baby the same meal over and over again to use it up! You could prepare enough food for each day of the week and freeze the rest so that you have a plan for Monday-Sunday for the next month if you wish. If you're going to the effort to cook or steam food, then it's worth taking the time to make a little extra and plan ahead. This is time saving in the long run and will save you standing at the stove preparing every meal they need.

When I was preparing my own baby food for my son, I would always set aside an hour or so on a Sunday. That way I was set up for the week and had all my portions in the freezer, knowing that I didn't need to do much else until the next month! If you desire to give your baby fresh refrigerated and non frozen food then you can just set aside a day a week to prepare this and keep your food for the next 3 - 4 days in the fridge. It's up to you what type of method you will employ and the best one is the one that works for you and your family. Either way you are feeding your little one fresh and home made food and giving them the best you possibly can.

Some parents get stuck into thinking if they try to use a batch cooking approach they have to make the same huge amount and don't think about the fact that they can change the amount to something that better suits their family. For example, you may only have a small freezer above your refrigerator so you will only have so much room for freezing baby food, along with everything else a typical family normally keeps in their freezer. So you will have to adjust how much extra you make to accommodate what you have to work with. These are all factors you should consider when cooking in batches and adjusting sizes according to your needs. It's okay to be flexible with your choices to make it work for your family.

Batch Cooking Methods

Steaming

Steaming involves boiling water and allowing foods to cook over this heat but not in it; this is probably the slowest way to cook foods but also the healthiest, as steaming maintains the most vitamins and nutrients in the foods and you do not use oils or butters. You will need a large pan and a steaming pan with holes to place over the top. Always remove foods carefully and check they are cooked through when cooking using this method.

Baking/Roasting

Baking in the oven requires the least attention and is still a healthy way of cooking as you can control the amount of oils you cook with, if any! Wrap fishes and meats and potatoes/sweet potatoes in foil or baking paper to keep as moist as possible and follow recommended cooking temperatures and timings. Always remove foods carefully and check they are cooked through when cooking using this method.

Boiling

Boiling is quicker than steaming but does take away some of the nutrients in fresh food. Use a large pan with a lid to boil fruit/veg and even poach meat.

Sautéing

When your baby moves on to solid knife and fork meals you may consider using a pan to sauté some foods. This is seen to be less healthy as often involves oils and butters to cook foods in. Choose a non-stick frying pan to avoid this problem and use healthier alternatives such as coconut oil when your baby is ready to eat coconut.

Freezing, Thawing and Reheating

So once you have made your baby food and placed what you plan on feeding this week in the refrigerator, you may have extra food that you would like to save for a later date The best storage method is freezing; extreme temperatures kill bacteria and keep anything harmful from being able to grow on the food. Your baby's immune system will still be developing so you should store frozen baby food for no more than about 3 months. Technically you can store their food for up to 6 months but they retain optimal nutritional levels in the first 3 months and quality can reduce after that.

There are a few ways you can thaw and reheat your baby's food after you have frozen it but there are a few rules you should follow for defrosting to keep it safe. Once thawed you can't refreeze baby food so don't take out more than 2 to 3 days at a time. After that amount of time bacteria has the opportunity to grow which could lead to sickness.

You should never defrost the food on the counter as room temperatures are a breeding ground for that pesky bad bacteria that we are trying to avoid: defrost in the fridge instead. There is no need to panic as long as you are careful with how you defrost your food and when you need to use it by. Make sure you plan accordingly when using this method of defrosting because it should take 12 hours to defrost depending on various factors, like the exact temperature of your fridge or the food you're defrosting. Just make sure you keep whatever container it's being defrosted in covered. This helps keep the food from becoming contaminated by anything that may be in the refrigerator.

Top tip for storing: Use labels to write the date of preparation on before freezing. You will be sure you haven't kept anything for longer than the recommended time of 3 months then! You can then add the date you take it out for defrosting to ensure you don't keep it beyond 3 days.

Another method for defrosting your baby food is using warm water for thawing or submersion. This is also a fairly easy method and takes about 10 to 20 minutes to accomplish -perfect if you need to defrost something but know you don't have 12 hours to wait before your baby gets hungry. Decant your baby food into a bowl and then place this bowl into a bowl of hot tap water. Not only can you defrost their food this way you can also gently heat it if they like their food warm. Every baby is different and some may like their food at room temperature. And remember, once served any leftovers should go into the bin. After a while you will get a hang of how much your baby tends to eat in one sitting and your servings will become more accurate, helping you to reduce waste.

You may not be a fan of using the microwave and some experts feel the microwave can sap nutrients from your foods. However, it is a great method when you're pressed for time. Your little one has decided they are hungry and they are hungry now. You have nothing defrosted and you know even the faster warm water method still won't be fast enough.

Top tip for microwaving: Always stir well and check food before you feed it to baby. The microwave can cause hot spots so stirring and testing can help you avoid any burns. You should also stick to glass; though some plastics are considered microwave safe, they can still breakdown slightly in the high temperatures used in the microwave. Besides being great for defrosting, you can also quickly provide your little one with the hot meal they may be craving.

The Microwave Argument

I want to dive a little further into the microwave argument. If this is something you're concerned about I would highly recommend talking with your pediatrician about it and doing some research of your own. I will discuss a few thoughts on the subject here but if it's an issue for you it's worth the effort to give you peace of mind in making the best possible decision.

In order for a microwave to function it essentially heats up the water molecules in your food by bouncing those molecules around rapidly and creating friction. This molecular friction, it is believed, causes structural changes in your food on a molecular level and as a result diminishes the nutrients in the food you're heating.

Additionally, some studies have been shown to link the reduction of the vitamin b-12 with microwave heating. It is also believed to affect breast milk when it is defrosted or heated using the microwave.

If you microwave a food wrapped in plastic, you can create carcinogens in your food. When you microwave any kind of plastic it breaks it down to some degree and will cause it to release certain toxins like BPA and benzene. When you eat your body absorbs the toxins that have made their way into the food that was cooked. There has also been research that suggests microwaves can change the make up of your blood, decreasing red blood cells and multiplying white blood cells and cholesterol.

There is no getting around the fact that if you microwave with plastics it can be unsafe. But microwave safe plastics are typically made without the chemicals that hurt us when they enter our bodies; you can even use glass containers that don't break down at all.

So let's look at the other side of the spectrum; we talked about how microwaves can essentially leach the nutrients out of your food. The best way to cook food, particularly fruits and vegetables is steaming, which retains the most nutritional value and it is my preferred method for cooking my son's food. When you cook in a microwave you are essentially steaming your food as well. When cooking on the stove you are in fact creating a similar process to that in the microwave - heating up the water molecules and creating friction to cook the food. Any time you cook food it will lose some of its nutrients as it is exposed to heat. Unfortunately, that's the way it goes if you want cooked food and steaming is no exception. When you cook food the best way to retain nutrients is to expose to heat for the smallest amount of time possible and use only a small amount of water. The more water you add the more nutrients that water is able to steal from your food. In theory the microwave allows you to do just that; you only need tiny amounts of water and it heats the food much faster than traditional methods. For an example if you boil spinach it loses up to 70% of its folic acid during the process but when you microwave it with just a little water it will keep almost all of its folic acid.

There are many people who believe cooking with the microwave can be safe and healthy and there is research out there to prove that side of the argument as well.

Top tip: Breast milk should be served at room temperature to avoid reducing the nutrients.

So should you use a microwave to heat up your baby's food? That's your call; of course microwaves are used across the world. I tend to use my microwave when absolutely necessary and use the hot water tip at other times. You should choose what methods work best for you when it comes to cooking, storing and reheating your baby's food.

The Every Day Batch Cooking Method

1. Plan ahead for the week
Work out what meals you will feed baby this week - see the helpful shopping lists provided for each stage of feeding to help you with this – and create a schedule.

2. Go shopping/order online
Remember to look out for the clean fruits and vegetables as well as organic versions of the toxic vegetables if possible (outlined earlier).

3. Get organized
Decide how you will cook each food. Have 4 categories – steam, bake, boil or puree raw.

4. Prepare your veg/meat
Clean with cold tap water and hands (use a scrubber on tough skins), peel if necessary, cut and chop as required.

5. Cook
Assemble your cooking tools, get your oven on, work out your timings for each vegetable/fruit/meat and start with the longest cooking time. Set your timer! Now put the next food on and set another timer if possible. Continue working through until all of your fruit and veg is cooking and keep an eye on the timing of each.

6. Puree, mash or chop
Depending on how young your baby is allow fruit and veg to cool, puree in a blender, mash with a fork or chop into small pieces with a knife.

7. Store it
Assemble your storage containers (if you haven't already), transfer baby food to containers, label and freeze or refrigerate. Just a reminder you can keep this in the fridge for up to 3 days or the freezer for up to 3 months.

8. Be smart
Add a note to your schedule to remove the meals you need 24 hours in advance to allow for thawing. This will take around an hour to prepare all in one go but will save you so much time later in the week.

chapter four

When the time is
RIGHT!

How to know when your baby is
ready for solids..

When the Time is Right

Your baby will be ready to start eating solids when it is right for them; there is no hard and fast rule on this. You need to listen to your baby and see if they are showing signs of being ready and wanting to start eating solid foods. I have some indicators that should help you to decide when they are ready. I would also recommend you discussing this with your pediatrician so that you can make the most informed decision possible.

As a general rule most research shows 4 to 6 months is around the time that an infant's digestive system is typically developed enough to be able to start processing solid food. As a parent you should watch your baby, not the calendar, when making the decision to start offering solid foods. Here are some of the things you should look for when deciding if it's time:

• They have lost their tongue-thrust reflex: this reflex of pushing the tongue forward when any foreign substance enters the baby's mouth is their way of protecting themselves from choking. This natural reflex is also what makes drinking easier for a baby as well. It will typically start to disappear around the 4 to 6-month period and will be the time that your baby is actually able to swallow food instead of pushing it back out with their tongue.

• They're able to hold their head up and sit up without assistance: when you no longer have to cradle their head to keep them up and they can sit upright alone, your baby is showing the strength to eat solid foods.

• They're able to indicate they are full: when a baby can show you signs that they are full such as turning their head away, it reveals that they are able to self regulate and know when they are full.

• They're at double their birth weight: this is a good indicator of when a baby is usually grown enough to eat solids.

• They're interested in what you're eating: babies first explore the world through their mouth, so this indicator can be confusing at times because they will reach an age where they want to just put everything in their mouth. But usually you can tell when they have a genuine interest in what you're eating as well as when this is happening often.

• They frequently wake up in the middle of the night after establishing a solid pattern: You may find your baby just doesn't stay full throughout the night. They may have a good established sleeping pattern that can become disrupted as they get hungry and need to eat more frequently to try and keep up with the demands their body is making.

Now that you have your basic indicators I also want to discuss some of the things you may hear from others; raising a child is hard and there will be many people in your life that will attempt to help you, thinking they are doing something good but not always realizing they are being pushy. I will reveal some of these myths on the next page in order to help you make your own decision about when to start your baby on solids.

Common Myths

1. "Your baby will sleep through the night if you start them on solids."

The idea behind this statement is there has been a correlation between infants who start eating solid foods and then begin sleeping through the night. In theory this makes sense; solids take longer to digest and therefore keep your baby sleeping and feeling full longer. But what's typically happening is a natural progression for your baby. As they age they will sleep for longer periods of time at night. That is simply the natural progression they take; this is also the time when many infants start eating solids. It doesn't necessarily mean they will sleep through the night simply because they are on solids. At around 8 months they can hit another growth spurt and you will be back to being woken up again by a hungry baby.

2. "It's okay to start your baby on solids early."

This is a common belief you may hear. Babies develop at such a variety of rates it's hard to have a rule about eating solids. Yes, there are certain milestones most babies pass at around the same time but even these vary. This is a decision you should make based on your child's development and not what others may tell you or what their children have done.

3. "Feed that kid some real food."

Some family members can be guilty of this and may even pressure you into giving your baby solid foods because they feel they need 'real' food and that they aren't getting enough from simply breast feeding or formula or purees. Just remember – formula, breast milk and purees are real food, simply in liquid form. They have everything your bouncy, happy baby needs to flourish and you shouldn't feel pressured into feeding them solids if you don't think they are ready. They can support your baby up to 1 year old and should still be given even with solids to help ensure that they get all the nutrients they need. So while others may tell you conflicting messages about when to start your baby on solids, based on their experiences and what they've heard, you will be able to look out for the right time for your own baby with the previous advice.

How to Introduce Solid Foods Onto Your Baby's Plate

So your little one is exhibiting all the signs of being ready to start eating solid food. You have talked with your pediatrician and they agree that they seem to be ready, so what is your next step as a parent? Where should you start?

I, along with your pediatrician and other friends, are likely to recommend starting with a single grain cereal like rice or oatmeal. Start off using formula or breast milk to mix with the cereal and keep it runny. You want it to just barely thicken the mixture and get your baby used to swallowing something thicker than milk. 1 tablespoon of cereal to 4 tablespoons of your chosen liquid is a good starting place. You may be tempted to feed this mixture to your baby in a bottle - but don't - use the spoon and get them used to eating from that as well.

As they improve you can start offering thicker versions and slowly more of it. Now that they have mastered cereal and the concept of eating and swallowing you can start to offer single foods. Stick to natural ones with no added sugar or salt: items like fruits, vegetables, and even meat. Again, I gave my son a variety at the recommendation of my pediatrician and just kept a close eye on his reactions to food after I had fed him. You may decide to give your baby the same food for a few days to keep an eye out for diarrhea, vomit, or rashes. If any of these signs develop you will be usually be able to pinpoint the food that doesn't agree with your son or daughter.

One of the great things about being a parent is that you get to choose what you feel is best for your child. As long as you stick to pureed food that is easy for your baby to swallow, then any plan is a good plan. For example, you could pick three different foods and serve them for the better part of a week, alternating between the three.

I like the idea my pediatrician recommended of serving my son different foods to keep him from assuming that food should always taste the same. I didn't want a picky eater but at the same time I wanted to be able to keep track of any reactions he might have. The advantage of being a parent is, I was able to take parts of different plans that I liked and combine them together to make a plan I felt most comfortable with.

I like to include examples like this because parenting isn't always black and white; it's something that morphs and changes to fit the values and beliefs you as a parent hold. Once your baby has mastered the purees you can change the texture of your foods, making them slightly chunkier while keeping an eye on how they handle it. You can also combine your foods once you have assessed how they react to individual foods. Once they start to show you that they are ready to chew, you can move on to finely chopped finger food. Cut them into small manageable bites; start with softer foods like fruits, cooked veggies, cheese and pasta. You can also start to give them smaller dry cereals at this point.

As your son or daughter progresses in what they are able to eat, you will also notice a change in how much they eat. They will probably start with tiny meals and mostly formula or breast milk but as they get bigger the amount of food will increase. You will find yourself cooking for them more and making fewer bottles. Once your little one hits 1 year old, many things about how you feed them will change. This is around the time you can start offering your little one whole milk and including more dairy foods into their diet. The bigger they get the more your options grow.

If you follow these steps, starting small and exposing them to more foods as they grow, you should be able to safely introduce solid foods to your little one and expand their little pallets as well. Listening to your baby and following the cues that they give you will always help you to make the best decisions for them. Every baby develops differently so look for the indicators that your son or daughter is ready and then take your time introducing them to solid food and textures to prepare them for the food they will be eating for the rest of their lives.

Age by Age Guide On What And How Much Your Baby Can Be Eating:

After so much research and my own experiences with Louis, I had to come to the conclusion that there is no hard and fast answer as to how much and how often you should be feeding your baby and therefore their eating habits are individual to them. Many different sources will provide conflicting information, and I for one know how stressful and frustrating this can be when you're trying to do what's best for your baby! These are the guidelines I used when feeding Louis and they seem to be a best fit of much of what I've researched. Use as approximate guidance and remember to listen to what your baby is telling you in terms of their hunger – they'll usually cry for more if they're still hungry, and turn their head if they're full. Consult your pediatrician for further advice.

0-4 months

What?

Breast Milk/Baby Formula – feed on its own

How much?
Formula approx.2-6 oz as your baby develops from 0-4 months.
When?
At this stage you can feed baby as often as they want to be fed and usually this is every hour or every couple of hours.

4-6 months

What?

Pureed fruit and veg and cereals

How much and when?
Continue milk on demand and start to introduce 1-2 tablespoons of cereals and pureed foods up to a maximum of 2 servings per day overall.

6-8 months

What?
Milk, pureed foods, cereals, meats
How much and When?
Continue milk 3-5 servings a day
Plus choose 2-3 options from the following servings:
2-3 tablespoons of cereals/fruit/veg up to 4x per day,
1-2 tablespoons of chicken, beef or pork up to 1x per day

8-12 months

What?

Milk, pureed foods, pasta, cereals and bread,

as well as meats and dairy.

How much and when?

Continue milk 3-4 servings a day
Plus: Choose 2-3 options from the following servings and increase as baby gets older:

2-4 tablespoons of cereals up to 3x per day
3-4 tablespoons of fruit up to 2x per day
3-4 tablespoons of veg up to 2x per day
3-4 tablespoons of chicken, beef or pork up to 2x per day
¼ cup of cheese (cottage or cheddar)

12 months+

What?
Whole milk, dairy, cereals, breads, pastas, egg, chunky foods and cereals as well as meats and dairy
How much and When?
½ cup whole milk 4x per day or breast milk on demand
½ cup grains 4-5 x per day
½ medium fruit 2x per day
½ cup of fresh veg/ ¼ cup frozen veg 4x per day
2 tablespoons meat/egg/beans 3-4 x per day
Finger food and small bites of food

chapter five

My First

FLAVOURS

Here are some of my favorite
4-6 month old
recipes to help and keep your
creative juices flowing!.

This is going to be the first of four chapters giving you great everyday recipes to guide you through making your own baby food. Thinking up new combinations for taste and nutritious variety can be a challenge. I certainly had times when I fell into a slump; I had a few baby food recipes that I knew how to make, so I kept making them, slightly intimidated with the idea of experimenting with what my son seemed to like. The problem with this was that he was missing out on other nutrients.

As well as this, his exposure to different food types was minimal and I worried that I was creating a fussy eater! So one day, about two months after I started making his food, I researched which natural foods could be steamed (my preferred method of preparing my homemade baby food) and then went to the grocery store and wandered down the produce area, selecting items that I hadn't used before for my baby food. Using various resources, I experimented with the new foods and my steamer, and started developing the recipes you will find in this book!

I have included 200 of my favorite recipes to help keep your creative juices flowing and once your baby is older than 6 months, there is no reason why you cannot continue to feed them the recipes from this chapter; just ensure you're continuing to give them a variety of foods and flavours and only moving onto the next chapters when they are ready. When your son or daughter is able to eat the thicker texture recipes then you can simply change the amount you blend the foods – less blending will provide a chunkier texture - which is great for your older babies and toddlers!

I have broken down these recipes into foods that are best for your baby to start with and then the recipes evolve to include foods, slightly more complex for them to digest. In this first chapter the recipes are typically considered stage one baby foods. The foods in the recipes are the lowest on the allergy scale and

easier to digest. When you first start feeding your baby, stick to the recipes in the beginning; these are single foods that will allow you to keep an eye on your baby's reactions as well as ensuring their digestive systems can adjust to the change from an all liquid diet to solid foods. Once they get used to eating you can get away with serving raw fruits for the most part as they are easily digestible but continue to cook the vegetables: the fiber in them is easier to break down when they are cooked.

There are a few more points I want you to keep in mind as you make your foods for this stage in your baby's life. First, you will want all these foods to be purees; they should be smooth, with no lumps or chunks that they could potentially choke on. This also means they should be a thin and runny consistency at first and as they develop you can make them thicker. The age ranges are given as a guide – just remember the signs to look for as to when your baby will be ready to progress to chunkier, solid foods. Most babies will fall into this feeding range but if they don't, I want you to look at this first chapter as where to start when introducing solids and work from there. It's all about paying attention to your son or daughter and following their cues. They will let you know when they are ready.

If you do choose to feed your baby only organic foods, just look out for organic options of the foods listed in each recipe. It is also worth remembering that fruits and vegetables that are in season and grown locally are better for the environment but I appreciate that such luxuries are not possible for everyone and emphasize that as long as you are feeding your baby healthy, natural ingredients (washed before use) then you're doing a great job! Also remember that creating your own baby food gives you the freedom to support and encourage your child to develop their eating habits, so don't be afraid to move ahead when you think they are ready. As always, if you are ever unsure, talk with your pediatrician, as they will be able to give you the best advice.

Shopping List

(Foods you can introduce...)

Fruits

Avocados
Apples
Bananas
Pears

Vegetables

Green Beans
Sweet Potatoes
Squash (Butternut/Acorn)

Grains

Barley
Oatmeal
Rice

Serving Size

1 - 2 tablespoons = 1 serving
Maximum of 2 servings per day

STARTER FOODS:
CEREALS

Rattle Rice Cereal

Starting your baby on rice cereals is normally recommended before you try other types of foods. This one is versatile and can be made with your choice of milk and then later added to fruit purees.

Ingredients

- 1/4 cup ground brown rice
- 1 cup water, breast milk or formula

How to make

- On a high heat, bring liquid to a boil and then add the rice.
- Simmer for 10 minutes while stirring constantly. Add liquid if needed to meet the correct consistency (start your baby off with a thin liquid and increase thickness as they get used to the texture).
- Serve warm.

OOOOO"- Oatmeal Cereal

Once your baby is fine with rice, try changing to oatmeal for a bit of a difference.

Ingredients

- 1/4 cup ground whole-meal oats (please do not use instant or quick cooking oats) ground in blender or similar
- 3/4 cup water, breast milk or formula

How to make

- Into a pan on a high heat, boil liquid and add oats.
- Simmer for 10 minutes while stirring constantly. You can choose to add more breast milk/formula for a creamier texture here.
- Serve warm.

Bouncy Barley Cereal

Another variety of cereal you can try out which tastes scrummy.

Ingredients

- 1/4 cup ground barley
- 1 cup water, breast milk or formula

How to make

- Place a pan on a high heat and bring liquid to a boil and then add the barley.
- Turn down and simmer for 10 minutes, stirring constantly.
- Add more liquid if needed to meet the correct consistency (start your baby off with a thin liquid and increase thickness as they get used to the texture).
- Serve warm.

Beautiful Bananas

High in fiber, Vitamin B6 and C, this first food is great especially if your baby has been suffering from diarrhea. It is easily digestible and full of slow releasing sugars to keep them fuller for longer – great at night time for a good night's rest!

Ingredients

- 1/2 banana
- 1/2 cup of water, breast milk or formula

How to make

- Peel the banana.
- Mash using a spoon or fork.
- Mix together with the liquid to form a smooth consistency.
- Once your baby has been introduced to single foods and is coping well, you can blend an avocado with the banana to form a delicious breakfast, lunch or dessert!

Precious Pear

Another high fiber fruit, rich in Vitamin C!

Ingredients

- 1 pear
- 1 tbsp breast milk or formula

How to make

- Peel and cut into chunks avoiding the seeds in the very center.
- If your baby is under 6 months steam gently for 10 minutes or until tender (save the water).
- If 6 months or older you may leave the pear raw if you wish.
- Blend until smooth.
- Use the liqiud if you need to thin out your puree, however pears tend to create a very runny puree anyway, making them excellent for your 4-6 month old!
- Add baby cereal to thicken if desired for older babies.

Grandpa's Green Beans

Aside from your baby's milk intake, green beans are a great calcium boost! It is usually suggested you wait until nearer the 6 month age range with green beans because of the tougher skins but buying frozen should reduce this problem.

Ingredients

- 1 cup of frozen green beans (fresh are a lot harder to puree)

How to make

- Place the green beans into a steamer.
- Steam for 15-20 minutes or until beans become very tender, keep an eye on your water level throughout cooking.
- Drain and set aside any extra water to use later.
- Blend until smooth (ensure all skins are pu reed).
- Add saved water as needed to get a smooth consistency.
- You could run the green beans through a strainer if required, to get rid of any skins.

Soothing Squash

Squash is very mild and tasty and what's more is packed with Vitamin A to help build strong bones. It also helps vision and skin, creating the best start to your baby's diet!

Ingredients

- 1 Medium butternut squash
- ½ cup of water, breast milk or formula

How to make

- Cut squash in half and scoop out the seeds.
- Peel and cut into cubes and layer with water in an oven dish.
- Bake squash cubes in oven at 400°F / 200°C / Gas Mark 6 for 30 minutes or until soft to the touch.
- Ensure you continue to top up water so that the squash doesn't dry out.
- Leave squash to cool.
- Blend until pureed.
- Note: a whole butternut squash will provide at least 4-5 servings for your baby so leave to cool and refrigerate (make sure you use within 3 days)or freeze (use within 3 months).

Angelic Apple Sauce

One of the first fruits baby can have and so versatile!

Ingredients

- 3 apples
- 3 cups of water

How to make

- Peel, core and cut apples into slices or chunks.
- Place into pan with shallow water just covering the apples.
- Boil or steam the apples for 15-20 minutes or until tender. Top up the water as necessary to ensure the apples don't stick or burn.
- Drain (keeping the water) and mash apples using a potato masher.
- If your baby is just starting out on single foods, blend the apples with the preserved water until runny. If not you can skip this step.

Avocado-licious

This fruit is a perfect start to your baby's diet as it is so rich in healthy fats, antioxidants and vitamin E – all great for building immune systems, fighting off disease and allowing your baby to grow healthy and happy.

Ingredients

- 1/2 ripe avocado
- 1 tbsp breast milk or formula

How to make

- Cut the avocado in half lengthways using a sharp knife.
- Remove the stone by gently nudging the knife underneath the stone and loosening it. It should pop right out if ripe enough.
- Scoop out the beautiful creamy flesh and mash using a spoon or fork.
- Mix together with the liquid to form a smooth consistency (a little like guacamole!)

Sophia's Special Sweet Potato

Similar in texture to squash, sweet potato is slightly easier to cook and as the name suggests, sweeter! It is packed full of goodness including Vitamin D – the vitamin we get from sunlight. This is particularly good for your baby's skin, hair and nails as well as for their immune system and energy levels.

Ingredients

• 1 sweet potato

How to make

- Wash the sweet potato and puncture the skin with a fork, creating pin pricks all over.
- Wrap in foil or baking paper.
- Place in oven on 400°F / 200°C / Gas Mark 6 and bake for 30 minutes or until very soft.
- Alternatively you can steam your sweet potato:
- Peel your sweet potato and cut into cubes.
- Place cubes of potato in to a pan of water, just enough to lightly cover them.
- Steam the potatoes until they are tender; make sure to keep an eye on the water level as you may have to top up.
- Drain and set aside any left over water for later.
- Blend sweet potato until pureed (if you baked your potatoes you will need to scoop out the flesh from the skins before blending).
- Add reserved water from steaming as needed whilst blending. You can use breast milk or baby formula here instead if wish.

MULTIPLE FOODS!

★ ★ ★ ★ ★

Baby's Bananapple

Once you have introduced single foods to your baby and are confident that they are not allergic or intolerant to certain ingredients, you can start to combine foods for more variety and enjoyment.

Ingredients

- 1 apple
- 1 ripe banana

How to make

- Peel, core and cut apple into slices or chunks.
- Place into pan with just enough water to slightly cover the apples.
- Boil or steam apples for 15-20 minutes until tender. Keep an eye on your water levels and make sure your apples don't become exposed.
- Drain and mash apples using a potato masher, you can also follow pureeing instructions from the apple sauce directions for a thinner consistency.
- Peel a ripe banana and mash with a fork in a separate bowl (you can heat the banana for a few seconds in the microwave to soften it if needed).
- Add applesauce to your mashed banana and serve.

Bedtime Banana Oatmeal

Oatmeal and banana combined forms a thicker consistency and a hearty meal for your son or daughter. The slow releasing carbohydrates are great to keep them fed and sleepy throughout the night or nap time and the banana adds a sweetness they'll love.

Ingredients

- 1/2 banana
- 3 tbsp of ground oatmeal
- 1/3 cup boiling water, breast milk or formula

How to make

- Peel and cut banana into slices.
- You may steam bananas for 10 minutes if you desire but it's not necessary.
- Mix boiling water and oatmeal in a separate bowl.
- Blend oatmeal and banana until you have a smooth consistency. You may add more water or oatmeal depending on your baby's preferred consistency.
- Serve warm, the boiling water should have cooled through this process but it's always best to test.

Starry-eyed Banana Barley

My son's favorite breakfast – the barley makes him energetic for the rest of the morning!

Ingredients

- 1/2 banana
- 3 tbsp of ground barley
- 1/3 cup boiling water

How to make

- Peel and cut banana into slices (save the other half for a snack later or just double the mixture for 2 servings).
- You may steam bananas for 10 minutes if you desire but it's not necessary.
- Mix boiling water and barley in a separate bowl.
- Blend barley and banana until you have a smooth consistency. You may add more water or barley depending on your baby's preferred consistency.
- Serve warm, the boiling water should have cooled through this process but it's always best to test.

Apply Oatmeal Fun

A winter warmer – I've been known to have a few sneaky mouthfuls of this one!

Ingredients

- 1/4 cup of peeled apple chunks
- 3 tbsp of ground oatmeal
- 1/3 cup boiling water, breast milk or formula

How to make

- Steam apples in a pan of shallow water for 20-25 minutes.
- Mix boiling water and oatmeal in a separate bowl.
- Blend apples and oatmeal until you have a smooth consistency.
- Serve warm (ensure the boiling water has cooled enough for your baby).

Banana-cado!

Now that your baby is used to both banana and avocado you can combine the two together to form a sweeter version of the avocado puree alone.

Ingredients

- 1/4 avocado
- 1/2 banana

How to make

- You can cook these in the microwave for 1 minute if you wish but both foods can be eaten raw.
- Mash together with a fork.
- Add a little breast milk or formula to create a smoother consistency.

Apple and Pear Delight

A fantastic sweet combo!

Ingredients

- 1/4 cup peeled apple cut into cubes
- 1/4 cup peeled pears cut into cubes

How to make

- Place apples and pears into a pan with an inch or two of water in the bottom.
- Steam or boil for 20-25 minutes or until tender, remove from heat and drain. Keep an eye on water levels, as you may need to top up.
- Set aside any leftover water for later.
- Place cooked pears and apples in appliance of your choice and puree. Add left over liquid as needed to achieve desired consistency.

Barley with Apple and Banana

Fruity and sustaining!

Ingredients

- 3 tbsp of ground barley
- 1/2 cup apple chunks, steamed
- 1/2 a banana
- 1/3 cup boiling water, breast milk or formula

How to make

- Mix boiling water and barley and fruit together.
- Blend until pureed.
- Serve warm: the boiling water should have cooled through this process and be the perfect temperature but it's always best to test.

Banana Sweet Potato

Perfect for lunch.

Ingredients

- 1/2 banana
- 1/3 cup sweet potato

How to make

- Peel and cut banana into slices.
- Wash, peel and cut up sweet potato into cubes.
- Steam sweet potato for 25-30 minutes or until very soft.
- Remove from heat and drain. Set aside any leftover water for later.
- Puree sweet potato with the banana in a blender - add left over liquid as needed to achieve desired consistency.

Apple Sweet Potato

Dinner time treat!

Ingredients

- 1/2 an apple, peeled and cubed
- 1/3 cup sweet potato peeled and cubed

How to make

- Steam the sweet potato and apple for 20-25 minutes or until tender.
- Remove from heat and drain. Set aside any leftover water.
- Blend together until pureed. Add liquid if needed whilst blending.

Green Beans and Apples

Although slightly unusual, the sugar from the apple sweetens the green beans and adds a pleasant taste for your baby's sweet tooth!

Ingredients

- 1/4 cup of apple, peeled and cubed
- 1/4 cup frozen green beans

How to make

- Steam apples for 20-25 minutes.
- Add the green beans to the steamer for the last 5-10 minutes and continue until all fruit is tender.
- Drain and set aside (save the water).
- Blend ingredients together to puree.

Delicious Autumnal Puree

This will create at least 4-5 servings to keep you organized and pre-prepared!

Ingredients

- 1 butternut squash – peeled, cubed & steamed
- 1 to 2 cups cooked brown rice cereal
- 1/2 cup applesauce

How to make

- Blend all ingredients together and serve.

chapter six

Trying new TEXTURES!

This chapter includes recipes
using foods that
your baby might
not have been able to digest
as easily in their 4-6 month stage. Now that you have
weaned them onto the basic foods including rice,
banana, sweet potato
and avocado,
you will be able to introduce
more variety into their diet!

Trying New Textures (6-8 Months Old)

This chapter includes recipes using foods that your baby might not have been able to digest as easily in their 4-6 month stage. Now that you have weaned them onto the basic foods including rice, banana, sweet potato and avocado, you will be able to introduce more variety into their diet. You can continue to use the purees from the first section and may now start to thicken them up with less liquid and extra ground brown rice or oatmeal. Continue to avoid chunks to eliminate choking hazards. Remember this is just a guideline and whilst they fit with many parents and their babies, it is always best to speak to your pediatrician to gain professional advice if you're unsure.

Foods you can introduce...

Fruits	Vegetables	Meat
Apricot	Carrots	Chicken
Mango	Parsnips	Turkey
Nectarine	Peas	Tofu (substitute)
Plums	Zucchini	
Peach		
Prunes		
Pumpkin		

Serving Size

Cereals, Fruit & Vegetables =
2-3 tablespoons = 1 serving
Maximum of 3 – 4 servings per day

Meat =
1-2 tablespoons = 1 serving
Maximum of 1 serving per day

Amazing Apricot Puree

Packed with a specific combination of vitamins and nutrients, these tiny little blushing fruits help to fight against heart disease and some cancers. You can start to introduce from around 6 months onwards.

Ingredients

- 3 apricots
- 2 cups water or breast milk/formula (sweeter)

How to make

- Bring liquid and fruit to a boil on a high heat and then simmer for 15 minutes or until completely soft and tender.
- Drain and reserve any liquid to use for puree.
- Blend with the juice until pureed.
- If freezing, pour into an ice cube tray and cover. You can pop one out and defrost thoroughly before serving next time!

Positively Yummy Peach Puree

This peach puree is delicious and can be used with baked or steamed peaches until after 8 months when it can be served with raw peaches.

Ingredients

- 3 peaches

How to make

- Steam or bake your peaches. Baking will make your fruit taste sweeter but steaming is always healthier as it contains more nutrients and vitamins than other methods of cooking.
- Steam/bake whole peaches in a pan with a thin layer of water. Steaming will need 10-15 minutes and baking 20-25 minutes on 375°F / 190°C /Gas Mark 5.
- Drain (save water) and allow to cool.
- Peel the skin from the fruit and remove the pit.
- Blend until pureed – add water from steaming if needed.

Magnificent Mango Puree

Mangoes are thought to contain a greater level of carotenoids than other fruits and these help battle the common cold! The puree also tastes delicious warm or cold and can be frozen for a summer time treat!

Ingredients

- 1 ripe mango
- ¼ cup water, breast milk or formula

How to make

- Cut mango lengthways along the side of the stone. You will now have 2 halves. On the side without the stone, use a sharp knife to cut criss-cross slices across the flesh and 'pop' this out by turning the skin inside out. Repeat on the other side once you've cut from the stone.
- You will now have cubes of mango.
- Blend mango until pureed.
- Add formula, breast milk, or water until a smooth puree is formed.
- You may wish to steam and mash the mango but your baby should be able to eat raw fruits by this stage. Again, consult your pediatrician if unsure. Once they have developed to the finger food, these cubes are great cut into smaller pieces as a snack!

Pretty Plum Sauce

Plums are super for helping your baby's digestion system along and are mouth-wateringly delicious! You could even try this sauce as a topping for the more basic rice cereals in chapter 5.

Ingredients

- 2 to 3 ripe plums
- 1 tbsp breast milk, formula or water

How to make

- Peel and pit your plums.
- Cut into small cubes.
- Plums, like other fruits at this stage, can be eaten raw but you may choose to steam for 5-10 minutes for a softer texture.
- Blend until pureed, adding liquid as necessary.

Prune Delight

Dried plums are also known as prunes and come with all the same benefits as their fresh counter-parts ! Just look out for natural prunes without sulphurs.

Ingredients

- ½ cup dried plums (prunes)

How to make

- Soak dried prunes in warm water until they plump up or steam gently for 5 minutes.
- Blend until pureed - adding water, breast milk or formula to achieve a smooth consistency.

Halloween Pumpkin Pie Puree

This giant fruit is low in fat and high in fiber. Along with its multiple vitamin and nutrient count, this puree is a super food of its kind – not just to be served on spooky evenings!

How to make

- Cut the pumpkin in half and scoop out the seeds (don't serve these to your baby as they are not recommended at this stage).
- Cut out the flesh and chop into cubes.
- Steam over water on a high heat for 35-40 minutes or until very soft.
- Blend until pureed – adding water, breast milk or formula to reach a smooth consistency.

Ingredients

- 1 medium cooking pumpkin, no heavier than 5 pounds (canned is fine but not pumpkin pie mix!)

Glow-in-the-Dark Carrot Puree

This old Wives' Tale actually has some substance! The Vitamin A content in carrots is what helps with vision in low lighting. So go ahead and try giving your baby carrots.

Ingredients

- 1 cup of peeled and chopped raw carrots

How to make

- On a high heat, steam the carrots in a pan with a little water for 25-30 minutes or until soft.
- Drain and discard the water (nitrate from the carrots are usually washed away during the steaming process and you shouldn't use this water for your baby's purees – don't worry the carrots themselves are fine).
- Blend until pureed, adding fresh water to reach a smooth consistency.

Pea-licious!

Peas are packed full of protein and other vitamins and minerals – they are great on their own or mixed with your baby's favorite vegetables.

Ingredients

- 1/2 cup fresh or frozen peas

How to make

- For fresh peas you will need to remove the peas from their pod. For frozen just cook straight from the packet!
- Steam peas for 5-10 minutes or until soft (or follow package guidelines).
- Drain and save water.
- Pour straight into cold or freezing water to retain vitamins and nutrients.
- Blend until pureed, using saved water until you reach a smooth consistency.
- Use a strainer to get rid of any skins if necessary.

Yummy Nectarine

Nectarines can now be introduced – remember to allow 4/5 days between each new food.

Ingredients

- 3 whole nectarines

How to make

- Wash the fruit clean and place in a pan with roughly an inch of water.
- Let the water boil and let the nectarines steam until tender.
- Remove nectarines, place water to one side and peel the skin and remove any seeds or pits.
- Place in blender and puree; add the reserved water as needed to achieve a smooth consistency.

Cheeky Chicken

Chicken can be introduced to your baby at this stage and is recognized for the benefits of providing protein and iron from a young age in order to help your baby grow strong and healthy. This also tastes delicious at dinner time as a savory option.

Ingredients

- 1 small chicken breast

How to make

- Cut chicken into small cubes.
- Preheat oven to 375°F / 190°C /Gas Mark 5 and bake in baking paper or tin foil for 25 minutes (ensure meat is completely cooked through by sticking a knife into the center – the juices should run clean and the meat should be white through-out).
- Blend until pureed and add a little water or un-salted chicken stock to achieve a smooth consistency.

Turkey-tastic!

Turkey, like chicken, is full of protein and iron and is one of the more easily digestible meats. Your baby can be introduced to turkey from 6 months but some parents choose to wait until 8 months. Again consult your pediatrician if unsure.

Ingredients

- 2 turkey breasts (skinless and boneless)

How to make

- Wash the turkey breast and slice into small cubes.
- Bring a pan of water to the boil before adding your turkey and bringing to a simmer for 15-20 minutes or until completely cooked through (juices should run clear when you insert a sharp knife into the meat and it should be white all the way through).
- Drain and allow to cool before blending until pureed. Again add a little water if needed to reach a smooth consistency.

Perfect Parsnip Puree

A source of calcium, these nutty delights whizz up into a delicious puree for your baby's savory meals.

Ingredients

- 1 cup of peeled, washed and cubed parsnips.

How to make

- Steam parsnips on a medium high heat for 15-20 minutes.
- Drain and set aside any leftover water for later.
- Blend until pureed.

Perfect Peaches and Pears

Blushing with goodness, these fruits combined will ensure your baby receives a host of vitamins.

Ingredients

- 1 peach
- 1/4 cup of peeled pear, cut into cubes

How to make

- Steam or boil fruit for 10-15 minutes or until tender, remove from heat and drain. Keep an eye on water levels, as you may need to top up.
- Set aside any leftover water for later.
- Place cooked peach and pear in appliance of your choice and puree. Add left over liquid as needed to achieve desired consistency.

Sweet Potato and Barley

A wonderfully filling meal, with a little sweetness from the sweet potato.

Ingredients

- 3 tbsp ground barley
- 1/2 cup steamed sweet potato cubes
- 1/3 cup boiling water, breast milk or formula

How to make

- Mix boiling water and barley together.
- Blend barley mix with sweet potatoes until pureed.
- Serve warm – remember to check the boiling water has cooled enough for your baby by testing it yourself.

Power Parsnip, Amazing Apple & Crazy Carrot Puree

Taste sensation!

Ingredients

- 4 parsnips
- 2 apples
- 4 carrots

How to make

- Peel the apples, parsnips and carrots and then chop them up into cubes.
- Steam the mix for 30 minutes until soft and tender.
- Add to a blender and puree until a smooth consistency is achieved.

Carroty Fruit Combo

Who says you can't eat carrot with fruit? Carrot cake is delicious and this is the closest thing you can get to that in the baby food world.

Ingredients

- 1 cup mango washed and cubed
- 2 apples, washed, peeled and cubed.
- 1 cup peeled and sliced carrot

How to make

- Steam carrots for 10-15 minutes.
- Blend all ingredients until pureed. Add your choice of water, breast milk, formula or even coconut water to loosen the mixture if needed.
- Serve cold.

Squashed Pear and Mango

Another combination of fruit and veg – this tastes delicious!

Ingredients

- 1/2 cup mango washed and cubed
- 2 pears washed, peeled and cubed.
- 1 cup squash washed, peeled, cubed and steamed

How to make

- Steam fruit and vegetables using guidelines from the single food recipe section. Mangos and pears do not necessarily need to be steamed if they are very ripe and you have introduced raw fruits already.
- Blend all ingredients until pureed. Add your choice of water, breast milk, formula or even coconut water to loosen the mixture if needed.
- Serve cold.

Turkey Rice and Carrot Dinner

A mini roast!

Ingredients

- 1/2 cup carrot washed, peeled and sliced
- 1 cup brown rice
- 1/2 cup of cooked turkey pieces

How to make

- Cook rice according to package directions.
- Place carrot in steaming basket with an inch or two of water in bottom of pan.
- Steam or boil for 10-15 minutes or until tender, remove from heat and drain. If you are steaming keep an eye on water level as you may need to top up.
- Set aside any leftover water for later.
- Blend ingredients in a food processor, adding water as necessary.
- Serve warm.

Garden Vegetable Supreme

Sometimes vegetarian fresh meals are the best.

Ingredients

- 1 summer squash washed, peeled and cubed
- 1 cup of green beans washed and sliced
- 1 cup of carrots washed, peeled and sliced
- 1 cup of peas washed

How to make

- Chop all vegetables into small pieces and combine together to steam. You can use fresh or frozen veggies.
- Add water to put with vegetables, just enough to cover the vegetables.
- Steam on a medium heat for 15 minutes or until tender.
- Drain and set aside left over water for later use.
- Place in appliance of your choice to puree the vegetables, using water set aside add to puree as needed to get desired consistency.

chapter seven

Spicing Things UP!

Now that your baby
has developed beyond single foods and multiple
they can start to be introduced to spices;
in this chapter I will introduce some
more acidic foods to the recipes.
This is also the stage in which you can
start to really introduce some texture into their foods;
at this point you may have gradually
made your baby food thicker,
even introducing some small chunks!

Spicing Things Up! (8-10 Months Old)

Now that your baby has developed beyond single foods and multiple they can start to be introduced to spices; in this chapter I will introduce some more acidic foods to the recipes. Up to this point we have made almost all your little one's foods with cooked ingredients (asides from some of the raw fruits). The cooking can cut down acidity in the fruits and vegetables and start the breaking-down process to make digestion easier. These "raw" foods will be a little more work for your baby's body but after being introduced to a wide variety of foods and learning to eat and process it all, they should be fine with the bigger variety of raw foods. This is also the stage in which you can start to really introduce some texture into their foods; at this point you may have gradually made your baby food thicker, even introducing some small chunks. Now you can continue to experiment with the texture by watching out for your baby's cues and speaking to your pediatrician for advice. I would advise sticking to foods that are soft and easy to mash during the next stage; once they go through the teething process, harder and solid foods can be introduced.

Foods to introduce at this stage...	Onions Peppers Rutabaga White Potatoes Turnips	Spices Anise Basil Nutmeg Vanilla*	*Curry Powder As with any new food, wait for 4-5 days to see how your baby reacts and only use tiny pinches to be on the safe side.
Fruits	Meat	Pepper	
Blueberry Cherries Citrus Coconut Cranberries Grapes Fig Kiwi Melon Papaya Persimmons	Beef Pork Grains Buckwheat Flax Kamut Pasta Quinoa	Garlic (powdered or minced) Rosemary Dill Oregano Lemon Zest Ginger Cinnamon Mint Curry powder*	*Vanilla pod/extract Use fresh vanilla pods where available. Look out for extracts that are not labeled 'pure' (often alcohol is used to preserve pure vanilla). However when cooking, alcohol is cooked out anyway so is okay to use for baking/cooking with. Serving Size
Vegetables Asparagus Broccoli Beets Cucumber Cauliflower Eggplant Kale Leeks	Dairy Cheese Cottage Cheese Cream Cheese Eggs Yogurt		Choose 2-3 options from the following servings and increase as baby gets older: 2-4 tablespoons of cereals up to 3x per day 3-4 tablespoons of fruit up to 2x per day 3-4 tablespoons of veg up to 2x per day 3-4 tablespoons of chicken, beef or pork up to 2x per day ¼ cup of cheese (cottage or cheddar)

Cuddly Coconut Crush

Now don't be alarmed! Though coconut milk sounds complicated and time consuming, it's actually really easy. It will take about 10 minutes and doesn't require any crazy equipment.

Ingredients

- 1 1/2 to 2 cups of shredded coconut, un sweetened
- 4 cups of water, breast milk, formula or coconut water

How to make

- Heat your water in a pan over a medium heat for 10 minutes - you don't want it to boil but it should be hot.
- Put the coconut in a blender or similar and add the water, blending on high until thick and creamy for a few minutes.
- Drain with a mesh colander to get the coconut pieces out then squeeze through a cloth to get any remaining solid traces out. A clean cloth is always recommended here.
- Serve immediately or store in the fridge and use within 3-4 days.
- You may find that it separates which is normal; shake before serving.

Cute Quinoa Cereal

Breakfast, lunch or dinner go-to.

Ingredients

- 1/4 cup ground quinoa
- 1 cup water, breast milk or formula

How to make

- On a high heat, bring liquid to a boil and then add the liquid.
- Simmer for 10 minutes while stirring constanly. Add liquid if needed to meet the correct consistency (start your baby off with a thin liquid and increase thickness as they get used to the texture).
- Serve warm.

Marvelous Melon

Melon is juicy and thirst-quenching and can be pureed at first and then cut into finger food as your baby develops.

Ingredients

- 1 melon (cantaloupe or honeydew)

How to make

- Cut melon into chunks, removing the rind at the same time.
- Place in steaming basket with an inch or two of water in the bottom of pan.
- Lightly steam for 20-25 minutes or until tender, remove from heat and drain. When steaming keep an eye on water level as you may need to top up.
- Set aside any leftover water for later.
- Place cooked melon in appliance of your choice and puree. Add left over liquid as needed to achieve your desired consistency.
- Serve.

Perfect Papaya Puree

Another tropical addition to your baby's diet.

Ingredients

- 1 ripe papaya
- ¼ cup water, breast milk or formula

How to make

- Peel, de-seed and cut the papaya into chunks.
- Blend papaya until pureed.
- Add formula, breast milk, or water and blend until you reach desired consistency.
- For a more sensitive stomach, steam the papaya for 10-15 minutes or until soft to break down the sugars and fibers, allowing for easier digestion.

Roaring Rutabaga

A cross between a turnip and a cabbage, rutabaga contains just as many benefits as turnips but allows you to mix and match with what you can find in the grocery store.

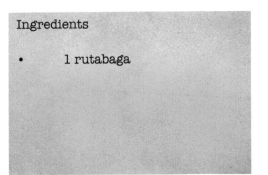

Ingredients

- 1 rutabaga

How to make

- Thoroughly wash before peeling the skin off, then cut into small chunks. Rutabagas can be slippery while you're cutting so don't be afraid to cut a small chunk off the bottom to give it a flat side for you to hold.
- Steam on a medium high heat for 15-20 minutes.
- Drain and set aside any leftover water for later.
- Blend until pureed.

Breakfast Blueberry Boost

Now that your baby has reached 8 months you can introduce blueberries – high in antioxidants these are bursting with goodness for your baby's defences!

Ingredients

- 1 cup of blueberries washed

How to make

- Wash your berries and remove any excess stems.
- Place in steaming basket with an inch or two of water in bottom of pan; you may also boil depending on your preference.
- Lightly steam for 5-10 minutes or until tender, and then remove from heat and drain. When steaming, keep an eye on water levels, as you may need to top up.
- Set aside any leftover water for later.
- Place cooked berries in appliance of your choice and puree. Add left over liquid as needed to achieve desired consistency.
- You don't need to steam your blueberries once you know your baby can tolerate them and can whizz up from raw – just ensure you've washed them carefully. Once they're able to eat solid foods, they can be given as a snack with no preparation.

Wonderful Watermelon Crush

Watermelon and cantaloupes can be introduced from 8 months onwards. Monitor your baby one food at a time just as you would when introducing any other food types. And remember to consult your pediatrician if you're unsure. Watermelon is wholesome and tasty and should be kept at room temperature until ready to serve.

How to make

Ingredients

- 1 watermelon

- On a chopping board, cut the watermelon in half lengthways (always remember to use a sharp knife and cut away from you).
- Now cut into quarters.
- Use your knife to make criss cross slices across the flesh of each piece (don't cut through the skin).
- Now lift up your quarter and slice along the skin, removing all the cubes of watermelon.
- Repeat for each quarter.
- Mush with a fork or blend until pureed. Once your baby is a little older you can use these cubes as finger food.

Krazy Kale Ketchup

Rich in Vitamin A and C – Kale is just bursting with goodness. Great on its own or as a dip when your baby graduates to finger food!

How to make

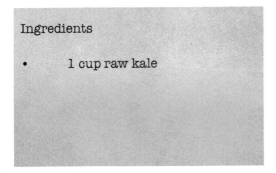

Ingredients

- 1 cup raw kale

- Wash kale and use a clean towel or kitchen paper to dry off excess water.
- Steam on a medium high heat for 10-15 minutes.
- Drain and set aside any leftover water for later.
- Blend until pureed, using liquid if needed.

Auntie's Homemade Yogurt

Some think that yogurt should not be served before 1 year old because of the dairy content, however this is more to do with milk, as experts are concerned that parents might replace breast milk or formula with cow's milk, which is unsuitable. Yogurt however is not seen as a substitute for milk time and so this is why it is allowed in this age range. Here is a recipe I've included which will allow you to make your homemade yogurt in batches, simply from a yogurt starter at least 4-5 times over – saving you money in the process and creating a much tastier alternative to commercial products.

Ingredients

- 3 tbsp yogurt starter (alternatively look for unflavored natural yogurt in the store) – this must contain active cultures
- 1.5 litre whole milk (breast milk can be used – see alternative options in instructions)
- You will need to buy a food thermometer for this which measures between 110-180°f

How to make

- Put a large pan of water (with a lid) on a high heat and bring to boiling point for 5 minutes. Add the thermometer and a spoon at this point to sterilize them.
- Now replace the water with the milk and warm on a medium heat until 185°f (this will ensure any 'bad' bacteria is killed). If using breast milk you do not need to warm through, as it is sterile anyway. Keep the lid off while you're doing this to keep an eye on the milk.
- Don't let the milk boil!
- Remove the pan from the heat and allow to cool until it
- decreases to 110-115°f.
- Once at optimum temperature, stir the yogurt into the milk until completely mixed in and place the lid on top of the pan.
- Move the pan to a warm place (wrapped in a thick towel or in the airing cupboard works well). Leave at a constant temperature for a minimum of 7 hours and check up on it. It will become thicker the longer it is left.
- Breast milk will need at least 10 hours to thicken, as it is a lot less creamy than whole milk.

Cherub's Cherry Choice

Heavenly delight – colorful and calcium-packed.

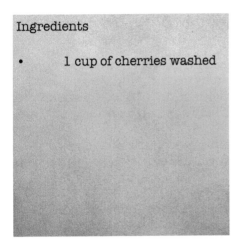

Ingredients

- 1 cup of cherries washed

How to make

- Remove stems and pit your cherries using a pitter (or buy pitted cherries if you can).
- Place in steaming basket with an inch or two of water in the bottom of pan, you may also boil depending on your preference.
- Gently steam for 10-15 minutes or until tender, and then remove from heat and drain. When steaming, keep an eye on water levels, as you may need to top up.
- Set aside any leftover water for later.
- Place cooked cherries in appliance of your choice and puree. Add left over liquid as needed to achieve desired consistency.
- Serve warm!

Easy Eggplant

Delicious and meaty in texture, eggplant is used the world over as a vegetarian dish. The vitamins and nutrients are abundant and it tastes brilliant too.

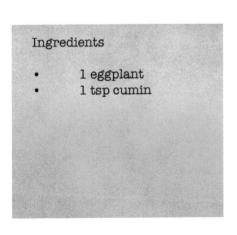

Ingredients

- 1 eggplant
- 1 tsp cumin

How to make

- Place in steaming basket with an inch or two of water in the bottom of pan, adding cumin to the water.
- Steam, bake or boil for 30-35 minutes or until tender, remove from heat and drain. If you are steaming keep an eye on water levels, as you may need to top up.
- Ensure flesh and skin (if remaining) is extremely soft.
- Set aside any leftover water for later.
- Place cooked eggplant in appliance of your choice and puree. Add left over liquid as needed to achieve desired consistency.

A-Z Zucchini

Fresh and nutritious, zucchini is a great addition to your baby's diet.

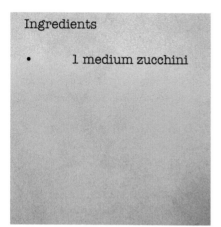

Ingredients

- 1 medium zucchini

How to make

- Wash, peel and cut zucchini into slices (when your baby is onto solid foods you may leave the skin).
- Place in steaming basket with an inch or two of water in the bottom of pan; you may also boil depending on your preference.
- Steam or boil for 5-8 minutes or until tender, remove from heat and drain. If you are steaming keep an eye on water levels, as you may need to top up.
- Set aside any leftover water for later.
- Place cooked zucchini in appliance of your choice and puree. Add left over liquid as needed to achieve desired
- consistency.

Kicking Kiwi

Kiwi is exotic and delicious and extremely hydrating. You can now introduce this; remember the 4-5 day rule to monitor new foods.

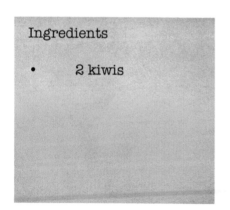

Ingredients

- 2 kiwis

How to make

- Peel and half the kiwis.
- Place in steaming basket with an inch or two of water in the bottom of pan.
- Steam gently for 5-10 minutes or until tender, and then remove from heat and drain.
- Set aside any leftover water for later.
- Place cooked kiwi in appliance of your choice and puree. Add left over liquid as needed to achieve desired consistency.
- You can serve kiwi raw, just cut into very small pieces – please note the seeds are fine to give to your baby, just use your judgment on their ability to handle textures.

Cheerful Cauliflower

Cauliflower is delightful and can be pureed at first and then cut into finger food as your baby develops.

Ingredients	How to make

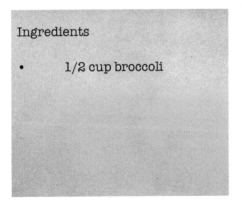

Ingredients

- 1/2 cup cauliflower florets

How to make

- Wash well.
- Place cauliflower in steaming basket with an inch or two of water in the bottom of pan; you may also boil depending on your preference.
- Steam or boil for 5-10 minutes or until tender, re move from heat and drain. If you are steaming keep an eye on water levels, as you may need to top up.
- Set aside any leftover water for later.
- Place cooked cauliflower in appliance of your choice and puree. Add left over liquid as needed to achieve desired consistency.

Brilliant Broccoli Breakfast

Broccoli aids the digestion system and is also high in Vitamin C! As with cauliflower, you can now introduce this vegetable to your baby's diet, bearing in mind it has the potential to make us a little gassy! Serve in moderation at first.

Ingredients

- 1/2 cup broccoli

How to make

- Wash well.
- Place in steaming basket with an inch or two of water in the bottom of pan; you may also boil depending on your preference.
- Steam or boil for 8-10 minutes or until tender, re move from heat and drain. If you are steaming keep an eye on water levels, as you may need to top up.
- Set aside any leftover water for later.
- Place cooked broccoli in appliance of your choice and puree. Add left over liquid as needed to achieve desired consistency.

Tremendous Turnip Treat

Once turnips are cooked they become softer and sweeter than raw: they're high in Vitamin C and fiber.

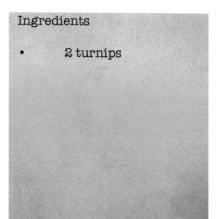

Ingredients

- 2 turnips

How to make

- Wash thoroughly, cut off greens and straggly roots, peel and chop into small chunks (the smaller your chunks the faster they will steam).
- Place in steaming basket with an inch or two in bottom of pan, you may also boil depending on your preference.
- Steam or boil on a medium heat for 20-25 minutes or until tender.
- Remove from heat and drain. If you are steaming keep an eye on water level, as you may need to top up.
- Set aside any leftover water for later.
- Place cooked turnip in appliance of your choice and puree. Add left over liquid as needed to achieve desired consistency.

Little Monster Mash

Simple comfort food.

Ingredients

- 1 whole baking potato
- ¼ cup of breast milk, formula or homemade yogurt p.76

How to make

- Peel, clean and chop potato into cubes.
- Steam for 25-30 minutes on a medium high heat until soft to the fork.
- Drain and save any leftover water for later.
- Allow to cool and then blend until smooth. You can add a liquid of your choice here to thin out the puree – yogurt gives the mash a lovely creamy texture without having to add butter!
- Serve warm.

A is for Asparagus!

One of my favorites as well as my son's! Actually a protein source, as well as a source of fiber and other vitamins. When your baby is a little older, try serving steamed asparagus stems as finger food. For now, see the recipe below.

Ingredients

- 4 stalks of asparagus

How to make

- Snap the base end of the asparagus off (this is very hard and will snap easily whilst using your fingers to bend the end).
- Place in steaming basket with an inch or two of water in the bottom of a pan, you may also boil depending on your preference.
- Steam or boil for 7-13 minutes or until tender, re move from heat and drain. If you are steaming keep an eye on water level as you may need to refill.
- Set aside any leftover water for later.
- Place cooked asparagus in appliance of your choice after cutting into smaller pieces and puree. Add left over liquid as needed to achieve desired consistency.

Cottage Cheese Delight

Calcium, healthy fats and protein are found in cottage cheese and can start to be introduced to your baby's diet now. If your baby has a known dairy or lactose intolerance wait until they are older before introducing cottage cheese and as always speak to your pediatrician to make sure.

Ingredients

- 1 tub of cottage cheese, unsweetened or salted
- ½ cup of apricot puree

How to make

- Place cheese in appliance of your choice and puree. Add liquid as needed to achieve desired consistency.
- You could decide to try and make your own cottage cheese, however most homemade recipes call for buttermilk, which isn't recommended at this stage.
- Serve only a few tablespoons of pureed cottage cheese, mixed with apricot puree (or one of your choice) to start with, it can be very rich for little tummies.

Beets

Your son or daughter will be sure to love the vibrant colors of beets, which makes for a really fun meal time!

Ingredients

- 2 beets

How to make

- Wash thoroughly and remove greens.
- Place in steaming basket with an inch or two of water in the bottom of pan, you may also boil depending on your preference.
- Steam or boil until tender, remove from heat and drain. If you are steaming keep an eye on water level as you may need to refill as you are steaming.
- Typically, you check for tenderness by stabbing your vegetable, try to avoid stabbing this one too much because they "bleed" every time you do – use the knife to check the 'springiness' of the skin instead.
- Once drained plunge them into cold water to stop cooking and so they are cool enough to handle.
- Once cool peel off the skins and then cut into small chunks.
- Place cooked beets in appliance of your choice and puree. Add liquid as needed to achieve desired consistency.

Peek-a-Boo Beef!

A meaty meal for baby who will certainly love this teamed with their favorite vegetable puree.

How to make

Ingredients

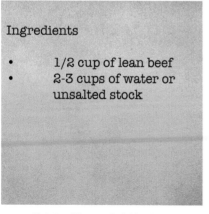

- 1/2 cup of lean beef
- 2-3 cups of water or unsalted stock

- Clean and cut beef into small chunks (again this can be seasoned if required but not with salt).
- In a saucepan add water or unsalted stock (enough to cover the beef) and bring to the boil.
- Cover and reduce to a simmer for 25-30 minutes.
- Once soft and cooked through, drain and remove from heat (save any leftover liquid).
- Allow to cool.
- Blend ingredients until pureed, adding liquid as needed.

Choosy Cherub's Chickpeas

A source of protein, fiber, vitamins and minerals. Lightly spiced and moreish!

Ingredients

- 1 cup of carrots washed, peeled, cubed and steamed.
- 1 cup of green beans washed and steamed.
- 1 cup of chickpeas, cooked
- A sprinkle of mild curry powder

How to make

- Blend all ingredients until pureed, using a little boiling water as you're blending.
- Serve– just ensure you've tested the temperature before feeding your baby!

Oregano Squash and Rice Soup

A little Italian meal.

Ingredients

- 1 cup butternut squash washed, peeled and cubed
- 1/2 cup coconut water
- 1/4 cup cooked brown rice
- 2 tbsp homemade yogurt
- 1 tsp oregano (dried or fresh)

How to make

- Preheat oven to 400°F / 200°C / Gas Mark 6.
- Bake butternut squash, sprinkled with oregano, for 35 - 40 minutes.
- Blend squash and coconut water until it begins to puree.
- Add rice and yogurt until pureed.
- Process ingredients to a consistency that baby will be happy with, typically on the runnier side.

Delicious Apple, Buckwheat and Mint Puree

The mint adds a fresh zinginess to this dish. Give it a go!

Ingredients

- 2 apples washed, peeled and cubed.
- 1 cup buckwheat, cooked
- 1 tbsp of mint

How to make

- Blend all ingredients until pureed. Add your choice of water, breast milk, formula or even coconut water to loosen the mixture if needed.
- Serve cold or heat using a little boiling water as you're blending – just ensure you've tested it before feeding your baby!

Amazing Cheesy Eggplant Puree

Greek-inspired!

Ingredients

- 1 eggplant
- 1 tbsp of grated cheese
- 1 tbsp of olive oil

How to make

- Preheat your oven to 375°F / 190°C /Gas Mark 5.
- Wash and slice your eggplant into baby-size pieces and lightly drizzle olive oil on the top.
- Bake in oven for 35 minutes or until really soft.
- Sprinkle cheese on the top and bake for a further 5 minutes.
- Allow to cool and puree.

Lovely Rosemary Chicken and Sweet Potato Stew

Hearty dish full of protein and nutrients.

Ingredients

- 2 cups sweet potato, washed, peeled and cubed
- 2 small chicken breasts, diced
- 1 sprig rosemary (fresh) or 1 tbsp dried rosemary

How to make

- Preheat oven to 400°F / 200°C / Gas Mark 6.
- Wrap chicken individually in baking paper or tin foil with the rosemary sprinkled inside.
- Place chicken on a baking tray for 20-25 minutes or until completely cooked through.
- Meanwhile steam sweet potato for 30 mins.
- Place cooked chicken and sweet potato in appliance of your choice and puree. Add liquid as needed to achieve desired consistency. You may use water or a splash of unsalted chicken stock for flavor.

Starry Chicken and Vegetable Soup

This can be combined to form a warming soup or blended completely to form a puree.

Ingredients

- 1/2 cup cooked and pureed chicken pg.63
- 1 cup star pasta
- 1 cup green beans and carrots (mixed), washed, peeled and sliced

How to make

- Cook pasta according to package instructions (add on 5 extra minutes to ensure the pasta is extremely soft).
- Steam the vegetables over the pasta for the last 10-15 minutes or until soft.
- Turn off the heat and leave pasta to sit in the water for an extra minute before draining (save the water).
- Very lightly blend vegetables or cut them into much smaller and more manageable pieces.
- Combine chicken, vegetables and pasta to make a delicious soup using the water from the pasta - you can blend this further to make it easier on baby.

Super Apple & Banana Quinoa

A healthy and hearty breakfast or lunchtime dish. Quinoa is a complete protein and wheat free!

Ingredients

- 1/4 cup of apple, peeled and cubed
- 1/2 banana
- 3 tbsp of ground quinoa
- 1/3 cup boiling water

How to make

- Steam apples for 20-25 minutes.
- Drain and set aside (save the water).
- Peel and cut banana into slices.
- Mix boiling water and quinoa in a separate bowl.
- Blend quinoa and fruit until pureed – add saved water if needed.
- Serve warm.

Amazing Apple & Blueberry Mix

Fruity and delightful.

Ingredients

- 1/2 cup of blueberries washed
- 2 apples washed, peeled and cut into small chunks
- 1 tbsp freshly chopped ginger (fresh or ground)

How to make

- Place fruit and ginger in steaming basket with an inch or two of water in the bottom of pan.
- Steam or boil for 20-25 minutes or until tender, remove from heat and drain. Keep an eye on water levels, as you may need to refill as you are steaming.
- Set aside any leftover water for later.
- Place cooked fruits in appliance of your choice and puree. Add left over liquid as needed to achieve desired consistency.
- Serve warm. Fold through homemade yogurt for a creamier treat.

Bountiful Banana and Berry Surprise

A Tropical Twist!

Ingredients

- 1 banana
- 1 cup berries

How to make

- Peel and slice banana, rinse berries well. Make sure to use berries that your little one has eaten already if you have allergy concerns.
- Place in steaming basket with an inch or two of water in the bottom of a pan, you may also boil depending on your preference. Your little one may be advanced enough to have berries without steaming them so use your judgment.
- Steam or boil for 5-10 minutes or until tender, remove from heat and drain. If you are steaming keep an eye on water level as you may need to refill.
- Set aside any leftover water for later.
- Place cooked fruits in appliance of your choice and puree. Add left over liquid as needed to achieve desired consistency.
- Serve warm or cold.

Victorious Vanilla and Pear Oatmeal

Vanilla is a natural extract which is great as an alternative for all of those added sugar baby foods you'll find in the stores.

Ingredients

- 1 vanilla pod or
- extract (don't use 'pure' vanilla extracts as they often contain alcohol)
- 3 tbsp ground oatmeal
- 1 washed, peeled and cubed pear
- 1/3 cup boiling water, breast milk or formula

How to make

- You may steam pears if you desire but as you have probably introduced pear by now, you are fine to use raw pear.
- Mix boiling water and oatmeal.
- Blend oatmeal mix with the pear (scrape the vanilla extract from the pod straight into the blender).
- Serve warm – remember to check the boiling water has cooled enough for your baby by testing it yourself.

Perfect Apple and Nutmeg Oatmeal

Nutmeg can soothe indigestion and relieve pain. It tastes great with its fruity friends, given that it didn't fall too far from the tree (nutmegs grow on evergreen trees).

Ingredients

- 6 tbsp ground oatmeal
- 1 tsp ground nutmeg (freshly grated or dried)
- 2 steamed or very ripe apples
- 2/3 cup boiling water, breast milk or formula

How to make

- Mix boiling water and oatmeal.
- Blend oatmeal mix with the apples (raw or steamed).
- Serve warm with a light dusting of nutmeg– remember to check the boiling water has cooled enough for your baby by testing it yourself.

Fruity Oaty Quinoa

Fruit goes wonderfully with quinoa and is so healthy!

Ingredients

- 4 tbsp ground oatmeal
- 1 cup washed blueberries (steamed)
- 2 tbsp ground quinoa
- 2/3 cup boiling water, breast milk or formula

How to make

- Mix boiling water, oatmeal and quinoa.
- Blend ingredients with the steamed blueberries.
- Serve warm– remember to check the boiling water has cooled enough for your baby by testing it yourself.

Fruity Flavorsome Yogurt

A lovely creamy yogurt recipe, perfect for breakfast or snack time.

Ingredients

- 1 cup washed and cooked blueberries
- 2 pears, washed, peeled and cubed
- ¼ cup of homemade yogurt (pg 76)
- 1 tsp of nutmeg
- 1 tbsp ground barley

How to make

- Blend blueberries and pears with the yogurt until pureed (once your baby is eating chunkier foods you can simply stir in the blueberries and finely chopped pear to make a quick and easy snack).
- Serve with a sprinkle of ground barley and nutmeg for a delicious crunchy finish.

Tasty Tropical Treat

Send your baby to the Caribbean with this exotic tasting wonder!

Ingredients

- 1 cup apricots (steamed)
- 2 peaches (steamed)
- 1 cup watermelon cubed (steamed)
- ¼ cup coconut water or milk

How to make

- Blend all ingredients until pureed.
- Serve cold!

Quinoa and Banana Oatmeal

A perfect breakfast treat!

Ingredients

- 2 tbsp ground oatmeal
- 1/2 cup chopped banana
- 1 tbsp ground quinoa
- 1/3 cup boiling water, breast milk or formula

How to make

- You may steam banana if you desire, rinse well prior to use.
- Mix boiling water, oatmeal and quinoa in a separate bowel.
- Blend oatmeal mixture and banana until pureed, adding the liquid as required.
- Serve warm – remember to check the boiling water has cooled enough for your baby by testing it yourself.

Bold Beef & Veg Puree

Iron and nutrients galore!

Ingredients

- ½ cup of ground beef
- ½ cup of peas
- ½ cup of chopped carrots

How to make

- Heat a pan on a medium to high heat and add the peas, carrots and ground beef. Then add just enough water to cover. Let the beef and veg cook until soft and tender which should be around 20-25 minutes.
- Remove the beef mix and place the leftover water to one side.
- Add the meat mix to a blender and puree adding the left over water until a smooth consistency is reached.

Quinoa Medley

Try sprucing up your baby's quinoa with a selection of their favorite fruits.

Ingredients

- 1/2 cup of apple chunks washed, peeled and cubed
- 1/2 avocado peeled and cubed
- 2 tbsp of ground oatmeal
- 1 tbsp of ground quinoa
- 2/3 cup boiling water, breast milk or baby formula

How to make

- You may steam apples if you wish, rinse them well prior to use.
- Mix boiling water, quinoa and oatmeal.
- Place oatmeal, quinoa and fruit in appliance of your choice and blend until you have a smooth consistency. You may add more water or oatmeal depending on your preference of consistency.
- Serve warm – test the water temperature yourself first!

Amazing White Popping Potato Puree

Creamy and flavorsome!

Ingredients

- 1 white potato

How to make

- Wash the potato and puncture the skin with a fork, creating pin pricks all over.
- Wrap in foil or baking paper.
- Place in oven on 400°F / 200°C / Gas Mark 6 and bake for 30 minutes or until very soft.
- Alternatively you can steam your potato:
- Peel your potato and cut into cubes.
- Place cubes of potato in to a pan of water, just enough to lightly cover them.
- Steam the potatoes until they are tender; make sure to keep an eye on the water level as you may have to top up.
- Drain and set aside any left over water for later.
- Blend potato until pureed (if you baked your potato you will need to scoop out the flesh from the skin before blending).
- Add reserved water from steaming as needed whilst blending. You can use breast milk or baby formula here instead if you wish.

Vanilla and Cinnamon Apple Yogurt

Fruity and spicy at the same time.

Ingredients

- 1 cup apple chunks washed, peeled and cubed
- 1 cup homemade yogurt (pg 76)
- 1 vanilla pod or essence (not the pure version from stores)
- 1 tsp cinnamon

How to make

- Place apple and vanilla in appliance of your choice and blend to a chunky consistency. You may need to add a bit of water if the apples aren't very juicy.
- Fold apple vanilla mixture into yogurt and serve with a sprinkle of cinnamon.

Delicious Broccoli & White Potato

Garlicky and delicious.

Ingredients

- 1 white potato, peeled and cubed
- 1 steamed chopped broccoli
- 1 tsp of minced garlic

How to make

- Get a pan and boil the white potatoes for 25 - 30 minutes until tender.
- Add the potato, garlic and broccoli to a processer and puree.

Bubbly Blueberry Oatmeal

Mouthwatering breakfast – adults enjoy this too!

Ingredients

- 1/4 cup of blueberries
- 3 tbsp of ground oatmeal
- 1/3 cup boiling water, breast milk or formula

How to make

- Rinse blueberries and steam for 5-10 minutes if you're just starting your baby with blueberries.
- Mix liquid and oatmeal together in a separate bowl.
- Blend oatmeal with blueberries until pureed.
- Serve warm – test on the back of your hand to make sure the boiling water has cooled enough.

Chunky Cinnamon Apple Oatmeal

Louis loved this one!

Ingredients

- 6 tbsp ground oatmeal
- 1 tsp of cinnamon
- 2 apples, peeled and cubed
- 2/3 cup boiling water

How to make

- You may steam apple if you desire, if they are very ripe and little one is used to eating at this point you can just blend them up raw.
- Mix boiling water and oatmeal in a separate bowl.
- Place oatmeal and apple in appliance of your choice and blend until you have a chunky consistency. You may add more water or oatmeal depending on your preference in thickness.
- Serve warm – remember to test.
- Sprinkle very lightly with cinnamon.

Wheat Germ and Mango Yogurt

Wheat germ is high in Vitamin E which has antioxidant properties. It tastes great with mango.

Ingredients

- 4 tbsp of wheat germ
- 1 teaspoon cinnamon
- 1/2 mango peeled and cubed
- 1 cup homemade yogurt (pg76)

How to make

- You may steam mango if you desire, if they are very ripe and little one is used to eating at this point you can just blend them up raw.
- Place wheat germ, cinnamon and mango in appliance of your choice and blend until you have a chunky consistency.
- Fold your mixture into the yogurt mixing well.

Berries and Beets

The combination of berries and beets is superb – this will form a beautiful deep purple puree which your baby will just love tucking into!

Ingredients

- 1 cup blueberries, washed
- 2 medium beets washed and steamed

How to make

- Blend beets and berries until pureed.
- Serve cold or warm through for 30 seconds in the microwave.

Amazing Peaches and Cream

Sweet and tempting.

Ingredients

- 2 peaches washed and chopped
- 2 apples washed, peeled and chopped
- 1 ripe banana
- 2 tbsp homemade yogurt (pg76)

How to make

- Peel and slice banana, apple and peach.
- Place apple and peach in steaming basket with an inch or two of water in bottom of pan.
- Steam for 20-25 minutes or until tender, remove from heat and drain.
- Set aside any leftover water for later.
- Place cooked or raw fruit and yogurt in appliance of your choice and blend, larger chunks are okay. Add left over liquid (you can also use coconut water for a nice twist) as needed to achieve desired consistency.

Oriental Coconut Chicken

A Taste of the Orient!

Ingredients

- 2 small chicken breasts
- 1/2 cup shredded un-sweetened coconut
- 1/4 cup coconut milk/ water

How to make

- Cut chicken into small chunks.
- Place chicken in a shallow pan and cook with a few drops of coconut oil (you may decide to boil the chicken depending on your preference).
- Cook or boil on a medium to high heat for 25-30 minutes or until cooked through and tender.
- Remove from heat and drain if needed.
- Blend cooled chicken with the coconut, adding coconut milk or water if needed to create a smoother consistency.

chapter eight

A Growing APPETITE

It is now time to introduce a few more foods as well as thickening the texture of your baby's meals even more. At this stage your baby will have more teeth and will be able to swallow foods more easily. They might even be starting to try to use a spoon themselves!

A Growing Appetite (10-12 Months)

It is now time to introduce a few more foods as well as thickening the texture of your baby's meals even more. At this stage your baby will have more teeth and will be able to swallow foods more easily. They might even be starting to try to use a spoon themselves – a great time to introduce small chunks!

Foods you can introduce..

Fruits

Strawberries

Vegetables

Beans (Lentils / Dried)
Corn
Spinach
Tomatoes

Meat

Fish

Dairy

Cow Milk

Serving Size

Choose 2-3 options from the following servings and increase as baby gets older:

2-4 tablespoons of cereals up to 3x per day
3-4 tablespoons of fruit up to 2x per day
3-4 tablespoons of veg up to 2x per day
3-4 tablespoons of chicken, beef or pork up to 2x per day
¼ cup of cheese (cottage or cheddar)

Strengthening Spinach Sauce

Containing calcium, iron and selenium which plays a key role in the metabolism, spinach can be introduced from 8 months old and upward. Use moderately at first until you are confident that it agrees with your baby.

Ingredients

- 1 cup fresh or frozen spinach (fresh is best but frozen will work just as well)

How to make

- Wash the fresh spinach and pat dry using a clean cloth or kitchen towel.
- Place in steaming basket with an inch or two of water in the bottom of pan; you may also boil depending on your preference.
- Steam or boil for 5 minutes until slightly wilted, remove from heat and drain. If you are steaming keep an eye on water levels, as you may need to top up.
- Set aside any leftover water for later.
- Place cooked spinach in appliance of your choice and puree. Add left over liquid as needed to achieve desired consistency.

Meaty Rice and Loving Lentils

Lentils are a great addition to most meats and keep your baby energized for longer.

Ingredients

- 2 cups of cooked brown rice (cook according to package instructions)
- 2 cups of cooked lentils (cook according to pack age instructions)
- 2 chopped apples
- 3 chopped carrots

How to make

- Get a saucepan and add the apples and carrots. Add water until the fruits are covered and place on the hob and cook for 25 - 30 minutes until fruits are tender .
- Remove the fruits from the saucepan and add to a blender along with the cooked brown rice and cooked lentils and puree. Add the left over water from the pan until the desired consistency is achieved.

Delicious Apple, Peach and Strawberry Jam

Sweet and tempting.

Ingredients

- 2 peaches washed and chopped.
- 2 apples washed, peeled and chopped.
- 1 ripe banana
- 2 tbsp homemade yogurt pg. 76
- 1 cup sliced strawberries

How to make

- Wash all fruit.
- Steam fruit if you wish although this is not necessary especially with very ripe fruits.
- Blend cooked or raw fruit until combined -larger chunks are okay. Use coconut water or milk to make a thinner consistency if you wish.
- Serve alone or as a yogurt topper.

Sunny Strawberry Beets

A delicious blend.

Ingredients

- 1 cup sliced strawberries
- 2 beets, peeled and sliced

How to make

- Prep beet and rinse strawberries.
- Place beet and strawberries in steaming basket with an inch or two of water in the bottom of pan. Steaming strawberries is optional.
- Steam for 15-20 minutes or until tender, remove from heat and drain. If you are steaming keep an eye on water level as you may need to refill as you are steaming.
- Remember not to poke your beet too much while you steam or your beet will "bleed".
- Drain and allow to cool (don't keep the water because of the nitrate levels as previously explained for carrots).
- Blend beets with strawberries.
- Serve cold or warmed through in microwave.

Sweet Corn Surprise

It is usually recommended to wait until at least 10 months to give your baby corn. The carbohydrate levels mean this is an energizing food, perhaps best served earlier in the day.

Ingredients

- 1 ear of corn (1 cup frozen sweet corn is also fine)

How to make

- Cut corn kernels away from cob or you may leave it whole and cut them away after cooking - the easiest way I have found to remove the kernels from the corn is to stand it up on its end, then holding it on a diagonal, cut the kernels off using a knife. Hold the blade flat cutting from one end to the other.
- Place in steaming basket with an inch or two of water in the bottom of pan - you may also boil depending on your preference.
- Steam or boil for 7-10 minutes or until tender, remove from heat and drain. If you are steaming keep an eye on water level as you may need to top up.
- Set aside any leftover water for later.
- Place cooked kernels in appliance of your choice and puree. Add left over liquid as needed to achieve desired consistency.

Quinoa Salad

So healthy and fulfilling – quinoa is a delicious complete protein so no need to add meat!

Ingredients

- 1 cup cooked quinoa
- ½ cup baked apples, chopped
- ½ cup butternut squash cooked and chopped
- ½ cup sweet potato cooked and chopped
- ½ avocado, peeled and chopped
- 1 beef tomato, peeled and chopped

How to make

- Combine all ingredients in a blender for 30 seconds and serve cold.

Super Sweetness

Herby and nutritious.

Ingredients

- 1 ear of corn
- 1 sweet potato
- 1 tsp finely chopped basil (fresh or dried)

How to make

- Cut corn kernels away from cob or you may leave it whole and cut them away after cooking.
- Clean, peel and cut sweet potato into chunks.
- Place corn and potato in steaming basket with an inch or two of water in the bottom of pan, you may also boil depending on your preference.
- Steam or boil for 25-30 minutes until tender, remove from heat and drain. Set aside any leftover water for later.
- Place basil, cooked kernels and sweet potato in appliance of your choice and puree. Add left over liquid as needed to achieve desired consistency.

Green Pepper, Black Bean & Sweet Potato

A multi-colored feast!

Ingredients

- 1 white onion
- 1 tbsp dried thyme
- 1 green pepper washed and finely chopped
- 2 cups washed, peeled and cubed sweet potatoes
- 1 cup black beans, drained and rinsed

How to make

- With a pan on a medium high heat, throw onion and thyme into a little olive oil and cook for 5 minutes until soft but not browned.
- Now add the pepper and sweet potato cubes for a further 10 minutes.
- Stir in beans and cook until potatoes are soft for another 5 minutes.
- Mash together to make this easier for baby to eat.
- Serve warm.

Moorish Cheesy Chicken Pasta

Deliciously creamy and satisfying.

Ingredients

- 1 cup cooked and finely chopped chicken
- 1/2 cup cottage cheese
- ¼ cup breast milk or formula
- 1 cup cooked and cooled pasta
- ¼ cup steamed and

How to make

- Preheat oven to 350°F / 180°C / Gas Mark 4.
- Mix cottage cheese and milk until lumps are smooth.
- Combine other ingredients in an oven dish.
- Pour over cheese milk.
- Bake in oven for 30 minutes or until slightly golden.
- Serve warm and ensure it is small enough for baby to eat.

Exotic Yogurt

This one includes a little coconut milk to sweeten up your yogurt – a lovely dessert or breakfast.

Ingredients

- 1 banana peeled and chopped
- 1 cup strawberries washed and sliced
- 1 cup homemade yogurt (p76)
- 1/2 cup homemade coconut milk (pg71)

How to make

- Prep and cut your strawberry and banana.
- With a fork mash your fruit into very small chunks. As long as your fruit is nice and ripe it should mash with no problem (you can also throw into the microwave for 15 seconds to help soften them up if you need).
- Mix your fruit, coconut milk and yogurt together to create a chunky and interesting yogurt with delicious and sweet fruit.
- If you wish to thicken it up use a little rice cereal.

Yummy Oregano and Corn Rice

Making your baby's rice more exciting.

Ingredients

- 2 ears of corn, washed and steamed
- 1 cup ground brown rice cooked
- 1 tsp finely chopped oregano (fresh or dried)

How to make

- Blend all ingredients until pureed, using a little boiling water as you're blending.
- Serve- just ensure you've tested the temperature before feeding your baby!

Green Greatness

Sweet and strengthening main meal or side dish once your baby gets a little older.

Ingredients

- 1 apple washed, peeled and sliced
- 2/3 cup raw or frozen spinach
- 2 kiwis

How to make

- Wash, peel and cut up apple and kiwi, rinse spinach.
- Place apples in steaming basket with an inch or two of water in bottom of pan, you may also boil depending on your preference.
- Steam or boil on a medium heat for 20-25 minutes until tender.
- Add the spinach to the steamer for the last 5-10 minutes. Remove from heat and drain.
- Set aside any leftover water for later.
- Place cooked fruit and spinach in appliance of your choice and puree. Add left over liquid as needed to achieve desired consistency.

Banana and Avocado Pancakes

Super healthy pancakes for little fingers.

Ingredients

- 1/2 ripe avocado
- 2 very ripe bananas
- 2 egg yolks
- ½ cup homemade yogurt (pg 76)

How to make

- Mix banana and avocado with egg yolks.
- Fold in the yogurt.
- In a pan, heat a little coconut oil on a low to medium heat.
- Use a teaspoon to pour tiny pancake portions into the pan.
- Cook for 1-2 minutes on each side until cooked through but not crispy (these should be soft enough for your baby to manage).

Yellow Lentil and Butternut Squash

Bursting with colour and flavor – your baby is sure to love this meal.

Ingredients

- 1 cup of butternut squash washed, peeled, cubed & steamed
- 1 cup of yellow lentils, washed and cooked
- 1 tbsp dill (fresh and finely chopped or dried)

How to make

- Blend all ingredients until pureed, using a little boiling water as you're blending.
- Serve– just ensure you've tested the temperature before feeding your baby!

Bouncy Banana, Apple, Strawberry

Pick-Me-Up!

Ingredients

- 1 cup strawberries sliced
- 2 apples, peeled and sliced
- 1 banana, peeled and sliced

How to make

- Steam fruit beforehand if you wish. Some parents like to continue steaming fruit, especially strawberries if concerned about these. Consult your pediatrician to make sure.
- Blend until pureed.
- If your baby is now eating chunkier foods you can just mash these fruits together for a quick and tasty snack.

Soothing Strawberry & Rutabaga

Sweet and savory works wonders.

Ingredients

- 2/3 cup strawberries sliced
- 1 cup rutabaga washed, peeled and cubed

How to make

- Thoroughly wash your rutabaga before peeling the skin off, then cut into small chunks. Remember rutabagas can be slippery while you're cutting so don't be afraid to cut a small chunk off the bottom to give it a flat side for you to hold.
- Wash and slice your strawberries.
- Place rutabaga in steaming basket with an inch or two of water in the bottom of a pan, you may also boil depending on your preference. You do not have to steam the strawberries if you don't want to.
- Steam or boil for 25-30 minutes until tender, remove from heat and drain.
- Set aside any leftover water for later.
- Place all your ingredients in an appliance of your choice and puree; choose between a smooth or chunky consistency. Add left over liquid as needed to achieve desired consistency.

Spiced Pumpkin and Red Lentil

A wonderful autumnal dish - full of vitamins and minerals.

Ingredients

- 1 cup of pumpkin washed, peeled , cubed and cooked
- 1 cup of red lentils washed, cooked

How to make

- Blend all ingredients until pureed, using a little boiling water as you're blending.
- Serve- just ensure you've tested the temperature before feeding your baby!

Lovely Strawberries and Cream

Strawberries and cream without the unwanted calories.

Ingredients

- 1 cup strawberries sliced
- 1 cup homemade yogurt (pg. 76)

How to make

- Wash and slice your strawberries.
- Place strawberries in appliance of your choice and blend to a nice smooth puree.
- Fold strawberries and yogurt together for a creamy and flavorful treat for your little one (you can also freeze this mixture and make your own popsicles when they're onto solid foods).

Energizing Cumin Black Beans and Butternut Squash

Another digestion aid, cumin also adds a marvelous flavor to vegetables.

Ingredients

- 1 cup of butternut squash washed, peeled , cubed and cooked
- A pinch of ground cumin (fresh or dried)
- 1 cup of black beans washed and cooked

How to make

- Blend all ingredients until pureed, using a little boiling water as you're blending.
- Serve with a pinch of cumin (a strong spice so use tiny amounts at first)-just ensure you've tested the temperature before feeding your baby!

Minty Strawberry Oatmeal

Yes strawberries and mint work well together! This will freshen your strawberries up and can be one of your baby's savory options.

How to make

Ingredients

- 6 tbsp ground oatmeal
- 4 tbsp homemade yogurt (p76) or coconut milk (pg71)
- 2/3 cup strawberries sliced
- 2/3 cup boiling water
- 1 tbsp finely chopped mint (fresh or dried)

- You may steam strawberries if you desire, if they are very ripe and little one is used to eating at this point you can just blend them up raw.
- Mix boiling water and oatmeal in a separate bowl.
- Place mint, oatmeal and strawberries in appliance of your choice and blend until you have a chunky consistency. You may add more water or oatmeal depending on your preference in thickness.
- Serve warm, folding tthrough yogurt or coconut milk.

Delicious Fresh Tomato & Rice Super Soup

This is a wholesome and filling soup dish.

Ingredients

- 1 large red onion, quartered and thinly sliced
- ¼ cup washed and finely chopped celery
- ¼ carrot washed, peeled and diced
- 8 large tomatoes, peeled, seeded, chopped
- 8 cups unsalted chicken stock
- 1/4 cup uncooked long-grain rice or rice blend
- 1 tbsp thyme finely chopped

How to make

- Add onion, carrots and celery to a large pan on a medium heat until softened (5-7 minutes).
- Now throw in the tomatoes and a splash of chicken stock.
- Turn down heat and leave to simmer for 15 minutes.
- Now add the remaining chicken stock, thyme and rice – simmer for a further 20-30 minutes or until rice is soft.
- Serve warm.

Sunny Banana, Mango & Sweet Potato Surprise

Unusual twist but tastes fantastic.

Ingredients

- 1 cup sweet potato washed, peeled and cubed
- 1 banana
- 1 cup mango peeled and cubed

How to make

- Steaming banana and mango is up to you.
- Place sweet potato in steaming basket with an inch or two of water in the bottom of a pan.
- Steam on a medium heat for 20-25 minutes until tender, remove from heat and drain.
- Set aside any leftover water for later.
- Blend sweet potato with fruit until desired consistency is reached.

Beginner Baby Pancakes

You won't be able to wait to get these ones started!

Ingredients

- 2 egg yolks beaten
- 2 ripe bananas
- 1 tbsp coconut oil

How to make

- Mix the banana with your beaten egg yolks until a smooth consistency is formed.
- Heat the coconut oil in a pan on a low to medium heat.
- Pour teaspoon size pancakes into the pan, cooking for 1-2 minutes on each side or until cooked through but not crispy.

Beautiful Blueberry Baby Pancakes

A classic for afters.

How to make

- Mix the banana with your beaten egg yolks until a smooth consistency is formed.
- Mix through the homemade yogurt.
- Blend mix with blueberries until smooth.
- Heat the coconut oil in a pan on a low to medium heat.
- Pour teaspoon size pancakes into the pan, cooking for 1-2 minutes on each side or until cooked through but not crispy.

Ingredients

- 1/2 cup homemade yogurt (pg.76)
- 2 egg yolks
- 1 very ripe banana
- 1 cup blueberries

Crazy Chicken, Brown Rice and Super Squash

Superfood salad.

Ingredients

- 2 small chicken breasts
- 1/2 cup cooked brown rice
- 1/2 cup squash washed, peeled, cubed

How to make

- Cut chicken into small chunks.
- Place chicken and squash in pan and cook with a few drops of olive oil (you may also boil or steam depending on your preference).
- Cook on a medium heat for 20-25 minutes or until chicken completely cooked through and squash is tender.
- Allow to cool.
- Blend cooked chicken, squash and rice for a slightly chunky consistency.
- Add liquid as needed to thin if required. You may use water or a splash of chicken stock for flavor.
- Serve hot.

Porky Pork and Angelic Apples

A dinner time delicacy!

Ingredients

- 1 cup cooked pork (lean cut)
- 1 cup apples, peeled and chopped

How to make

- Pre-cook your pork in the oven according to package guidelines. No need to add oil.
- Once cooled blend pork with apple until you achieve your desired consistency.

Amazing Apple and Sweet Beets

Your baby will love the fruity flavors mixed with the beets.

Ingredients

- 1 cup sliced strawberries
- 2 beets washed and steamed
- 2 apples washed and steamed

How to make

- Combine ingredients in a blender until smooth. If your baby's eating chunky foods by now you can simply mash together the strawberries with the steamed beets and apples.

Delicious Grainy Apple and Sweet Potato

So sweet!

Ingredients

- 1 cup apple washed, peeled and cubed
- 1 cup sweet potato washed, peeled and cubed
- 1/2 cup quinoa or barley (cooked)

How to make

- Prep and cut your apple and sweet potato.
- Place apple and sweet potato in steaming basket with an inch or two of water in bottom of a pan.
- Steam for 20-25 minutes or until tender, remove from heat and drain.
- Set aside any leftover water for later.
- Blend apple, sweet potato, grains and 1/3 cup of leftover water (still very hot).
- Add more left over liquid or grains as needed to achieve desired consistency

Kicking Spicy Tomato Pasta

A little twist on a baby favorite.

Ingredients

- 1 cup dried pasta
- 3 cups water
- 1 cup chopped tomatoes (no added sugar or salt)
- 1 tsp mild curry powder

How to make

- On a high heat, boil water and add pasta to pan, following package instructions for cooking time.
- Turn off the heat and allow pasta to sit in water for an extra few minutes once cooked before draining (this lets pasta get softer for your baby's mouth).
- Drain the water from the pan, reserving a tiny amount in the bottom.
- Stir through the chopped tomatoes and curry powder on a low heat and stir until heated through.
- Serve warm.

My First Mac and Cheese

Speaks for itself!

Ingredients

- 1 cup pasta (macaroni pieces or shells)
- 1 cup cheese (of your choice)
- 1/2 cup of breast milk or formula
- 1 tbsp butter (unsalted)
- 4 cups of water

How to make

- Boil your water and cook pasta according to package directions. You can add a few more minutes to make pasta extra tender for little mouths.
- Drain pasta when done and return to pot.
- Mix in milk, cheese and butter. Stir well.
- Serve warm.

Mediterranean Pasta Medley

A taste of the Mediterranean Sea in your baby's dinner bowl!

Ingredients

- 2 beef tomatoes, chopped
- ½ cooked and chopped zucchini
- ½ cooked eggplant
- 1 cup of pasta (any shape)
- 1/2 teaspoon of coconut oil
- 1 minced garlic clove

How to make

- Boil water and cook pasta according to package directions. You can add a few more minutes to make pasta extra tender for little mouths.
- Clean and cut your tomato, (you can boil it with the pasta, if you wish).
- Drain pasta when done and return it to the pot you cooked it in.
- Mix in tomatoes, garlic, zucchini, eggplant and coconut oil, stirring on a meduim heat for 5 minutes.
- Serve warm.

Brilliant Banana, Pear & Sweet Potato

So sweet!

Ingredients

- 1 banana
- 1 cup of pears washed, peeled and chopped
- 1 cup of sweet potato steamed and cubed

How to make

- Blend until a chunky consistency is formed. Alternatively just use a fork to mash the ingredients and serve.

Kicking Chicken and Rice Broth

Wintery and delicious!

Ingredients

- 1/2 cup cooked chicken pieces
- 1 cup brown rice
- 4 cups unsalted chicken stock

How to make

- Bring 2 cups of chicken stock to a boil on a high heat and add brown rice.
- Turn down to a medium high heat and continue to cook for 20 minutes or until rice is cooked through.
- Remove from the heat and add remaining 2 cups of chicken stock.
- Add cooked chicken, return to the heat, and heat through completely.
- Serve warm as a chunky broth or blend if needed.

Tasty Turkey and Vegetable Soup

Protein and nutrient-bursting soup.

Ingredients

- 1/2 cup cooked turkey pieces
- 1 cup brown rice
- 1 cup green beans and carrots
- 4 cups of chicken stock (unsalted)

How to make

- Bring 2 cups of chicken stock to a boil on a high heat and add brown rice.
- Turn down to a medium high heat and continue to cook for 20 minutes or until rice is cooked through.
- Remove from the heat and add remaining 2 cups of chicken stock.
- Add cooked turkey and vegetables and heat through for another 10 minutes or until heated through completely.
- Serve warm as a chunky broth or blend if needed.

chapter nine

Everyday
BABY FOOD

Hooray! Your little one has
reached a new milestone. This is around the
time they will really be able to sink
their teeth into whatever you're
making. It's always good to start them off
with softer finger foods and solids
and then work them up to more solid foods later;
this will allow your baby
to try new foods gradually and continue their progression
from the last stage of eating chunkier foods and even pastas.

Everyday Baby Food (12+ Months)

Hooray! Your little one has reached a new milestone. This is around the time they will really be able to sink their teeth into whatever you're making. It's always good to start them off with softer finger foods and solids and then work them up to more solid foods later; this will allow your baby to try new foods gradually and continue their progression from the last stage of eating chunkier foods and even pastas. Your son or daughter may already be trying to feed themselves and when you're able to add in finger foods they really start to feel empowered. They'll want to be just like their mommy or daddy, so they'll be showing an interest in your foods and starting to copy you - they'll be so happy when they get to do the same as you! In this chapter I will also be introducing new foods that were previously a little too risky to give your baby. As always, leave a 4-5 day wait between introducing new food types so you can monitor reactions and always consult your pediatrician. I wish you and your baby many happy meal times for years to come and hope these recipes will get you started.

Foods you can introduce..

Fruits

Raspberries

Honey

Nuts (if no family history of allergic reactions)

Citrus

Lovely Chicken and Pineapple Rice

Another tropical fusion – once your baby is able to manage solid foods you can serve this in small chunks and let them chomp away!

Ingredients

- 2 small chicken breasts
- 1/2 cup cooked brown rice
- 1/2 cup pineapple chopped

How to make

- Cut chicken into small chunks.
- Prep and cut your pineapple and prepare the rice according to the package directions.
- Place chicken and pineapple in a pan on a medium to high heat and cook with a few drops of coconut oil for 25-30 minutes or until cooked right through (you may decide to boil the chicken depending on your preference).
- Allow to cool.
- Blend chicken with pineapple and cooked rice. You may use water or a splash of chicken stock, pineapple juice or coconut water for flavor.
- Serve hot but check it won't burn baby.

Punchy Pineapple Sweet Potato

Creamy and nutty with a boost of citrus!

Ingredients

- 1/2 cup pineapple cubed
- 1 medium sweet potato washed, peeled and cubed

How to make

- Prep and cut sweet potato and pineapple.
- Place fruit and potato in steaming basket with an inch or two of water in the bottom of a pan (steaming pineapple is up to you).
- Steam for 20-25 minutes or until tender, remove from heat and drain.
- Set aside any leftover water for later.
- Blend, adding left over liquid or plain water (you can also use coconut water for a nice twist) as needed to achieve desired consistency.

Warming Cinnamon and Honey Oatmeal

As your baby will already be used to oatmeal, the addition of the sweet, runny honey will be a real surprise for their tiny taste buds! Consider waiting until 18 months+ to feed your baby this one as some experts advise this as an extra-precaution to the typical suggestion of 12 months. As with any new foods, always consult your pediatrician if unsure.

Ingredients -

- 8 tbsp ground oatmeal (or unground at this stage)
- 1 tsp of cinnamon
- 2 tsp honey
- 2/3 cup boiling water, breast milk or formula

How to make

- Combine oatmeal and boiling liquid.
- Use unground oats for a thicker consistency here.
- Stir in honey.
- Sprinkle with cinnamon.
- Check temperature before you serve – it can also be a great idea to make this into a fun time to teach your little one to blow on their hot food before eating.

Lovely Pear and Raspberry Oats

Another great snack or breakfast.

Ingredients

- 1/2 cup pear washed, peeled and chopped
- 1/2 cup raspberries washed
- 1 cup ground oats
- 2/3 cup boiling water

How to make

- Peel, wash and cut pear.
- Wash raspberries well.
- Mix oats and boiling water in a separate bowl.
- You can steam your pear but if you're using a ripe one you should be able to mash it up with a fork along with the raspberries.
- Mix oats and fruits together, the boiling water should be cooled by now and your little one will have a nice warm mash to enjoy.

Funny Pasta

Fresh and zingy!

Ingredients

- 2 beef tomatoes, finely chopped
- 1/2 lemon, juiced
- 1 cup of pasta (any shape)
- 1/2 teaspoon of coconut oil
- 1 tsp tarragon

How to make

- Boil water and cook pasta according to package directions (you can add a few more minutes to make the pasta extra tender for little mouths).
- Drain pasta when done and return it to the pot you cooked it in.
- Mix in the tomatoes, coconut oil, lemon juice and tarragon
- Mix well and serve immediately.

Thoughtful Banana, Nutmeg and Flaxseed

Fruity and wholesome.

Ingredients

- 1 banana
- 1 tsp nutmeg, grated or dried
- 1 tsp milled flaxseed

How to make

- Mash all ingredients together with a fork and serve! Tastes great with a little homemade yogurt.

Pear, Banana, Raspberry and Flax Seed

A great fruity punch for your beautiful baby.

Ingredients

- 1 cup raspberries
- 2 pears
- 1 ripe banana
- 2 tsp milled flax seeds

How to make

- Peel and slice banana and pear.
- Steam fruit if you wish although this is not necessary
- especially with very ripe fruit. Place cooked or raw fruit and flax seeds in appliance of your choice and blend (larger chunks are okay).
- You can add coconut water for a nice twist to achieve desired consistency.

Lovely Homemade Muesli Bircher

A European favorite – this sweet and tasty snack is so satisfying and packed with goodness.

Ingredients

- 2 tbsp ground oatmeal (unsweetened)
- 2 tbsp. ground barley
- 1/2 cup unsweetened grape juice
- ¼ cup raisins
- 1/2 cup homemade yogurt (pg76)

How to make

- Mix ingredients well and transfer to a sealed container.
- Refrigerate overnight and serve in the morning for breakfast. The cereal should be nice and soft by now.

Caribbean Coconut and Pineapple Breakfast Oatmeal

This Caribbean inspired meal is going to give your baby energy for the whole day.

Ingredients

- 6 tbsp ground oatmeal
- 2/3 cup cubed pineapple
- 4 tbsp homemade coconut milk. (pg71)
- 2/3 cup boiling water

How to make

- Optional – steam pineapple on a medium heat for 15-20
- minutes or until soft.
- Meanwhile mix boiling water and oatmeal in a separate bowl.
- Blend oatmeal, pineapple and coconut milk until smooth (you can leave this slightly chunky now that your baby is older).
- Serve warm - it's always best to test.
- You can add additional fruit and yogurt toppings to suit your baby's appetite!

Homemade Tropical Breakfast Cereal

Breakfast is the most important meal of the day!

Ingredients

- 3 tbsp ground oatmeal
- 1 tsp flax seed
- 1/2 cup mango
- 1/2 cup pineapple
- 2/3 cup boiling water

How to make

- You may steam fruit if you desire.
- Mix boiling water and oatmeal in a separate bowl.
- Place oatmeal, flaxseed and fruit in appliance of your choice and blend until you have a chunky consistency.
- Serve warm – remember to test before giving to your baby!

Tot's Homemade Ice Cream

Shop bought ice cream is a no-go for your baby but the good news is you can treat them to your own delicious homemade version!

Ingredients

- 4 very ripe bananas, peeled and sliced
- 1 avocado peeled and cut into small pieces
- ½ cup raspberries
- 1 vanilla pod (optional)
- 2/3 cup homemade coconut milk (pg71)
- 4 tsp coconut oil.

How to make

- Blend all ingredients in a blender until smooth and then place in a sealed container in the freezer for at least one hour.
- Take out and serve.

Coconut and Pineapple Breakfast Barley

Another tasty start to the day!

Ingredients

- 6 tbsp ground barley
- 2/3 cup cubed pineapple
- 4 tablespoons homemade coconut milk (pg71)
- 2/3 cup boiling water
- 1/4 cup of raisins

How to make

- Mix boiling water and barley in a separate bowl.
- Blend barley, pineapple, raisins and coconut milk until smooth (you can leave this slightly chunky now that your baby is older).
- Serve warm.

Delicious Pineapple & Avocado Puree

Very tasty!

Ingredients

- 1 cup pineapple (fresh)
- 1 avocado

How to make

- Wash, remove skins and cut pineapple and avocado.
- Blend pineapple with avocado until pureed.
- If your baby is now eating small finger foods or chunkier foods you can simply mush these two ingredients together with a fork.

Nutty Nutmeg & Pineapple with Banana

Taste bud sensation!

Ingredients

- 1 cup pineapple
- 1 banana
- 1 tsp nutmeg (dried or freshly grated)
- 1 tsp of honey

How to make

- Prep and cut pineapple and banana.
- Blend pineapple with banana until desired consistency is reached. Top with nutmeg & drizzle with honey to serve.

Vanilla Pineapple and Pear

Soft and creamy pud!

Ingredients

- 1 cup pineapple
- 2 pears
- 1 vanilla pod

How to make

- Prep and cut pineapple and peel and cut pears.
- Steam pineapple and pears if you wish.
- Blend fruits with the vanilla from the pod, until desired consistency is reached.

Dreamy Pineapple and Papaya Yogurt

Fresh and fruity dessert!

Ingredients

- 1 cup pineapple peeled and cubed
- 1 cup papaya peeled and cubed
- 1 cup homemade yogurt (pg 76)

How to make

- Wash and cut up your pineapple and papaya.
- Steam pineapple and papaya if you wish.
- Blend fruits together until desired consistency is reached.
- Fold into yogurt.

Fruity Fruit Smoothie

A refreshing drink for your little one!

Ingredients

- 1/4 cup mango
- 1/4 cup raspberry
- 1/4 cup homemade yogurt (pg 76)

How to make

- Prep all your fruits with necessary washing and cutting.
- Place all your fruit, raw or cooked in appliance of your choice with yogurt and blend.
- You may need to add a little coconut water, as this mixture can get thick. Blend it all together for a delightful drink for your baby

Cuddly Cottage Cheese and Pineapple

Great for lunch time!

Ingredients

- 1 cup pineapple
- 1 cup cottage cheese

How to make

- Prep and cut your pineapple in chunks.
- Place pineapple in appliance of your choice and blend to a chunky mixture.
- Mix together the pineapple and cottage cheese.
- Serve.

Super Strawberry, Pineapple and Yogurt

Super baby food!

Ingredients

- 1/2 cup strawberry slices
- 1/2 cup pineapple chunks
- 1 cup yogurt

How to make

- Wash and cut strawberries and pineapple.
- Place strawberries and pineapple in appliance of your choice and blend to a nice smooth puree or a chunky consistency - both will work for this recipe.
- Mix everything together with your yogurt and serve.

Amazing Apple, Pineapple & Sweet Potato

Fresh and fun!

Ingredients

- 1 cup sweet potato washed, peeled and cubed
- 2 apples washed, peeled and cubed
- 1/2 cup pineapple cubed

How to make

- Steaming pineapple and apple is up to you, remember if your little one is okay with raw fruit they will get more nutrients than they would if you cooked it.
- Place sweet potato in steaming basket with an inch or two of water in the bottom of a pan.
- Steam on a medium heat for 20-25 minutes until tender, remove from heat and drain.
- Set aside any leftover water for later. Blend sweet potato with fruit until desired consistency is reached, adding a little water as needed and serve.

Woodland Berry and Black Beans

Berries and beans combine to create a thicker textured puree which is very filling & tasty.

Ingredients

- 2 cups blackberries, washed and steamed
- 2 apples washed, peeled and cubed.
- 1 cup cooked black beans, cooked
- 1 tbsp all spice

How to make

- Blend all ingredients until pureed. Add your choice of water, breast milk, formula or even coconut water to loosen the mixture if needed.
- Serve cold or heat using a little boiling water as you're blending – just ensure you've tested it before feeding your baby!

Spicy Lamb Meatballs

This can be made for the whole family!

Ingredients

- 1 small red onion, finely chopped
- 1 tbsp olive oil
- 1 garlic clove, crushed
- ½ tsp curry powder
- 2 cups of lean minced lamb
- 2 tsp chopped fresh parsley leaves
- 1 tsp clear honey
- 1 egg yolk

How to make

- Beat the eggs in a bowl and mix in garlic, herbs and spices.
- Use your hands to roll small meatball size balls of minced lamb and onions and dip in the egg mix to bind it together.
- On a medium heat, drizzle a little olive oil into a shallow pan.
- Plop the meatballs into the pan and brown on all sides.
- Continue to cook for 25-30 minutes or until completely cooked through. Make sure there is no pink meat left in the middle.
- Serve warm with a wholemeal pitta or cooked pasta of your choice.

The Mighty Bolognaise

Another dinner time staple.

Ingredients

- 1 cup of cooked wholemeal pasta or spaghetti
- 1 tsp olive oil
- ¼ onion finely diced
- 2 cups of lean minced beef
- ½ cup of tomatoes chopped
- ¼ cup unsweetened stock.
- 1 tsp basil finely chopped

How to make

- On a medium high heat, drizzle a little olive oil into a shallow pan.
- Cook the onions for 5 minutes or until softened.
- Now add the minced beef, stirring until completely browned.
- Stir in the tomatoes and a splash of unsweetened stock.
- Stir in the sauce, cover and cook covered for 2 minutes.
- Add the basil and turn down to a simmer, allowing to cook through for a further 25 minutes or until completely done.
- Serve on top of pasta.

Porky Pork with Spinach and Lentils

Flavorsome and healthy.

Ingredients

- 1 pork fillet
- 1/2 cup spinach
- 1 cup lentils
- 1 tbsp homemade yogurt (pg. 76)

How to make

- Cook pork to packet instructions and chop into very small pieces.
- Meanwhile, steam lentils for 20-25 minutes or until cooked through.
- Add spinach to steamer/pot for last 5 minutes until wilted.
- Mix spinach and pork into cooked lentils and top with a serving of homemade yogurt – yum!

Homemade Bean Stew

A vegetarian dish, also delicious enough for meat-eaters!

Ingredients

- 1/4 cup butterbeans cooked
- ¼ cup of chickpeas cooked
- 2 beef tomatoes chopped
- ½ red onion finely chopped
- 1 garlic clove, minced
- 1 tsp oregano
- 1/2 fresh lime

How to make

- Drizzle a little olive oil in a pan on a medium heat and sweat onions and garlic for 10 minutes until softened.
- Add in the beans and chickpeas and stir through until hot.
- Now time to add the chopped tomatoes, oregano and a splash of water.
- Turn the heat to a simmer and allow to thicken for 15
- minutes.
- Serve with the juice of ½ lime and some freshly chopped herbs of your choice.

Lovely Chicken Tray Bake

Mediterranean-inspired.

Ingredients

- 2 chicken breasts, diced
- 1/2 zucchini chopped
- 1 red onion chopped
- 1 cup chopped tomatoes
- 1 tsp dried thyme
- ½ cup sweet potato peeled and cubed

How to make

- Preheat oven to 375°F / 190°C /Gas Mark 5.
- In a baking dish, throw in all of your ingredients and toss with a little olive oil.
- Top up with water to just cover ingredients.
- Cover and place in oven for 45-50 minutes until chicken and vegetables are cooked through.
- Cut up into manageable pieces and serve warm.

Kicking Turkey Curry

Spicy and delicious!

Ingredients

- 2 tsp coconut oil
- 1 white onion, finely diced
- thumb-size piece of fresh ginger, grated
- 1 garlic clove, finely chopped
- 1 tbsp mild curry powder
- ½ cup unsalted chicken stock
- 1 cup coconut milk
- ½ cup cooked and diced sweet potato
- 1 cup cooked turkey breast, diced

How to make

- In a deep saucepan, heat oil on a medium high heat.
- Sauté the onion, garlic and ginger.
- Add the turkey, stirring until heated through and then add stock and coconut milk.
- Sprinkle in curry powder and add sweet potato.
- Bring to the boil.
- Turn down slightly and allow to simmer for 20 minutes or until sweet potato soft.

Friday Fish Supper

Not necessarily just for Fridays – boosts baby's omega 3 levels.

Ingredients:

- 2 fillets of cod or other white fish (boneless)
- 1/4 cup whole milk
- 1/4 cup cooked and mashed peas
- 1/4 cup cooked and mashed carrots
- Sprinkle of finely chopped parsley

How to make

- Check your fish for any bones that may still be remaining.
- On a medium to high heat, poach fish in milk & parsley for 20 minutes or until cooked through.
- In last 10 minutes steam your veg over the fish until cooked through and soft.
- Break up cooked fish and check again for any bones.
- Serve warm with the mashed veg.
- This can also be blended for a soup for younger babies.

Beautiful Chicken Pasta

Heartwarming!

Ingredients:

- 1 cup macaroni shapes
- ½ cup carrots and peas
- 1 cup of cooked chicken, shredded
- 2 cups water or unsalted chicken stock

How to make

- Boil water in a pan over a medium high heat and cook macaroni shapes for 15-20 minutes or until soft.
- Add veg to steam for the last 10 minutes.
- Drain the pasta and combine macaroni and vegetables in the pan.
- Add the chicken and cover with water or stock.
- Turn down to a simmer and leave for a further 10 minutes or until heated through.
- Serve warm.

Mr Rabbit's Delicious Sweet Potatoes & Butternut Squash Medley

Autumnal treat!

Ingredients:

- 3 medium sweet potatoes
- 1 small butternut squash

How to make

- On a medium to high heat, steam squash and sweet potatoes together for 30-35 minutes or until tender.
- Mash or chop with a fork and serve alone or as a side to baby's favorite meat dish.

Heartwarming Buttery Pasta

A creamy treat that your baby can eat whole. So easy to whip up!

Ingredients

- 1 cup of pasta
- 1 tbsp of butter
- A pinch of minced or powdered garlic

How to make

- Boil water on a high heat and cook pasta according to package directions.
- You can add a few more minutes to make pasta extra tender for little mouths.
- Drain pasta when done and return it to the pot you cooked it in.
- Mix in butter and garlic.
- Mix well and serve warm.
- This is a very simple pasta dish that can appeal to your baby's picky pallet.

Super Scrambled Eggs

Now that your baby is one, you can start to feed them the whole egg and this is a quick snack loaded with protein- a great way to start your baby's day.

Ingredients

- 2 eggs
- 1/2 cup of whole milk
- ¼ cup steamed spinach

How to make

- Beat eggs in a bowl breaking the yoke and mix in milk.
- Spray pan with cooking spray and heat on a medium heat.
- Pour eggs into the pan and beat slowly to get delicious and fluffy eggs – ensure you cook through and eggs are not too runny when serving.
- Mix through the steamed spinach.
- Serve warm.

Ridiculously Amazing Ribs

Yes- ribs! Go on...

Ingredients

- 1/2 rack of ribs
- 1 bottle of bbq sauce very mild (no extra sugar or salt or preservatives)

How to make

- Preheat oven to 375°F / 190°C /Gas Mark 5.
- Place ribs in a pot of water and boil on a high heat until they start to get tender.
- Place in a baking dish and smother with sauce.
- Bake for 1-2 hours. The pork should reach an internal temperature of 160°f (you will need the thermometer you used for your yogurt here pg76).
- Remove from oven and serve once cooled down.
- Use a fork to flake off the meat before serving.

Scrummy Sausage Casserole

I accidentally found out that my son loved this dish as he was peering over my shoulder when eating with my husband one evening! I gave him a bite and he wanted more and more.

Ingredients

- 1 cup cooked and sliced sausage
- 1 cup sliced bell peppers
- 1 cup sliced zucchini
- 1 tbsp coconut oil
- 1 cup chopped tomatoes

How to make

- Over a medium high heat warm coconut oil.
- Ensure sausage and veggies are sliced small enough for your baby to manage in one bite.
- Add sausage and vegetables and cook for 10-15 minutes until both areheated through (veggies should be tender).
- Add chopped tomatoes and allow to simmer for a further 20 minutes.
- Serve warm.

Amazing Apple & Pumpkin Granola

Yum!

Ingredients

- 1/2 cup of apple, washed and chopped into small pieces
- 1/2 cup of pumpkin, washed, chopped & cooked
- 1/4 cup of oatmeal
- ¼ cup barley
- 1 cup of boiling water

How to make

- Blend apple and pumpkin until smooth.
- Combine boiling water, oatmeal and barley together in a separate bowl.
- Mix together oatmeal and apple pumpkin mixture.
- Serve warm.

Lovely Broccoli and Cheddar Cheese

Bubbly and cheesy and delicious!

Ingredients

- 2 cups broccoli washed and cut into florets
- 1 cup grated cheddar or similar
- 1/4 cup of plain flour
- 2 cups whole milk or similar
- 1 knob of butter

How to make

- Preheat oven to 375°F / 190°C /Gas Mark 5.
- Steam the broccoli on a medium high heat for 10 minutes until soft.
- Meanwhile, on a medium heat, place your butter into the nearest side of a pan (try and keep it from running across the whole circumference).
- Sift your flour into the pan next to the butter and gradually mix the flour into the butter until you have formed a thick paste.
- Now slowly add the milk to the mixture, stirring continuously (this will be very lumpy at first but continue to stir for at least 5-10 minutes and a lovely thick creamy sauce will form – trust me!)
- Now add your cheese and stir until smooth.
- Layer the broccoli into an oven dish and pour the cheese sauce over the top.
- Place in oven for 10 minutes or so or until slightly golden and delicious.
- Allow to cool enough for baby before serving an individual portion.

Mexican Baby Tortilla

A Mexican style treat for Baby!

Ingredients

- 200g self raising flour
- 150ml warm water
- 3 tbsp extra virgin olive oil or coconut oil
- 1 cup cooked ground beef
- 1/2 cup shredded lettuce
- 1/2 cup diced tomato
- 1/2 cup shredded cheese

How to make

- Sift your flour into a large bowl.
- Pour the water and oil into a measuring jug or separate bowl and mix well.
- Now add to the flour, stirring until doughy.
- Lightly flour your work surface and knead the dough with your fists for a few minutes.
- Divide into 8 and roll each quarter into small circles.
- Allow to rest for a few minutes.
- On a medium heat, heat some coconut oil and cook each tortilla for 1 minute on each side.
- Look out for a slight golden brown colour.
- Now fill with your fillings, roll and fold.
- Place under the grill on a medium heat until golden. These tortillas will be small but you may need to cut up for your baby if they are just starting out with finger foods.

Amazing Apple Raspberry Avocado

Liven up your avocado with other fruits to add sweetness – the avocado provides an almost yogurt texture.

Ingredients

- 1/2 apple washed, peeled and cubed
- 1/4 cup raspberries washed
- 1 avocado peeled and cubed

How to make

- Wash and peel fruit accordingly – you can steam at this stage if you haven't yet introduced raw fruits.
- Remove avocado pulp and cut apple into chunks.
- Mash or blend together to reach the appropriate consistency.

Noodle Beef Surprise

Full of great vitamins and iron to keep your baby going!

Ingredients

- 1 cup cooked and diced beef
- 1 cup cooked egg noodles
- ½ cup cooked carrots and corn
- 2 cups unsalted beef stock
- 1 tsp tomato paste

How to make

- Heat a pan on a medium high heat and add stock.
- Throw in your cooked ingredients and heat through for 10 minutes or until thoroughly hot throughout.
- Add tomato paste close to the end to thicken.
- Serve warm as a dish (ensure you've cut it into small enough pieces for your baby's stage of eating).

Tasty Chicken and Amazing Avocado Wrap

Tasty dinner time fun for the family.

Ingredients

- 200g self raising flour
- 150ml warm water
- 3 tbsp extra virgin olive oil or coconut oil
- 1 cup shredded cooked chicken
- 1/2 avocado crushed
- 1/2 cup tomatoes washed and chopped
- 1/2 cup lettuce shredded

How to make

- Sift your flour into a large bowl.
- Pour the water and oil into a measuring jug or separate bowl and mix well.
- Now add to the flour, stirring until doughy.
- Lightly flour your work surface and knead the dough with your fists for a few minutes.
- Divide into 8 and roll each quarter into small circles.
- Allow to rest for a few minutes.
- Fill wrap with chichen and salad. Add a squeeze of lemon juice and a dollop of homemade yogurt if you wish.
- Cut into bitesize pieces and serve.

Baby Rice Pudding

Doesn't need to taste like your old school dinners! This one is sweet and fruity.

Ingredients

- 1 cup pudding rice
- 3 cup whole milk
- 1 - 2 tbsp honey
- 1 tbsp strawberry puree
- 1 vanilla pod or ½ tsp vanilla essence

How to make

- In a pan, add the rice, milk and honey and vanilla.
- Bring the milk to the boil and then turn down and simmer (lid on) for 30 minutes. (Keep stirring whilst cooking every now and then).
- Serve warm with strawberry puree mixed through.

Red Pepper Lamb and Apricot Tagine

I came about this one after a trip to Morocco – Louis couldn't get enough!

Ingredients

- 1 tsp olive oil
- ½ white or red onion, finely chopped
- 1/2 red pepper, finely chopped
- 1/2 zucchini, finely chopped
- 2 cups stewing lamb, diced
- 4 cups water
- 1 tsp ground cumin
- 10 dried apricots

How to make

- Preheat oven to 400°F / 200°C / Gas Mark 6.
- On a medium heat, sauté the onions and vegetables with a little olive oil for 10 minutes until softened.
- Sprinkle cumin over vegetables and sauté for a further 5 minutes.
- Add your lamb and brown each side.
- Transfer ingredients to a tagine or deep oven dish.
- Add water and bake for 45-50 minutes or until lamb completely soft and tender.
- Serve warm, with your baby's favorite rice of potato.

Salmon and Dill Pasta

Fresh and mouth watering.

Ingredients

- 1 fillet of salmon
- 1/2 cup whole milk
- 1 tbsp finely chopped dill
- 1 cup pasta of your choice

How to make

- Steam or fry salmon on a medium high heat for 25 minutes or until completely cooked through.
- Meanwhile, cook your chosen pasta according to package directions. Rice works well with this dish too!
- Remove salmon from heat and allow to cool before flaking.
- Once pasta is cooked, remove and drain and stir in salmon flakes.
- Now add milk and dill and allow to simmer for another 10 minutes or until heated through – a dollop of homemade yogurt will thicken it up a bit.

Easy Cream Cheese and Asparagus Pasta

So easy.

Ingredients

- 3 tbsp creamed cheese
- 5 cooked asparagus stems, chopped into small pieces
- 1 cup pasta of your choice

How to make

- Cook pasta according to packet instructions.
- Drain and stir through cream cheese and asparagus.
- Season with a little black pepper and a squeeze of fresh lemon juice to serve.

FINGER FOODS

Gorgeous Homemade Chicken Nuggets

Every child's favorite!

Ingredients

- 2 chicken breasts
- 1 cup of wholemeal or brown bread crumbs
- 4 free-range egg yolks
- 1 cup of milk (of your choice)
- 1 tsp rosemary (finely chopped fresh or dried)

How to make

- Preheat oven to 350°F / 180°C / Gas Mark 4
- Cut your chicken into easy bite-size pieces for little fingers.
- Whisk egg and milk in a bowl.
- Layer breadcrumbs in a shallow dish.
- Dip a chicken piece into the milk and egg mixture, making sure it's thoroughly coated.
- Dip the chicken into the breadcrumb mixture, coating all over.
- Repeat for each piece of chicken or place your egg-covered chicken in a container with the breadcrumbs and shake well.
- Place chicken onto oven dish and bake for 25 minutes or until cooked through (test the biggest nugget first).
- Allow to cool for a few minutes before serving.
- Serve with the Kale Ketchup you made earlier! (pg103)

Finger Lickin' Fish Fingers

A dinner time treat and way better homemade than shop-bought!

Ingredients

- 2 fillets of white fish (ensure this is completely deboned)
- 1 cup of wholemeal or brown bread crumbs
- 2 free-range egg yolks
- 1 tsp dill (finely chopped fresh or dried)
- 1 cup of milk (your choice)

How to make

- Preheat oven to 350°F / 180°C / Gas Mark 4.
- Thoroughly wash and slice fish fillets into baby-friendly finger shapes.
- Whisk egg and milk in a bowl.
- Layer breadcrumbs in a shallow dish.
- Firstly dip fish finger into the egg mixture and then the breadcrumb mixture, coating all over.
- Repeat for each piece of fish or place your egg-covered fish pieces in a container with the bread crumbs and shake well.
- Place onto oven dish and bake for 25 minutes or until cooked through.

Sweet Corn Fritters

A healthy snack!

Ingredients

- 1 cup of cooked corn
- 1 white potato cooked and mashed
- 1 tsp coconut oil
- 1 tsp chilli powder

How to make

- Mix mashed potato, corn and chilli powder.
- Using the palms of your hands, shape potato mix into patty shape pieces.
- Heat coconut oil in a pan over a medium high heat.
- Cook for a few minutes each side until lightly browned and then turn down heat and continue to cook for further 10 minutes or until hot all the way through.
- Allow to cool and serve alone or with side vegetables of your choice.

Tofu Treats

Vegetarian friendly and very delicious.

Ingredients:

- 1 pack of firm tofu
- 1/4 cup flour
- 2 egg yolks
- 1 cup wholemeal bread crumbs
- 1 tsp garlic powder
- 1 tsp cumin

How to make

- Preheat oven to 350°F / 180°C /Gas Mark 4.
- Remove tofu from packet and place on a chopping board; place another chopping board on top and a heavy item on the top of this. Allow to sit for as long as you can to remove any excess water from the tofu. This will make it easier to cook and less runny.
- Slice tofu into squares.
- On a flat plate, dust with flour.
- In a separate bowl, beat the eggs and mix in the rest of the ingredients.
- Dip the tofu into the flour and coat each side.
- Now dip into the egg mixture until covered.
- Place onto a baking sheet and cook for 15-20 minutes until crisp. Alternatively heat in a pan on a medium to high heat until cooked through and starting to crisp.
- Serve alone as finger food when cool enough or with noodles/rice as a dinner.

Caribbean Popping Plantain

An exotic option for finger food time.

Ingredients

- 1 plantain
- 1 tbsp honey

How to make

- Peel plantain and slice in half lengthways.
- Heat a pan on a medium heat and add honey.
- Place the plantain slice into the pan and fry for 5-6 minutes on each side or until soft.
- Serve warm.

Italian Cheese Pizza Bites

A party snack that your baby will enjoy into childhood.

Ingredients

- 2 slices soft whole meal or brown bread
- 1/2 cup of chopped tomatoes
- 1/4 cup shredded mozzarella cheese
- A pinch of basil, finely chopped

How to make

- Preheat grill on a medium heat.
- Prep a baking tray by spraying with olive oil.
- Slice your bread into finger size slices and place under the grill for a few minutes each side or until golden.
- Meanwhile, heat your chopped tomatoes with a little basil either over a medium heat on the hob or in the microwave for 1 minute.
- Carefully remove your bread slices from under the grill and spread a thin layer of the tomatoes over each slice (leave one end free for your baby's fingers).
- Top with a sprinkle of mozzarella on each and place back under the grill for a couple of minutes until the cheese has melted.
- Remove from grill and leave to cool to a warm temperature before serving.

Tasty Turkey and Apple Fruit Loaf

A healthy alternative to bread.

Ingredients

- 2 cups minced turkey
- 1 whole egg
- 1/2 cup carrot puree
- 1/4 cup apples puree
- 1/4 cup ground oatmeal
- 1/4 cup wholemeal breadcrumbs

How to make

- Preheat oven to 350°F / 180°C /Gas Mark 4.
- In a mixing bowl, mix turkey, egg, purees and dry ingredients.
- Puree can continue to be added to ensure this mix is not too dry.
- Spray a bread tin or similar with cooking spray and pour mixture in.
- Cover with foil.
- Cook for 40-45 minutes or until cooked through (check that a knife inserted into the middle of the loaf comes out clean).
- Remove from oven and allow to cool.
- Slice into soldiers.

Funky Fresh Fruit Salad

Now that your baby has most likely tried all of the fruits raw, try introducing small pieces for them to snack on. They'll benefit from all of the vitamins and nutrients in their best possible form this way.

Ingredients

- 1/4 cup of blueberries, washed
- 1/4 cup of raspberries, washed
- 1/4 cup of strawberries, washed and sliced
- 1/4 cup of bananas, washed and sliced

How to make

- Mix everything together in a bowl and feed to your little one.
- If they're just starting out with finger foods, try giving them individually to prevent a clumsy accident as well as to help them get used to eating foods without a spoon.
- You don't want to make too much fruit salad in advance as it will start to brown quite quickly.

Fantastic French Toast

A healthy version of this indulgent snack – perfect for your little one.

Ingredients

- 2 slices of soft wholemeal or brown bread
- 2 free-range egg yolks
- 1/4 to 1/2 cup of whole milk
- 1 to 2 teaspoons of cinnamon

How to make

- Cut your bread into finger shaped slices.
- In a shallow bowl mix the milk and egg together.
- Dip the bread fingers in the egg and milk mixture then place in a pan with a little coconut oil.
- Cook on a medium heat for 4-5 minutes on each side or until they are a nice golden brown.
- Ensure that the egg is cooked all the way through by checking for that golden brown color.
- Leave to cool slightly and dust with cinnamon if you wish.
- Serve warm.

Sophia's Mini Blueberry Muffins

Soft and fluffy, these muffins are a wonderful treat.

Ingredients

- 1 cup flour
- 3/4 tsp baking powder
- 1/4 tsp cinnamon
- 1/4 tsp of salt
- 1 large egg yolk
- 1/3 cup coconut oil
- 2/3 cup whole milk
- 2/3 cup honey
- 1 vanilla pod (not essential)
- 1/2 cup blueberries, washed

How to make

- Preheat oven to 375°F / 190°C /Gas Mark 5.
- Prepare a mini muffin dish with 24 muffin holes, spray with cooking oil or similar.
- Mix the dry ingredients into a large bowl, leaving blueberries and honey for now.
- In a separate bowl, whisk the wet ingredients with honey.
- Fold in blueberries.
- Using a spoon scoop small amounts into the muffin tin so they are about 3/4 of the way full.
- Bake for 15 to 20 minutes. Test by poking a sharp knife into the center (it will come out clean when cooked).
- Remove from oven and transfer onto cooling rack for 5 minutes.
- These can be frozen for later or served immediately.

Lovely Mini Banana Muffins

Amazing flavor!

Ingredients

- 1 cup flour
- 3/4 tsp baking powder
- 1/4 tsp of ground nuts (optional)
- 1/4 tsp of salt
- 1 large egg yolk
- 1/3 cup coconut oil
- 2/3 cup whole milk
- 2/3 cup honey
- 1 vanilla pod (not essential)
- 1 sliced ripe banana

How to make

- Preheat oven to 375°F / 190°C /Gas Mark 5.
- Prepare a mini muffin dish with 24 muffin holes, spray with cooking oil or similar.
- Mix the dry ingredients into a large bowl, leaving banana and honey for now.
- In a separate bowl, whisk the wet ingredients with honey.
- Fold in banana.
- Using a spoon scoop small amounts into the muffin tin so they are about 3/4 of the way full.
- Bake for 15 to 20 minutes. Test by poking a sharp knife into the center (it will come out clean when cooked).
- Remove from oven and transfer onto cooling rack for 5 minutes.
- These can be frozen for later or served immediately.

Homemade Sweet Potato Wedges

Make a whole batch of these and freeze to avoid opting for the fast food option.

Ingredients

- 8 medium to large sweet potatoes
- 1 tsp rosemary

How to make

- Preheat oven to 400°F / 200°C / Gas Mark 6.
- Thoroughly wash sweet potatoes, leaving the skin on if baby is used to skin.
- Cut into thin wedges.
- Spread out on a baking tray and add finely chopped rosemary and a drizzle of olive oil.
- Bake for 30-45 minutes or until soft.
- Allow to cool enough for baby and serve as finger food or with their favorite meat/fish.

Scrumptious Chicken and Rosemary Pizza Bites

Try adding meat to your baby's pizza bites for an extra mouthwatering dimension.

Ingredients

- 2 slices soft wholemeal or brown bread
- 1/2 cup of chopped tomatoes
- 1/4 cup shredded mozzarella cheese
- 1/4 cup of chicken, cooked and diced into tiny pieces
- A pinch of rosemary, finely chopped

How to make

- Preheat grill on a medium heat.
- Prep a baking tray by spraying with olive oil.
- Slice your bread into finger size slices and place under the grill for a few minutes each side or until golden.
- Meanwhile, heat your chopped tomatoes with a little rosemary either over a medium heat on the hob or in the microwave for 1 minute.
- Carefully remove your bread slices from under the grill and spread a thin layer of the tomatoes over each slice (leave one end free for your baby's fingers).
- Top with chicken and a sprinkle of mozzarella on each and place back under the grill for a couple of minutes until the cheese has melted.
- Remove from grill and leave to cool before serving.

Happy Egg and Soldiers

Fun time breakfast.

Ingredients

- 1 egg
- 1 slice of bread

How to make

- Boil water in a pan on a high heat.
- Place egg in pan and turn heat off, place lid on and leave for 7-8 minutes for medium boiled and 10-12 minutes for hard boiled.
- Lightly toast sliced bread and then cut into 'soldiers' or thin strips.
- Take egg off of the heat and run under a cold tap.
- Tap with a sharp knife to crack the shell and then carefully pull off the shell.
- Place egg in an egg cup and cut the top off.
- Let baby have fun dipping their soldiers into the egg and then they can pick up what's left and enjoy!

Bubba Baby Potato Skins

Amazing flavor!

Ingredients

- 1 potato type of your choice
- 1/4 cup of cheddar cheese
- 1/4 cup of ham (sliced)

How to make

- Preheat oven to 375°F / 190°C /Gas Mark 5.
- Wash and then bake whole potato in oven for 30-40 minutes or until soft all the way through.
- After your potato is cooked and tender, scoop out the insides (reserving the skin) and mash well mixing cheese and ham.
- Refill the potato skins and place back in oven until the cheese is melted and slightly golden.
- Serve with a spoonful of homemade yogurt and cut into small pieces if your baby is just starting out with solid foods.

Lovely Homemade Bread

Easier than you think!

Ingredients

- 1 cup milk
- 8 tablespoons melted butter
- 2/3 cup stevia
- sprinkle of salt
- 6 1/2 cups bread flour
- 4 large eggs
- 2 tablespoon of instant yeast

How to make

- Preheat oven to 400°F / 200°C / Gas Mark 6.
- Ensure you bring your ingredients to room temperature.
- Starting with liquids, mix ingredients together well into a large bowl and then slowly add dry ingredients (yeast should be last).
- Kneed your mixture by hand until it is smooth and well mixed (15 minutes should do the trick).
- Leave your dough to rise (in a bowl covered with a towel) for 1-2 hours.
- Shape bread into a loaf or oval shape as best as you can (it doesn't need to be perfect!) and place in oven on an oven tray sprayed with a little cooking spray.
- Bake for about 25 to 35 minutes. Keep an eye on it without opening the oven door – look out for a golden brown color and check its done by cutting through (the knife should come out clean).
- Break off small pieces for baby and serve warm.

TREATS

Sweet Cinnamon & Raisin Bread

For a sweet tooth.

Ingredients

- 1 cup milk
- 8 tablespoons melted butter
- 2/3 cup stevia
- sprinkle of salt
- 6 1/2 cups bread flour
- 4 large eggs
- 2 tablespoon of instant yeast
- 1 vanilla pod
- 1/2 cup raisins
- 1 tablespoon cinnamon

How to make

- Preheat oven to 400°F / 200°C / Gas Mark 6.
- Ensure you bring your ingredients to room temperature.
- Starting with liquids, mix ingredients together well into a large bowl and then slowly add dry ingredients (yeast should be last).
- Kneed your mixture by hand until it is smooth and well mixed (15 minutes should do the trick).
- Leave your dough to rise (in a bowl covered with a towel) for 1-2 hours.
- Now fold in the cinnamon, vanilla and raisins and allow to rise for a further 3- minutes.
- Shape bread into a loaf or oval shape as best as you can (it doesn't need to be perfect!) and place in oven on an oven tray sprayed with a little cooking spray.
- Bake for about 25 to 35 minutes. Keep an eye on it without opening the oven door – look out for a golden brown color and check it's done by cutting through (the knife should come out clean).
- Break off small pieces for baby and serve warm.

Rip Roaring Honey Cakes

Indulgent.

Ingredients

- 3 1/2 cups all-purpose flour
- 1 teaspoon baking soda
- 1 tablespoon baking powder
- 4 teaspoons cinnamon
- sprinkle of salt
- 1/2 teaspoon ground cloves
- 1 cup coconut oil
- 1 cup honey
- 3 egg yolks
- 1 vanilla pod
- 1/2 cup of orange juice

How to make

- Pre-heat oven to 350°F / 180°C / Gas Mark 4.
- Prep your cake tin (cupcake) with paper cases or cooking spray.
- In a large bowl whisk together the baking soda, baking powder, spices, salt and flour.
- Make a well in the centre and pour in eggs, vanilla, orange juice, honey, and oil.
- Using a mixer on slow or a whisk, combine the ingredients making a thick mixture and ensuring there are no lumps.
- Spoon the mixture into the cake tray and place in oven for 15-20 minutes.
- Keep an eye on them without opening the oven door – look out for a golden brown color and check it's done by cutting through (the knife should come out clean).
- Remove cakes from oven and let sit for 15 minutes on a wire rack to finish cooling.

Delicious Oatmeal & Raisin Baby Cookies

Baking can be fun.

Ingredients

- 1/2 cup softened butter
- 1 cup honey
- 1 egg
- 1 cup flour
- 1 cup rolled oats
- 1 cup raisins
- 1/2 teaspoon cinnamon (optional)
- 1/2 teaspoon salt
- 1 teaspoon baking powder

How to make

- Preheat oven to 350°F / 180°C /Gas Mark 4.
- In large bowl cream together butter and honey together with electric mixer or whisk.
- Add egg and continue until mixed thoroughly. Add baking powder, salt and cinnamon and continue mixing.
- By hand, mix in flour, then raisins, then oats and combine until sticky.
- Pour small cookie shape pieces onto a lightly oiled baking tray.
- Bake for about 9 minutes or until cookies are lightly browned.
- Remove and allow to cool before serving.

Mini Baby Doughnuts

For a special occasion..

Ingredients

- 1/2 teaspoon baking powder
- 2/3 cup all purpose flour
- 1/8 teaspoon salt
- 1/4 teaspoon ground nutmeg
- 1/4 cup whole milk
- 1/2 tsp vanilla extract
- 5 tbsp softened butter
- 1 egg
- 1 tsp honey
- Piping bag

How to make

- Preheat oven to 350°F / 180°C /Gas Mark 4.
- Get a muffin tin and spray with cooking spray or similar.
- In bowl 1, combine nutmeg, salt, flour and baking powder.
- In bowl 2, combine milk and vanilla.
- In bowl 3, combine butter and honey and stir until smooth, then add the egg and beat.
- Gradually combine all 3 bowls into a large bowl (add a little of each bowl's mixture at a time until smooth).
- Get your piping bag and squeeze mixture inside. Cut your hole and squeeze out circle shapes onto your muffin tin.
- Bake for 10 to 12 minutes (check they're done by inserting a knife into the center- it should come out clean).
- Leave to cool before serving.

Delicious Strawberry, Pear and Lime Baby Popsicle

Great for a hot summer's day!

Ingredients

- 1 to 2 cups strawberry washed and cubed
- 1 to 2 cups pear washed and cubed
- Ice cube tray or similar
- Juice of 1 lime
- Popsicle sticks

How to make

- Puree strawberry and pear and lime juice until liquid.
- Pour your fruit puree into an ice cube tray.
- Freeze for 30 minutes or until slushy.
- Place popsicle sticks into each ice cube and place back in freezer for 1 hour or until set.

Tasty Apple Cinnamon Treats

Halloween treat.

Ingredients

- 2 apples
- 2 tbsp honey
- 1 tsp cinnamon
- 1 tbsp butter

How to make

- Wash and core apples (leave skin on).
- Cut into slices.
- Heat a pan on a medium heat and cook apples in the butter for 10-15 minute.
- Sprinkle cinnamon and drizzle honey over apples and continue cooking for another 1- minutes or until softened and slightly caramelized.
- Don't allow your apples to burn! Remove from pan once done and leave to cool.
- Serve for a one-off treat!

Honey Candied Sweet Potatoes

Try with sweet potato or apple!

How to make

- Preheat oven to 375°F / 190°C /Gas Mark 5.
- Prick holes in the skin of your sweet potatoes with a fork and bake in the oven for 25-30 minutes.
- Once cooked, cut potato into wedges.
- Place a pan on a medium heat and melt butter and then combine with honey and cinnamon.
- Toss sweet potatoes in mixture and add to oven again.
- Heat through for 10 minutes or so or until starting to caramelize.
- Allow to cool and serve.

Ingredients

- 2 large sweet potatoes
- 1 tbsp honey
- 1 tsp cinnamon
- 1 tbsp butter

Seasonal Cinnamon and Sultana Barley

When introducing new spices, ensure you wait for 4-5 days to monitor your baby's reaction to these. That being said, baby food needn't be bland forever and by adding herbs and spices from a young age, many believe babies will be less fussy as a result of such variety. Your pediatrician will help advise you on this if you're at all worried.

Ingredients

- 6 tsp ground barley
- 1 tsp cinnamon
- 1/2 cup of sultanas
- 2/3 cup boiling water, breast milk or formula

How to make

- Mix boiling water and barley well.
- Blend the barley mix with the sultanas until pureed, adding the liquid as required.
- Serve warm with a dusting of cinnamon for a festive touch; although this is great anytime of the year.

Cheeky Animal Crackers

Fun for play time

Ingredients

- 1/4 cup buttermilk
- 2 tsp honey
- 1/4 cup butter, softened
- 1/4 tsp salt
- 1/4 tsp baking soda
- 1/2 cup rolled oats (ground)
- 3/4 cup flour, all purpose

How to make

- Preheat over to 400°F / 200°C / Gas Mark 6.
- Get a mixing bowl and add the flour, baking soda, salt and oats.
- Mix together and then add the butter . Use your fingers to rub the butter into the mixture until all blended in and the mixture has formed small rounded shapes almost like breadcrumbs.
- Now mix the buttermilk and honey until you form a dough.
- Lightly dust your work surface with flour and use a rolling pin to roll out your dough until about 1cm thick.
- Cut out using animal cutters (or baby's favorite shapes).
- Bake in the oven for 6 to 7 minutes.
- Remove from oven to cool.
- Serve!

Sweet Pear and Raisin Yogurt Crunch

Wake your baby up the right way and try this delicious breakfast first thing!

Ingredients

- 4 tbsp of ground oatmeal
- 4 tbsp of ground barley
- 4 tbsp raisins
- 2 apples washed, peeled and cubed
- 2 pears washed, peeled and cubed
- 1 cup homemade yogurt (pg. 76)
- 1/2 cup hot water

How to make

- Mix hot water and oats and barley in a separate bowl.
- Place granola, raisins, pears and apple in appliance of your choice and blend until you have a chunky consistency.
- Fold your mixture into yogurt mixing well.

Delicious Watermelon Popsicles

Refreshing and hydrating on a hot summer's day!

Ingredients

- 2 cups watermelon chunks washed and cubed
- Ice cube tray or similar
- Popsicle sticks

How to make

- Puree watermelon cubes into a smooth liquid.
- Pour watermelon puree into your ice cube tray.
- Place in the freezer for 30 minutes – the puree will have started to set.
- Set each popsicle stick into each ice cube so that they are sticking upright.
- Return to freezer for another hour or until popsicles are solid and hold their shape.

12
QUICK AND EASY
30 *sec*
FINGER FOODS

Quick And Easy 30 Second Finger Foods!

This section is dedicated to finger food ideas – I didn't think they needed a recipe for each one as they are so simple. I hope these get you started with inspiration for small foods to feed your loved one and that you can continue to experiment and be creative in the kitchen while your baby's appetite grows!

Strawberry Slices

Banana Slices

Cheese and Pineapple bites

Raisin and Apple Bites

Mango Wedges

Papaya Wedges

Cucumber Slices

Mandarin Orange Segments

Corn On the Cob

Halved Grapes

Pitted Cherries

Watermelon Bites

the best is yet to COME!

Well- we've made it!

Congratulations on putting in the time, effort and dedication to preparing your own baby food.

I know when I first started to make my son's baby food it became a chore very quickly and I soon wanted to give up. I felt it was time consuming and I just wasn't sure if it was worth my efforts nutritionally or financially for my little one. Part of my problem was I had no idea what I was doing, a lot of my cooking was trial and error and it was frustrating. The books I had read didn't give me step by step instructions, nor did they give recommended suggestions for different ages.

Hopefully you and your baby have enjoyed every single one of the homemade baby food recipes in this book. I certainly know that Louis and I had fun steaming, blitzing and playing around with all the different colors and textures. You're likely better off because of your hard work and effort and more importantly your son or daughter will be healthy and happy from having eaten homemade, fresh foods everyday.

With any luck you will have found out how easy it is to prepare and cook and freeze your own baby food recipes, as well as noticing how nice it is not to have hundreds of glass jars lying around the house waiting to be recycled! You've probably saved a lot of money in the process too!

If you have a bad day and things don't seem to be going quite so well as they usually are, don't despair and give up forever – just get back to it the next day! Once your baby is used to solid foods and lumps and chunks, you can simply whizz up your family's meals (it might also encourage healthier eating for the rest of the family!)

I wish you all the happiness and health, for you and your family, each and every day!

Sophia

Index

Lightning Source UK Ltd.
Milton Keynes UK
UKOW07f0146211016

285749UK00006B/35/P